Fourteenth Edition

# Essentials of Real Estate Finance

David Sirota, PhD • Doris Barrell, GRI, DREI, CDEI

President: Dr. Andrew Temte
Chief Learning Officer: Dr. Tim Smaby
Executive Director, Real Estate Education: Melissa Kleeman-Moy
Development Editor: Kari Domeyer

ESSENTIALS OF REAL ESTATE FINANCE FOURTEENTH EDITION

Published by DF Institute, Inc., d/b/a Dearborn Real Estate Education
332 Front St. S., Suite 501
La Crosse, WI 54601



Printed in the United States of America
First revision, March 2016
ISBN: 978-1-4754-2839-1 / 1-4754-2839-1
PPN: 1557-1015

# Contents

# Preface

Welcome to the intriguing and exciting world of real estate finance. The past few years have seen tremendous changes in the real estate financing market. New programs seemed to appear almost daily as everyone from those in the Oval Office to the local corner bank worked to keep homeowners from losing their homes to foreclosure.

In October 2008, Congress passed the first of the rescue bills aimed at easing the great credit crunch that was brought about by the burst bubble of the burgeoning real estate markets of the early part of this century. The new bill directed $700 billion to help lenders dispose of their worthless defaulted loans and to restart their lending activities. Over the next three years, the government created numerous programs designed to assist homeowners at risk of foreclosure due to increased monthly payments and unemployment. The recovery, now in process, is again based on long-term, fixed-interest-rate loans made to qualified borrowers financing reasonably evaluated real estate properties.

Although loans can still be secured through the internet, underwriters will be screening these loans carefully to make sure the borrowers have verifiable credit histories, and the collateral properties are evaluated accurately. Nothing-down, interest-only, and variations of subprime loans are no longer acceptable. Lenders must now adhere carefully to the underwriters' requirements in order to sell their real estate loans in the secondary markets.

To a great extent, the U.S. economy depends on the ability of many individuals to comprehend and use real estate finance. Each participant need not know everything about all phases of financing real estate, but those who do understand the process are more likely to achieve success.

People have depended, in ever-increasing numbers, on banks, thrift institutions, and life insurance companies to lend them the dollars with which to buy a piece of America. Some people bought large pieces, and some grouped together to buy even larger ones, but most people just bought the little piece they call home.

In this new edition, you will find numerous revisions and additions that reflect the many changes that have occurred in the real estate financial market in recent years. The most commonly used forms have been moved to the appendices, including the new Loan Estimate and Closing Disclosure forms, which have been mandated for use on August 1,

2015. Of course there will always be new changes, especially as the market slowly works its way out of the overwhelming foreclosure problem. It is critically important for instructors and students to keep up-to-date with their own research. The websites listed in each chapter provide excellent resources.

Doris Barrell
David Sirota

## In Memoriam

On October 2, 2014, the world of real estate lost one of its finest educators, practitioners, and authors. Dr. David S. Sirota passed away in Green Valley, Arizona, where he had enjoyed several years of retirement with his wife, Roslyn. His influence on thousands of students can never be fully measured, and he will be greatly missed by his many friends, former students, and colleagues throughout the real estate industry.

## ACKNOWLEDGMENTS

Dr. David Sirota had a combined 40 years of field experience as a real estate agent, broker, appraiser, and consultant, plus an academic background culminating in a PhD from the University of Arizona in Area Development. He has said, "To be extraordinarily successful, it's not enough to know how the system works, but why it does. Then you can be in a position to utilize it for your own highest benefits."

Dr. Sirota taught real estate subjects at the University of Arizona in Tucson, the University of Nebraska in Omaha, Eastern Michigan University in Ypsilanti, National University in San Diego, and California State University in Fullerton. He held the Real Estate Chair at Nebraska and was a visiting professor at the University of Hawaii. He was involved as a consultant in the development of a congregate care center in Green Valley, Arizona, and acted in a consultant capacity for individuals and developers. He was a founding member of the Real Estate Educators Association, securing one of its first DREI designations. Dr. Sirota was also the author of *Essentials of Real Estate Investment* and coauthor of *California Real Estate Finance.*

Doris Barrell, GRI, DREI, CDEI, has been in the real estate business for over 30 years, working first for a builder/developer, next as a general brokerage agent, and then for nine years as managing broker for a 60-agent office in Alexandria, Virginia. She became a full-time instructor in 1996, bringing her wealth of real-life experience into the classroom, where she taught courses in finance, agency, fair housing, ethics, and legislative issues.

In addition to *Essentials of Real Estate Finance*, Ms. Barrell is the author of *Real Estate Finance Today*, *Ethics in Today's Real Estate World*, *Know the Code,* and *Everyday Ethics in Real Estate*; coauthor of *Reaching Out: The Financial Power of Niche Marketing* and *Fundamentals of Marketing for the Real Estate Professional*; and consulting editor for *Reverse Mortgages* and *Virginia Practice and Law*. She served as a teaching consultant to the International Real Property Foundation, bringing real estate education to countries in Eastern Europe and Southeast Asia for over 10 years. Ms. Barrell recently retired "with honors" from NeighborWorks® America, where she prepared course materials and taught classes at NeighborWorks® Training Institutes throughout the United States. She also developed the "Expanding Housing Opportunities" course for NAR, which she taught in addition to Train the Trainer classes for NAR instructors.

## CONTRIBUTORS

Our gratitude must begin with the many students who have insisted through the years, "Teachers, you should write that down." To them we say, "Thank you for supplying the necessary motivation."

For their contribution to earlier editions of the text, thanks are extended to Joseph L. Barrett, associate professor, Essex Community College; Bruce Baughman; W. Frazier Bell, Piedmont Virginia Community College; George Bell, DREI, George Bell Productions, Ltd.; Robert J. Bond; John Bonin, NeighborWorks® America National Faculty; Lynn Brown, PhD, professor, Jacksonville State University; Thomas Cary, real estate instructor/coordinator, Wadena Technical Institute; Adrij W. Chornodolsky, MA, CMA Valuation, LLC; Kelly W. Cassidy; Maurice Clifton, GRI, DREI, ERA West Wind-Boise; Gerald R. Cortesi, Triton College; Richard D. Cowan, North Carolina Academy of Real Estate; Dr. Arthur Cox, University of Northern Iowa; Lee Dillenbeck, real estate coordinator, Elgin Community College; Barbara Drisko, Real Estate Training and Education Services (RETES); Ed Elmer, Denver Financial Group; Calvin Ferraro, GRI, Coldwell Banker Real Estate; Gloria Fisher, Senior Loan Officer, Source One Mortgage Services, Green Valley, Arizona; Donald A. Gabriel; Bill Gallagher, DREI, GRI, CCDS, CBR, Mingle School of Real Estate; Arlyne Geschwender; Gerald N. Harris, Asheville Professional School of Real Estate; Janet Heller, Berks Real Estate Institute; Carl Hemmeler III, Columbus State Community College; Steve Hummel, Ohio University—Chillicothe; Carl M. Hyatt; John Jeddeloh; Glenn Jurgens; F. Jeffery Keil, J. Sargeants Reynolds Community College; Mike Keller; John W. Killough, Blue Ridge Community College; Rick Knowles, Capital Real Estate Training; Melvin S. Lang, National Institute of Real Estate; Craig Larabee, director, Larabee School of Real Estate and Insurance; "Doc" Blanchard LeNoir, PhD, Cedar Valley College; Thomas E. LoDolce, Financial Estate Institute; Lucy Loughhead; Laurie S. MacDougal, Laurmac Learning Center, Inc.; Jon C. McBride, Wake Technical Community College; Justin H. McCarthy, Minneapolis Technical Institute; Colin F. McGowan, Frederick Academy of Real Estate; Timothy C. Meline, Iowa Realty Company, Inc.; Stephen C. Messner; T. Gregory Morton; William E. Nix, UCLA Extension; Henry J. Olivieri, Jr., Real Estate Education Company; Charles E. Orcutt, Jr., attorney at law and adjunct faculty, Babson College; Nick J. Petra, CFP, CRB, Priority One Education Systems; Paul R. Pope, real estate education consultant, University Programs, Inc.; Dr. Wade R. Ragas, University of New Orleans; Mike Rieder, Gold Coast School of Real Estate, A Gimelstob Company; John F. Rodgers III, Catonsville Community College; Jerome D. Rutledge, North Texas Commercial Association of REALTORS®; Nancy Seago, GRI, Nancy Seago Seminars; Charles V. Sederstrom, III, Randall School of Real Estate; Dan South, Columbus State Community College; Paul C. and Margaret E. Sprencz; Ronald Stark, Northwest Mississippi Community College; Phyllis Tonne, Dayton Area Board of REALTORS®, Audrey May Van Vliet, Academy of Real Estate Education, Inc.; Richard Zemelka, Maplewood Area JVS Branch, John Carroll University; and Roger Zimmerman, faculty, Polaris Career Center and Cuyahoga Community College.

Chapter

# The Nature and Cycle of Real Estate Finance

## LEARNING OBJECTIVES

When you've finished reading this chapter, you will be able to

- evaluate the importance of the construction industry to the national economy;
- define and illustrate the concepts of collateralization, hypothecation, and leverage;
- differentiate between the primary and secondary financing markets;
- list important factors that affect real estate cycles; and
- discuss government plans for stimulating the economy.

**American Recovery and Reinvestment Act of 2009 (ARRA)**
**American Taxpayer Relief Act of 2012 (ATRA)**
**baby boomers**
**collateral**
**Consumer Financial Protection Bureau (CFPB)**
**disintermediation**
**echo boomers**
**equitable title**
**Generation X**
**Home Affordable Modification Program (HAMP)**
**Home Affordable Refinance Program (HARP)**
**hypothecation**
**leverage**
**mortgage-backed securities (MBSs)**
**Mortgage Forgiveness Debt Relief Act of 2007**
**primary market**
**real estate cycle**
**robo-signing**
**secondary market**
**shadow inventory**
**short sale**
**subprime market**
**Taxpayer Relief Act of 1997 (TRA '97)**
**Wall Street Reform and Consumer Protection Act (Dodd-Frank Act)**

There is no getting away from real estate: We farm on it, live on it, work on it, build on it, fly away from and return to it, and we ultimately are buried in it. No one can question the importance of real estate in our lives.

Complementing its physical importance is the economic impact of real estate on our lifestyles. The industrial and commercial activities of our nation are completely dependent on the land and its natural resources for their very existence. Our society cannot function without food, lumber, minerals, water, and other parts and products of our land.

Many of us are involved, either directly or indirectly, in some activity concerning real estate. Salespersons, brokers, farmers, miners, engineers, surveyors, land planners, homebuilders, furniture manufacturers, and paint purveyors—all of these people and more depend on real estate and its use for their livelihood. Millions of persons are engaged directly in construction activities in the United States, with literally millions more providing them with the materials and peripheral services essential to their work.

Nowhere is the economic impact of the real estate market better shown than during the economic crisis that began in 2007. As the overall real estate market began to decline and it became impossible for many people to sell or refinance their homes, the rate of foreclosures began to climb all over the country. The overall picture remained grim until 2012 when the housing market began to show some signs of renewal in many parts of the country. With the exception of the "sand belt"—Florida, Arizona, and Nevada—and the states affected by Hurricane Sandy, the rate of foreclosures began to decline and continued into 2013 and 2014. This was partially due to a higher acceptance of short sales by lenders. Unlike recoveries from previous recessions, the rate of employment has remained low, but there has been a gradual increase in the number of housing starts, which is an essential element to the overall economic picture.

## THE NATURE OF REAL ESTATE FINANCE

The construction industry is vital to our country's economic well-being and is therefore a significant factor in real estate finance. Any changes in its activities soon affect everyone. A building slowdown results in layoffs and cutbacks, while increased activity stimulates production and services in the many areas associated with the industry. Little construction is attempted that is not paid for by loans secured from the various sources of money for real estate finance. In fact, most real estate activities rely on the availability of borrowed funds.

The popular saying "as goes the construction industry, so goes the economy" was illustrated in the economic crisis that began with the downturn in the housing market in 2007. The number of housing starts kept falling, especially for new single-family homes. The first hopeful signs of a return to safe financial ground were not seen until 2013–2014 when single-family building began to slowly increase and multifamily starts actually reached their highest level since 1998.[1]

---

1 Joint Center for Housing Studies of Harvard University, "The State of the Nation's Housing Report 2013," Joint Center for Housing Studies, www.jchs.harvard.edu/sites/jchs.harvard.edu/files/son2013.pdf (accessed October 28, 2014).

## Credit System Economy

We all recognize that our society is credit oriented. We postpone paying for our personal property purchases by using credit cards and charge accounts. Credit expands our ability to own goods that in turn enhance our lives.

The credit concept of enjoying the use of an object while still paying for it is the basis of real estate finance. Financing a real estate purchase involves large sums of money and usually requires a long time to repay the loan. Instead of revolving charge accounts or 90-day credit loans for hundreds of dollars, real estate involves loans of thousands of dollars, repayable for up to 40 years.

The long-term nature of real estate loans complements the holding profile of the major financial lenders. Furthermore, the systematic repayment of real estate loans, usually in regular monthly amounts, creates the rhythm that enables lenders to collect savings and redistribute funds to implement continued economic growth.

However, this rhythm can be interrupted when there is a prolonged period of **disintermediation**; that is, when more funds are withdrawn from financial institutions than are being deposited. This results in a net loss of deposits, a cutback in lending, and a slowdown in the economy. There is continuous, vigorous competition for the use of money among individuals, industry, and government. That is why we need the Federal Reserve (the Fed) and the secondary markets to redistribute funds nationally and provide a constant flow of cash.

## Financing Relationships

The nature of the financing relationship can be described in three ways. In its simplest form, real estate finance involves pledging real property as **collateral** to back up a promise to repay a loan. As illustrated in Figure 1.1, a building and the land on which it stands are pledged to a lender as the borrower's guarantee that the terms of a loan contract will be satisfied. If a borrower defaults on repayment promises, the lender is legally able to foreclose on the real estate and sell it to try to recoup the loan balance.

*FIGURE 1.1* **Financing Real Estate with Collateral**

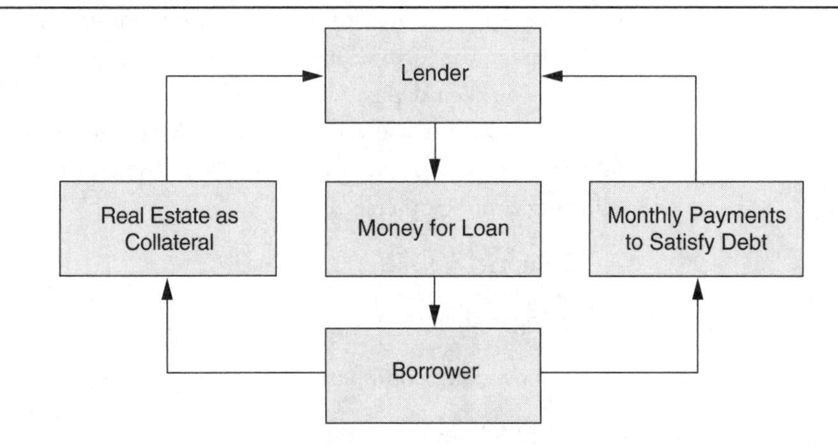
Lender
Real Estate as Collateral
Money for Loan
Monthly Payments to Satisfy Debt
Borrower
Until the borrower repays the lender in full, the real estate is the borrower's collateral or security that the debt will be repaid.

A second way to describe real estate finance is **hypothecation**. The borrower remains the legal owner and retains rights of possession and control while the lender secures a "bare title," a "naked title," or an **equitable title** in the property. An equitable title confers no rights to the lender except after a loan default when the legal title may be attained through foreclosure. In other words, under hypothecation, the lender has only a security, or equitable, interest in the collateral property, which ends when the loan is paid in full.

Hypothecation is found in other situations as well. A tenant may pledge leasehold rights as collateral for a loan. A lender may pledge rights in a receivable mortgage, deed of trust, or contract for deed as collateral for another loan. A life tenant can acquire a loan on beneficial rights as well as remainder rights. A farmer can pledge unharvested crops as collateral for a loan. In each of these cases, and others of similar design, the borrower retains possession, control, and use of the collateral but capitalizes on its value by borrowing against it.

**Leverage** is the third way to describe real estate finance. Leverage is the use of a proportionately small amount of money to secure a large loan for the purchase of a property. Buyers invest a portion of their money as a down payment and then leverage by borrowing the balance needed toward the full purchase price.

The quality and quantity of leverage are important topics. Buyers may be asked to invest 3, 5, 10, or even 20% of the purchase price before being eligible to borrow the balance. As a result of tightened qualifying standards due to the financial crisis, today's buyers may be asked to provide a much larger down payment than in the past. The minimum down payment for most conventional loans today is 5%, although FHA remains at 3.5%. The degree of leverage depends on the specific situation and the type of loan desired. These varying cash requirements dramatically affect a buyer's ability to purchase property. The use of leverage to purchase investment property generally increases the return on cash invested to an amount substantially higher than paying all cash.

## MORTGAGE LENDING ACTIVITIES

Underlying and forming the foundation for mortgage lending is the concept of savings. These savings are loaned to borrowers from whom additional earnings are produced for the lenders in the form of interest. These earnings are then used in part to pay interest to the savers on their deposits.

Most loans for real estate are made by financial institutions designed to hold individuals' savings until they are withdrawn. These primary market institutions include the following, among others:

- Commercial banks
- Savings banks
- Life insurance companies
- Credit unions

*FIGURE 1.2* **Mortgage Debt Outstanding, End of Q1 2014 (Millions of Dollars)**

| | |
|---|---|
| **By Type of Property** | |
| One- to four-family residence | $9,851,321 |
| Multifamily residence | 939,036 |
| Nonfarm, nonresidential | 2,294,141 |
| Farm | 183,000 |
| **Total** | **$13,267,498** |
| **By Type of Holder** | |
| Major financial institutions | $4,421,126 |
| Federal and related agencies | 4,977,000 |
| Mortgage pools and trusts | 2,907,125 |
| Individuals and others | 962,247 |
| **Total** | **$13,267,498** |

Source: www.federalreserve.gov/econresdata/releases/mortoutstand/current.htm

The loans originated by the primary market lenders are then packaged and sold to the secondary market, which includes the following:

- Fannie Mae
- Freddie Mac
- Ginnie Mae
- Federal Home Loan Bank
- Private investors

The scope of the mortgage lending activities of various sources of funds is shown in Figure 1.2.

The total amount of mortgage loans outstanding at the end of Q1 2014 was more than $13 trillion, down from a total of $14 trillion in 2009. Notice that almost 75% of all loans are made for one- to four-family residential properties, a dramatic testimony to the importance of housing in the real estate market.

The price of real estate fluctuates over time, depending on changing market conditions. Most buyers do not have the cash required for real estate purchases. They must borrow to complete their acquisitions. If the sources for these loans were to be limited to any large extent, fewer properties would be developed and fewer would be sold. Shortages of funds for mortgage lending affect every level of the construction industry, with serious ramifications throughout the total national economy.

## Interest Rates

In the late-1980s, interest rates on real estate loans were at double-digit levels, as shown in Figure 1.3. This effectively eliminated a major portion of the participants in the real estate market. To meet this emergency, a broad range of creative financing arrangements were

*FIGURE 1.3* **30-Year Fixed-Rate Mortgage Interest Rates**

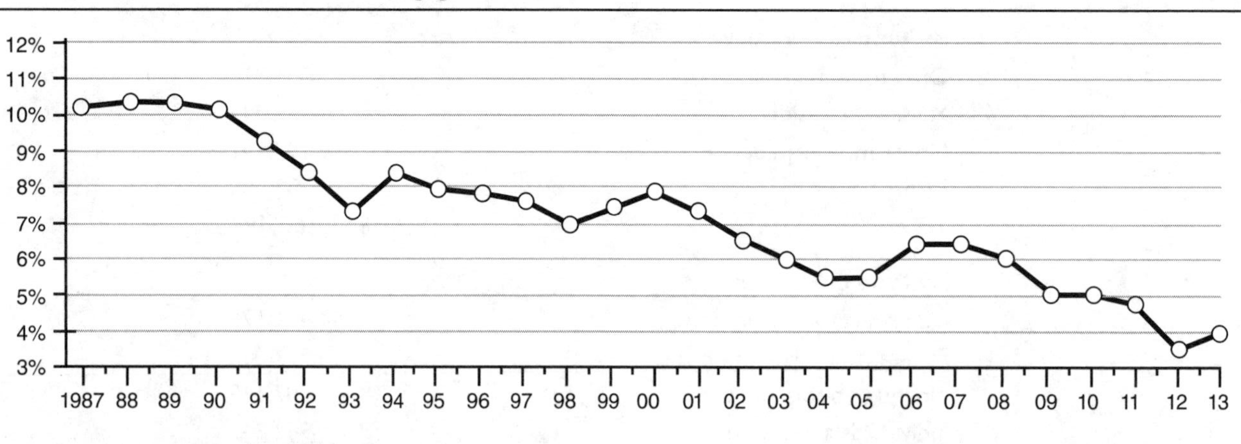


Source: www.freddiemac.com

invented to allow market continuity. These arrangements included partnerships between lenders and borrowers (called participation financing, which is used mostly in commercial real estate), variable-interest-rate loans, and variable-payment loans, all designed to relieve borrowers' burdens and permit lenders to stay in business. As the decade progressed, interest rates fell almost as rapidly as they had risen, and the demand for basic fixed-rate mortgages returned. This reduction in interest rates, to between 6 and 8%, resulted in a sharply increased demand for mortgage refinancing, and the focus of the lenders shifted from loans for purchasing property to loans for refinancing existing high-interest adjustable-rate and fixed-rate loans. In addition, relatively low interest rates fueled a sharp rise in real estate activity. As interest rates continue to drop in the second decade of the 2000s and there are more loan modifications with these lower interest rates, lenders were once again swamped with refinancing requests. Midway through 2014, the average interest rate for a fixed-rate, 30-year mortgage is slightly over 4%.

## Financial Crisis

In the late 1990s and early 2000s, the **subprime market** more than doubled offering higher qualifying ratios, hybrid ARMs with artificially low initial payment schedules, and more liberal qualifying standards. Fannie Mae and Freddie Mac conforming loans also became available in many different forms using liberal qualifying standards and long-term risky loan products.

As the overall housing market boom began to decline in 2006, the subprime market was the first to crash, but by 2007, Fannie Mae and Freddie Mac were also in trouble. Borrowers found themselves unable to pay their sharply increased mortgage payments as adjustable-rate mortgages began to reset at higher rates. Refinancing was no longer an option because housing values were declining, and the slow market made it very difficult to sell. By 2007, more than 1% of all households were facing foreclosure, with projections of at least 3% by 2010. A Mortgage Bankers Association survey in August 2008 showed 9.2% of all U.S. mortgages were either delinquent or in foreclosure. By September 2009, this had risen to 14.4%. On a more optimistic note, in April 2010, RealtyTrac® reported a 2% drop in foreclosures from the previous year, the first annual decline in five years.

The decline continued in 2011 but was mainly attributed to the slowdown in the way many lenders handled foreclosure documentation after being criticized for taking shortcuts such as **robo-signing** (in which a bank official signs thousands of documents without verifying the information). As the banks began to move past these problems, the rate of foreclosures began to once again increase. According to financial analysts from CoreLogic, as of June 30, 2011, 22.5% of U.S. homeowners were "underwater" (i.e., they owed more than their house was worth) on their mortgage. The U.S. Foreclosure Market Report, published by RealtyTrac®, showed that one in every 213 U.S. housing units had a foreclosure filing in the third quarter of 2011.

The National Association of REALTORS® forecast for 2013 showed that the **shadow inventory** (i.e., houses that were delinquent or in foreclosure) represented about one-third of the market in 2010 and 2011. This number dropped to around 25% in 2012 and was projected to fall to single digits by 2014. In the January 10, 2014, issue of *REALTOR® Magazine*, Mark Fleming, the CEO of CoreLogic, was quoted as saying that the shadow inventory, which is also referred to as the "pending supply," had fallen to its lowest level since August 2008, down 24% from the previous year.

The National Mortgage Settlement, announced in February 2012, is believed to have played a major role in the drop in the number of foreclosures. This was a joint state/federal settlement with five of the largest mortgage servicers in the country: Ally/GMAC, Bank of America, CitiMortgage, JPMorgan Chase, and Wells Fargo. The settlement, which provided nearly $25 billion in relief to distressed borrowers and direct payments to states and the federal government, was the largest multi-state settlement since the tobacco settlement in 1998.

Another major factor in the reduction of foreclosures was the growing acceptance by lenders of short sales. After careful analysis, many lenders realized that accepting a determined loss from a **short sale**, in which the lender accepts less than the actual payment due, could result in a lesser amount of loss than carrying the property through foreclosure with limited prospects for resale.

## Plans for Stimulus to the Ailing U.S. Economy

On February 17, 2009, President Obama signed into law the **American Recovery and Reinvestment Act of 2009 (ARRA)**, which is also called the Stimulus Bill. Important components of the act included federal tax cuts, expansion of unemployment benefits, other social welfare provisions, and domestic spending in education, health care, and infrastructure. Some of the credits and provisions of the act that were due to expire at the end of 2010 were extended by the Tax Relief and Job Creation Act of 2010 and again later by the American Taxpayer Relief Act of 2012.

On February 18, 2009, President Obama announced his Homeowner Affordability and Stability Plan, which included the Making Home Affordable (MHA) program. The MHA program offered assistance to seven to nine million homeowners making a good-faith effort to make their mortgage payments through loan modification or refinancing. The **Home Affordable Modification Program (HAMP)** is a key component of the MHA initiative and has been extended through 2015.

The original HAMP actions taken included

- expanding the Fannie Mae, Freddie Mac, and FHA loans limits up to $729,750;
- launching a $23.5 billion Housing Finance Agencies initiative to help state and local housing finance agencies;
- supporting the First-Time Homebuyer Tax Credit; and
- providing over $5 billion in support for affordable rental housing through low-income housing tax credit programs and $2 billion in additional support for the Neighborhood Stabilization Program (NSP) to restore neighborhoods hardest hit by concentrated foreclosures.

On February 19, 2010, the government announced the $1.5 billion Hardest-Hit Fund for state housing financing agencies (HFAs) in the nation's hardest-hit housing markets ($600 million more were added on March 29, 2010, for an additional five HFAs).

In April 2010, enhancements were made to HAMP. The program modifications expanded flexibility for mortgage servicers and originators to assist more unemployed homeowners and those who owe more on their mortgage than the home is worth because of large declines in home values in their local market. This second chance was anticipated to help three to four million struggling homeowners in 2012. The **Home Affordable Refinance Program (HARP)** provides refinancing assistance for some homeowners who are not eligible for HAMP. This program has been extended to December 31, 2015.

In July 2010, President Obama signed into law the **Wall Street Reform and Consumer Protection Act (Dodd-Frank Act)**. This lengthy piece of legislation contains many provisions that are anticipated to restore responsibility and accountability to the financial system. Title III of the act abolished the Office of Thrift Supervision, transferring its power of holding companies to the Federal Reserve, state savings associations to the FDIC, and other thrifts to the Office of the Comptroller of the Currency. The amount of deposits insured by the FDIC and the National Credit Union Share Insurance Fund was permanently increased to $250,000.

Title X of the act established the Bureau of Consumer Financial Protection, also called the **Consumer Financial Protection Bureau (CFPB)**. The CFPB is housed within the Federal Reserve but operates independently. Its mission is to set rules and regulations for any business that provides financial services for consumers. The CFPB will be discussed in more detail in Chapter 3.

For more information on the Dodd-Frank law, see http://banking.senate.gov/public/.

## Local Markets

Real estate is a local market in that it is fixed in place. It is impossible to move a parcel of land. As a result, any activities are done to and on the property. A building is constructed on the lot. Utilities are brought to the property and taxes are imposed on it. A real estate loan is made on a property, usually by a local lender or the local representative of a national lender.

The activities of the local real estate market, especially as they influence property values, are vital to the activities of the local real estate lenders. Regional, national, and international economic and political events have an indirect effect on specific real property values. However, the immediate impact of local activities on individual properties most directly affects their value.

For example, police power decisions involving zoning regulations can dramatically raise individual property values, while just as dramatically lowering neighborhood property values. Political decisions concerned with community growth or no-growth policies, pollution controls, building standards, and the preservation of coastline and wildlife habitats can significantly alter a community's economic balance and property values.

In times of economic distress, as evidenced by high interest rates and/or unemployment, local financial institutions decrease their mortgage-lending activities. This decrease adds to the downward cycle. In good times, their lending activities increase to serve the growing demand.

### National Markets

When the demand for mortgage money is great, local lenders may deplete available funds. In an economic slump, these lenders may not have any safe outlets for their excess funds. A national mortgage market was developed to balance these trends.

Fannie Mae, Freddie Mac, and Ginnie Mae are the major participants in a viable national market for real estate mortgages. They, and other groups of investors, are collectively known as the **secondary market**. Loans created by local lenders, thrifts, banks, mortgage bankers, and others, known as the **primary market**, are purchased by these "second" owners who, in turn, often package these loans into mortgage pools. Proportionate ownership of these mortgage pools is then sold to investors in the form of securities called **mortgage-backed securities (MBSs)**.

In this manner, the secondary mortgage market participants act to stabilize the real estate market by shifting funds from capital-excess areas to capital-deficient areas. Although they were originally designed to provide safe investments for the purchasers of their securities, recently this has not necessarily been the case. The purchase of packages of "junk" loans that did not provide a safe investment was a major contributing factor to the economic crisis that started in 2007.

## REAL ESTATE CYCLES

The ups and downs of real estate activities are described as **real estate cycles**. The word *cycle* implies the recurrence of events in a somewhat regular pattern. By studying past real estate market activities, researchers can develop prognoses for future investment plans.

### Supply and Demand

Real estate cycles are affected by many variables, all of which, either directly or indirectly, are influenced by the economic forces of supply and demand. Real estate cycles can be short term or long term. In the short-term cycle, the general business conditions that produce the earnings needed to create an effective demand usually trigger the real estate market's activity. In a growth area where business is good and demand is higher than the available supply of real estate, the prices of properties available for sale increase. This active demand generally encourages more building, and the supply of real estate tends to increase until there is a surplus. When the supply exceeds the demand, prices decrease. Any new construction becomes economically unsound. The cycle repeats itself as soon as the demand again exceeds the supply.

## In Practice

An elderly couple lives in a small town. They have decided to sell their home of 34 years and move to a retirement community. Unfortunately, the local factory, the only real business in town, recently closed its doors, putting 300 people out of work. Most of the families who worked there have to relocate as there are no jobs available in the immediate area, even at lower salaries.

Even though the couple isn't directly affected by the factory shutdown, they will suffer the effects of a declining real estate cycle. Their home is now one of many on the market at a time when there are very few potential buyers. The price they will be able to get for their property today is much less than they could have expected a year ago.

Another variable affecting the short-term real estate cycle is the supply of money for financing. Tight money circumstances develop when competitive drains on the money supply occur or the Fed takes certain actions to restrict the supply of money. The two largest competitors for savings are the federal government, with its gargantuan budgetary commitments, and industry, which taps the money markets to finance additional inventory or plant expansion. Any continuing deficits in its budget force the government into the borrowing market, reducing funds available for real estate finance.

In the short term, the market responds to current economic conditions, while in the long term, the time variables associated with real estate development prevail. It takes time to put a real estate project on the ground. From the creation of the idea to the acquisition of the land; through its possible rezoning, engineering, and preparation; during its construction, promotion, and sales, years sometimes pass. During this interval, the markets are fluctuating, and the developer may not achieve the anticipated profit.

Short-term real estate cycles generally run from three to five years. In the long term, they generally run from 10 to 15 years. The ability to examine the causes of the cycles and to forecast their movements in order to anticipate the markets is important to a real estate investor's success.

### Population Characteristics

An important factor involved in making real estate development decisions is the makeup of this country's population and how it changes over time. Both financial investors in commercial real estate and real estate professionals in the residential market need to be aware of changing demographics in their local area in order to provide a solid basis for marketing planning. Census information continues to show that the majority of U.S. households live in officially designated metropolitan areas, and mostly in the suburbs.

The number of homeowner households has remained steady since 2007 in the range of 75 million. Single-person households now account for over one-third of the market. The number of rental households increased from 35 million in 2007 to nearly 40 million in 2012. This increase is attributed to two factors: (1) the number of households in foreclosure has forced many into renting, and (2) tightened qualifying standards have made it more difficult to obtain a home mortgage loan. Ironically, the national Housing Affordability Index (a measure of how many households with median income can afford a house of median price) reached an all-time high in 2012; however, the tighter lending standards still made it very difficult to obtain a loan.

Harvard's *State of the Nation's Housing Report 2013* anticipates that in 2015, minorities will make up 36% of U.S. households with 46% in the 25–34 age group. This group represents half of first-time homebuyers. The demographic distribution shows a slight drop in ownership by white persons, with minimal change in ownership by African-Americans, and an increase in ownership by Hispanics and Asian-Americans. The Harvard report estimates growth in the decade of 2015–2025 of between 11 and 13 million, depending on immigration. This would be in line with the annual averages from the 1980s, 1990s, and 2000s.

## Who Is Buying What

The U.S. Census Bureau description of a median home has enlarged slightly over the last decade and now consists of more than 1,800 square feet (2,200 for new construction) with five or six rooms, three of which are bedrooms. About half have two or more bathrooms. Two-thirds of these households have no children younger than 18. About 30 million persons live alone. The median house value in 2012 was $181,400. Median household income was $53,046.

According to the 2013 Census estimate, the population of the United States is 316,128,839. (The census.gov website keeps a daily tally that shows the population as of September 14, 2014, as 318,875,946.) This represents around a 10% increase since 2000. The 2013 population is 50.8% female and 49.2% male, with the rate of growth faster in the older age groups. The median age increased from 35.3 in 2000 to 37.2 in 2010. Maine and Vermont have the highest median age, surpassing the leaders in 2000, which were West Virginia and Florida. Utah remained the state with the lowest median age of 29.2.

A 2004 interim report published by the U.S. Census Bureau projected a new total population in 2050 of 419.854 million, distributed as shown in Figure 1.4. These numbers may all be less, however, as a result of a potential drop in the number of persons immigrating in the next four decades.

Minorities are still expected to make up one-third of the U.S. population by 2016 and were originally expected to account for more than two-thirds of the net increase in households between 2010 and 2020. However, the economic crisis created a decline in the national homeownership rate from a high of 69% in 2004 to 65% in 2014 and also impacted the number of new immigration households. The total number of foreign-born households, which continuously increased in the past, actually started to decline in 2007.

*FIGURE 1.4* **Projected U.S. Population in 2050**

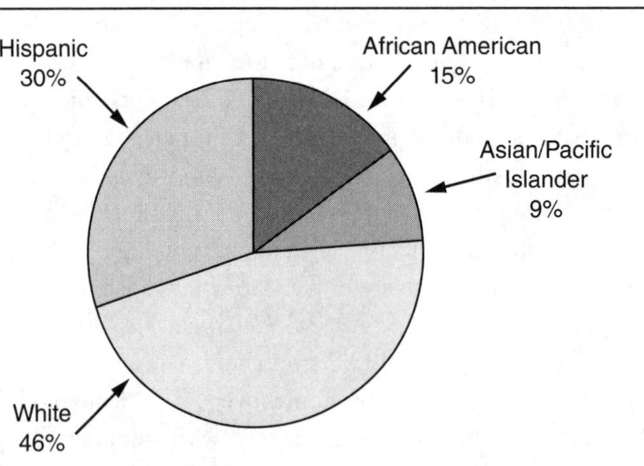


Source: U.S. Census Bureau

## An Aging Population

Our population is also aging. The 78 million **baby boomers** born between 1946 and 1964 are creating a middle-aged bulge in population demographics. Unlike the previous generation, boomers are living longer and healthier lives and many continue to work at least part time past the typical retirement age due to the erosion of retirement savings and the loss of acquired home equity. This generation tends to "age in place" and may look to make improvements or modifications in order to remain in their present home or to demand more services and amenities designed for senior citizens in one of the many independent or assisted living options. Harvard's *State of the Nation's Housing Report 2013* indicates that the number of households over age 65 will increase by 10.7 million by 2025.

The next age group, those born between 1965 and 1979 and often called **Generation X**, tend to marry later, have a higher divorce rate, and a lower remarriage rate, making the single-person household the fastest-growing household type. According to the Harvard study, persons living alone are expected to account for 36% of household growth between 2010 and 2020.

Then there are the **echo boomers**, those born in the 1980s and early 1990s. There are five million more of them than their parents' generation. They should be just entering their most productive buying years but are inhibited by current economic conditions, and a large percentage of them continue, or have returned, to live at home. In general, they tend to be interested in green and environmentally friendly types of housing.

The Census Bureau shows our population divided as follows:

- Married couple household: 51.7%
- Two or more people, nonfamily: 6.1%

- Female householder, other family: 12.2%
- Male householder, other family: 4.2%
- Single householder, nonfamily: 25.8%

## Social Attitudes

Changing social attitudes also influence real estate cycles. Historically, fast growth was the goal of many U.S. communities, and some still favor this approach today. Local governments often offer concessions to induce industry to move to their towns. Nevertheless, many communities promote an attitude of planned growth, legally limiting new construction activities to satisfy voters' demands.

Throughout the United States, many communities are striving for smart growth, with proper planning a prerequisite for allowing new development. A no-growth policy leads to a downturn in the economy, but rampant overgrowth leaves communities lacking in schools, police and fire protection, and adequate transportation. There is also a growing concern today for energy conservation and other environmental issues.

## Tax Issues

The constantly changing federal income tax structure also affects real estate cycles. In 1986, Congress imposed dramatic restrictions on the use of excess losses from real estate investments to shelter other income under the Tax Reform Act of 1986 (TRA '86). Special treatment for capital gains and excessive depreciation deductions were also introduced.

Effective May 7, 1997, Congress again fine-tuned the income tax laws by passing the **Taxpayer Relief Act of 1997 (TRA '97)**, providing homeowners with broad exemptions from capital gains taxes on profits made from the sale of personal residences. Replacing the one-time exemption of $125,000 for sellers older than age 55, TRA '97 exempts up to $500,000 of profits from taxes for a married couple filing jointly (or up to $250,000 for a single person) who have lived in the property as a primary residence for more than two years in the five years previous to the sale.

TRA '97 eliminated the necessity to purchase another residence at a price equal to or higher than that of sold property. It also eliminated keeping records of repairs, additions, or other changes to the sold property's tax basis unless the gain from the sale exceeds the exemptions. These tax benefits may be taken every two years, and Internal Revenue Service (IRS) regulations now stipulate that if the property meets the entire exclusion, the transaction need not be reported at all.

Investors in real estate received additional benefits from TRA '97. The long-term maximum capital gains tax rate was reduced to 15% (5% for investors in the 10% and 15% income brackets). The depreciation recapture tax on the amount that has been depreciated over the years is charged at 25%. Note that the property must be held a minimum of 12 months. In 2001, this rate dropped to 18% (8% for those in the 15% tax bracket) for assets acquired after January 2001 and held for five years or longer.

The reduced 15% tax rate on qualified dividends and long-term capital gains was scheduled to expire in 2008 but was extended through 2010 and again through 2012. From 2008 to 2012, the tax rate was 0% for those in the 10% and 15% tax brackets.

Since 2012, dividends are taxed at the taxpayer's ordinary income tax rate, and the long-term capital gains tax rate is 20% (10% for those in the 15% tax bracket). Also after 2012, the qualified five-year 18% capital gains rate (8% for taxpayers in the 15% tax bracket) was reinstated.

The **Mortgage Forgiveness Debt Relief Act of 2007** provided a benefit for homeowners who had lost a home to foreclosure. In the past, the IRS counted any write-off amount on a loan as taxable income to the borrower. Under this act, any income realized as a result of modification of the terms of the mortgage such as recasting of the loan for a lesser amount, or as a result of foreclosure on a principal residence, was not counted as income. The act was extended through the end of 2013.

## American Taxpayer Relief Act of 2012

The **American Taxpayer Relief Act of 2012 (ATRA)** was signed into law on January 2, 2013. The bill extended the mortgage debt cancellation relief that had been granted under the Mortgage Forgiveness Debt Relief Act of 2007 through 2013. The act also extended the deduction for mortgage insurance premiums for tax filers making less than $110,000. Both of these extensions expired January 1, 2014, and remain in congressional limbo. It has been suggested that the slight drop in the number of short sales in 2014 may be due to the uncertainty over the debt relief. Another extension awaiting further action is the 10% tax credit, up to $500, for homeowners making energy efficient improvements to an existing home.

Current tax rates were extended for households earning less than $450,000 or $400,000 for individual filers. For households earning more than these limits, tax rates reverted to 2003 numbers, resulting in taxpayers in the highest income bracket paying at a rate of 39.5%, up from 35%.

The tax rate on capital gains remains the same, at 15%, for most households, with an increase to 20% for the higher income bracket. The exclusion from taxes for gains on a principal residence remains the same unless the sellers are in the higher income bracket.

A key change in estate tax is the requirement that estates be taxed at a top rate of 40%, with the first $5 million in value exempted for individual estates and $10 million for family estates.

For more information, see the IRS website at www.irs.gov.

## Property Value Fluctuations

Although some properties display a character of their own and run counter to prevailing trends, most properties are carried along in a cyclical action. Generally, in the long run, most real property values rise. In the short run, property values rise and fall.

In the past, the stabilizing influences of Fannie Mae, Freddie Mac, and Ginnie Mae calmed some of the volatile short-term reactions of localized booms and busts. At the same time, the financial management policies of the Federal Reserve and the U.S. Treasury largely soothed long-term reactions to these cycles. These latter federal government agencies were expected to control the supply of money in circulation. The financial crisis that began in 2007 challenged every aspect of mortgage financing, from the federal government to the local bank on the corner.

Traditional real estate cycles can be moderated by better market information and by increasing openness about real estate dealings, financing, and new construction. The following four key groups are largely responsible for providing this important market information:

- Bond analysts and rating agencies submit highly detailed information to investors who participate in mortgage-backed securities.
- Real estate investment trust (REIT) analysts provide full disclosure of the data in the field that now controls a substantial percentage of the commercial real estate market.
- Bank and insurance analysts publish essential underwriting market data.
- Information providers on the internet act as important sources of the vast amount of data available.

## IMPACT OF THE FINANCIAL CRISIS

After years of spectacular growth in the single-family housing market with concomitant increases in property values, the housing market boom came to an abrupt halt in mid-2008. Upon the discovery that lenders all over the country had issued thousands of subprime loans to unqualified borrowers on properties with super-inflated values, the financial markets froze and stopped making loans.

Even Fannie Mae and Freddie Mac were caught up in the lending disaster, having purchased thousands of "worthless" loans that they bundled and sold to international investors. The federal government stepped in to rescue these government-sponsored enterprises from bankruptcy, confiscating their assets and firing managers.

Now in conservatorship under the Federal Housing Finance Agency (FHFA), Fannie Mae and Freddie Mac have reinstated their basic standards, which real estate lenders must carefully observe if they wish to sell their new loans to these secondary market operators. The tighter qualifying standards have driven many potential borrowers to government-owned or guaranteed loans. FHA became the primary lender for low down payment loans, accounting for 80% of the market in 2012. USDA Section 502 guarantees for homes in rural areas also increased significantly. In 2014, a new cycle may be starting as more private investment returns to the real estate financing market. The percentage of conventional loans sold to Fannie Mae and Freddie Mac continues to rise, and the percentage of FHA loans is decreasing slightly. Discussion continues on the future of Fannie Mae and Freddie Mac, but the FHFA expects business as usual for at least a few more years.

## SUMMARY

Millions of persons are involved in some form of activity related to real estate. When flourishing, the construction industry directly employs millions of people. Innumerable additional workers are engaged in providing this industry its materials and peripheral services.

Most real estate activities are financed. Monies accumulated by thrifts, banks, life insurance companies, pension funds, and other formal financial intermediaries are loaned to builders and developers to finance their projects. Other loans are made to buyers of already existing structures, providing the financial institutions a continuing opportunity for investments of their entrusted funds. These investments produce returns and new funds available for loans to stimulate additional growth.

These financing activities are based on the simple premise of real estate being pledged as collateral to guarantee the repayment of a loan. An owner of a property borrows money from a lender and executes a promise to repay this loan under agreed-upon terms and conditions. The real estate is pledged as collateral to back up this promise. The borrower continues to be able to possess and use the collateral real estate during the term of the loan. The ability to maintain control of the property while borrowing against it is called hypothecation. It is also a manifestation of leverage, by which a small amount of money can provide the means for securing a large loan for the purchase of property. If the promise to repay the loan is broken, the lender can acquire the collateral and sell it to recover the investment.

Generally, the majority of loans on real estate are made by local financing institutions, using deposits accumulated by persons in the community. However, a national market for real estate finance operates under the auspices of Fannie Mae, Freddie Mac, Ginnie Mae, the Federal Home Loan Bank, and private investors. These agencies provide a secondary market for buying and selling mortgages on a national level.

The overall cycle of real estate economics and finance is modified by the forces of supply and demand. Excess demand normally leads to increased production until excess supply reverses the cycle. Mirroring these forces of supply and demand is the availability of money for financing at reasonable costs. Other variables that affect real estate cycles include population changes in terms of numbers, age, and social attitudes; changes in political attitudes governing community growth policies; and changes in the federal income tax structure.

Complementing the secondary market activities that balance national level mortgage loan funding sources are the much broader controls exercised by the Federal Reserve (the Fed) and the U.S. Treasury. By controlling the amounts of money in circulation and the cost of securing mortgage funds, these agencies attempt to balance the fluctuations of the national money market.

The general decline in the housing market in 2006 started the domino effect of people unable to sell or refinance their homes and going into foreclosure. Purchases of packages of "junk" loans led to further financial collapse on the secondary market. Hopefully, the housing market will be able to lead the road to economic recovery over the next decade.

## INTERNET RESOURCES

Fannie Mae
*www.fanniemae.com*

Federal Housing Finance Agency
*www.fhfa.gov*

Freddie Mac
*www.freddiemac.com*

Ginnie Mae
*www.ginniemae.gov*

Joint Center for Housing Studies of Harvard University
*www.jchs.harvard.edu*

Internal Revenue Service
*www.irs.gov*

RealtyTrac®
*www.realtytrac.com*

U.S. Census Bureau
*www.census.gov*

## REVIEW QUESTIONS

1. This country's economic well-being would be substantially affected by a slowdown in which industry?
   a. Farm
   b. Steel
   c. Construction
   d. Garment

2. A financial institution experiencing disintermediation is *BEST* described as
   a. a form of dispute resolution.
   b. more funds being withdrawn than deposited.
   c. an involuntary stock takeover.
   d. an excess of subprime loans.

3. A situation where the borrower retains possession of the property while the lender has a security interest is called
   a. disintermediation.
   b. collateral.
   c. hypothecation.
   d. leverage.

4. A buyer makes a very small down payment and borrows the balance needed to purchase real property. This is called using
   a. leverage.
   b. collateral.
   c. hypothecation.
   d. equitable title.

5. The largest holder of mortgage loan debt for one- to four-family units are
   a. major financial institutions.
   b. mortgage pools and trusts.
   c. individuals and others.
   d. federal and related agencies.

6. Which activity would have the *MOST* effect on property values in a moderately sized Midwestern city?
   a. Crash of the Japanese stock market
   b. Decline in the NASDAQ stock exchange
   c. Closing of the largest factory in the city
   d. Extensive hurricane damage in the South

7. According to the U.S. Census Bureau, the largest percentage of households today are
   a. married couples.
   b. female heads of household.
   c. two unrelated persons.
   d. single people.

8. A city is experiencing 28% growth in population this year as a result of three new industries moving into the area. Based on supply and demand, this population growth will probably lead to
   a. a decline in home prices.
   b. an increase in home prices.
   c. an increase in property taxes.
   d. a decrease in property taxes.

9. The population demographics of the United States are changing in all categories *EXCEPT*
   a. an increase in Asian and Hispanic households.
   b. baby boomers reaching middle age.
   c. an increase in number of elderly households.
   d. a higher birth rate.

10. In order to qualify for the $500,000 exemption from capital gains tax on the sale of their home, a couple must have
    a. lived there the two years prior to selling.
    b. lived there an aggregate of two years out of the past five years.
    c. lived there two years plus be at least 55 years old.
    d. never used the residence as a rental property.

Chapter 2

# Money and the Monetary System

## LEARNING OBJECTIVES

When you've finished reading this chapter, you will be able to

- describe the activities of the Federal Reserve System;
- explain the role of the U.S. Department of the Treasury as the nation's fiscal manager;
- discuss the role of the Federal Home Loan Bank System (FHLB); and
- outline the responsibilities of the Federal Deposit Insurance Corporation (FDIC).

**annual percentage rate (APR)**
**commercial paper**
**discount rate**
**Federal Deposit Insurance Corporation (FDIC)**
**federal funds rate**
**M1, M2, M3**
**open-market operations**
**prime rate**
**quantitative easing (QE)**
**Regulation Z**
**reserve requirements**
**securities**
**Treasury bonds**
**Treasury bills**
**Treasury notes**
**Troubled Asset Relief Program (TARP)**
**Truth in Lending Act (TILA)**

An understanding of mortgage lending requires knowledge of how the mortgage market functions within our monetary system. The federal government is deeply involved in our financial systems, beginning with the creation and distribution of money. The government also provides a number of regulatory agencies to supervise the actions of financial institutions and their representatives to insure and protect a multitude of depositors. The federal participants in the monetary system, which control to a great degree the activities in the real estate financial markets, are the Federal Reserve (the Fed), the U.S. Treasury, and the Federal Home Loan Bank (FHLB) System. These agencies will be reviewed in this chapter, as will the **Federal Deposit Insurance Corporation (FDIC)**.

## WHAT IS MONEY?

### Definition

Money allows us to convert our physical and mental efforts into a convenient method of exchange. Thus, we can define money as

- a medium of exchange or means of payment,
- a storehouse of purchasing power, and/or
- a standard of value.

In primitive societies, money is anything that is generally accepted as a means of exchange, such as beads, salt, shells, and so on. Money can also be represented by coins, bills, or checks, which are currently our convenient, acceptable, representative means for exchanging value.

Today's system of money is based on confidence. As long as the public can exchange symbolic paper money for commodities of like value, the system works. When that confidence is shaken, as in countries suffering economic or political turmoil, the ability of money to command commodities of like value diminishes.

Most people strive to acquire money for the goods and services it can purchase. Our efforts to acquire money are related directly to satisfying our need for food, clothing, and shelter. After we have acquired these essentials, we strive to accumulate money to satisfy our need for additional security, pleasure, or power, depending on individual motivations.

### The Supply and Costs of Money

Economic stability is linked directly to the supply of money and the cost of money. As shown in Figure 2.1, the larger the supply of money in circulation, the greater the economic activity. When the economy is infused with more spendable cash, the possibility for an increase in spending activity is enhanced. Increased spending requires increased production to replenish depleted inventories. With increased production come more jobs; more people are employed and are spending money.

*FIGURE 2.1* **The Supply of Money and Economic Activity**

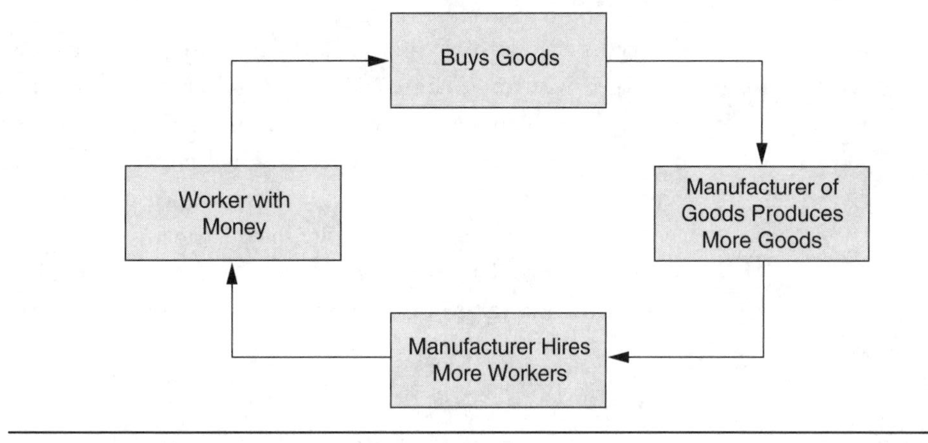


If this economic cycle is true, then the reverse condition, the withdrawal of funds from circulation, should result in a slowdown of economic activity.

The three measures of the total money supply are known as the monetary aggregates of M1, M2, and M3. The M stands for money, and the numbers represent increasing levels of liquidity.

- **M1** is money easily obtainable: cash in public hands, private checking accounts at commercial banks, credit union share accounts, and demand deposits at thrift institutions. (The amount of money held by the Federal Reserve is subtracted from this amount.)
- **M2** is assets less liquid: all of M1 plus money market funds (except those in IRAs or Keogh accounts), retirement accounts, and deposits of less than $100,000.
- **M3** is assets even less liquid: all of M2 plus deposits over $100,000, money held in banks abroad, institutional money market funds (including pension fund deposits), and deposits with non-bank institutions. (The Federal Reserve no longer makes data on M3 available to the public.)

Considering the cost of money in terms of the interest charged for borrowed funds, it would appear that the higher the cost, the lower the borrowing activity and the slower the economic activity. The reverse situation, the lowering of interest rates, should raise the demand for borrowed funds and produce increased economic activity.

Theoretically, then, manipulations of the supply and cost of money should result in economic balance. The reality is that a balanced economy is largely shaped by the federal agencies empowered to control the supply and cost of money (e.g., the Federal Reserve System, the U.S. Treasury, and the Federal Home Loan Bank System). Although their efforts at balancing the national economy are not always successful, resulting in part from time lags and consumer resistance, these agencies have a profound effect on national real estate finance.

# THE FEDERAL RESERVE SYSTEM (THE FED)

The Federal Reserve System (the Fed) is this nation's monetary manager. The Fed is charged with the maintenance of sound credit conditions to help counteract inflationary and deflationary movements. It also has a role in creating conditions favorable to high employment, stable values, internal growth of the nation, and rising levels of consumption. The Fed keeps the public informed of its activities through its website at www.federalreserve.gov. The website includes many topics, such as a survey of consumer finances, statistical releases on a variety of subjects including household finance, and reports from meetings of the Federal Advisory Council and Board of Governors.

## Purpose

The Fed was established in 1913 when President Woodrow Wilson signed the Federal Reserve Act. This act's original purpose was to establish facilities for selling or discounting commercial paper and to improve the supervision of banking activities. Its full impact on our monetary system has broadened over time to include influence over the availability and cost of money and credit (interest rates).

As the central bank of the United States, the Fed attempts to ensure that money and credit growth over the long run is sufficient to provide a rising standard of living for all U.S. citizens. In the short run, the Fed seeks to adapt its policies in an effort to combat deflationary or inflationary pressures; as a lender of last resort, it has the responsibility of using policy instruments available to it in an attempt to forestall national liquidity crises and financial panics.

In response to the financial crisis that emerged in the summer of 2007, the Fed used special programs designed to address severe liquidity strains in key financial markets, to provide credit to troubled important institutions, and to lower longer-term interest rates. An important first step was the lowering of the target federal funds rate from 5¼% to effectively zero. On September 13, 2012, the Fed announced that it would keep that rate at zero until 2015 and below 2% into 2016. Other programs were initiated to support the liquidity of financial institutions and to create improved conditions in financial markets. The Fed expanded its traditional tool of open market operations by purchasing long-term securities, such as agency-guaranteed, mortgage-backed securities (MBS) and long-term (10-year) Treasury notes. This program was referred to as **quantitative easing (QE)** and was planned to continue until unemployment fell below 6.5% or inflation rose above 2.5%. From 2008 to 2011, the Fed spent more than $2 trillion in the purchase of bank and government debt. It also committed to trillions more in insuring and loaning money to banks for money market funds and to purchase commercial paper. By mid-2014, the goals of the QE program were close to being realized. On October 29, 2014, the Fed announced it would no longer purchase bonds and ended the program. As long as the bonds already purchased remain with the Fed, the interest rates should remain low.

Under the Dodd-Frank Act that was signed on July 21, 2010, the Fed assumed new regulatory powers. In addition to supervising approximately 3,000 member banks, the Fed is also responsible for approximately 17,000 other depository institutions, including nonmember commercial banks, savings banks, savings and loan associations, and credit unions. Although not formally part of the Federal Reserve System, these institutions are subject to system regulations, including reserve requirements, and they have access to system payment services. The Fed also houses the Consumer Financial Protection Bureau. The act limits the Fed's emergency lending authority by requiring approval from the Secretary of the Treasury for any lending program.

## Organization

The Fed is a central banking system composed of 12 Federal Reserve districts. Each is served by a district Federal Reserve Bank, coordinated and directed by a single seven-member board of governors housed in Washington, DC. These districts and their branch territories are shown in Figure 2.2.

The Federal Reserve banks are not under the control of any governmental agency, but each reserve bank is responsible to a board of directors. Each board is composed of nine members representing their Federal Reserve district. The organization of the Fed is shown in Figure 2.3. Members are drawn from the 12 districts to form three statutory advisory councils that advise the board on matters of current interest: the Federal Advisory Council, the Consumer Advisory Council, and the Thrift Institutions Advisory Council.

*FIGURE 2.2* **The Federal Reserve System (Boundaries of Federal Reserve Districts and Their Branch Territories**

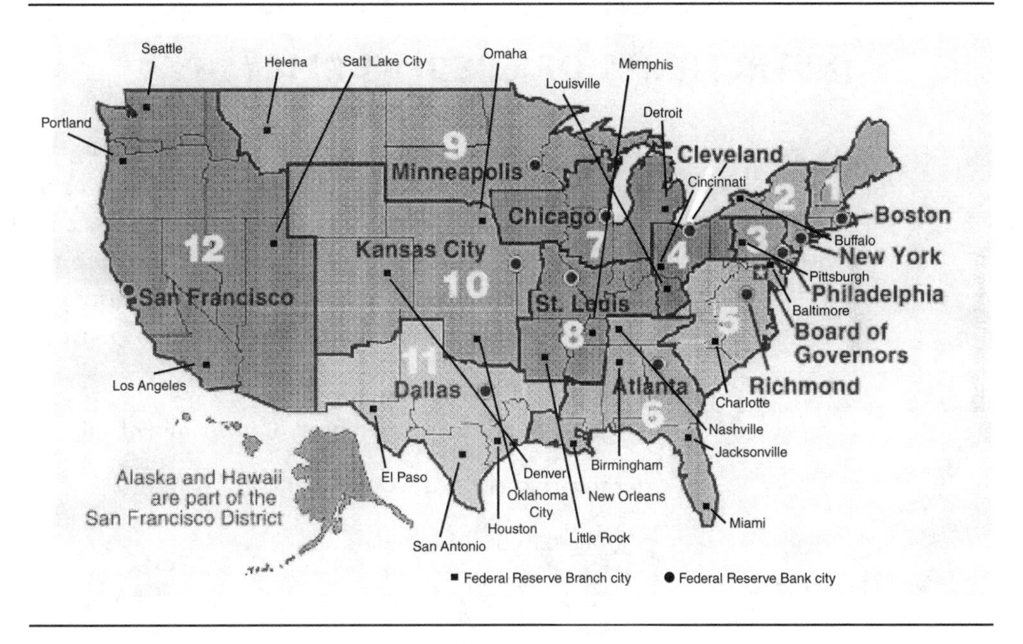


## Member Banks

All nationally chartered commercial banks must join the Fed while state-chartered banks may also become members of the system. Each member bank is required to purchase capital stock in its Federal Reserve district bank to maintain sufficient monetary reserves to meet the Fed's requirements and to clear checks through the system. In addition, they must comply with other rules and regulations imposed by the Fed for governing loans made by member banks and maintaining the stability of our monetary system by insuring

*FIGURE 2.3* **Organization of the Federal Reserve System**

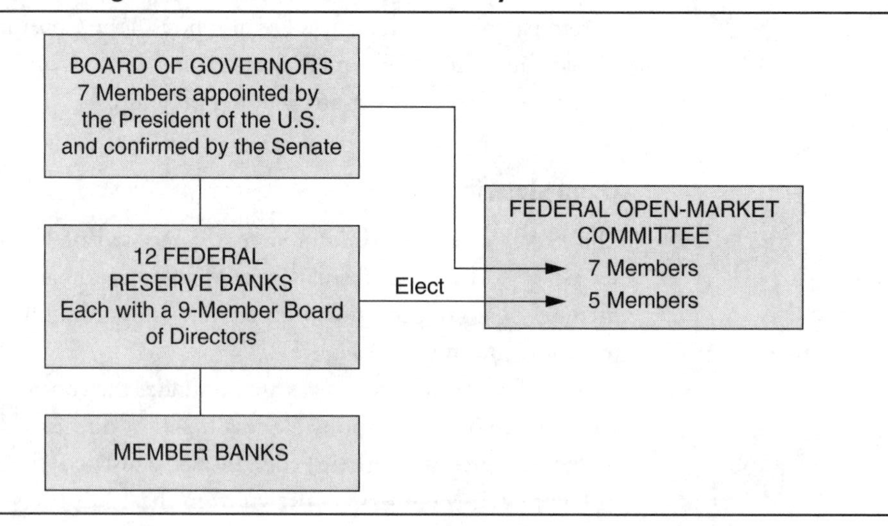


their deposits. Member banks may borrow money from their federal district bank when in need of funds, share in the informational systems available, and generally engage in all banking activities under the protective umbrella of the Fed.

# INSTRUMENTS OF CREDIT POLICY

The Fed has numerous functions, among which are issuing currency in the form of Federal Reserve notes (paper money), supervising and regulating member banks, clearing and collecting their checks, and administering selective credit controls over other segments of the economy. Other functions include acting as the government's fiscal agent in holding the U.S. Treasury's principal checking accounts and assisting in the collection and distribution of income taxes. However, the four functions most closely related to real estate finance are

- the Fed's regulation of the amount of its member banks' reserves,
- determination of the discount rates,
- open-market operations, and
- supervision of the Truth in Lending Act (Regulation Z).

## Reserve Requirements

Each of the Fed's individual member banks is required to keep reserves equal to a specified percentage of the bank's total funds on deposit with its federal district bank. These **reserve requirements** are designed to protect bank depositors by guaranteeing that their funds will be available when they need them. More important, though, is the Fed's ability to manage the national money market by adjusting the amount of reserves required from time to time. By raising the reserve requirement (and thereby limiting the amount of money available to the member banks for making loans), the Fed can frequently cool down a hot money market and slow the economic pace. By lowering the reserve requirements, the Fed can permit more money to enter a sluggish economy. Member banks can retain a larger percentage of their total assets, allowing more money to become available for loans. Managing the reserve requirements is one way the Fed serves its purpose of balancing the national economy.

## In Practice

What would happen if figures were released showing almost a 2% increase in inflation for the quarter plus a sharp drop in unemployment? Although this might seem more like good news than bad news, this combination would be a matter of concern to the Fed. The Fed is responsible for maintaining a stable economy and, ironically, the Fed must be as concerned when things are going too well as when things seem to be slowing down. The Fed must take quick action to prevent a spiraling effect into a run-away economy. If unemployment is low, employment is high. In order to attract good employees from a shrinking pool of job seekers, a company may have to pay higher salaries. In order to pay the higher salaries, the company raises prices. Higher prices lead to inflation.

The Fed has several tools it may use to slow things down, but the most likely one in this situation would be an announcement that the federal discount rate will be increased. The discount rate is the interest charged by the Fed to its member banks. When this rate is increased, even if only by a quarter of a percent, there is usually an immediate reaction in the financial world. A slight "tap on the brakes" by the Fed can slow down the acceleration, heading off more serious problems later. Sometimes just a casual hint from the Fed's chairperson that rates may be going up will achieve the desired effect.

The amounts of reserves vary from 3 to 22% of the member banks' funds, depending on the type of these deposits and the location of the member banks (since 2008, the reserve rate has remained low). For instance, more reserves are required for checking accounts than for savings deposits, reflecting the short-term quality of the former versus the long-term quality of the latter. In addition, more reserves are required from a city bank than a country bank because of the increased banking activities expected from numerous urban depositors as opposed to a smaller number of rural depositors.

### Discount Rates

Commercial banks operate primarily to finance personal property purchases and short-term business needs. The loans they issue are called **commercial paper**. The Fed operates a market for selling this paper at a discount, providing member banks with additional funds for continued lending activity. This is done at the "discount window," which is either open or closed to control the money supply. When the window is open, money is added to the system, and vice versa.

Although discounting commercial paper may appear to have little significance for real estate finance, the process enables members to expand their lending activities. The banks actually borrow funds from their district federal reserve bank and pledge their commer-

*FIGURE 2.4* **Discount and Prime Rates**

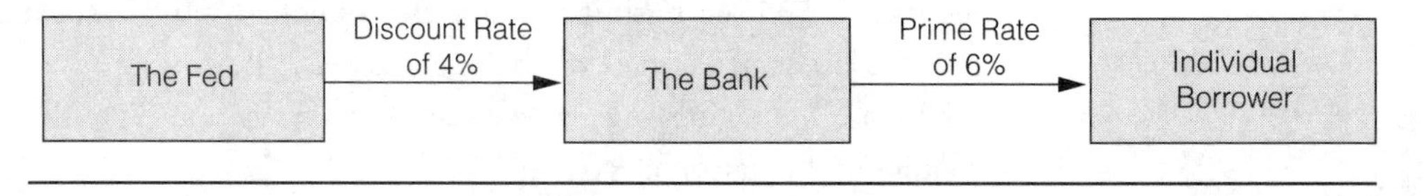


cial paper as collateral. In effect, the Fed charges the borrowing bank interest on its loan, interest that is considered to be the **discount rate**, which can also be interpreted as the cost of borrowed funds to the borrower bank. Thus, the individual bank has a basic or primary interest rate against which it can measure the interest it must charge its borrowers. As illustrated in Figure 2.4, the Fed discount rate is used by many major banks to set their **prime rate**, prime simply meaning the rate a commercial bank charges its most creditworthy customers or its prime customers. Now the implications for real estate finance become clearer. The higher the Fed's discount rate charged to the bank, the higher its prime will be, and, consequently, the higher the rate of interest to the real estate borrower.

In mortgage lending, these discounts establish the base interest charges for short-term mortgage loans. Borrowers, depending on their credit standings, can expect to pay the prime rate or higher, as circumstances dictate. For example, many construction loans are secured from commercial banks at "two points above prime," or 2% above the prime rate. If the prime rate is 6% when the construction loan is made, the interest rate charged under this formula would be 8%. Thus, by adjusting the rate of its discount, the Fed exerts a great deal of control over the amount of money or credit available throughout the system.

When the Fed raises its discount rate, member banks slow their sales of commercial paper and obtain fewer additional funds. Therefore, less credit becomes available at the local level, and, theoretically, the economy is slowed. Of course, the reverse process occurs when the discount rate is lowered. The Fed's discount rate can be found daily in the *Wall Street Journal* and other financial publications.

## Federal Funds Rate

The Fed also lends money to its member banks without requiring any collateral. These loans are usually made for short periods of time, and the rate of interest that is charged to the borrowing banks is known as the **federal funds rate**. It is the rate that banks charge each other for short-term funding, often overnight loans. The banks use this interbank borrowing to meet the Fed's requirements for cash liquidity in the bank's portfolio. The federal funds rate is published daily in financial journals and becomes another benchmark against which the banks can base interest charges to their customers.

## Open-Market Operations

The Fed relies on its **open-market operations** as another important tool to achieve its goal of balancing the economy. These activities involve the purchase or sale of government securities in lots, which consist primarily of U.S. Treasury issues, and also include securities issued by the federally sponsored housing and farm credit agencies, the Federal Home Loan Bank system, the Federal Housing Administration (FHA), Ginnie Mae, and others.

Open-market bulk trading in securities generally averages several billion dollars per day. Special dealers authorized to handle these transactions over the counter manage the purchase and sale of these securities. Dealers and their customers are linked by a national communication system of services that facilitate the transfer of tremendous quantities of securities.

The Fed's open-market operations are directed and regulated by the system's Federal Open-Market Committee (FOMC), which meets monthly to decide on current policies. This committee is composed of 12 members. All seven members of the Federal Reserve's board of governors serve on FOMC, giving them the majority. The president of the Federal Reserve Bank of New York and four other district reserve bank presidents are elected to serve one-year terms on a rotating basis.

A decision by FOMC to buy or sell securities has an immediate and important impact on the availability of money for economic activities. When FOMC sells securities, the economy slows down, as money available for credit is withdrawn from the market. When FOMC buys securities, it is in effect pumping money into the economic system, thereby encouraging growth and expansion. The impact of these procedures on the availability of money for real estate is quite similar to the impact caused by raising or lowering the discount rate.

## Truth in Lending Act (TILA, Regulation Z)

The Federal Reserve is responsible for supervising the **Truth in Lending Act (TILA)**, Title I of the Consumer Protection Act of 1968. The Fed's board of governors was given the responsibility at that time to formulate and issue a regulation, called **Regulation Z**, to carry out the purposes of this act. Rulemaking authority for TILA regulations was transferred to the Consumer Financial Protection Bureau (CFPB) on July 21, 2011, pursuant to the Dodd-Frank Wall Street Reform and Consumer Protection Act. The exemption threshold was raised from $25,000 to $50,000 and is to be adjusted annually based on the percentage increase in the Consumer Price Index. The threshold as of January 1, 2015, will be $54,600.

Each of the following three loan types is covered by the act if the loan is to be repaid in more than four installments or if a finance charge is made:

- Real estate loans
- Loans for personal, family, or household purposes
- Consumer loans for $50,000 or less

In the final analysis, however, Regulation Z is nothing more than a law requiring that lenders reveal total loan costs through the use of a standard measurement of interest rates, called an **annual percentage rate (APR)**. This is not an interest rate per se, but simply a rate that will reflect the effective rate of interest on a loan.

■ **FOR EXAMPLE** Assume a borrower needs $1,000 for one year at 8% interest. If, at the end of the year, the borrower repays the $1,000 plus the $80 interest, the annual percentage rate (APR) and the interest rate will be the same ($80 ÷ $1,000 = 8%). However, if the lender collected a $25 service charge in advance, the borrower would receive

$975 instead of $1,000 and pay $105 instead of $80. The APR would be calculated as follows: $105 ÷ $975 = 10.77%.

In addition to the finance charge and the APR, the Regulation Z disclosure statement must include the creditor's identity; the amount financed; the number, amount, and due dates of the payments; the notice of the right to receive an itemization of the amount financed; the late payment and prepayment provisions and penalties; a description of the security; and whether the loan can be assumed by a subsequent purchaser.

The CFPB was charged with developing a form that combined the disclosures required by the Real Estate Settlement Procedures Act (Regulation X) and the Truth in Lending Act (Regulation Z). After a lengthy study period, the two new integrated mortgage disclosure forms will go into effect on August 1, 2015. The Loan Estimate will replace both the RESPA and the TILA disclosure forms. The Closing Disclosure form will replace the HUD-1 Settlement Statement.

## Advertising

Prior to the passage of the Truth in Lending Act, residential real estate lenders and arrangers of credit frequently included only the favorable loan aspects in advertisements, thus distorting the actual cost of obtaining credit. Now, advertising is strictly regulated by the law, and advertisers are required to disclose all financing details if any one item is disclosed. The advertising requirements apply to television, handbills, signs, and, as shown in Figure 2.5, newspapers.

Advertising terms that would require complete disclosure include "Only 5% down!"; "Why pay the landlord when you can own for $550 per month?"; "30-year financing available"; or "Assume a 9.5% VA loan." Advertising terms that would not require complete disclosure include "Low down payment"; "Easy monthly payments"; "10% APR loans available"; or "FHA and VA loans."

## Right of Rescission

Under Regulation Z, if a consumer obtains a loan (refinancing, remodeling, or equity) that is secured by a principal residence, the borrower has the right to rescind the transaction up to three business days following the loan application or delivery of the disclosure statement, whichever comes later. Because borrowers have the three-day rescission period, lenders usually do not release funds until the rescission period has passed.

A major exception to the right of rescission applies to a loan that is used for the purchase or initial construction of the borrower's principal residence. Consequently, there is no right of rescission in a typical residential real estate purchase.

Any lender or arranger of credit who intentionally violates the requirements of the Truth in Lending Act is subject to a fine of up to $5,000 and/or imprisonment for up to one year. However, if the lender or arranger of credit unintentionally violates the law, the lender or arranger could be liable to the borrower for actual and punitive damages equal to twice the finance charge, up to a maximum of $1,000. A summary of the Fed's credit policy tools is shown in Figure 2.6.

*FIGURE 2.5* **Newspaper Advertisement**

*FIGURE 2.6* **Relation to Credit Policy Tools of the Federal Reserve System**

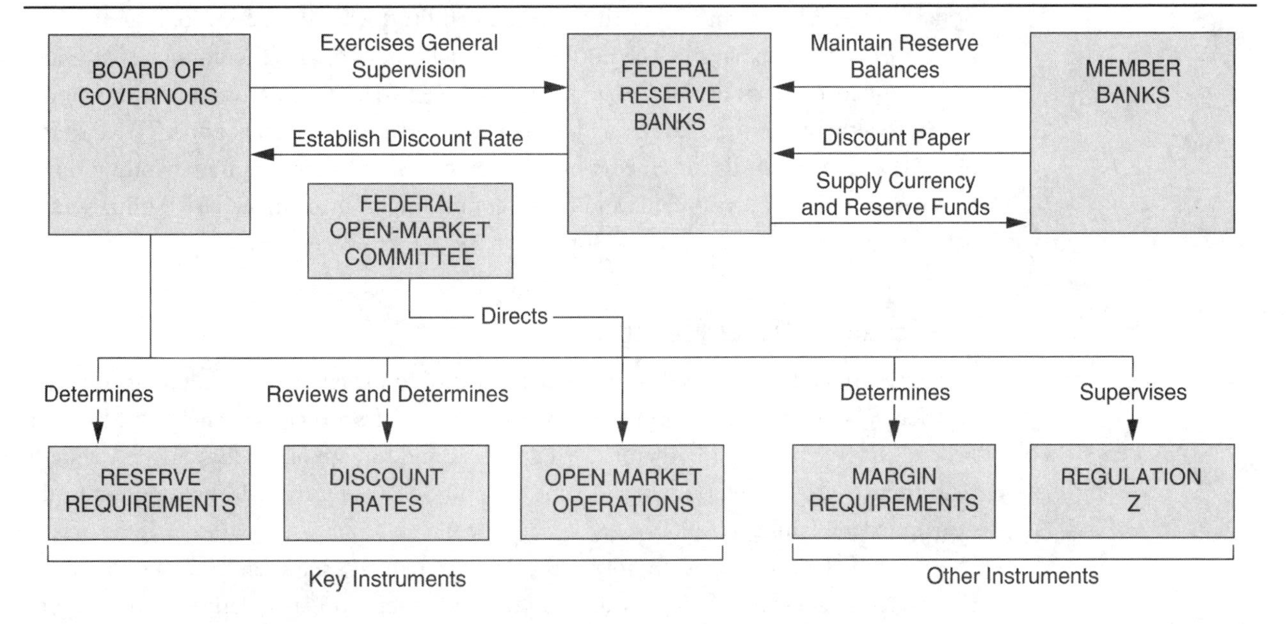


Source: Federal Reserve Board

# THE U.S. TREASURY

Although the Fed regulates money and credit, the U.S. Treasury is also involved in maintaining the nation's economic balance. The Fed may be called the nation's monetary manager. The Treasury serves as the nation's fiscal manager and is self-described as "the steward of U.S. economic and financial systems" (see www.treasury.gov/about/role-of-treasury/). The Department of the Treasury is responsible for advising the president on economic and financial matters, encouraging economic growth within the country, and improving governance in financial institutions. The Secretary of the Treasury has played a significant role in working towards a resolution of the economic crisis starting in 2007. How effectively the Treasury balances the government's income against its long-term and short-term debt instruments has a direct effect on the monetary and credit climate of the country.

The basic functions of the Department of the Treasury include

- collecting taxes, duties, and monies paid to and due to the United States;
- paying all bills of the United States;
- producing currency and coinage;
- supervising national banks and thrift institutions;
- enforcing federal finance and tax laws; and
- investigating and prosecuting tax evaders, counterfeiters, and forgers.

Under 2008's **Troubled Asset Relief Program (TARP)**, the Treasury was authorized to spend $700 billion to purchase assets and equity from financial institutions in trouble with a cost to the taxpayers of as much as $300 billion. In March 2011, the Congressional Budget Office stated that the actual expenditure would be $432 billion at a cost of $19 billion to taxpayers. The authority to make new financial commitments under TARP ended on October 3, 2010. As of July 31, 2014, cumulative collections under TARP, together with the Treasury's additional proceeds from the sale of non-TARP shares of AIG, exceed total disbursements by $15 billion. The Treasury is now winding down its remaining TARP investments and is also continuing to implement TARP initiatives to help struggling homeowners avoid foreclosure.

## The Nation's Fiscal Manager

The Treasury collects funds for government operating expenses from federal income tax payments, Social Security receipts, and other sources. These receipts are held on deposit in Federal Reserve banks and other insured domestic and foreign banks. Employers regularly send their payroll deductions for income tax and Social Security withholding tax to the nearest federal bank.

When federal revenues do not keep pace with federal spending, in either volume or timing, a deficit occurs. Often the amount of government funds on deposit in the nation's banks is not sufficient to make the payments required to keep the ongoing federal agencies in operation. The Treasury then has to borrow money to offset these shortages.

From time to time, short-term or long-term debt instruments, called **securities**, may be issued and sold by the Treasury to generate the cash it requires. These securities are guaranteed by the full faith and credit of the U.S. government, whose financial stability is backed by its taxing power. It is not so much the total amount of the national debt that is the measure of our economic health as it is the willingness of our citizens to pay for it by buying government security issues.

The national debt is composed of smaller component debts of varying denominations, drawn at different interest rates and due at various times. The Treasury's long-term debt instruments, called **Treasury bonds**, mature in 30 years; its intermediate-length obligations, for two to ten years, are called **Treasury notes**; and its short-term securities are called **Treasury bills**. As existing debt instruments become due, they are either repaid, reducing the balance of the overall debt, or refinanced by a new issue of bonds, notes, and/or bills. At the same time, Treasury officials must meet their continuing regular fiscal obligations, which include federal payrolls and Social Security payments.

## The Treasury's Role

The Treasury mixes its issues of short-term and long-term debt instruments to repay or refinance the securities periodically coming due. How it keeps the government in funds directly influences the money supply and indirectly affects sources of funds for real estate finance. Theoretically, issuing more securities should remove money from a "hot" economy and act to slow it down, just like the selling operations for FOMC. Likewise, repaying some securities issues as they become due should pump more money into a sagging economy.

Sometimes, because of purely fiscal pressure, the Treasury's efforts run counter to the Fed's goals. For instance, in an attempt to speed up a sluggish economy, the Fed will reduce its reserve requirements and discount rates to pump money into the economy. Simultaneously, the Treasury will float a huge securities issue to meet unusually large deficits. By removing funds from the market, the Treasury is counteracting the Fed.

Historically, the Treasury has assumed a continuing role as supplier of funds for practically all federal agencies. This role makes the Treasury a primary contributor to the success of many important national programs for real estate financing. The Treasury's participation in establishing Fannie Mae and Ginnie Mae created a national secondary mortgage market. The Treasury's funding of the federal land bank system has been of immeasurable and sustained help to farmers.

Due to the economic crisis, the U.S. Treasury added $200 billion to its commitment for Fannie Mae and Freddie Mac. The Treasury continues to work with the Fed and the FDIC to assist in the recovery of the U.S. financial system.

Further discussion of the various roles of the Treasury Department may be explored on www.treasury.gov.

## Office of the Comptroller of the Currency (OCC)

An important bureau of the U.S. Department of the Treasury is the Office of the Comptroller of the Currency (OCC). It was organized in 1863 in large part to establish a national currency to finance the Civil War. The current role of the OCC is to charter, regulate, and supervise all national banks. In regulating national banks and federal thrifts, the OCC has the power to

1. examine the national banks and thrifts;
2. approve or deny applications for new charters, branches, capital, or other changes in corporate or banking structure;
3. take supervisory actions against national banks and federal thrifts that do not comply with laws and regulations or otherwise engage in unsound practices (possible actions include removing officers and directors, negotiating agreements to change banking practices, and issuing cease and desist orders as as civil money penalties); and
4. issue rules and regulations, legal interpretations, and corporate decisions governing investments, lending, and other practices.

Its operations are funded primarily by assessments on the national banks with additional revenue from investment in U.S. Treasury securities. See www.occ.treas.gov for more information.

### Office of Thrift Supervision (OTS)

Similarly, the Office of Thrift Supervision (OTS) was created to charter, regulate, and supervise the nation's thrift (savings) associations. Many of the new charters approved by OTS were issued to nonbanks such as insurance companies and other large financial entities. A federal charter from the OTS preempted state laws and allowed banking operations in all 50 states. On July 21, 2011, as part of the Dodd-Frank Act, the OTS was merged with the Office of the Comptroller of the Currency. The OCC now regulates both national banks and federal savings associations (thrifts).

### The Bureau of Engraving and Printing

The **Bureau of Engraving and Printing (BEP)** is also part of the Department of Treasury. The bureau produces security documents along with billions of Federal Reserve notes for delivery to the Federal Reserve System each year. These notes are produced at facilities in Washington, DC, and Fort Worth, Texas. Over the past few years, the bureau has worked on a program to redesign Federal Reserve notes in an effort to discourage counterfeiting, and several new bills have been created. The most recent is the $100 bill that features the 3-D security ribbon and the bell in the inkwell.

In addition to U.S. currency, the BEP also produces portions of U.S. passports, materials for Homeland Security, military identification cards, and Immigration and Naturalization Certificates.

## THE U.S. MINT

Congress created the **U.S. Mint** in 1792. Its primary mission is to produce an adequate volume of circulatory coinage for the nation to conduct its trade and commerce. Its recent activities include producing up to 20 billion coins annually in addition to maintaining physical custody and protection of the nation's billions of dollars of gold and silver assets.

The Mint also produces commemorative coins and medals for the general public as well as selling platinum, gold, and silver bullion coins. It has production and storage facilities in Denver, Philadelphia, San Francisco, West Point, and Fort Knox.

## THE FEDERAL DEPOSIT INSURANCE CORPORATION (FDIC)

The Federal Deposit Insurance Corporation (FDIC) was created as an independent agency in 1933 in response to the thousands of bank failures that occurred during the Great Depression. Initially, bank deposits were insured up to $5,000 for each account. This coverage climbed steadily over the years to its present level of $250,000 per title per account. The FDIC insures all accounts in member depository institutions, both banks and savings associations (thrifts). Since the beginning of the FDIC program, no depositor has lost any money due to a bank failure.

The FDIC receives no Congressional appropriations. It is funded by premiums that are paid by banks and thrifts and from earnings from U.S. Treasury securities. As of 2014, the FDIC insures more than $7 trillion of deposits in virtually every bank and thrift in the country. FDIC does not insure securities, mutual funds, stocks, bonds, or insurance or annuity products.

The FDIC is managed by a five-person board of directors appointed by the President of the United States with senate approval, with no more than three from the same political party. The FDIC regularly examines and supervises more than half of the institutions in the banking system for operational safety and soundness. The banks are also examined for compliance with consumer protection laws like the Fair Credit Reporting Act, Fair Debt Collection Practices Act, and Community Reinvestment Act (CRA).

The FDIC responds immediately when a bank or thrift fails. The institution is usually closed by its chartering authority, which is the state or the OOC (or the OTS until it was transferred to the OCC). The two most common methods employed by the FDIC in cases of insolvency or illiquidity are the following:

- Purchase and Assumption Method—all deposits are assumed by an open bank. That bank may purchase the failed bank's assets or they may be auctioned online.
- Payout Method—insured deposits are paid by the FDIC, which attempts to recover the funds by liquidating the estate of the failed bank. The FDIC determines the insured amount for each depositor, including any accrued interest.

The FDIC has been busy during the recent financial crisis, arranging numerous takeovers of banks that were in jeopardy of failing. They have kept all deposits intact during these adjustments to offset any panic, and the entire system continues to function normally.

## THE FEDERAL HOME LOAN BANK (FHLB) SYSTEM

Organized in 1932 to bring stability to the nation's savings associations, the Federal Home Loan Bank (FHLB) was designed to provide a central credit clearing facility for all member savings associations and to establish rules and regulations for its members.

### Organization

Patterned after the Fed, the FHLB includes 12 regional Federal Home Loan Banks (FHLBanks). These district banks are distributed throughout the states and are owned by the regulated financial institutions from all 50 states. When the Federal Home Loan Bank Board was disbanded by the Financial Institutions Reform, Recovery, and Enforcement Act of 1989 (FIRREA), the new Federal Housing Finance Board (FHFB) became the regulator of the 12 FHLBanks. Under the Housing and Economic Recovery Act of 2008 (HERA), the FHFB was replaced with the Federal Housing Finance Agency (FHFA). The Federal Home Loan Bank is a government-sponsored enterprise (GSE) like Fannie Mae and Freddie Mac but managed to survive the recent economic crisis with minimal losses.

For more information on the FHLB, see www.fhlbanks.com.

### Activities

Although member associations may borrow money directly from their district home loan banks for up to one year without collateral, the longer-term loans necessary for real estate finance must have collateral pledged by the borrowing association. Acceptable collateral may include government securities or established real estate mortgages held in the association's investment portfolio. If thrifts capitalize on their stock in trade, real estate mortgages, they can obtain additional funds to expand their activities, just as commercial banks can discount their commercial paper with their Federal Reserve district banks.

The thrifts throughout this country play an important role in the single-family home loan market while also participating in other forms of real estate loans. The intensity of their lending activities depends on the amount of accumulated savings, as well as reserve requirements set by the FHLB.

## SUMMARY

Our monetary system is based primarily on confidence rather than on gold or silver. Money is identified as a medium of exchange; its value is largely its ability to command the purchase of goods and services. When money is available at relatively low interest rates, the economy booms. The reverse is also true.

The federal government's role in mortgage lending permeates every phase of financial activity. The federal agencies charged with determining the quantity of funds circulating in our monetary system—and, as a result, the amount of credit available and the rates of interest in effect—are the Federal Reserve System (the Fed) and the U.S. Treasury. The Fed functions as a manager of money, regulating its member banks' reserves, determining discount rates, operating in the open market for buying and selling government securities, supervising the Truth in Lending Act, and regulating and controlling all facets of the country's commercial banking system. The actions of the Fed have a strong influence on the number and dollar amounts of mortgage loans made.

The U.S. Treasury also plays an important role in real estate finance. The Treasury's primary purpose is to manage the national debt and balance the federal budget. Budget deficits are offset by issuing and selling government securities to raise funds. The amount of Treasury securities for sale determines to a large degree the quantity of money available for other investments, such as mortgages.

In addition, the Treasury is now involved in supervising all of this nation's depository institutions through the Office of the Comptroller of the Currency (OCC). All consumer deposits up to $250,000 per account are protected by the Federal Deposit Insurance Corporation (FDIC). The Federal Home Loan Bank (FHLB) system, operating similarly to the Fed, provides funds for both short-term and long-term needs of its members at favorable interest rates. The FHLB determines its members' reserve requirements and provides its members with an important secondary source of funds.

## INTERNET RESOURCES

Federal Deposit Insurance Corporation
*www.fdic.gov*

Federal Home Loan Bank System
*www.fhlbanks.com*

Federal Housing Finance Agency
*www.fhfa.gov*

Federal Reserve
*www.federalreserve.gov*

Office of the Comptroller of the Currency
*www.occ.treas.gov*

U.S. Treasury Department
*www.treasury.gov*

## REVIEW QUESTIONS

1. The ability to exchange symbolic paper money for commodities in the United States is based primarily on
   a. the gold standard.
   b. the silver standard.
   c. confidence.
   d. the Federal Reserve.

2. When the Fed recommends an increase in interest rates, what is *MOST* likely to happen?
   a. More money will flow into the economy, increasing spending.
   b. Less money will flow into the economy, decreasing spending.
   c. Production will increase, creating more jobs.
   d. The demand for products will increase.

3. The *MOST* significant short-term goal of the Fed is to
   a. act as a check clearing house for banks.
   b. combat inflationary or deflationary pressures.
   c. sell discounted commercial paper.
   d. raise the overall standard of living.

4. When the Fed lowers the reserve requirements for commercial banks, what is *MOST* likely to happen?
   a. Banks will cut back on lending.
   b. Banks will retain less of their total assets.
   c. More money will become available for lending.
   d. The economy will experience a slowdown.

5. Commercial banks are able to borrow funds from the district federal reserve bank, pledging commercial paper as collateral. The interest charged is called the
   a. prime rate.
   b. discount rate.
   c. federal funds rate.
   d. open-market rate.

6. The Fed is responsible for administering the
   a. Fair Housing Act.
   b. Equal Credit Opportunity Act.
   c. Real Estate Settlement Procedures Act.
   d. Truth in Lending Act.

7. A borrower secures a new loan at 0.75 points above prime. If the prime rate is 8%, what is the rate of interest?
   a. 0.75%
   b. 7.25%
   c. 8.00%
   d. 8.75%

8. The government agency that serves as the nation's fiscal manager is the
   a. Federal Reserve.
   b. U.S. Treasury.
   c. HUD.
   d. OTS.

9. The U.S. Treasury's long-term debt instruments (for more than ten years) are called
   a. Treasury bills.
   b. Treasury notes.
   c. Treasury bonds.
   d. Treasury mortgages.

10. The FDIC insures accounts up to $250,000 deposited in
    a. commercial banks only.
    b. thrifts only.
    c. both commercial banks and thrifts.
    d. neither commercial banks nor thrifts.

Chapter 3

# Additional Government Influence

## LEARNING OBJECTIVES

When you've finished reading this chapter, you will be able to

- list the responsibilities and activities of HUD and the CFPB;
- explain the criteria for selling property under the Interstate Land Sales Full Disclosure Act;
- identify important acts of federal legislation that affect real estate finance; and
- describe the operation of the Farm Credit System.

**Community Development Block Grant Program (CDBG)**
**Community Reinvestment Act (CRA)**
**entitlement communities**
**Equal Credit Opportunity Act (ECOA)**
**Good Faith Estimate (GFE)**
**Home Mortgage Disclosure Act (HMDA)**
**Housing Choice Voucher Program**
**Housing and Economic Recovery Act of 2008 (HERA)**
**HUD-1 Settlement Statement**
**Interstate Land Sales Full Disclosure Act (ILSFDA)**
**Neighborhood Stabilization Program (NSP)**
**property report**
**Real Estate Settlement Procedures Act (RESPA)**
**statement of record**
**tax increment financing**

Over the years, the federal government has established special departments and programs to regulate trends in the U.S. housing market. Some of the most significant of these will be covered in this chapter along with important federal legislation directly affecting real estate practice.

This chapter begins with a discussion of the activities of the Department of Housing and Urban Development (HUD) and the new Consumer Financial Protection Bureau (CFPB). One of HUD's primary duties is to supervise the Federal Housing Administration (FHA). HUD is also responsible for the Government National Mortgage Association (Ginnie Mae) and interstate land sales in addition to administering a variety of housing programs focused on social improvement, including low-rent housing projects, urban renewal, and rehabilitation programs.

The Consumer Financial Protection Bureau was established in 2010 as part of the Dodd-Frank Wall Street Reform and Consumer Protection Act. Its central mission is to make consumer financial products and services work better for Americans—whether applying for a mortgage, selecting a credit card, or using any other type of consumer financial products. Rulemaking authority for several consumer financial protection laws was transferred from seven federal agencies to the CFPB as of July 21, 2011.

This chapter also reviews current federal legislation that regulates the complex real estate marketplace. This legislation includes the Equal Credit Opportunity Act (ECOA), the Real Estate Settlement Procedures Act (RESPA), and its various disclosure requirements. It examines the role of various agencies that assist communities in attracting new industry, improving the housing of their citizens, and regulating the fair application of real estate loans.

Finally, this chapter reviews the cooperative Farm Credit System (FCS), which is designed to serve the particular financial needs of farmers and ranchers. The FCS provides funding for land acquisition, home and accessory buildings, equipment purchases, and general farm and ranch operations. The U.S. Department of Agriculture Rural and Community Development Program complements the Farm Credit System by providing funds for farmers and ranchers who are unable to secure credit from other sources.

## U.S. DEPARTMENT OF HOUSING AND URBAN DEVELOPMENT (HUD)

The Department of Housing and Urban Development (HUD) was given cabinet status in 1965. It consolidated a number of older federal agencies.

HUD is the federal agency responsible for national policy and programs that address America's housing needs, improve and develop U.S. communities, and enforce fair housing laws. HUD's mission is to help create a decent home and suitable living environment for all U.S. citizens.

As illustrated in Figure 3.1, HUD's primary activities include

- supervising the Federal Housing Administration (FHA),
- directing Ginnie Mae,
- enforcing the Fair Housing Act,
- managing the Housing Choice Voucher Program (formerly Section 8 Housing),
- managing the Indian Housing Act, and
- supervising public housing projects.

*FIGURE 3.1* **The Primary Supervisory Activities of HUD**

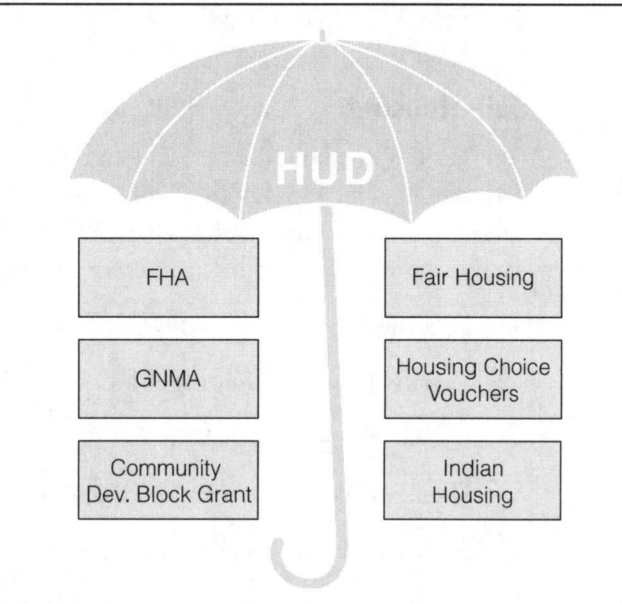


As part of the **Housing and Economic Recovery Act of 2008 (HERA)**, HUD authorized the Neighborhood Stabilization Program (NSP). This program was designed to stabilize communities suffering from large numbers of abandoned homes and foreclosures by providing funds to all states and selected local governments to acquire and redevelop those properties. Under the American Recovery and Reinvestment Act of 2009 (ARRA), the NSP was expanded to include grants to nonprofit organizations. A third round of NSP funding was included in the Dodd-Frank Act of 2010.

In the past, HUD was also responsible for overseeing Fannie Mae and Freddie Mac operations. Regulation of these government-sponsored enterprises now falls under the Federal Housing Finance Agency (see Chapter 4). The enforcement of RESPA regulations was transferred to the CFPB in 2011.

One of the important functions of HUD is to provide information on home ownership to the public. The HUD website (www.hud.gov) is a tremendous resource for the public and for real estate practitioners.

Working under the stated mission to "create strong, sustainable, inclusive communities and quality affordable homes for all," HUD's Strategic Framework for 2014–2018 emphasizes the following strategic goals:

- Strengthen the nation's housing market to bolster the economy and protect consumers
- Meet the need for quality affordable rental homes
- Use housing as a platform for improving quality of life
- Build inclusive and sustainable communities free from discrimination

Each of the strategic goals are backed up with strategic objectives that are specific to each goal. The complete 2014–2018 plan is available at www.hud.gov.

The Federal Housing Administration (FHA) is covered in Chapter 8, and Ginnie Mae is covered in Chapter 4. Additional HUD responsibilities will be covered in this chapter.

## Fair Housing

The HUD Office of Fair Housing and Equal Opportunity (FHEO) enforces the Fair Housing Act (Title VIII of the Civil Rights Act of 1968 prohibiting discrimination in the sale, rental, and financing of dwellings based on race, color, national origin, religion, sex, familial status, and disability) and other civil rights laws, including

- Title VI of the Civil Rights Act of 1964,
- Section 109 of the Housing and Community Development Act of 1974,
- Section 504 of the Rehabilitation Act of 1973,
- Title II of the Americans with Disabilities Act of 1990,
- the Age Discrimination Act of 1975,
- Title IX of the Education Amendments Act of 1972, and
- the Architectural Barriers Act of 1968.

In some cases, fair housing complaints are handled at the state level when the state has an equivalent enforcement program.

## Community Development Block Grant (CDBG)

The **Community Development Block Grant (CDBG)** program is one of HUD's longest continuously run programs. Since its inception in 1974, the CDBG program has helped communities with economic development, job opportunities, and housing rehabilitation. CDBG funds have been used to construct and improve public facilities such as water, sewer, streets, and neighborhood centers; to purchase real property; and to assist private businesses.

CDBG funds are split between states and **entitlement communities**, defined as metropolitan cities with populations of at least 50,000 and urban counties with populations of at least 200,000. States distribute to non-entitlement communities. Annual grants are provided to 1,209 general units of state and local government. The amount of each grant is determined based on a formula made up of different measures of community needs such as the poverty level, population data, age, and density of housing. Seventy percent of CDBG funds must benefit low-income and moderate-income families.

## Neighborhood Stabilization Program (NSP)

The **Neighborhood Stabilization Program (NSP)** was established to help stabilize communities that have suffered from foreclosed and abandoned homes. NSP funds authorized under the Housing and Economic Recovery Act (HERA) (called NSP1 funds) provided grants to states and selected local governments to purchase and redevelop such properties. NSP2 funds were authorized under the American Recovery and Reinvestment Act

(ARRA) to include nonprofit entities on a competitive basis for grants and to fund $50 million to national and local technical assistance providers. NSP3 funds were authorized under the Dodd-Frank Act of 2010 to provide a third round of grants to states and local governments on a formula basis.

## Interstate Land Sales

The **Interstate Land Sales Full Disclosure Act (ILSFDA)**, passed by Congress in 1968, established the informational criteria for marketing residential land to potential buyers. Designed to reduce fraud in the sale of land by developers, the law requires that anyone selling or leasing 25 or more lots of unimproved land as part of a common plan in interstate commerce must comply with the act's provisions. The exceptions include subdivisions of five acres or more, cemetery land, commercial and industrial land, and any residential subdivision marketed exclusively in the state where it is located.

A developer must provide HUD with a **statement of record** that includes explanations and descriptions of existing and proposed encumbrances, improvements, utilities, schools, recreation areas, roads, and all services to be provided for the residents' use. A **property report** must be delivered to the buyer prior to the purchase of the property. The seller must have a signed receipt from the buyer indicating the buyer received the property report. If a property report is received within 48 hours prior to signing, the buyers have the right to change their minds within seven days, cancel their contract, and receive a return of any deposits made. However, if the report is not received within the allotted time, the buyers may legally rescind their contract at any time.

Although the ILSFDA was once a subagency of HUD, its enforcement has been shifted to the new Consumer Financial Protection Bureau. New regulations and guidelines will be provided by the CFPB.

## Urban Renewal

HUD sponsors urban renewal projects that encompass entire neighborhoods as well as specific properties. Neighborhood renewal involves large-scale planning, including site acquisition, site clearance, construction, and disposition. Urban renewal originates at the community level, where a workable plan is developed and then sent to HUD for approval and sponsorship.

In addition to providing funds for slum clearance, HUD makes loans and grants to owners and tenants in depressed areas for rehabilitating their properties. Grants are also available to demolish structures unfit for habitation.

## Public Housing

HUD provides financial assistance to local authorities for acquisition and operation of properties for public housing programs. This assistance includes grant monies, housing subsidies, and other means of support. HUD also helps finance public housing agency projects to integrate public housing into surrounding communities and to provide residents the skills to contribute to their communities.

### Housing Choice Voucher Program

The HUD **Housing Choice Voucher Program** is the federal government's major program for assisting very-low-income families, the elderly, and the disabled to obtain safe and affordable housing. The program was originally only for rental subsidy and was called Section 8. Families seeking assistance apply through their local public housing agency. Tenants have the freedom to select housing where they want to live within a standard rent range. The rent subsidies are paid to owners and consist of the difference between what the tenant can pay and the contracted rent.

Under legislation passed in 2001, individual Public Housing Authorities (PHA) have the option to use a portion of their Housing Choice Vouchers to assist first-time homebuyers. PHAs individually make the determination of how much of their funding they wish to allocate to this Homeownership Voucher Program. FHA sets minimum income and employment requirements, but other eligibility requirements are set by the PHA. For example, recipients may be required to attend a homeownership and housing counseling program.

### Native American Housing

Through the **Office of Native American Programs (ONAP)**, HUD promotes providing decent, safe, and affordable housing for lower-income Native American, Alaska Native, and Native Hawaiian families. ONAP works closely with tribes and tribally designated housing entities to administer their own programs.

### Other Programs

HUD offers monetary support to state and local governments and to nonprofit organizations to assist homeless individuals and families to move from the streets to temporary shelters to supportive housing and, ideally, back into the mainstream of American life. HUD also helps fund cooperative housing for low-income persons, housing for the elderly, mortgage interest subsidies, relocation assistance, college housing, disaster area reconstruction, and housing in isolated areas.

HUD provides a Good Neighbor Next Door sales program for law enforcement officers, pre-kindergarten through 12th-grade teachers, firefighters, and emergency medical technicians. A discount of 50% of the sales price is provided in return for a commitment to live in the property for a minimum of 36 months.

For full details on all of HUD's special programs, see www.hud.gov.

## CONSUMER FINANCIAL PROTECTION BUREAU

The CFPB was charged by the Dodd-Frank Act to issue rules that combine the disclosures required in the Good Faith Estimate and the Truth-in-Lending Disclosure. In November 2013, the CFPB released the 1,900-page RESPA-TILA Integrated Disclosures final rule. Under the new rule, there are two disclosures: the three-page Loan Estimate (replaces the GFE and initial TILA forms) and the Closing Disclosure (replaces HUD-1 and the final TILA disclosure). The new forms are mandated to go into effect on August 1, 2015.

Applications taken right up until July 31, 2015, must use the old forms. (See Appendices A and B.)

## Loan Estimate

The Loan Estimate provides a summary of the loan terms, estimated loan costs, other closing costs, and additional application disclosures. This form could be used to compare different loan products. The Loan Estimate must be provided to the borrower within three business days from application. *Application* is now defined by the CFPB as the submission of six pieces of information: (1) the consumer's name, (2) the consumer's income, (3) the consumer's Social Security number to obtain a credit report, (4) the property address, (5) an estimate of value of the property, and (6) the mortgage loan amount sought. This is slightly different from the original requirements of Regulation X – RESPA. A business day is defined as a day that the lender's offices are open. (See Appendix L.)

## Closing Disclosure

The Closing Disclosure provides a summary of the actual loan terms, the loan costs, other settlement costs, and additional closing disclosures. The Closing Disclosure must be provided to the consumer at least three business days before closing. If there are significant changes, an updated Closing Disclosure must be prepared and there will be another three-day waiting period. The three business days are defined, as in Regulation Z – TILA, as any day other than a Sunday or legal holidays. Changes that would require a new three-day waiting period are (1) changes to the APR greater than ⅛ of a percent, (2) changes to the loan product, or (3) the addition of a prepayment penalty. (See Appendix M.)

The CFPB has provided a September 2014 revised edition of the *TILA-RESPA Integrated Disclosure Rule, Small Entity Compliance Guide* that includes sample forms. It is available at www.consumerfinance.gov.

The CFPB released new rules that took effect on January 10, 2014, on how mortgage servicers must treat borrowers. The rules apply to all mortgage servicers with 5,000 or more loans. The goal of the new regulations is to make sure that servicers cannot take advantage of borrowers who fall behind on their payments. Despite concern in the mortgage lending industry regarding the thousands of pages of rules and new processes that are now required, most lenders were able to develop coping strategies and to implement the new regulations in a timely fashion.

The new rules require the servicer to

1. provide billing information in writing;
2. provide at least two months' warning if there is going to be a change in an adjustable-rate mortgage interest rate that will change the payment amount;
3. promptly credit mortgage payments;
4. respond quickly when asked about paying off a loan;
5. not charge for insurance that is not needed or over-charge for force-placed insurance;
6. quickly resolve complaints and share information;

7. have and follow good customer service policies and procedures;
8. contact the borrower to help when the borrower is having trouble making payments;
9. work with the borrower who is having trouble paying the mortgage before starting or continuing foreclosure; and
10. allow the borrower to seek review of the mortgage servicer's decision about a loan workout request.

The CFPB has prepared a brochure for consumers that provides contact information for anyone who does not believe that their mortgage servicer is following the new rules. The brochure and other CFPB news is available at www.consumerfinance.gov.

## SIGNIFICANT FEDERAL LEGISLATION

In the past, real estate transactions were virtually unregulated, and each party was assumed to be knowledgeable about the facts and conditions surrounding the sale and financing of a property. As the marketplace evolved and became more complex, it also became clear that many purchasers or sellers were not well informed. As a result, some significant federal legislation was passed that has become standard practice in every real estate transaction.

### The Federal Equal Credit Opportunity Act (ECOA)

The **Equal Credit Opportunity Act (ECOA)** is Title VII of the Consumer Protection Act. It prohibits lenders from discriminating against credit applicants on the basis of race, color, religion, national origin, sex, marital status, age, or dependency on public assistance. The basic provisions of the act include the following:

- The lender may not ask if the applicant is divorced or widowed. However, the lender may ask if the borrower is married, unmarried, or separated. The term *unmarried* denotes a single, divorced, or widowed person and, in a community property state, is of particular interest to local lenders.
- The lender may not ask about the receipt of alimony or child support unless the borrower intends to use such income to qualify for the loan. The lender may ask about any obligations to pay alimony or child support.
- The lender may not seek any information about birth control practices or the child-bearing capabilities or intentions of the borrower or co-borrower.
- The lender may not request information about the spouse or former spouse of the applicant unless that person will be contractually liable for repayment or the couple lives in a community property state.
- The lender may not discount or exclude any income because of the source of that income.

- The lender must report credit information on married couples separately in the name of each spouse.
- The lender may ask about the race or national origin of the applicant, but the borrowers can refuse to answer without fear of jeopardizing their loan.

The ECOA also prohibits lenders from discriminating against credit applicants who exercise their rights under truth-in-lending laws. In addition, lenders and other creditors must inform all rejected applicants in writing of the principal reasons why credit was denied or terminated. The focus of the ECOA is to ensure that all qualified persons have equal access to credit.

Both the Justice Department and HUD are charged with protecting borrowers from discrimination in lending practices under the fair housing laws and ECOA. An example of ECOA's effectiveness is the case against the Chevy Chase Federal Savings Bank in Washington, DC, which was accused of violating the racial discrimination standards. The bank denied all allegations but agreed to invest $11 million to open at least one new branch in an African American area of the city. The bank also agreed to provide eligible borrowers discounted interest rates and grants equaling 2% of the loan down payments.

## The Real Estate Settlement Procedures Act (RESPA)

Formerly administered under the FHA, but now under the CFPB, the **Real Estate Settlement Procedures Act (RESPA)** is designed to protect the participants in a real estate transaction by providing closing cost information so they better understand the settlement procedures. RESPA covers the sale of residential properties and the acquisition of mortgage loans, including home equity loans, second mortgages, and refinancing loans on residential properties.

Violations of RESPA are subject to severe penalties such as triple damages, fines, and even imprisonment. RESPA covers almost every service provider involved in the purchase of a home, including

- real estate brokers and agents,
- mortgage brokers and mortgage bankers,
- title companies and title agents,
- home warranty companies,
- hazard insurance agents,
- appraisers,
- flood insurers and tax service suppliers, and
- home and pest inspectors.

Real estate brokers or agents are prohibited from receiving anything "of value" for referring business to another real estate service provider or from splitting fees received for settlement services unless the fee is paid for an actual service. Exemptions to the referral restrictions are (1) promotional and educational activities, (2) payment for goods provided or service performed, and (3) affiliated business arrangements. For a detailed description of each of the exempt categories and to see examples of permissible activities and payments, see www.hud.gov.

In 2012, the House passed a bill that would have taken home warranty companies off of the RESPA list, but the Senate failed to take action, so it remains in place.

**Disclosures Under RESPA.** In order to protect participants in a real estate transaction, RESPA requires all service costs to be disclosed at various times during the process. Disclosures must be made during the time of a loan application, before settlement/closing, at settlement, and after settlement.

**Disclosure at the Time of a Loan Application.** At the beginning of the mortgage loan process, the lender must provide the borrower the following three items:

- A Special Information Booklet containing information on real estate settlement services must be provided.
- Within three business days, a **Good Faith Estimate (GFE)** of settlement costs listing the charges the borrower is likely to pay at closing and indicating whether the borrower has to use a specific settlement service must be provided. A new GFE form developed by HUD went into effect on January 1, 2010 (see Appendix A). The new GFE gives specific details on all loan terms, closing costs, and related fees, giving the borrowers a better opportunity to compare different loan products. The new GFE has zero tolerance for any change to significant aspects of the estimate. This GFE is being replaced as of August 1, 2015, with the new Loan Estimate form.
- A mortgage servicing disclosure statement informing the borrower whether the lender intends to keep the loan or transfer it to a different lender for servicing, in addition to information on how the borrower can resolve complaints, must be provided.

**Disclosures Before Settlement/Closing.** Prior to settlement, an Affiliated Business Arrangement (AFBA) Disclosure is required whenever a settlement service provider refers the borrower to a firm with which the servicer has any connection, such as common ownership. The service usually cannot force a borrower to use a connected firm. A preliminary copy of a **HUD-1 Settlement Statement** (see Appendix B) is required if the borrower requests it 24 hours prior to closing. This form estimates all settlement charges that must be paid by the participants. The borrower must also receive a copy of the truth-in-lending statement prior to closing that discloses the annual percentage rate and total costs of credit involved in the transaction. The HUD-1 form is being replaced with the Closing Disclosure form as of August 1, 2015. The form must be provided to the consumer three days prior to closing. The new form also replaces the final truth-in-lending statement.

**Disclosures at Settlement.** The HUD-1 Settlement Statement is distributed at closing and shows the actual charges incurred by the participants. In addition, an initial escrow statement is required at closing or within 45 days of closing. This statement itemizes the estimated taxes, insurance premiums, and other charges that must be paid from the escrow account during the first year of the loan. RESPA limits the amount of "cushion" the lender may require in the escrow account to two months of payments. It is now federal law to include a lead-based paint disclosure on all properties built before 1978. The new HUD-1 form became effective January 1, 2010, and lists the actual costs side-by-side with the estimated costs, giving borrowers documentation for their records plus protection from possible fraud or predatory lending practices. This information will not be included in the new Closing Disclosure form. If there are significant changes, an updated form must be prepared with a new waiting period of three days.

**Disclosures After Settlement.** After settlement, an Annual Escrow Statement must be delivered by the loan servicer to the borrower. This document enumerates all escrow deposits and payments during the past year. It indicates any shortages or surpluses in the escrow account and informs the borrower how to remedy them. If the loan service is transferred to another servicer, a Servicing Transfer Statement is delivered to the borrower.

## Truth in Lending Act (TILA)—Regulation Z

The Truth in Lending Act, Title I of the Consumer Credit Protection Act of 1968, requires that all costs of financing be disclosed to the consumer. The intent of this act is to ensure that consumers can compare the cost of making a purchase using credit to the cost of making the same purchase with cash. Important TILA disclosures that relate to mortgage lending are listed in the following:

- The annual percentage rate (APR) discloses the true yield achieved by the lender through a combination of the stated rate of interest, any discount points, and additional lender fees. The APR must be disclosed to the consumer prior to making the loan and in all advertising.
- Regulation Z requires full disclosure of all elements of financing. Disclosure of any one of the "trigger" terms—rate of interest, number of payments, term of the loan, amount of monthly payment, down payment amount, or percentage—requires full disclosure of all of the terms.
- Adjustable-rate mortgages must include disclosure of all potential rate increases.

TILA disclosures are always required for credit extended for the purchase of real property. If credit is to be extended for the purchase of personal property in excess of $25,000, or if repayment will be made in more than four installments, TILA disclosure is required. There is sometimes a misconception on the part of the public that all credit agreements have a three-day right of rescission. There is no right of rescission for credit extended for the purchase or construction of real property. Credit extended for a home equity loan or refinancing does have the three-day right of rescission.

## In Practice

A real estate licensee recently represented a buyer as her buyer agent for the purchase of a new town house. The licensee recommended three different loan officers for the buyer to contact regarding obtaining a home mortgage loan. The buyer picked one and was very happy with him, until this morning, when she received a truth-in-lending statement in the mail. She immediately called the licensee, obviously very upset. "You and the loan officer both assured me that I was getting a 6.5% loan and that I was going to be able to borrow $200,000. Today I get this statement in the mail saying that the interest rate will be 6.82% and that I'm only borrowing $194,000. Now I don't know what or who to believe."

This is not an uncommon reaction to receipt of the truth-in-lending statement. Fortunately, the licensee has dealt with this many times before and was quickly able to calm the buyer down. He then explained to her that the Truth in Lending Act requires the lender to disclose exactly how much they are earning on the loan, including any loan fees and discount points that may have been charged. Because there were three points on this $200,000 loan, the lender only sends a check for $194,000 to the settlement table (they receive the other $6,000 in points, paid by the buyer, seller, or both). When the discount points and additional loan fees of $500 are calculated, the lender's actual yield becomes 6.82%.

### The Community Reinvestment Act (CRA)

The **Community Reinvestment Act (CRA)**, passed by Congress in 1977, ensures that financial institutions pursue their responsibilities to meet both the deposit and the credit needs of members of the communities in which they are chartered. Each institution is required to delineate its community, specify the types of credit services it offers, post a public notice stating that the institution is being reviewed by a federal supervisory agency, and prepare a community reinvestment statement to be made available to the public. The act covers the majority of U.S. financial institutions. The federal supervisory agency would include the Comptroller of the Currency and the board of governors of the Fed, the FDIC, and the new Consumer Financial Protection Bureau.

The 1990s were a period of strong CRA enforcement due to the number of mergers and acquisitions taking place. The act was revised in 1995 and again in 2005.

### The Home Mortgage Disclosure Act (HMDA)

Under the **Home Mortgage Disclosure Act (HMDA)**, all mortgage originators are required to report information relating to income level, racial characteristics, and gender of mortgage applicants. This includes loans originated as well as applications rejected.

## STATE AND LOCAL PROGRAMS

Various states have established agencies to provide financial assistance at the community level for special real estate developments. These agencies are grouped into categories—one to assist local communities in attracting new industry and another to improve the housing of its citizens. A complete discussion of bond programs that may be used by states or local governments can be found in Chapter 5. Another source of funding for state and local redevelopment programs are the Neighborhood Stabilization Program grants previously described in this chapter.

## Industrial Development Agencies

Under legislation from the state government, communities have organized industrial development agencies empowered to purchase and improve land for industrial and office parks. These activities are funded by industrial revenue bonds (IRBs) backed by a state's bonding credit. Some funds are also raised through voluntary contributions from citizens interested in expanding the economic base of their community.

Community growth is the ultimate goal behind the development of industrial land. By offering preplanned industrial park sites, as well as other amenities and incentives, a community can attract new industrial activities. IRBs can create new jobs and more commercial activity in the local area, with commensurate increases in profits for businesses and tax revenues for the community. Many U.S. communities have used the IRB approach to achieve growth and have been successful in attracting new industries. The interest paid on these bonds is federally income tax free to the bond purchaser, thus providing a lower borrowing interest rate to the developer.

## Mortgage Insurance Programs

Some states have developed special real estate mortgage insurance programs of their own, funded by the state itself. The state sells either general obligation bonds repaid from state income tax collections or, more frequently, revenue bonds repaid from the mortgage insurance premiums collected. The funds raised from the sale of these bonds are used primarily as reserves for backing specific development projects. For instance, if a community wished to embark on a rehabilitation project, money could be secured from private sources to pursue this objective. If the project were approved, the state would issue insurance for repayment of the funds so the work could proceed.

Money raised from the sale of state bonds might also be used for direct loan purposes, such as special loans for the purchase of farm or ranch land. In Virginia, the Virginia Housing Development Authority (VHDA) provides funding for low- to moderate-income first-time homebuyers in the state through the sale of bonds and securities. Other states with special housing programs include California, Indiana, Michigan, South Dakota, Tennessee, Texas, and Wisconsin. Some of these socially oriented programs include programs for veterans and for low-income housing projects.

## Community Redevelopment Agencies

Local governments may establish community redevelopment agencies for expansion of the supply of low-income housing. These agencies are supervised by city council members and can acquire property by eminent domain. Any building program must agree to allocate 30% of the rental units for low-income tenants before it can be approved. Replacement housing must be provided within or outside the redevelopment area for every person displaced by the project.

**Tax Increment Financing.** Projects of community redevelopment agencies are funded in large part with **tax increment financing**. This technique allocates the increased property tax revenues derived from redevelopment to pay the debts incurred in improving the area. It requires that property taxes be frozen as of the date the redevelopment plan is adopted, with any excess taxes applied directly to satisfy the debt or used as security for the sale of bonds. After the debts have been satisfied, the taxes may rise to current levels, offsetting additional community costs brought about by the improvements.

## AGRICULTURAL LENDING

Farm loans have special cyclical requirements. The values of farm and ranch lands depend on productivity, and productivity in turn depends on management expertise and climatic conditions. Although management skills can be evaluated based on past experience, nobody can estimate the influence of nature on each season's crops, and farm and ranch loans acquire a unique risk factor.

Agricultural loans have to be designed with as much flexibility as possible. Rather than following a rigid payment pattern, their design must allow the farmer-borrowers the opportunity to pay when they can. It is essential, for instance, that the principal amount is not due in a bad crop year. The terms of the loans need to be lengthened, up to 40 years in some cases, to allow for those years when crops fail and no payments can be made. Farmer-borrowers also need an opportunity to pay larger portions of the principal, in addition to the interest required, during a good year so that they can repay their loans in full over the longer time period.

Farmer-borrowers need to be able to extend, expand, and otherwise adjust their loans depending on unforeseen circumstances. The extension and expansion techniques designed to satisfy the special problems of the farmers are defined as open-end mortgages. As a last resort for a distressed farmer-borrower, a moratorium on payments occasionally is used to offset imminent foreclosures brought on by situations outside the borrower's control. Open-end mortgages and moratoriums will be discussed in later chapters of this book.

### The Farm Credit System (FCS)

The Farm Credit System (FCS) was created by Congress in 1916 to provide American agriculture with a source of sound, dependable credit at competitive rates of interest. Through approximately 90 local Farm Credit associations and five Farm Credit Banks, more than $160 billion in credit and related services have been provided to farmers, ranchers, producers, and harvesters of aquatic products, rural homeowners, timber harvesters, agricultural cooperatives, rural utility systems, and agribusinesses.

The FCS banks do not take deposits. The funds used for lending are raised through the sale of bonds and notes in national capital markets. The Federal Farm Credit Banks Funding Corporation manages the sale of system-wide debt securities. Purchasers of these securities are assured of timely payment of principal and interest by the Farm Credit System Insurance Corporation (FCSIC).

Long-term mortgage loans are generally made by Farm Credit Banks, Federal Land Bank Associations, or Federal Land Credit Associations. Short-term and intermediate-term loans are usually made by Production Credit Associations. In some cases, these entities have combined to form Agriculture Credit Associations that provide both long- and short-term loans. The Farm Credit Administration (FCA) is an independent federal regulator responsible for examining and ensuring the soundness of all FCS institutions.

See www.agfirst.com and www.fca.gov for more information on the Farm Credit System.

### Federal Agriculture Mortgage Corporation (Farmer Mac)

The Federal Agriculture Mortgage Corporation, known as Farmer Mac, was created by Congress to provide a secondary market for agricultural and rural housing mortgage loans. In the Farmer Mac I Program, Farmer Mac purchases qualified loans from agricultural mortgage lenders, thereby replenishing the lenders' source of funds to make new loans. The loans are then packaged and sold as securities. In the Farmer Mac II Program, Farmer Mac purchases guaranteed portions of USDA loans. Farmer Mac also purchases qualified rural utility loans or guarantees payment of interest and principal of securities backed by pools of such loans.

Although both the Farm Credit System and Farmer Mac were created and chartered by Congress, neither is funded by taxpayers. Farmer Mac securities are sold on the over-the-counter desk of the New York Stock Exchange. See www.farmermac.com for more information on the program.

### The U.S. Department of Agriculture Rural and Community Development Program (USDA Rural Development)

The activities of the Farm Credit System are complemented by the USDA. This governmental unit was created in 1994 to combine the Farmers Home Administration (FmHA), the Rural Development Administration, the Rural Electrification Administration, and the Agricultural Cooperative Service.

The USDA Rural and Community Development Program [Rural Housing Service (RHS)] forges new partnerships with rural communities to reverse the downward spiral of rural job losses, out-migration, and diminishing services. The program funds projects that bring housing, community facilities, utilities, and other services to rural areas. The USDA also provides technical assistance and financial backing for rural businesses and cooperatives to create quality jobs in rural areas. The USDA has released new maps showing areas that are eligible for rural development housing programs.

See www.rurdev.usda.gov for more information on the program.

## SUMMARY

This chapter examined the Department of Housing and Urban Development (HUD), which participates actively in real estate finance. In addition to supporting the FHA and Ginnie Mae, HUD promotes various urban renewal projects, area rehabilitation ventures, and open-space developments. Among its other socially oriented housing activities are public housing programs, cooperative housing for low-income persons, mortgage interest subsidies, relocation aid, disaster area construction, and isolated area housing. The new Consumer Financial Protection Bureau is also covered in this chapter.

Federal legislation regulating real estate finance was examined, including the Equal Credit Opportunity Act (ECOA), the Community Reinvestment Act (CRA), the Real Estate Settlement Procedures Act (RESPA), and the Truth in Lending Act (TILA). ECOA prohibits lenders from discriminating against credit applicants on the basis of race, color, religion, national origin, sex, marital status, age, or dependency on public assistance. The Community Reinvestment Act requires all federally regulated financial institutions to expand their responsibilities to meet the needs of all citizens of a community. RESPA is designed to prevent abuses of buyers and sellers by providing estimated costs of a real estate transaction before closing to avoid any last-minute shocks, and TILA requires a full disclosure of all costs of credit.

Most states have established financing agencies of their own to help develop industry in various communities and provide the means to improve the housing requirements of their citizens. These agencies frequently use bond issues to raise funds for their programs, some of which are repaid with tax increments.

The last section of this chapter reviewed the Farm Credit System, which originated under the federal Farm Loan Act of 1916 and serves the particular financial needs of farmers, ranchers, producers and harvesters of aquatic products, rural homeowners, and selected farm-related businesses. Complementing the various agencies of the Farm Credit System, the U.S. Department of Agriculture Rural and Community Development makes loans to farmers and ranchers unable to secure credit from other sources.

## INTERNET RESOURCES

Consumer Financial Protection Bureau
*www.consumerfinance.gov*

Department of Housing and Urban Development
*www.hud.gov*

Fannie Mae
*www.fanniemae.com*

Farm Credit Administration
*www.fca.gov*

Farm Credit Bank
*www.agfirst.com*

Federal Agricultural Mortgage Corporation
*www.farmermac.com*

Freddie Mac
*www.freddiemac.com*

Ginnie Mae
*www.ginniemae.gov*

U.S. Department of Agriculture
*www.usda.gov*

USDA Rural Development
*www.rurdev.usda.gov*

## REVIEW QUESTIONS

1. HUD is responsible for all of the following *EXCEPT*
   a. FHA.
   b. Ginnie Mae.
   c. Fannie Mae.
   d. Community Development Block Grants.

2. A developer is planning a new subdivision of building lots. In which case will it be subject to the Interstate Land Sales Full Disclosure Act?
   a. If all lots will be 10 acres
   b. If the subdivision will consist of 20 individual lots
   c. If the subdivision will be marketed out of state
   d. If the subdivision will be marketed locally

3. The Housing Choice Voucher Program allows a public housing authority to use a portion of its available funds to
   a. provide rehabilitation funds for depressed areas.
   b. improve public water and sewer systems.
   c. provide mortgage payment subsidies for qualified applicants.
   d. build psychiatric hospitals.

4. While taking a loan application from a married couple, a loan officer inquired about the wife's ability to have more children. Which federal act is the lender violating?
   a. RESPA
   b. ECOA
   c. TILA
   d. HMDA

5. RESPA does *NOT* require that the lender provide a borrower with a
   a. Good Faith Estimate.
   b. truth-in-lending statement.
   c. HUD-1 closing statement.
   d. right of rescission.

6. The disclosure of all elements of financing in advertising is required under
   a. APR.
   b. GFE.
   c. CRA.
   d. Regulation Z of TILA.

7. The Community Reinvestment Act requires a lender to
   a. provide housing voucher certificates when requested.
   b. offer credit to all qualified members of the community served.
   c. build low-cost housing.
   d. become a member of the Federal Reserve system.

8. Selling industrial revenue bonds (IRBs) backed by the state's bonding credit is one way for a local community to
   a. build a new high school.
   b. purchase and improve land for an industrial or office park.
   c. rehabilitate the city jail.
   d. provide street lights throughout the downtown area.

9. The Neighborhood Stabilization Program provides grants for the
   a. purchase and redevelopment of foreclosed properties.
   b. development of low-cost rental projects.
   c. construction of public facilities.
   d. exclusive benefit of low-income families.

10. The Farm Credit System network of financial institutions may provide credit to farmers and ranchers for all *EXCEPT* the
    a. processing and marketing of goods.
    b. purchase of farm equipment.
    c. rehab of farm outbuildings.
    d. purchase of a home in an urban area.

Chapter 4

# The Secondary Mortgage Market

## LEARNING OBJECTIVES

When you've finished reading this chapter, you will be able to

- describe the original purpose and organization of Fannie Mae and Freddie Mac and how they have evolved since then;
- explain the role of the Federal Housing Finance Agency (FHFA);
- list underwriting guidelines that must be followed in order to sell mortgage loans to Fannie Mae or Freddie Mac;
- explain the role of Ginnie Mae in the secondary market; and
- briefly describe the function of the FHLB, Farmer Mac, and REMICs.

**administered price system**
**collateralized mortgage obligation (CMO)**
**conforming loan**
**Desktop Originator® (DO)**
**Desktop Underwriter® (DU)**
**Fannie Mae**
**Federal Home Loan Bank (FHLB)**
**Federal Housing Finance Agency (FHFA)**
**Freddie Mac**
**Ginnie Mae**
**government-sponsored enterprise (GSE)**
**jumbo loans**
**Loan Prospector®**
**nonconforming loan**
**par**
**participation certificates (PCs)**
**pass-through certificates**
**premium**
**primary lender**
**qualified residential mortgage (QRM)**
**real estate mortgage investment conduits (REMICs)**

The secondary mortgage market is designed to deal in real estate mortgages, buying them from loan originators and selling them to investors or pooling them to enlarge the markets for these types of securities. When mortgages are purchased from

**primary lenders** (such as banks, thrifts, and mortgage companies), also known as loan originators, the money generated acts to replenish the supply necessary for continued lending activities. When mortgages are sold to investors such as Fannie Mae, Freddie Mac, and other financial institutions, funds are recirculated nationally making credit available to borrowers in all geographic locations.

## MAJOR PARTICIPANTS IN THE SECONDARY MARKET

The major participants in the secondary mortgage market are Fannie Mae (formerly the Federal National Mortgage Association), Freddie Mac (formerly the Federal Home Loan Mortgage Corporation), and Ginnie Mae (formerly the Government National Mortgage Association). Other participants include the Federal Home Loan Bank (FHLB), the Federal Agricultural Mortgage Corporation (Farmer Mac), and many private real estate mortgage investment conduits (REMICs) that use mortgage-backed securities (MBSs) to collateralize their own securities.

The financial market for real estate loans is based on the ability of loan originators to dispose of their new loans as quickly as possible in the secondary market as they need to replenish funds and strive to manage the interest rate risk that arises from long-term, fixed-rate mortgages. This results in loan originators having to closely follow the loan guidelines established by the secondary market investors.

This chapter examines the participants in the secondary mortgage market and how their activities facilitate the national distribution of funds to the primary markets. Figure 4.1 illustrates an example of how the process works.

### Collateralized Mortgage Obligation (CMO)

The trend toward selling real estate loans has led to the development of a major new group of secondary market investors. Based on the concept of collateralization—the pooling together of homogenous types of mortgages to use as collateral for issuing marketable securities—private companies have emerged to challenge the dominant positions of Fannie Mae and Freddie Mac. Wall Street developed a market for these **collateralized mortgage obligation (CMO)** loans tied to short-term interest rates. These adjustable-rate mortgages were often sold to the consumer on the premise that they could always refinance before the initial rate increased. Subprime lending doubled and tripled as these high-risk types of loans were originated, often based on lax underwriting standards. When Fannie Mae and Freddie Mac saw their market shares drop, they too began purchasing these "exotic" loans. Operating as real estate mortgage investment conduits (REMICs), life insurance companies, pension funds, securities dealers, and other financial institutions

*FIGURE 4.1* **The Secondary Mortgage Market**

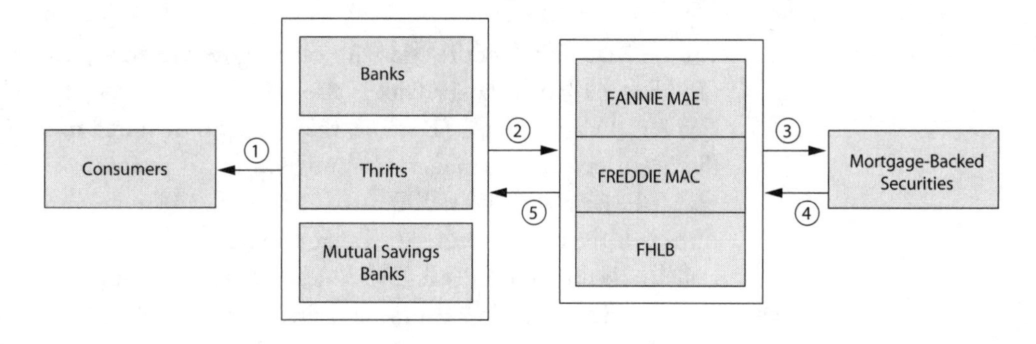


Step 1: Primary Market Lenders (Banks, Thrifts, Mutual Savings Banks, etc.) Provide Mortgages to Consumers.

Step 2: Primary Market Lenders Sell Loan Packages to Fannie Mae, Freddie Mac, and Federal Home Loan Bank.

Step 3: Fannie Mae, Freddie Mac, and FHLB Sell Mortgage-Backed Securities on the Open Market.

Step 4: Monies Received through the Sale of Mortgage-Backed Securities Provide Fannie Mae, Freddie Mac, and FHLB with Funds to Purchase More Loan Packages from the Primary Lenders.

Step 5: By Purchasing More Loan Packages, Fannie Mae, Freddie Mac, and FHLB Provide the Primary Market Lenders with Additional Money to Fund More Mortgage Loans for Consumers.

began creating new loans for their own portfolios, as well as buying and selling loans from other originators.

**...and the walls came crashing down!** Inevitably, the bubble burst. As housing prices began to decline in 2006 and borrowers were unable to refinance due to lowered property values, the rate of foreclosure went up throughout the country, and by 2007, both Wall Street and Main Street were in trouble.

Almost all of the subprime lenders went under and by 2011, most of the private mortgage insurance companies were headed for failure. In September 2008, Fannie Mae and Freddie Mac were both placed in conservatorship under the Federal Housing Finance Agency (FHFA). The conservatorship has continued far longer than was originally anticipated and was still in place in 2014. One of the primary goals of the FHFA was to stabilize the operations of Fannie Mae and Freddie Mac in order to continue the functions of the secondary market. By 2013, that phase appears to have been successful. The second goal focused on foreclosure prevention efforts. Over 2.7 million foreclosure prevention actions indicate that the second phase is also having some success.

Much discussion has taken place about whether or not Fannie Mae and Freddie Mac should continue at a corporate level in the secondary market. The new director of FHFA, Melvin Watt, indicated that Fannie Mae and Freddie Mac should remain in place with no reduction in current loan limits until the level of private investors increases. The FHFA will continue the government's role in the mortgage finance market.

The following section will discuss the background and history of Fannie Mae and Freddie Mac with a brief description of some of their loan products.

## THE GOVERNMENT-SPONSORED ENTERPRISES (GSEs)

**Fannie Mae** and **Freddie Mac** are called **government-sponsored enterprises (GSEs)**. (The Federal Home Loan Bank is also a GSE but will be covered separately later in this chapter.) Due to their GSE status, they were not required to register their securities with the Securities and Exchange Commission or to pay state and local corporate income tax. They were also allowed to carry a large line of credit with the Treasury Department. Although their debt securities and mortgage-backed securities (MBSs) were never officially backed by the federal government, there was a public conception that the government would never allow Fannie and Freddie to default on their obligations.

Over four decades, Fannie Mae and Freddie Mac grew rapidly and dominated the secondary market for **conforming loans** (loans that fit their qualifying standards). They both developed numerous loan products that enabled more potential homebuyers to obtain mortgage loans at low interest rates. Unfortunately, when the overall housing market began to decline in 2006, housing prices dropped and made it impossible for at-risk homeowners to either sell or refinance. The two GSEs suffered large losses in areas of their portfolios such as subprime loans and mortgage-backed securities issued by private companies.

The **Federal Housing Finance Agency (FHFA)** was established under the Federal Housing Reform Act of 2007 as an independent agency to regulate Fannie Mae, Freddie Mac, and the Federal Home Loan Bank (FHLB). At that point, these three enterprises had $5.4 trillion of guaranteed mortgage-backed securities (MBSs) and debt outstanding with an 80% market share of all new mortgages. Despite the best efforts of the enterprises to provide liquidity to the conforming mortgage market while raising and maintaining capital, their ability to fulfill their mission deteriorated, raising concern over both safety and soundness issues.

By September of 2008, Fannie Mae and Freddie Mac had outstanding guarantees of $3.8 trillion, and there were serious doubts as to whether they would be able to cover the potential losses. On September 6, 2008, acting under the Housing and Economic Recovery Act of 2008, FHFA placed Fannie Mae and Freddie Mac into conservatorship. The Treasury was given the authority to provide them with unlimited capital by purchasing their stock in order to keep them solvent. At this point, the government officially backed their debt securities and MBS guarantees. Under the conservatorship, both entities operate business as usual but with stronger backing for the holders of mortgage-backed securities (MBSs) and other debt. FHFA assumed the power of the board of directors and management. Common stock and preferred stock dividends were eliminated, but all common and preferred stock remains outstanding.

By 2009, the two GSEs owned or guaranteed approximately half of the outstanding mortgages in the country and financed almost 75% of all new mortgages that year. By the fall of 2011, the GSEs had provided more than $5.7 trillion in funding for U.S. mortgage markets.

In July 2010, Fannie Mae and Freddie Mac were delisted from the New York Stock Exchange; they are currently traded in the over-the-counter (OTC) market. They are quoted on the OTC Bulletin under the symbols *FNMA* and *FMCC*. The Congressional Budget Office estimated that nearly $400 billion in tax dollars would eventually be needed to cover losses on the trillions of dollars' worth of mortgage-backed securities they own or guarantee.

As conservator of Fannie Mae and Freddie Mac, FHFA is taking aggressive steps in an effort to recover losses on both Fannie and Freddie loan portfolios. In July 2011, USB Americas was sued for making material misstatements and omissions about mortgage loans packaged under its private-label MBS. In September 2011, FHFA announced that it was suing 17 different financial institutions for misrepresenting the quality of mortgage-backed securities sold to Fannie or Freddie. As of September 2014, 15 of the original 17 lawsuits had been settled for a total of more than $17.5 billion.

A major challenge for Congress over the next few years will be to develop a structure for the secondary mortgage market to achieve its original two purposes:

- Help ensure a steady supply of financing for residential mortgages.
- Provide subsidized assistance for mortgages on housing for low- and moderate-income families.

## FHFA Actions

FHFA establishes the conforming loan limits and sets goals for the percentage of loans to be made to low- and moderate-income households each year. On October 24, 2011, changes to the Home Affordable Refinance Program (HARP) were announced that made the program available to more homeowners who were underwater in their mortgages. The program eliminated some risk-based fees, removed the current 125% loan-to-value ceiling, eliminated the need for a new appraisal, and extended the end date for HARP until December 31, 2013, for loans sold to Fannie Mae or Freddie Mac on or before May 31, 2009. HARP has now been extended through the end of 2015.

Under the terms of the Housing and Economic Recovery Act (HERA), the baseline limit for conforming loans must be adjusted each year to reflect changes in the national average home price, though the act prohibits any decline. Regardless of some ups and downs in average home prices between 2009 and 2014, the baseline limit remains at $417,000 for one-unit properties in the contiguous United States. Loan limits are higher for multi-unit properties. In high-cost areas and in Alaska, Hawaii, Guam, and the U.S. Virgin Islands, the limit is 150% of the baseline limit. The local limit is based on 115% of the FHA median house price for an area, which is well below $417,000 in most parts of the country. In no case can it exceed $625,500 (150% of $417,000).

The 2014 loan limits are shown in Figure 4.2.

*FIGURE 4.2* **2014 Conforming Loan Limits**

| | *General* | *High Cost** |
|---|---|---|
| Single unit | $417,000 | $625,500 |
| Duplex | $533,850 | $800,775 |
| Triplex | $645,300 | $967,950 |
| Fourplex | $801,950 | $1,202,925 |

*These high-cost limits also apply to Alaska, Hawaii, Guam, and the U.S. Virgin Islands. The loan limits are based on 115% of local median price established by FHFA up to the maximum limits shown above.

## FANNIE MAE

Fannie Mae was established by congressional charter in 1938 as the Federal National Mortgage Association (FNMA) to expand the flow of available mortgage money throughout the country by creating a secondary market for the purchase of FHA-insured mortgages. The scope of operations was broadened in 1944 to include purchasing VA-guaranteed loans. The purchase of the FHA and VA loans was made at **par**; that is, at full face value, making Fannie Mae an important and sought-after provider for the real estate mortgage market.

### Empowerment to Sell Mortgages

In 1954, Fannie Mae was rechartered as a national secondary mortgage market clearinghouse to be financed by private capital. Fannie Mae was empowered to sell its mortgages as well as purchase new FHA and VA loans. Fannie Mae's purchases were no longer made at par but at whatever discounted price would develop a reasonable rate of return. This profit attitude was consistent with the reorganizational goal of private ownership. Fannie Mae did not have to purchase every mortgage submitted to it, only those mortgages that met its standards for marketability.

In other words, Fannie Mae imposed its own criteria for acceptance of mortgages submitted for sale, which sometimes created animosity among mortgage originators. It was argued that one federal agency should accept another's standards. Fannie Mae countered with the argument that the FHA and VA standards for credit and appraisal were minimum standards and insisted that all mortgages submitted to Fannie Mae would have to meet its own standards for quality, yield, and risk. The quality and level of stability of guaranteed and insured loans were raised in order to meet these new requirements.

When Fannie Mae purchases mortgages, a servicing agreement is executed allowing the loan originator-seller to act as a collection agent for a specified fee. This fee, a rate of approximately one-fourth to three-eighths of 1% of the mortgage amount, creates a substantial source of income for the originator, depending on the size of its mortgage loan portfolio.

Loan originators derive a large portion of their mortgage investment income from origination and collection fees. In many cases, especially with the mortgage bankers who issue the bulk of FHA and VA loans, the more loans that can be created, the higher the potential profits. Thus, the Fannie Mae secondary mortgage market allows loan originators an opportunity to roll over their money. By selling their mortgages, these originators can secure more funds for making additional loans, thereby collecting more origination fees.

When Fannie Mae sells its mortgages, it does so in open-market transactions in which the purchasers are required to pay current prices for the securities.

### Reorganization Under HUD

The Housing and Urban Development Act of 1968 changed the Fannie Mae organization once again. Based on its successful operation in preceding years as a quasi-public, profitable corporation, Fannie Mae was reorganized as a fully private corporation. All

Treasury-owned stock was redeemed, and a like amount of over-the-counter common stock was offered to the general public. Fannie Mae became a separate, privately owned corporation subject to federal corporate income tax and exempt from state income taxes. It retained the benefit of government sponsorship, which includes a line of credit with the U.S. Treasury, and was called a GSE.

The 1968 reorganization was meant to enhance Fannie Mae's ability to participate in the secondary market and to encourage new money to enter the real estate mortgage market. Fannie Mae could now purchase mortgages at a **premium** (in excess of par) and was allowed to expand its own borrowing ability by floating securities backed by specific pools of mortgages in its portfolio.

The Emergency Home Finance Act of 1970 gave Fannie Mae the additional authority to purchase mortgages other than FHA-insured or VA-guaranteed loans, mostly conventional loans. This further expanded Fannie Mae's impact on national real estate finance.

## Administered Price System

In the past, Fannie Mae's mortgage-purchasing procedures had been handled under a free-market-system auction. Lenders offered to sell Fannie Mae their loans at acceptable discounts, with Fannie Mae buying the lowest-priced loans—those with the deepest discounts. This system was replaced by an **administered price system** in which Fannie Mae adjusted its required yields daily in accordance with market factors and its financial needs.

Under the administered price system, lenders call a special Fannie Mae rate line to secure current yield quotes and then a separate line to place an order to sell. Lenders may order a mandatory commitment whereby delivery of loans to Fannie Mae is guaranteed or a standby commitment in which the lender retains the option to deliver the loans or not, depending on the price at time of delivery.

## Fannie Mae Mortgage-Backed Securities (MBSs)

When Fannie Mae purchases mortgage loans from mortgage companies, savings institutions, credit unions, or commercial banks, they are generally packaged into mortgage-backed securities (MBSs) and sold in international capital markets. In June 2005, Fannie Mae announced that first lien fixed-rate (and some adjustable-rate) mortgages for a term of up to 40 years would be eligible for inclusion in its MBS pools. Fannie Mae also issues a variety of short- and long-term debt securities to meet investor needs. The Universal Debt Facility Offering Circular is a legal document that provides detailed information on Fannie Mae's available Debt Securities: Benchmark Bills®, Benchmark Bonds®, and Benchmark Notes®. The Offering Circular clearly states that the securities are not guaranteed by nor constitute any debt or obligation of the United States.

For more detailed information, visit www.fanniemae.com and search for "Understanding Fannie Mae Debt."

## Underwriting Standards

Lenders wishing to sell their conventional loans to Fannie Mae must subscribe to its guidelines, which are revised from time to time. Fannie Mae provides two versions of its automated underwriting system, the **Desktop Underwriter® (DU)** for lender servicers and the **Desktop Originator® (DO)** for independent mortgage broker-agents. Lenders access Fannie Mae's sophisticated loan analysis system through the software they offer customers. Selling Guides are available on www.efanniemae.com, along with a full guide to underwriting, which includes specific details on reporting borrower income and assets, debts and other liabilities, maximum interest rates, and loan amounts allowed for different types of loan products. After all of the borrower information is submitted to DU, a response is received with regard to both credit risk and eligibility for the loan. Ideally, the response will be approved/eligible.

Some Fannie Mae loan products require manual underwriting for loans that do not meet the guideline requirements as provided under automatic underwriting. The requirements for manual underwriting are also available online.

Typical Fannie Mae guidelines include the following:

- Any loan with a loan-to-value (LTV) ratio of more than 80% must carry private mortgage insurance; cost varies according to the amount of down payment and the borrower's credit history.
- A 20% down payment may be entirely from gift funds; gift funds are also permitted with less than 20% down, but 5% will be required from borrowers' own funds.
- The seller can contribute up to 3% of the sales price toward borrower's closing costs with a 5% down payment and up to 6% with a 10% down payment. (Six percent may be allowed on MyCommunityMortgage®.)
- Homebuyer Education and counseling is required for first-time homebuyers obtaining a MyCommunityMortgage®, those depending on non-traditional credit, or those purchasing a two-, three-, or four-unit property.
- Specific ratios for the total amount allowed for housing expenses (principle, interest, real estate taxes, property insurance, and any homeowner association or condominium fees) and for total monthly debt vary according to the type of loan product, but a conservative estimate would be 28% of gross monthly income (GMI) for housing and 36% of GMI for total debt, including housing expenses. The ratios are higher for special loan products such as the MyCommunityMortgage®.
- A minimum down payment of 5% is preferred, but there are still some loan products that only require a 3% down payment. A 2014 change now allows gifts and grants for a down payment.

Effective since 2011, a prospective borrower who has experienced a prior foreclosure may have to wait seven years before being eligible for a Fannie Mae loan. If the home was sold as a short sale where the bank accepted less than the total amount due, the waiting period is a minimum of two years. In the past, monthly debt like a car payment that would be paid off in less than ten months may not have counted as part of the total debt. As of 2014, all debt will be counted regardless of the months remaining.

See www.fanniemae.com for an eligibility matrix with information on both desktop and manual underwriting for fixed-rate and adjustable-rate mortgages plus HomeStyle Renovation®, Manufactured Housing, and MyCommunityMortgage®.

## In Practice

A savings bank has just closed on $5 million worth of home mortgage loans. The loans are all for 30 years at an interest rate of 8%. Although these loans will provide the bank with a steady stream of income for many years, the bank is now faced with a dilemma—no more funds available to make additional mortgage loans.

One way to achieve more capital would be to sell the mortgages to Fannie Mae or Freddie Mac. Of course, the bank would have to make sure that it followed the Fannie Mae/Freddie Mac guidelines with regard to the current maximum loan amount, down payment, qualifying ratios, seller contribution to purchaser's closing costs, and any private mortgage insurance requirements. As long as these guidelines are met, the $5 million package of loans can be sold, though there will be a discount on the total. The bank can maintain the level of yield it desires, however, by passing along the discount to the borrowers in the form of discount points.

**Conforming and Nonconforming Loans.** The terms *conforming* and *nonconforming* are used by lenders to define loans that conform to the Fannie Mae/Freddie Mac qualifying guidelines. Loans that do not meet the conforming guidelines, including maximum loan amount and down payment requirements, are called **nonconforming loans**. Although there is a conforming loan limit, buyers may pay any price for a property, making up the difference in cash. Maximum loan limits are established to set a standard for these types of loans so that they become homogeneous packages for securitization in the secondary market. Loans issued in excess of these amounts are nonconforming. They are called **jumbo loans** and may be held by lenders for their own investment portfolios or sold to the secondary market. Any loan that does not meet all of the Fannie Mae/Freddie Mac guidelines is considered nonconforming, even though the loan amount may be very small.

**Credit Scoring.** Included in the automated underwriting process is the applicant's credit score, an objective method of assessing credit risk based on the statistical probability of repayment of the debt. The applicant's score is based on data included in the national repository files maintained by the credit bureaus Experian, Equifax, and TransUnion. The actual numerical score is derived from FICO scoring system.

Credit scores reflect the combination of many risk factors. In some instances, a borrower who has had a bankruptcy with an otherwise clean history of making payments may have a better credit score than another borrower who has not had a bankruptcy but has a long history of delinquent payments. A credit score of 620 to 680 may be acceptable with a larger down payment, but 720 is preferred for any LTV greater than 90%.

FICO and credit scoring will be discussed in greater detail in Chapter 9.

### Establishing Non-Traditional Credit

Fair Isaac Credit Services, Inc., offers a FICO Expansion Score to assess credit risk. The secondary market has responded to this need by establishing guidelines for a Non-Traditional Mortgage Credit Report (NTMCR). Fannie Mae will only allow an NTMCR if a traditional credit score is not available from any of the three major credit repositories. Fannie Mae uses a three-tier approach for those unable to obtain a traditional credit score: Tier I credit includes rent, utilities, and telecommunication payments; Tier II includes direct insurance payments; and Tier III includes payments to local stores for durable goods, medical bill payments, and payments for school tuition or childcare. The goal is to obtain a 12-month history from four sources, preferably from Tier I. Freddie Mac has similar guidelines but includes union dues payments and regular payments to a savings or stock purchase plan.

### Fannie Mae Mortgage Loan Products

Fannie Mae offers both fixed- and adjustable-rate mortgage loans in a variety of different loan products. For current information on mortgage loans eligible for purchase by Fannie Mae, visit www.fanniemae.com and www.efanniemae.com. Fannie Mae also purchases home construction and renovation loans as well as the FHA reverse mortgage for seniors called the Home Equity Conversion Mortgage. The 97% LTV Flexible Mortgage has been eliminated.

Fannie Mae offers a low-down-payment option for properties owned by Fannie Mae called the HomePath loan. The HomeStyle Renovation loan is for the purchase and cost of renovations with a down payment as low as 3%. It is available for the purchase of a primary residence, second home, or investment property.

Fannie Mae's MyCommunityMortgage® loans offer more flexibility in qualifying guidelines and credit history and have special options for teachers, police officers, firefighters, health care workers, and those with disabilities. There are also special loan products for rural housing and Native Americans.

See Fannie Mae's *Selling Guide*, available at www.fanniemae.com, for information on all Fannie Mae loan products.

## FREDDIE MAC

The credit crunch of 1969 and 1970 gave rise to the Emergency Home Finance Act of 1970, which created, among other things, the Federal Home Loan Mortgage Corporation (FHLMC), now known as Freddie Mac. Freddie Mac was organized specifically to provide a secondary mortgage market for conventional loans originated by the savings associations and thrifts that are members of the Federal Home Loan Bank System.

### Organization

Freddie Mac was established with an initial subscription of $100 million from the 12 Federal Home Loan Banks and placed under the direction of three members of the Federal Home Loan Bank Board. Freddie Mac was given the authority to raise additional funds by floating its own securities, which were backed by pools of its own mortgages. Since 1989, Freddie Mac has become an independent stock company and is a GSE like Fannie Mae.

As a major player in the secondary market, Freddie Mac buys mortgages that meet stated guidelines and product standards, packages the loans into **participation certificates (PCs)**, and sells the securities to investors on Wall Street.

As part of the Housing and Economic Recovery Act of 2008, Freddie Mac came under the supervision of FHFA and, in September 2008, was placed in conservatorship along with Fannie Mae.

## Underwriting Standards

Freddie Mac generally follows the same conforming loan standards as Fannie Mae. One exception is that Freddie Mac only looks at total debt-to-income ratio with no set percentage for housing expense. The amount of down payment and qualifying ratios varies with different loan products.

**Electronic Underwriting System.** Freddie Mac provides its own automatic underwriting service, called **Loan Prospector®**, to participating lenders, mortgage insurers, mortgage bankers and brokers, and others in the real estate market.

The Loan Prospector® software evaluates a borrower's creditworthiness using statistical models and judgmental rules. The credit evaluation indicates the level of underwriting and documentation necessary to determine the investment quality of a loan. It includes the borrower's credit reputation and financial capacity as well as the estimated value of the property. The credit analysis uses information from the loan application and credit searches. The value of the property is derived from statistical models or from a traditional appraisal.

## Freddie Mac Loan Products

Freddie Mac purchases both fixed- and adjustable-rate loans for a predetermined amount of time from 15-year, 20-year, 30-year, and, in some cases, 40-year terms. Loans may be for the purchase or refinance of owner-occupied single-family dwellings, condominiums, planned unit developments (PUDs), and manufactured homes. Loans are also available for one- to four-unit primary residence and investment properties and single-unit second homes. As of September 2010, Freddie Mac no longer accepts interest-only mortgages.

Freddie Mac's Home Possible® mortgages offer a low down payment option for first-time and low- to moderate-income homebuyers and provide additional flexibility for teachers, firefighters, law enforcement officers, health care workers, and members of the U.S. armed forces. Homeownership education is required for first-time homebuyers using Home Possible mortgages. The debt-to-income ratio may be as high as 45%.

For a full description of the variety of loan products that can be purchased by Freddie Mac, see www.freddiemac.com.

### Qualified Residential Mortgage (QRM)

The Consumer Financial Protection Bureau (CFPB) has been working on developing rules and regulations for establishing the **qualified residential mortgage (QRM)** program. Under this potential new program, a QRM would have a 20% down payment (no mortgage insurance), follow 28/36 income and debt ratios, and allow only borrowers with an above-average credit score. For any loan that doesn't meet QRM standards that is to be sold to Fannie Mae or Freddie Mac, the lender would have to retain a 5% interest in any mortgage securities.

After strong opposition from the National Association of REALTORS® (NAR), congressional leaders, and consumer and industry groups, the CFPB reproposed the QRM rule and aligned the definition of QRM with the same standards of a QM (qualified mortgage). The QM rule ensures that lenders only make loans to borrowers who have the ability to repay the loan. The QM rule prohibits loans with negative amortization, interest-only payments, balloon payments, terms of more than 30 years, and all "no doc" loans. Additional requirements are that points and fees paid by the consumer may not exceed 3% of the loan amount, and the debt-to-income ratio may not exceed 43%. No prepayment penalties are allowed.

There is a special provision regarding balloon-payment USDA loans in rural areas.

## GINNIE MAE

The Government National Mortgage Corporation, known today as **Ginnie Mae**, was created in 1968 as a government-owned corporation under the direction of the Department of Housing and Urban Development (HUD) to provide financing for special assistance programs and operate the securities pool. Its stated mission is to expand affordable housing in America by linking domestic and global capital markets to the nation's housing markets.

Ginnie Mae does not buy or sell loans or issue MBSs but instead guarantees that investors will receive timely payments of principal and interest on MBSs backed by federally insured (FHA) or guaranteed (VA) loans. Other eligible loans for Ginnie Mae MBSs include those originated by the Department of Agriculture Rural and Community Housing (RHS) and HUD's Office of Native American Programs (ONAP). Ginnie Mae MBSs are fully modified pass-through securities guaranteed by the full faith and credit of the U.S. government. Regardless of whether the mortgage payment is made, the investor receives the full principal and interest payment.

### Ginnie Mae Mortgage-Backed Securities

Mortgage-backed securities are pools of mortgages used as collateral for the issuance of securities, commonly called **pass-through certificates**, as the principal and interest payments are "passed through" to the investor. The interest on the security is lower than the interest rate on the loan to cover the cost of servicing and the guaranty fee. There are two types of Ginnie Mae MBSs available. The Ginnie Mae I MBS requires that all mortgages in the pool be the same type (e.g., single-family) and that the mortgages remain insured or guaranteed by FHA, VA, RHS, or ONAP with a minimum pool size of $1 million. Payment is made on the 15th of the month.

The Ginnie Mae II MBS provides for multiple-issue pools that allow for more geographic dispersal. Higher servicing fees are allowed, and the minimum pool size is $250,000 for multilender pools and $1 million for single-lender pools. Payment is made on the 20th of the month to allow time for payments to be consolidated by a central paying agent.

**Ginnie Mae Platinum Securities.** The Platinum Securities program allows investors to combine Ginnie Mae MBSs pools into a single security and receive one payment each month rather than separate payments from individual pools. See www.ginniemae.gov for more information on this program.

**Ginnie Mae Real Estate Mortgage Investment Conduits (REMICs).** Ginnie Mae administers a real estate mortgage investment conduits (REMICs) program. REMICs direct principal and interest payments from underlying mortgage-backed securities to classes with different principal balances, interest rates, average lives, prepayment characteristics, and final maturities. REMICs allow investors with different investment horizons, risk-reward preferences, and asset-liability management requirements to purchase MBSs tailored to their needs.

Unlike traditional pass-throughs, the principal and interest payments in REMICs are not passed through to investors pro rata; instead they are divided into varying payment streams to create classes with different expected maturities, differing levels of seniority, or subordination or other characteristics. The assets underlying REMIC securities can be either other MBSs or whole mortgage loans.

Ultimately, REMICs allow issuers to create securities with short, intermediate, and long-term maturities, flexibility that in turn allows issuers to expand the MBS market to fit the needs of a variety of investors.

## FEDERAL HOME LOAN BANK (FHLB)

The 12 banks of the **Federal Home Loan Bank (FHLB)** system (referred to at FHLBanks) are owned by over 8,100 regulated financial institutions from all over the United States. Equity in the FHLBanks is held by the owner-members and is not publicly traded. FHLBanks are self-capitalizing and exempt from state and local income taxes but receive no direct taxpayer assistance. The mission of the FHLBanks is to provide cost-effective funding to the members for use in housing, community, and economic development; to provide regional affordable housing programs; to support housing finance through advances and mortgage programs; and to serve as a reliable source of liquidity for its membership.

As a government-sponsored enterprise (GSE), the FHLB is now regulated by the Federal Housing Finance Agency (FHFA). A major function of the FHLB is to provide its members a national market for their securities. The FHLB purchases loans from its member banks and provides strong competition in the secondary market. A recent update from the FHFA reports that the FHLBanks have emerged from the financial crisis in generally good condition. They are profitable and have strengthened capital positions with their 2012 annual earnings being their highest since 2007.

## FARMER MAC

This program was originally created by Congress with the Agricultural Credit Act of 1987 as the Federal Agricultural Mortgage Corporation (FAMC). Known now as Farmer Mac, its mission is to improve the availability of long-term credit at stable interest rates to America's farmers; ranchers; and rural homeowners, businesses, and communities. This mission is accomplished by purchasing qualified loans from agricultural mortgage lenders, thus providing them with funding to make additional loans. Farmer Mac is the secondary market for agriculture loans in the same way that Fannie Mae and Freddie Mac are for conventional and government loans. See www.farmermac.com for more information on the program.

## REAL ESTATE MORTGAGE INVESTMENT CONDUITS (REMICS)

**Real estate mortgage investment conduits (REMICs)** were established under the Tax Reform Act of 1986, and they are companies that hold pools of mortgages that back up securities collateralized by the mortgage cash flows. Mortgage-backed securities are broken into different classes called tranches, which direct principal and interest to predetermined groups of investors. REMICs are structures for the private securitization of real estate mortgages and contributed to the opening of the general capital markets to real estate lenders. Fannie Mae, Freddie Mac, and Ginnie Mae all offer REMIC multiclass, mortgage-backed securities.

REMICs offer several tax advantages that were not previously available on mortgage-backed securities. A REMIC may have various sources of income, but ownership comes in two categories: regular interests and residual interests. Regular interests are those offered to most investors. They are bond-like instruments with a face value equal to the share of the REMIC's underlying assets. Residual interests collect payments made in excess of those needed to pay the regular interests and any reserve funds set up initially.

A popular REMIC is the commercial mortgage-backed securities (CMBSs) pool. Prior to the development of this REMIC, commercial loan originators had no option but to keep these loans in their own portfolios. Very large loans were divided among several lenders. The CMBS industry continues to expand its participation in the U.S. mortgage loan market with over $1 trillion securitization of commercial loans.

## SUMMARY

This chapter examined the roles of the various major agencies involved in the secondary mortgage market for real estate finance, including Fannie Mae, Freddie Mac, Ginnie Mae, and the Federal Home Loan Bank.

Based on electronic procedures that are uniform in the evaluation of credit and collateral, a huge market for trading in securities has evolved. Local originators of loans sell them to secondary investors, thereby freeing local capital for making more loans. In addition to FHA and VA loans, the secondary mortgage market has expanded to include conventional loans on homes, condominiums, multifamily projects, and commercial developments. Operating as warehousers of money, Fannie Mae and Freddie Mac effectively redistribute funds from money-rich areas to money-poor areas.

Fannie Mae was organized in 1938 as a federal agency involved primarily in purchasing and managing FHA-insured loans. The association evolved into a private, profit-making corporation dealing in every type of residential real estate mortgage loan. To raise funds for the purchase of these mortgages, Fannie Mae charges fees and has the authority to borrow from the U.S. Treasury. Fannie Mae markets its own securities. Freddie Mac was created in 1970 to provide a secondary mortgage market for the nation's savings associations. Through the years, it evolved into a private corporation, buying and selling all types of loans and adding to the effectiveness of the secondary market. As a result of the financial crisis that started in 2007, Fannie Mae and Freddie Mac were placed in conservatorship under the Federal Housing Finance Agency in 2008.

Created as a wholly owned government corporation in 1968, Ginnie Mae is under the jurisdiction of HUD. It finances special assistance programs and participates in the secondary market through its guarantee of FHA and VA mortgage-backed securities. In addition to the three major participants in the secondary market, other public and private agencies and companies have begun developing under the concept of collateralization. This concept pools existing mortgages together in homogeneous packages that are then pledged as collateral to issue mortgage-backed securities (MBSs). These MBSs are, in turn, sold to investors.

Additional secondary market participants are the Federal Home Loan Bank, Farmer Mac (which deals in farm and ranch loans), and the various real estate mortgage investment conduits (REMICs).

## INTERNET RESOURCES

Fannie Mae
*www.fanniemae.com*
*www.efanniemae.com*

Federal Agricultural Mortgage Corporation
*www.farmermac.com*

Federal Home Loan Bank
*www.fhlbanks.com*

Federal Housing Finance Agency
*www.fhfa.gov*

FICO
*www.fico.com*

Freddie Mac
*www.freddiemac.com*

Ginnie Mae
*www.ginniemae.gov*

National Association of REALTORS®
*www.realtor.org*

## REVIEW QUESTIONS

1. Fannie Mae and Freddie Mac are able to replenish their own funds, enabling them to purchase loans from primary lenders by
   a. borrowing from the Federal Reserve bank.
   b. borrowing from each other.
   c. requesting grant funds through HUD.
   d. selling mortgage-backed securities.

2. Lenders may order either a mandatory or standby commitment to sell loans to Fannie Mae through the
   a. federal open market.
   b. stock exchange.
   c. free market auction.
   d. administered price system.

3. Which of the following statements regarding Fannie Mae guidelines is *TRUE*?
   a. Loans with a higher than 80% LTV require private mortgage insurance.
   b. Maximum loan limits are set annually by each individual lender.
   c. The seller may contribute up to 6% towards borrower's closing costs on all loans.
   d. Homebuyer education and counseling is required of all borrowers.

4. The *BEST* description of a nonconforming loan is one that
   a. exceeds loan limit set annually by Fannie Mae and Freddie Mac.
   b. does not meet Fannie Mae and Freddie Mac qualifying guidelines.
   c. is restricted to four-family units.
   d. is limited to low-income housing.

5. All of the following are government-sponsored enterprises *EXCEPT*
   a. Fannie Mae.
   b. Freddie Mac.
   c. Ginnie Mae.
   d. the Federal Home Loan Bank.

6. Freddie Mac was originally chartered to
   a. compete with Fannie Mae.
   b. provide a secondary market for conventional loans (not FHA or VA).
   c. purchase government loans.
   d. provide mortgage loans for qualified applicants.

7. The agency established to ensure the financial safety and soundness of Fannie Mae and Freddie Mac is the
   a. Federal Deposit Insurance Corporation (FDIC).
   b. Office of Thrift Supervision (OTS).
   c. Federal Reserve System (FED).
   d. Federal Housing Finance Agency (FHFA).

8. The *MOST* important role played by Ginnie Mae today is
   a. originating FHA loans.
   b. purchasing VA loans.
   c. oversight of Fannie Mae and Freddie Mac.
   d. guaranteeing FHA and VA mortgage-backed securities.

9. The duties of the Federal Housing Finance Agency include all of the following *EXCEPT*
   a. establishing conforming loan limits.
   b. setting the percentage of loans to be made to low- and moderate-income borrowers.
   c. regulating Fannie Mae and Freddie Mac.
   d. supervising FHA.

10. The Tax Reform Act of 1986 established an entity that can issue multiclass securities. This entity, which has added to the activities of the secondary market, is the
    a. REIT.
    b. REMT.
    c. REMIC.
    d. RESPA.

Chapter 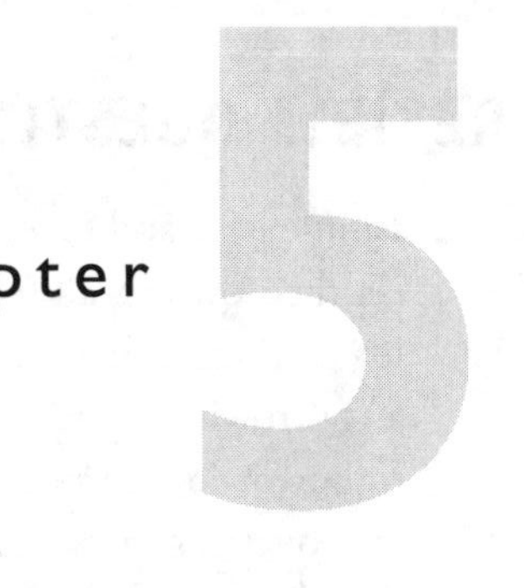

# Sources of Funds: Institutional, Non-Institutional, and Other Lenders

## LEARNING OBJECTIVES

When you've finished reading this chapter, you will be able to

- describe the types of loans offered by a commercial bank;
- explain the services of a mortgage broker and a mortgage banker;
- identify the various types of bonds used in real estate finance; and
- describe the role of private and foreign investors in real estate.

**bearer bonds**
**correspondents**
**coupon bonds**
**debentures**
**demand deposits**
**fiduciary responsibility**
**financial intermediaries**
**general obligation bonds**
**industrial development bonds**
**industrial revenue bonds (IRBs)**
**interim financing**
**junior financing**
**mortgage bankers**
**mortgage brokers**
**mortgage revenue bonds**
**municipal bonds**
**origination fee**
**participation financing**
**real estate investment trust (REIT)**
**real estate mortgage trust (REMT)**
**registered bonds**
**revenue bonds**
**Secure and Fair Enforcement Mortgage Licensing Act (SAFE Act)**
**thrifts**
**warehouse of funds**
**zero-coupon bonds**

Money available to finance real estate emanates from a long list of traditional and not so traditional lenders. The range of loan sources extends from the banks, thrifts, and life insurance companies, through the mortgage bankers and brokers to the private lending companies, and finally to the sellers who carry back loans to sell their own properties.

This chapter examines the following listed sources that make real estate loans. Collectively, they are called **primary lenders** or **financial intermediaries**. These lenders manage and guard entrusted funds over a period of time. The funds must be protected so they are available to their owners, dollar for dollar, when called for according to established arrangements. Because of certain characteristics, such as value, durability, and fixity, real property attracts much of this capital. Each of those listed will be described in detail, starting with institutional lenders, followed by non-institutional lenders:

| ***Institutional Lenders*** | ***Non-Institutional Lenders*** |
|---|---|
| Commercial banks | Life insurance companies |
| Mutual savings banks | Pension and retirement programs |
| Savings associations/thrifts | Credit unions |
| Mortgage brokers | Real estate bonds |
| Mortgage bankers | Private lenders |
| Real estate trusts | Foreign lenders |

## COMMERCIAL BANKS

As the name implies, commercial banks are designed to be safe depositories and lenders for a multitude of commercial banking activities. Although they have other sources of capital, including savings, loans from other banks, and the equity invested by their owners, commercial banks rely mainly on **demand deposits**, better known as checking accounts, for their basic supply of funds.

### Mortgage Loan Activities

Commercial banks were originally designed primarily to make loans to businesses to finance their operations and inventories. In more recent years, they often diversify into loans on real estate. In the past, they concentrated on industrial and commercial property real estate loans, but commercial banks are also active today in the one- to four-family home loan market.

Much of their real estate–related loan activities include construction loans, also known as **interim financing**; home improvement loans; and manufactured housing loans. These loans are all relatively short term and match the bank's demand deposit profile.

Construction loans run from three months to three years, depending on the size of the project. Home improvement loans may run up to five years and include financing the cost of additions, modernization, swimming pool construction, or other similar improvements. Manufactured home loans range from ten years to a longer term, usually depending on how permanently the home is attached to the property. These longer manufactured home loans usually include insurance from the Federal Housing Administration (FHA) or guarantees from the Department of Veterans Affairs (VA).

Today, most large commercial banks participate fully in home mortgages. Some of these loans may be kept in the bank's own portfolio, but most often the loans are packaged and sold in the secondary market to Fannie Mae, Freddie Mac, or other investors. Some smaller banks serve their select customers by providing them with long-term mortgage money on their homes. Other banks participate to some degree in the secondary money market by either selling home loans that they originate or buying packages of home loans to round out their own investment portfolios. Some commercial banks make loans to farmers for the purchase or modernization of their farms or for financing farm operations.

## Other Bank Activities

Loans to borrowers based on the equity in their homes are a popular product for commercial banks. The Internal Revenue Service (IRS) eliminated tax deductions for interest paid on consumer loans but preserved the deductions for interest paid on home loans. As a result, banks compete vigorously for equity loan business. Borrowers may use the monies generated by equity loans to purchase personal property, pay for education expenses or vacations, and even buy additional real estate. Excesses in the creation of these equity loans, many known as subprime loans, contributed greatly to the recent financial crisis.

Commercial banks also participate in real estate financing through at least three other avenues: by operation of their trust departments; by acting as mortgage bankers (including the ownership of mortgage banking companies); and by direct or indirect ownership of other lending businesses.

Commercial banks' trust departments supervise and manage relatively large quantities of money and property for their beneficiaries. They act as executors or coexecutors of estates, as conservators of the estates of incompetent persons, as guardians of the estates of minors, as trustees under agreements entered into by individuals or companies for specific purposes, and as trustees under insurance proceeds trusts. They also act as escrow agents in the performance of specific escrow agreements; as trustees for corporations in controlling their bonds, notes, and stock certificates; and as trustees for company retirement or pension funds.

In keeping with their **fiduciary responsibilities** to obtain maximum yields at low risks, trust departments usually take a conservative approach when making investments with funds left in their control. The primary role of the trustees is to preserve the value of the property entrusted to their management. Real estate loans made from these trust accounts are only one possibility in a long list of investment opportunities.

In addition to acting as originating and servicing agents for their own mortgages, many commercial bank mortgage loan departments originate and service loans for other lenders. Acting in the role of mortgage bankers, commercial banks represent life insurance companies, real estate investment or mortgage trusts, or even other commercial banks seeking loans in a specific community. In this capacity, a mortgage loan department secures an origination fee and a collection fee for servicing the new account, adding earnings to its overall profit picture.

Finally, some commercial banks participate, either directly or indirectly, as owners of real estate mortgage trusts (REMTs) or as members in a regional bank-holding company. These expanded investment opportunities add great flexibility to the real estate mortgage loan activities of commercial banks. Some larger banks make loans on commercial real estate developments, such as apartment projects, office buildings, or shopping centers. These larger loans usually are placed through bank-holding companies or subsidiary mortgage-banking operations.

Despite a movement toward the consolidation of banks, there is a countermovement of small bank start-ups. Many new small banks have been chartered, often organized by bankers who lost their jobs through mergers. These new banks seek business from the customers generally overlooked by the larger banks—small business owners, elderly depositors, and persons disenchanted with large bank anonymity.

The banking world continued to fight for the right to conduct general real estate brokerage up until March 11, 2009, when President Obama signed into law the FY2009 Omnibus Appropriations Act that permanently prohibits banks from entering the real estate brokerage and management businesses.

## MUTUAL SAVINGS BANKS

Formed to provide savings services for the emerging class of thrifty workers in the U.S. industrial expansion of the mid-19th century, mutual savings banks are concentrated in the eastern United States. Although a few of these financial institutions are located in the states of Alaska, Oregon, and Washington, most are found in Connecticut, New York, and Massachusetts. Others are located in Delaware, Indiana, Maryland, Minnesota, New Jersey, Ohio, Pennsylvania, and Wisconsin.

These banks are organized as mutual companies in which depositors-owners receive profits as interest or dividends on savings accounts, and leading local business people make up the boards of directors. The boards maintain their integrity and continuity by controlling the appointments of new directors. They generally take a strongly conservative investment attitude, reflecting the safety requirements of their depositors.

Mutual savings banks play an active and important role in local real estate financing activities, providing long-term mortgage loans. This is a consequence of the nature of their organization, for these banks are actually savings institutions. More than 70% of their assets are derived from savings accounts, which by definition have a long-term quality.

Mutual savings banks prefer to make real estate loans on properties located near their home offices so that the loans can be supervised efficiently. In those instances where a bank's funds exceed local mortgage market demands, out-of-state mortgage outlets are sought, mostly through mortgage bankers.

Mutual savings banks generally are limited in their lending activities by their charters. These limitations vary from state to state and are also further affected by specific bank policies. Usually, only 60 to 70% of total savings deposits may be invested in real estate mortgages and then mostly within restricted lending boundaries and predominantly in residential properties. These area restrictions were originally imposed to ease loan servicing requirements, among other purposes. Although mutual savings banks play a relatively small role in actual dollar amounts in the total national real estate loan market, they do provide important local real estate loan support, and they were the prototype for the savings associations/thrifts.

## SAVINGS ASSOCIATIONS/THRIFTS

Legend has it that the savings and loan associations, now known as savings banks or **thrifts**, were born when ten friends got together, each of them contributing $1,000 to a pot. Each contributor then drew a number from a bowl, with number one having the use of the $10,000 for a prescribed time period, then number two, and so on. This legend is not too far from the truth; early institutions were established as building and loan associations, with the specific purpose of providing loans to their depositors for housing construction.

### In Practice

A local builder wishes to obtain financing to build six houses. He first checks with his own credit union—it is a fairly small credit union and they do not finance construction or home mortgage loans.

He then calls his insurance agent and finds that the agent is only interested in much larger projects—in which the insurance company might actually acquire some ownership interest. His own home mortgage loan is with a local savings bank, so he meets with a loan officer there. He finds that the savings bank would be interested in providing loans for the eventual buyers of the six properties, but the savings bank is not interested in construction financing.

The builder finally goes to a large commercial bank and is successful in acquiring a construction loan. In fact, the commercial bank offers him a construction/permanent loan product that will provide the construction financing now and guarantee the availability of permanent financing for the mortgage loans required by the buyers of the finished properties.

Thrifts are organized as either stock or mutual companies. Many mutual associations have converted to stock companies to attract more capital. These thrifts were relatively free from public regulation until the creation of the Federal Home Loan Bank (FHLB) System in 1932. Paralleling the Federal Reserve System for the commercial banks, the FHLB was chartered to regulate member organizations, determine their reserve requirements, set discount rates, and provide insurance for their depositors.

The FHLB operates the 12 district banks that are now regulated by the Federal Housing Finance Agency. The member savings associations were chartered and regulated by the Office of Thrift Supervision (OTS), which now falls under the Comptroller of the Currency (OCC). The accounts are insured up to $250,000 per title per account by the Federal Deposit Insurance Corporation (FDIC).

All savings banks must be chartered, either by the OCC or by the state in which they are located. All federally chartered savings banks are required to participate in the FDIC insurance program.

### Mortgage Lending Activities

Of all the financial institutions, the thrifts have the most flexibility in their mortgage lending operations. Although some limitations are imposed by federal or state regulations, savings banks can make conventional mortgage loans for up to 100% of a property's value. More commonly, though, the loans are based on an 80% loan-to-value ratio (LTV) with private mortgage insurance (PMI) required for any loan with higher than an 80% LTV. Any limitation on the area in which loans can be made has been virtually eliminated by the ability of savings banks to participate in the national mortgage market through Freddie Mac and Fannie Mae. The thrifts also participate in the FHA-VA loan market.

Paralleling the growing movement in small commercial bank start-ups was a marked increase in applications to the OTS for charters to operate new savings banks. The only way for companies that were not commercial banks to enter into the full service banking business was to secure a savings bank charter. This charter could be owned by any type of company, and a federal charter enabled the new savings bank to operate in all 50 states.

## LIFE INSURANCE COMPANIES

Although the largest share of savings in the United States today is in securities and mutual funds, life insurance still plays a major role. According to the Department of Commerce, the insurance industry is one of the largest industries in terms of tax revenue on both the state and federal level. Insurance companies invest in municipal bonds, provide businesses with capital for research or expansion, and invest in commercial real estate.

Although there are no national laws concerning life insurance or casualty insurance companies, each state regulates these companies under their insurance departments. Life insurance and casualty companies can raise premium rates with permission from these state agencies, based on the amount needed to pay current claims and the earnings of the portfolio for future claims.

Life insurance companies are less concerned with the liquidity than with the safety and long-term stability of an investment. They prefer to finance larger real estate projects like shopping centers, leaving smaller loans such as home mortgages and construction financing to other lenders.

Many life insurance companies try to enhance the profitability and safety of their positions by insisting on equity positions in any major commercial project they finance. As a condition for such a loan, the company requires a partnership arrangement with the project developer. This type of financing is called **participation financing**, and it serves to expand the life insurance companies' investment portfolios. Life insurance companies also purchase blocks of single-family mortgages or securities from the secondary mortgage market.

The continuing popularity of term insurance provides life insurance companies billions of dollars on which they do not pay dividends. This allows these companies to participate competitively in the real estate mortgage market, and life insurance companies play an indispensable role in providing funds for real estate developments.

## PENSION AND RETIREMENT PROGRAMS

Monies held in pension funds are similar to the premiums collected and held by life insurance companies. Pension monies are collected routinely, usually from payroll deductions, and are held in trust until needed at retirement. They are not usually distributed in a lump sum but in regular payments, mostly on a monthly basis. This gives the pension fund managers a substantial amount of fixed funds together with a continuous flow of new monies. Over the last decade, a larger portion of U.S. savings have been in pension and other retirement programs.

Historically, pension monies were invested in government securities and corporate stocks and bonds, with little going into mortgage lending. Since the advent of the secondary mortgage market, pension fund managers have increasingly been purchasing blocks of mortgage-backed securities. The impact of this approach due to the economic crisis of 2007 is still to be determined.

## CREDIT UNIONS

Federally chartered credit unions were originally authorized by President Roosevelt in 1934. Credit unions experienced years of tremendous growth after the National Credit Union Administration (NCUA) was created in 1970 as an independent federal agency to charter and supervise federal credit unions, and the National Credit Union Share Insurance Fund (NCUSIF) was established to insure credit union deposits. The NCUSIF was recapitalized in 1985 by requiring all credit unions to deposit 1% of their shares into the Share Insurance Fund, which was backed by the full faith and credit of the United States. Since that time, credit unions have continued to grow and provide their members with a source of funding for personal property such as autos or furniture, home improvements, home equity loans, and real estate.

As the insurer and regulator of federally chartered credit unions, the NCUA acts in a similar way to the FDIC with the ability to place a credit union in conservatorship. This became necessary several times during the financial crisis due to losses on investments in mortgage-backed securities.

As of July 2014, there are over 8,000 federally insured credit unions with government agency securities as the largest component of the industry's investment portfolio, the largest being the Navy Federal Credit Union based in Vienna, Virginia.

Under the Credit Union Membership Access Act, which became effective in January 1999, credit unions were allowed to solicit new members from much wider criteria. These changes have allowed small business groups to join credit unions, as well as any person who resides in a member's household, including unmarried couples, live-in housekeepers, nursing care professionals, or anyone who contributes support to the household. Moreover, all immediate family members may also be eligible to join, greatly expanding credit unions' growth.

Credit unions present competition to the banking industry. They generally are not governed by federal, state, or local banking regulations, providing them greater flexibility in making loans. Although credit unions specialize in personal property loans, they continue to expand their participation in real estate finance as they offer competitive interest rates and low loan placement fees. The credit unions are also involved in the secondary markets by pooling their mortgage loans into various real estate mortgage investment conduits (REMICs).

## MORTGAGE BROKERS AND BANKERS

Financial intermediaries often lack the monetary capacity to expand beyond their local markets. When this occurs, these institutions look to the regional and national mortgage markets provided by Fannie Mae, Ginnie Mae, and Freddie Mac for expanded investment opportunities. These institutions also use the services of mortgage brokers and mortgage bankers.

Likewise, life insurance companies and pension fund managers enlist the aid of mortgage brokers or mortgage bankers to originate and service some of their real estate loans at the local level, rather than maintain an expensive network of branch offices.

Most lenders charge the borrower a placement or **origination fee** to cover the cost of creating the new loan—for the loan officer, processing, underwriting, closing, and all materials needed.

### Mortgage Brokers

Much as stockbrokers or real estate brokers act to bring buyers and sellers together to complete a transaction for which the brokers are duly compensated, **mortgage brokers** join borrowers with lenders for real estate loans. The successful completion of the loan entitles the mortgage broker to earn a placement fee.

Unlike the major lenders, a mortgage broker seldom invests capital in a loan and does not service a loan beyond its placement. After a loan "marriage" is completed, specific arrangements are made for the collection of the required payments. Usually, these payments are made directly to the lender, but often they are collected by a local escrow collection service. The mortgage broker fulfills all obligations when the loan is completed.

It is important for mortgage brokers to assume a large part of the responsibility for qualifying borrowers and investigating the soundness of an investment. In fact, their very business lives depend on the quality of the loans recommended. A borrower seeking the services of a mortgage broker depends on the broker's access to the many institutions that participate in real estate lending. A mortgage broker's success is a function of two things: (1) accessibility to the offices of the major real estate lenders and (2) the ability to "sell" the loan to these lenders. If the loan appears initially to be a poor risk, a broker would be destroying the broker's long-run effectiveness by recommending it.

The Association of Mortgage Professionals, formerly called the National Association of Mortgage Brokers, is the trade organization for this group. Emphasizing adherence to a strict code of ethics, this association promotes a full range of educational programs for its members. See www.namb.org for more information.

## Mortgage Bankers

Many lenders seek to make real estate loans on properties located far from where they can personally supervise the loans. However, it is desirable to observe the physical condition of the collateral carefully, as well as to be available in the event of loan collection difficulties. Therefore, mortgage lenders, also called investors, seek the services of local intermediaries, called **mortgage bankers** or **correspondents**. These intermediaries not only originate new loans but also collect payments, periodically inspect the collateral involved, and supervise a foreclosure, if necessary. Mortgage bankers literally manage real estate loans.

### Operation

Mortgage banking is not banking in the traditional sense. There are no tellers, cashiers, checking accounts, savings accounts, safe deposit boxes, or depositors. Some banks and bank holding companies own subsidiary mortgage banking companies to expand their latitude in creating and servicing their loans. Some larger companies are even going public, but most mortgage banking companies are privately owned. As private entrepreneurs, they derive income from fees received for originating and servicing real estate loans. The more loans they make, the greater their income. Therefore, mortgage bankers are under constant pressure to secure new business with which to earn substantial origination fees and increase service collection accounts.

Most mortgage bankers maintain a high community profile, taking active roles in social, political, and humanitarian efforts within their geographic regions. They also cultivate friendships with local land developers, builders, and real estate brokers to establish mutually beneficial associations. At the same time, most successful mortgage bankers develop a retinue of mortgage loan investment companies, which they represent in a specific locale. Thus, the mortgage banker assumes the role of an intermediary, searching out and developing new mortgage business, originating loans, selling the loans to investors, and collecting the payments on the loans for the benefit of the investors. Some of the larger mortgage banking companies maintain hazard insurance and escrow departments in addition to their loan origination and servicing divisions.

Although the mortgage banking industry is regulated under specific state laws, it is less regulated than banks because, in effect, mortgage bankers are not lending depositors' monies. Mortgage bankers often lend their own monies, or monies that they borrow from banks, to place new loans. These loans are then pooled into homogeneous packages that satisfy the requirements of specific loan investors as to loan amounts and property locations. Such packages are then sold to these investors, while the mortgage banker retains the servicing contract.

Mortgage bankers are involved with every type of real estate loan. They can finance every stage of a real estate development—from providing funds to a developer to purchase, improve, subdivide the land, and construct buildings to providing the final, permanent long-term mortgages for individuals to buy these homes. In fact, a mortgage banker provides the expertise, money, and commitment necessary for the success of many real estate projects, both residential and commercial.

## In Practice

A loan officer works for a lending company, which is a subsidiary of a savings bank. She is currently working with a young couple that is trying to purchase their first home. Unfortunately, they are deeply in debt and don't have the best credit.

However, the loan officer feels that there are some significant compensating factors that should make it possible for them to get their loan approved. Because she is a loan officer for the lending company, she is well aware of the qualifying standards required by the investor and will be able to work directly with the underwriter to try to make this loan work. If the loan officer worked for a company acting as a mortgage broker, she would not have such direct access to the source of funding for the loan and might not be as successful in working with the underwriter. On the other hand, as the mortgage banker is limited to its primary source of funding, there might not be as wide a range of programs available as there would be if the loan officer worked for a mortgage broker where she would be able to shop around to find a loan product that would fit the young couple's needs.

The mortgage banker's financial activities are based largely on the investors' commitments as to the quantity and required yields of mortgages to be placed in a particular community.

For example, a large life insurance company may want to invest $50 million in multiunit apartment projects in a specific community. The company may specify a certain interest rate and also that no single mortgage may be less than $10 million or more than $20 million. Its representative mortgage banker would then seek to lend these funds on economically feasible projects to qualified borrowers. The mortgage banker must first negotiate, document, appraise, analyze, submit, and seek approval for a particular loan from the insurance company that, in turn, issues a mortgage commitment to the mortgage banker, who then issues a commitment to the developer.

The mortgage banker in this example typically might begin by making a commitment to a builder for a permanent loan on the apartment buildings to be built. This commitment would be based on the value of the property as estimated from the builder's plans and specifications. The banker would stipulate that a certain sum of money be loaned under the specific terms and conditions of payment, interest, and time.

On the strength of this commitment, the builder would be able to obtain a construction loan from a commercial bank. This construction loan would be repaid from the permanent loan proceeds when the project was completed. When the total of these loans satisfied the $50 million commitment of the insurance company, they would be sold as a package to this investor, who would then reimburse the mortgage banker, who would retain the servicing contracts.

Mortgage bankers often lack the financial capacity to lend the monies necessary to develop a package for their final investors because these investors will not send the mortgage banker any funds until the packages are accumulated. The mortgage banker will usually seek the aid of a commercial banker, who will, in turn, make a commitment to the mortgage banker to lend certain sums of money during the construction period until funds are received from the investors for mortgage settlements. This is called a **line of credit**. These short-term loans fit perfectly into the commercial banks' requirements, and, essentially, these banks become warehouses for mortgage money. Now the mortgage banker can draw down on the committed **warehouse of funds**, paying the commercial bank's interest requirement until the final funding from the investor satisfies the warehouse commitment. For example, the mortgage banker could borrow the monies from a commercial bank to close the loans with various borrowers until such time as the insurance company took delivery of the loans and funded them.

There is substantial and constant competition in the mortgage lending business. Depending to a great degree on the status of the money markets, the mortgage bankers compete with local savings banks, commercial banks, real estate investment trusts, and other mortgage bankers for a share of the market. The Mortgage Bankers Association (MBA) is active in promoting homebuyer education, often cooperating with local or state housing organizations. See www.mortgagebankers.org for more information.

### The SAFE Act

The **Secure and Fair Enforcement Mortgage Licensing Act (SAFE Act)** was signed into law in 2008 as part of the Housing and Economic Recovery Act (HERA) and applies to all mortgage brokers and mortgage bankers. The SAFE Act was designed to provide more consumer protection and reduce fraud by encouraging states to establish minimum standards for the licensing and registration of state-licensed mortgage loan originators (MLOs). All mortgage loan originators were required to register with the Nationwide Mortgage and Licensing System and Registry (NMLSR) by July 29, 2011. The original standards for state licensing and registration were issued by HUD in June 2011, and responsibility for the SAFE Act was moved to the Consumer Financial Protection Bureau (CFPB) in July of that year.

Loan processors and underwriters are not subject to licensing requirements as long as they perform under the direction and supervision of a state-licensed and registered loan originator. A real estate professional who is only describing the terminology and the loan process is not subject to the SAFE Act requirement for licensure.

## REAL ESTATE TRUSTS

Born under the provisions of the Real Estate Investment Trust Act of 1960, real estate trusts are designed to provide vehicles by which real estate investors can enjoy the special income tax benefits already granted to mutual funds and other regulated investment companies. The earnings of regular corporations are taxed at the corporate level and then again at the individual level when distributed as dividends to stockholders. The real estate trusts have only a single tax, imposed at the beneficiary level. A **real estate investment trust (REIT)** is sold like stock on the major exchanges. Some REITs may invest in a particular type of property (such as a shopping mall); others may concentrate on a specific area of the country.

There are three types of REITs:

- Equity REIT: invests in real estate; income derived from rents or sale of property
- Mortgage REIT: lends money for mortgages or purchases mortgages or mortgage-backed securities; income derived from interest earned
- Hybrid REIT: combines equity REITs and mortgage REITs by investing in both property and mortgage

To qualify for the advantages of being a pass-through entity for U.S. corporate income tax, a real estate investment trust must

- be structured as a corporation, trust, or association;
- be managed by a board of directors or trustees;
- have transferable shares or certificates of interest;
- be taxable as a domestic corporation;
- not be a financial institution or insurance company;
- be jointly owned by 100 or more persons;
- have 95% of its income derived from dividends interest or property income;
- have no more than 50% of the shares held by five or fewer individuals during the last half of each taxable year (5/50 rule);
- have at least 75% of its total assets invested in real estate;
- derive at least 75% of its gross income from rents or mortgage interest;
- have no more than 20% of its assets invested in taxable REIT subsidiaries; and
- distribute at least 90% of its taxable income to shareholders annually in the form of dividends.

The value of a beneficiary interest in a real estate trust is a measurement of the profitability of that enterprise. If the trust is a successful entity, the beneficiaries profit accordingly. However, if the investment trust fails, the beneficiary's investments are lost. Thus, high risks ride in tandem with potentially high profit investments.

## Equity REIT

Designed to deal in equities, equity REITs are owners of improved income properties, including apartments, office buildings, shopping centers, and industrial parks. As an equity trust, the REIT can offer small investors opportunities to pool their monies to participate as owners of larger and, hopefully, more efficient and profitable real estate investments. The REIT's income is derived from two sources: (1) the net profits secured from its rental activities and (2) the capital gains made when these rental properties are sold. All profits are subject to income tax but only at the participant's level.

As REITs are designed as a form of mutual fund, they pass rental income directly through to shareholders with no tax imposed at the REIT level. In exchange for avoiding the double income taxes paid by business corporations and their stockholders, REITs are expected to be strictly passive investors.

Under the REIT Modernization Act (RMA) of 2001, the industry has been allowed to expand its earnings opportunities to include owning up to 100% of the stock of a normally taxable subsidiary company that can provide services to REIT tenants and others without disqualifying the rents that a REIT receives from its tenants. Thus, a REIT can now own companies that provide management and ancillary services for its buildings and tenants. REITs have grown to be a significant participant in the real estate market. They own over $300 billion of investments, composed of office, retail, industrial, and hotel properties in addition to health care and specialty real estate. REIT yields are currently averaging around 6.18% annually. See www.reit.com for more information.

### Mortgage REIT

More significant to mortgage lending are the **real estate mortgage trusts (REMTs)**. Attracting millions of dollars through the sale of beneficial shares, REMTs expand their financial bases with strong credit at their commercial banks and make mortgage loans on commercial income properties. Many of these are properties constructed for the investment portfolios of REITs. In fact, many REMTs are owned by either a parent company REIT or a commercial bank.

The REMTs' main sources of income are mortgage interest, loan origination fees, and profits earned from buying and selling mortgages. Although these trusts participate in long-term permanent financing, they are more inclined to invest in short-term senior and junior loans, where higher potential profits prevail.

### Combination (Hybrid) Trusts

The combination or hybrid trusts join real estate equity investing with mortgage lending, thus earning profits from rental income and capital gains as well as mortgage interest and placement fees. REITs chartered today seek approval to invest in real estate and finance real estate.

Detailed information on real estate investment trusts can be found on the National Association of Investment Trusts website at www.reit.com.

## REAL ESTATE BONDS

Bonds can be used to secure funds for financing real estate projects in two distinct ways. One is the issue and sale of mortgage bonds by business firms, usually corporations, to raise capital. The second is the issue and sale of bonds issued by states, local governments, school districts, and other forms of government to finance community improvements, such as schools, parks, bridges, hospitals, paving, sewers, and renewal projects. Bonds in the latter group are termed collectively **municipal bonds**. The interest paid on municipal bonds is exempt from all federal income tax and, in many cases, from state income taxes.

Figure 5.1 illustrates various types of bonds used in mortgage lending.

The administration of funds raised by a bond sale is left in the hands of a *trustee,* who acts as an intermediary between the borrower (issuer) and the bond owners (purchaser-lenders). The trustee supervises the collection of payments from the borrower and makes disbursements to the appropriate bondholders.

If the borrower defaults on a real estate bond, the trustee files a notice with the borrower that the entire balance and the interest are immediately due in full. At the same time, upon declaration that the borrower cannot or will not satisfy the debt, the trustee may enter the property, dispossess the borrower, and manage or sell it. All income or sales proceeds will apply to the benefit of the bond owners.

*FIGURE 5.1* **Bonds Used in Mortgage Lending**

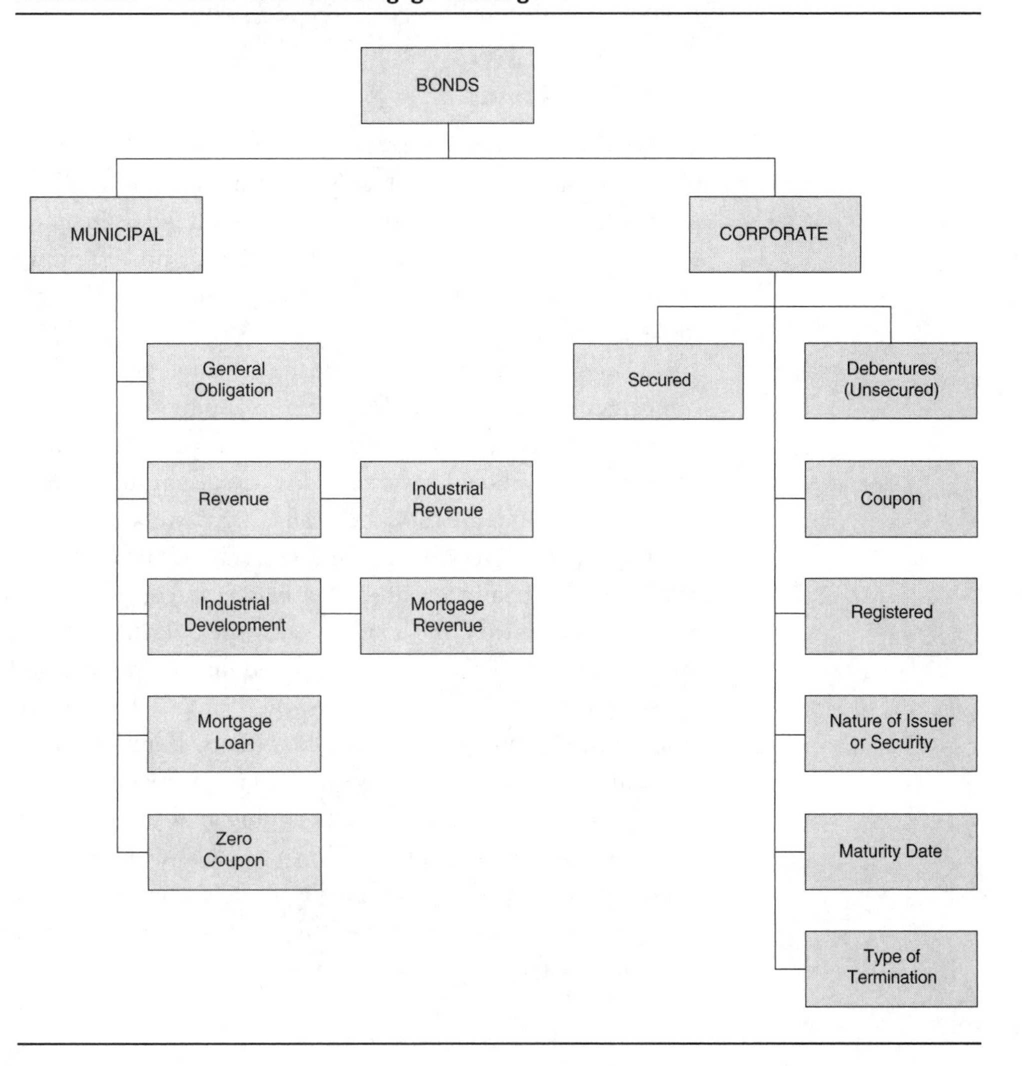

## The Nature of Bonds

Corporate bonds are credit instruments used to raise long-term funds. When these bonds are backed by a mortgage on specifically described real property, they are called secured bonds. When a company issues bonds that are a claim against its general assets, they are called unsecured bonds or **debentures**.

Corporate bonds are also classified according to their method of payment. **Coupon bonds** have interest coupons attached, which are removed as they become due and are cashed by the bearer. Interest is paid to the person possessing the coupon, so these bonds are also called **bearer bonds**. **Registered bonds** are issued to a specific owner and cannot be transferred without the owner's endorsement. Under this form of bond, interest is paid to the last registered owner.

Bonds can be classified further as to the nature of the issuer—for instance, railroad bonds, industrial bonds, or corporate bonds. They are often described by the nature of their security, such as mortgage bonds, income bonds, or guaranteed bonds, or by their maturity date, as in long-term, short-term, or perpetual bonds. In addition, bonds may be classified by their type of termination—for instance, convertible, redeemable, serial, or sinking fund bonds. Finally, they may be classified by their purpose—for example, refunding, construction, equipment, or improvement bonds.

## Corporate Bonds

The issue of corporate bonds to raise funds for real estate capital improvements, such as plant expansion or new equipment acquisition, is a relatively costly approach when compared to the use of mortgages. To float a new bond issue successfully, a corporation must secure the services of an investment banker or broker, print bonds (usually in $1,000 denominations), and pay fees in advance to the appropriate regulating agencies as well as to the issuing brokerage house.

A large company could easily float a debenture or unsecured bond issue, while smaller companies would have difficulty even in issuing secured bonds. The investment broker is responsible for advising which bonds to market, what interest rates to pay, and what prices the bonds should have, according to specific money market conditions.

After the bonds are sold, their values fluctuate with the money market. For instance, if market interest rates rise, the value of the bonds issued at a lower interest rate decreases accordingly. To compete with higher market interest rates, the face value of these bonds would be discounted if the bond owner wished to sell them. The reverse is also true; when interest rates drop below those being paid on existing bonds, their value increases above their face amount. Bonds may be worth 95% of their face value at one time and 105% at another, depending on market conditions. Bonds are rated according to the financial security of their issuers. Investment rating services, such as Standard and Poor's and Moody's, constantly watch the major companies and report their financial conditions as they reflect on the companies' ability to pay their debts when due. Bonds with the highest ratings are considered by buyers to be safe investments and thus are not discounted to any major degree. Bonds with lower ratings usually are traded at greater discounts to reflect their higher risks.

## Municipal and Private Bonds

A popular use for real estate bonds is to finance municipal improvement projects. By issuing **general obligation bonds**, guaranteed by the taxing power and the full faith and credit of the community, governments can raise funds for financing schools, street improvements, sewer installations, park developments, and other civic improvement projects.

A variation on this theme is the issue of **revenue bonds** to fund a specific community improvement project. These bonds will be repaid from the revenues generated by the improvements. For instance, a toll bridge could be constructed using the money raised from the sale of revenue bonds, and the repayment of the bonds would be designed to match the revenue secured from the tolls collected.

An illustration of the role of such revenue bonds in mortgage lending is their possible use in developing employment centers for a community. For instance, a city could float revenue bonds to develop an industrial park or construct buildings that might be leased to commercial tenants. These bonds are known as **industrial revenue bonds (IRBs)**. The rental income from the buildings would be adequate to repay the bonds over a long period of time. By this process new jobs are created, new taxes are generated, and generally an impetus of growth is infused into the community. Additional revenue bonds and other incentives can then be used by these growth-oriented communities to attract more businesses to their industrial parks.

## Industrial Development Bonds

Unlike industrial revenue bonds, which are issued by a municipality for public improvements, **industrial development bonds** allow private investors an opportunity to finance apartment and commercial developments by using tax-exempt, and thus relatively inexpensive, funds. The developer prepares an application for approval by a local city or county Industrial Development Authority (IDA). This application includes the plans for the apartment or commercial development and a statement describing the need for these units to enhance the community's welfare. The bond attorney for the IDA reviews the application and makes a recommendation to the all-volunteer board.

If approval is secured, the developer hires a bond broker and floats a new issue. The interest rate is determined by the broker as a function of the market with the earnings exempted from federal, and often state, income taxes.

## Mortgage Revenue Bonds

**Mortgage revenue bonds** are a form of industrial development bond. The bond issue is tax exempt because it is offered by state and local governments through their housing financing agencies. Use for the proceeds of the bond sales is limited to financing segments of the housing markets, such as low-income buyers, first-time buyers, and so on. Other limitations are imposed as well, such as the prices of homes eligible for participation in the bond program and the income of the borrowers.

The government agency transfers the proceeds of the bond sale to the lender, who then makes a mortgage loan to the developer of the project. Because of the tax exemption on income derived by the bondholders, interest to the borrower is lower than market rates, and rents can be lowered accordingly. In addition, 20% of the units must be allocated for low-income renters for ten years or half the life of the loan, whichever is longer.

A significant portion of the senior housing market, assisted-living care facilities, can now be financed with tax-exempt revenue bonds so long as the project does not provide continual or frequent medical or nursing services according to IRS rule 98-47. The ruling states that these are residential rental properties and eligible for the bonding finance.

### Zero-Coupon Bonds

**Zero-coupon bonds** represent an old approach to bond buying. They are patterned after World War II savings bonds, which were sold for $18.75 and redeemed after ten years for $25. A buyer writes a check for a bond at a discounted price and holds this bond until maturity or until it is sold, with interest compounding regularly. Interest must be reported each year for tax purposes even though it is not collectible until the bond matures.

### Mortgage Loan Bonds

Some states issue income-tax-free bonds to secure funds for relatively low-cost mortgage loans. These loans are available to eligible persons to help them acquire houses and condominium units. The interest income from these bonds is tax exempt at both the federal and state levels, so their purchasers can buy them at lower rates than would be required on taxable investments. These savings are passed along to the borrowers, who will pay slightly higher interest rates on their loans than are paid to the bondholders to cover operational costs.

## PRIVATE LENDERS

Another group of lenders that provides funds for mortgage lending is the private lenders. This group includes individuals and private loan companies. Little data is available about the impact of these private lenders on the overall realty money market because of the privacy of the participants' transactions. Because these lenders invest their own funds, they owe no duty to others and can maintain complete discretion over their activities.

Despite this comparative freedom, most lenders observe conservative limitations. No one invests to lose money, and good underwriting procedures are followed. In the entire field of real estate lending, these private lenders have the most flexibility and can take the most risks. This often makes them the only source of funds for certain real estate projects.

### Individuals

When other financing is not available, the sellers of property often have to provide the funds to close the deal. Arrangements for seller financing are usually made in the negotiations directly between the buyer and seller.

## Sellers as Lenders

The single most important source of private finance funds consists of the sellers who finance a portion of the sales price with carryback loans. In fact, seller financing has become the only way some sales can be consummated. Using junior loans, contracts for deed, wraparounds, and other creative financing devices (described in later chapters), sellers often help finance a portion of a property's sales price.

Some loans made directly between buyers/borrowers and sellers/lenders involve first mortgages. For instance, when the property being sold is held free and clear of any debt, the seller might agree to carry back a new first mortgage from the buyer for most of the purchase price. However, if a house is selling for $180,000 and the current balance on the existing mortgage is $140,000, the seller might agree to carry back $20,000 of the $40,000 equity as a second mortgage if the buyer agrees to pay $20,000 as a cash down payment. Most individual financial agreements involve junior financing where the seller carries back a portion of the equity in the property.

Sellers agreeing to carry back a portion of their equity as a junior loan subject to an existing senior loan must be aware of the risk that the buyers may not keep up the payments on the senior loan. This would put the sellers in jeopardy of losing their junior loan equity. To offset this risk, a collection escrow could be established at the time of the sale where the buyers would send both the senior and junior loan payments to the collection agent with directions for immediate notification to the sellers if these payments are not forthcoming.

## Family Members as Lenders

Homebuyers, especially those with small children, may find they do not have the funds necessary to meet down payment requirements. They may look to their parents or other family members for help. Under these circumstances, a letter from the donors indicating the amount of the gift is delivered to the loan officer who is preparing the new loan package. In some cases, the donors are required to cosign the mortgage documents in order to include their own financial resources as additional collateral.

These arrangements often can be established as partnerships in which the parents, as co-owners, make the down payment and the children agree to make all the monthly payments on the mortgage. If the property is refinanced or sold in the future, the partners will share in the proceeds.

Based on current law, anyone can make an annual tax-free gift of up to $13,000 to any individual. A married couple could present up to $52,000 in tax-free gifts every year to their two children ($13,000 from each parent to each child).

## Private Loan Companies

Private loan companies range from the large national company with branches in almost every city to the individual entrepreneur who may personally buy and sell loans. These private lenders deal primarily in **junior financing** arrangements that use a borrower's equity in real property as collateral. These companies make loans from their own funds or monies borrowed from their commercial banks, act as mortgage brokers in arranging loans between other lenders and borrowers, and buy and sell junior financing instruments, usually at a discount. In this latter capacity, these private loan companies help create a secondary market for junior loans.

Private real estate loan companies usually charge more than other lenders. They attempt to offset the risks inherent in their junior lien position by charging the maximum interest rates allowable by law and imposing high loan placement fees. Many states have developed laws regulating the activities of private lenders. Besides requiring loan companies to obtain licenses and performance bonds, some states limit the amount of fees that these lenders can charge for their services.

## FOREIGN LENDERS

The United States has been considered safe for foreign investment for many years. At any given time, there may be billions in foreign monies deposited in U.S. commercial banks. Short-term funds have little impact on mortgage lending, although funds left on deposit for relatively long periods of time can have an effect on the monies available for mortgage lending. Foreign investors also bought heavily into mortgage-backed securities, which caused serious problems as a result of the financial crisis of 2008.

As many countries throughout the world teeter on the brink of financial collapse, the United States still attracts foreign money. On June 20, 2011, the *Chicago Tribune* reported that foreign investment in the United States had risen 49% in 2010 over the previous year. Over 90% of that investment came from Canada, Europe, and Japan, with less than 1% from China. However, the *New York Times* reported in July 2011 that Chinese investment rose to $5 billion in 2010, with the anticipation of over a trillion more in this decade. FoxBusiness reports over $14 billion in 2013. A direct impact on real estate can be seen in New York City, where Chinese investors have poured billions into real estate development. These investors are buying luxury apartments and investing in commercial and residential projects throughout the city. The latest data from the National Association of REALTORS® shows that foreign buyers purchased over $68 billion of single-family homes in the United States in the year ending March 2013—about 7% of the total U.S. market. The fastest growth was buyers from China and Canada, and the majority of purchases were in Arizona, California, Florida, New York, and Texas.

## SUMMARY

The major financial intermediaries are commercial banks, mutual savings banks, savings associations or thrifts, life insurance companies, pension and retirement funds, and credit unions. They usually display conservative investment attitudes compatible with their roles as guardians and protectors of their depositors' and premium payers' money.

Commercial banks have traditionally participated in real estate finance mainly as short-term lenders, preferring to maintain their liquidity while at the same time maximizing their earnings by trading in commercial paper. Through their mortgage loan departments, however, commercial banks have become very active in the home mortgage loan market in addition to construction loans, home improvement loans, and manufactured home mortgages—all relatively short-term investments. In addition, through their trust departments, mortgage banking facilities, and ownership of real estate investment trusts, commercial banks participate to some degree in long-term real estate investments.

Mutual savings banks are designed to participate extensively in local realty mortgage markets. Because savings by definition have a long-term nature, these institutions are able to make long-term loans, predominantly in real estate finance.

Savings banks engage actively in owner-occupied, single-family residential mortgages. Some savings banks also participate in regional and national mortgage markets by buying and selling blocks of securities from and to the secondary market.

Life insurance companies accumulate large reservoirs of monies to be held for long periods of time. Their real estate investments complement this profile and include the larger mortgages on major national commercial and industrial real estate developments. Although life insurance companies invest only a portion of their total assets in real estate finance, the huge dollar amounts of these assets make their contribution to real estate financing and the success of large-scale construction projects significant.

Pension and retirement funds have substantially increased their assets in recent years and have the potential to become a major source of mortgage lending. In the past, however, pension funds have mostly been invested in government and corporate securities.

Another type of financial intermediary that participates to an increasing degree in mortgage lending is the credit union. Although involved primarily in financing members' personal property purchases, many credit unions are now financing equity loans and first mortgages.

Mortgage brokers act as catalysts in the process of matching borrowers and lenders, a service for which they earn a finder's fee. Fees on residential loans are related to an origination fee and compensation for the servicing of the loan. Fees on commercial loans are related to the time and effort expended in the loan's successful presentation. Once a loan has been finalized, the broker's responsibilities are usually completed.

Mortgage bankers, on the other hand, not only generate new mortgage loans between the major fiduciary lenders and individual borrowers but continue to function as intermediaries. They collect mortgage payments, inspect the condition of collateral, counsel delinquent borrowers, and foreclose when necessary. In addition, mortgage bankers often invest their own funds or borrow money from their banks to finance site acquisitions, land improvements, construction costs, and permanent mortgages in order to complete a full development program. The real estate trusts, much like the stock market's mutual funds, are depositories for small investors who pool their monies for greater investment flexibility. The investors take a passive role in management and allow the trust's directors to decide on the investment policy.

Some real estate trusts are involved exclusively in equity holdings. These equity trusts are described as real estate investment trusts (REITs), and they purchase property for its income and potential growth in value. Other real estate trusts, defined as real estate mortgage trusts (REMTs), invest primarily in real estate mortgage loans. Some real estate trusts are hybrids that combine equity participation and mortgage investments.

The issue and sale of real estate bonds is an additional source of funds for mortgage lending. Corporations issue bonds to secure money for plant expansion, equipment purchases, and operational expenses. Various governmental bodies may issue bonds to raise funds for improvements, such as schools, parks, streets, industrial developments, bridges, hospitals, and sewage plants. The administration of funds raised by a bond sale is left in the hands of a trustee, who supervises the collection of payments from the borrower-issuer and the distribution of dividends to the investors/purchasers.

Private lenders often provide the funds required to close many real estate transactions. Without their ability to make independent decisions and take extra risks, many real estate transactions would be impossible to complete.

Foreign investment into the general economy has been increasing, especially from China. These investments are directly impacting real estate development in New York City.

## INTERNET RESOURCES

Mortgage Bankers Association
*www.mortgagebankers.org*

The Association of Mortgage Professionals
*www.namb.org*

National Association of Real Estate Investment Trusts
*www.reit.org*

National Credit Union Administration
*www.ncua.gov*

## REVIEW QUESTIONS

1. What is the main source of capital for the supply of funds needed by a commercial bank?
   a. Interbank loans
   b. Savings accounts
   c. Federal Reserve deposits
   d. Checking accounts

2. All of the following are usually short-term mortgage loans *EXCEPT*
   a. construction loans.
   b. home improvement loans.
   c. single-family home loans.
   d. manufactured home loans.

3. A local builder wishes to obtain financing to build four houses. His *BEST* source would be a
   a. savings association.
   b. commercial bank.
   c. credit union.
   d. life insurance company.

4. Mutual savings banks are located primarily in the
   a. West.
   b. Northeast.
   c. Midwest.
   d. South.

5. Which is *NOT* a prominent role of life insurance companies in real estate?
   a. Purchasing blocks of mortgages on the secondary market
   b. Financing large commercial projects like office buildings or shopping centers
   c. Originating individual home mortgage loans
   d. Financing major industrial projects

6. A mortgage broker may do all *EXCEPT*
   a. receive a placement fee.
   b. service the loan.
   c. investigate soundness of the investment.
   d. bring together the borrower and the lender.

7. A couple has applied for a mortgage loan. The loan officer will prequalify the couple, match them with an appropriate loan product, carry their case through to loan approval, and continue to service the loan. The loan officer's company is a
   a. mortgage banker.
   b. mortgage broker.
   c. financial fiduciary.
   d. financial investor.

8. A mortgage company is preparing a package of loans for sale to an investor. In order to have adequate funds to originate the number of loans required by the investor, the company may need to establish a line of credit with a local commercial bank. This is called
   a. warehousing.
   b. direct deposit lending.
   c. participation financing.
   d. correspondents.

9. An individual has invested in a real estate trust that will derive income using the net profits from rent and sale of rental properties. He has invested in a
   a. REIT.
   b. REMT.
   c. hybrid.
   d. joint venture.

10. An individual has invested in a real estate trust deriving income from mortgage interest, loan fees, and profits from buying and selling mortgages. She has invested in a
    a. REIT.
    b. REMT.
    c. hybrid.
    d. joint venture.

11. A county is issuing bonds for sale to fund a new consolidated high school. These bonds are termed
    a. corporate bonds.
    b. trustee bonds.
    c. municipal bonds.
    d. debentures.

12. A woman recently lost a briefcase containing several different types of bonds. She is very concerned that someone finding the briefcase will be able to cash in her bonds. She need *NOT* be concerned if the bonds are
    a. coupon bonds.
    b. bearer bonds.
    c. registered bonds.
    d. unsecured bonds.

13. Which is *TRUE* regarding the value of a bond?
    a. The value never changes throughout the term of the bond.
    b. The value is guaranteed to increase over the term of the bond.
    c. The value will fluctuate with the money market.
    d. The value is established by Standard and Poor's rating service.

14. The *MOST* significant feature of a REIT is its
    a. ownership by at least five investors.
    b. continuous growth in value.
    c. elimination of double taxes.
    d. fiduciary relationship to its investors.

Chapter 6

# Instruments of Real Estate Finance

## LEARNING OBJECTIVES

When you've finished reading this chapter, you will be able to

- give examples of encumbrances and liens on a property;
- compare a mortgage and a deed of trust;
- discuss the possible uses for a contract for deed and precautions that should be taken;
- describe a junior loan used as a home equity loan and how it may be used; and
- identify special clauses that may be used in mortgage lending instruments.

**acceleration clause**
**assumed**
**beneficiary**
**carryback loan**
**contract for deed**
**cross-defaulting clause**
**deed of trust**
**defeasance clause**
**due-on-sale clause**
**encumbrance**
**equitable right of redemption**
**equity loan**
**exculpatory clause**
**granting clause**
**involuntary lien**
**lien theory**
**lifting clause**
**mortgagee**
**mortgagor**
**nonrecourse clause**
**note**
**note and mortgage**
**novation**
**power of sale**
**prepayment clause**
**release clause**
**second mortgage**
**subject to**
**subordination**
**title theory**
**trust deed**
**trustee**
**trustor**
**usury**
**vendee**
**vendor**
**voluntary lien**

Although many aspects of mortgage lending change frequently, the instruments for executing a real estate loan have remained basically the same. This chapter reviews the broad legal aspects of pledging real estate as collateral for a loan, and it examines the form and content of the three instruments used to finance real estate. Each state may have its own statutes stipulating the form and content of these instruments. The actual financing documents are usually prepared by the lender; the deed conveying interest in the property is prepared by the settlement attorney or agent.

This chapter examines a number of special provisions that can be included in financing instruments to serve the needs of both borrowers and lenders. The final section reviews the instruments used to establish junior financing relationships.

## ENCUMBRANCES AND LIENS

An **encumbrance** is a right or interest in a property held by one who is not the legal owner of the property. Encumbrances that affect the physical condition of a property may be imposed on a parcel of land without destroying the owner's estate. These physical encumbrances do not prevent the owner from using the property or transferring it. Encumbrances of this type include easements, public and private restrictions, and encroachments.

Almost every parcel of real property has some form of physical encumbrance imposed on it. The most common is the utility easement that provides the accessibility, both under and over the land, for the installation of water, gas, electric, telephone, and sewer services. These easements are recorded agreements between the property owner, usually the original subdivider, and the appropriate agency responsible for the services indicated. These recorded physical encumbrances become "covenants that run with the land" and follow the title through its various owners.

A property's title may also be affected by a financial encumbrance called a lien. A lien is a charge against a specific property where the property is made the security for the performance of a certain act, usually the repayment of a debt. Thus, deeds of trust, mortgages, and contracts for deed are all forms of liens.

Unlike physical encumbrances, liens are personal in quality, relating owners' economic situations with their real property. Liens can be either **voluntary liens**, such as financing instruments, or **involuntary liens** imposed by law, such as liens for taxes or assessments, mechanics' (construction) liens, and judgment liens. General liens apply to all nonexempt property, while specific liens apply only to a single property of the debtor.

### In Practice

A married couple is purchasing their first house for $150,000. They are making a down payment of $15,000 with a mortgage loan of $135,000. The mortgage establishes a financial encumbrance on the property. This encumbrance is called a *lien*. Prior to settlement, they are informed by the title company handling the closing that there are several other encumbrances on the property:

- The local electric utility company has an easement across the front edge of the property where they have power lines buried that serve that entire block.
- The homeowners association has restrictions against any fencing in the front yard of the house.
- The next-door neighbor's fence is encroaching on the property by four inches on one side of the property.

Should any of these be of concern to the couple? The title company agent explains that the electric company's gross easement and the homeowners association's private restriction are covenants that run with the land; in other words, they have been previously granted and automatically transfer along with the conveyance of the property. The question of the neighbor's fence encroaching on their property will probably need to be resolved before title insurance will be issued.

A mortgage loan secured by a parcel of real estate becomes a specific voluntary lien against the subject property at the time it is recorded at the courthouse of the county where the property is located. Deeds of trust, mortgages, and contracts for deed will be signed by all appropriate parties, acknowledged by a notary, and usually recorded. This recording process is designed to give public notice that a lender has certain lien rights in the property described in the loan instrument.

Lenders' rights are invariably superior to the rights of other subsequently recorded lienholders, with certain special exceptions. These exceptions include the specific liens imposed by local or state governments for nonpayment of property taxes. Otherwise, based on the doctrine of "first in time, first in right," lenders establish a priority lien position on the date their loan document is recorded. In the event of a foreclosure and sale of the collateral, the proceeds of the sale are distributed per the priority of the liens existing against the subject property. Lenders whose loans have the earliest recording dates are said to be in senior lien positions, and their rights take priority over those of all subsequent lienholders.

## LOAN SECURED BY A REAL ESTATE INTEREST

Any interest in real property can be security for a real estate loan. Most common to real estate finance is the pledge of a fee simple ownership as collateral to back up a promise to repay a money debt. Real property can also be pledged as collateral to secure financial lines of credit or ensure the specific performance of a contract. Fee simple ownership can be enjoyed by individuals, corporations, and various forms of partnerships. Individuals, their assigns, and their heirs can pledge their titles and interests in real estate in exchange for loans. Corporations, as legally created entities, may own real property and can pledge it as collateral for financing purposes. Likewise, various combinations of individuals and corporations that have joined into partnerships to own real properties can pledge their interests in these properties in order to borrow money.

Less-than-freehold interests, such as rental income from property or the leasehold rights of a tenant, can also be used as collateral for a loan. The parties to a life estate can pledge their interests for loans, even though these interests are not fully vested when the loan is secured. Most lenders are aware of the risks involved with such loans.

Other interests in real property can be owned independently from the land itself. Rights to the use of the airspace over a parcel of property fall into this latter category, as do the rights to the use of water and the extraction of oil and minerals from the earth. These rights can be pledged as collateral for a loan, either singly, collectively, or jointly with other properties.

In some instances, personal property is required as additional security to real property pledged as collateral for a loan. Thus, loans for houses might include furnishings as collateral, in addition to the real estate. Commercial property loans might include trade fixtures as mortgage loan collateral.

## Title, Lien, and Intermediate Theories

Originally, most real estate loans were designed to allow the lender to take actual physical possession of the land until the principal sum of the loan and any agreed-upon interest was obtained from the proceeds of the land's production. For all intents and purposes, the lender was the owner of the land until the debt was satisfied, at which time ownership and possession were returned to the borrower. Simply put, the lender held title to the collateral.

As the system evolved, the procedure was changed to allow borrowers to remain in possession of the land, so long as they kept the terms of the loan agreement. However, the borrower was still required to transfer legal ownership to the lender by placing title to the property in the lender's name. Thus, the lender secured legal title, and the borrower retained equitable rights in the property.

Concern about who held title to collateral property stemmed from lender demand for guarantee of the return of funds loaned or, at least, a property with value adequate to substitute for funds lost. Here the rights of a lender were superior to the rights of a borrower. The lender could dispossess the borrower without notice at the first default of the loan agreement. No compensation was made for any monies already paid to the lender. This concept has evolved into the **title theory** of mortgage lending, which has been adopted in some states.

As time progressed, the laws were modified to reflect the borrower's legal right to redeem property within some reasonable time after default. This right, called an **equitable right of redemption**, gave defaulting borrowers time to protect their interests, but it ceased when the property was sold at a foreclosure sale.

To complement these equitable redemption rights, more than half the states have adopted periods for redemption after the foreclosure sale. These statutory periods of redemption vary from three months to two years, depending on the state.

Through the years, the competition between lenders' and borrowers' rights has shifted dramatically to borrowers. Most states have adopted the **lien theory**, which recognizes the rights of lenders in collateral property as equitable rights, while borrowers retain their legal rights in their property. Thus, a borrower maintains legal interest in property while pledging it as collateral to a lender who acquires a lien, or an equitable interest, in the collateral property in return for the funds lent. In effect, the lien theory allows a defaulted borrower to retain possession, title, and all legal rights in the property until the lender perfects the lien against the collateral property, according to legal foreclosure procedures that recognize the borrower's redemption rights. This theory shows quite a shift in the priority of rights.

However, just as excessive power gave rise to abuses by lenders prior to the development of equity of redemption, lien theory, when coupled with the concept of statutory redemption, provides the opportunity for borrowers to become abusive. Whereas lenders previously were able to dispossess their borrowers arbitrarily, now defaulted borrowers are often able to remain in possession of their properties for long periods of time without making loan payments. Longer statutory redemption periods have resulted in endless problems for lenders trying to recover their collateral and minimize their losses within a reasonable time.

Therefore, some states have taken a modified position between the title and lien theories. This intermediate position allows a lender to take possession of collateral property in the event of a loan default, often without having to wait until foreclosure proceedings have resulted in a possessory judgment. However, the lender does not receive title until after the expiration of statutory redemption periods prescribed by law.

## General Requirements for a Finance Instrument

Regardless of the theory practiced in a particular state, all borrowers and lenders throughout the United States must observe the same general requirements to protect their rights when making a loan transaction. Real estate loans are contractual agreements that must contain certain basic elements to be valid. All terms of the loan transaction must be formalized in writing. They must include accurate descriptions of the interest and property being pledged as collateral and a complete statement detailing the loan repayment. The parties to the agreement must be legally competent; their consent must be indicated by their signatures, properly attested and affixed to the loan agreement, and a sufficient consideration must be paid.

The three basic instruments used to finance real estate—the note and deed of trust, the note and mortgage, and the contract for deed—all share the requirements listed previously, but each has its own unique form and content.

# THE NOTE AND DEED OF TRUST (TRUST DEED)

A trust is described as a right of property, real or personal, being held by one party for the benefit of another. The parties to a trust include a **trustor**, who grants rights to a **trustee**, who holds the property in trust for a **beneficiary**. In all cases involving the establishment of a real estate trust, an instrument called a **trust deed** is executed by the trustor in order to transfer legal fee ownership, to be held for the beneficiary, in the name of the trustee. Note: The trustee and the beneficiary may sometimes be the same person/entity.

When a trust deed is used for financing real estate, it is called a **deed of trust**. The lender/beneficiary usually selects a trustee who secures title to the collateral from the trustor/borrower as well as the power to foreclose if necessary.

In title theory states, a deed of trust transfers the title of the collateral to the name of a third-party trustee, who retains this "ownership" position until the terms of the loan are satisfied. In lien and intermediate theory states, title remains with the borrower (trustor), and the trustee acquires only lien rights. If the loan goes into default, the trustee is empowered to foreclose on the collateral property. These foreclosure powers are described in Chapter 10.

## Note Used with a Deed of Trust

The **note** that accompanies a deed of trust includes the borrower's promise to pay the lender a designated sum under the terms and conditions specified. It also refers to the security of a specific deed of trust given to the trustee as collateral for the loan.

In the event of a default under a note for a deed of trust, borrowers have assigned their defenses to the automatic action of the laws governing foreclosure of the debt instrument, known as the **power of sale**. This gives lenders the opportunity to secure more readily full legal title to the collateral, even when borrowers abandon their property and disappear. However, borrowers' rights are still protected by law. Lenders are required to give adequate notice to borrowers and allow them an appropriate period in which to redeem their property. This increased foreclosure power is the distinguishing feature between the deed of trust and the mortgage.

A note for a deed of trust must be signed by the borrowers and accepted by the trustees, acknowledging their role as holders of the deed of trust until the terms of the note are fulfilled. This note will not be acknowledged, and only one copy will be signed.

## Deed of Trust

In a deed of trust (see Appendix C), the borrower (trustor) conveys property as collateral to a trustee that will hold title on behalf of the lender (the beneficiary) until the terms of the loan are satisfied. When the loan is paid in full, the trustee will reconvey the property to the trustor, as directed by the **release clause**. If the loan goes into default, the trustee will foreclose on the collateral to secure full legal title and will sell the property to recover the balance of monies due to the lender. Examine the uniform covenants itemized in the Note and Deed of Trust Purchase Agreement (found in Appendix D) to understand more fully the legal relationships between the parties to this loan agreement.

## NOTE AND MORTGAGE

Another real estate financing instrument is the **note and mortgage**. The note is the promise to pay a debt, while the mortgage is the pledge of real estate as collateral to secure this promise. A mortgage instrument, although executed separately, invariably has a copy of the note attached to it or at least a reference to the note's conditions incorporated into the mortgage form. While a note by itself is legal evidence of a debt, a mortgage always needs a note in order to be a legally enforceable lien against the collateral.

### The Note

A note is a contract complete in itself. Its terms specify the amount of money borrowed and under which conditions the debt will be repaid. After being signed by a borrower—without any additional signatures or acknowledgments—it becomes a legally enforceable and fully negotiable instrument of debt when in the possession of its bearer. If the terms of a note are met, the debt is discharged. If the terms of a note are broken, a lender may choose either to sue on the note or foreclose on the note's collateral if a mortgage has been arranged as security for the note.

A note does not need to be tied to a mortgage. When a note is used as a debt instrument without any related collateral, it is described as an unsecured note. Unsecured notes are often used by banks and other lenders to extend short-term personal loans. However, a real estate loan, described as a secured loan, always includes a mortgage with a note, often called a security.

A note generally includes the following provisions.

**Date Signed.** The date of a note's origination is clearly delineated in the form. Accurate dates are vital to every legally enforceable contract because time is always of the essence in identifying chronological order of priority rights.

**Participants' Identities.** The participants engaged in a loan contract are identified, and their relationship as borrower and lender is established. Some preprinted note forms identify the borrower as "the undersigned," and the lender's name is printed on the form.

**Promise to Pay.** The words *promise to pay* establish the precise legal obligation of the borrower. The fulfillment of the promise is the satisfaction of the obligation; a broken promise entitles the lender to seek legal remedies to recover any damages that might occur.

**Payment Due Dates.** The specific schedule of payments must be incorporated into the note. A systematic repayment program of principal and interest over the life of the loan is described as amortization. A plan can be designed for a number of time intervals, such as for monthly, quarterly, semiannual, or annual payments. Semi-amortized notes call for periodic payments of principal and interest, with a large principal amount, called a balloon payment, due at the end of the loan term. Notes can also be designed to be paid at a monthly or annual rate of interest only with a single lump-sum principal payment due at some future time. This form of finance is described as a term loan. In all cases, a note will specify when the payments will start, on which dates they will be due, and when they will stop.

**Amount and Terms.** The amount of the payments depends on the terms of a loan. If a term loan for $1,000 for one year at 6% interest per annum is designated, the note will stipulate a payment of $1,060, including principal and interest, to be due in full one year from the date of its inception.

The payments due on an amortized note will be based on the length of time involved and the agreed-upon interest rate. For example, a $150,000 note payable in monthly installments over a 30-year time span at 6% annual interest would require a $599.56 regular monthly payment to satisfy the obligation. This sum represents only the monthly principal and interest amounts due the lender. If hazard insurance premiums and property taxes are to be included in the monthly payment, these additional requirements must be described in the mortgage form. Only the scheduled amount of principal and interest owed to the lender is specified in the note.

The terms and conditions for the repayment of a loan can be as flexible and varied as a particular situation demands. However, the note is always the determining instrument in interpreting the intentions of the parties to a loan.

**Reference to Security.** After the terms of a loan are specified, a referral is made in the note that it is secured by a mortgage upon real property. This reference to a security is formalized when a copy of the note is attached to its mortgage, thereby firmly and legally establishing the security.

The mortgage is the liening document, the life of which depends on the note. The note is a freestanding contract personally obligating the borrower for the debt. A lender may sue for damages on the note instrument in the event the borrower defaults. The mortgage is the lender's final protection and may be foreclosed if a borrower cannot fulfill the obligation under the note. Thus, the note is the power instrument in this realty lending design.

**Signatures and Endorsements.** Although several copies of the note are prepared and distributed to the parties in the loan transaction, only one copy is signed. This signed copy is delivered to the lender, to be held until the debt is satisfied. This is important to a borrower because each signed note is a negotiable instrument in itself. Only one note should be signed in any loan transaction.

A note requires only the borrower's signature. The delivery of the signed note to the lender is adequate evidence of ownership. A note signed by a borrower is a negotiable instrument; a lender can assign it to another person by simply endorsing it on its back, much like a check. If a mortgage is involved, the process is more complicated, but the note itself is a viable, negotiable instrument. A transfer does not affect either terms or conditions of the original agreement, except that the place to which the borrower sends payments may change. When the loan is repaid, the lender marks *paid in full* across the face of the original note, signs under this comment, and returns the original to the borrower.

**Cosigners.** The lender who once made the statement that "there can never be too many signatures on a note" was referring to the fact that all signers on a note are individually and collectively responsible for its repayment. If a married couple is securing a loan, a lender will require both husband and wife to sign the note. Sometimes a lender may require the signatures of persons other than the borrower to provide additional guarantees that the obligation will be repaid. These additional signatures are usually the borrower's family or friends whose credit has been considered in qualifying the borrower for a loan. These cosigners share personal liability with the original maker of the note in the event of a default.

The number of signatures on a note does not have to conform with the number of persons who sign the accompanying mortgage. Because the property in question is being pledged as collateral to back up a specific note, only the property owners sign. Thus, a note may have more or fewer signatures than its mortgage. In fact, the signatures on both instruments may be different, although this would be rare. (A sample note is shown in Appendix C.)

## The Mortgage

Mortgage provisions vary, depending on the policies of individual lenders and the circumstances in a particular transaction. The components covered in this section are standard to most mortgage forms (see Appendix E for a sample mortgage form).

**Recording Information.** A mortgage is a lien on a specific property or properties to secure the fulfillment of a promise—usually a promise to repay a debt. The only way a lender has to notify the world that there is a lien on a specific property is to record the mortgage at the office of the recorder in the county where the property is located.

Without the recording of the mortgage lien, only the borrower and the lender would know of the transaction. Other parties having an interest in the property would not receive notice of the lien. Thus, for its protection, a lender will insist on recording the mortgage. Generally, this recording will take place before the proceeds of a loan are distributed, although this technique varies from state to state. By holding back the disbursement of a loan until after recording, a lender or escrow agent has a last-minute opportunity to recheck the public records about the condition of the collateral property's title.

Most standard mortgage forms have a space at the top of the first page devoted to specific county recording information. Others leave a blank space elsewhere on the form to be filled in at the recorder's office. This lien vests at the date and time stamped on the mortgage document by the recorder's clock stamp.

**Participants.** The participants to a mortgage include a borrower, the **mortgagor**, and a lender, the **mortgagee**. In exchange for a certain consideration, usually a sum of money, a mortgagor will pledge property as collateral to back up the promise to repay a mortgage. The proper names of both mortgagor and mortgagee must appear on the mortgage form.

**Pledge.** Any rights owned by a mortgagor in real estate may be pledged as collateral for a loan. Most mortgages include the pledge of a property's fee simple ownership, although leasehold, mineral, water, and other rights less-than-a-freehold interest can be pledged.

The portion of the mortgage that pledges the mortgagor's rights is called the **granting clause**. It includes the words "grant, bargain, sell, and convey," which are the same words that appear on the face of a deed that transfers the ownership of a property from a grantor to a grantee. These words of conveyance in the mortgage form actually transfer a quasi-legal, or equitable, form of ownership to the mortgagee, creating a lien that the mortgagee will either release when the loan is satisfied or perfect into a full legal fee if there is a default.

**Property Description.** All property pledged as collateral in a mortgage must be described accurately to prevent any future controversies. A description used in prior transactions is usually an adequate reference, and it can be copied onto the new forms. However, whenever a new subdivision is involved in a loan or some complication arises concerning a property description, it may be necessary to retain a surveyor to provide a precise legal description.

In addition to the real property described, most mortgage forms include the pledge of

> ". . . all buildings and improvements now or hereafter placed thereon; all rents, issues, and profits thereof; all classes of property now, or at any time hereafter, attached to or used in any way in connection with the use, operation, or occupation of the above-described property; all property rights and privileges now or hereafter owned by a mortgagor . . . All of the foregoing shall be deemed to be, remain, and form part of the realty and be subject to the lien of this mortgage."

Thus, the real property, anything that is permanently attached to it, and all of the mortgagor's rights in it are pledged as collateral for the loan.

**Covenant of Seisin.** The covenant of seisin is the clause stating that the mortgagors have title to the property described and that they have the authority to pledge the property as collateral. This covenant goes one step further by specifying that the mortgagors will warrant this title and guarantee that it is being pledged free and clear of any encumbrance not described in the mortgage document.

Although this clause is found in most standard mortgage forms, it is of little practical consequence because a mortgagor's warranty would be useless in the event of default. As a result, most mortgagees rely on a careful title examination and title insurance to protect against misrepresentation.

**Note Attachment.** It is not necessary to describe all terms and conditions of a note in the body of a mortgage. In fact, the parties to a loan often prefer not to reveal this information and merely indicate a reference to the note, using the phrase "this mortgage is given to secure the payment of a certain indebtedness evidenced by a note payable to the order of the mortgagee," or words to that effect.

However, some forms provide a space for the attachment of a true copy of the note. Whatever the case, the borrower agrees in the mortgage to pay the full sum due according to the terms of the note.

**Property Taxes.** In addition to being obligated to repay a mortgagee according to the terms and conditions of the promissory note, a mortgagor must pay all property taxes, assessments, adverse claims, charges, and liens that may jeopardize the priority position of the mortgagee. Any negligence on the part of a mortgagor to pay these claims technically puts a mortgage into default.

Depending on specific circumstances, mortgagees may protect their interests by including as a condition of the loan contract that the mortgagor pay a proportionate share of the annual taxes with each monthly payment of principal and interest. These tax payments would then be held in a special impound or escrow account to accumulate over the year and be paid to the tax collector, usually the county treasurer, when they are due. This procedure has eliminated many of the problems connected with mortgagors who simply were not conditioned to putting aside the funds necessary for annual property taxes. In most commercial loans and some residential loans, however, the mortgagors still retain control over these tax payments, and they are not impounded by a mortgagee.

A mortgagee will closely supervise the prompt payment of all current property taxes because a tax lien takes a priority position over any other liens, recorded or not.

**Insurance.** Just as mortgagees must protect themselves by supervising the prompt payment of property taxes, they must also specify in their mortgage contracts that the homeowners insurance that includes both hazard and liability is to be provided and paid for by the mortgagor in an amount adequate to and under terms adequate to protect the mortgagee's interest in the property. In most cases, a copy of the insurance policy must be submitted to the lender a few days prior to closing. The insurance agency chosen by the mortgagor is subject to approval by the mortgagee. Due to the occurrence of numerous natural disasters in recent years, obtaining homeowners insurance has become more difficult. Lenders may require proof of insurance much earlier in the process.

Not only must adequate coverage be provided, the mortgagee must also be named as a coinsured party. The original policy must be deposited with the mortgagee, and proportionate shares of the insurance premiums must be included together with the monthly payment of principal, interest, and taxes. These hazard insurance payments are deposited in the impound account, together with the property taxes collected, and the funds accumulated are used to pay the insurance premiums when they become due. In this manner, a mortgagee supervises the current status of the insurance coverage of the collateral.

If a loss occurs, the check for the insurance proceeds is issued either to the mortgagee only or to the mortgagor and the mortgagee jointly, the latter having an opportunity to inspect the repairs prior to endorsing the check. In the former case, the mortgagee usually retains the right to apply the proceeds to the amount of the indebtedness or make the necessary repairs. Thus, a mortgagee can protect the value of the collateral during the entire life of the loan.

**Maintenance of the Collateral.** As a further protection of the mortgagee's interests, a mortgagor is required by the terms of a mortgage to preserve the value of the premises by maintaining its physical condition. A mortgagor is charged "not to permit or commit waste on said premises" and "to preserve and repair said property."

**Defeasance Clause and Acceleration.** A mortgage usually includes a **defeasance clause**. It "defeats" foreclosure by stating that the mortgagor will regain full, free, and clear title upon the repayment of the debt. It has also become standard procedure to include an **acceleration clause** that outlines the consequences of failure to pay on the part of the mortgagor. The acceleration clause usually states the following:

> "In the event of nonpayment of any sum of money, either principal, interest, assessments . . . adverse claims, encumbrances, charges or liens, premiums of insurance when due or failure to maintain said premises or to keep or perform any other agreement, stipulation, or condition herein contained, then the whole principal sum of said note, at the option of the mortgagee, shall be deemed to have become due, and the same, with interest thereon at the rate contracted, shall thereupon be collectible in a suit at law *or* by foreclosure of this mortgage, as if the whole of said principal sum were payable at the time of any such failure."

This acceleration clause is at the heart of a mortgage in relation to a mortgagee's protection. Any of the neglects mentioned can result in a default of the contract's provisions and allow a mortgagee to accelerate the mortgage, granting the right to take the appropriate legal steps to recover the investment. A mortgagee can elect to sue on the note and pursue a mortgagor personally for any balance due or sue for foreclosure on the property pledged as collateral. In most jurisdictions, a mortgagee cannot pursue both actions at the same time. In most cases, the mortgagee forecloses against the collateral and files a subsequent suit against the mortgagor for any deficiency incurred from the sale of the collateral. In any event, in the absence of an acceleration clause, a mortgagee would have to sue on each payment as it became delinquent, not the entire debt. The full consequences of a default are examined in Chapter 10.

**Signatures and Acknowledgment.** Like the note, a mortgage must be signed by the mortgagors accepting the conditions of the contract. These signatures must also be dated and acknowledged by a notary public, attesting to their authenticity, because unacknowledged instruments are not accepted by a county recorder and are not admissible in a court as true evidence.

**Release of Mortgage.** When a mortgage loan is paid in full, it is removed from the records by recording a satisfaction of mortgage form, executed by the lender, indicating that the loan terms have been met.

## CONTRACT FOR DEED (LAND CONTRACT)

Alternately known as a real estate contract, a land contract, a contract for sale, an agreement for deed, an installment sale, and articles of agreement, a **contract for deed** has as many forms as it has synonyms. A contract for deed does not have an accompanying note; it is a single, complete financing and sales agreement executed between a buyer and a seller. A contract for deed should not be considered a mortgage or deed of trust, even though the same basic conditions are incorporated into its form. These conditions include the pledge of specific property as collateral for the loan, the terms and conditions for the loan's repayment, the enumeration of the borrower's responsibilities, and a statement of the consequences of a default.

The contract for deed is an agreement drawn up between two parties, a buyer/borrower, the **vendee**, and a seller/lender, the **vendor**. Under a contract for deed, the seller remains the legal fee owner of the property, which is one major distinction between this form of financing instrument and the mortgage and deed of trust. Although the buyer agrees to pay the seller a specific price under certain terms and conditions, thereby gaining possession of the property, the buyer does not receive full legal title until the terms of the contract are met. This procedure provides the seller, who is financing the sale of the property, added protection in case of the buyer's default. Because every contract for deed is drawn up as a specific contract, no example is given here.

## Components of a Contract for Deed

Because a contract for deed does not have a note accompanying it, all conditions of the sale are described in the contract form, including the purchase price and the terms of the loan. The contract specifies the buyer's responsibilities to pay the payments when due, as well as the taxes, special assessments (if any), and hazard insurance premiums. The contract also describes the deed that the seller will deliver to the buyer upon fulfillment of the contract or deposit with an escrow—if an escrow is used—to be held until the terms of the agreement have been met. The delivery and subsequent recording of this deed serve as proof of the satisfaction of the contract debt.

The contract directs the buyer to take possession of the subject property and maintain possession so long as the agreed-upon terms of the contract are met. In the event of a contract breach, all payments made by the buyer are forfeited. The seller may then elect to bring an action against the buyer for specific performance of the agreement or may choose to use any other legal remedies granted in the contract for recovery of the property and any losses incurred.

A contract for deed is both a sale and financing agreement in one instrument; both the buyer and seller sign the document and have their signatures notarized in anticipation of recording.

## Foreclosure Power

The contract for deed goes one step further than the deed of trust. It places even more foreclosure power into the hands of the seller/lender in the event of a default. In fact, a lender under a contract for deed may be able to recover property pledged as collateral in as little as 30 days. When compared to the much longer property recovery periods of up to two years specified in the mortgage form—and up to four months under the deed of trust—the short term provided by a contract for deed gives the seller/lender significant additional security in case of default.

Some states, such as Colorado and Florida, require the seller/lender to foreclose a contract for deed as if it were a mortgage or deed of trust. Most frequently, the contract for deed form is used between individuals in the purchase and sale of real property when other means of financing are not readily available. Contracts for deeds are frequently junior financing instruments, established between a buyer and seller, to close a particular sale when the buyer does not have sufficient cash or credit to secure a new senior mortgage or trust deed loan.

Despite its seeming simplicity, the contract for deed form of financing real estate is relatively complicated. It must be recorded to protect the vendee's rights in the property. A collection escrow should be established to make sure the payments on the underlying loan or loans are made on time and that proper records are kept. Provisions must be made at the outset for delivery to the vendee of the deed when the contract is paid in full. This deed should be fully executed at the time of establishing the contract and deposited with the collection escrow. Because of these complexities (and others) in establishing a contract for deed, competent legal advice should be sought.

## JUNIOR FINANCE INSTRUMENTS

When special problems or needs arise in the financing of real estate, junior financial instruments are often used as part of the solution. Generally, when a deed of trust, mortgage, or contract for deed is used as a second encumbrance, the loan involves a higher risk, and the lender should be aware of this circumstance.

Under normal conditions, most real estate sales are finalized when a buyer secures a new first deed of trust or mortgage from a financial institution to cover the major portion of a property's purchase price. The balance, if any, is usually paid in cash as a down payment. Frequently, however, a buyer who has insufficient cash for the entire amount of the required down payment will make an offer to purchase a property based on the condition that the seller carry back a portion of the sales price in the form of a purchase-money second mortgage or deed of trust (called a **carryback loan**).

Mortgage brokers, mortgage bankers, and various small loan companies operating on direct lines of credit from commercial banks also arrange junior loans. Some companies buy and sell these second securities on a regular basis. In addition to financing the purchase of commercial and residential properties, junior financing often provides funds for land developers to pay for off-site improvements such as streets, sidewalks, sewers, and other utility installations. A lender advances the funds necessary for these improvements and accepts a lien on all of the property involved. Such a lien usually is in second position behind a developer's purchase-money loan. Once the land is subdivided, improved, built on, and sold, the underlying first lien and the junior lien for improvements are replaced by individual conventional or guaranteed loans executed by the buyers of the buildings constructed on the developed land.

### Second Mortgage or Deed of Trust

As its name implies, a **second mortgage** or deed of trust is a lien on real property that is second, or junior, in position behind an existing first lien. Just as the senior loan requires the execution of a note specifying the terms and conditions of the promise to pay, the junior loan calls for such a promissory note. In addition, the junior loan form itself is exactly the same as the senior loan form, except that the junior instrument includes—typed boldly on its face—the word *SECOND* to identify its junior priority position. The property that is described as collateral for the junior loan is the same property that is pledged as collateral for the existing senior loan.

Because the second loan is in a subordinate position, the junior lienholder is in a relatively high-risk position. If the senior encumbrance is not paid according to its terms and conditions, the senior lienholder may foreclose on the collateral property and sell it to recover as much of the outstanding senior debt as possible. This foreclosure process could effectively eliminate the junior lienholder's position in the subject property without commensurate compensation. After costs, the proceeds from the sale would be allocated to the senior lienholder first and then to the junior lienholder or lienholders, according to their priority positions. If the property did not sell for a price sufficient to satisfy the senior lender, no funds would be left to distribute to the junior lienholder(s).

In the event of a default, a senior lender knowing of the existence of a junior lien gives the junior lender a chance to step in and make the delinquent payments. The junior lender then forecloses against the collateral property, but the primary lender must be protected and will pursue any legal means available to maintain the value of the investment.

**Clauses.** Certain provisions can be incorporated into a junior lending instrument to protect the position of the junior lienholder against that of the senior lender. A clause can be included that grants the junior lender the right to pay property taxes, insurance premiums, and similar charges for a borrower who is not making these payments. These charges can then be added to the total debt in anticipation of foreclosure. Another clause can require the borrower to pay into escrow the funds for taxes, insurance, and the first mortgage payments to offset any possible delinquencies. The junior lender can also reserve the right to cure any default on the first mortgage.

Some junior mortgages include a **lifting clause** that allows a borrower to replace an existing first mortgage without disturbing the status of the junior mortgage. The amount of the new first mortgage cannot exceed the specific amount of the original first mortgage outstanding at the time the second mortgage was established. Finally, if a **cross-defaulting clause** is included in the junior mortgage provisions, a default on the first mortgage automatically triggers a default on the second mortgage.

**Pledging Equity.** Junior financing is often used by owners who have accumulated measurable equity in their property through a pay-down of the first mortgage principal balance, an inflationary rise in a property's value, or both. The property is pledged as collateral to secure funds over short-term periods. When these **equity loans** come due, borrowers frequently refinance to secure a new loan adequate to pay off all liens.

Owners may pledge their equity to secure funds for home improvements. Improvement loans are somewhat safer than other types of junior financing because they are secured not only by the equity pledged but also by the enhanced value of the improved property. Home equity loans face significant defaults when the economy slows. Particularly at risk are the high-yield loans amounting to more than 100% of the value of the collateral.

**Third Mortgage.** There are also third mortgages and deeds of trust, but these are relatively rare and used only occasionally. For example, a real estate broker may accept a third mortgage for the amount of a commission behind an already existing first mortgage and a purchase-money second mortgage carried back by the seller.

**Junior Loan Interest Rates.** Junior loans secured from mortgage brokers and bankers, fiduciary lenders, and small loan companies usually carry relatively high interest rates to offset to some degree the possibility of loss due to default. It is interesting to observe, however, that junior carryback loans issued by sellers intent on completing the sales of their property may actually provide a below-market interest rate.

As a practical matter, there can never be an effective legal limitation on the amount of interest that can be charged on a loan. If the law stipulates a specific interest rate that would constitute **usury**, a lender can circumvent the restriction by charging points or raising the principal amount to reach a desired effective yield. The imposition of usury limitations on real estate loans is currently obsolete.

## SPECIAL PROVISIONS IN MORTGAGE LENDING INSTRUMENTS

All three instruments for real estate financing may be enhanced and expanded by a multitude of provisions designed to serve the specific requirements of individual loans. Some of the provisions to be reviewed in this chapter have already become standard practice and are incorporated regularly into loan instruments (e.g., prepayment privileges and/or penalties and due-on-sale clauses). Some special provisions are used only rarely and under unique circumstances, such as lock-in clauses, subordination, or release clauses.

### Late Payment Penalty

Many real estate loans include a clause that imposes a penalty, called a late charge, on the borrower for any late payments. Although most lenders accept payments up to 10 days or 15 days after they are due without penalizing a borrower, later payments incur a penalty charge—usually 4 or 5% of the total payment or a flat fee of some previously specified amount. The penalty rate may vary by state.

### Prepayment Privilege

A prepayment privilege, or a **prepayment clause**, usually allows a borrower to repay the balance of a loan at any time without any restriction or penalty. Some loans include a provision permitting certain portions of the balance to be paid in specific years. For instance, a note might include a prepayment privilege of no more than 10% of the original principal amount to be paid in any one year. Other loans might stipulate a fixed sum of money that can be paid in addition to the regular payments in a single year.

### Prepayment Penalties

Normally, a lender does not want a borrower to prematurely repay a high-yield loan. If a borrower with a high-interest loan seeks to refinance the property, the existing mortgage would be repaid in full, and the lender will lose the opportunity for high earnings.

One way to control this is by including a prepayment penalty clause in the loan contract. This penalty usually constitutes a certain percentage of the original face amount of the loan, a percentage of the outstanding balance of the loan, or some fractional penalty, such as three months' interest. For example, if a contract includes a prepayment penalty clause of 3% of the remaining loan amount, the owner of a property will be charged $1,500 to repay an existing $50,000 principal balance prior to its normal amortization.

A lender may wish to enforce the prepayment penalty when an existing loan is being replaced by a new loan at lower interest or by a loan secured from another lender. With the exception of jumbo ARMs, few loans today have a prepayment penalty. Some states have abolished the prepayment penalty entirely and FHA, VA, and most loans purchased by Fannie Mae and Freddie Mac do not permit any prepayment penalties.

## Lock-in Clause

The most drastic form of prepayment control is a lock-in clause whereby a borrower is actually forbidden to pay a mortgage loan in full before a specific date, sometimes for as long as ten years after its inception. It seems obvious that this lock-in clause would be imposed primarily on very high-yield mortgage loans in order to preserve a lender's earning position for a prescribed time period.

Often combinations of the prepayment privilege, prepayment penalty, and lock-in clause are included in a single loan. For example, no prepayment would be allowed at all for a specified period of time from the date of the loan's inception. Then proportionate amounts of the loan would become payable in advance according to an agreed-upon schedule, with some penalty imposed if the loan were repaid after the three years but before its regularly scheduled time.

## Due-on-Sale Clause

Many financing arrangements include a **due-on-sale clause**, also known as a call clause or right-to-sell clause. This condition stipulates that a borrower "shall not sell, transfer, encumber, assign, convey, or in any other manner dispose of the collateral property or any part thereof, or turn over the management or operation of any business on the collateral property to any other person, firm, or corporation, without the express prior written consent of the lender." The due-on-sale clause further stipulates that if any of the foregoing events should occur without the lender's consent, the loan balance becomes immediately due in full, with the threat of foreclosure if it is not paid.

In reviewing a new buyer's request for permission to assume a loan, lenders can insist on certain terms and conditions before approving such an assumption. Depending on the circumstances, a lender could require additional cash as a larger down payment, adjust the interest rate on the existing balance to reflect the current market rate more accurately, charge a fee for the assumption, or impose any or all of these conditions, as well as others.

These practices by lenders caused a great deal of consternation regarding the legality of the due-on-sale clause. Various state supreme courts upheld its validity, while others denied its enforceability. Some state courts ruled differently in cases involving federally chartered lenders versus state-chartered lenders.

On June 28, 1982, in the California case of *Fidelity Federal Savings and Loan Association v. de la Cuesta,* the U.S. Supreme Court settled those controversies and ruled in favor of the ability of federally chartered banks and savings institutions to enforce the due-on-sale provisions. Assumption of conventional (non-government) loans has been rare since that time. The Garn-St. Germain Act of 1982 limited the enforcement of the due-on-sale clause in special situations, such as divorce settlements and the passing of title by inheritance.

## Assumption Versus Subject To

In the absence of a due-on-sale clause, deeds of trust, mortgages, or contracts for deed are assumable by buyers of the collateral property. A buyer may arrange with a seller to purchase a property, assume an existing encumbrance, and make any arrangements for financing the difference between the balance of the existing loan and the purchase price. This difference can be paid for either in cash or by some form of junior financing or both.

There are two ways for a buyer to arrange responsibility for an existing loan. The loan can be **assumed** or the property purchased **subject to** any existing encumbrances. If a loan is assumed, the buyer, along with the original borrower and any intervening buyers who have also assumed the loan, becomes personally liable to the lender for its full repayment. In the event of a default, the lender will foreclose, sell the collateral, and sue the original maker of the note and mortgage, as well as all subsequent persons who assumed it, for any deficiencies incurred.

On the other hand, a buyer may purchase a property with an existing encumbrance but stipulate the purchase is subject to the lien of the debt. This approach eliminates the buyer's contingent personal liability in the event of a deficiency judgment. Only the original borrower and any subsequent assumers are liable. Under the subject to format, a buyer may simply walk away from the property, forfeit any equity that has accumulated, and avoid any future responsibility in the transaction.

Knowledge of the difference between the two approaches can be extremely useful under certain circumstances. For instance, a seller in a low-down-payment transaction would insist the buyer assume the underlying mortgage to bind more tightly the responsibility for the mortgage payments. Conversely, a buyer making a substantial down payment would insist on the subject to approach eliminating any contingent liability.

Whether the buyer assumes the loan or buys subject to the lien, the original maker of the note and mortgage remains primarily responsible to the lender until the loan is paid in full or a buyer goes through a process of full substitution.

**Novation.** **Novation** is a technique where the seller of a property can end personal legal liability as the originator of a real estate loan when the loan is being assumed. The original borrower, as seller, submits a request to the lender to be replaced with the new buyer as maker on the loan instrument. After the new buyer completes the qualifying process, including a credit analysis, and is accepted by the lender, the old borrower is completely released from liability. The transfer of obligation is completed by executing an amendment to the original loan contract. The new agreement is recorded to maintain the appropriate continuity of the property's title.

Although FHA and VA loans remain assumable with borrower qualification, most conventional loans are only assumable with lender permission and rarely occur today.

When interest rates are low, there is little incentive for a purchaser to attempt to assume an existing loan.

## Subordination Clause

To subordinate means to place in a lower order, class, or rank. In real estate finance, **subordination** involves placing an existing encumbrance or right in a lower-priority position to a new loan secured by the same collateral property.

Any real estate finance instrument can be designed to provide for its subordination to the rights of some future lien. For example, a loan created to finance the sale of vacant land to a developer could include a subordination clause granting the developer an opportunity to secure new financing to construct houses on a portion of the already encumbered land. Because the construction lender for the houses would insist on being in first lien position, the existing loan given to buy the land would have to be subordinated on those specific portions to be financed with construction mortgages. The land mortgage would then be in a junior lien position to the first mortgagee on those specific parcels on which houses were to be built. The wording used to establish this type of subordination could be, "The mortgagee shall, upon written request from the mortgagor, subordinate the lien of this mortgage on the lot or lots specified in order of release, to the lien of a new construction loan or loans from a recognized lending institution." Subordination is also employed with land leases where the interests of a landlord are subordinated to a new mortgage secured by a tenant in order to develop a parcel of land (see Chapter 7 – Leasehold Mortgage).

## Release Clause

When two or more properties are pledged as collateral for a loan, some provision for releasing a portion of the collateral as certain amounts of the loan are repaid is usually incorporated into the financing instrument. An analysis of release clauses is included in Chapter 7.

## Exculpatory Clause

When securing a new real estate loan, some borrowers require that their assets, other than the property being financed, be protected from attachment in the event of a future foreclosure. This limited personal liability can be established by the inclusion of an **exculpatory clause** in the loan contract. This clause stipulates that the borrower's liability under the loan is limited to the property designated in the legal description. In the event of a default, the lender is limited to the recovery of the collateral property only and cannot pursue any deficiency judgments against the borrower's remaining assets.

## Nonrecourse Clause

Real estate loans are often sold in the financial market (see Chapter 4). When a **nonrecourse clause** is included in the sale's agreement, the seller of the security is not liable if the borrower defaults. The buyer of the security must take action to recover the unpaid balance of the loan from the borrower or foreclose on the collateral. However, if a real estate loan is sold with recourse, the seller of the security is obligated to reimburse the buyer if the borrower defaults.

### Extensions and Modifications

Some loan instruments include provisions for extensions or modifications under special circumstances. Sometimes a lender will allow an extension of time for a financially troubled borrower to continue payments beyond a specific due date. Other lenders may make adjustments and modifications in loan contracts in order to meet particular problems arising after a loan has been in effect for some time. These modifications could include adjustments in payments, interest rates, due dates, or, in extreme cases, payment moratoriums.

In response to the financial crisis starting in 2007, the government provided several different loan modification programs in an effort to help at-risk homeowners avoid foreclosure. The most recent programs are Home Affordable Modification Program (HAMP) and Home Affordable Refinance Program (HARP). Under HAMP, the monthly mortgage payment may be reduced by as much as 40%. Refinancing under HARP lets the homeowner take advantage of current low interest rates.

Two major problems arise from an extension or modification of a real estate loan instrument. The first concerns the rights of an intervening lien or who may move into a priority position when an existing loan is recast. Lenders usually require a complete title examination prior to modifying their loans in order to meet such contingencies. The second problem is the possibility of negating the insurance or guarantee that a mortgage may have under its original form. In the event of any modifications to an insured loan, the guarantee may be lost.

Under some circumstances, such as a delinquent construction loan, the lender usually continues to carry the loan until the builder can sell the property to a qualified buyer. The delinquency is preferred to a modification and recasting of the loan, which might jeopardize mechanic's lien priorities.

## SUMMARY

A person can borrow money by pledging interests in real estate as collateral to guarantee the promise to repay. Usually, a borrower's ownership interest in property is encumbered to a lender for this purpose. However, other property interests can also be pledged as collateral for a loan—interests such as leaseholds; life estates; and mineral, air, and water rights.

One instrument of real estate finance is the deed of trust, which pledges the subject property as collateral for a loan drawn in favor of a third-party trustee. A deed of trust includes a power of sale clause, and if a default occurs, the trustee can sell the property to recover any losses in as little as four months.

Another real estate financing instrument is the note and mortgage. A note is a promise to pay, while a mortgage is the pledge of a specific parcel of real property as collateral to secure this promise. A note signed by a mortgagor is a negotiable instrument that specifies the terms and conditions for the repayment of a debt. A mortgage signed by both mortgagor and mortgagee establishes a lien on the collateral property as of the date it is recorded. When a mortgage debt is paid in full, the mortgagee marks the note *paid in full*, signs it, and returns it to its maker, along with a satisfaction of mortgage form, which will clear the record of the mortgage lien.

A contract for deed is, at the same time, both a sales agreement and a financing instrument between the buyer/borrower/vendee and the seller/lender/vendor. The full terms of the sale, as well as the manner in which the loan will be repaid, are elaborated in this contract financing form. The buyer is granted possession and control of the property during the term of the payments under the conditions specified in the contract. When the terms of the contract are satisfied, the seller delivers a deed to the buyer, which transfers full legal title. The contract for deed form of real estate financing is used primarily when other financing means are not available.

When a prospective property buyer does not have enough cash to satisfy the down payment requirement, a second mortgage, second deed of trust, or junior contract for deed may be carried back by the seller to finance the difference. Owners often pledge their equity as collateral for home improvement loans or personal needs. Junior instruments of finance are second in priority to an existing senior loan.

All three financing instruments may be expanded by a variety of provisions designed to serve the needs of individual borrowers and lenders. Real estate loans may include special provisions to allow for the prepayment of portions of the principal from time to time. Other loans impose prepayment penalties if the loan is paid prior to its regularly scheduled completion date. A lock-in clause prohibits any prepayment for certain specified time periods. Penalties imposed to inhibit prepayments are usually designed to preserve a lender's earnings position, and these penalties are generally included in high-interest rate loans.

Although some federally insured or guaranteed mortgages are assumable without the consent of their lenders, most conventional mortgages include a due-on-sale clause, which stipulates that a borrower cannot sell the collateral property or transfer it in any manner without the prior written consent of the lender. In the absence of a due-on-sale clause, property may be sold with the existing loan remaining in effect. The buyer has two ways in which to arrange responsibility for an existing loan. It can be "assumed," in which case the buyer along with the original borrower becomes personally liable for the loan. The buyer can also make the purchase "subject to" this encumbrance. The latter technique eliminates the buyer's personal liability on the loan, although the originator of the loan remains personally liable until the loan is paid in full. Infrequently, a seller requires a buyer to pursue a process of novation, which, upon its successful completion, substitutes the buyer for the seller on an existing loan contract.

To subordinate a finance instrument is to change its priority lien position in relation to subsequent loan instruments. Lending instruments may also be extended or modified to solve unforeseen financial problems. With the written agreement of all parties to a loan contract, a payment can be altered or waived for a certain time period.

## INTERNET RESOURCES

Examples of various contract forms can be seen at the following websites:

*www.uslegalforms.com*

*www.findforms.com*

*www.lawdepot.com*

Some state or local associations of REALTORS® may also have sample forms available.

## REVIEW QUESTIONS

1. Which circumstance would create a voluntary lien?
   a. Mortgage on the property
   b. Overdue property taxes
   c. Unpaid contractor who installed a swimming pool
   d. Judgment from an unpaid hospital bill

2. *First in time, first in right* generally gives the first mortgage lender a priority lien position, the only exception being
   a. a mechanic's lien.
   b. a judgment lien.
   c. a second mortgage lender.
   d. an unpaid property tax.

3. A lender may prefer to have a deed of trust instead of a mortgage because
   a. foreclosure is accomplished more easily and quickly.
   b. a deed of trust takes less paperwork.
   c. a deed of trust has no redemption period.
   d. a deed of trust does not require foreclosure.

4. Which statement regarding a note is *FALSE*?
   a. A note is a promise to pay a debt.
   b. A note is a complete contract.
   c. A note must be tied to either a mortgage or deed of trust.
   d. A note is a fully negotiable instrument.

5. When the mortgage loan is fully paid, the borrower (mortgagor) regains full and clear title to the property based on which clause in the mortgage?
   a. Acceleration clause
   b. Power-of-sale clause
   c. Defeasance clause
   d. Exculpatory clause

6. A homeowner sells his property to an individual, retaining title to the property until the loan has been paid in full. The homeowner has executed a
   a. purchase contract with note and deed of trust.
   b. purchase contract with note and mortgage.
   c. contract for deed.
   d. purchase contract with note only.

7. A seller was willing to allow a purchaser to assume his current conventional loan, but the lender would not allow it. The lender was exercising his rights under the
   a. due-on-sale clause.
   b. release clause.
   c. prepayment penalty clause.
   d. acceleration clause.

8. A buyer was able to purchase her new home, taking over the payments from the current owner. Although the buyer is responsible for making the payments, in the event she should default on the loan, the lender will look to the original borrower for payment of the balance due. The home was bought
   a. on a land contract.
   b. subject to the debt lien.
   c. by assuming the first mortgage.
   d. with an FHA assumption.

9. Although a developer now has a loan with his local bank for the eight properties he is building, he must be able to give clear title to each property as they are sold. In order not to be required to pay off the entire loan before conveying each individual property, the mortgage *MUST* include
   a. an acceleration clause.
   b. a subordination clause.
   c. a release clause.
   d. an exculpatory clause.

10. Lenders may be willing to waive payments temporarily but are usually reluctant to modify, or recast, the original loan agreement due to their concern that
    a. the borrower may no longer be qualified.
    b. an intervening lienholder may move into the priority position.
    c. it takes too much paperwork.
    d. they would rather foreclose on the property.

Chapter 7

# Real Estate Financing Programs

## LEARNING OBJECTIVES

When you've finished reading this chapter, you will be able to

- provide an example of both a 30-year and a 15-year loan for a specific amount, comparing the difference in payment and in interest paid over the life of the loan;
- list the basic guidelines for conventional conforming loans;
- describe the components of an adjustable-rate mortgage;
- explain the concept of private mortgage insurance and how it protects the lender; and
- differentiate between subprime and predatory lending.

**adjustable-rate mortgage (ARM)**
**ad valorem**
**amortization**
**balloon payment**
**blanket mortgage**
**boot**
**buydown**
**completion bond**
**draws**
**escrow funds**
**fixed-rate loan**
**hazard insurance**
**homeowners insurance**
**Home Equity Line of Credit (HELOC)**
**impound funds**
**interest-only loans**
**interest rate factor**
**Internal Revenue Code Section 1031**
**lease option**
**lease purchase**
**loan-to-value (LTV) ratio**
**manufactured housing**
**negative amortization**
**package mortgage**
**piggy-back loan**
**point**
**private mortgage insurance (PMI)**
**predatory lending**
**reverse annuity mortgage (RAM)**
**right of first refusal**
**split loan**
**stop date**
**Streamlined Modification Program (SMP)**
**subprime lenders**

Real estate loans can be as flexible and adaptable as needed to satisfy market demands. Contemporary financing techniques offer an opportunity to provide for most contingencies by varying one or more of the four basic characteristics of a real estate loan—the principal amount, the interest rate, the payment schedule, and the repayment terms. Each loan lends itself to a number of variations, limited only by the imaginations of those involved. This chapter begins with a discussion of interest and how it applies to mortgage lending then continues with an explanation of many different types of lending programs.

## INTEREST

From a borrower's point of view, interest can be described as rent paid for the use of money. A lender views interest as money received or earned from a loan investment. Just as rent is paid and received for the use of an apartment, house, office, or store under the special conditions of a lease, real estate finance can be considered the process by which interest and principal are paid and received under the terms and conditions of a loan agreement. Money is borrowed (leased) at a certain interest rate (rent) for a specified time period during which the amount borrowed is repaid.

The amount of rent that a landlord can charge for the use of property depends on the rental market for that particular type of real estate. Similarly, the rate of interest that a lender can charge depends on the money market as it affects that particular type of loan. A rational borrower will not pay a lender more interest than the lowest interest rate available on a specific loan at a particular time.

### Simple Interest

Most loans made on real estate are established at a simple rate of interest. Simple interest is rent that is paid only for the amount of principal still owed. When money is repaid to the lender, rent for that money stops.

The formula for computing simple interest is the following:

$$I = PRT$$

where

I = Interest

P = Principal

R = Rate

T = Time

■ **FOR EXAMPLE** Using this formula, the interest on a $1,000 loan to be repaid in one year at 8% is $80.

I = PRT

I = $1,000 × 0.08 × 1

I = $80

## Interest Rate Factor

The **interest rate factor** represents the dollars required to pay off $1,000 of a loan for a set number of years on a fully amortized loan that will be paid off at the end of the loan term. Figure 7.1 illustrates how the factor changes according to the rate of interest and the term of the loan. Note that the interest rate and the factor are the same only at a rate of 6% for a 30-year loan.

## Interest-Only Loans

**Term Loan.** Also known as a straight loan or bullet loan, a term loan requires payments of interest only with the entire principal being repaid at a specified time, called the **stop date**. The loan is then paid in full with a **balloon payment** of the principal plus any interest still owed.

■ **FOR EXAMPLE:** Consider a term loan of $10,000 at 8% per annum, payable interest only monthly, to be paid in full in three years.

| | |
|---|---|
| Loan Amount | $10,000 |
| Interest Rate | × 0.08 |
| Annual Interest | 800 |
| Pro Rata Months | ÷ 12 |
| Monthly Interest Payment | = 66.66 |
| Final Principal Payment | +10,000 |
| Balloon Payment | $10,066.66 |

*FIGURE 7.1* **Monthly Payment Required to Amortize a $1,000 Loan**

| *Years* | *5%* | *5.5%* | *6%* | *6.5%* | *7%* | *7.5%* | *8%* |
|---|---|---|---|---|---|---|---|
| 5 | 18.88 | 19.11 | 19.34 | 19.57 | 19.81 | 20.04 | 20.28 |
| 10 | 10.61 | 10.86 | 11.11 | 11.36 | 11.62 | 11.88 | 12.14 |
| 15 | 7.91 | 8.18 | 8.44 | 8.72 | 8.99 | 9.28 | 9.56 |
| 25 | 5.85 | 6.15 | 6.45 | 6.76 | 7.07 | 7.39 | 7.72 |
| 30 | 5.37 | 5.68 | 6.00 | 6.33 | 6.66 | 7.00 | 7.34 |

To compute the monthly principal and interest, multiply the number of thousands in the loan by the appropriate factor. For example; $150,000 30-year loan at 7% interest: 150 × 6.66 = $999 per month

When residential real estate prices reach new highs, qualifying borrowers for higher mortgage payments on larger loans becomes a serious problem. In order to reduce monthly payments, the use of **interest-only loans** emerges as an alternative type of loan.

When you examine the fixed-rate loan payment schedule in Figure 7.1, the regular monthly payment of $999.00 includes an amount for principal and interest and is designed to pay the debt of $150,000 at 7% in full over the 30-year time period.

To reduce this payment, the only portion that can logically be waived is the principal amount, reducing the payment to interest only. To reduce this payment any further would be paying less than interest only, which would result in the loan balance increasing each month by the difference, resulting in **negative amortization**.

There are several alternatives for interest-only loans. One option is to establish a five-year stop date with a balloon payment as described previously. These monies can be received from refinancing the property, which, hopefully, will have retained or increased its value over time. Another plan would be to establish a series of smaller balloon payments over time to gradually whittle the balance down to zero. A variation of the interest-only loan is a loan with interest-only payments for 15 years, with the remaining payments adjusted to cover the total interest and principal needed to repay the loan over the remaining term. Borrowers have the option to prepay the principal at any time.

Before the financial crisis of 2008, the interest-only loan was employed as a financing device on loans that equaled or exceeded the full purchase price of the collateral property, creating risky portfolios. As long as the housing market enjoyed an inflationary movement, these lenders were protected. However, the significant downturn in the market resulted in many loan defaults and foreclosures.

## Points

A **point** is 1% of the total loan amount. For example, one point of a $200,000 loan is $2,000. Lenders charge discount points as up-front interest to lower the interest rate for the borrower while raising the yield for the lender. The number of points charged varies according to market conditions. A loan may be quoted as "5.5% with 3 points." One of the points is usually for the origination fee, which pays for the lender's processing expenses.

## Permanent/Temporary Buydown Plan

A **buydown** is money paid by someone (e.g., seller, builder, employer, buyer) to a lender in return for a lower interest rate and monthly payment. The buydown payment is essentially interest paid in advance and may lower the borrower's payments for the entire loan term (a permanent buydown) or for a lesser period of time, usually one to three years (a temporary buydown). Each percentage of buydown is quoted as a point. Buydowns are often used as a selling tool for new home builders.

■ **FOR EXAMPLE** Assume a $100,000 loan for 30 years at 8%. To apply a temporary buydown of 2-1-0 would cost $2,432.04 or approximately two and one-half points.

| *Payment* | *Rate* | *Reg. P&I* | *Effective Rate* | *P&I* | *Difference* |
|---|---|---|---|---|---|
| 1st year | 8% | $733.77 | 6% | $599.56 | $134.21 |
| 2nd year | 8% | 733.77 | 7% | 665.31 | 68.46 |
| 3rd year | 8% | 733.77 | 8% | 733.77 | 0.00 |
| Etc. | | | | | |

| | | |
|---|---|---|
| Buydown Cost 1st Year | $134.21 × 12 = | $1,610.52 |
| Buydown Cost 2nd Year | $68.46 × 12 = | 821.52 |
| Total Buydown Costs | | $2,432.04 |

In most cases, it is not economically feasible for a borrower to pay for a buydown. Before making this decision, the buyer should calculate how long it would take to recover the additional cost at settlement.

## Amortization

The most common payment format for a real estate loan is a system of regular payments made over a specified period. These payments include portions for both principal and interest. The process is called **amortization**. Amortization tables are available in text form and online.

■ **FOR EXAMPLE** Consider a loan of $90,000 at 7% for 30 years. The monthly payment of principal and interest is $599.40. The rate factor is 6.66.

| | |
|---|---|
| Number of Thousands | 90 |
| Payment Factor (Figure 7.1) | × 6.66 |
| Monthly Payment P&I | $599.40 |

**Note:** There will be a slight difference between a payment calculated by calculator and one calculated from a factor table due to rounding.

**Distribution of Principal and Interest.** Intrinsic in the amortization design is the distribution of the level payments into proportionate amounts of principal and interest.

■ **FOR EXAMPLE** Consider the $90,000 loan at 7% interest for 30 years with a monthly principal and interest payment of $599.40.

| *Payment No.* | *Balance* | *Interest* | *Principal* |
|---|---|---|---|
| 1 | $90,000.00 | $525.00 | $74.40 |
| 2 | 89,925.60 | 524.57 | 74.83 |
| 3 | 89,850.77 | 524.13 | 75.27 |
| 4 | 89,775.50 | 523.69 | 75.71 |
| Etc. to 360 | | | |

The schedule in the previous example can be extended for the full period of 360 months to show the complete distribution of principal and interest and the remaining balance of the loan at any time. These amortization schedules can be prepared on computer printouts and are often presented by lenders to borrowers so they can follow the progress of their payments. Amortizing schedules are also available to the public online.

**Interest Adjustment.** Mortgage payments are normally paid in arrears. For example, a payment made on May 1 covers the principal due on that day plus the interest charged for the month of April. At closing, interest is usually charged to the borrower to cover the period from the closing date to the end of that month. The next full payment will not be due until the following month. For example, the closing is on June 15, interest is charged from June 15 to June 30, and the next payment is due on July 1.

## TYPES OF LOANS

There are two general categories of real estate loans: conventional and government. Conventional loans can be conforming (conforming to guidelines set by Fannie Mae and Freddie Mac) or non-conforming (those that do not meet the Fannie/Freddie guidelines). Government loans are those insured by the Federal Housing Administration (FHA), guaranteed by the Veterans Administration (VA), provided by the U.S. Department of Agriculture (USDA), or provided by special programs created by individual states or local jurisdictions. Most originators of conventional loans do not keep them for their own portfolios but sell them in the secondary market. They frequently keep the collection responsibilities and the commensurate fees for servicing the loans. Packages of loans are sold on the secondary market to Fannie Mae, Freddie Mac, the Federal Home Loan Bank, and private investors.

The majority of real estate loans originated over the past two decades were conventional loans; however, as a result of the financial crisis in the mortgage lending industry that began in 2007, a large number of borrowers have turned to FHA financing. Both conventional and government loans are available in different variations. The most common ones are described here.

### Fixed-Rate Loans

The most traditional loan product is the **fixed-rate loan**, in which the interest rate remains constant over the term of the loan. Fixed-rate loans may be amortized over a specific number of years in equal monthly payments, including principal and interest. The most popular fixed-rate loan is the 30-year mortgage, where the principal and interest portion of the payment remains the same with only slight annual changes in the portion set aside for escrow funds to pay property taxes and homeowner insurance. Even though the amount paid towards principal is very small at first, the result of this payment format is that the borrower begins to build equity with the first monthly payment. In most cases, the borrower is allowed to pay off the loan early if so desired.

■ **FOR EXAMPLE** Consider a 30-year, fixed-rate, self-amortizing loan for $100,000 at 7%.

| *Month* | *Fixed Payment* | *Interest* | *Principal* | *Balance* |
|---|---|---|---|---|
| 0 | | | | $100,000.00 |
| 1 | $665.31 | $583.33 | $81.98 | 99,918.02 |
| 2 | 665.31 | 582.85 | 82.46 | 99,835.56 |
| 3 | 665.31 | 582.37 | 82.94 | 99,752.62 |
| 4 | 665.31 | 581.89 | 83.42 | 99,669.20 |
| 5 | 665.31 | 581.40 | 83.91 | 99,585.29 |
| Etc., to 360 | | | | |

Fixed-rate loans for 15 years are also popular with borrowers who wish to have their home paid for within a 15-year period. Lenders like them because of their relatively short amortization time, and they market these loans on the basis of the borrower being able to save significant amounts of interest, compared with the 30-year loan. A 15-year loan is usually offered at 25 to 50 basis points below market rates (there are 100 basis points in 1%, so 25 basis points equal one-fourth of 1%, and 50 basis points equal one-half of 1%). However, the monthly payment required on the 15-year loan is approximately 20% higher than the payment on the 30-year loan, which limits the number of borrowers who can afford the higher payment.

■ **FOR EXAMPLE** Consider a 15-year, fixed-rate, self-amortizing loan for $100,000 at 7%.

| *Month* | *Fixed Payment* | *Interest* | *Principal* | *Balance* |
|---|---|---|---|---|
| 0 | | | | $100,000.00 |
| 1 | $898.83 | $583.33 | $315.50 | 99,684.50 |
| 2 | 898.83 | 581.49 | 317.34 | 99,367.16 |
| 3 | 898.83 | 579.41 | 319.42 | 99,047.74 |
| 4 | 898.83 | 577.77 | 321.06 | 98,726.68 |
| 5 | 898.83 | 575.90 | 322.93 | 98,403.75 |
| Etc., to 180 | | | | |

## Impound or Escrow Funds

In addition to the principal and interest, the lender often collects monthly amounts needed to pay annual taxes and insurance. These amounts, called **impound funds** or **escrow funds** in different parts of the country, are determined by dividing the total amounts due each year by 12. Although the principal plus interest payment remains constant over the life of the loan, the amount needed to pay the taxes and insurance may vary, resulting in a change in the total monthly payment. At the end of the year, some adjustment may need to be made if the escrow fund is either over or under the allowed amount.

On rare occasions, a property owner may be charged an assessment lien for off-site improvements such as a sewer or street paving. Because these improvement district bonds are a priority lien, the lender may insist that a proportionate monthly amount be escrowed (impounded) along with the taxes and insurance.

## Property Taxes

Property taxes are charged to property owners as a basic source of funds to pay for public services of state, county, city school district, and other local governmental jurisdictions. Because liens for non-payment of property taxes take priority over other liens, lenders require the escrowing of funds to ensure that funds are available when needed.

The taxing process begins by determining the funds needed to satisfy the specific budgetary requirements of each governing body within the taxing district for the following fiscal year. At the same time, every county assessor must maintain a current inventory of the fair market value of all privately owned real property within the county's boundaries. Thus, the term coined for this form of taxation is **ad valorem** (i.e., according to value). Most counties apply an assessor's factor to the fair market value, which reduces this amount to an assessed valuation of all taxable property within the county.

The tax rate to be applied to individual properties is derived by dividing the total budgetary requirements of the taxing district by the total value of the taxable property within the jurisdiction. The tax rate is usually expressed in terms of so many mills (thousandths of a cent) or dollars per thousand dollars of assessed value.

■ **FOR EXAMPLE** A taxable property having a fair market value of $200,000 in a jurisdiction that applies a 35% assessor's factor would have a $70,000 assessed valuation. If the tax rate on this particular property is $50 per $1,000 of assessed value, also described as a $50-mill rate, the tax to be paid for the year is $3,500. This owner would pay $291.67 monthly for the property tax impound ($3,500 ÷ 12 = $291.67).

## Hazard/Homeowners Insurance

In addition to the property tax impound, a lender usually requires that a proportionate share of the homeowner insurance premium be included in the monthly payment. **Hazard insurance** premiums are based on risk—the higher the risk, the higher the insurance premium. The insurance rate for a wood-frame house located in a rural area far from any possible fire-fighting service would be higher than the rate for a brick home situated two blocks from a fire station. Also, if an area is vulnerable to hurricanes, tornadoes, excessive floods, or other natural disasters, insurance rates will reflect these risks.

**Homeowners insurance** includes both hazard and liability and is generally preferred by the lender. It also provides the best protection for the homeowner. Whatever method is used to determine the insurance rate, one-twelfth of the annual premium will be included in the monthly payment. A homeowners insurance policy with a $360 annual premium will require an additional $30 per month be included in the payment.

## Variable Payment Mortgages

Traditionally, most loans are fairly standard in their payment schedules, requiring a certain sum to be paid at regular intervals over a prescribed time period. However, some real estate loans are designed to vary the required payments and interest to reflect more accurately the financial capabilities of a borrower, as well as the current state of the economy.

These alternative mortgage instruments allow a lender's return to keep pace with prevailing interest rates while simultaneously providing a borrower the opportunity to qualify for larger mortgage amounts.

## Adjustable-Rate Mortgage (ARM)

The interest rate of an **adjustable-rate mortgage (ARM)** is adjusted in accordance with a prearranged index. The ARM usually includes an annual interest rate cap to protect the borrower from volatile interest rate fluctuations. In addition, there usually is an overall interest rate cap over the entire term of the loan. A large part of the blame for the financial crisis starting in 2007 was laid on the consequences of borrowers with ARMs where the payments escalated beyond the borrower's ability to pay. Reasonable annual and life-of-loan caps may have prevented some of those losses.

Components of an ARM that should be considered when selecting an adjustable-rate mortgage include the following.

**Adjustment Periods.** This indicates the frequency of interest rate adjustments with concomitant payments. For example, the interest on a one-year ARM can change every year, while the interest on a three-year ARM can only change every three years.

**Initial Rate.** Sometimes called the teaser rate, it will always be below the market rate in order to attract borrowers to this type of loan.

**Note Rate.** The note rate or the calculated rate is the adjusted rate (index plus margin), imposed from time to time at the adjustment period.

**Qualifying Rate.** Because ARM interest rates fluctuate from time to time, the rate at which to qualify a borrower often creates problems. If the initial loan rate is low but is expected to increase in the near future, the borrower may not be able to make the higher payments. Lenders may require a borrower making less than 20% down payment to qualify at the maximum second-year rate. However, all interest rate adjustments on the loan will be made from the initial loan rate.

**Index.** The index is the starting point to adjust a borrower's applicable interest rate. Lenders must use an index that is readily available to the borrower but beyond the control of the lender. Some indexes are more volatile than others. Those most frequently used are the

- one-year constant-maturity Treasury (CMT) securities,
- Eleventh District Cost of Funds Index (COFI), and
- London Interbank (LIBOR) interest rates.

**Margin.** Each lender adds a margin percentage rate to the index at every adjustment period to derive the new note rate. Individual lenders set their own margins based on their estimated expenses and profit goals. The margin percentage rate may not change throughout the life of the loan. Typical margins range from 2 to 3%.

**Interest Rate Caps.** Most variable rate loans include an annual cap applied to the adjusted interest rate. This cap limits interest rate increases or decreases over a stated period of time and varies from lender to lender and ranges from one to two percentage points per year. Most lenders also include a life-of-the-loan interest cap ranging up to 6%. This combination of caps should provide the borrower protection against debilitating payment increases.

**Payment Caps.** Some lenders use annual payment caps instead of interest rate caps. The most common payment cap is 7.5% of the initial payment. This is equivalent to a 1% change in the interest rate. This means a payment of $750 per month, principal and interest, could not vary up or down more than $56.25 per month in one year's time. These payment caps are also combined with life-of-the-loan caps in some plans.

Most variable-rate loans do not include a prepayment penalty. Without this penalty, a borrower can more easily refinance to a fixed-rate mortgage. Some lenders also include a convertible loan feature that allows a variable-rate loan to be changed to a fixed-rate loan after the initial adjustment periods have been completed. A sample fixed-/adjustable-rate note appears in Appendix F.

All ARM originations from federally insured lending institutions must comply with disclosure regulations. Under an amendment to Regulation Z, the borrower must receive

- a descriptive ARM brochure;
- details of the specific loan program; and
- an illustrative example, based on a $10,000 loan, showing how the payments and loan balance have been affected by historical changes in the index.

## Graduated-Payment Mortgage (GPM)

A graduated-payment mortgage is designed with lower payments in the early years of a loan. These payments increase gradually until they are sufficient to amortize the loan fully. A GPM may specify less-than-interest-only early payments. This results in negative amortization, and the principal amount owed increases over time by the amount of the deficiency. This type of loan is rarely seen today.

## Low Documentation Loans

Some major lenders have offered a program for those with good credit and steady income who wished to avoid the hassle of providing documentation to be approved. Sometimes called a low-doc loan, this program was especially appealing to self-employed and commission-income borrowers. In most cases, a high credit score was required, and the interest rate may have been slightly higher. As mortgage qualifying standards have become tighter since 2008, low-doc loans are rarely available.

## Home Equity and Home Equity Line of Credit (HELOC)

When the Tax Reform Act of 1986 eliminated the tax deduction for interest paid on everything except home mortgages, the home equity loan became an important financing tool for many Americans. In most cases, the interest paid is tax deductible, and the funds may be used for any purpose. A home equity loan is usually made at a lower rate of interest than credit card or other short-term financing and can be either a fixed-rate or adjustable-rate loan. The amount that can be received is based on a percentage of the equity in the home and is limited to a combined loan-to-value (CLTV) ratio of the first mortgage plus the equity loan (most commonly 90 or 95%). In almost all cases, the home equity loan establishes a second mortgage as collateral for the loan, and closing costs can be rolled into the loan. An obvious disadvantage of the home equity loan is that the borrower is using up the equity established in the home in the present and will reduce the amount to be received upon an eventual sale of the property. As a result of the recent financial crisis, the percentage of the CLTV is likely to be lower with most banks.

A popular version of the home equity loan is the **home equity line of credit (HELOC)**. The line of credit is set up in the same way as the home equity loan, but rather than the borrower receiving the maximum amount as a lump-sum payment at closing, the borrower can write an access check, make a withdrawal with a VISA access card, or transfer funds online for any amount up to the approved limit whenever funds are needed for almost any purpose. Each lender establishes its own criteria, but, generally, the draw period ranges from 10 to 20 years and has been up to 90 or 95% of combined LTV, although the percentage is likely to be lower today. As house prices have declined, some banks have even lowered the amount available on an existing HELOC. Closing costs may be charged, and an appraisal of the property is usually required. No interest is paid until funds are withdrawn; however, many HELOCs have adjustable-rate interest and could become expensive if rates escalate.

## Home Ownership and Equity Protection Act of 1994

The Home Ownership and Equity Protection Act of 1994 (HOEPA) addresses certain deceptive and unfair practices in home equity lending. The law was strengthened by the Federal Reserve with an amendment to the Truth in Lending Act (TILA) in Section 32 of Regulation Z. Under this amendment, home loans are covered if the annual percentage rate exceeds the rate of Treasury securities of comparable maturity by more than eight percentage points (10% for second mortgages) or the fees and points paid by the borrower exceed $592 (2011 figure), including the cost of credit insurance and other debt protection products paid at closing. The amount is adjusted annually by the Federal Reserve Board, based on the Consumer Price Index. For more information on the types of loans covered, required disclosures, and prohibited practices, go to www.ftc.gov/bcp/edu/pubs/consumer/homes/rea19.pdf.

## Reverse Annuity Mortgage (RAM)

This plan is based on a borrower's ability to capitalize on accumulated equity and is designed to enhance the income of the elderly. Many senior citizens own their homes free and clear but face the problem that their incomes are fixed and relatively low. Thus, the **reverse annuity mortgage (RAM)** allows them to use their equities, with the lender paying the borrower a fixed annuity.

The property is pledged as collateral to a lender, who may provide funds to the borrower in one of the following three ways:

- Funds may be provided with regular monthly checks to the borrower until a stipulated balance has been achieved with no cash payment of interest required. The increase in the loan balance each month represents the cash advanced, plus interest on the outstanding balance.
- An initial lump-sum payment may be provided.
- A line-of-credit on which checks may be drawn may be provided. When the maximum loan amount is reached, the borrower is obligated to start repayment. In some cases, this requires the sale of the property.

■ **FOR EXAMPLE** An eligible couple (at least 62 years old) owns a $37,500 house free and clear, but they need additional money to supplement their retirement income. With a RAM, a lender could make monthly payments of $147 to the couple for ten years. At the end of the term, the couple would have received a total of $17,607 and would owe $30,000 plus all interest and fees involved. If the couple lived beyond the ten-year period, they could sell their home and move to other living quarters. Most participants in RAMs anticipate the need for a change in housing by the time the repayment requirements mature.

Under the HUD reverse mortgage program, known as the Home Equity Conversion Mortgage (HECM), the monthly payments continue for as long as the borrowers live in the home, with no repayment required until the property is sold (see Chapter 8 for more information on the HECM program).

## Conventional Conforming Loan Products

A conventional conforming loan is one that follows the Fannie Mae/Freddie Mac qualifying guidelines. Loans that do not meet the criteria set up by Fannie Mae and Freddie Mac are considered to be nonconforming loans and will not be purchased by Fannie Mae or Freddie Mac on the secondary market. The following four basic Fannie Mae and Freddie Mac guidelines are generally used to qualify borrowers for conventional loans. The actual percentage ratios shown for both housing (Rule 1) and debt (Rule 2) are not as significant today because most underwriting is done by computer.

Rule 1. Principal, interest, taxes, property insurance, private mortgage insurance, and any applicable condominium or homeowner association fees shall not exceed 28% of borrower's gross monthly income.

Rule 2. All of the previously listed plus monthly debts shall not exceed 36% of borrower's gross monthly income.

Rule 3. Borrower must have good credit.

Rule 4. Borrower must have stable employment.

It is important to know that loan underwriters have flexibility in applying these guidelines in specific cases and that the rules can be changed from time to time. For example, special affordable loan products such as Fannie Mae's MyCommunityMortgage® and Freddie Mac's Home Possible® mortgages often have higher qualifying ratios. The worksheet shown in Figure 7.2 is based on basic standard ratios of 28% of gross monthly income (GMI) for total housing expense and 36% of GMI for total debt to income.

*FIGURE 7.2* **Conventional Loan Borrower Qualification Worksheet**

| | | |
|---|---|---|
| Mortgage | $ ________ | |
| Gross Monthly Income | $ ________ | (A) |
| | | |
| Housing Expense | | |
| Principal and Interest | $ ________ | |
| Property Taxes | ________ | |
| Homeowners Insurance | ________ | |
| Monthly PMI Premiums | ________ | |
| Association Fees | ________ | |
| Total | $ ________ | (B) |
| | | |
| Debts | | |
| Installment Obligations | $ ________ | |
| Revolving Charges (Minimum Payment) | ________ | |
| Auto Loans | ________ | |
| Child Support/Alimony Payable | ________ | |
| Child Care Expenses | ________ | |
| Other | ________ | |
| Total Debts | $ ________ | (C) |

| | |
|---|---|
| (B ÷ A) × 100 = ________ % | Housing expense (B) should be less than 28% of gross monthly income (A) |
| [(B + C) ÷ A)] × 100 = ________ % | Housing expense (B) plus long-term debt (C) should be less than 36% of gross monthly income (A) |

■ **FOR EXAMPLE** The borrowers have a combined gross monthly income of $5,000. The loan amount applied for is $100,000 at 7.5% for 30 years payable at $699.22 per month principal and interest. The monthly property taxes are $300, insurance is $30, PMI premium is $62.50, and the neighborhood association fee is $20 per month. In addition, the borrowers have a monthly installment obligation of $100, a minimum revolving charge payment of $50, an auto loan payment of $175, child care expenses of $200 per month, and other monthly charges of $100. They have stable jobs and good credit. Do they qualify under rules number 1 and 2?

| | |
|---|---|
| Combined Monthly Gross Income | $5,000.00 |
| Housing Expenses: | |
| Principal and Interest | $699.22 |
| Property Taxes | 300.00 |
| Hazard Insurance | 30.00 |
| PMI Premium | 62.50 |
| Association Fees | 20.00 |
| Total: | $1,111.72 ÷ 5,000 = 22.23% OK |
| Debt Expenses: | |
| Installment Payments | 100.00 |
| Revolving Charges | 50.00 |
| Auto Loan | 175.00 |
| Child Care | 200.00 |
| Other | 100.00 |
| Total: | 625.00 |
| Plus Housing Expenses | 1,111.72 |
| Grand Total: | $1,736.72 ÷ 5,000 = 34.73% OK |

■ **FOR EXAMPLE** A single parent's gross monthly income is $3,000. The loan amount applied for is $75,000 at 7.5% for 30 years with a monthly principal and interest payment of $524.42. The property taxes are $200 per month, insurance is $20, and the PMI is $60. Installment obligations are $100 per month, the auto loan payment is $80, child care is $100, and other payments cost $100 per month. Does the borrower qualify under rules 1 and 2?

| | |
|---|---|
| Monthly Gross Income | $3,000.00 |
| Housing Expenses: | |
| Principal and Interest | $524.42 |
| Property Taxes | 200.00 |
| Hazard Insurance | 20.00 |
| PMI Premium | 60.00 |
| Total: | $804.42 ÷ 3,000 = 26.81% OK |
| Debt Expenses: | |
| Installment Payments | 100.00 |
| Auto Loan | 80.00 |
| Child Care | 100.00 |
| Other | 100.00 |
| Total: | 380.00 |
| Plus Housing Expenses | 804.42 |
| Grand Total: | $1,184.42 ÷ 3,000 = 39.48% Not OK |

To qualify, this borrower will have to pay off some of the debt.

### Fannie Mae/Freddie Mac Maximum Loan Limits

The conforming loan limit is now set by the Federal Housing Finance Agency (FHFA). The limit for 2013 and 2014 remained at $417,000 for most areas, with a special provision for high-cost areas. These limits are set equal to 115% of local median house prices and cannot exceed 150% of the standard limit ($417,000 in 2014 or $625,500 for high-cost areas). According to provisions of the Housing and Economic Recovery Act of 2008 (HERA), the national loan limit is set based on changes in house prices over the previous year, but it cannot decline from year to year. New loan limits are generally published at the end of each calendar year for the coming year. For more information on current loan limits see www.hud.gov. For specific Fannie Mae and Freddie Mac loan products, see www.fanniemae.com and www.freddiemac.com.

### Jumbo Loans

Any loan exceeding the current Fannie Mae/Freddie Mac conforming loan limits is considered a jumbo loan. Each lender is free to set their own qualifying standards, although the Fannie Mae/Freddie Mac guidelines are often used. Jumbo loans may be up to whatever amount a lender is willing to risk.

## PRIVATE MORTGAGE INSURANCE

**Private mortgage insurance (PMI)** is required on conventional loans when the **loan-to-value (LTV) ratio** is in excess of 80% as stated in the Fannie Mae and Freddie Mac guidelines. The insurance covers the amount of the loan in excess of the 80% LTV ratio. Private mortgage insurance programs vary in the need for coverage and amount of coverage required. Rates can also vary depending on the private mortgage insurance carrier and on the credit standing of the borrower.

Mortgage insurance is issued to protect the lender in case the borrower defaults on the loan payments. If a property is foreclosed, the insurance company either pays the lender in full and acquires the property or pays the lender in accordance with the terms of the insurance plan plus expenses, and the lender acquires the property.

Although some borrowers may choose to pay part or all of the private mortgage insurance at closing, it is more common for the annual renewal fee to be paid monthly and added to the principal, interest, taxes, and insurance (PITI) payment. The annual premium is calculated as a percentage of the loan amount (generally ranging from 0.65% to 1.25%, depending on the amount of the down payment and the borrower's credit status) divided by 12 and added to the monthly mortgage PITI payment, as seen in the following.

$100,000 fixed rate, 30-year loan with 10% down (90% LTV)
Premium: 0.75% of loan amount
Calculation: $100,000 × 0.75 = $750 annual premium
$750 ÷ 12 = $62.50 added to monthly PITI payment

There are also PMI payment plans in which the costs are financed. This is accomplished by adding the lump-sum premium amount to the loan balance to be repaid over the life of the loan. There is also a plan where the lender pays the PMI, but the borrower pays a higher interest rate on the PMI portion of the loan. One advantage to the borrower is that all of the interest is deductible. The disadvantage is that the higher interest rate remains for the life of the loan.

Private mortgage insurance on loans originated between 2007 and 2012 was deductible under the Mortgage Forgiveness Debt Relief Act of 2007. The full deduction was available for families with an adjusted gross income of $100,000 or less. Families with incomes over $100,000 were eligible for a partial deduction. The deduction was not limited to first-time homebuyers and could be claimed for the principal residence of the taxpayer plus one other residence, such as a vacation home. The act was extended through the end of 2013. A further extension remains under consideration by Congress.

The financial crisis that began in 2007 resulted in disaster for the PMI companies, with many insurers going out of business. Despite billions of losses, four of the major companies survived and are beginning to show their first profits in several years. The private mortgage insurance business has benefited from the government loan modification programs that have prevented many foreclosures and also from the gradual shift back to conventional financing from FHA loans, which had taken over approximately 80% of the market after the housing bubble burst. The four surviving PMI companies, plus two new companies, have formed a new trade association called the U.S. Mortgage Insurers (USMI), which has replaced the Mortgage Insurance Companies of America (MICA), which closed in early 2014. Members of the new association are Arch Mortgage Insurance Ltd., Essent Group Ltd., Genworth Financial, MGIC Investment Corporation, National Mortgage Insurance Corp., and Radian Group Inc.

## PMI Guidelines

In response to the declining market in 2007, private mortgage insurers re-evaluated their guidelines for approval. From time to time, a PMI company may designate certain states as severely declining and enforce additional underwriting restrictions. Factors that can be affected are the minimum credit score, the maximum loan amount, and the debt-to-income ratio.

The Federal Housing Finance Agency (FHFA), as conservator for Fannie Mae and Freddie Mac, is working with the GSEs to revise, expand, and align their risk management requirements in order to incorporate a new, risk-based framework that will ensure a sufficient level of liquid assets is always available to pay claims. According to MICA, the PMI companies paid over $22 billion in claims to Fannie Mae and Freddie Mac, reducing taxpayer liability by over 14% during the recent crisis period.

## Termination of PMI Payments

PMI premiums continue until the lender releases the coverage, which depends not only on the increased equity position of the borrower, but on the payment history as well. Once the LTV ratio reaches 80%, the insurance company is no longer liable for any losses due to default by the borrower, and the insurance premium payments should stop. Usually the borrower must initiate the release.

Under the Homeowners Protection Act of 1998, PMI premiums must be terminated automatically when the LTV ratio reaches 78% of the property's original value, not its current market value. Termination is required only if the loan payments are current. Borrowers may also request to have the PMI canceled when the LTV ratio reaches 80%, if their recent payment history is unblemished and there is no other debt on the property. Fannie Mae and Freddie Mac require that mortgage lenders and servicers doing business with them automatically terminate PMI premiums on all existing loans that are halfway through their term. They also require lenders to drop the PMI once a homeowner reaches 20% equity. They calculate this figure by including the value of the home improvements and market appreciation. However, this approach is not automatic. The borrower must have a record of timely payments and formally request such an action.

### Split or Piggy-Back Loan

One way for a borrower to avoid paying a PMI premium is called a **split loan** or a **piggy-back loan**, involving a first and second mortgage executed simultaneously. The arrangement can be for an 80/10/10 split, an 80/15/5 split, or even an 80/20/0 split, although this would be rare today. In each case, the first mortgage remains at 80% LTV, which requires no PMI. The second number represents a second mortgage that is held by the same lender but at a slightly higher rate and shorter term. The last number represents the down payment. The actual monthly payment may be less than it would have been with a 95% or 97% LTV, and all of the interest is deductible. For refinancing purposes, the sum of the two mortgages is considered the original loan amount.

## REFINANCING EXISTING CONVENTIONAL LOANS

With mortgage interest rates at relatively low levels for the past few years, many homeowners have considered refinancing their existing loans as a method for saving money by lowering their monthly payments. The amount of this saving may not be cost-effective for everyone, however. The costs of refinancing are unregulated and vary dramatically among lenders. A new loan may require an application fee, title insurance, an appraisal, an attorney, and probably some discount points where one point equals 1% of the loan amount. It is important to determine the total costs before making a decision to refinance.

For example, assume a balance exists on a 30-year amortizing loan of $100,000 at 8% with a monthly payment of $733.77, including principal and interest. To refinance this amount with a new 30-year loan at 7% interest will require a monthly payment of $665.31, a savings of $68.46 per month. If the cost of securing this new financing total is $3,500, it will take about 51 months to recover the costs ($3,500 ÷ $68.46 = 51.12 months). It is generally accepted that a rule-of-thumb to use in analyzing the advisability of refinancing is that the costs of the new loan should be recovered over a two-year to three-year period. Thus, when the owner continues to occupy the property for a longer period of time, a savings will be achieved.

Before making the decision, it is important to discuss a loan modification with the existing lender. It may offer a lower interest rate with minimal transaction fees eliminating the need for refinancing. In an effort to help homeowners avoid foreclosure, several new refinancing programs were introduced in 2008 as part of the Making Home Affordable (MHA) initiative. The most recent plan for refinancing is the Home Affordable Refinancing Program (HARP).

The monies received from refinancing, even if they exceed the price paid for the property, are known as realized capital gains and are not taxable until they become recognized capital gains when the property is sold.

## Streamlined Modification Program (SMP)

In November 2008, the FHFA announced a **Streamlined Modification Program (SMP)** that Fannie Mae and Freddie Mac could offer to seriously delinquent borrowers in an effort to prevent foreclosure. The SMP allows a lender to modify an existing loan to provide the borrower with an affordable monthly payment at no more than 38% of gross monthly income. This can be done by reducing the interest rate, extending the term to 40 years, or forbearing part of the principal. The program was available for borrowers who occupy the property as a permanent resident, have missed at least three monthly payments on loans that were originated on or before January 1, 2008, and have not filed for bankruptcy. The loan-to-value (LTV) ratio must be at least 90% based on an appraisal, a valuation provided by Fannie Mae or Freddie Mac.

In March 2013, the FHFA announced a new Streamlined Modification Initiative, which requires eligible borrowers to make three on-time trial payments, after which the mortgage will be permanently modified. The program went into effect July 1, 2013, and expires August 1, 2015. Requirements of the new plan are as follows:

1. The loan must be owned or guaranteed by Fannie Mae or Freddie Mac.
2. The loan must be 90 days to 24 months delinquent.
3. The first-lien mortgage must be at least 12 months old with an LTV equal to or greater than 80%.

Loans that have been modified at least two times previously are not eligible. The key difference from the original SMP program is that borrowers will not be required to document their hardship or financial situation.

## Home Affordable Modification Program (HAMP)

On March 4, 2009, the Home Affordable Modification Program (HAMP) was introduced as a part of the Making Home Affordable Program. The Treasury department partnered with financial institutions to reduce homeowners' monthly payments to a 31% front-end ratio. Special incentives were offered to both loan servicers and borrowers under this program. In order to be eligible, the borrowers must

- be delinquent on the mortgage or at imminent risk of default,
- occupy the property as a principal residence, and
- have a mortgage that originated on or before Jan. 1, 2009, with an unpaid balance of less than $729,750.

The lender may take the following steps for an eligible borrower to achieve the 31% ratio:

- Reduce the interest rate to as low as 2%
- If necessary, extend the loan term to 40 years
- If necessary, defer a portion of the principal until the loan is paid off, waiving the interest on the deferred amount
- Elect to forgive principal in order to achieve the target monthly payment

As of June 1, 2012, the HAMP program was expanded to include

- homeowners who currently rent their home,
- homeowners who did not previously qualify for HAMP because their debt-to-income ratio was 31% or lower,
- homeowners who previously defaulted on a HAMP trial period, and
- homeowners who previously defaulted on a HAMP modification.

The HAMP program has been extended through the end of December 2015.

Homeowners may also be eligible for the Home Affordable Refinance Program (HARP) subject to the following criteria:

- The mortgage must be owned or guaranteed by Freddie Mac or Fannie Mae.
- The mortgage must have been sold to Fannie Mae or Freddie Mac on or before May 31, 2009.
- The mortgage cannot have been refinanced under HARP previously.
- The current loan-to-value ratio must be greater than 80%.
- Borrowers must be current on their mortgage with a good payment history for the past 12 months.

A limited number of lenders have chosen to participate in HARP 2.0, which has the following revisions:

- There is no longer a 125% LTV cap.
- Borrowers with mortgage insurance can refinance.
- Appraisals are waived with most Fannie Mae loans and some Freddie Mac loans.
- A low credit score is accepted if automated underwriting approves it.
- The debt-to-income ratio can be up to 50%.

The HARP program is scheduled to end on December 31, 2015.

For more information, see www.makinghomeaffordable.gov and www.hmpadmin.com.

## SUBPRIME AND PREDATORY LENDING

In the financial world, mortgage loans are designated as A, B, C, or D paper. Ideally, all borrowers would be rated "A." There are cases, however, where the loan is considered "B" quality—showing definite credit problems; "C" quality—indicating borrowers with very marginal or poor credit; or even "D" quality—indicating a very high risk on the loan. A category of "A minus" may be used to describe those applicants who are very close to "A" but have minor credit or qualifying problems. Lenders who provide loans or even specialize in the B, C, or D paper are called **subprime lenders**.

Subprime lending is credited with making home ownership possible for many immigrants, first-time homebuyers, and those suffering from temporary financial setbacks and was a contributing factor to the record 69% rate of homeownership reached in 2004. Unfortunately, the percentage of homeownership has been slowly declining as a result of the increased rate of foreclosures occurring throughout the country. Overuse of subprime lending products is also considered to have been a contributing factor to the downfall of the mortgage lending market, beginning in 2007.

In the Center for Responsible Lending's *Lost Ground, 2011: Disparities in Mortgage Lending and Foreclosures* report, it is stated that of mortgages made between 2004 and 2008, 6.4% have ended in foreclosure and that another 8.3% are at risk (see www.responsiblelending.org/mortgage-lending/research-analysis/Lost-Ground-2011.pdf). The report also says that foreclosure rates are consistently worse for borrowers who received high-risk loan products largely promoted by the subprime market (e.g., loans with prepayment penalties, hybrid adjustable-rate mortgages, and option ARMs).

The terms *subprime* and *predatory* are not synonymous. Subprime loans are made to persons with less-than-perfect credit ratings and usually carry higher interest rates and fees than the prime loans offered to applicants with no credit problems.

A subprime loan may range from 1 to 5% above the current market rate, depending on the extent of the potential borrower's credit problems. Borrowers should beware of predatory lending when the quoted interest rate is in excess of these percentages or the rate seems competitive but the annual percentage rate (APR) is much higher than the quoted rate.

There has always been a need for a subprime market to meet the needs of special case buyers who do not qualify for traditional mortgage loans. Unfortunately, the rapid expansion of the subprime market to thousands of homebuyers who did not fully understand the implications of possible future changes in the amount of monthly payment due led to financial disaster for both the borrowers and the subprime lending companies.

### Predatory Lending

Billions of dollars are lost by consumers every year due to predatory mortgages, payday loans, and other lending abuses, such as overdraft loans, excessive credit card debt, and tax refund loans. HUD, VA, Fannie Mae, Freddie Mac, the Mortgage Bankers Association, and the Association of Mortgage Professionals have all worked very hard to combat the prevalence of predatory lending. Unfortunately, the predatory lender may be someone well-known and trusted by the potential borrower. It is suggested that a borrower check out any lender being considered with the local Chamber of Commerce, the Better Business Bureau, and either the Mortgage Bankers Association or the Association of Mortgage Brokers. The problem is especially difficult when the borrowers do not speak English and are literally being preyed upon by a lender of their particular ethnic-language group.

**Predatory lending** is generally defined as the practice of charging interest rates and fees that are higher than justified by risk-based financing. Fees on a typical mortgage loan average around 1%; on a predatory loan, fees totaling 5% or more are common. Because points and fees can be financed as part of the loan, they may be disguised or downplayed by the lender. Often, borrowers are placed in a loan that is not only expensive in terms of rate and fees, but it may also be difficult, if not impossible, to pay back. The result can be the loss of the home or continued refinancing of the loan, called loan flipping. Another common practice is charging abusive prepayment penalties. Only a small percentage of regular home loans contain any prepayment penalty, but the predatory lender may include a prepayment clause in the note that prohibits the borrower from paying off this high-interest loan for three years or more and charges more than six months' interest as a penalty. One of the most reprehensible forms of predatory lending is where a lender entices a homeowner to take out a home equity loan, knowing full well that there is no way that the loan can be repaid and that it will eventually lead to foreclosure on the property.

In communities across America, borrowers have lost their homes because of the actions of predatory lenders, appraisers, mortgage brokers, and home improvement contractors. Other predatory lending practices include

- lending on properties for more than they are worth using inflated appraisals;
- encouraging borrowers to lie about their income, expenses, or cash available for down payment;
- knowingly lending more money than a borrower can afford to repay;
- charging high interest rates to borrowers based on their race or national origin;
- charging fees for unnecessary or nonexistent products and services;
- pressuring borrowers to accept higher-risk balloon or interest-only loans, or loans with steep prepayment penalties or possible negative amortization;
- stripping homeowners' equity from their homes by convincing them to refinance again and again when there is no benefit to the borrower;
- using high-pressure sales tactics to sell home improvements and single-premium mortgage insurance; and
- steering the borrower into a subprime mortgage when the borrower could have qualified for a mainstream loan. Fannie Mae has estimated that up to one-half of borrowers with subprime mortgages could have qualified for loans with better terms.

Two types of loans that are not necessarily predatory but could be if the borrower does not understand the implications of the loan are the following:

- Balloon loan requiring full payment at the end of the initial term
- Interest-only loan with balance of principal plus interest due at end of term

## Mortgage Fraud Red Flags and Best Practices for Prevention[1]

It is important for real estate professionals to be aware of common fraud schemes to help protect their clients and their business.

**Foreclosure Rescue Scheme.** This type of fraud takes advantage of homeowners who have fallen behind on their monthly mortgage payments. Some of the red flags to look out for are:

- The borrower is buying the property as an investment while continuing to rent.
- The borrower is buying multiple rental properties simultaneously.
- The borrower is buying the property as a primary residence while already owning a home of a higher value.
- The borrower is unable to contribute to funds to close.

**False Stated Income Fraud.** In a stated income loan, the income that is put on the loan application is not fully verified. In a false stated income loan, the borrower's income is misstated for qualification purposes. Use the following best practices to help all of the parties to the transaction avoid this type of fraud:

- Try to ensure that the most experienced underwriters on the lending team underwrite stated income loans.
- Review the borrower's age, education, experience, and job position, and then compare them against the income listed on Form 65.
- Evaluate the borrower's accumulation of assets and consider the borrower's debt.
- Refer to online tools and databases that provide income and employment data by zip code.
- If a W-2 wage earner is qualifying under a stated income program because the borrower has additional income that is not documented, Form 65 should specifically state which portions of the borrower's income are earned from each source.
- If the borrower does not qualify based on traditional income documentation, the originator may not place the borrower into a stated income loan.
- The income of a non-qualifying spouse or partner should never be added to the borrower's income for qualifying purposes under a stated income loan.

---

1 Source: http://www.freddiemac.com/singlefamily/preventfraud/redflags.html

**Cash-Out Purchases and Illegal Property Flipping.** Property flipping with a cash-out purchase becomes fraudulent when a buyer/borrower approaches the seller with an offer that is considerably higher than the list price. The offer will include a stipulation that the additional amount over the list price will be given to the buyer/borrower at closing. An inflated value charged to non-existent home improvements will be used to support the inflated sales price. Although difficult to detect, some of the red flags to look out for with this type of scheme are:

- The home may have been on the market for an extended period of time.
- The sales contract may have been modified or may include an addendum regarding the payment to the borrower.
- The appraisal may include red flags symptomatic of inflated value.
- Many of the red flags that are found with a traditional flip also apply to this type of fraud (e.g., straw buyer, false source of funds, and false occupancy).
- The preliminary HUD-1 form may already indicate a portion of the net proceeds going back to the borrower.

## State Legislation and Predatory Lending

Many states have initiated predatory lending legislation. The first of these was North Carolina in July of 1999. Other states soon followed, and today almost every state, including the District of Columbia, has some type of antipredatory lending law. Unfortunately, these laws vary greatly from state to state, creating compliance difficulties for large national lenders. Specific updated information by state can be found on the Mortgage Bankers Association website at www.mbaa.org.

## Federal Legislation and Predatory Lending

Other than the traditional Real Estate Settlement Procedures Act (RESPA), Truth in Lending Act (TILA), and Homeowner and Equity Protection Act (HOEPA), there has been little federal legislation specifically prohibiting predatory lending. The new Consumer Financial Protection Board will be taking steps to address the problems of predatory lending in all areas of personal finance.

HUD has taken action to combat one form of predatory lending in HUD 24 CFR Part 203 "Prohibition of Property Flipping" in HUD's Single Family Mortgage Insurance programs. This regulation was passed to prevent a home being purchased with an FHA-insured loan and then flipped within a short period of time for a considerable profit. In some cases, this was being done with collusion between the lender and an appraiser.

In May 2010, in an effort to speed the sale of foreclosed homes, FHA dropped the 90-day requirement as long as the property is being sold by a lender after foreclosure.

## VARIATIONS IN FORMATS

The deed of trust, note and mortgage, and contract for deed are flexible and, therefore, adaptable to many situations by using creative design. Almost every realty financing contingency can be solved to the satisfaction of all the participants. Not only can specific terms and conditions be designed to meet particular requirements, but special forms of these three lending instruments can also be developed to finance unique real estate situations.

### Open-End Mortgage

An open-end mortgage allows a borrower to secure additional funds from a lender—funds that, in many instances, represent the principal already paid by the borrower. The funds advanced by this process are repaid by either extending the term of the mortgage loan or increasing the monthly payments by the amount appropriate to maintain the original amortization schedule. The interest rate can also be adjusted accordingly, and appropriate fees can be charged.

Open-end mortgages are often used by farmers to raise funds to meet their seasonal operating expenses. Similarly, builders use the open-end mortgage for their construction loans in which advances are made periodically while the building is being completed. In addition, many private loan companies are offering customers an opportunity to draw down on a line of credit backed by the collateral of their home equity.

A basic legal problem associated with open-end financing is one of securing future advances under an already existing debt instrument and, at the same time, preserving its priority against any possible intervening liens. For example, an advance made under a construction mortgage that sets forth a specific pattern of draws is interpreted to have priority over a construction (mechanic's) lien that may have been filed in the period prior to the last advance.

Under the laws of those states that have adopted the Uniform Commercial Code, any personal property security agreements for the purchase of goods that become fixtures on the collateral property have a priority lien over future advances made under an original mortgage. Suppose a homeowner signs a financing contract to purchase and install a central air-conditioning system in June, and the agreement is recorded. In December, the owners secure an advance on their open-end mortgage to build an addition to their home. Because the central air-conditioning system is now a fixture, the appliance company's lien will take priority over any future advances made by the original mortgagee.

### Construction Mortgage

A construction mortgage, also called an interim financing agreement, is a unique form of open-end mortgage. It is a loan to finance the costs of labor and materials as they are used during the course of constructing a new building. An interim mortgage usually covers the period from the commencement of a project until the loan is replaced by a more permanent form of financing at the completion of construction. This financial format is unique because the building pledged as part of the collateral for the loan is not in existence at the time that the mortgage is created. The value of the land is the only available collateral at the loan's inception, a condition that requires the lender to seek some form of extra protection.

The procedure for protecting the lender is both logical and practical. Although the full amount to be loaned is committed at the start of construction, the funds are distributed in installments as the building progresses, not as a lump sum in advance. The outstanding loan balance is matched to the value of the collateral as it grows.

**Application and Requirements.** To obtain a construction loan, the borrower submits plans and specifications for a building to be constructed on a specific site to a loan officer for analysis. Based on the total value of the land and the building to be constructed thereon, a lender will make a commitment for a construction loan, usually at the rate of 75% of the property's total value.

For example, a $100,000 project would be eligible for a $75,000 construction loan. This amount normally would be adequate to cover most of the costs of construction, with the $25,000, or 25% equity, representing the value of the free and clear lot. In a case where the lot is encumbered by an existing mortgage, the mortgagee must subordinate that interest to the lien of the new construction mortgage before the loan can be granted.

Construction loans are available for projects of all sizes, and the charges imposed vary according to the lender. Typically, there is at least a 1-point placement fee plus interest at 2 points above the prime rate charged to AAA-rated borrowers. Interest rates and placement fees fluctuate as a function of business cycles, borrowers' credit ratings, and individual situations.

**Pattern of Disbursements.** Disbursement of funds under a construction loan usually follows one of two basic patterns. A construction loan may be designed to include a schedule for disbursing funds in a series of **draws** as construction progresses. In a five-stage plan, an interim financier distributes 20% of the funds each time the building reaches another one-fifth of completion.

In the $75,000 example, $15,000 is distributed to the builder when the first stage is accomplished, with subsequent $15,000 draws until completion, when the final draw is paid. This final $15,000 might be withheld pending the full payment of all labor and materials as evidenced by lien waivers from each of the contractors and subcontractors of the job, receipt of a certificate of completion and approval for occupancy issued by a building inspector, or expiration of the statutory time to file a construction lien.

Another pattern of disbursement under a construction loan requires the borrower to submit all bills for subcontracted labor and materials to the lender, who then pays these bills and charges the loan account accordingly. This plan gives the lender greater control over the possibility of intervening construction liens.

The pattern of disbursement, in the form of either draws to the builder or direct payments from the lender, effectively matches the value of the collateral to the amount of the loan outstanding at a particular time. If there is a default at any point during construction, the lender can foreclose and recover the collateral in its unfinished condition. It can then be sold "as is" or completed to recover the investment.

Interest is charged on these monies only after they are disbursed following each inspection of the work's progress. The accumulated interest charges and the entire construction loan principal are paid in full within some relatively short period of time after completion of the project. Usually, a construction loan is replaced by a permanent, long-term senior loan for which the builder has arranged in advance.

**Lender Protection.** There are no insurance plans for guaranteeing the payments on construction loans. As additional protection, many construction financiers insist their borrowers/builders secure a **completion bond** from an insurance company, naming the lender as the primary beneficiary. The bond is drawn in the amount of the total construction cost and is exercised only if the builder is unable to complete the construction. Under this circumstance, the lender can step in and use the bond proceeds to pursue the completion and subsequent sale of the property to recover the interim loan funds. Often small building companies cannot qualify for bonding and must pledge other assets as additional collateral for a construction loan.

Construction loans are drawn for relatively short time periods—six months to a year for a house and up to three years for larger projects. The interim lender needs to be paid in full at the end of these periods and is vitally concerned with making provisions in advance for the security and satisfaction of the construction loan. The borrower is equally concerned with this payback and is eager to be relieved of the heavy interest burden imposed during the loan period. Therefore, provisions for a permanent, long-term mortgage are made prior to the origination of the construction loan to satisfy or "take out" the interim financier at the completion of construction.

**Sources of Funds.** The relatively short-term nature of construction loans closely matches the investment profile of commercial banks, which take an active role in this form of financing. However, some lenders that generally deal in long-term loans also participate in interim financing. For example, they will provide money for construction and then simply convert these interim mortgages to permanent mortgages for eligible borrowers. In other words, these lenders have created an in-house loan package, called a construction/permanent loan.

While construction loans are tailored to the investment needs of commercial banks, permanent long-term takeout loans match the investment designs of thrift institutions and life insurance companies. All types of investment groups can participate in the various stages of construction financing.

## Blanket Mortgage

Depending on the terms of a specific transaction, a lender may require a borrower to pledge more than one parcel of property as collateral to back up a mortgage. The debt instrument used in this situation is called a **blanket mortgage** and can take any of the financing forms discussed previously. When the properties encumbered by a blanket mortgage are located in more than one county, the debt instrument must be reproduced and recorded at the courthouse in each county where a subject property is located.

**Release Clause.** When two or more properties are pledged as collateral for one loan, it is often necessary to provide some means for relinquishing an individual parcel as payments are made. Such a tool is called a release clause. In exchange for some action, such as a designated amount of repayment, a specific property or portion of a property can be freed from the lien of a blanket mortgage.

Blanket mortgages are often used to purchase large tracts of land for development, and a release clause usually is incorporated into these financing instruments. The absence of a release clause requires the payment in full of the entire balance due before any portion of the land can be sold lien free. The alternative is to sell a portion of the land without satisfying the underlying blanket mortgage or contract for deed. This latter technique could create many difficulties for the buyer of a small parcel. If the payments on the underlying encumbrance are not made on time by the developer, the small parcel owner may be wiped out in a foreclosure. Unfortunately, some early land promotion developments in this country were designed on this no-release basis, with concurrent losses to individual buyers.

**Recognition Clause.** Most responsible land developers secure a special recognition clause from their underlying financiers that protects individual small parcel owners. This clause specifies that in the event of a default and a resultant foreclosure, the underlying financier will recognize and protect the rights of each individual lot owner. Many states require not only full disclosure of the physical attributes of the land involved in such a development but also a description of all financing terms. These state disclosure laws closely parallel those of the federal government for interstate land sale promotions.

## Leasehold Mortgage

Tenants are able to pledge their leasehold interests as collateral for leasehold mortgages. Some of these mortgages are eligible for FHA and VA insurance and guarantees, and national banks have been authorized to make such loans provided that the lease term extends for a sufficient interval after the expiration of the leasehold mortgage.

The major sources of funds for leasehold mortgages are life insurance companies, mutual savings banks, and commercial banks. Any primary lender must be in first priority lien position so that full title to the collateral property may be secured in the event of a default. Thus, a leasehold mortgage arrangement usually includes the landlord's pledge of the legal fee in the property as well as the tenant's pledge of the improvements as collateral for the loan. The landlord's pledge of the fee simple legal rights in the land is called subordination.

As a consequence, if a loan default occurs that necessitates a foreclosure action, a lender will be protected by having the legal right to recover both the land and the building. Most leasehold mortgages are designed to include both land and buildings as collateral, requiring the landlord's subordination of the legal fee to the new lien.

## Package Mortgage

When personal property is included with the sale of real estate, it is possible to use a single financing instrument called a **package mortgage**. It includes as collateral not only the real estate but certain fixtures attached to the property and/or other items of personal property described in the mortgage document. Most installations, such as heating units, plumbing fixtures, and central air systems, when attached to the real estate, become real property and are automatically included under the lien. However, other fixtures not normally considered real property, such as ranges, ovens, refrigerators, freezers, dishwashers, carpets, and draperies, may be included in a home purchase financing agreement to attract buyers. This inclusion will enable homebuyers to stretch the payments for these items over the entire term of the mortgage, as opposed to the shorter term of a consumer installment loan.

An additional incentive to use the package loan is that the interest on a home loan is tax deductible whereas the interest on a consumer loan is not. Many commercial rental properties, including condominiums, apartment rentals, office buildings, and clinics are specifically designed to include package financing.

## Manufactured Housing Mortgage

In 1974, HUD was designated as the agency to oversee the Federal Manufactured Housing Program. All **manufactured housing** (formerly known as mobile homes) must be built to HUD standards in a controlled atmosphere manufacturing plant. The structures are then transported in one or more sections on a permanent chassis to a building site.

Are manufactured homes real or personal property? The lender is obviously concerned that there is sufficient collateral to justify financing the purchase of the home. There is little doubt that a travel trailer attached by a hitch to an automobile or set onto the bed of a pickup truck or a van-type travel home is clearly identifiable as personal property. Many larger homes manufactured as factory-built housing units are legally transportable only by professional movers. These units are permanently attached to lots in rental parks that cater to long-term tenancies or are installed on property purchased by the owner of the home. When long-term leases are involved or a homeowner has title to the lot on which the unit is permanently affixed, real estate financing is possible. Most manufactured homes are eligible for FHA or VA financing.

## Purchase-Money Mortgage

The term *purchase-money mortgage* is usually used to refer to when a seller carries back a portion or all of the sales price as a loan to a buyer. A purchase-money mortgage can be either a senior or junior lien on the property.

## Bridge Loan

A bridge loan is an equity loan designed to serve a specific purpose, usually for a relatively short period of time. For example, owners of one property wishing to purchase another might seek a short-term bridge loan on their equity to be able to close the purchase. This loan would be satisfied when the old property was sold or at a specified time, whichever came first. The bridge loan is usually an interest-only term loan, requiring a balloon payment at its conclusion.

## Wraparound Loan

A wraparound loan is a special instrument created as a junior financing tool that encompasses an existing debt. Adopting any of the three basic financing forms, these encumbrances are used in circumstances where existing financing cannot be prepaid easily due to a lock-in clause or a high prepayment penalty. They are also used where the interest rate on the existing mortgage allows a lender to secure a higher yield by making a wrap loan.

■ **FOR EXAMPLE** The sale of a $100,000 property with a $10,000 cash down payment and an assumable first mortgage balance of $70,000 at 6% interest can only be financed by a seller who would carry back a new wraparound loan for $90,000 at 7% interest. This wraparound would require the purchaser/mortgagor to make payments on the $90,000 of $6,300, while the seller/wraparound-mortgagee would retain responsibility for making the required payments on the undisturbed existing $70,000 first mortgage of $4,200, leaving $2,100 as a yield on the $20,000 wrap equity or 11%.

The use of the wrap has diminished dramatically as most existing real estate loans cannot be easily assumed. Some lenders might offer their borrowers an opportunity to secure additional funds on the equities in their properties at less-than-market interest rates by arranging to wrap the existing loans at a one-point or two-point override.

### Option to Buy

An option to buy gives the buyer, also known as the optionee, the absolute right (but not the obligation) to acquire certain real estate during the option period, provided the option payments are kept current.

### Lease with Option to Buy

A variation of the option to buy is a **lease option** to buy. In this case, the buyer agrees to purchase the property at a price negotiated within the lease. Often, a portion of the rent is applied to the purchase price as an incentive for closing the transaction. Contemporary lease-options include a **right of first refusal** clause instead of an outright option. Here, the price is not fixed at the outset; market conditions dictate the final value to be accepted by both parties. A variation that is regaining popularity since it has become more difficult to obtain mortgage financing is the **lease purchase**. Unlike the lease-option, there is an actual sales contract that includes the sales price, provisions for the amount of rent to be paid, any credit to be given back to the purchaser at time of settlement, and a projected settlement date. Financing is usually arranged 30 to 60 days prior to the projected settlement date.

## PARTICIPATION AGREEMENTS

### Mortgage Participation

There are three types of mortgage participation. One is a partnership among several mortgagees, a second includes the teaming of several mortgagors, and a third establishes a partnership between a mortgagee and a mortgagor.

**Partnership of Mortgagees.** In the first type, a mortgage participation involves more than one mortgagee as the owner of the instrument designed to finance a real estate project. It is used in large project financing. Several mortgagees join together, each advancing a proportionate share of the monies required and receiving a commensurate share of the mortgage payments.

Mortgage-backed securities are in reality a form of mortgage participation. Individual investors may purchase shares in a designated group, or pool, of mortgages (e.g., Ginnie Mae guarantees mortgage-backed securities or other real estate mortgage investments conduits [REMICs]).

In addition to the private partnerships among several mortgagees on a single loan and the Ginnie Mae mortgage-backed securities program, real estate mortgage trusts (REMTs) also offer opportunities for mortgage partnerships. Trusts are formed where investors purchase beneficial shares under special terms. Using the pool of monies acquired by the sale of these beneficial interests, mortgage trust managers invest in real estate mortgages and distribute the profits according to a prearranged formula. The private ownership quality of REMTs allows them to invest in high-risk loans such as junior loans or construction financing. Sometimes, as a result of adverse financial conditions, REMTs are inadvertently converted to real estate investment trusts (REITs) when they foreclose on their delinquent mortgagors and end up owning the properties they financed.

**Partnership of Mortgagors.** The second type of mortgage participation involves several mortgagors sharing responsibility for a single mortgage on a multifamily property, called a cooperative.

A cooperative vests ownership in a corporation that issues stock to all purchasers, giving them the right to lease a unit from the corporation. This proprietary lease is drawn subject to the rules and restrictions established by the corporation, and management is in the hands of a board of directors elected by the stockholders. The major weakness of the cooperative form of mortgage participation is that each cooperative participant is dependent on the other owners to prevent a default of the mortgage. A financially irresponsible tenant or units that remain unsold for long periods create a financial strain on the remaining tenants who are still liable for making the total mortgage payments.

**Partnership of Mortgagees and Mortgagors.** The third type of participation, called a participation mortgage, is engendered when a mortgagee becomes a partner in the ownership of a project on which a loan will be placed. When a developer requests a commitment for a participation mortgage on a substantial commercial real estate project, a lender may accept a higher loan-to-value ratio, lower the interest rate, or make other concessions in return for a percentage of the project's ownership as a condition for issuing the loan commitment. These mortgagee ownerships range from 5 to 50% or more and simultaneously make the lender a partner in the development as well as its financier.

## Shared Appreciation Mortgage

Lenders sometimes can expand their earning possibilities by participating in a real estate transaction as both owners and financiers. In addition to the Shared Appreciation Mortgage (SAM), where the lender reduces the initial interest rate in exchange for a share of the property's future increased value, there are other variations of this type of participation financing.

## Joint Ventures

The most complete form of equity participation is a joint venture, in which the lender puts 100% of the funds needed for a development up front in exchange for the expertise and time of the developer. The lender then becomes an investor in full partnership with the developer.

Some joint venture partnerships are expanded to include the landowner, the construction company, the financier, and the developer, who supervises the entire project from its inception until it is completely rented and sometimes even beyond as a permanent manager. Passive investors in joint venture partnerships cannot use a loss from passive investment to protect their active income.

## Sale-Leaseback

The sale-leaseback is a useful tool of real estate finance and is used primarily for larger projects. In this situation, the owner of the property sells it to an investor and leases it back at the same time. This financing arrangement is used when companies with considerable cash tied up in their real estate want to free this capital for more speculative ventures. The lease used for this method is usually a fully net lease that extends over a period long enough for the investor to recover invested funds and to make a fair profit on the investment.

The sale-leaseback approach to real estate finance is generally applied to commercial properties because rents paid by businesses and professional persons are deductible expenses in the year in which they are incurred. Using this approach, a seller/lessee enjoys many benefits, including the following:

- The seller/lessee retains possession of the property while obtaining the full sales price, in some cases keeping the right to repurchase the property at the end of the lease, in effect freeing capital frozen in equity.
- The seller/lessee maintains an appreciable interest in realty that can be capitalized by subleasing or by mortgaging the leasehold.
- The seller/lessee gets a tax deduction for the full amount of the rent, equivalent to being able to take depreciation deductions for both the building and the land.

The cash secured from the sale might be used for plant expansion, remodeling, or investing in other opportunities. In addition, a lease appears as an indirect liability on a firm's balance sheet, whereas a mortgage shows up as a direct liability and adversely affects the firm's debt ratio in terms of obtaining future financing.

The advantages to the investor/landlord in this type of arrangement include a fair return *on* and *of* the investment in the form of rent during the lease term and ownership of a depreciable asset already occupied by a good tenant. In other words, the investor is buying a guaranteed income stream that can mostly be sheltered through the proper use of interest and depreciation allowances. When determining the rent to be paid on the lease, the investor can actually manage the risk by the amount of rent received. The rent for a quality tenant will normally be lower than the rent for a high-risk tenant.

When the lease includes an option for the tenant to repurchase the property at the end of the lease term, it is called a sale-leaseback-buyback. However, care must be taken to establish the buyback price at the fair market value at the time of sale. Otherwise the arrangement is considered a long-term installment mortgage, and any income tax benefits that might have been enjoyed during the term of the lease will be disallowed by the Internal Revenue Service. Also, a fair market purchase option can only be included if the property is a new acquisition and the lessee has never been in the title chain.

### Sale-Buyback

Under this variation of the sale-leaseback technique, a lender, usually a life insurance company or a pension fund, agrees to purchase a completed project from the developer and sell it right back on an installment sale contract for deed. The lender retains legal title to the property and profits by including a kicker in the payment to cover a participation return of the investment as well as regular interest on the investment. The developer profits through 100% financing and the depreciation shelter that comes with gaining equitable title to the property.

These contracts may be designed to extend 10 years longer than a normal mortgage term, with the payments made during the time of an average mortgage loan being sufficient to repay the purchase price. The additional 10 years of payments are added compensation to the lender/participator. If a contract runs for 30 years, it might include payments for 20 years, sufficient to amortize the sales price, then continue for an additional 10 years at a higher interest rate to satisfy the kicker requirement.

### Split-Fee Financing

A more common form of lender participation than the sale-buyback form is split-fee financing. In this plan, the lender purchases the land and leases it to the developer while financing the improvements to be constructed on the leasehold as well.

The land lease payments can be established at an agreed-upon base rate plus a percentage of the tenant's income above a specified point. Under this arrangement, the lender/investor benefits by receiving a fixed return on the investment plus possible overages, while maintaining residual property rights through ownership of the fee. The developer has the advantage of high leverage and a fully depreciable asset because she owns the leasehold improvements but not the land.

## TAX IMPACTS IN MORTGAGE LENDING

All homeowners receive the benefit of being able to deduct the interest paid on their mortgage loan as long as they itemize deductions on their Federal Income Tax. Points paid in the year of the origination of a mortgage loan are also deductible regardless of who pays for them. The tax benefits derived when selling a home were previously described in Chapter 3.

*FIGURE 7.3* **Two-Party Exchange**

Step 1. Balancing Equities

| ***Property A*** | | ***Property B*** |
|---|---|---|
| $100,000 | EXCHANGE PRICE | $150,000 |
| – 60,000 | EXISTING MORTGAGE | – 80,000 |
| 40,000 | OWNER'S EQUITY | $ 70,000 |
| + 30,000 | CASH REQUIRED | |
| $ 70,000 | | |

Step 2. Deriving Realized Gain

| | | |
|---|---|---|
| $100,000 | EXCHANGE PRICE | $150,000 |
| – 70,000 | ADJUSTED BASIS | – 90,000 |
| $ 30,000 | REALIZED GAIN | $ 60,000 |

Step 3. Deriving Recognized Gain

(Recognized gain equals the sum of unlike properties.)

| | | |
|---|---|---|
| -0- | CASH RECEIVED | $30,000 |
| -0- | BOOT | -0- |
| -0- | MORTGAGE RELIEF | +20,000 |
| -0- | RECOGNIZED GAIN | $50,000 |

Step 4. Determining Tax Impact

(Taxable income is the realized gain or the recognized gain, whichever is less)

| | | |
|---|---|---|
| $30,000 | REALIZED GAIN | $60,000 |
| -0- | RECOGNIZED GAIN | 50,000 |
| -0- | TAXABLE GAIN | $50,000 |

(Note: A will pay no tax. B will pay income tax on $50,000.)

*FIGURE 7.3* **Two-Party Exchange (continued)**

Step 5. Reestablishing Book Basis

| | A | B |
|---|---|---|
| Old Basis | $ 70,000 | $ 90,000 |
| New Mortgage | 80,000 | 60,000 |
| Cash and Boot Paid | 30,000 | -0- |
| Recognized Gain | + -0- | + 50,000 |
| Total: | $180,000 | $200,000 |
| Less | | |
| Old Mortgage | $60,000 | $ 80,000 |
| Cash and Boot Received | + -0- | + 30,000 |
| Total: | $60,000 | $100,000 |
| New Basis | $120,000 | $90,000 |

Step 6. Allocating New Basis
Each individual will decided which portions of the individual's new basis to allocate to land and to improvements in order to establish new depreciation schedules.

## Installment Sales

A special financing tool designed to postpone capital gains income taxes on properties that do *not* qualify for special exemptions available under the income tax laws is called an installment sale plan.

A gain on an installment sale is computed in the same manner as is the net capital gain on a cash sale: gross sales price minus costs of sale minus adjusted book basis equals net capital gain. However, under an installment sale, the seller can elect either to pay the total tax due in the year of the sale or to spread the tax obligation over the length of the installment contract. The installment plan allows a seller to pay tax in amounts proportionate to the gain collected each year. A seller whose tax bracket decreases over the term of an installment contract will pay less tax than if he had elected to pay the full tax in the year of the sale. This arrangement is particularly advantageous to a seller nearing retirement age who will enter a lower tax bracket during the term of the installment contract. On the other hand, there is the possibility that a seller's tax bracket could rise over the installment term, which would lead to the payment of more tax. Consequently, a seller is allowed to pay the amount of tax due on a capital gain whenever it becomes expedient during the installment contract period.

## Exchanges

Another method often employed to postpone tax on capital gains is the property exchange technique. **Internal Revenue Code Section 1031** provides for the recognition of gain to be postponed under the following conditions:

- Properties to be exchanged must be held for productive use in a trade or business or for investment.
- Properties to be exchanged must be of like kind to each other; that is, their nature or character must be similar. Like kind is only limited to another income-producing property. A rental condo could be exchanged for a delicatessen; a rental town house could be exchanged for a gas station or marina. One property may be exchanged for several properties; it is not limited to one.
- Properties must actually be exchanged.

Property held for productive use in a trade or business may include machinery, automobiles, factories, and rental apartments. Property held for investment may include vacant land and antiques. Like kind includes a machine for a machine or real estate for real estate. Improvements on the land are considered to be differences in the quality of the real estate, not in the type. Thus, a vacant lot can be exchanged for a store property. Unlike property, called **boot**, is often included in an exchange and must be accounted for separately.

There are at least six basic mathematical computations involved in the exchange process:

1. Balancing the equities
2. Deriving realized gain
3. Deriving recognized gain
4. Determining tax impact
5. Reestablishing book basis
6. Allocation of new basis

These computations are illustrated by the two-party exchange recorded in Figure 7.3.

It is rare to make a straight two-party exchange. More frequently, there are three-party exchanges or more, as well as delayed (Starker) exchanges requiring definite time limits—45 days to select and 180 days to settle.

Generally, the investor who is trading up benefits by not being required to pay taxes, while the downside exchanger is taxed on gains. A prudent investment program provides for trading up during an investor's acquisition years and trading down after retirement, when tax brackets are lower.

## SUMMARY

There are two general categories of real estate loans: conventional and government. There are many variations of conventional loans. Those that meet the qualifying guidelines of Fannie Mae and Freddie Mac are called conforming loans, and they may be either fixed or adjustable rate. Other types of conventional loans include jumbo, home equity, and reverse mortgages. For conventional loans with less than a 20% down payment (80% LTV), private mortgage insurance is required. Government loans include FHA insured, VA guaranteed, USDA for rural housing, and other state or local government programs.

Subprime lending meets the needs of those who do not qualify for "A" paper loans. Although not necessarily predatory, a subprime loan may become predatory when excessive interest rates or fees are charged. Another form of predatory lending exists when a lender forces a borrower into a subprime loan unnecessarily or encourages the homeowner to enter into a home equity loan with no possible hope of repayment.

There are many variations in format for conventional loans, including open-end, construction, blanket, leasehold, manufactured housing, purchase-money, bridge, and wraparound. There are also numerous ways available for both mortgage and equity participation in a purchase.

A major source of tax-free dollars becomes available through the refinancing of the equity accumulated in real property. As borrowed money, refinancing proceeds are not taxable income but will be taxed when the property is sold.

A useful commercial property financing arrangement is the sale-leaseback. This plan involves selling real estate to an investor and, at the same time, leasing it back. As an alternative to financing a large commercial real estate development, some financiers participate in the profits by purchasing the entire project and then reselling it to the developer on a long-term installment contract. Probably the most complete example of equity participation is the joint venture, in which a financier joins with a developer as a full partner in a commercial project.

There are numerous tax advantages to owning real estate, including installment sales and Internal Revenue Code Section 1031 exchanges.

## INTERNET RESOURCES

Department of Housing and Urban Development, Predatory Lending
*http://portal.hud.gov/hudportal/HUD?src=/program_offices/housing/sfh/pred/predlend*

Fannie Mae
*www.fanniemae.com*

Freddie Mac
*www.freddiemac.com*

Internal Revenue Code Section 1031
*www.irs.gov*

Manufactured Housing Institute (MHI)
*www.manufacturedhousing.org*

U.S. Mortgage Insurers
*www.usmi.com*

## REVIEW QUESTIONS

1. Traditionally, the *MOST* popular type of mortgage loan is the
   a. 15-year fixed rate.
   b. 30-year fixed rate.
   c. adjustable rate.
   d. interest only.

2. Current legislation requires that private mortgage insurance be automatically dropped when the equity position reaches what percentage of the property's original value?
   a. 20
   b. 22
   c. 78
   d. 80

3. A couple is purchasing a $300,000 home. In order to avoid paying private mortgage insurance, they have opted for an 80/15/5 split loan. Their second mortgage will be in the amount of
   a. $15,000.
   b. $45,000.
   c. $60,000.
   d. $240,000.

4. Using standard Fannie Mae/Freddie Mac qualifying ratios of 28/36, a couple with a combined annual income of $80,000 would be allowed what total amount to cover all housing expense plus long-term debt?
   a. $1,867
   b. $2,400
   c. $22,400
   d. $28,800

5. A subprime lender is one who
   a. specializes in "A" quality mortgage loans.
   b. offers below-prime interest rate loans.
   c. is also called a predatory lender.
   d. makes higher-interest rate mortgage loans available to those with poor credit.

6. Refinancing is generally worth considering when
   a. the market rate has dropped by any amount.
   b. the market rate has dropped 2%.
   c. bank offers no closing costs.
   d. the cost of the new loan can be recovered in two years or less.

7. An adjustable-rate mortgage based on a LIBOR index of 4%, with a margin of 2%, note rate of 6%, and initial rate of 3.5% with 2/6 caps, could increase to what rate in a five-year period?
   a. 4%
   b. 6%
   c. 9.5%
   d. 11.5%

8. An elderly couple has lived in their home for more than 30 years. The husband and the wife are both in their 70s and have experienced extremely large medical bills. They desperately need cash. A feasible solution for them could be
   a. an ARM.
   b. a RAM.
   c. a GPM.
   d. a GEM.

9. Funds are dispersed on a construction loan
   a. at settlement.
   b. on completion of the building.
   c. in increments called draws.
   d. whenever requested by the builder.

10. An individual is selling her home to a young couple. The couple has agreed to pay her $10,000 as a down payment. They will also pay her a total of $6,000 per year at 8% interest for ten years. The young couple and the seller have transacted which of the following?
    a. An option to buy
    b. A lease with an option to buy
    c. An installment sale
    d. A Section 1031 exchange

11. An individual has agreed to buy a farmhouse for $60,000. He will pay $500 per month rent for one year with a credit back to him of $200 per month, payable at time of settlement on the property. The buyer and the seller have executed
    a. an option to buy.
    b. a lease-purchase.
    c. a right-of-first-refusal.
    d. a Starker exchange.

12. Which condition is *NOT* required in an Internal Revenue Code Section 1031 exchange?
    a. Properties exchanged must be held for productive use in trade or business.
    b. Properties exchanged must be of like kind.
    c. Properties exchanged must be of equal value.
    d. Properties must actually be exchanged.

13. The owner of a 15-acre parcel of land, a local real estate developer, the owner of a construction company, and the president of a savings association are making plans for a new shopping center to be located near the edge of town. They are *MOST* likely entering into a
    a. shared-appreciation mortgage.
    b. sale-buyback.
    c. split-fee financing.
    d. joint venture.

Chapter

# Government Loans

## LEARNING OBJECTIVES

When you've finished reading this chapter, you will be able to

- explain the most important components of the major FHA programs;
- calculate the down payment and loan amount for an average-priced home;
- calculate the complete PITI plus MIP payment for a given loan amount;
- determine how eligibility for VA entitlement is derived;
- list the options available if a property appraises at less than the sales price; and
- describe the assumption process for a VA loan, including release of liability and substitution of entitlement.

**allowable closing costs**
**certificate of eligibility**
**certificate of reasonable value (CRV)**
**direct endorsement program**
**Energy Efficient Mortgage (EEM)**
**entitlement**
**funding fee**
**Home Equity Conversion Mortgage (HECM)**
**housing ratio**
**mortgage insurance premium (MIP)**
**partial entitlement**
**rehabilitation loan FHA 203(k)**
**release of liability**
**residual income**
**substitution of entitlement**
**total obligations ratio**

The Federal Housing Administration (FHA) was established under the provisions of the National Housing Act of 1934. It was organized to stimulate new jobs by increasing activities in the construction industry; to stabilize the real estate mortgage market; and to facilitate the financing of repairs, additions, and sales of existing homes and other properties. A system of mortgage loan insurance was developed to accomplish these goals. In this system, the credit of the U.S. government is placed squarely behind the credit of an individual borrower. The FHA has insured over 40 million home mortgages since it began in 1934.

It long has been the custom in the United States to acknowledge the needs of the men and women who serve in the armed forces. They and their dependents receive special consideration in terms of educational opportunities, medical care, and housing allowances. The Department of Veterans Affairs (VA) supervises a vast network of programs designed to aid U.S. war veterans.

In 1944, shortly before the end of World War II, Congress passed the Serviceman's Readjustment Act, more commonly known as the GI Bill of Rights. This program was designed to provide returning veterans medical benefits, bonuses, and low-interest loans to help them readjust more easily to civilian life. Title III of this act provides guarantees to lenders making real estate loans to eligible veterans that these loans will be repaid regardless of any borrower default. Special finance programs have been established to provide funds to eligible veterans, reservists, and members of the National Guard to enable them to purchase homes, farms, or ranches and to improve these properties.

## FEDERAL HOUSING ADMINISTRATION (FHA)

The FHA operates entirely from its self-generated income through the proceeds of mortgage insurance premiums paid by borrowers. Although the variety of attractive conventional loan programs available over the past several years had lowered the FHA share of the mortgage market, it has once again become the loan of choice in response to the mortgage lending crisis. The FHA loan is a viable product for first-time homebuyers, borrowers with credit issues who may have trouble qualifying for a conventional loan, and for the purchase of manufactured housing.

### Organization and Requirements

Since 1965, the FHA has operated under the direction of the Department of Housing and Urban Development (HUD) Office of Housing with headquarters in Washington, DC, and four regional centers located in Atlanta, Denver, Philadelphia, and Santa Ana. Through these offices, the FHA closely supervises the issuance of mortgage loans bearing its insurance.

Any lender participating in the FHA insurance program must grant long-term, self-amortizing loans at interest rates established in the marketplace. There is no limit on the number of points that may be paid by the borrower, although they must be reasonable. The FHA designates qualified lenders to underwrite loans directly without submitting applications to the FHA. These lenders participate in the **direct endorsement program**.

Every loan application is reviewed carefully to determine the borrower's financial credit and ability to make payments. In addition, a comprehensive written appraisal report is made on the condition and value of the property to be pledged as collateral for the loan. All property must meet certain minimum standards of acceptability. After qualifying the borrower and the property, the FHA issues a conditional commitment for mortgage insurance to the lender reflecting the value of the property. This commitment is valid for six months on existing property and for nine months on new construction.

Since September 1999, FHA requires appraisers evaluating property for FHA-insured loans to be state licensed or certified. In addition to providing an estimate of value, the appraisal provides an examination of the property for any visible, obvious, or apparent deficiencies. The appraisal must contain the statement, "FHD/FHA MAKES NO WARRANTIES AS TO THE VALUE AND/OR CONDITION OF ANY FHA-APPRAISED PROPERTY." The buyers are advised to have the house inspected by a professional home inspector. Every FHA borrower is required to receive a form entitled *For Your Protection: Get a Home Inspection.* A sample of this form is available at http://portal.hud.gov/hudportal/documents/huddoc?id=92564-cn.pdf.

As of 2010, all condominium developments must be re-approved for FHA financing every two years. Spot approvals for individual condo units no longer exist. The *Condominium Project Approval and Processing Guide* is available online at http://portal.hud.gov/hudportal/documents/huddoc?id=12-18ml.pdf. The guide was designed to provide guidance for approving condominium projects under Section 203(b) insurance.

In the past, it has often been difficult to obtain FHA financing for condominiums because of the limitations on the percentage of investor owners. In September 2012, FHA made the following temporary approval provisions to the *Condominium Project Approval and Processing Guide*:

- A developer or single investor may own up to 50% of the total units at the time of the project approval.
- Mixed-use developments are defined as developments with a combination of any of the following: commercial, residential, retail, office, or parking spaces.
- No more than 15% of the units can be in arrears.
- The Project Owner's Certification document has been revised.

For more details, see www.hud.gov.

## FHA-INSURED LOAN PROGRAM

The FHA is designed as a program of mortgage insurance, so it does not make direct loans to borrowers, except in very special circumstances involving the resale of properties acquired by the FHA as a result of foreclosure. Even under these circumstances, the FHA usually requires a buyer of a foreclosed property to secure financing elsewhere and pay the FHA cash for the property. Although FHA lenders are required to make every effort to offset a possible foreclosure, in the event of a default and subsequent foreclosure, an insured lender will look to the FHA to recover the unpaid balance of the mortgage and any costs involved in the foreclosure action.

By designing a program of mortgage insurance funded by mortgage insurance premiums (MIPs), the FHA has reduced the down payment obstacle for cash-short buyers. By insuring 100% of the loan amount, the insurance program eliminates lenders' risks and preserves their fiduciary profiles by ensuring that FHA lenders will not lose any money on loans they make to eligible borrowers. This FHA insurance helps stabilize the mortgage market and develops an active national secondary market for FHA mortgage loans.

## Existing FHA Programs

The National Housing Act of 1934 provided for Title I and Title II insurance programs that are still in use today, along with additional sections that have been added to reflect consumer needs and market conditions. Changes to both Title I and Title II under the Housing and Economic Recovery Act of 2008 (HERA) are reflected in the following material.

**Title I.** Title I, Section 2 provides insurance for loans to finance light or moderate rehabilitation of properties, including the construction of nonresidential buildings. Loans on single-family homes may be used for alterations, repairs, and site improvements. Loans on multifamily structures may only be used for building alteration and repairs.

Maximum Loan Amount:

- Single-family house—$25,000
- Manufactured house on permanent foundation—$25,090
- Manufactured house (classified as personal property)—$7,500
- Multifamily structure—average of $12,000 per unit, up to $60,000

Maximum Loan Term:

- Single-family house—20 years
- Manufactured house on permanent foundation—15 years
- Manufactured house (classified as personal property)—12 years
- Multifamily structure—20 years

The interest rate is based on the common market rate and is negotiable between lender and borrower. Any loan over $7,500 must be secured by a mortgage or deed of trust on the property. There is no prepayment penalty. The structure must have been completed and occupied for at least 90 days.

**Manufactured Home Financing.** Since 1969, Title I, Section 2 provided insurance loans used for the purchase or refinancing of a manufactured home, a developed lot on which to place a manufactured home, or a combination of lot and home. Title I Manufactured Housing as created under HERA replaced the existing program effective April 1, 2009, with new insurance coverage, premiums, underwriting guidelines, and loan limits. Highlights of the program currently in place are included here.

Maximum loan amounts as of 2014 are as follows:

- Manufactured home only—$69,678 20-year term
- Manufactured home lot—$23,226 15-year term
- Manufactured home and lot—$92,904 20-year term
- Multi-section manufactured home and lot 25-year term

The maximum loan limit for lot and combination loans may be as much as 85% higher in designated high-cost areas. Loan limits may be adjusted annually based on manufactured housing price data collected by the U.S. Census Bureau.

Manufactured homes must comply with the Model Manufactured Home Installation Standards and all applicable state and local requirements governing the installation and construction of the foundation system. The home must be installed on a suitable home site that meets local standards and has adequate water supply and sewage disposal facilities. The site may be a rental site in a manufactured home park meeting FHA guidelines or on an individual site owned or leased by the borrower. Built-in appliances, equipment, and carpeting may also be financed. Financing under Title I mortgage loans is provided by FHA-approved lenders. Credit is granted based on the borrower's credit history and ability to repay the loan in regular monthly installments. The up-front mortgage insurance premium may not exceed 2.25% with annual premiums of not more than 1% of the original insured obligation.

**Title II.** Title II originally established two basic mortgage insurance programs: Section 203 for one- to four-family homes and Section 207 for multifamily projects such as rental housing, manufactured home parks, and multifamily housing projects. Many additional programs have been added over the years. The most frequently used Title II insurance programs are described in more detail later in the chapter. Changes made under the Housing and Economic Recovery Act of 2008 (HERA) are reflected here:

- Section 203(b)—mortgage insurance for one- to four-family homes, including single units in a condominium project
- Section 203(h)—mortgage insurance for disaster victims (100% financing available; must file within one year after declaration of disaster)
- Section 203(k)—mortgage insurance for purchase plus rehabilitation
- Section 203(n)—mortgage insurance for purchase of a unit in a cooperative housing project
- Section 221(d)(3) and (4)—mortgage insurance for multifamily rental or cooperative projects
- Section 223(e)—mortgage insurance for older, declining areas
- Section 234(c)—mortgage insurance for condominium projects
- Section 251—mortgage insurance for adjustable-rate mortgages

- Section 255—mortgage insurance for Home Equity Conversion Mortgage (reverse mortgage)
- Section 811—supportive housing for persons with disabilities (provides direct funding to nonprofit organizations to support housing for low-income adults with disabilities)

## Special HUD/FHA Programs

Special programs to assist buyers and homeowners are available through HUD/FHA, including the following.

**Energy Efficient Mortgage (EEM).** The EEM can be used to finance the cost of adding energy-efficient features to new or existing houses in conjunction with a Section 203(b) or 203(k) loan. It can also be used with the Section 203(h) program for victims of presidential-declared disasters. The cost of the energy-efficient improvements that are eligible for financing into the mortgage is the greater of 5% of the property's value or 115% of the median sales price for the area, or 150% of the conforming Freddie Mac loan limit. The money for the improvements is placed in an escrow account at closing and released after an inspection verifying that the improvements are installed and that energy savings will be achieved. The total loan amount can exceed the FHA loan limit by the amount of the energy-efficient improvements.

**Home Equity Conversion Mortgage (HECM).** FHA's mortgage insurance makes HUD's **Home Equity Conversion Mortgage (HECM)** reverse mortgage program less expensive and more attractive for homeowners 62 and older who wish to borrow against the equity in their homes. No monthly payments are required, and there are no asset or income requirements or limitations. Homeowners may receive a percentage of the value of the home's equity in a lump sum, on a monthly basis (either for life or for a fixed term), or as a line-of-credit. No repayment of the loan plus interest and other fees is due until the surviving homeowner leaves the home. The FHA insurance provides the assurance that the funds will continue as long as one surviving member remains in the home and that in the event that the eventual sale does not cover the balance due the lender, there will be no debt carried over to the estate or heirs.

New provisions added under HERA include the following:

- Seniors can purchase and obtain a HECM loan in a single transaction as long as the home is to be a primary residence.
- All applicants for a HECM loan must receive counseling by trained and tested counselors who follow uniform protocols. The FHA uses a portion of the mortgage insurance premiums to fund such counseling.
- Lenders are prohibited from requiring the borrower to purchase insurance, an annuity, or other additional product as a requirement or condition of eligibility for a HECM loan (exceptions are title insurance, hazard, flood, or other peril insurance).
- HECM origination fees are limited to 2% of maximum claim amount (MCA), up to $200,000 and 1% of MCA over $200,000. (For homes valued less than $125,000, the fee is limited to $2,500.)

- Cooperatives may now be insured under HECM program (condominiums were already allowed).
- The single loan limit of $417,000 applies nationwide, up to $625,500 in high-cost areas.
- The annual mortgage insurance premium for all HECM loans is 1.25%. An initial MIP ranging from 0.5% to 2.5% may be charged depending on the type of disbursements.

**Good Neighbor Next Door.** The Officer Next Door program has been expanded to include law enforcement officers, pre-kindergarten through 12th grade teachers, firefighters, and emergency medical technicians. Under this program, HUD offers a discount of 50% from the list price of the home with a down payment of $100. The borrower must commit to live in the property for at least 36 months. Available homes are listed by state on the internet. If more than one person makes an offer on a property, selection is made by a random lottery. If the property needs repairs, a 203(k) mortgage may be used.

**Homeownership Vouchers.** The Housing Choice Voucher program, formerly known as Section 8, has expanded its rental assistance program to allow participants to use Homeownership Voucher funds to assist in meeting monthly homeownership expenses such as mortgage payments, real estate taxes and insurance premiums, utilities, maintenance costs, and repairs. Applicants must be first-time homeowners, have at least one member of the family employed, and meet minimum income requirements. Interested applicants should contact their local Public Housing Authority for more information.

**Native American Housing.** Under Section 184 Indian Housing Loan Guarantee Program, HUD offers homeownership and housing rehabilitation opportunities for American Indian and Alaska Native families and tribes. FHA will also insure mortgage loans for Native Americans under the Section 248 program for properties on tribal lands.

**Title II Manufactured Home Financing.** If a higher loan amount than is provided under Title I is required, the FHA does offer financing for manufactured homes under Title II. The mortgage must cover both the manufactured home and its site with a term on not more than three years. There are some additional requirements, including the following:

- Have a floor area of not less than 400 square feet
- Be constructed after June 15, 1976
- Be classified as real estate
- Be built and remain on a permanent chassis
- Have a finished grade elevation at or above the 100-year elevation

**Disaster Relief.** In November 2013, FHA issued the following guidance for FHA borrowers struggling to repair or rebuild after disasters (such as Hurricane Sandy):

- There is a 90-day moratorium on foreclosures.
- Servicers must consider a full range of benefits, such as mortgage modifications, partial claims, FHA-HAMP or other refinance options, and a waiver of late charges.
- Lenders are to release homeowner insurance proceeds to the borrower.

Refer to HUD Section 203(h) and 203(k) for further information.

## Underwriting Guidelines

Like Fannie Mae and Freddie Mac, the FHA has its own set of guidelines to qualify eligible borrowers for acceptable loans. These requirements include all of the following elements.

**Maximum Loan Limitations.** As part of the **Housing and Economic Recovery Act of 2008**, the FHA established a set formula for mortgage loan limits. FHA loan limits were to be set at 115% of the median house price in a given area but could not be lower than 65% of the conforming loan limit. In November 2011, Congress raised the loan limit for FHA high-cost areas to $729,750, while leaving the limit for Fannie Mae and Freddie Mac at $625,500. However, in 2014 the loan limit for high-cost areas was adjusted back to the original 2008 amount of $625,500.

FHA loan limits for 2014 are shown in Figure 8.1.

The maximum loan amounts for a geographical area may be found at https://entp.hud.gov/idapp/html/hicostlook.cfm.

**Down Payment Requirements.** The FHA has greatly simplified its formula for calculating the down payment required on its insured loans. As of January 1, 2009, the purchaser must provide 3.5% of either the sales price or appraised value (whichever is less) from their own funds; a family gift; or a grant from a local, state, or nonprofit down payment assistance program that does not receive any financial benefit from the transaction. In most cases, this is applied as the down payment. For some special programs that allow for a higher loan-to-value (LTV) ratio, a part of the 3.5% may go towards approved closing costs.

*FIGURE 8.1* **CY2014 FHA Maximum Loan Limits**

| *Type of Property* | *Standard* | *High-Cost Areas* |
|---|---|---|
| Single-Family | $271,050 | $625,500 |
| Duplex | $347,000 | $800,715 |
| Triplex | $419,425 | $967,950 |
| Four Units | $521,250 | $1,202,925 |

(All limits are 150% higher in Alaska, Guam, Hawaii, and the U.S. Virgin Islands.)

**Borrowers' Income Qualifications.** The FHA qualifies borrowers based on two ratios (the borrowers must qualify under both ratios):

- The **housing ratio** of 31% is one way borrower qualifications are tested. A borrower's total monthly housing expenses may not exceed 31% of the total gross monthly income. Included in these expenses are mortgage, principal, and interest; property taxes; home insurance premiums; mortgage insurance premiums; and homeowners' or condominium association fees if applicable.

  The housing ratio may be raised if the borrowers have certain compensating factors, such as

  - low long-term debt,
  - a large down payment,
  - minimal credit use,
  - excellent job history,
  - excellent payment history for amounts equal to or higher than new loan payment, or
  - additional income potential.

- The **total obligations ratio** of 43% is the other measure the FHA uses to gauge borrower qualifications. A borrower's total monthly obligations may not exceed 43% of the total monthly gross income. Included in these obligations are monthly housing expenses plus monthly debt payments. Debts that will be paid in full within ten months are sometimes not included. Alimony and child support payments are deducted from monthly gross income before calculating the qualifying ratio.

■ **FOR EXAMPLE** Assume that borrowers want to qualify for a $200,000 FHA-insured home loan at 6% interest for 30 years. The up-front MIP of 1.75% is added to the loan amount. The principal and interest plus MIP payment is $1,220 per month, property taxes are $300 per month, hazard insurance premium is $30 per month, and the monthly MIP payment is $220.46 ($203,500 × 1.30% = $2,645.50 ÷ 12 = $220.46). The borrowers pay $600 per month on other long-term debt. (All numbers are rounded off.)

| | |
|---|---|
| $1,220 | Principal and interest + Up-front MIP ($200,000 + $3,500 = $203,500 @ 6%) |
| 300 | Property taxes |
| 30 | Hazard insurance |
| 220 | Monthly MIP |
| $1,770 | Housing cost ÷ 0.31 = $5,710 |
| + 600 | Other debts |
| $2,370 | Total obligations ÷ 0.43 = $5,512 |

To qualify for this loan, the borrowers would need to earn at least $5,710 in combined gross monthly income ($68,520 annually). The required gross monthly income must meet the requirements of the housing ratio unless the total of other debts makes the required amount even higher.

**Non-Traditional Credit and Credit Scoring.** In some cases, the FHA may allow a lender to develop a non-traditional mortgage credit report (NTMCR) to document a borrower's payment history in cases where a credit bureau score cannot be derived. A 12-month history of timely payments for rent, utilities, telephone and cellular phone services, and cable television is preferred. Additional sources that may be given consideration include insurance coverage (medical, auto, or life insurance), childcare payments, and other documented history of payments or savings.

Borrowers with a credit score of 500 or less are not eligible for an FHA loan. Generally, a score of 620 is preferred.

**Mortgage Insurance Premium (MIP).** When the FHA issues an insurance commitment to a lender, it promises to repay the balance of the loan in full if the borrower defaults. This guaranty is funded by imposing a **mortgage insurance premium (MIP)** that must be paid by the borrower when obtaining an FHA-insured loan. It can be paid in cash or financed even if the loan plus the MIP exceeds the maximum loan limit.

As of February 2012, the up-front MIP premium of 1.75% of the loan amount is charged on all FHA loans, including those for condominiums.

FHA borrowers must also pay an annual premium, which is payable monthly and is included in the regular PITI payment. This MIP applies to all types of FHA loans.

As of June 2013, the annual premium is as follows:

- LTV less than 95% — 30-year loan — 1.30%
- LTV greater than 95.01% — 30-year loan — 1.35%
- LTV less than 78% — 15-year loan — 0.45%
- LTV 78.01% to 90% — 15-year loan — 0.45%
- LTV greater than 90.01% — 15-year loan — 0.70%

FHA monthly insurance payments will no longer be automatically terminated when an LTV of 78% is reached. MIP will only be canceled under the following conditions:

- For mortgage terms of more than 15 years with an original LTV of less than 90%, the annual MIP will be canceled when the loan-to-value ratio reaches 78%, provided the mortgagor has paid the annual premium for at least 11 years.
- For mortgage terms of 15 years or less and with original loan-to-value ratios of 90% or less, annual premiums will be canceled when the loan-to-value ratio reaches 78%, provided payments have been made for at least 11 years.

## In Practice

A loan officer is working with a married couple who have a combined monthly gross income of $4,000. They have $5,000 in savings and monthly debts of $600. They have found a 20-year-old, three-bedroom house with a large yard in an older neighborhood just 15 miles from downtown where they both work. They love the house, but the sales price of $150,000 seems to be out of their range. The loan officer has suggested they look into an FHA loan. The loan officer is meeting with the couple today to go over the FHA guidelines. The loan officer tells them that he has 5.5% financing for a 30-year loan with no points. Factors that will be taken into consideration include the following:

- Maximum loan amount: The maximum loan amount for their geographic area is $160,000. With a $5,250 down payment, they will only need to borrow $144,750 so they fit within the maximum loan amount limits.
- Down payment: Purchasers must provide 3.5% of the sales price for a down payment of $5,250. The couple is confident they can add $250 to their present savings of $5,000, which will cover the down payment. Because they do not have additional funds for closing costs, they will ask the seller to contribute the 6% of the sales price allowed by the FHA to be used for their closing costs.
- Qualifying ratios: The FHA allows 31% of gross monthly income for housing and 43% for total debt obligation. Their combined monthly gross income of $4,000 × 31% = $1,240; $4,000 × 43% = $1,720.

Deducting the $600 monthly debt from the $1,720 allowed for total debt leaves $1,120 for PITI (principal, interest, taxes, and insurance). Subtracting 30% for taxes, homeowners insurance, and mortgage insurance leaves $784 ($1,120 – $360). The dollars available for PITI must be divided by the rate factor for a 5.5% loan: $784 ÷ $5.68 (rate factor for 5.5%) = $138,000 able to be borrowed. Because they need to borrow $144,750, they would not qualify to buy the house. If they could reduce the monthly debt obligation from $600 to $400, they would stay within the guidelines and be able to use the $1,240 (31% of GMI) for PITI ($1,720 – 400 = $1,320). $1,240 – 30% (372) = $868 for PI. $868 ÷ 5.68 = $152,820 able to be borrowed. The final calculations for the couple's house are as follows:

| | |
|---|---|
| Sales price | $150,000 |
| Down payment | – 5,250 |
| Loan amount | 144,750 |
| Plus 1.75% up-front MIP ($2,533) | $2,533 |
| | $147,283 |
| Monthly PI | $ 836.26 |
| Taxes and insurance | 230.00 |
| Annual MIP (1.30%) | 160.46 |
| Total PITI payment | $1,226.72 |

$1,226.72 ÷ 4,000 = 31% (qualifies under FHA ratio of 31%)

| | |
|---|---|
| Plus long-term debt | 400.00 |
| | $1,626.72 |

$1,626.72 ÷ 4,000 = 41% (qualifies under FHA ratio of 43%)

**Allowable Closing Costs.** The FHA has strict guidelines defining **allowable closing costs** that may be charged to a borrower. The amounts may differ by geographic area but must be considered to be reasonable and customary. All other costs in the transaction are generally paid by the seller when purchasing a new home or by the lender in the case of a refinance.

The seller may contribute for the borrower up to 6% of the sales price to cover discount points and other allowable closing costs.

The allowable closing costs are

- appraisal fee and any inspection fees;
- actual costs of credit reports;
- lender's origination fee;
- deposit verification fee;
- home inspection service fees up to $200;
- cost of title examination and title insurance;
- document preparation (by a third party not controlled by the lender);
- property survey;
- attorney's fees;
- recording fees, transfer stamps, and taxes; and
- test and certification fees, water tests, and so on.

The allowable costs in a refinance are

- courier fees,
- wire transfer fees,
- fees to pay off bills, and
- reconveyance fees.

**Second Mortgages/Buydowns.** In some cases, the FHA will allow a second mortgage to be acquired on the collateral property. There are certain conditions, however, including the following:

- The total of the first and second mortgages must not exceed the allowable maximum LTV ratio.
- The borrower must qualify to make both payments.
- There can be no balloon payment on the second mortgage if it matures before five years.
- The payments on the second mortgage must not vary to any large degree.
- The second mortgage must not contain a prepayment penalty.

The FHA allows mortgage buydowns when the borrower or seller can make an advance cash payment to lower the interest rate for a period of time. This effectively reduces the corresponding monthly payments. The FHA also allows the borrower the advantage to qualify for the loan at the bought-down interest rate, not the contract interest rate.

**Assumptions.** FHA loans originated prior to December 1989 are generally assumable without qualifying, but the original borrower retains some responsibility in the event of a default. For FHA loans originated after December 1989, all sellers are released from liability under an assumption. Buyers have to qualify under the current 31% and 43% rule and must occupy the property. The FHA currently prohibits the assumption of loans by investors.

**FHA TOTAL Scorecard.** The FHA TOTAL Scorecard was developed by HUD to evaluate the credit risk for loans that are submitted to an automated underwriting system (AUS). The Scoreboard recommends levels of underwriting and documentation to determine a loan's eligibility for FHA insurance. There are two risk classifications: "Accept/Approve" or "Refer." An "Accept/Approve" indicates that the FHA will ensure the loan with reduced documentation; "Refer" means the lender must manually underwrite the loan.

**FHA-HAMP Guidelines.** FHA's Loss Mitigation Program was established in 1996 to ensure that distressed FHA mortgagors were given an opportunity to retain their homes and minimize losses to the FHA Mutual Mortgage Insurance Fund. Changes were made to the FHA version of HAMP in 2012 to

- eliminate the requirement for a back-end debt-to-income ratio of 55%,
- eliminate the requirement that the mortgage be no more than 12 months past due, and
- permit only one loan modification in 24 months.

## Most Frequently Used FHA Loans

**Section 203(b): One-Family to Four-Family Mortgage Insurance.** This mainstay of the FHA single-family insurance programs remains an important financing option for first-time homebuyers, persons who may have trouble qualifying for a conventional loan, or those living in underserved areas. The low down payment, higher total debt ratio, and consideration of compensating factors may make it possible for owner-occupants to achieve their dream of homeownership. FHA 203(b) loans can also be used for the purchase of condominium and cooperative units.

**Section 203(k): Rehabilitation Mortgage Insurance.** The Section 203(k) loan makes it possible for the purchaser to obtain a single long-term loan (either fixed or adjustable rate) to cover both the acquisition and rehabilitation of a property. The 203(k) is also available for refinancing a property that is at least one year old. The value of the property is limited by the FHA mortgage loan limits for the area and is determined by either the value before rehabilitation plus the cost of rehabilitation or 110% of the appraised value after rehabilitation, whichever is less.

Other features of the **rehabilitation loan FHA 203(k)** include the following:

- Rehab costs must be at least $5,000.
- The borrower pays only taxes and insurance during the first six months.
- The rehab funds are paid to the borrower in draws.
- The rehab costs and installation time must be approved by the lender before the loan can be granted.
- Basic energy efficiency and structural standards must be met.

The FHA 203(k) program is not available to investors. A list of the types of improvements that may be made under 203(k) financing and other information regarding eligible properties and applicants may be found on the HUD website at http://portal.hud.gov/hudportal/HUD?src=/program_offices/housing/sfh/203k.

The Streamlined 203(k) Limited Repair Program permits homebuyers to finance up to an additional $35,000 into their mortgages to improve or upgrade their homes before move-in. The cash can be used to pay for property repairs or improvements identified by a home inspector or FHA appraiser.

**Section 251: Insurance for Adjustable-Rate Mortgage.** The FHA adjustable-rates mortgages (ARMs) are available to owner-occupants of one- to four-family dwelling units. The down payment, maximum loan amount, and qualifying standards are the same as for 203(b) and may be written for 30 years. The FHA offers a standard one-year ARM and four hybrid ARM products with an initial interest rate that is constant for the first three, five, seven, or ten years. After the initial period, the interest rate will adjust annually. FHA ARMs have both annual and life-of-the-loan caps on the amount that the interest rate can go either up or down at each adjustment period.

The different interest rate caps are as follows:

- One- and three-year ARMs have annual caps of 1% and life-of-loan caps of 5%.
- Five-, seven-, and ten-year hybrid ARMs have annual caps of 2% and life-of-loan caps of 6%.

The FHA ARMs are fully assumable, and buydowns are permitted. When qualifying at the buydown rate of interest, it is possible for the borrower to afford a larger loan amount. When interest rates are low, a fixed-rate loan may be preferable to an ARM, especially when the up-front and monthly mortgage insurance premiums are factored in.

**Streamline Refinance.** Since 1980, FHA has permitted insured mortgages to be streamline refinanced. The amount of documentation and underwriting is greatly reduced, although closing costs still apply. These costs can be included in the new mortgage amount with sufficient equity in the property as determined by an appraisal. The basic requirements for a streamline refinance are

- the mortgage must already be FHA insured;
- the mortgage must be current, not delinquent;

- the refinance must result in lowering of monthly principal and interest payment; and
- no cash may be taken out.

### Direct Endorsement

Under the **direct endorsement program**, applications for the FHA's single-family mortgage insurance programs can be underwritten by an approved lender that certifies the mortgage complies with applicable FHA requirements. The lender performs all appraisal duties and analyzes the borrower's credit. Direct endorsement leaves FHA with the risk of loss from default but gives it control through its ability to remove the lender from the program. The majority of all FHA mortgage insurance applications are now being processed under its format.

## FHA CONTRIBUTIONS TO REAL ESTATE FINANCE

Every financier recognizes the significance of the FHA's major contributions to the stabilization of the real estate mortgage market. These contributions are summarized in the following:

- *The FHA instituted basic standards for qualifying borrowers.* Because credit applications and borrower creditability criteria are standardized, all lenders who issue FHA-insured loans use the same basic language and tools.
- *The FHA instituted standards for appraising property.* Minimum construction standards are established that must be met before a property can qualify for an FHA-insured loan. These standards apply to both new and used buildings, and they are measured by an FHA appraisal of the potential collateral.
- *The long-term amortized loan was used.* Prior to the FHA's long-term amortization design, in which a borrower has from 15 to 30 years to repay a loan in equal monthly payments, most mortgage loans had to be *paid in full* or *refinanced* approximately every five years. This created hardships for both borrowers and sellers and contributed to the many foreclosures during the depression years. Currently, the FHA monthly payments include an amount for principal, interest, property taxes, homeowners insurance, and, if required, property improvement assessments and FHA mortgage insurance premiums.
- *The FHA lending standards and amortization design provided the foundation for a national market in mortgage securities.* By developing reliability and safety in mortgage loan investments, the FHA enables financial investors from all over the world to trade in these securities.

## VA LOAN GUARANTEE PROGRAM

Originally, the amount of guarantee was for 50% of the loan's balance, not to exceed $2,000. In 1945, Congress increased the guarantee to 60% against $4,000 and has gradually increased these limits. The conforming loan limit is adjusted each year by the Federal Housing Finance Agency (FHFA). In 2012, the VA guarantee is $104,250, or 25% of the current Freddie Mac loan limit of $417,000 (see Figure 8.2)

Because the lender regards this guaranteed amount the same as a 25% down payment, the lender will loan four times the guaranty for a single-family home. A lender would be willing to loan a qualified veteran borrower up to $417,000. The maximum loan amount would be 50% higher for first mortgages in Alaska, Hawaii, Guam, and the U.S. Virgin Islands.

The maximum loan may also be higher in certain high-cost areas. A county-by-county list for 2014 can be viewed at www.benefits.va.gov.

### Program Application

In general, the VA is concerned with guaranteeing loans made by institutional lenders, such as commercial banks, thrift organizations, life insurance companies, and mortgage bankers and brokers. It tries to eliminate any risks taken by these lenders when they make loans on real estate to eligible veterans. If a veteran cannot continue to meet the required payments, the lender is compensated by the VA for any losses incurred in the foreclosure and subsequent sale of the property, up to the limit of the guarantee. The operations of the VA real estate loan guarantee program are managed by nine regional centers located throughout the country. The program is not designed to be used indiscriminately. Each loan application is reviewed carefully to determine the veteran's eligibility, credit history, and ability to pay. The value of the property is firmly established by an appraisal, and assurances are secured that the veteran will occupy the premises as the major residence. Poor risks are denied loans and are referred to other programs. The VA guarantees close to 200,000 loans per year.

Several veterans, related or not, may purchase one-family to four-family homes as partners, as long as they intend to occupy the property. A veteran and a nonveteran who are not married may purchase a home together as co-borrowers, although the VA will not guarantee the nonveteran's portion of the loan. However, the VA does qualify common-law marriages without reduction of the loan guarantee for the nonveteran, as long as proper documentation has been supplied.

The VA guarantees mortgage loans for single-family homes, condominiums, cooperative units, manufactured housing, and farm homes.

*FIGURE 8.2* **VA Loan Guarantee Periods**

| | |
|---|---|
| December 28, 1945 | $ 4,000 |
| July 12, 1950 | 7,500 |
| May 7, 1968 | 12,500 |
| December 31, 1974 | 17,500 |
| October 1, 1978 | 25,000 |
| March 1, 1988 | 36,000 |
| December 20, 1989 | 46,000 |
| October 13, 1995 | 50,750 |
| January 1, 2005 | 89,912 |
| January 1, 2006, to present | 104,250 |

## Eligibility/Entitlement

A veteran's eligibility or **entitlement** to participate in the program is derived from the following active-duty criteria:

- More than 90 days of continuous active duty, discharge because of a service-connected disability, or separation under other-than-dishonorable conditions during any of the following wartime periods:

| | |
|---|---|
| World War II | September 16, 1940, to July 25, 1947 |
| Korean Conflict | June 27, 1950, to January 31, 1955 |
| Vietnam War | August 5, 1964, to May 7, 1975 |
| Persian Gulf War | August 2, 1990, to undetermined date |

- More than 181 days of continuous active duty for other than training purposes, discharge because of a service-connected disability, or separation under other-than-dishonorable conditions during the following peacetime periods:

| | |
|---|---|
| Post-World War II | July 26, 1947, to June 26, 1950 |
| Post-Korean Conflict | February 1, 1955, to August 4, 1964 |
| Post-Vietnam War | May 8, 1975, to September 7, 1980 (enlisted) |
| | May 8, 1975, to October 16, 1981 (officer) |

- For enlisted personnel, two years of continuous active duty or separation under other-than-dishonorable conditions during the peacetime period from 1980 to the present. For officers, two years of continuous active duty or separation under other-than-dishonorable discharge during the peacetime period from 1981 to the present.
- At least six years of continuous active duty as a reservist in the Army, Navy, Air Force, Marine Corps, Coast Guard, or National Guard. Active duty service personnel are eligible after serving 181 days of continuous activity (90 days during the Gulf War).

Unremarried spouses of veterans may be eligible for VA loans if the veteran died of a service-connected injury or illness or is listed as missing in action.

## Certificate of Eligibility

One of the most important documents needed for a loan application by a veteran is a **certificate of eligibility**. To receive this certificate, the veteran must secure forms to determine eligibility as well as an available loan guarantee entitlement. These forms must be accompanied by evidence of military service. At present, veterans receive their certificate of eligibility with their discharge from service.

There is no time limit on the entitlement, and it remains in effect until completely used up. This loan guarantee must be used in the United States, its territories, and its protectorates. A certificate may be requested on VA Form 26-1880 and submitted along with the DD Form 214 (Certificate of Release or Discharge) through the local VA office. It can also be ordered online at www.ebenefits.va.gov or through a local lender. After using the VA guarantee for a real estate loan, the veteran may gain the restoration of eligibility when the loan is paid in full and the property has been conveyed to another owner (there is a one-time exemption of the conveyance requirement).

## Partial Entitlement

Veterans who have used their benefits in the past may be eligible for another VA loan if they have any remaining entitlement. With a **partial entitlement**, a veteran may pay cash down to the maximum loan amount and still benefit accordingly.

To determine any remaining entitlement, examine Figure 8.2 and subtract the amount used previously from the amount currently in effect. This is the amount available for the guarantee. Finally, to determine the maximum VA loan allowed under a partial entitlement, take 75% of the appraised value and add the remaining entitlement amount.

■ **FOR EXAMPLE** Consider a veteran who purchased a house in 1989 using the entitlement of $46,000. In 1999, the veteran decided to purchase a new house but wanted to keep the original residence for an income property. With the new house appraised for $150,000, a new VA loan of $117,250 was acquired using the following process:

| | |
|---|---|
| Maximum 1999 entitlement | $ 50,750 |
| 1989 entitlement | – 46,000 |
| Remaining entitlement | 4,750 |
| 75% of $150,000 | +112,500 |
| | $117,250 |

To complete the transaction, the veteran paid $32,750 as a cash down payment.

## Certificate of Reasonable Value (CRV)

The VA requires a VA-assigned certified real estate appraiser to submit a formal estimate of the value of the property to be financed. The appraiser issues a **certificate of reasonable value (CRV)**, stating the amount of the appraisal. This CRV is valid for 6 months for existing properties and 12 months for new construction. It may not be extended.

If a sale is made subject to a CRV and the appraisal comes in at less than the sale price, the following may occur:

- The buyer can make up the difference in cash.
- The seller can accept the lower amount as the sale price.
- The buyer and seller can compromise.
- The transaction can be canceled.

In the purchase of a home in excess of the maximum guaranteed VA loan amount with no money down, the difference is required to be paid in cash. The VA reserves the right to approve the source of the cash. This is to ensure that the veteran is not borrowing an additional amount that would adversely affect the total debt ratio.

## Interest

In the past, the VA specified the interest rate the lender could charge the veteran. Now, however, the VA allows the borrower the opportunity to shop the marketplace and negotiate the best rate available. Thus, all types of mortgage loans are competitive as to interest rates, leveling the financing market.

## Qualifying Requirements

The VA uses only one ratio to analyze a borrower's ability to qualify for the loan payment. This ratio is 41% of the borrower's gross monthly income and includes principal, interest, taxes, insurance, utilities, maintenance, repairs, and other monthly obligations. The VA provides maintenance and utilities guidelines for all states using the following formula:

Square feet of living area × $0.14 per square foot

For example, 1,500 sq. ft. × 0.14 = $210 per month. The VA also provides the lender with a table of required **residual income** amounts based on geographic region and family size. Staying within the residual income guidelines is more important than meeting the 41% ratio.

The following is an example of the calculation of residual income (maintenance and utility costs are not used in this calculation):

| | |
|---|---|
| Total monthly income: | $2,500 |
| | × 41% |
| 41% of income | $1,025 |
| Less housing costs (PITI) | (800) |
| Less recurring debts | (200) |
| Total residual income | $25 |

Like the FHA, the VA will sometimes allow for compensating factors such as

- excellent credit history,
- conservative use of consumer credit,

- minimal consumer debt,
- long-term employment,
- significant liquid assets,
- sizable down payment,
- existence of equity in refinancing loans,
- little or no increase in shelter expense,
- high residual income,
- low debt-to-income ratio,
- tax credits for child care, and
- tax benefits of home ownership.

Under no circumstances will compensating factors offset unsatisfactory credit.

■ **FOR EXAMPLE** A veteran applies for a VA loan of $100,000 at 5% interest for 30 years. The monthly principal and interest payment is $537. Other monthly costs include $70 for taxes, $25 for insurance, $214 for maintenance and utilities, and $200 for other obligations. The veteran's total gross monthly income will have to be at least $2,673 ($32,078 annually) to qualify for this loan.

| | |
|---|---|
| Principal and Interest | $ 537 |
| Property Taxes | 70 |
| Homeowner Insurance | 25 |
| Maintenance and Utilities | 214 |
| Other Payments | 200 |
| Total Obligations | $ 1,096 |
| VA Income Ratio | ÷ 0.41 |
| Gross Monthly Income Required | $ 2,673 |
| | × 12 |
| Gross Annual Income Required | $ 32,078 |

## Closing Costs

Closing costs may not be included in VA loans and must be paid in cash at closing. The only costs that may be charged to the veteran include the following:

- 1% of the loan amount charged by lender as loan origination fee
- Discount points as determined by market
- VA funding fee
- Reasonable and customary charges for appraisal, credit report, recording fees and/or taxes, taxes and/or assessments chargeable to borrower, initial deposit for tax and insurance escrow account, hazard insurance including flood insurance, survey if required, title examination, and title insurance

The seller may pay all of the borrower's closing costs plus an additional 4% of the loan amount to be used for the funding fee or to pay off borrower's debt to allow borrower to qualify for the loan.

## Funding Fee

Although the VA does not charge a mortgage insurance premium, it does charge a **funding fee**, which may be used to cover expenses in case of borrower default. The funding fee may be paid in cash or included in the loan amount, even in excess of the CRV. However, the addition of the funding fee to the original loan amount may not exceed the maximum allowable loan. The funding fee is required on all VA loans except from veterans receiving compensation for service-connected disabilities, from veterans receiving retirement pay in lieu of disability compensation, from spouses of veterans who died in service or died from service-connected disabilities, and in some transactions in which a large down payment is made (see Figure 8.3).

■ **FOR EXAMPLE** The funding fee charged on a $100,000 VA loan where the veteran makes no down payment is $2,150:

$100,000
× 0.0215
$ 2,150

■ **FOR EXAMPLE** The funding fee charged on a $100,000 VA loan where the veteran makes a 10% down payment is $1,250:

$100,000
× 0.0125
$ 1,250

■ **FOR EXAMPLE** The funding fee charged on a $100,000 VA loan secured for refinancing is $500:

$100,000
× 0.005
$ 500

## Second Mortgages

The VA will allow second mortgages to be placed on the collateral property under the following conditions:

- The second mortgage document must be approved by the VA legal department prior to loan closing.
- The total of the first and second mortgage liens may not exceed the value of the property.
- The interest rate on the second mortgage may not exceed the interest rate on the first.

*FIGURE 8.3* **Schedule of Funding Fees for VA Loans**

| *Down Payment* | *First-Time Use* | *Subsequent Use* | *Reservist/ National Guard* | *Subsequent Use (Reservist/ National Guard)* |
|---|---|---|---|---|
| None | 2.15% | 3.30% | 2.40% | 3.30% |
| 5% up to 10% | 1.50% | 1.50% | 1.75% | 1.75% |
| 10% or more | 1.25% | 1.25% | 1.50% | 1.50% |
| Cash-out refinance | 2.15% | 3.30% | 2.40% | 3.30% |

| *First Time or Subsequent—All Categories of Service* | |
|---|---|
| Assumptions | 0.50% |
| Rate reduction refinancing | 0.50% |
| Manufactured home | 1.00% |

- The second mortgage may not have a prepayment penalty or a balloon payment.
- The second mortgage must be amortized for at least five years.

### Buydowns

Buydowns are allowed only on VA loans issued with level payments. A buydown is an amount of money paid in advance, accepted by the lender, to reduce the interest rate on the loan. The buydown fee may be paid by the seller, the buyer, or family members. The borrower must qualify at the first year's payment rate.

### Assumptions

Prior to March 1988, VA loans were fully assumable without prior lender approval of the buyer's credit. For VA loans made after this date, the buyer's credit must be approved by the lender prior to the assumption of an existing loan. Any unauthorized assumption may trigger a technical default, and the loan balance can be called in full. In any approved assumption, the loan interest rate will not be changed.

## In Practice

Sally Green's real estate office is located very close to a military base, and she is currently working with four clients who are all interested in obtaining VA loans to purchase new houses. Sally is trying to determine their eligibility status. Mark Brown served for one year between March 1985 and March 1986 and has been told that only 180 days are required. Sam Jones served for 90 days during the Persian Gulf War. Michael Green served for eight years in the National Guard. John Smith used his VA eligibility in 1989.

Sally finds that Mark will not be eligible because two years of active service are required after 1980 (except for the Gulf War period). Sam and Michael should have full eligibility.

John Smith may have a partial entitlement. The entitlement in 1978 was $25,000. As of January 2005, the entitlement is $89,912, which would leave him with a $64,912 partial entitlement. The banks will generally lend four times that amount for a no-money-down loan. If John wants to purchase a house costing $250,000 the bank will lend 75% of the appraised value, plus the partial entitlement ($250,000 × 75% + $64,912 = $252,412). John will not be required to make a down payment.

John may be pleasantly surprised to find that he has his full entitlement back. By checking with his regional VA office, he finds that the house that he purchased in 1978 and sold in 1984, letting the purchaser assume his loan, has been subsequently sold with all new conventional financing. John will have regained his entitlement at the current amount of $104,250. He can now obtain a VA loan for up to $417,000, as long as he meets all qualifying standards. He will have to pay a 3.3% funding fee this time, unless he is receiving disability payments from the VA.

## Release of Liability/Novation

The original makers of a VA loan remain liable until it is paid in full or the veteran receives a **release of liability** or a **substitution of entitlement** from a cooperating buyer. The release of liability relieves the veteran-seller of the responsibility for repayment and any deficiencies resulting from a default on the loan.

Although it is unusual for a veteran to have more than one VA loan in effect at any one time, it is not unusual for a veteran to secure a complete release from the liability of a previous VA loan and a restoration of eligibility for a new maximum guarantee. General requirements for restoration of entitlement by the VA call for the veteran to sell the property and repay the debt in full. The VA does allow for a one-time-only provision for restoration of entitlement with repayment of the debt without having to dispose of the property. In addition, a veteran can qualify to ask the VA for a substitution of entitlement if the home is sold to another qualified veteran willing to assume the loan.

In cases in which a veteran's loan is assumed by a purchaser who is not a veteran, the VA will not allow the seller-veteran to regain maximum entitlement. The purchaser, however, can agree to assume the veteran's liability to reimburse the VA in case of default, and the buyer and seller can then petition the VA to release the veteran from all obligations. This full substitution technique is called novation. If the new buyers meet the credit requirements of the old lender, the VA may accept them in lieu of the veteran and release the veteran's liability on the loan. Note, however, that release of a veteran's liability does not restore eligibility for the maximum guarantee amount. It will not be restored until the loan is finally paid off by the purchaser.

# ADDITIONAL VA LOAN PROGRAMS

## Adjustable-Rate Mortgage

The Veteran's Benefits Act of 2008 extended the VA Adjustable-Rate Mortgage (ARM) program through September 30, 2012, and then in August of that year it was made a permanent loan product. Following are the key features of this program:

- Annually adjusted interest rate
- Interest rate adjustments limited to increase or decrease 1% per year
- Interest rate adjustments cannot exceed 5 percentage points over life of the loan
- ARM loan must be underwritten at 1% above initial rate

## Refinancing

Three types of refinance programs are available to veterans:

- *VA Streamline Refinance.* Refinance for a lower interest rate with no out-of-pocket closing costs, no appraisal required, and no income or credit check needed. There is a 0.50% funding fee. (This is also referred to as the IRRRL program.)
- *Cash Out Refinance.* Refinance using existing equity to take out cash or pay off debts up to 90% of the value of the property. A funding fee is required.
- *Conventional to VA Mortgage.* Refinance up to 100% of the value of the property into a VA mortgage from a conventional loan with a maximum loan of $417,000. A funding fee is required but may be financed. No private mortgage insurance is required, there are no out-of-pocket closing costs, and the new interest rate may be lower.

## Special Programs

- *Section 184 for Indian Housing.* Loan product designed to meet needs of Native Americans on tribal lands.
- *Energy Efficient Mortgage (EEM).* Allows up to $6,000 to be added to mortgage for energy-efficient improvements to the home.
- *Assistance to Veterans in Default.* The VA provides supplemental servicing assistance to help cure the default.

## SUMMARY

The Federal Housing Administration (FHA) was established under the provisions of the National Housing Act of 1934 and is under the jurisdiction of the Department of Housing and Urban Development (HUD). Under FHA insurance, borrowers enjoy low down payments, a variety of loan arrangements, no due-on-sale clauses, fully assumable loans, and no prepayment penalties. Up-front insurance premiums are required.

The FHA collects monthly payments for annual renewal premiums on all newly issued loans. These premiums constitute the reserves from which the FHA pays the lenders for defaulted loans. As of April 2011, HUD is allowed to make changes in the MIP premiums.

The FHA provides insurance for loans on single-family dwellings, one- to four-family apartment units, medical clinics, and hospitals. The FHA also provides special subsidized programs to pay interest or rent for low- to moderate-income families.

The FHA requires borrowers to qualify for loan payments with monthly housing expense limited to 31% of their total monthly gross income, and the total housing plus long-term debt expense cannot exceed 43% of gross monthly income. Compensating factors may be taken into account.

The FHA has special programs, such as the Good Neighbor Next Door and 203(k) rehabilitation loan programs, that provide funds to repair newly purchased homes. Making Home Affordable programs have been developed to help borrowers struggling to make their mortgage payments by refinancing with an FHA mortgage loan.

The Serviceman's Readjustment Act, or the GI Bill of Rights, guarantees lenders making real estate loans to eligible veterans that the Department of Veterans Affairs (VA) will pay if the borrower defaults. To be eligible for the loan guarantee, a veteran must meet specific guidelines as to time of service in war and peace time. Reservists and National Guard members are also included, as are unremarried spouses of deceased veterans.

The VA guarantees the top 25% of the current conforming loan limit. In the event of a default, the lender would receive the guaranteed amount from the VA and sell the property to recover the balance owed.

The VA allows the borrower to negotiate for market interest rates. In addition, the borrower may finance all funding fees. Either borrowers or sellers can pay the discount points, and the seller can pay all closing costs. A VA appraisal is provided under a certificate of reasonable value. This appraisal is valid for 6 months for an existing property and 12 months for new construction.

To qualify for a VA loan, the veteran's monthly payments, including PITI, utilities, maintenance, repairs, and other monthly obligations, cannot exceed 41% of the month's total gross income with an amount set aside as residual income. The veteran may be released from liability on a VA loan by paying it in full, securing a release of liability from the VA, securing a substitution of entitlement from another eligible veteran, or pursuing the full substitution process of novation.

## INTERNET RESOURCES

Federal Housing Administration (FHA)
*www.fha.gov*
*www.hud.gov*

Department of Veterans Affairs
*www.va.gov*
*www.benefits.va.gov/homeloans/*

## REVIEW QUESTIONS

1. The important aspect of FHA loans introduced in 1934 that made them attractive to lenders was that
   a. a purchaser could make a very small down payment.
   b. a purchaser could borrow additional funds for closing costs.
   c. the government insured the full amount of the loan.
   d. the government established qualifying standards for the property.

2. The FHA is under the direct administration of
   a. Fannie Mae.
   b. HUD.
   c. Congress.
   d. Ginnie Mae.

3. The FHA protects itself against the risk of defaulting borrowers by requiring
   a. a higher rate of interest.
   b. a larger down payment.
   c. a mortgage insurance premium.
   d. low qualifying ratios.

4. The 3.5% of the sales price that must be provided by the borrower may come from any of the following sources *EXCEPT*
   a. the borrower's savings.
   b. a gift from a family member.
   c. a grant from a nonprofit assistance program.
   d. the seller.

5. An elderly couple who needs extra monthly income but does not want to have to sell their home could apply for
   a. an Energy Efficient Mortgage.
   b. a Home Equity Conversion Mortgage.
   c. a Good Neighbor Next Door Mortgage.
   d. a Housing Choice Voucher program.

6. The annual renewal premium for any FHA loan is
   a. paid up front at closing.
   b. financed over the life of the loan.
   c. paid monthly as part of the PITI payment.
   d. paid by the seller.

7. A young woman has applied for a FHA 203(k) loan. She is likely
   a. planning to purchase and rehab a property.
   b. looking for lower payments in the first year.
   c. seeking an Officer Next Door loan.
   d. planning to refinance her home mortgage.

8. Even with a 0% down payment, VA loans are acceptable to lenders because
   a. they are insured by the VA.
   b. the interest rates are set higher by the VA.
   c. it is faster to obtain loan approval.
   d. the VA guarantees the first 25% of the allowable loan.

9. The amount of entitlement for which the veteran is eligible is shown on the
   a. DD 214.
   b. VA Form 1068.
   c. Certificate of Eligibility.
   d. discharge papers.

10. If the certificate of reasonable value (CRV) is less than the contract sales price, the seller has the option to
    a. require the veteran to pay the contract price.
    b. accept the CRV value as the sales price.
    c. carry back a second mortgage for the difference.
    d. submit an independent appraisal.

11. A retired Air Force colonel wants to buy a new home using a VA loan. She used her VA guarantee of $46,000 in 1989 when she purchased her first home. Based on a guarantee of $104,250, she will be able to use her partial eligibility to obtain a VA loan with no money down in the amount of
    a. $58,250.
    b. $233,000.
    c. $359,650.
    d. $439,120.

12. The VA protects itself from the risk of borrower default by charging
    a. a mortgage insurance premium.
    b. private mortgage insurance.
    c. a funding fee.
    d. an extra point origination fee.

Chapter

# Processing Real Estate Loans

## LEARNING OBJECTIVES

When you've finished reading this chapter, you will be able to

- discuss the impact of credit scoring on obtaining loan approval;
- describe the direct sales comparison, cost, and income capitalization approaches and how an appraiser may reconcile them to determine value;
- define a cloud on the title and how it is resolved;
- identify the costs that may be involved in the closing of a real estate loan;
- define impound (or escrow) funds and how they are collected; and
- explain the types of title insurance and how payment is made.

**abstract of title**
**actual notice**
**appraisal**
**assets**
**broker price opinion (BPO)**
**capitalization rate**
**Closing Disclosure**
**cloud on the title**
**constructive notice**
**cost approach**
**credit report**
**credit score**
**depreciation**
**direct sales comparison approach**
**drive-by appraisal**
**FICO**
**financial statement**
**gross rent multiplier (GRM)**
**income approach**
**liabilities**
**Loan Estimate**
**market value**
**net worth**
**reconciliation**
**suit to quiet title**
**survey**
**title insurance**
**title report**
**Torrens Certificate**
**tri-merge credit report**
**underwriting**
**value in exchange**
**value in use**
**weighted average**

Processing a loan for mortgage lending includes at least four basic procedures:

1. Determine the ability of a borrower to repay the loan.
2. Estimate the value of the property being pledged as collateral to guarantee this repayment.
3. Research and analyze the marketability of the collateral's title.
4. Prepare the documents necessary to approve and close the loan transaction (see Figure 9.1).

In the past, students of real estate finance frequently debated the order of importance of the first two procedures. Some said that the ability of a borrower to make payments should be the determining factor in granting a loan. Others insisted that because a borrower's payment ability can fluctuate with attitude, health, luck, and other events beyond the borrower's control, that the value of the collateral is the only truly consistent input and should be the pivotal factor in all real estate loan decisions. Recently, the emphasis has shifted to a risk assessment of the borrower's history of making timely payments on all financial obligations.

*FIGURE 9.1* **The Loan Approval Process**

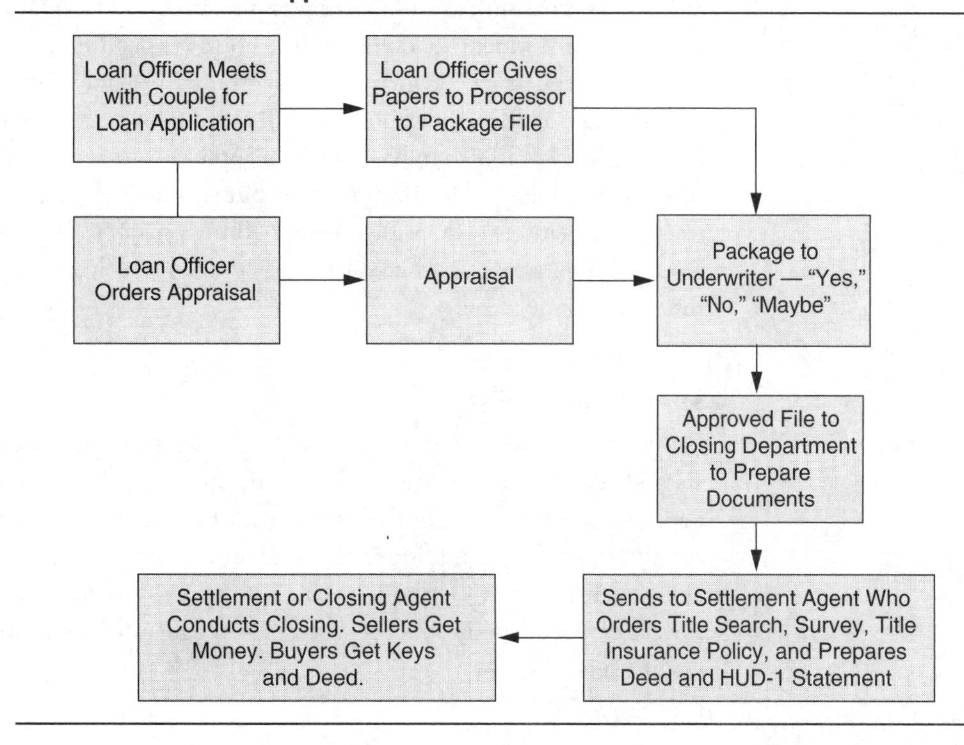

Loan **underwriting** is the evaluation of the risks involved when issuing a new mortgage or deed of trust. This process determines whether a particular borrower and the subject property meet the minimum requirements established by the lender, investor, or secondary market in which the loan will probably be sold.

## QUALIFYING THE BORROWER

Prior to the advent of high loan-to-value (LTV) ratios and long-term loan amortization, little emphasis needed to be placed on a borrower's ability to repay a real estate loan. Loans were created at 50 to 60% of a collateral property's value and were based on a payment of interest only for certain short specified periods, usually one to five years. The entire principal was due in full at the stop date. If the principal could not be paid in full, partial payment could be made and the balance of the loan amount recast for an additional five years. This five-year rollover pattern could continue until the debt was paid in full. However, if a borrower did not meet the payment obligations promptly and in the amount called for in the contract, the collateral was quickly foreclosed and sold for an amount sufficient to recompense the lender.

This repayment pattern has not changed much despite the 30-year amortization schedules and regular monthly payments of principal and interest that are the framework of our current real estate financing system. The average age of a real estate loan is still only seven to eight years. What has changed, and quite dramatically, are the LTV ratios. From the original 50% LTV, this ratio grew to up to 100% or more of a property's value. One outcome of the 2007 financial crisis was a return to lower LTV ratios, requiring larger down payments. In most cases, conventional loans now require a minimum of 5% down, and mortgage insurance is required for any loan with an LTV higher than 80%. The lenders' emphasis has shifted from relying on the successful foreclosure sale of the collateral to protect the investment to looking to the borrower's ability to repay the loan.

While lenders under guaranteed or insured programs of real estate finance do not directly bear the risks of default, they still must follow the guidelines of their guaranteeing agencies. They must carefully screen loan applicants to derive some reasonable estimate of not only the ability of borrowers to pay but also their attitudes about meeting their contractual obligations responsibly. A great effort is made to thoroughly check and evaluate a potential borrower's past credit history and current financial status in order to predict future economic stability.

### Loan Application

Every formal real estate loan processing procedure begins with a borrower completing a standardized loan application form and submitting it to a prospective lender. All loan application forms identify the property to be pledged, the borrower, and the amount of money requested. Additional facts about the prospective borrower are also included, along with information about the loan sought. Most loan applications show the borrower's employment and income record, a statement of assets and liabilities, and a list of credit references.

An application for a commercial or an industrial loan requires even more information than one for a residential loan. The borrower might be requested to supply such data as rent schedules or tenants' lease terms. In cases of commercial and industrial borrowers, the application form will usually outline every phase of the borrower's present business, such as management; sales; production; purchasing; research and development; personnel, plant, and equipment, and include financial statements and audits of the total operations of each phase. A Dun & Bradstreet credit report might be required. These financial statements would go back a number of years to give perspective to the general market profile of the borrower corporation and show the pattern of asset-liability ratios over a sufficient length of time. From these past profit and loss statements, the lender should be able to assess the corporation's profitability, the effectiveness of its management, and the prospects for future corporate growth.

All loan applications are designed to reveal a borrower's financial ability to meet the basic obligations of the loan agreement (see Appendix G for a typical residential loan application). The bulk of the application is devoted to securing personal information from the borrower about family size and ages of dependent children, sources of income, employment history, and a comprehensive financial statement.

**Financial Statement.** **Financial statements** follow a standard format that lists all assets and liabilities. This enables a lender to measure the current financial status of an applicant quickly and efficiently.

**Assets** consist of all things of value, encumbered or not, owned by the applicant—and cash heads the list. Cash consists of money in hand, money on deposit in checking and savings accounts, and the cash given as a deposit on the property being purchased. Lenders place great weight on a borrower's cash position as a reflection of liquidity and money management habits. A strong cash balance develops a sense of confidence in a borrower's ability to maintain payments and meet other obligations, even in the event of temporary setbacks.

Next in the financial statement asset column, all monies invested in stocks and bonds, notes or accounts receivable, personal business ventures, and other real estate are listed. The value of the applicant's automobiles, surrender value of life insurance policies, other personal property, and all other assets are enumerated. The dollar amounts assigned to these items must reflect their realistic current value, not their purchase price or some imagined value.

When more than one bond, stock, or parcel of real estate is owned, additional spaces are provided for their itemization. Should the applicant need more space than is provided, additional pages will be affixed to this inventory to fulfill these important requirements.

**Liabilities** consist of all monetary obligations of the borrower-applicant. Heading the list of liabilities are any notes payable because these are considered a priority claim against cash assets. Next in order of importance are all installment accounts, such as charge accounts and automobile payments. Other accounts payable, such as medical bills or insurance premiums, follow the list of installment accounts. Remaining long-term liabilities are then enumerated: alimony and child support payments, any encumbrances on the real estate listed as assets, accrued and unpaid real estate property and/or income taxes, security obligations on personal property such as furniture, loans on the life insurance policies listed as assets, and any other debts for which the applicant is responsible.

It is hoped that the total of the assets will exceed the total of the liabilities, with the difference being an applicant's **net worth**. The amount of net worth is added to the total liabilities in order to balance both sides of the financial statement. A two-to-one current ratio indicates that the applicant has twice as many current assets as current liabilities and is a good credit risk. If total liabilities exceed an applicant's total assets, a loan would probably be denied at this point and the file closed. Assuming an applicant has a positive net worth, a series of related actions begin.

## Data Verification

Under Fannie Mae's automatic underwriting system, Desktop Underwriter®, and Freddie Mac's Loan Prospector®, much of the data involved in analyzing a potential loan is available from credit reporting agencies like Experian, Equifax, and Transunion. Some larger lenders, such as Wells Fargo, use their own automated underwriting systems (AUSs), programmed to meet Fannie Mae's and Freddie Mac's approval.

The loan officer charged with processing the loan verifies the information included in the application by actually checking with the various references given, the banks where deposits are held, and the applicant's employer. Some lenders will accept alternate documentation, pay stubs, bank statements, and so on, to speed up processing.

**Deposits.** The borrower is obliged to sign deposit verification forms (see Appendix H) that authorize the bank to reveal to the lender the current balances in the borrower's accounts. Without a verification form, such confidential information could not be released by the bank under the Federal Right to Privacy Act.

A deposit verification permission form must be signed by the borrower for each bank account to enable the loan processor to ascertain all the current balances. The knowledge that the loan processor can verify account amounts is usually enough incentive for the borrower to be truthful in reporting financial information. When the deposit balances are verified, the appropriate entries are made in the applicant's file. In some cases, the lender will accept two months of current bank statements.

**Employment.** Likewise, an applicant is required to sign an employment verification form (see Appendix I). It authorizes the employer to reveal confidential information concerning the applicant's job status. Not only are an applicant's wages and length of employment verified, but the employer is requested to give a prognosis for continued employment and prospects for advancement.

**Credit Report.** Simultaneously, with the gathering of financial and employment information, a loan processor sends a formal request for a borrower's **credit report** to a local company offering this service. Within a few days if the applicant is a local resident, or longer if out-of-town credit must be checked, the credit search company sends the loan officer a confidential report on its findings. See Appendix J for a sample credit report.

The credit report is an itemization of the status of current accounts. In addition, it indicates the quality and dates of the payments made and their regularity, delinquency, or any outstanding balances. This payment history is the most important part of the entire report. Credit managers and loan officers frequently state that a person's future attitude is in most cases a reflection of past behavior in meeting financial obligations. Research tends to reinforce these opinions, indicating that slow and erratic payers generally retain those attitudes when securing new loans, and prompt and steady payers are also consistent in meeting their future obligations.

When a credit report is returned revealing a series of erratic and delinquent payments, the loan is usually denied at this point and the file closed. If there are only one or two unusual entries in a group of otherwise satisfactory transactions, the applicant is asked to explain these variations, noted in writing to be kept for future reference.

As with many standardized procedures, credit reporting has become computerized, dramatically shortening the time needed for completing a check. Credit reports should be used only by the persons or institutions requesting the information and only for the purposes stated.

Most credit agencies insist on seeing a buyer's written permission before issuing any information in order to protect the buyer's confidentiality. After the deposit and employment verifications are returned with acceptable information and a favorable credit report is obtained, the lending officer makes a thorough credit evaluation of the data collected.

## Credit Score

**Credit scores** are not based on age, race, gender, religion, national origin, marital status, current address, or receipt of public assistance. As shown in Figure 9.2, credit scores are based on factors such as how you pay your bills, how much outstanding debt you have, what type of credit and how long you have had established credit, and how many times you have had inquiries relative to extending credit.

The **FICO** score (named after Fair, Isaac and Company, the San Rafael, California-based firm that created the test) assigns relative risk rankings to applicants based on statistical analyses of their credit histories. FICO scores range from 300 to 850, with most people scoring in the 600s or 700s. As shown in Figure 9.3, applicants who always pay their bills on time and make moderate use of their credit cards receive the highest scores—700 to above 800. Applicants who are late in paying bills present greater risks and receive lower scores, ranging from 400 to 620.

*FIGURE 9.2* **Factors That Influence an Applicant's Credit Score**

Payment History—How has the applicant paid debt?

Outstanding Debt—How many loans and open charge accounts does the applicant have?

Credit History—How long has the applicant had credit?

Credit Inquiries—How many times has the applicant authorized a credit check?

Types of Credit—What types of credit does the applicant have?

Source: www.fanniemae.com

*FIGURE 9.3* **Credit Scoring and Applicant Characteristics**

| ***Low 400s to Low 600s*** | ***620 to High 800s*** |
|---|---|
| • Late in paying bills | • Pays bills on time |
| • Has many credit cards | • Makes moderate use of credit card(s) |
| • Too many credit inquiries | • Pays off debt rather than moving to another card |
| • Has "maxed out" credit cards | |

The FICO score is based on the following percentages:

- Payment history = 35%; late payments, bankruptcies, and other negative items hurt score, but on-time payments help score.
- Amount owed = 30%; amount owed on all accounts, number of accounts with balances, and how much of available credit is being used.
- Length of credit history = 15%; longer credit history increases score, but shorter history not detrimental if good credit record established.
- New credit = 10%; multiple search for mortgage loan should be done within 30 days.
- Other factors = 10%; mix of credit types (credit cards, mortgage or car loan, and personal lines of credit can add to score, while maxed out credit cards can lower score).

Another result of tightened qualifying standards is the requirement for a higher credit score. Just as lenders are raising the acceptable credit score, millions of potential homebuyers are seeing a significant drop. FICO reports that over 50 million consumers saw anywhere from a 20 to 50 point drop in their score in 2008 and 2009. Being three months late on a loan could cost 130 points, and a short sale with a deficiency balance could cost up to 160 points. FICO also reports that it can take as much as 30 to 36 months to recover a 70- to 110-point drop in score. In November 2011, the National Association of REALTORS® released a survey stating that 33% of members surveyed reported contract failures, mostly due to credit issues. This was a jump from 8% in a similar survey taken just a year previously.

According to Ken Harney, real estate reporter for *The Washington Post* Writer's Group, average FICO scores for loans originated for sale to Fannie Mae or Freddie Mac in 2011 ranged at 760 or above. Even borrowers using FHA mortgages are showing average scores of around 700.

FICO has announced plans to start using a new credit formula in 2014 that may help bring up scores. Some of the changes include the following:

- A debt that goes to collection and is paid off will no longer affect the score.
- Medical debts in collection will not count as heavily as in the past.
- New methods will be employed for those without a long history of borrowing.

## Obtaining Your Credit Report

As of September 2005, everyone has the right to one free credit report per year from each of the three major credit reporting agencies:

| | | |
|---|---|---|
| Equifax | 800-685-1111 | www.equifax.com |
| Experian | 866-200-6020 | www.experian.com |
| TransUnion | 800-888-4213 | www.transunion.com |

Congress has established the Annual Credit Report Request Service to make it easier for consumers to obtain credit reports and credit scores (see www.annualcreditreport.com). By ordering one report every four months, a consumer can receive all three free reports within one year. To receive the actual credit score, a small fee must be paid.

FICO also offers free newsletters with product discounts, free educational presentation, and timely topics dealing with credit issues through its website at www.myfico.com.

Lenders may order credit scores electronically at relatively low cost from credit repositories or bureaus. Most lenders today order a **tri-merge credit report** containing information from all three of the major credit repositories. In most cases, the numerical credit score will be different on all three reports due to variations in time and content from creditors. Generally, the lender will use the middle score, not an average.

Potential misuse of credit scoring has prompted the following rules on their use:

- Never automatically disqualify applicants because of a subpar credit score (credit scores may not single out or prohibit low- to moderate-income borrowers from becoming homeowners).
- Be aware of potential errors in electronic credit files.
- With a subpar score, look hard at the score factor codes and work with the applicant to clear fixable items.

## Income Evaluation

Not only is the quantity of an applicant's income evaluated for loan qualification, its quality is evaluated as well. The lender is looking for income that is stable, regular, and recurring. Thus, income from all sources is added together to find an acceptable total on which to apply the qualifying ratios.

In a normal transaction, the wages and earnings of the co-borrowers are considered. In the event a cosigner is involved, this person's income is included as well. Extra income is considered if it is received regularly and for a period of at least three years; thus, bonuses and overtime pay can be included if they fit this criterion. Pensions, interest, and dividends are treated as regular income, although it is recognized that interest and dividends do fluctuate over time and may cease if the investment is cashed out.

A second or part-time job is accepted as part of the regular monthly income if it can be shown that the job has existed for approximately two years and there is good reason to believe it will continue. Child support can also be included in the determination of monthly income, but only if it is the result of a court order or has a proven track record. Also, under the Equal Credit Opportunity Act (ECOA), government entitlement funds must be considered. Self-employed borrowers, including commissioned wage earners, need at least two years of established income to qualify for a mortgage loan.

Divorced buyers are required to submit a copy of their decree to inform lenders which party is responsible for liabilities, how the assets are divided, and whether there are support and/or alimony obligations. For alimony to be considered as income, most lenders require a one-year history of payment receipts and reasonable assurance that payments will continue for at least three years from the date of the loan application.

On the other hand, alimony or child support payments are considered a debt of the borrower responsible for these and must be included in the financial analysis.

On the Verification of Employment, an applicant's employer is asked for an opinion of job stability and possible advancement. Length of time on the job no longer carries the heavy clout it once did. Applicants whose employment records show frequent shifts in job situations that result in upward mobility each time are given full consideration. Lenders will, however, be wary of an applicant who drifts from one job classification to another and cannot seem to become established in any specific type of work.

**Loan Qualifying Income Ratios.** When analyzing the borrower's ability to make the required loan payments, loan underwriters generally apply the following pairs of income ratios (although higher ratios may be considered with different loan products):

| ***Loan Type*** | ***Housing Ratio*** | ***Total Debt Ratio*** |
|---|---|---|
| Conventional loans | 28% | 36% |
| FHA loans | 31% | 43% |
| VA loans | — | 41% |

The front-end, or housing ratio, refers to the total of principal, interest, taxes, insurance, and homeowners' or condominium association fees as a percentage of gross monthly income. The back-end, or total debt ratio, refers to the total of the mortgage payment plus other monthly installment obligations, such as car, credit card, or student loan payments, as a percentage of gross monthly income. Some flexibility exists in this latter category, such as eliminating a scheduled payment that will end in ten months or less.

■ **FOR EXAMPLE** Consider a conventional loan of $250,000 at 6% interest for 30 years using 28/36 ratios. The property taxes are $3,600 per year, and the homeowners insurance premium is $480. The homeowners association fee is $240 for the year. The borrowers have a car payment of $400 per month, with two years left to pay.

| $250,000 @ 6% for 30 years: | |
|---|---|
| Principal and Interest | $1,498.90 |
| Property Taxes | 300.00 |
| Homeowners Insurance | 40.00 |
| HOA Fee | 20.00 |
| Monthly Payment | $1,858.90 |
| Housing Expense Ratio | ÷ 28% |
| Required Gross Monthly Income | $6,638.93 |

| | |
|---|---|
| Monthly Payment | $1,858.90 |
| Car Payment | 400.00 |
| Total Housing + Debt Payment | $2,258.90 |
| Total Debt Ratio | ÷ 36% |
| Required Gross Monthly Income | $6,274.72 |

Because the required income to satisfy the total debt ratio is less than that required by the housing expense ratio, the $6,638.93 would apply. The housing expense may not exceed the given ratio. The total debt ratio only affects the required monthly income if the additional long-term debt is higher.

If the borrowers had $800 in car payment debt, the Total Housing + Debt Payment would be $2,658.90; divided by 36% = $7,385.83 required monthly income.

■ **FOR EXAMPLE** The following is an example of a VA loan using the same total housing and debt payment. Divided by the VA 41% ratio, the required monthly income is less.

| | |
|---|---|
| Monthly Payment | $1,858.90 |
| Car Payment | 400.00 |
| Total Housing + Debt | $2,258.90 |
| VA Housing and Debt Ratio | ÷ 41% |
| Required Monthly Income | $5,509.51 |

Because VA loans only use one ratio of 41%, less income is required. Neither of the previous examples takes into account mortgage insurance or a VA Funding Fee. Most conventional loans are based on automated underwriting and may result in higher ratios than the 28/36 standard.

After reviewing all the information provided in the loan application and making the appropriate ratio analyses of the income and expense data, plus the borrower's FICO score, the loan officer collects all pertinent papers and sends the package to the company underwriters for a final determination. If a special report of unusual circumstances is warranted, it is included. During the borrower's qualification process, an appraiser is evaluating the collateral, and this appraisal report is included in the submission.

## QUALIFYING THE COLLATERAL

Despite the current trend toward emphasizing a borrower's financial ability as the basic loan-granting criterion, real estate lenders and guarantors are practical and fully understand that life is filled with unpredictable, uncontrollable events. A family's breadwinner can die. Negative economic activities in a particular geographical area can exert devastating financial impacts. Applicants can be left unemployed due to layoffs. Personal decisions can result in bankruptcies and divorces, often damaging or destroying credit in the process. To hedge these risks and others, real estate lenders look to the value of the collateral as the final assurance for recovery of their investments in a default situation. Therefore, an accurate estimate of the value of this collateral becomes another pivotal point in the lending process.

## Definition of Value

Value is defined as the ability of an object to satisfy, directly or indirectly, the needs or desires of human beings. As such, economists call it **value in use**. When the value of an object is measured in terms of its power to purchase other objects, it is called **value in exchange**.

From these definitions, it is apparent that value is a function of use and demand. As such, value is subjective by its very nature. A seller may have an entirely different idea of a property's value than a potential buyer. A condemning agency would probably offer a different opinion of a property's value than its owner. Tax assessors and property owners disagree about a particular property's value, as do many other persons under varying circumstances. However, an appraiser must make an objective estimate of value based on supply and demand in the marketplace.

## In Practice

A married couple recently made an offer on a house near the husband's office. Their offer of $140,000 was accepted with a $7,000 down payment and a 95% LTV mortgage loan of $133,000. As first-time homebuyers, the couple thought that was all they needed to start packing for the move to their new home. Over the past few weeks, they have learned a lot about the possible pitfalls between the time of a contract acceptance and a successful closing.

First, in qualifying for their loan, they were surprised to learn that they have accumulated too much credit card debt. The lender is requiring that they pay off the outstanding balances and close out three of their credit cards.

They never realized that the property itself had to qualify. When the appraisal came in at $138,000, the lender was no longer willing to give them a mortgage loan of $133,000. As the couple does not have the extra cash to make up the difference, they were greatly relieved when the seller eventually agreed to reduce the sales price to $138,000, leaving the down payment at $7,000 with a $131,000 loan.

With settlement only four days away, the couple thought they were all set when an unexpected call came from their agent telling them that the title search had come up with a cloud on the title—an outstanding mechanic's lien for $3,500 was still recorded on the property. Fortunately, the sellers have cancelled checks showing that the contractor who replaced the roof three years ago was in fact paid in full, although there had been lengthy arguments about the quality of the work, which had delayed payment.

Finally, 30 days since acceptance of their offer, the couple is scheduled for settlement with borrowers, collateral, and title all satisfactorily qualified.

There can be only one market value for a specific real property at any given point in time. **Market value** is the price a property would most likely bring if it were exposed for sale in the open market for a reasonable period of time. Implicit in this definition is that both buyer and seller are well informed and under no undue pressure to influence the decision of either party.

In terms of market value, it is important to note the fine distinctions that exist among cost, price, and value. Cost, a measure of past expenses, may not reflect current market value, especially if a building is fairly old. Price, on the other hand, is a present measure but one that may be affected by some unusual circumstances of a specific transaction. Unique financing terms or a temporarily active local housing market in which potential buyers briefly exceed available properties may cause prices to rise. Therefore, each parcel of property pledged for collateral must be inspected and appraised carefully to estimate its fair market value because this amount will be employed as the basis for determining the mortgage loan amount. Depending on the type of loan to be issued and its concurrent LTV ratio, either the amount of the formal appraisal made as part of the loan process or the purchase price, whichever is less, will determine the amount of the loan.

## Appraiser Independence Requirements

An **appraisal** is the estimate of a property's value at a specific point in time. It must be reported in writing, in accordance with the *Uniform Standards of Professional Appraisal Practice (USPAP)*, using the Uniform Residential Appraisal Report (see Appendix K), by competent individuals whose professional integrity is beyond reproach.

As of October 15, 2010, all conventional, single-family (one- to four-unit) loans must comply with the Appraiser Independence Requirements (AIR). AIR applies only to loan origination, not to foreclosure, workouts, or any type of mitigation. All lenders are required to select an appraiser who meets the following:

- Selected in compliance with AIR
- Certified or licensed in the state where the property is located
- Familiar with the local market, competent to appraise the subject property type, and has access to the data sources needed

Lenders can choose from a rotating roster of appraisers, but this is not required. Appraisers may also be selected from a preapproved list or panel as long as any employee of the lender involved in the selection is independent of the loan production staff.

The Federal Housing Finance Agency (FHFA) issued new appraisal standards that took effect in July of 2012. The Uniform Appraisal Dataset (UAD) was created to improve the quality and consistency of appraisals on mortgages to be sold to Fannie Mae and Freddie Mac. The FHA and the VA are expected to adopt the UAD or something similar. There are a number of appraisers' associations: the Appraisal Institute, the American Society of Appraisers, the National Association of Independent Fee Appraisers, and the National Association of Review Appraisers and Mortgage Underwriters. Some of these groups maintain active education programs and award achievement designations for completing a number of formal courses and for serving a number of years as an appraiser. For example, the Appraisal Institute offers the Member Appraisal Institute (MAI), Senior Residential Appraiser (SRA), Senior Real Estate Appraiser (SREA), and Senior Real Property Appraiser (SRPA) designations.

The methods of appraisal are predominantly mathematical. Nevertheless, an appraiser relies on personal interpretive skills to a great degree. Appraising is, therefore, a science that is artfully interpreted.

## The Appraisal Process

In most appraisals, the appraiser comprehensively examines the property and provides a detailed description of its attributes and shortcomings. Sometimes an appraiser performs a **drive-by appraisal** of the property when more detail is not required. Drive-by appraising involves the appraiser literally driving by the property for a quick inspection to form an opinion of its outward appearance. If it appears to be well-kept and in good condition, it is assumed that the interior is also well-maintained, and the appraisal will be made on the square footage and location. If, on the other hand, the property looks worn and not well-kept, the drive-by appraiser's report would reveal this information and include a recommendation for a more comprehensive examination or even a denial of the loan. In some cases, a lender may request a **broker price opinion (BPO)**, which is not to be confused with an appraisal. A BPO may consist of a drive-by appraisal plus available computer information.

The appraisal process generally includes defining the appraisal problem, determining the purpose for the appraisal, examining the neighborhood and property being appraised, collecting the pertinent data, applying the appropriate approaches to estimate value, reconciling these value estimates, and preparing the appraisal report.

The single most important skill in appraising is the collection of data pertinent to the problem. The appraiser estimates value primarily by carefully examining the subject property and comparing it with properties that have like features (comparables, or comps). The appraiser must not only seek to find properties similar to the subject property in age, size, physical condition, location, and zoning, but must gather recent relevant data about these comparable properties to help estimate the value. The estimate of value will be based on the appraiser's opinion of the subject property's probable worth as a result of skillfully interpreting the data acquired from the most appropriate appraisal approach.

Three basic approaches are used to arrive at an estimate of a property's value. These three techniques—the direct sales comparison approach, the cost approach, and the income approach—will be described in general terms here.

## Direct Sales Comparison Approach

The **direct sales comparison approach** is based on a comparison of the subject property with similar properties in the same locale that have sold recently. An appraiser searches the records of the county recorder's office and the various multiple listing services and maintains a comprehensive and current filing system. Thus, the appraiser is usually able to discover the sales prices and terms involved in recent transfers of properties similar to the property being appraised (see Figure 9.4).

The proficiency of an appraiser is never more clearly tested than in the direct sales comparison approach. Training and experience must be employed artfully to interpret, evaluate, and reconcile the data collected from comparable sales into a dollar amount that represents the subject property's value. No two properties are exactly alike; the appraiser must make many subjective adjustments to the sales prices of the comparable properties (comps) to more clearly reflect the subject property's worth. The reasons for the various differences in the sales prices of comps must be determined and their prices adjusted to reflect what they would have sold for had they more exactly matched the subject property.

*FIGURE 9.4* **Sales Comparison Approach to Value**

| | | Comparable Properties | | |
|---|---|---|---|---|
| | ***Subject Property*** | ***A*** | ***B*** | ***C*** |
| ***Sales price*** | | ***$260,000*** | ***$252,000*** | ***$265,000*** |
| Financing concessions | none | none | none | none |
| Date of sale | | current | current | current |
| Location | good | same | poorer +6,500 | same |
| Age | 6 years | same | same | same |
| Size of lot | 60' × 135' | same | same | larger –5,000 |
| Landscaping | good | same | same | same |
| Construction | brick | same | same | same |
| Style | ranch | same | same | same |
| No. of rooms | 6 | same | same | same |
| No. of bedrooms | 3 | same | poorer +500 | same |
| No. of baths | 1½ | same | same | better –500 |
| Sq. ft. of living space | 1,500 | same | same | better –1,000 |
| Other space (basement) | full basement | same | same | same |
| Condition—exterior | average | better –1,500 | poorer +1,000 | better –1,500 |
| Condition—interior | good | same | same | better –500 |
| Garage | 2-car attached | same | same | same |
| Other improvements | none | none | none | none |
| Net adjustments | | –1,500 | +8,000 | –8,500 |
| Adjusted value | | $258,500 | $260,000 | $256,500 |

Note: The value of a feature that is present in the subject but not in the comparable property is *added* to the sales price of the comparable. Likewise, the value of a feature that is present in the comparable but not in the subject property is *subtracted*. A good way to remember this is: CBS stands for "comp better subtract"; and CPA stands for "comp poorer add." The adjusted sales prices of the comparables represent the probable range of value of the subject property. From this range, a single market value estimate can be selected.

For instance, the appraiser must be able to estimate what the sales price of a comp would be if it were the same age, condition, style, floor plan, size, location, and material as the subject property and also what price it would bring on the day of the appraisal, rather than at the time of its actual sale, six months or a year ago. The appraiser must make these adjustments, all of which involve judgments based on experience, in order to estimate the subject property's value more accurately. An appraiser's efforts depend on the magnitude of the loan and the degree of risk involved. These efforts can expand from a mere impression of value, as discerned by a drive-by examination of the subject property and a recollection of other similar properties recently sold, to a massive report based on 10 comparables, 15 comparables, or even more. Each comparable is adjusted for significant variables to reflect the subject's value. These comprehensive appraisals are made easier by the increasing use of computer technology.

Because of the current credit crisis, appraisers are cautioned to pay particular attention to foreclosed properties and their impact on the values of other properties in the neighborhood when applying the direct sales comparison approach.

## Cost Approach

The cost approach method of estimating a property's value is based on the current value of its physical parts. In the **cost approach** an appraiser examines and evaluates the subject property, its improvements, amenities, and land value. This technique includes an estimation of the current cost to reproduce the improvements, an estimate of the improvements' depreciation, and an estimate of the land value as derived by using the direct sales comparison approach.

An appraiser accumulates data about the current cost of building the subject property. If the property is actually newly constructed, its plans and specifications are reviewed and analyzed to estimate its value. An older property requires an examination of its design and composition to estimate its current reproduction cost. Obviously, the cost approach works best with recently built or unique properties, such as a church or museum.

When used properties are appraised, a depreciation allowance must be applied to the costs of reproduction. This depreciation adjustment is based on the rule of substitution, which states that no rational, economical person would pay the same price for a used property as for the same property when new.

**Depreciation** is a lessening in value from physical deterioration, functional obsolescence, or economic obsolescence. An example of physical deterioration is an older roof that may need patching or replacement. Functional obsolescence describes a situation in which access to one bedroom is available only through an adjoining bedroom. An example of economic obsolescence is a location downwind from a sewage treatment plant. The appraiser must include in the adjustments a consideration of the present physical condition of the improvements, their functional utility, and the effects of forces outside the property on its value.

After the reproduction cost is calculated and adjusted to allow for depreciation of the improvements, the value of the land, as determined by the direct sales comparison approach, is added to the depreciated figure to arrive at an estimate of the total property value. The cost approach in formula form is as follows:

Current replacement cost of improvements
− Depreciation
______________________________
Estimate of current value of improvements
+ Amenities and land value
______________________________
Estimate of current value of property

■ **FOR EXAMPLE** A 10-year-old house with an estimated 50-year life consists of 1,800 square feet, with a current reproduction cost factor of $100 per square foot. If the lot is worth $50,000, the estimate of property value using the cost approach is $194,000.

| | |
|---|---|
| 1,800 | Square feet |
| × 100 | Reproduction cost |
| 180,000 | Value of improvements when new |
| × 0.80 | Straight-line depreciation reciprocal |
| 144,000 | Depreciated value of improvements |
| +50,000 | Lot value |
| $194,000 | Estimated property value |

## Income Capitalization Approach

The income approach measures the value of a property on the basis of its ability to generate income by capitalizing the net annual income using a current market **capitalization rate**. In other words, the **income approach** actually measures the present worth of a property's income stream based on an investor's required rate of return.

This method is best suited to estimating the value of apartments, stores, shopping centers, and office buildings. The first factor an appraiser determines is the property's annual gross market income. Although a subject property may have an established rental income, an appraiser must verify whether this income is based on market rents or rents that are higher or lower than the market rate. Thus, the direct sales comparison approach is first employed to locate similar properties and analyze their rental schedules.

After the gross annual rental income has been determined, an appropriate amount must be deducted for operating expenses such as property taxes, insurance, maintenance, vacancy allowances, management, utilities, pest control, snow removal, accounting services, and advertising. Although depreciation is not considered an operating expense per se, most appraisers will include an item called reserves for replacements or reserves for major repairs. An income property should be able to support itself in every way to substantiate its value.

A net annual market rental income is derived when the operating expenses are deducted from the gross annual market rent. This net rental income is the amount that is capitalized into an estimate of the property's value using the formula:

$$\text{Value} = \frac{\text{Net Income}}{\text{Capitalization Rate}}$$

■ **FOR EXAMPLE** Consider an apartment house generating $250,000 gross annual income. Operating expenses, including vacancies, total 45% of this income. In a market that supports a 10% capitalization rate, this property is worth $1,375,000 using the income approach.

| | |
|---|---|
| Gross Annual Income | $250,000 |
| Operating Ratio Reciprocal | × 0.55 |
| Net Operating Income | 137,500 |
| Capitalization Rate | ÷ 0.10 |
| Estimate of Value | $1,375,000 |

## Gross Rent Multiplier (GRM)

When estimating the value of single-family or small commercial and industrial properties, a **gross rent multiplier (GRM)** is often used. The GRM is derived by locating comparable properties that have sold recently, then dividing their sales prices by a monthly market gross rent to derive the multiplier. For an example of a GRM, see Figure 9.5.

## Reconciliation of Data and Opinion of Value

After applying the preceding approaches pertinent to the estimate of a particular property's value, an appraiser reviews the results, reconciles or correlates the different values derived, and renders a written opinion of the property's value. This opinion may place more emphasis on one approach than another. For instance, the cost approach is more reliable when appraising a newer property than an older one. The income approach is more valid with true income property rather than with houses or vacant land on which an appraiser must impute a fictitious "rent" before this approach can be applied. The direct sales comparison approach supplies the balancing aspect to an appraisal, frequently providing the middle value in a spectrum where the cost approach is invariably high and the income approach is usually low. The direct sales comparison approach is also an integral part of the other two approaches. It is used in the cost approach to determine the value of the land and in the income approach to help derive the net annual market rental income

*FIGURE 9.5* **Gross Rent Multiplier**

| *Comparable No.* | *Sales Price* | *Monthly Rent* | *GRM* |
|---|---|---|---|
| 1 | $280,000 | $1,800 | 155.55 |
| 2 | 243,000 | 1,350 | 180.00 |
| 3 | 287,000 | 2,000 | 143.50 |
| 4 | 262,500 | 1,675 | 156.72 |
| Subject | ? | 1,750 | ? |

Note: Based on an analysis of these comparisons, comparables 1 and 3 show extremes. Based on monthly rent between comparables 1 and 4, a GRM of 156.72 seems reasonable for homes in this area. In the opinion of an appraiser, the estimated value of the subject property would be $1,750 × 156.72, or $274,260.

to be capitalized. One way of **reconciliation** is to apply the **weighted average** technique, which assigns percentages to illustrate the importance of one approach over another.

■ **FOR EXAMPLE** If an appraiser finds that the market, cost, and income approaches indicate $200,000, $210,000, and $220,000, respectively, and the appraiser weights them 50%, 30%, and 20%, respectively, the reconciliation will be $207,000.

| | |
|---|---|
| $200,000 × 0.50 = | $100,000 |
| 210,000 × 0.30 = | 63,000 |
| 220,000 × 0.20 = | 44,000 |
| | $207,000 |

When an appraisal is completed, it is delivered to the loan officer to aid in the final loan decision. As noted previously, a loan amount is based on the lesser of either this appraised value or the sales price of the property.

# QUALIFYING THE TITLE

Anticipating a new loan, the loan processor secures a **title report** on the collateral, which includes a search of the records to determine all the interests in a property. Normally, property interests are perfected through the appropriate filing and recording of standard notices. A recorded deed notifies the world that a grantee has the legal fee title to the property. A recorded construction lien is notice of another's interest in a property. These forms of recording are described as **constructive notices**, an express revelation of a fact.

Another form of notice, one that is imputed by law, is described as an **actual notice**. Even if a buyer does not actually inspect the house that is in the process of being purchased, its occupants have displayed their claim to certain rights merely through their physical possession of the property, even if they have not recorded that interest. The buyer is presumed to know of the occupants' interest in the property, as this information is available through ordinary inquiry. Similarly, even if a person does not actually view the recorded information, it is presumed to be known by actual notice because it is there for the viewing.

At least three methods are employed for obtaining assurance of good title—the abstract and opinion, title insurance, and the Torrens system. Whichever method is used, the title report on the collateral provides the loan officer and the lender's attorney all recorded information relevant to the legal status of the subject property, as well as any interests revealed by actual notice. This title search requirement is yet another manifestation of a lender's efforts to protect the loan investment.

## Abstract and Opinion of Title

An **abstract of title** is described as a synopsis of the current recorded condition of a property's title. Abstracting is the process of searching the records to accumulate information that is then distilled by the abstractor and presented as a formal report.

An abstract is not considered an official document because it makes no pretense of disclosing any hidden title hazards. The abstractor is responsible only for an accurate portrayal of documents of record pertinent to a property's title status. If the loan officer wants a more complete analysis of a title, a request is made for an opinion on the condition of the collateral's title from a lawyer. This opinion is based on the facts revealed in the abstract, and all defects in the title are brought to the loan officer's attention. However, neither the abstractor who searches the title nor the lawyer who renders an opinion of the title's condition issues a guarantee or insures against defects. If the lender requires additional protection against hidden defects or possible errors in the abstracting process, a title insurance policy must be secured.

## Title Insurance

**Title insurance** is based on risk elimination rather than risk assumption. A title insurance policy insures the quality of title on real estate as it exists on the date of the policy, but it does not insure against future events (e.g., a lien filed after the date of settlement). Consequently, most of the premium goes to investigating the history of the title.

Title companies combine the abstracting process with a program of insurance that guarantees the validity and accuracy of the title search. A purchaser of **title insurance** can rely on the assets of the insurance company to back up its guarantee of a property's marketable title. These guarantees are evidenced by policies of title insurance. Most institutional lenders require that a title policy be issued to them for the full face amount of the loan.

When a title insurance policy is issued to a lender (the insured), it is usually in the American Land Title Association (ALTA) form. While a standard title policy insures against items overlooked in the search of the recorded chain of title, an ALTA policy expands this standard coverage to include many unusual risks. Among these risks are forgeries, incompetency of parties involved in issuing documents pertaining to the transfer of ownership, legal status of parties involved in the specific loan negotiations, surveying errors, and other possible off-record defects. Some additional risks can be and usually are covered by special endorsements to an insurance policy. These might include protection against any unrecorded easements or liens, rights of parties in possession of the subject property, mining claims, water rights, and additional negotiated special items pertinent to the property involved. The expanded ALTA policy is usually required by participants in the secondary mortgage market—Fannie Mae, Freddie Mac, and Ginnie Mae—for the added protection it provides. Practitioners use the phrase "an ALTA policy" when describing an extended coverage policy.

## Title Commitment

Because the wording of a title commitment may vary by state, it would be helpful to obtain a sample copy from a local title company that could be reviewed in detail. The commitment for title insurance will be based on the information obtained in the abstract of title and a search of recorded documents related to the property in question.

## Torrens System

The Torrens system of title guarantees is designed to shorten the time needed to search the title. It places the insurance process in the hands of the state. Essentially, under the Torrens plan, a title is searched only as far back as the previous search. It is assumed in the process that all transactions prior to the last search were accurate and legal and that any problems that might have been revealed were resolved satisfactorily. A **Torrens Certificate** is issued, which includes the state as guarantor of the title in the event of a claim. A charge is made for this certificate to cover the costs of the search, and, in some states, an additional premium is charged to provide a reserve fund to cover any contingent losses.

The Torrens system has some advantages over the regular recording system, including saving time, eliminating the accumulation of large quantities of title evidence, and lowering the costs of title examining and insuring. Only a few states today allow registration under the Torrens Act, including Colorado, Georgia, Hawaii, Illinois, Massachusetts, Minnesota, New York, North Carolina, Ohio, Virginia, and Washington.

## Title Faults

Whether the abstract and opinion, the title insurance policy, or the Torrens system is used, in all cases a property's title is searched by an experienced abstractor, who prepares a report of those recorded documents that clearly affect the current quality of ownership. In addition, a survey is sometimes required. If a fault is found, called a **cloud on the title**, the loan process will not continue until this cloud is cleared to the lender's satisfaction. Such a cloud could be an unsatisfied construction lien, an income tax lien, a property tax lien, an encroachment, or a zoning violation. Sometimes a borrower's name is not legally correct on the deed, or the deed has a faulty acknowledgment or lacks the appropriate signatures. Because of the many complexities in a real estate transaction, there are innumerable possibilities for faults to appear in a title search and property survey. It is the abstractor's responsibility to discover and report them.

In certain instances where clouds are difficult to remove by ordinary means, they will need to be cleared by the seller of the property or by the borrower filing a **suit to quiet title**. After appropriate evidence has been submitted, a judge removes or modifies an otherwise damaging fault in a title, and the loan process can continue. The assurance of good title is as essential to a loan's completion as the credit of the borrower and the value of the collateral. The sales of foreclosed properties create complexities that require scrupulous examination and careful documentation of the title's condition.

## Surveys

Although many loan closings require delivery of a plat to identify the location of buildings on the lot, some lenders may require a full **survey** of the collateral property as a condition for a new loan. Although many properties are part of subdivisions that have been engineered and described by licensed and registered surveyors and engineers, some owners might have enlarged their homes or added to the improvements since the original survey. These might not meet the various setback restrictions required in the local zoning laws. Some properties might have been re-subdivided, while others might now have an encroachment problem.

Surveys often reveal errors in legal descriptions or discover encroachments and easement infractions. A few interesting lawsuits have developed as a result of the wrong property being encumbered by a new real estate loan.

## CLOSING THE LOAN

Once a borrower's credit has been approved, the collateral's value is acceptable, and the legal title to the collateral is clear, the loan underwriter approves the loan and preparations for closing begin. An approved loan commitment is communicated to all interested parties, obligating the lender to issue the loan under the terms and conditions stipulated. This commitment remains in force for only a limited time, preventing any delay in the closing.

The lender's closing department prepares the various loan documents and establishes the escrow or impound account. The documents are then sent to the settlement or escrow agent who prepares the deed and the HUD-1 Settlement Statement, which shows the allocation of all charges and credits to both buyer and seller (see Appendix B).

At the closing, the settlement agent prepares the HUD-1 Settlement Statement that shows all charges and credits to both buyer and seller and the deed conveying title. After all documents are recorded, monies are distributed.

The actual closing may be handled differently in different parts of the country. In the western states (influenced by Spanish law), closing is done in escrow, with one escrow officer preparing all documents and disbursing funds and keys to the appropriate parties. In the middle and eastern states (influenced by British law), closing may be done by either an attorney or a title company settlement agent. Both buyers and sellers attend the settlement, along with the real estate agents and any additional attorneys, plus loan officers in some cases.

### Additional Charges and Requirements

The seller usually pays the real estate broker's commission, although in some cases the buyers may pay for the buyer agent directly. Many states charge a transfer tax, which is a percentage of the new money involved and is paid by the seller. Both the seller and the buyer pay their appropriate share of recording fees and payment to the settlement agent.

While the borrower likely paid in advance for the appraisal, credit report, homeowners insurance, and any other required special insurance policies (such as flood insurance), these items still show up on the HUD-1 form marked POC (paid out of closing). The borrower will pay for the lender's title insurance policy and for the owner's policy, unless the property is in a state where the seller is obligated to pay for it.

Interest on the loan, property taxes, and homeowners' or condominium associations fees are all prorated to the day of settlement. In the case of income property, deposits may need to be collected and rents prorated. Some states such as Florida and Virginia hold the buyer responsible for the closing day, but in most states the seller is still considered the owner.

## Servicing the Loan

Most loans today are sold or assigned in the secondary market, though the original lender often remains as the servicer for the loan. The new owner must be notified of where, when, and how mortgage payments are to be made. Usually, a coupon book is provided indicating the amount due if paid by the required date and a higher amount if paid late. The servicer collects the payments, maintains the escrow account, makes timely payments for both property taxes and homeowners insurance, and contacts the borrower in case of any default. If the loan is sold, the lender must provide the borrower with a Loan Transfer Disclosure statement containing all new information needed for timely payment on the loan.

## New Rules from the Consumer Financial Protection Bureau (CFPB)

The CFPB released new rules on how mortgage servicers must treat borrowers. These rules took effect on January 10, 2014, and apply to all mortgage servicers with 5,000 or more loans. The goal of the new regulations is to make sure that servicers cannot take advantage of borrowers who fall behind on their payments.

## HUD-1 Settlement Statement

The HUD-1 form summarizes the charges and credits and shows the amount due from the buyer and credit to the seller, usually required to be in certified funds. No monies are generally paid out until after the recording of the loan documents and the deed. All parties concerned are notified of the date and place of the closing. After all documents have been signed, the deed has been transferred, the loan has been recorded, and the monies have been paid, the loan process is completed.

## Required Lender Notices

Sections 1098 and 1100A of the Dodd-Frank Act directed the CFPB to publish rules and forms that would combine the disclosures that consumers receive in connection with applying for and closing on a mortgage loan under the Truth in Lending Act (Regulation Z) and the Real Estate Settlement Procedures Act (Regulation X). Consistent with this act, the CFPB amended Regulations X and Z to establish new disclosure requirements and forms in Regulation Z for most closed-end consumer credit transactions secured by real property. The final rule also provides extensive guidance for lenders regarding compliance with the requirements. The new TILA-RESPA Integrated Disclosure Rule has combined the Good Faith Estimate (GFE) and the initial truth-in-lending disclosure (TIL) into a new form, the **Loan Estimate** (see Appendix L). The new form is designed to provide disclosures helpful to consumers in understanding the key features, costs, and risks of the mortgage loan for which they are applying. The form must be supplied to potential borrowers no later than the third business day after loan application is made.

The second new form is the **Closing Disclosure** (see Appendix M), which is a combination of the HUD-1 Settlement Statement and the truth-in-lending disclosure. This form must be provided to the consumer at least three business days before settlement. The new forms are mandated for use as of August 1, 2015. Prior to that date, the GFE, TIL, and HUD-1 remain in use.

## SUMMARY

This chapter described the process of obtaining a real estate loan, including qualifying the borrowers, evaluating the collateral, and determining the status of the property's legal title.

Beginning with an application to secure a loan, the borrowers' credit is analyzed to determine their ability to honor debts and repay the loan as agreed. Current assets and employment are verified and a credit rating is obtained. Other basic criteria used to determine the applicants' creditworthiness include gross monthly earnings adequate to meet the required monthly mortgage payment, stability of earnings, and a good prognosis for continued employment and advancement.

The value of the real estate to be pledged as collateral is analyzed by a certified or licensed appraiser conforming to Appraiser Independence Requirements (AIR). A formal appraisal report is submitted to the loan processor. This estimate of value is derived from the appraiser's application of one or more of the three basic appraisal techniques—the direct sales comparison approach, the cost approach, and the income approach.

The direct sales comparison approach for estimating the value of real property matches the subject property to other, similar properties sold recently to make a value comparison. Because there are no perfect comparables, adjustments must be made to the sales price of those comparables that most closely resemble the subject property. The adjusted sales prices for the comps then indicate the subject property's market value.

The cost approach examines the total worth of a property in terms of the current value of its component parts. The current prices of the bricks, lumber, plumbing fixtures, nails, roofing, electrical fixtures, and so on, are added together to estimate the value of the building if it were to be reproduced as closely as possible to its present condition. If the property is not new, its reproduction cost is depreciated by an appropriate amount. This depreciated value for the improvements, when added to the market value of the lot, establishes an estimate of the total property value.

The income approach measures the value of a property on the basis of the amount and quality of its income stream. An appraiser using the income approach divides the net annual income from the property by a market capitalization rate to derive an estimate of the property's value.

After collecting all data pertinent to the subject property and deriving value estimates by using the various approaches, the appraiser reconciles these estimates and renders an opinion of the property's value. This appraised value is compared to the sales price; the loan is made on the basis of the lower figure.

After a borrower's credit and the collateral's value are verified, the current status of the property's title is examined. The abstract is delivered to the lender's attorney for an opinion of accuracy and validity. Lenders usually require title insurance to guarantee the status of the title.

After the borrower and the collateral are qualified and the title is complete, the loan is ready to be closed. The actual closing may be handled by an attorney, escrow agent, or title company, depending on the part of the country in which the property is located.

## INTERNET RESOURCES

American Land Title Association (ALTA)
*www.alta.org*

American Society of Appraisers (ASA)
*www.appraisers.org*

Appraisal Institute
*www.appraisalinstitute.org*

Dun & Bradstreet Credibility Corporation
*www.dandb.com*

National Association of Independent Fee Appraisers
*www.naifa.com*

Fair Isaac Corporation
*www.myfico.com*

## REVIEW QUESTIONS

1. The first basic procedure usually followed in processing a loan is to
   a. determine the borrower's ability to repay the loan.
   b. estimate the value of the property to be used as collateral.
   c. research the marketability of the title.
   d. prepare the documents for closing.

2. The average life of a real estate loan is
   a. 15 years.
   b. 30 years.
   c. 7 to 8 years.
   d. 10 years.

3. A financial statement lists all assets and liabilities of the prospective borrower. A comfortable ratio of assets to liabilities would be
   a. 2 to 1.
   b. equal.
   c. 1 to 1.
   d. irrelevant.

4. The *MOST* important aspect of a credit report is that it shows
   a. the person's attitude toward handling credit and debt.
   b. how many accounts the person currently has.
   c. what the outstanding balances on accounts are.
   d. the number of late payments.

5. An appraiser has just completed a search of the records for comparable residential properties that have sold within the last six months. He is using the
   a. direct sales comparison approach.
   b. cost approach.
   c. income approach.
   d. gross rent multiplier.

6. An appraiser assigned the task of appraising a unique property like a church would probably use the
   a. direct sales comparison approach.
   b. cost approach.
   c. income approach.
   d. gross rent multiplier.

7. A recorded deed, or recorded note and mortgage, is considered to be
   a. actual notice.
   b. constructive notice.
   c. a title abstract.
   d. an opinion of title.

8. In which circumstance would an ALTA title insurance policy *NOT* protect both the lender and the new owner?
   a. If the signature has been forged
   b. If there is an error on the survey
   c. If a mechanic's lien is filed a year after settlement
   d. If there is an unrecorded easement

9. A type of title insurance that includes the state as the guarantor of title is called
   a. an ALTA policy.
   b. a standard title insurance policy.
   c. the Torrens system.
   d. an abstract and opinion of title.

10. A cloud on the title that is difficult to remove may require that
    a. an affidavit of release be signed by the seller.
    b. a suit to quiet title be filed.
    c. a second opinion on the title search be obtained.
    d. the price on the property be raised.

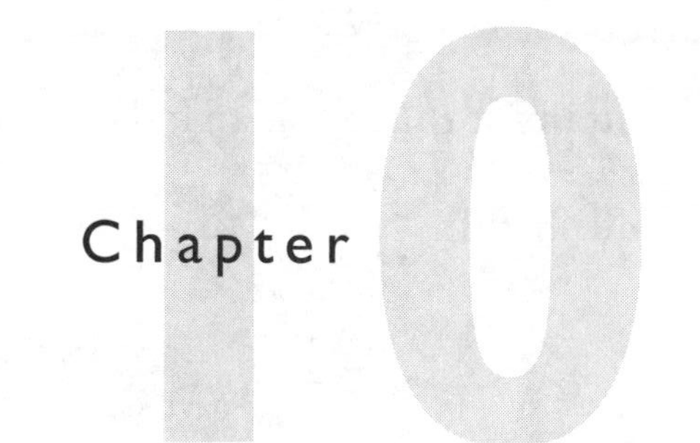


Chapter

# Defaults and Foreclosures

## LEARNING OBJECTIVES

When you've finished reading this chapter, you will be able to

- describe the various causes for default on a mortgage loan;
- define the various actions that a lender could take to help the borrower avoid foreclosure;
- differentiate between equitable and statutory redemption periods and how they are used; and
- compare the non-judicial power-of-sale foreclosure with the judicial foreclosure on a mortgage.

| | | |
|---|---|---|
| **deed in lieu of foreclosure** | **grace period** | **recast** |
| **default** | **HOPE NOW** | **statutory period of redemption** |
| **deficiency judgment** | **judgment decree** | **strict foreclosure** |
| **equitable redemption period** | **judicial foreclosure** | **subrogation** |
| **eviction** | **moratorium** | **upside down or underwater** |
| **forbearance** | **power-of-sale method** | **workouts** |

The basic responsibilities of the parties to a real estate financial contract are relatively clear-cut. In exchange for money loaned, a borrower is obligated to repay the loan according to conditions stipulated in the contract as well as preserve the value of the collateral and the priority lien position of the lender. In the event the borrower breaches these obligations, the lender can exercise its power of acceleration and insist that the loan balance, accrued interest, and costs incurred be paid immediately and in full.

In an ideal real estate financing arrangement, a comfortable rhythm of lending and repayment is established between the participants, with few unusual circumstances occurring to cause a breach in the loan agreement. The lender establishes a real estate loan on the basis of availability of funds, general economic conditions, local economic stability, and competitive lenders' actions, as well as the borrower's financial position and the property's value. Unfortunately, the ideal arrangement was sorely misused in the early years of the 21st century, leading to the highest rate of foreclosures ever seen in this country. The government initiated a number of programs administered through the U.S. Treasury and Department of Housing and Development (HUD) in an effort to help millions of struggling homeowners. The Making Home Affordable Program, which included the Home Affordable Modification Program (HAMP) and the Home Affordable Refinancing Program (HARP), was discussed in Chapter 1. One additional program is Home Affordable Foreclosure Alternatives (HAFA), which enabled some homeowners to participate in a short sale or deed in lieu of foreclosure. HAFA was discontinued on December 31, 2013.

**HOPE NOW** is an alliance of counselors, servicers, investors, and other market participants to maximize outreach efforts to at-risk homeowners. These homeowners are encouraged to call the HOPE Hotline at 888-995-4673 (HOPE) to talk to HUD-approved credit counselors to guide them through possible options such as a loan workout or modification. For more information on government programs, see www.makinghomeaffordable.gov.

## Equity Building

Except for infrequent periods in U.S. economic history when severe depressions or recessions created serious financial difficulties (as seen in the economic crisis period starting in 2007), a borrower who pledged realty as security for a loan generally enjoyed the benefits of a steady inflation in the economy that usually increased the value of the property. At the same time, the balance owed on the loan was being paid down. The interaction between this growth in value and the lessening of the loan balance increases the protection against risk for the lender. The slow and steady increase of an equity position encourages the borrower to continue payments on the loan to protect the growing investment. However, when the equity position is eroded and borrowers become upside down or underwater in their mortgages, foreclosure rates begin to climb.

## Loan Failure

When a real estate loan fails, it is often the result of events that are beyond the control of the parties to the loan. There are circumstances under which individuals and companies suffer personal or financial setbacks that may jeopardize their ability to maintain normal payment patterns. Some of the more readily recognized problems include loss of employment, illness, divorce, bankruptcy, loss of tenants' rent as a result of local economic setbacks (e.g., overbuilding of income properties), or ordinary mismanagement. Under such conditions, real estate loan payments usually cannot be met. Defaults and foreclosures result.

The financial crisis beginning in 2007 led to an alarming increase in the number of foreclosures throughout the country. The resetting of subprime loans was largely blamed for many homeowners' inability to make their mortgage payments, though other factors such as the high rate of unemployment were also significant. A report by the Center for Responsible Lending showed a direct link between the higher number of foreclosures and loans originated by brokers such as hybrid-adjustable mortgages, option ARMs, and other subprime loan products.

Realty Trac®, a leading online source for real estate data, released a 2014 Foreclosure Market Report that showed a 23% decrease in the number of foreclosures from the first half of 2013. Daren Blomquist, vice president of RealtyTrac® was quoted in the report as saying, "Nationwide foreclosure activity in June 2014 reached an important milestone, dropping to levels not seen since before the housing price bubble burst in August 2006." He anticipates that foreclosures should return to consistent historic levels within a year.

# DEFAULTS

A **default** is the breach of one or more of the conditions or terms of a loan agreement. When a default occurs, the **acceleration clause** contained in all loan contracts is activated, allowing the lender to declare the full amount of the debt immediately due and payable. If the borrower cannot or will not meet this requirement, the lender may foreclose against the collateral to recover any loss. Although legally any default in a loan contract enables the lender to accelerate the debt, most lenders seek to avoid foreclosure and arrange a plan with the borrower to protect the interests of both parties and avoid costly, time-consuming court procedures. These efforts are called **workouts** and take the form of payment waivers, refinancing, or other arrangements designed to avoid foreclosure.

## Delinquencies

Most loan defaults occur when the borrower falls behind in making payments, in paying taxes, insurance premiums, or other lien payments.

**Principal and Interest.** The most common form of default occurs when the payment of principal and interest is not made when due, called **delinquency**. Loan agreements stipulate that the regular payment is due "on or before" a specified date, but most lenders will allow a reasonable **grace period**, usually up to 15 days, in which to receive the regular payment. Most loan arrangements include a **late payment charge** of some specific amount that is applied if the borrower exceeds the grace period. Most lenders are not disturbed by payments made within grace periods, but they will take remedial action when an account consistently incurs late charges or when a borrower exceeds a 30-day delinquency period. Late charges generally range from 3 to 5% of the amount due and may be regulated by state law.

## In Practice

A man has made some poor choices on the stock market and now finds himself two months behind on his mortgage payment with no hope of catching up or even being able to continue the regular payment, at least until he is able to sell his house and car.

He is tempted to just lock the door and walk away, but he has always had a good credit rating in the past and believes that this would severely affect his credit score and prevent him from qualifying for future loans. A friend who is a real estate licensee encourages him to discuss his situation with his lender and look for any possible solution other than foreclosure.

The man is pleasantly surprised to learn that the bank is willing to work with him and that the bank, in fact, is not interested in having to foreclose—the lender just wants its money. The man's licensee friend had suggested giving the bank the keys and the deed to the property (in lieu of foreclosure), but the bank does not want to sell the house. Instead, the lender suggests a three-month moratorium where no payment is required. This should give the man time to sell the house and car, giving him the funds to make the loan current. If for some reason this does not work, the bank will consider extending the term of the loan by the extra three months, with the man resuming regular payments at the end of the moratorium period. As a last resort, the bank might consider recasting the loan for a new period of time, resulting in a lower monthly payment.

The important issue here is that the man contacted the lender as soon as he realized he was in trouble. Too often people wait until it really is too late to avoid foreclosure—a no-win situation for both borrower and lender.

**Property Taxes.** Another cause for default is the nonpayment or late payment of property taxes. Although this situation is not very prevalent with residential loans because of the effectiveness of the impounding technique in which the lender collects funds for taxes and insurance (as described in Chapter 7), it becomes a more serious problem with commercial real estate financing, in which impounds generally are not required.

Property taxes represent a priority lien over most existing liens on real estate. If a tax lien is imposed, the lender's position as priority lienholder is jeopardized. If a lender is unaware of a property tax delinquency and, thus, is not protected, the collateral property may be sold for taxes, eliminating the safe lien position. As a consequence, all realty loan agreements include a clause stipulating a borrower's responsibility to pay property taxes in the amount and on the date required. Otherwise the lender is notified by the county treasurer, and the loan goes into default and may be accelerated.

**Other Liens.** Defaults may also occur when a borrower allows other liens that have priority over the loan to vest against the collateral property. Such liens might be imposed for nonpayment of federal, state, or local income tax. In some jurisdictions, construction and materialmen's (mechanics') liens can take priority over any preexisting liens. Under these circumstances, a lender may consider a loan in default and pursue appropriate legal remedies.

**Homeowners Insurance.** Another cause for default is the nonpayment of homeowners insurance premiums required by the lender for the protection of the value of the improvements on the collateral property. Again, the impounding technique prevents most of the possible difficulties in this area. However, some realty loan arrangements allow the borrower to pay insurance premiums outside the framework of the regular payment structure, contingent on the mortgagee's prior approval of the insurance carrier and the terms of the policy. Where this independent payment flexibility is granted, the borrower is obligated to make the premium payments on time to prevent any lapse of coverage and is usually required to provide the lender with a copy of the paid invoice as evidence of this accomplishment.

The lender is named in the insurance policy as a coinsured along with the borrower/property owner. If any losses are incurred by reason of fire, windstorm, or other insurable circumstance, the lender's collateral position must be preserved. The damages will be repaired to the lender's satisfaction, or the insurance proceeds will be applied to reduce the balance of the loan to match the reduced value of the collateral. Due to several recent natural disasters, such as Hurricanes Katrina and Sandy and numerous earthquakes, obtaining homeowners insurance is no longer a simple transaction. Lenders may require proof of insurance much earlier in the process than they did in previous years.

### Poor Property Management

Often lenders include a provision in a formal real estate loan agreement that requires a borrower to maintain the collateral property in such a manner that its value will not diminish to the point of undermining the lender's security position. A breach of this covenant creates a technical default of the terms of the loan. It is difficult to assess the amount of waste that creates such a defaulting situation, especially as its discovery would depend on constant inspection by a lender, an impractical task where many loans are being serviced. Usually, a lender will rely on a borrower's pride of ownership to protect the collateral, but a serious violation can result in a loan default and acceleration of the debt.

## ADJUSTMENTS AND MODIFICATIONS

A final foreclosure action is studiously avoided whenever possible. Before a lender decides to foreclose, full consideration is taken of the amount of the borrower's equity in the property, the general state of the current real estate market, and the positions of any junior lienholders. The lender also judiciously weighs the circumstances that caused the default and the attitude of the borrower concerning the repair of the breach in the contract.

The only time a foreclosure should ever be considered is when the current market value of the collateral property is actually less than the balance of the indebtedness and the borrower can no longer make the payment. Even under these extreme circumstances, a borrower should be aware that a foreclosure is not mandatory and that a **deed in lieu of foreclosure** is a possible option if the lender will accept it. A deed in lieu of foreclosure still has a negative impact on the borrower's total credit rating.

The greatest risk to a lender making a real estate loan is that a property pledged as collateral will be abandoned by the borrower. Although this risk is considerably less when unimproved land is the collateral, any improved property left vacant becomes an immediate and irritating source of concern for a lender.

Frustration may cause a borrower to blindly seek retaliation and perhaps even physically damage the collateral. Even if an abandoned property is left in good condition, a vacant building is often an invitation for vandalism. When investigating their delinquent accounts, many lenders have discovered empty shells of buildings. In the final analysis, many borrowers should be able to negotiate with their lenders from positions of strength rather than weakness. Lenders may be willing to make adjustments to the terms and conditions of the real estate loan contract to reflect emergency needs. Many lenders today are also willing to accept a short sale if they can determine that their loss will be less than it would be from a foreclosure.

## Short Sales

As the year 2012 drew to a close, more lenders and homeowners began to view a short sale as a better alternative than letting the home go to foreclosure.

A short sale occurs when a property is sold and there will not be sufficient funds to satisfy the outstanding mortgage lien and other liens secured by the property. The seller must seek agreement from the lender and other lienholders to be released from part of the debt in order to sell the property and convey good title. Generally unheard of in the past, this is now an everyday part of real estate practice. In a short sale, the seller may be referred to as an *upside down* or *underwater seller.*

## Moratoriums and Recasting

As discussed earlier, the most common default on real estate loans is delinquent payments.

Most lenders will attempt to cooperate with those borrowers who have legitimate excuses for failing to make payments. Sometimes a lender will waive a portion of the payment, usually the principal amount, to help a delinquent borrower regain financial balance. At other times the interest portion of the payment is waived as well and added to the balance owed toward that time when the borrower regains financial stability. These partial or full payment waivers, described as **forbearance** or **moratoriums**, originated during the Great Depression monetary crises. A lender expects that during the moratorium period the borrower can solve the problem by securing a new job, selling the property to a buyer qualified to make the loan payments, or finding some other acceptable solution.

A forbearance arrangement will usually require that a borrower add extra money to the regular payments when they are reinstated. These extra monies will be applied to satisfy the bubble of principal and interest that accrued during the moratorium.

For a defaulted borrower just recovering sound economic footing, an increase in payments may present too great an additional burden. In order to offset any possible hardships that these extra payments might create, a lender may choose to extend the term of the loan by a time interval equal to the moratorium period. Then the borrower can continue to make regularly scheduled monthly payments at the same amount but for a longer period of time. Another alternative is for the lender to require one balloon payment for all the monies accrued during the moratorium, to be payable at the loan's scheduled expiration date.

Delinquent loans can also be **recast** to lower the payments to suit a borrower's damaged financial position. When a loan has been paid down over a period of time (e.g., five years) and a default is imminent as a result of a borrower's financial crisis, the lender may redesign the balance still owed into a new loan, extending the original time period. This recasting would effectively reduce the payments required and relieve the pressure on the borrower.

Recasting invariably requires a new title search to discover if any intervening liens or second encumbrances have been recorded. This is especially necessary in the case of a delinquent borrower who might have sought aid from other sources. A lender may also require additional collateral and/or cosigners for the new financing agreement.

The government loan modification programs HAMP and HARP (described in Chapter 1) have provided a solution for some lenders and homeowners to resolve the problem without resorting to foreclosure. For some homeowners who are **upside down or underwater** on their mortgage (meaning they owe more than the property is now worth), another option could be a short sale.

A short sale may be the best option if the homeowner does not qualify for either the HAMP or HARP program and there is no hope that the property would sell for enough to pay off the existing debt. Since the lender would be required to accept an amount of money that is less than the amount actually owed, the lender has to give approval for such a sale. Obviously, this would not be the lender's first choice, but many lenders have found their loss would be even greater if they proceed with a foreclosure with multiple carrying costs and no guarantee of a future sale at any price.

The Federal Housing Finance Agency (FHFA) has required both Fannie Mae and Freddie Mac to issue new guidelines to enhance and streamline the short sale process. Eligibility based on hardship has been increased, and improvements have been made to the valuation process for the property.

## Voluntary Conveyance of Deed

When all efforts at adjusting the terms of a loan to solve a borrower's problems have failed and the property cannot be sold to a buyer willing and able to assume the loan's balance, a lender may seek to secure a **voluntary transfer of deed** from the borrower. This action prevents the costly and time-consuming process of foreclosure. By executing either a quitclaim deed or a regular deed, a borrower can eliminate the stigma of a foreclosure, maintain a respectable credit rating, and hopefully avoid the possibility of a deficiency judgment. On some applications for a new loan, the borrowers are asked if they have ever executed a voluntary deed in lieu of foreclosure.

A deed in lieu of foreclosure is a mutual agreement in which the delinquent owners of a property deed it to the lender in return for various considerations, usually a release from liability under the terms of the loan. It can be completed quickly, without the cost of a foreclosure, and the rights of third parties having interests in the property are left undisturbed.

However, the lender must take care to be protected against any future claims of fraud or duress by the borrower. Note that some lenders consider a voluntary conveyance of deed as bad as a regular foreclosure with regard to the borrower's credit rating. In times of financial crisis, as has been the case in the recent decade, banks are very reluctant to accept a deed in lieu. The last thing they want is one more house to have to sell.

### FHA and VA Foreclosures

Under the 1964 Housing Act, the FHA required that lenders provide relief in situations in which default is beyond a borrower's control. For example, a lender might recast or extend the mortgage of a borrower who has defaulted because of unemployment during a serious illness. The VA also requires leniency in the case of a borrower who is willing but unable to pay. The VA itself may pay for such delinquencies in order to keep a loan current for a veteran, although these payments do not reduce the debtor's obligation. The VA retains the right to collect these advances at a future date.

## AUCTIONS

The use of an **auction** to dispose of foreclosed properties is not a new concept, having been used extensively for years in farm and ranch finance. Originally, an auction was held to determine the true value of a property. Today, however, the major reason for the use of auctions is the pressure of the carrying costs for holding defaulted properties. Auctions often allow them to be sold quickly.

Carrying costs include those for mortgage insurance, maintenance, management, property taxes, and other related expenses. Usually, these costs will not be recouped in the form of a higher selling price. Add to these costs the interest rates in the current market and you can see that holding foreclosed properties creates an enormous burden on lenders.

## TYPES OF FORECLOSURES

When all else has failed, a lender pursues foreclosure to recover the collateral in order to sell it and recoup the investment. By definition, to foreclose means to shut out, exclude, bar, or deprive one of the right to redeem a mortgage, deed of trust, or land contract. **Foreclosure**, then, is not only a process to recover a lender's collateral but also a procedure whereby a borrower's rights of redemption are eliminated, and all interests in the subject property are removed.

Under old English law a borrower had few, if any, rights in property beyond possession. If the borrower did not pay on time and in the amount called for, any property rights were immediately forfeited and full ownership was vested in the lender.

This instantaneous and often capricious deprivation of property rights aroused widespread criticism and eventually was brought before the monarch, who assigned the adjudication of these grievances to a court of equity. Certain hardship cases were ruled on according to their merit, rather than on legal technicalities. Gradually, a system developed wherein a distressed borrower was allowed extra time to raise the funds necessary to protect property rights. This relief was called an **equitable redemption period**. Under this ruling, a borrower could secure a certain period beyond the default time in order to redeem the property. This could be accomplished by either bringing the payments current or repaying the total amount of the principal due in addition to interest owed and any court costs incurred.

As time passed, borrowers began to abuse their equitable redemption rights. Some defaulted borrowers remained in possession of their property beyond the redemption period and otherwise created great difficulties for lenders trying to reclaim the forfeited collateral. Complaints to the court of equity resulted in the decree of foreclosure, a legal process whereby the equitable period of redemption could be terminated under appropriate conditions. This became known as **strict foreclosure** or **strict forfeiture**.

Our present-day redemption and foreclosure processes have evolved from these medieval court decisions. However, during the 1800s, when the U.S. economy was still basically agrarian, many states expanded the strict foreclosure procedure to include additional protection for borrowers' equity interests in anticipation of better harvests in the following year. At the end of the equitable redemption period, the mortgagee was directed to sell the property at public auction rather than automatically take title to the collateral. It was hoped that the foreclosure sale would obtain a fair market value for the property and save part of the borrower's equity. In addition, the defaulted borrower was given another redemption period after the sale to recover the property before title to the collateral was transferred.

This additional time period is called the **statutory period of redemption** because it came into being as a result of the enactment of state statutes. During the entire redemption period, the defaulted borrower is allowed to retain possession of the property. The foreclosure methods and redemption periods vary from state to state.

## Judicial Foreclosure and Sale

A common foreclosure procedure, called the **judicial foreclosure** and sale process, involves the use of the courts and the consequent sale of the collateral at public auction. This foreclosure procedure is used in all states where a mortgage is used to establish collateral for a loan. States that use deeds of trust instead of a mortgage to establish collateral for a loan use a nonjudicial process, which is described later in this chapter.

**Conventional Mortgages.** Before a lender forecloses on a conventional first mortgage, the delinquent mortgagor is notified of the default and the reasons for it. An immediate solution is required, and all efforts must be expended to solve the problem as soon as possible. However, if all attempts fail, a complaint is filed by the mortgagee in the court for the county in which the property is located, and a summons is issued to the mortgagor, initiating the foreclosure action.

Simultaneous with this activity, a title search is made to determine the identities of all parties having an interest in the collateral property, and a **lis pendens** is filed with the court, giving notice to the world of the pending foreclosure action. Notice is sent to all parties having an interest in the property, requesting that they appear to defend their interests, or else they will be foreclosed from any future rights by judgment of the court. It is vitally important for the complainant/mortgagee to notify all junior lienholders of the foreclosure action lest they be omitted from participation in the property auction and, thus, acquire the right to file suit on their own at some future time.

Depending on the number of days required by the jurisdiction for public notice to inform any and all persons having an unrecorded interest in the subject property that a foreclosure suit is imminent, and depending on the availability of a court date, the complaint is eventually aired before a presiding judge. In most instances, the defendant/mortgagor does not appear in court unless special circumstances are presented in defense of the default. Those creditors who do appear to present their claims are recognized and noted, and a sale of the property at public auction by a court-appointed referee or sheriff is ordered by means of a **judgment decree**.

A public sale is necessary in order to establish the actual market value of the subject property. Essentially, the lender sues for foreclosure under the terms of the mortgage. The auction does not usually generate any bids in excess of the balance of the mortgage debt. If the proceeds from the auction sale are not sufficient to recover the outstanding loan balance plus costs, in most states the mortgagee may alternatively sue on the note for the deficiency. Most lenders do not pursue the deficiency, however, because of the apparent financial straits of the defaulted mortgagor. The mortgagee makes the opening bid at the auction in an amount equal to the loan balance plus interest to date and court costs, and then the lender hopes that someone else will bid at least one dollar more. If there are any junior lienholders or other creditors who look to the property as collateral for their loans, they now have the opportunity to step in and bid to protect their priority positions. Their bids obligate them to repay the first mortgagee. When no junior lienholders or creditors enter a bid, the auction closes at the first mortgagee's bid price. Any interests that these junior creditors may have in the property are effectively eliminated. However, if any other person bids an amount above the first mortgage, after the first lien is paid, the excess funds are distributed to the junior lienholders in order of their priority, with any money left over going to the defaulted mortgagor.

**Conventional Insured Mortgages.** Under the terms of the insurance policies of most private mortgage insurance companies, a default is interpreted to be nonpayment for four months. Within ten days of default, the mortgagee is required to notify the insurer, who then decides whether to instruct the mortgagee to foreclose.

When a conventional insured mortgage is foreclosed, the first mortgagee is the original bidder at the public auction of the collateral property. Under these circumstances, the successful bidder/mortgagee files notice with the insurance company within 60 days after the legal proceedings have transpired. If the insurance company is confident of recovering the losses by purchasing the collateral property from the mortgagee and then reselling it, it will reimburse the mortgagee for the total amount of the bid and secure title to the property. If, however, the company does not foresee any possibility for this recovery, it may elect to only pay the mortgagee the agreed-upon specific amount of insurance, and the mortgagee will retain ownership of the property. The collateral is then sold to recover any balance still unpaid.

In cases of judicial foreclosure and sale, any ownership rights acquired by the successful bidder at the foreclosure auction are still subject to any redemption rights of the defaulted mortgagor. A full fee simple absolute title cannot vest in the bidder until these redemption rights have expired.

**FHA-Insured Mortgages.** Foreclosures on FHA-insured mortgages originate with the filing of Form 2068, Notice of Default, which must be given to the local FHA administrative office within 60 days of default. This notice describes the reasons for the mortgagor's delinquency, such as death, illness, marital difficulties, income depletion, excessive obligations, employment transfers, or military service.

In many cases involving delinquent FHA-insured mortgages, counselors from the local FHA offices will attempt to design an agreement between the mortgagee and the mortgagor for adjustments to the loan conditions in order to prevent foreclosure. The most common technique used in circumstances where a default is beyond the mortgagor's control but deemed curable is forbearance of foreclosure.

If the problems causing the default are solved within a one-year period, the mortgagee informs the local FHA office of the solution. If not, a default status report is filed, and the mortgagee must initiate foreclosure proceedings. If the bids at the auction are less than the unpaid balance, the mortgagee is expected to bid the debt, take title, and present it to the FHA along with a claim for insurance, which may be paid in cash or in government debentures. In some cases, with prior FHA approval, the mortgagee may assign the defaulted mortgage directly to the FHA before the final foreclosure action in exchange for insurance benefits. In any case, if the property can be sold easily at a price that will repay the loan in full, the mortgagee simply will sell the property after bidding at the auction and will not apply for FHA compensation. If the FHA ends up as the owner of the property, the collateral will be resold "as is" or repaired, refurbished, and resold at a higher price to help minimize the losses to the FHA. Public notice of HUD-owned properties for sale is made through local newspapers and online.

**VA-Guaranteed Mortgages.** Unlike the FHA-insured mortgages, whereby a lender's entire risk is recovered from the insurance benefits, a VA loan is similar to a privately insured loan in that a lender receives only the top portion of the outstanding loan balance. In the event of a delinquency of more than three months on a VA loan, the mortgagee must file proper notification with the local VA office, which may then elect to bring the loan current if it wishes, with **subrogation** rights to the mortgagee against the mortgagor for the amount advanced. This means that the VA claim against the defaulted veteran takes priority over the rights of the mortgagee to these funds.

Much like the FHA, VA lenders are required to make every effort to offset a foreclosure through forbearance, payment adjustments, sale of the property, deed in lieu of foreclosure, or other acceptable solutions. Actual foreclosure is considered only as a last resort.

In the event of a foreclosure, the mortgagee is usually the original bidder at the auction and submits a claim for losses to the local VA office. The VA then has the option either to pay the unpaid balance, interest, and court costs and take title to the collateral or to require that the mortgagee retain the property and the VA will pay only the difference between the determined value of the property on the date of foreclosure and the mortgage balance. The latter alternative is usually chosen when the property is badly deteriorated, accenting the importance for a mortgagee to properly supervise the collateral.

**Junior Mortgages.** Defaults of junior mortgages are handled in exactly the same manner as senior mortgages. Here, however, the relationship is usually between two individuals rather than between an institutional lender and an individual borrower.

A junior lender usually seeks the counsel of an attorney to manage the foreclosure process. The delinquent borrower is requested to cure the problem within a certain time period. If a cure cannot be accomplished, notice is given to all persons having an interest in the property, and the attorney then files for foreclosure.

The junior lender is generally the bidder at the public sale and secures ownership of the collateral property subject to the balance of the existing senior loan. This loan is usually required to be paid in full because the foreclosure triggers the due-on-sale clause, unless other solutions are negotiated ahead of time.

## Nonjudicial Foreclosure and Sale

An alternative to the judicial foreclosure process is the **power-of-sale method** of collateral recovery. Under this form, a lender or the trustee has the right to sell the collateral property upon default without being required to spend the time and money involved in a court foreclosure suit. In fact, under this form of lender control, a borrower's redemption time frame is shortened considerably by the elimination of the statutory redemption period granted in the judicial process.

**Deeds of Trust.** The most common application of the power-of-sale foreclosure process is by exercise of the trustee's responsibility created in a deed of trust. In the event of a default, the beneficiary (lender) notifies the trustee in writing of the trustor's (borrower's) delinquency and instructs the trustee to begin the foreclosure by sale process.

Notice of default is recorded by the trustee at the county recorder's office within the jurisdiction's designated time period, usually 90 days, to give notice to the public of the intended auction. This official notice is accompanied by advertisements in public newspapers that state the total amount due and the date of the public sale. Unlike the notice given in the judicial process, notice need not be given to each individual junior lienholder when the power-of-sale process is enforced. However, the trustor/borrowers must be given special notice of the situation so they have full benefit of the redemption period.

During the equitable redemption period preceding the auction, the trustors or any junior lienholders may cure the default by making up any delinquent payments together with interest and costs to date. However, if such payments are not made, the property is placed for sale at public auction shortly after the expiration of the redemption period, and absolute title passes to the successful bidder.

**Mortgage.** The power-of-sale foreclosure process may be incorporated into the standard mortgage contract in approximately one-third of the states where the trust deed is not in use.

The procedure for foreclosing a mortgage under a power of sale is essentially the same as the one used to foreclose a deed of trust, except that in most states allowing this foreclosure format, the mortgagee is prohibited from bidding at the sale. In addition, the amount that the mortgagee may recover by suing for a deficiency judgment on the note is limited. The purchaser at a mortgagee's sale acquires the same type of title that would be acquired at a judicial auction and steps into the mortgagor's interest in the property.

## Strict Foreclosure

Although judicial and nonjudicial foreclosure procedures are the prevailing practices, in some states (Connecticut, New Hampshire, and Vermont) it is still possible for a lender to recover the collateral through a strict foreclosure process. After appropriate notice has been given to the delinquent borrower and the proper papers have been filed and processed, the court establishes a specific time period during which the balance of the defaulted debt must be paid in full by the borrower. If this is not done, the borrower's equitable and statutory redemption rights are eliminated, and full legal title is awarded to the lender.

Using strict foreclosure, it is possible for a lender to secure ownership to a property with a value in excess of the loan's balance. Because of the possible inequities that might arise from the foreclosure of a property when no value is established, the strict foreclosure method is seldom used and, in fact, has been abolished by statute in some states.

The only effective surviving use of the strict foreclosure method still allowed in many states is under the contract for deed form of financing. By wording a land contract appropriately and carefully observing and following all of the legal steps required for adequate notice to the errant vendee and to the public, a vendor may exercise a strict foreclosure in certain low-equity loan arrangements.

## Other Foreclosure Processes

As with a number of laws concerning real estate, many states have established their own unique methods for foreclosing on defaulted mortgages, most of which are variations of the strict foreclosure procedure. Although a legal process in certain states, they usually only occur as a backup plan to the more traditional judicial or nonjudicial foreclosure processes.

**By Advertisement.** Foreclosure by advertisement is a method whereby a mortgagee notifies the mortgagor of default and advertises that the property will be sold at public auction. The successful purchaser at the auction is awarded an ownership certificate rather than legal possession of the property. To gain possession of the newly acquired property, in most states recognizing this foreclosure process, the successful bidder has to bring an action for **eviction**, which legally dispossesses a defaulted borrower from the premises after a court hearing. The extra cost and trouble associated with this foreclosure procedure keep it from being a popular form for recovering a mortgagee's collateral.

**By Entry and Possession.** Maine, Massachusetts, New Hampshire, and Rhode Island recognize the power of a mortgagee to petition the court for the right to take actual physical possession of the collateral pledged on a defaulted loan. The entry for possession must be peaceable, made before witnesses, and attested to by a certificate filed with the court. Full legal ownership vests in the mortgagee after a period of time during which the mortgagor may redeem the property by repaying the mortgage lien plus costs. Entry by Possession may be paired with a Power of Sale, allowing the lender to sell the house at a trustee sale.

**By Writ of Entry.** Maine, Massachusetts, and New Hampshire also allow a mortgagee to initiate a court action whereby a writ of *entry only* is granted. The writ specifies the delinquent amounts due from the mortgagor and the time in which such funds must be paid. If the debt is not paid in accordance with these requirements, the mortgagee receives full legal title to the property. A summary of foreclosure processes is shown in Figure 10.1.

*FIGURE 10.1* **Summary of the Foreclosure Process**

| ***Judicial*** | ***Power of Sale*** | ***Strict Foreclosure*** |
|---|---|---|
| Notice | Notice | Notice |
| Lis pendens | Publication | Redemption period |
| Hearing | Public sale | Repossession |
| Decree | No redemption | |
| Public sale | | |
| Redemption period | | |
| ***By Advertisement*** | ***Entry and Possession*** | ***Writ of Entry*** |
| Notification | Court petition | Court petition |
| Public sale | Repossession | Eviction |
| Ownership certificate | Eviction | |
| Eviction | | |

## DEFICIENCY JUDGMENTS

If a lender receives less money than the entire loan balance, interest to date, and costs incurred as a consequence of a default after the delinquency, default, and foreclosure processes have been completed, the lender may pursue the borrower for these losses. The lender sues on the note and secures a **deficiency judgment** from the court, including an unsecured blanket lien, which may be perfected against any property currently owned or acquired in the future by the foreclosed borrower or any other signatories to the note. As mentioned previously, in most cases a defaulted borrower does not have any assets to make up this deficiency; therefore, deficiency judgments are practically unenforceable.

No deficiency judgments are allowed by the FHA, and while it is possible to obtain a deficiency judgment under a VA-guaranteed loan, the VA discourages this practice. In general, there is little evidence that deficiency judgments are feasible as a means for recovering a lender's losses, and many states have totally eliminated them.

## TAX IMPACTS OF FORECLOSURE

In a foreclosure, there may be an unexpected tax consequence for the person or entity that has borrowed the money. In the normal course of events, paying off a real estate loan has no tax consequences. When the last payment is made, all principal borrowed has been returned, plus interest. However, in a foreclosure, the loan is retired without being paid in full.

A tax is due when the property's adjusted book value is less than the balance of the loan. As far as the IRS is concerned, a foreclosure is considered a sale; if the amount of the defaulted loan exceeds the tax basis of the property, the IRS considers that a gain has been made.

The **Mortgage Forgiveness Debt Relief Act of 2007** allowed taxpayers to file a Form 982 with their tax returns through 2012, which excluded any canceled debt that was forgiven or canceled by a lender as part of a modification of the mortgage or foreclosure on a principal residence. The act was extended through 2013 but remains in legislative limbo in 2014. Concern over whether it will continue has led to a slight drop in short sales throughout the country. More information on obtaining and filling out the form is available at www.irs.gov.

## SUMMARY

This chapter summarized the consequences of defaults in real estate finance. Generally, most realty financing arrangements do not result in problems leading to foreclosure. Rising property values coupled with the systematic repayment of loans create measurable equity positions for the borrower that usually inhibit the loss of property because of loan default. However, when the overall housing market began to decline in 2007, the options for an at-risk borrower became very limited. The government initiated numerous loan modification programs as homeowners struggled to make their monthly mortgage payments and the rate of foreclosure began to climb.

Under less dramatic circumstances, a lender usually attempts to adjust the conditions of a loan in order to help a troubled borrower over short-term difficulties. Delinquent loan payments are the most common cause for a default, although the nonpayment of taxes or homeowners insurance premiums, lack of adequate maintenance, and allowing priority liens to vest are also defaultable conditions. To offset the possibility of a foreclosure on delinquent loans, lenders have several workout options, including forbearance or a moratorium on the full payments. Other adjustments in the terms of a delinquent loan that might aid the defaulted borrower include an extension of time or a recasting of the loan to reflect the borrower's current ability to pay. Short sales have become a popular alternative to foreclosure.

A loan is foreclosed only if there are no alternatives. Under a judicial foreclosure proceeding, the lender notifies the defaulting borrower and arranges the advertisement necessary to inform the public that the foreclosure is in process so that all creditors having an interest may be alerted. At the foreclosure sale, the lender usually bids the outstanding balance, hoping that someone will bid one dollar more and repay the loan. When the defaulted mortgage is a conventional loan, the lender assumes the risks of ownership and attempts to sell the property to minimize losses. When the defaulted loan is FHA-insured, the lender recovers any balance owed from the FHA insurance benefits. When the loan is VA-guaranteed or privately insured, the lender will recover the top portion of the loan up to the insured amount and will sell the property to recover the balance.

The foreclosure process is designed to eliminate a borrower's rights in the collateral property. However, the laws of redemption grant the delinquent borrower certain specified times during which the property may be redeemed. Not until the redemption periods expire does the new buyer of the property receive title to it.

A junior lender follows essentially the same procedures in foreclosing a delinquent loan, except that the integrity of the existing senior lender's priority position must be maintained by seeing that the first-mortgage payments, property taxes, and insurance premiums are paid.

Some mortgages and all deeds of trust contain a power-of-sale provision that allows a lender to pursue a somewhat faster foreclosure process than under the judicial process. Under a power of sale, a trustee is entitled to sell a defaulted collateral property with reduced redemption times allotted to the borrower. This nonjudicial foreclosure tool must follow definitive notification and advertisement procedures to be legally valid.

Strict foreclosure proceedings are used only rarely, mostly with contracts for deed. In fact, many states have declared this foreclosure process illegal in their jurisdictions. In effect, the strict foreclosure process quickly eliminates a defaulted borrower's total redemption rights in property.

Other unique foreclosure processes are used in a few states. Foreclosure by advertisement, by entry and possession, and by writ of entry are additional means enabling lenders to recover their collateral.

After all the various processes have been exhausted and a lender sells the collateral, but does not accumulate funds in an amount adequate to cover the investment and costs, the borrower may be sued under the note, and the lender can secure a deficiency judgment for the amount of the loss. Some states have eliminated or reduced the impact of a deficiency judgment. Often it is a practical impossibility to actually secure these funds, and in the event of a foreclosure, most lenders will look to the sale of the collateral property as their ultimate security.

## INTERNET RESOURCES

Center for Responsible Lending (CRL)
*www.responsiblelending.org*

Department of Housing and Urban Development (HUD)
*www.hud.gov*

Internal Revenue Service (IRS)
*www.irs.gov*

Mortgage Bankers Association®
*www.mbaa.org*

RealtyTrac®
*www.realtytrac.com*

## REVIEW QUESTIONS

1. The slow but steady increase in the equity position on mortgaged property is a benefit to
   a. the borrower.
   b. the lender.
   c. both borrower and lender.
   d. neither borrower nor lender.

2. When a breach in one of the terms or conditions of a loan agreement results in a default, which clause in the contract is activated?
   a. Alienation
   b. Acceleration
   c. Defeasance
   d. Subordination

3. When a lender agrees to waive a portion or all of the monthly payment for a specified period of time, this is called a
   a. grace period.
   b. forbearance or moratorium.
   c. deed in lieu of foreclosure.
   d. recasting of the loan.

4. An early English court of equity established an equitable redemption period that allowed for the
   a. lender to immediately take possession of property on a defaulted loan.
   b. borrower to have a specified amount of time to clear the default.
   c. lender to sell the property.
   d. borrower to remain in the property after it was sold.

5. A mortgage company recognizes there is little point in attempting to sue a homeowner for a deficiency judgment due to his extreme financial difficulties. The mortgage company will therefore
   a. sue on the note.
   b. sue on the terms of the mortgage.
   c. not bid at the auction.
   d. bid slightly less than the balance due.

6. The *MOST* common technique used in delinquent FHA mortgages where it is determined that the default was caused by circumstances beyond the borrower's control is
   a. forbearance of foreclosure for a one-year period.
   b. recasting of the loan.
   c. moratorium on payments for one year.
   d. immediate assignment of the loan to the FHA.

7. In the case of a VA loan that goes to foreclosure, the lender receives
   a. the full amount of the balance due.
   b. the amount of the entitlement at the present time.
   c. the top portion of the loan.
   d. immediate title to the property.

8. The biggest benefit to a lender using the power-of-sale method to foreclose on a property is that it
   a. guarantees repayment of the loan.
   b. lengthens the statutory redemption period.
   c. does not require judicial (court) procedure.
   d. does not require notice to the public.

9. In strict foreclosure, the court sets a specific time period for the borrower to pay the balance due or else the lender receives full legal title to the property. This usually is found today in which type of real estate financing?
   a. Note and mortgage
   b. Note and deed of trust
   c. Contract for deed
   d. Deed in lieu

10. The only instance in which there would be a tax consequence to a foreclosure is when the
    a. amount of the defaulted loan is less than the tax basis on the property.
    b. amount of the defaulted loan exceeds the tax basis on the property.
    c. proceeds of the auction pay off the balance due on the loan.
    d. proceeds of the auction are insufficient to pay off the balance due.

# Appendix A: Good Faith Estimate (GFE)

# Good Faith Estimate (GFE)

OMB Approval No. 2502-0265

| | |
|---|---|
| Name of Originator | Borrower |
| Originator Address | Property Address |
| Originator Phone Number | |
| Originator Email | Date of GFE |

**Purpose**

This GFE gives you an estimate of your settlement charges and loan terms if you are approved for this loan. For more information, see HUD's *Special Information Booklet* on settlement charges, your *Truth-in-Lending Disclosures,* and other consumer information at www.hud.gov/respa. If you decide you would like to proceed with this loan, contact us.

**Shopping for your loan**

Only you can shop for the best loan for you. Compare this GFE with other loan offers, so you can find the best loan. Use the shopping chart on page 3 to compare all the offers you receive.

**Important dates**

1. The interest rate for this GFE is available through ☐. After this time, the interest rate, some of your loan Origination Charges, and the monthly payment shown below can change until you lock your interest rate.
2. This estimate for all other settlement charges is available through ☐.
3. After you lock your interest rate, you must go to settlement within ☐ days (your rate lock period) to receive the locked interest rate.
4. You must lock the interest rate at least ☐ days before settlement.

**Summary of your loan**

| | |
|---|---|
| Your initial loan amount is | $ |
| Your loan term is | years |
| Your initial interest rate is | % |
| Your initial monthly amount owed for principal, interest, and any mortgage insurance is | $ per month |
| Can your interest rate rise? | ☐ No ☐ Yes, it can rise to a maximum of %. The first change will be in . |
| Even if you make payments on time, can your loan balance rise? | ☐ No ☐ Yes, it can rise to a maximum of $ |
| Even if you make payments on time, can your monthly amount owed for principal, interest, and any mortgage insurance rise? | ☐ No ☐ Yes, the first increase can be in and the monthly amount owed can rise to $ . The maximum it can ever rise to is $ . |
| Does your loan have a prepayment penalty? | ☐ No ☐ Yes, your maximum prepayment penalty is $ . |
| Does your loan have a balloon payment? | ☐ No ☐ Yes, you have a balloon payment of $ due in years. |

**Escrow account information**

Some lenders require an escrow account to hold funds for paying property taxes or other property-related charges in addition to your monthly amount owed of $☐.
Do we require you to have an escrow account for your loan?
☐ No, you do not have an escrow account. You must pay these charges directly when due.
☐ Yes, you have an escrow account. It may or may not cover all of these charges. Ask us.

**Summary of your settlement charges**

| | | |
|---|---|---|
| A | Your Adjusted Origination Charges *(See page 2.)* | $ |
| B | Your Charges for All Other Settlement Services *(See page 2.)* | $ |
| A + B | Total Estimated Settlement Charges | $ |

Understanding your estimated settlement charges

## Your Adjusted Origination Charges

| | |
|---|---|
| 1. **Our origination charge**<br>This charge is for getting this loan for you. | |
| 2. **Your credit or charge (points) for the specific interest rate chosen**<br>☐ The credit or charge for the interest rate of ☐ % is included in "Our origination charge." (See item 1 above.)<br>☐ You receive a credit of $ ☐ for this interest rate of ☐ %. This credit **reduces** your settlement charges.<br>☐ You pay a charge of $ ☐ for this interest rate of ☐ %. This charge (points) **increases** your total settlement charges.<br>The tradeoff table on page 3 shows that you can change your total settlement charges by choosing a different interest rate for this loan. | |
| **A** Your Adjusted Origination Charges | $ |

## Your Charges for All Other Settlement Services

*Some of these charges can change at settlement. See the top of page 3 for more information.*

| | |
|---|---|
| 3. **Required services that we select**<br>These charges are for services we require to complete your settlement. We will choose the providers of these services.<br>*Service* *Charge* | |
| 4. **Title services and lender's title insurance**<br>This charge includes the services of a title or settlement agent, for example, and title insurance to protect the lender, if required. | |
| 5. **Owner's title insurance**<br>You may purchase an owner's title insurance policy to protect your interest in the property. | |
| 6. **Required services that you can shop for**<br>These charges are for other services that are required to complete your settlement. We can identify providers of these services or you can shop for them yourself. Our estimates for providing these services are below.<br>*Service* *Charge* | |
| 7. **Government recording charges**<br>These charges are for state and local fees to record your loan and title documents. | |
| 8. **Transfer taxes**<br>These charges are for state and local fees on mortgages and home sales. | |
| 9. **Initial deposit for your escrow account**<br>This charge is held in an escrow account to pay future recurring charges on your property and includes ☐ all property taxes, ☐ all insurance, and ☐ other ☐. | |
| 10. **Daily interest charges**<br>This charge is for the daily interest on your loan from the day of your settlement until the first day of the next month or the first day of your normal mortgage payment cycle. This amount is $ ☐ per day for ☐ days (if your settlement is ☐ ). | |
| 11. **Homeowner's insurance**<br>This charge is for the insurance you must buy for the property to protect from a loss, such as fire.<br>*Policy* *Charge* | |
| **B** Your Charges for All Other Settlement Services | $ |
| **A + B** Total Estimated Settlement Charges | $ |

# Instructions

## Understanding which charges can change at settlement

This GFE estimates your settlement charges. At your settlement, you will receive a HUD-1, a form that lists your actual costs. Compare the charges on the HUD-1 with the charges on this GFE. Charges can change if you select your own provider and do not use the companies we identify. (See below for details.)

| These charges **cannot increase** at settlement: | The total of these charges **can increase up to 10%** at settlement: | These charges **can change** at settlement: |
|---|---|---|
| ■ Our origination charge<br>■ Your credit or charge (points) for the specific interest rate chosen *(after you lock in your interest rate)*<br>■ Your adjusted origination charges *(after you lock in your interest rate)*<br>■ Transfer taxes | ■ Required services that we select<br>■ Title services and lender's title insurance *(if we select them or you use companies we identify)*<br>■ Owner's title insurance *(if you use companies we identify)*<br>■ Required services that you can shop for *(if you use companies we identify)*<br>■ Government recording charges | ■ Required services that you can shop for *(if you do not use companies we identify)*<br>■ Title services and lender's title insurance *(if you do not use companies we identify)*<br>■ Owner's title insurance *(if you do not use companies we identify)*<br>■ Initial deposit for your escrow account<br>■ Daily interest charges<br>■ Homeowner's insurance |

## Using the tradeoff table

In this GFE, we offered you this loan with a particular interest rate and estimated settlement charges. However:

- If you want to choose this same loan with **lower settlement charges,** then you will have a **higher interest rate.**
- If you want to choose this same loan with a **lower interest rate,** then you will have **higher settlement charges.**

If you would like to choose an available option, you must ask us for a new GFE.

*Loan originators have the option to complete this table. Please ask for additional information if the table is not completed.*

| | The loan in this GFE | The same loan with lower settlement charges | The same loan with a lower interest rate |
|---|---|---|---|
| Your initial loan amount | $ | $ | $ |
| Your initial interest rate[1] | % | % | % |
| Your initial monthly amount owed | $ | $ | $ |
| Change in the monthly amount owed from this GFE | No change | You will pay $ **more** every month | You will pay $ **less** every month |
| Change in the amount you will pay at settlement with this interest rate | No change | Your settlement charges will be **reduced** by $ | Your settlement charges will **increase** by $ |
| How much your total estimated settlement charges will be | $ | $ | $ |

[1] *For an adjustable rate loan, the comparisons above are for the initial interest rate before adjustments are made.*

## Using the shopping chart

Use this chart to compare GFEs from different loan originators. Fill in the information by using a different column for each GFE you receive. By comparing loan offers, you can shop for the best loan.

| | This loan | Loan 2 | Loan 3 | Loan 4 |
|---|---|---|---|---|
| Loan originator name | | | | |
| Initial loan amount | | | | |
| Loan term | | | | |
| Initial interest rate | | | | |
| Initial monthly amount owed | | | | |
| Rate lock period | | | | |
| Can interest rate rise? | | | | |
| Can loan balance rise? | | | | |
| Can monthly amount owed rise? | | | | |
| Prepayment penalty? | | | | |
| Balloon payment? | | | | |
| **Total Estimated Settlement Charges** | | | | |

## If your loan is sold in the future

Some lenders may sell your loan after settlement. Any fees lenders receive in the future cannot change the loan you receive or the charges you paid at settlement.

# Appendix B: Settlement Statement (HUD-1)

OMB Approval No. 2502-0265

# A. Settlement Statement (HUD-1)

**B. Type of Loan**

| | | | |
|---|---|---|---|
| 1. ☐ FHA 2. ☐ RHS 3. ☐ Conv. Unins.<br>4. ☐ VA 5. ☐ Conv. Ins. | 6. File Number: | 7. Loan Number: | 8. Mortgage Insurance Case Number: |

**C. Note:** This form is furnished to give you a statement of actual settlement costs. Amounts paid to and by the settlement agent are shown. Items marked "(p.o.c.)" were paid outside the closing; they are shown here for informational purposes and are not included in the totals.

| | | |
|---|---|---|
| D. Name & Address of Borrower: | E. Name & Address of Seller: | F. Name & Address of Lender: |
| G. Property Location: | H. Settlement Agent: | I. Settlement Date: |
| | Place of Settlement: | |

**J. Summary of Borrower's Transaction**

| **100. Gross Amount Due from Borrower** | |
|---|---|
| 101. Contract sales price | |
| 102. Personal property | |
| 103. Settlement charges to borrower (line 1400) | |
| 104. | |
| 105. | |
| **Adjustment for items paid by seller in advance** | |
| 106. City/town taxes to | |
| 107. County taxes to | |
| 108. Assessments to | |
| 109. | |
| 110. | |
| 111. | |
| 112. | |
| **120. Gross Amount Due from Borrower** | |
| **200. Amount Paid by or in Behalf of Borrower** | |
| 201. Deposit or earnest money | |
| 202. Principal amount of new loan(s) | |
| 203. Existing loan(s) taken subject to | |
| 204. | |
| 205. | |
| 206. | |
| 207. | |
| 208. | |
| 209. | |
| **Adjustments for items unpaid by seller** | |
| 210. City/town taxes to | |
| 211. County taxes to | |
| 212. Assessments to | |
| 213. | |
| 214. | |
| 215. | |
| 216. | |
| 217. | |
| 218. | |
| 219. | |
| **220. Total Paid by/for Borrower** | |
| **300. Cash at Settlement from/to Borrower** | |
| 301. Gross amount due from borrower (line 120) | |
| 302. Less amounts paid by/for borrower (line 220) | ( ) |
| **303. Cash** ☐ **From** ☐ **To Borrower** | |

**K. Summary of Seller's Transaction**

| **400. Gross Amount Due to Seller** | |
|---|---|
| 401. Contract sales price | |
| 402. Personal property | |
| 403. | |
| 404. | |
| 405. | |
| **Adjustment for items paid by seller in advance** | |
| 406. City/town taxes to | |
| 407. County taxes to | |
| 408. Assessments to | |
| 409. | |
| 410. | |
| 411. | |
| 412. | |
| **420. Gross Amount Due to Seller** | |
| **500. Reductions In Amount Due to seller** | |
| 501. Excess deposit (see instructions) | |
| 502. Settlement charges to seller (line 1400) | |
| 503. Existing loan(s) taken subject to | |
| 504. Payoff of first mortgage loan | |
| 505. Payoff of second mortgage loan | |
| 506. | |
| 507. | |
| 508. | |
| 509. | |
| **Adjustments for items unpaid by seller** | |
| 510. City/town taxes to | |
| 511. County taxes to | |
| 512. Assessments to | |
| 513. | |
| 514. | |
| 515. | |
| 516. | |
| 517. | |
| 518. | |
| 519. | |
| **520. Total Reduction Amount Due Seller** | |
| **600. Cash at Settlement to/from Seller** | |
| 601. Gross amount due to seller (line 420) | |
| 602. Less reductions in amounts due seller (line 520) | ( ) |
| **603. Cash** ☐ **To** ☐ **From Seller** | |

The Public Reporting Burden for this collection of information is estimated at 35 minutes per response for collecting, reviewing, and reporting the data. This agency may not collect this information, and you are not required to complete this form, unless it displays a currently valid OMB control number. No confidentiality is assured; this disclosure is mandatory. This is designed to provide the parties to a RESPA covered transaction with information during the settlement process.

**L. Settlement Charges**

| 700. Total Real Estate Broker Fees | Paid From Borrower's Funds at Settlement | Paid From Seller's Funds at Settlement |
|---|---|---|
| Division of commission (line 700) as follows : | | |
| 701. $ to | | |
| 702. $ to | | |
| 703. Commission paid at settlement | | |
| 704. | | |
| **800. Items Payable in Connection with Loan** | | |
| 801. Our origination charge $ (from GFE #1) | | |
| 802. Your credit or charge (points) for the specific interest rate chosen $ (from GFE #2) | | |
| 803. Your adjusted origination charges (from GFE #A) | | |
| 804. Appraisal fee to (from GFE #3) | | |
| 805. Credit report to (from GFE #3) | | |
| 806. Tax service to (from GFE #3) | | |
| 807. Flood certification to (from GFE #3) | | |
| 808. | | |
| 809. | | |
| 810. | | |
| 811. | | |
| **900. Items Required by Lender to be Paid in Advance** | | |
| 901. Daily interest charges from to @ $ /day (from GFE #10) | | |
| 902. Mortgage insurance premium for months to (from GFE #3) | | |
| 903. Homeowner's insurance for years to (from GFE #11) | | |
| 904. | | |
| **1000. Reserves Deposited with Lender** | | |
| 1001. Initial deposit for your escrow account (from GFE #9) | | |
| 1002. Homeowner's insurance months @ $ per month $ | | |
| 1003. Mortgage insurance months @ $ per month $ | | |
| 1004. Property Taxes months @ $ per month $ | | |
| 1005. months @ $ per month $ | | |
| 1006. months @ $ per month $ | | |
| 1007. Aggregate Adjustment -$ | | |
| **1100. Title Charges** | | |
| 1101. Title services and lender's title insurance (from GFE #4) | | |
| 1102. Settlement or closing fee $ | | |
| 1103. Owner's title insurance (from GFE #5) | | |
| 1104. Lender's title insurance $ | | |
| 1105. Lender's title policy limit $ | | |
| 1106. Owner's title policy limit $ | | |
| 1107. Agent's portion of the total title insurance premium to $ | | |
| 1108. Underwriter's portion of the total title insurance premium to $ | | |
| 1109. | | |
| 1110. | | |
| 1111. | | |
| **1200. Government Recording and Transfer Charges** | | |
| 1201. Government recording charges (from GFE #7) | | |
| 1202. Deed $ Mortgage $ Release $ | | |
| 1203. Transfer taxes (from GFE #8) | | |
| 1204. City/County tax/stamps Deed $ Mortgage $ | | |
| 1205. State tax/stamps Deed $ Mortgage $ | | |
| 1206. | | |
| **1300. Additional Settlement Charges** | | |
| 1301. Required services that you can shop for (from GFE #6) | | |
| 1302. $ | | |
| 1303. $ | | |
| 1304. | | |
| 1305. | | |
| **1400. Total Settlement Charges (enter on lines 103, Section J and 502, Section K)** | | |

| Comparison of Good Faith Estimate (GFE) and HUD-1 Charrges | | Good Faith Estimate | HUD-1 |
|---|---|---|---|
| **Charges That Cannot Increase** | **HUD-1 Line Number** | | |
| Our origination charge | # 801 | | |
| Your credit or charge (points) for the specific interest rate chosen | # 802 | | |
| Your adjusted origination charges | # 803 | | |
| Transfer taxes | # 1203 | | |

| Charges That In Total Cannot Increase More Than 10% | | Good Faith Estimate | HUD-1 |
|---|---|---|---|
| Government recording charges | # 1201 | | |
| | # | | |
| | # | | |
| | # | | |
| | # | | |
| | # | | |
| | # | | |
| | # | | |
| | **Total** | | |
| | **Increase between GFE and HUD-1 Charges** | $ or | % |

| Charges That Can Change | | Good Faith Estimate | HUD-1 |
|---|---|---|---|
| Initial deposit for your escrow account | # 1001 | | |
| Daily interest charges $ /day | # 901 | | |
| Homeowner's insurance | # 903 | | |
| | # | | |
| | # | | |
| | # | | |

**Loan Terms**

| | |
|---|---|
| Your initial loan amount is | $ |
| Your loan term is | years |
| Your initial interest rate is | % |
| Your initial monthly amount owed for principal, interest, and any mortgage insurance is | $ includes<br>☐ Principal<br>☐ Interest<br>☐ Mortgage Insurance |
| Can your interest rate rise? | ☐ No ☐ Yes, it can rise to a maximum of %. The first change will be on and can change again every after . Every change date, your interest rate can increase or decrease by %. Over the life of the loan, your interest rate is guaranteed to never be **lower** than % or **higher** than %. |
| Even if you make payments on time, can your loan balance rise? | ☐ No ☐ Yes, it can rise to a maximum of $ |
| Even if you make payments on time, can your monthly amount owed for principal, interest, and mortgage insurance rise? | ☐ No ☐ Yes, the first increase can be on and the monthly amount owed can rise to $ . The maximum it can ever rise to is $ . |
| Does your loan have a prepayment penalty? | ☐ No ☐ Yes, your maximum prepayment penalty is $ |
| Does your loan have a balloon payment? | ☐ No ☐ Yes, you have a balloon payment of $ due in years on . |
| Total monthly amount owed including escrow account payments | ☐ You do not have a monthly escrow payment for items, such as property taxes and homeowner's insurance. You must pay these items directly yourself.<br>☐ You have an additional monthly escrow payment of $ that results in a total initial monthly amount owed of $ . This includes principal, interest, any mortagage insurance and any items checked below:<br>☐ Property taxes ☐ Homeowner's insurance<br>☐ Flood insurance ☐<br>☐ ☐ |

**Note:** If you have any questions about the Settlement Charges and Loan Terms listed on this form, please contact your lender.

# Appendix C: Promissory Note Secured by Deed of Trust

# PROMISSORY NOTE SECURED BY DEED OF TRUST

$__________________ ______________, Arizona Date: ______________

For value received, ________________________________________________ maker,

promises to pay to ________________________________________________, holder

or order, the sum of ______________________________________________ DOLLARS

payable as follows:

**Payments:**
Payable in regular monthly payments of $__________________, or more, on or before the _____ day of every month beginning ________________ , with interest on all unpaid principal at the rate of ______% per annum from ______________ , the interest to be first deducted from the regular payment(s) and the remainder to be applied upon the principal.

**Late Charge:**
Any above noted payment which is at least ________ days past due, shall be subject to a late charge of $_________. If said late charge is not paid with the delinquent payment, said late payment shall be accepted by the Servicing Agent and the unpaid late charge(s) shall be accumulated as a separate balance that shall not accrue interest.

If the final payment is late, then the late fee per day will be $_____________.

This note may be prepaid in part or in full without pre-payment penalty.

**Due on Sale:**
It is understood and agreed by the parties hereto that the maker shall not assign or otherwise transfer any right, title or interest in or to these premises or this encumbrance during the life of this encumbrance, without the written consent of the holder to such assignment or transfer. In the event of such assignment or transfer without written consent, the entire unpaid principal balance, accrued late penalties and all accrued interest shall, at the option of the holder, become all due and payable.

Should default be made in payment of any payment when due, the whole sum of the principal and interest shall become immediately due at the option of the holder of this note.

Principal and interest payable in lawful money of the United States.

The makers and endorsers hereof waive presentment, demand, notice of dishonor and protest.

If suit be brought to recover on this note, the Maker (Payor) agrees to pay such sum as the Court may fix as attorney's fees.

This Note is secured by a Deed of Trust, of even date herewith, upon real property.

**Having reviewed, accepted, and approved this Note with all its terms and conditions, this Note shall supercede any and all other agreements, and is hereby accepted in its final form.**

ACCEPTED AND APPROVED:

______________________________
Maker (Payor)

______________________________
Maker (Payor)

______________________________
Holder (Payee)

______________________________
Holder (Payee)

DO NOT DESTROY THIS NOTE

**Do Not Destroy this original Note: When paid, this original note, together with the Deed of Trust securing same must be surrendered to Trustee for Cancellation and retention before reconveyance will be made.**

# Appendix D: Note & Deed of Trust Purchase Agreement

THIS IS A SAMPLE DOCUMENT ONLY AND IS NOT INTENDED FOR USE.

Disclaimer. We are not attorneys and not licensed to advise you on the law or prepare legal forms for you. Please have an attorney or title company (if applicable) prepare important legal documents.

**NOTE & DEED OF TRUST**

**PURCHASE AGREEMENT**

**(Without Recourse)**

___ ____, 20__

**(1)** **DESCRIPTION**. The undersigned Purchaser, and/or assigns, hereby agrees to purchase, and the undersigned Seller hereby agrees to sell and assign, without recourse as to the future financial performance of the Grantor(s), that certain Note and Deed of Trust described as follows:

**Date of Note:** _, 20

**Payor:**

**Payee:**

**Original Principal Amount:** $

**Current Balance:** $

**Interest Rate:** _%

**Amortization Period:**

**Balloon:**

**Balloon Date:** _, 20

**Balloon Amount:** $

**Monthly Payments:**

**Payment Amount:** $

**Due Date of Payments:**



Source: www.mortgage-investments.com

**1st Payment Made:** _, 20

**Last Payment Made:** _, 20

**Next Payment Due:** , 20

**Number of Payments Made:**

**Payments Remaining:**

**Date of Deed of Trust:___________**, 20

**Recording Date of Trust Deed:** , 20

**Place of Recording:**

**Book & Page:** BK_PG(S)

**Type of Real Estate:**

**Address of Real Estate:**

**Legal Description of**

**Real Estate:** See Attached Exhibit "A"



The Seller warrants and represents that all of the above information is true and correct. The security interest described above shall also be assigned to the Purchaser herein.

**(2) PRICE AND FINANCING.** The purchase price for the above-described Note and Deed of Trust shall be: $_, payable as follows:_. This Agreement is contingent upon Purchaser obtaining financing to purchase the Seller's interest in the aforesaid Note and Deed of Trust, upon financing terms satisfactory to Purchaser.

**(3) INTERIM PAYMENT RECEIPTS.** Seller shall keep any payments that are received during the pendency of this Agreement; however, any such payments shall be deducted from Seller's proceeds at time of closing.

**(4) REQUIRED DOCUMENTATION.** Seller agrees to provide to Purchaser, within 10 (ten) days of the date of this Agreement, the following "checked" (X) documents:

(X) Copy of Original Note

(X) Copy of Original Recorded Deed of Trust

(X) Amortization Table

(X) Title Policy (ALTA Loan Policy Commitment)*

(X) Copy of Hazard Insurance Policy

(X) Credit Report on Payor of Note*

(or Credit Report Authorization)

(X) Payment History (Affidavit Form)*

(X) Copy of all Underlying Notes, Deed of Trusts, and/or other Liens, along with payoff amounts for each

(X) Appraisal of Real Estate*

(X) Copy of Original Closing Statement

(X) Executed Grantor Estoppel Affidavit*

(X) Executed Beneficiary Estoppel Affidavit*

(X) Picture of Real Estate

(X) Corporate/Partnership Resolution, if applicable

( )

( )

------------

* Purchaser to obtain or prepare

------------

Seller agrees to provide original Note, Deed of Trust and Closing Statement at closing.

**(5) <u>REVIEW AND INSPECTION CONTINGENCY</u>.** This Agreement is contingent, at the exclusive option of Purchaser only, upon the receipt and satisfactory review of the above-checked items and upon a physical inspection of the real estate securing the aforesaid Note and Deed of Trust.

**(6) CLOSING.** The parties agree that the Closing for the transaction contemplated herein shall occur on or before 15 (fifteen) business days after receipt of all of the above-checked items and completion of the physical inspection of the real estate. The Closing shall be held at a title company of the Purchaser's choosing located in or near the County of , State of , or at such other place as may be designated by the parties hereto.

**(7) COSTS.** The Purchaser shall be responsible for all costs of Closing, including but not limited to: credit report fees, appraisal fees, attorney fees (exclusive of attorney fees incurred by Seller on his own behalf), title examination, title insurance and binder/commitment fees, and any other costs incident to the Closing of the transaction contemplated herein; provided, however, in the event that the property does not appraise at a fair market value of at least $_, and/or in the event that the title examination discloses any defects or other liens or encumbrances not previously disclosed in writing to the Purchaser, then the Seller shall reimburse Purchaser for all costs incurred pursuant to this Agreement. To ensure Seller's performance hereunder, Seller shall deposit a "Commitment Application Fee" of $ 350.00 with Purchaser, said fee to be refunded in full to Seller upon the successful closing of the transaction specified in this Agreement; otherwise said fee shall be retained by Purchaser and applied toward the costs which Purchaser may have incurred hereunder.

**(8) SECURITY INTEREST.** To secure Purchaser's interest in and under this Agreement, Seller hereby grants a security interest in the Deed of Trust and Note described in paragraph (1) of this Agreement; Seller further agrees to execute any and all documents now or hereafter required to fully perfect Purchaser's security interest and/or to fully consummate the transaction contemplated herein.



**(9) CANCELLATION FEE.** Should the Seller wish to cancel this Agreement prior to Closing, Seller paying to the Purchaser by means of a certified check, cashier's check or money order, an amount equal to 5% of the current balance due on the Note as specified in Paragraph (1) herein, plus any costs incurred or advanced by Purchaser, including earnest monies. Upon receipt of said sum by Purchaser, all rights and interest in and under this Agreement shall be extinguished forever, and Seller and Purchaser shall both be released of any and all obligations or liabilities hereunder.

**(10) DEFAULT.** Should Seller default under this Agreement, Seller shall be liable to Purchaser for all expenses, damages, losses, attorneys fees, and other costs which Purchaser may incur, in addition to the cancellation fee stated in paragraph (9).

**(11) SELLER'S REPRESENTATIONS AND WARRANTIES.** The Seller hereby covenants, represents and warrants as follows:

(a) That the Deed of Trust is a good and valid instrument and constitutes a valid lien against the real property described therein.

(b) That the Seller is vested with a full and absolute title to said Deed of Trust and Note and has authority to assign and transfer the same which are presently free and clear of all encumbrances, except:_.

(c) That the real property secured by the Deed of Trust has a fair market value of at least $_.

(d) That the original principal face amount of the Deed of Trust and Note has been advanced to or on behalf of the Grantor; that the Grantor received consideration for the Note and Deed of Trust; and that there are no defaults existing at the present time under any of the covenants contained in the said Deed of Trust and Note except the following:_.

(e) That the Deed of Trust and Note were not originated or closed in a manner which violated, or now violates, any Federal, State or Local laws, ordinances, regulations or rulings including, without limitation, Federal and State truth-in-lending laws and any other consumer protection laws, any applicable State usury laws, the requirements of the Real Estate Settlement Procedures Act of 1974, the applicable requirements of the Servicemen's Readjustment Act of 1944, and the National Housing Act.



(f) That there are no undisclosed agreements between the Grantor and the Seller concerning any facts or conditions whether past, present or future which might in any way affect the obligations of the Grantor(s) to make timely payments thereon.

(g) That the Seller has no knowledge of any valid legal defenses which would adversely affect the collectibility or enforceability of the Deed of Trust and/or Note.

(h) That the Deed of Trust and Note documents were executed by person(s) purported to be the Grantor(s) and contain no forged or unauthorized signatures, and that the parties named therein were of full age and capacity to contract.

(i) That the Note and Deed of Trust and any other documents, instruments, or records representing, evidencing, or relating thereto, are true, correct, undisputed, and reflect full, correct, and accurate information as to the balance and the status thereof; and that no credit heretofore has been given the Grantor(s) which was gratuitous or was given for a payment made by an employee or agent of the Seller, or which has arisen from a renewal granted for the purpose of concealing or restructuring a delinquency.

(j) That the Deed of Trust and Note are free of the claim or defense of usury and free from any set-off, claim, counterclaim, or defense of any nature whatsoever; that no settlement, payment or compromise has been made with respect to the Deed of Trust and Note; and that no special promise or consideration has been made to the Grantor.

(k) That all other information contained within this Agreement is true, correct, and accurate, in all respects.

**(13) INDEMNIFICATION.** Seller agrees to indemnify and save Purchaser harmless from and against any and all loss, damage, liability and expense (including its reasonable attorney's fees and cost of litigation) sustained or incurred by Purchaser arising out of, or based upon, the inaccuracy or breach of any warranty or representation made by Seller or its agent(s) under this Agreement or of any covenant to be performed by Seller under this Agreement.



**(14) SOLE AGREEMENT.** This Agreement sets forth the entire agreement of the parties with respect to the subject matter hereof and it supersedes and cancels any and all prior negotiations, arrangements, agreements, and understandings, whether oral or written between the parties respecting the subject matter hereof. This Agreement shall survive the Closing.

**(15) TIME AND BINDING EFFECT.** Time shall always be of the essence and this Agreement shall inure and be binding upon the respective heirs, representatives, successors and assigns of the parties hereto.

**(16) ASSIGNMENT WITHOUT RECOURSE.** The Seller agrees to sell and assign the said Note and Deed of Trust without recourse as to the future financial performance of the Grantor(s) and assumes no responsibility or liability relating thereto. However, as to all other terms, conditions, representatives, warranties, and covenants of this Agreement, the Seller agrees to assume personal responsibility and liability therefore.

**(17) DISCLAIMER.** The parties hereto acknowledge that the Purchaser is NOT an agent of the Seller; nor does the Purchaser have any fiduciary obligation to the Seller. The Purchaser is acting as an independent investor and/or dealer in this transaction, with the expectation of profit; the Seller disclaims any representative relationship and disclaims any interest in the Purchaser's profit.

**(18) <u>OTHER TERMS, CONDITIONS, OR CONTINGENCIES</u>:**

**IN WITNESS WHEREOF**, this Agreement was executed by the parties hereto on the date first above mentioned.

**SIGNED:**

**BUYER(S):**

-

**Witness**

-

**Witness**

-

**Witness**

-

**SELLER(S):**



-

**Witness**

-

**Witness**

-

**Witness**

**Address of Seller(s):**

**Phone:**

-

**Address of Buyer(s):**

**Phone:**

(State of , County of ) SS:

Before me, a Notary Public in and for said state and county, personally came , the Buyer in the above instrument, who acknowledged the execution of same to be (his, her) free and voluntary act and deed.

In testimony whereof, I have hereunto subscribed my name and affixed my notarial seal at , , on this day of , 20.

Notary Public

(Seal)

(Exp. Date)

(State of , County of ) SS:



-

Before me, a Notary Public in and for said state and county, personally came , the Buyer in the above instrument, who acknowledged the execution of same to be (his, her) free and voluntary act and deed.

In testimony whereof, I have hereunto subscribed my name and affixed my notarial seal at , , on this day of , 20 .

(Seal) Notary Public

(Exp. Date)

(State of , County of ) SS:

Before me, a Notary Public in and for said state and county, personally came , the Seller in the above instrument, who acknowledged the execution of same to be (his, her) free and voluntary act and deed.

In testimony whereof, I have hereunto subscribed my name and affixed my notarial seal at , , on this day of , 20 .

(Seal) Notary Public

(Exp. Date)

(State of , County of ) SS:

-

Before me, a Notary Public in and for said state and county, personally came , the Seller in the above instrument, who acknowledged the execution of same to be (his, her) free and voluntary act and deed.

In testimony whereof, I have hereunto subscribed my name and affixed my notarial seal at , , on this day of , 20 .

(Seal) Notary Public

(Exp. Date)

**EXHIBIT A**

(Legal Description of Mortgaged Property)

# Appendix E: Note & Mortgage Purchase Agreement

THIS IS A SAMPLE DOCUMENT ONLY AND IS NOT INTENDED FOR USE.

Disclaimer. We are not attorneys and not licensed to advise you on the law or prepare legal forms for you. Please have an attorney or title company (if applicable) prepare important legal documents.

**NOTE & MORTGAGE**

**PURCHASE AGREEMENT**

**(Without Recourse)**

___ ____, 20__

**(1) DESCRIPTION**. The undersigned Purchaser, and/or assigns, hereby agrees to purchase, and the undersigned Seller hereby agrees to sell and assign, without recourse as to the future financial performance of the mortgagor(s), that certain Note and Mortgage described as follows:

**Date of Note:** _, 20

**Payor:**

**Payee:**

**Original Principal Amount:** $

**Current Balance:** $

**Interest Rate:** _%

**Amortization Period:**

**Balloon:**

**Balloon Date:** _, 20

**Balloon Amount:** $

**Monthly Payments:**

**Payment Amount:** $

**Due Date of Payments:**



Source: www.mortgage-investments.com

**1st Payment Made:** _, 20

**Last Payment Made:** _, 20

**Next Payment Due:** , 20

**Number of Payments Made:**

**Payments Remaining:**

**Date of Mortgage:** ______________, 20

**Recording Date of Mortgage:**______, 20

**Place of Recording:**

**Book & Page:** BK_PG(S)

**Type of Real Estate:**

**Address of Real Estate:**

**Legal Description of**

**Real Estate:** See Attached Exhibit "A"



The Seller warrants and represents that all of the above information is true and correct. The security interest described above shall also be assigned to the Purchaser herein.

**(2) PRICE AND FINANCING.** The purchase price for the above-described Note and Mortgage shall be: $_, payable as follows:_. This Agreement is contingent upon Purchaser obtaining financing to purchase the Seller's interest in the aforesaid Note and Mortgage, upon financing terms satisfactory to Purchaser.

**(3) INTERIM PAYMENT RECEIPTS.** Seller shall keep any payments that are received during the pendency of this Agreement; however, any such payments shall be deducted from Seller's proceeds at time of closing.

**(4) REQUIRED DOCUMENTATION.** Seller agrees to provide to Purchaser, within 10 (ten) days of the date of this Agreement, the following "checked" (X) documents:

(X) Copy of Original Note

(X) Copy of Original Recorded Mortgage

(X) Amortization Table

(X) Title Policy (ALTA Loan Policy Commitment)*

(X) Copy of Hazard Insurance Policy

(X) Credit Report on Payor of Note*

(or Credit Report Authorization)

(X) Payment History (Affidavit Form)*

(X) Copy of all Underlying Notes, Mortgages, and/or other Liens, along with payoff amounts for each

(X) Appraisal of Real Estate*

(X) Copy of Original Closing Statement

(X) Executed Mortgagor Estoppel Affidavit*

(X) Executed Mortgagee Estoppel Affidavit*

(X) Picture of Real Estate

(X) Corporate/Partnership Resolution, if applicable

( )

( )

------------

* Purchaser to obtain or prepare

------------

Seller agrees to provide original Note, Mortgage and Closing Statement at closing.

**(5)** **<u>REVIEW AND INSPECTION CONTINGENCY</u>.** This Agreement is contingent, at the exclusive option of Purchaser only, upon the receipt and satisfactory review of the above-checked items and upon a physical inspection of the real estate securing the aforesaid Note and Mortgage.

**(6) CLOSING.** The parties agree that the Closing for the transaction contemplated herein shall occur on or before 15 (fifteen) business days after receipt of all of the above-checked items and completion of the physical inspection of the real estate. The Closing shall be held at a title company of the Purchaser's choosing located in or near the County of , State of , or at such other place as may be designated by the parties hereto.

**(7) COSTS.** The Purchaser shall be responsible for all costs of Closing, including but not limited to: credit report fees, appraisal fees, attorney fees (exclusive of attorney fees incurred by Seller on his own behalf), title examination, title insurance and binder/commitment fees, and any other costs incident to the Closing of the transaction contemplated herein; provided, however, in the event that the property does not appraise at a fair market value of at least $_, and/or in the event that the title examination discloses any defects or other liens or encumbrances not previously disclosed in writing to the Purchaser, then the Seller shall reimburse Purchaser for all costs incurred pursuant to this Agreement. To ensure Seller's performance hereunder, Seller shall deposit a "Commitment Application Fee" of $ 350.00 with Purchaser, said fee to be refunded in full to Seller upon the successful closing of the transaction specified in this Agreement; otherwise said fee shall be retained by Purchaser and applied toward the costs which Purchaser may have incurred hereunder.

**(8) SECURITY INTEREST.** To secure Purchaser's interest in and under this Agreement, Seller hereby grants a security interest in the Mortgage and Note described in paragraph (1) of this Agreement; Seller further agrees to execute any and all documents now or hereafter required to fully perfect Purchaser's security interest and/or to fully consummate the transaction contemplated herein.

**(9) CANCELLATION FEE.** Should the Seller wish to cancel this Agreement prior to Closing, Seller paying to the Purchaser by means of a certified check, cashier's check or money order, an amount equal to 5% of the current balance due on the Note as specified in Paragraph (1) herein, plus any costs incurred or advanced by Purchaser, including earnest monies. Upon receipt of said sum by Purchaser, all rights and interest in and under this Agreement shall be extinguished forever, and Seller and Purchaser shall both be released of any and all obligations or liabilities hereunder.

**(10) DEFAULT.** Should Seller default under this Agreement, Seller shall be liable to Purchaser for all expenses, damages, losses, attorneys fees, and other costs which Purchaser may incur, in addition to the cancellation fee stated in paragraph (9).

**(11) SELLER'S REPRESENTATIONS AND WARRANTIES.** The Seller hereby covenants, represents and warrants as follows:

(a) That the Mortgage is a good and valid instrument and constitutes a valid lien against the real property described therein.

(b) That the Seller is vested with a full and absolute title to said Mortgage and Note and has authority to assign and transfer the same which are presently free and clear of all encumbrances, except:_.

(c) That the real property secured by the Mortgage has a fair market value of at least $_.

(d) That the original principal face amount of the Mortgage and Note has been advanced to or on behalf of the mortgagor; that the mortgagor received consideration for the Note and Mortgage; and that there are no defaults existing at the present time under any of the covenants contained in the said Mortgage and Note except the following:_.

(e) That the Mortgage and Note were not originated or closed in a manner which violated, or now violates, any Federal, State or Local laws, ordinances, regulations or rulings including, without limitation, Federal and State truth-in-lending laws and any other consumer protection laws, any applicable State usury laws, the requirements of the Real Estate Settlement Procedures Act of 1974, the applicable requirements of the Servicemen's Readjustment Act of 1944, and the National Housing Act.



(f) That there are no undisclosed agreements between the mortgagor and the Seller concerning any facts or conditions whether past, present or future which might in any way affect the obligations of the mortgagor(s) to make timely payments thereon.

(g) That the Seller has no knowledge of any valid legal defenses which would adversely affect the collectibility or enforceability of the Mortgage and/or Note.

(h) That the Mortgage and Note documents were executed by person(s) purported to be the mortgagor(s) and contain no forged or unauthorized signatures, and that the parties named therein were of full age and capacity to contract.

(i) That the Note and Mortgage and any other documents, instruments, or records representing, evidencing, or relating thereto, are true, correct, undisputed, and reflect full, correct, and accurate information as to the balance and the status thereof; and that no credit heretofore has been given the mortgagor(s) which was gratuitous or was given for a payment made by an employee or agent of the Seller, or which has arisen from a renewal granted for the purpose of concealing or restructuring a delinquency.

(j) That the Mortgage and Note are free of the claim or defense of usury and free from any set-off, claim, counterclaim, or defense of any nature whatsoever; that no settlement, payment or compromise has been made with respect to the Mortgage and Note; and that no special promise or consideration has been made to the mortgagor.

(k) That all other information contained within this Agreement is true, correct, and accurate, in all respects.

**(13) INDEMNIFICATION.** Seller agrees to indemnify and save Purchaser harmless from and against any and all loss, damage, liability and expense (including its reasonable attorney's fees and cost of litigation) sustained or incurred by Purchaser arising out of, or based upon, the inaccuracy or breach of any warranty or representation made by Seller or its agent(s) under this Agreement or of any covenant to be performed by Seller under this Agreement.



**(14) SOLE AGREEMENT.** This Agreement sets forth the entire agreement of the parties with respect to the subject matter hereof and it supersedes and cancels any and all prior negotiations, arrangements, agreements, and understandings, whether oral or written between the parties respecting the subject matter hereof. This Agreement shall survive the Closing.

**(15) TIME AND BINDING EFFECT.** Time shall always be of the essence and this Agreement shall inure and be binding upon the respective heirs, representatives, successors and assigns of the parties hereto.

**(16) ASSIGNMENT WITHOUT RECOURSE.** The Seller agrees to sell and assign the said Note and Mortgage without recourse as to the future financial performance of the mortgagor(s) and assumes no responsibility or liability relating thereto. However, as to all other terms, conditions, representatives, warranties, and covenants of this Agreement, the Seller agrees to assume personal responsibility and liability therefore.

**(17) DISCLAIMER.** The parties hereto acknowledge that the Purchaser is NOT an agent of the Seller; nor does the Purchaser have any fiduciary obligation to the Seller. The Purchaser is acting as an independent investor and/or dealer in this transaction, with the expectation of profit; the Seller disclaims any representative relationship and disclaims any interest in the Purchaser's profit.

**(18) OTHER TERMS, CONDITIONS, OR CONTINGENCIES:**

-

-

-

-

-

-

-

**IN WITNESS WHEREOF**, this Agreement was executed by the parties hereto on the date first above mentioned.

**SIGNED:**

**BUYER(S):**

-

**Witness**

-

**Witness**

-

**Witness**

-

**SELLER(S):**

-

**Witness**

-

**Witness**

-

**Witness**

**Address of Seller(s):**

**Phone:**

-

**Address of Buyer(s):**

**Phone:**

(State of , County of ) SS:

Before me, a Notary Public in and for said state and county, personally came , the Buyer in the above instrument, who acknowledged the execution of same to be (his, her) free and voluntary act and deed.

In testimony whereof, I have hereunto subscribed my name and affixed my notarial seal at , , on this day of , 20.

Notary Public

(Seal)

(Exp. Date)

(State of , County of ) SS:

-

Before me, a Notary Public in and for said state and county, personally came , the Buyer in the above instrument, who acknowledged the execution of same to be (his, her) free and voluntary act and deed.

In testimony whereof, I have hereunto subscribed my name and affixed my notarial seal at , , on this day of , 20 .

(Seal) Notary Public

(Exp. Date)

(State of , County of ) SS:

Before me, a Notary Public in and for said state and county, personally came , the Seller in the above instrument, who acknowledged the execution of same to be (his, her) free and voluntary act and deed.

In testimony whereof, I have hereunto subscribed my name and affixed my notarial seal at , , on this day of , 20 .

(Seal) Notary Public

(Exp. Date)

(State of , County of ) SS:

-

Before me, a Notary Public in and for said state and county, personally came , the Seller in the above instrument, who acknowledged the execution of same to be (his, her) free and voluntary act and deed.

In testimony whereof, I have hereunto subscribed my name and affixed my notarial seal at , , on this day of , 20 .

(Seal) Notary Public

(Exp. Date)

**EXHIBIT A**

(Legal Description of Mortgaged Property)

# Appendix F: Fixed/Adjustable Rate Note

# FIXED/ADJUSTABLE RATE NOTE

**(LIBOR One-Year Index (As Published In *The Wall Street Journal*)–Rate Caps)**

**THIS NOTE PROVIDES FOR A CHANGE IN MY FIXED INTEREST RATE TO AN ADJUSTABLE INTEREST RATE. THIS NOTE LIMITS THE AMOUNT MY ADJUSTABLE INTEREST RATE CAN CHANGE AT ANY ONE TIME AND THE MAXIMUM RATE I MUST PAY.**

____________________, ______ ____________________ ____________________
[City] [State]

______________________________________________________________
[Property Address]

## 1. BORROWER'S PROMISE TO PAY

In return for a loan that I have received, I promise to pay U.S. $______________ (this amount is called "Principal"), plus interest, to the order of Lender. Lender is ______________________________. I will make all payments under this Note in the form of cash, check or money order.

I understand that Lender may transfer this Note. Lender or anyone who takes this Note by transfer and who is entitled to receive payments under this Note is called the "Note Holder."

## 2. INTEREST

Interest will be charged on unpaid principal until the full amount of Principal has been paid. I will pay interest at a yearly rate of __________%. The interest rate I will pay may change in accordance with Section 4 of this Note.

The interest rate required by this Section 2 and Section 4 of this Note is the rate I will pay both before and after any default described in Section 7(B) of this Note.

## 3. PAYMENTS

### (A) Time and Place of Payments

I will pay principal and interest by making a payment every month.

I will make my monthly payments on the first day of each month beginning on __________________, ____. I will make these payments every month until I have paid all of the principal and interest and any other charges described below that I may owe under this Note. Each monthly payment will be applied as of its scheduled due date and will be applied to interest before Principal. If, on __________________, ____, I still owe amounts under this Note, I will pay those amounts in full on that date, which is called the "Maturity Date."

I will make my monthly payments at ______________________________________________ or at a different place if required by the Note Holder.

### (B) Amount of My Initial Monthly Payments

Each of my initial monthly payments will be in the amount of U.S. $______________. This amount may change.

**(C) Monthly Payment Changes**

Changes in my monthly payment will reflect changes in the unpaid principal of my loan and in the interest rate that I must pay. The Note Holder will determine my new interest rate and the changed amount of my monthly payment in accordance with Section 4 of this Note.

**4. ADJUSTABLE INTEREST RATE AND MONTHLY PAYMENT CHANGES**

**(A) Change Dates**

The initial fixed interest rate I will pay will change to an adjustable interest rate on the first day of ____________________, ____, and the adjustable interest rate I will pay may change on that day every 12th month thereafter. The date on which my initial fixed interest rate changes to an adjustable interest rate, and each date on which my adjustable interest rate could change, is called a "Change Date."

**(B) The Index**

Beginning with the first Change Date, my adjustable interest rate will be based on an Index. The "Index" is the average of interbank offered rates for one-year U.S. dollar-denominated deposits in the London market ("LIBOR"), as published in *The Wall Street Journal*. The most recent Index figure available as of the date 45 days before each Change Date is called the "Current Index."

If the Index is no longer available, the Note Holder will choose a new index that is based upon comparable information. The Note Holder will give me notice of this choice.

**(C) Calculation of Changes**

Before each Change Date, the Note Holder will calculate my new interest rate by adding ______________ percentage points (___________%) to the Current Index. The Note Holder will then round the result of this addition to the nearest one-eighth of one percentage point (0.125%). Subject to the limits stated in Section 4(D) below, this rounded amount will be my new interest rate until the next Change Date.

The Note Holder will then determine the amount of the monthly payment that would be sufficient to repay the unpaid principal that I am expected to owe at the Change Date in full on the Maturity Date at my new interest rate in substantially equal payments. The result of this calculation will be the new amount of my monthly payment.

**(D) Limits on Interest Rate Changes**

The interest rate I am required to pay at the first Change Date will not be greater than ___________% or less than ___________%. Thereafter, my adjustable interest rate will never be increased or decreased on any single Change Date by more than two percentage points from the rate of interest I have been paying for the preceding 12 months. My interest rate will never be greater than ___________%.

**(E) Effective Date of Changes**

My new interest rate will become effective on each Change Date. I will pay the amount of my new monthly payment beginning on the first monthly payment date after the Change Date until the amount of my monthly payment changes again.

**(F) Notice of Changes**

The Note Holder will deliver or mail to me a notice of any changes in my initial fixed interest rate to an adjustable interest rate and of any changes in my adjustable interest rate before the effective date of any change. The notice will include the amount of my monthly payment, any information required by law to be given to me and also the title and telephone number of a person who will answer any question I may have regarding the notice.

**5. BORROWER'S RIGHT TO PREPAY**

I have the right to make payments of Principal at any time before they are due. A payment of Principal only is known as a "Prepayment." When I make a Prepayment, I will tell the Note Holder in writing that I am doing so. I may not designate a payment as a Prepayment if I have not made all the monthly payments due under this Note.

I may make a full Prepayment or partial Prepayments without paying any Prepayment charge. The Note Holder will use my Prepayments to reduce the amount of Principal that I owe under this Note. However, the Note Holder may apply my Prepayment to the accrued and unpaid interest on the Prepayment amount before applying my Prepayment to reduce the Principal amount of this Note. If I make a partial Prepayment, there will be no changes in the due dates of my monthly payments unless the Note Holder agrees in writing to those changes. My partial Prepayment may reduce the amount of my monthly payments after the first Change Date following my partial Prepayment. However, any reduction due to my partial Prepayment may be offset by an interest rate increase.

**6. LOAN CHARGES**

If a law, which applies to this loan and which sets maximum loan charges, is finally interpreted so that the interest or other loan charges collected or to be collected in connection with this loan exceed the permitted limits, then: (a) any such loan charge shall be reduced by the amount necessary to reduce the charge to the permitted limit; and (b) any sums already collected from me that exceeded permitted limits will be refunded to me. The Note Holder may choose to make this refund by reducing the Principal I owe under this Note or by making a direct payment to me. If a refund reduces Principal, the reduction will be treated as a partial Prepayment.

**7. BORROWER'S FAILURE TO PAY AS REQUIRED**

**(A) Late Charges for Overdue Payments**

If the Note Holder has not received the full amount of any monthly payment by the end of __________ calendar days after the date it is due, I will pay a late charge to the Note Holder. The amount of the charge will be __________% of my overdue payment of principal and interest. I will pay this late charge promptly but only once on each late payment.

**(B) Default**

If I do not pay the full amount of each monthly payment on the date it is due, I will be in default.

**(C) Notice of Default**

If I am in default, the Note Holder may send me a written notice telling me that if I do not pay the overdue amount by a certain date, the Note Holder may require me to pay immediately the full amount of Principal that has not been paid and all the interest that I owe on that amount. That date must be at least 30 days after the date on which the notice is mailed to me or delivered by other means.

**(D) No Waiver By Note Holder**

Even if, at a time when I am in default, the Note Holder does not require me to pay immediately in full as described above, the Note Holder will still have the right to do so if I am in default at a later time.

**(E) Payment of Note Holder's Costs and Expenses**

If the Note Holder has required me to pay immediately in full as described above, the Note Holder will have the right to be paid back by me for all of its costs and expenses in enforcing this Note to the extent not prohibited by applicable law. Those expenses include, for example, reasonable attorneys' fees.

**8. GIVING OF NOTICES**

Unless applicable law requires a different method, any notice that must be given to me under this Note will be given by delivering it or by mailing it by first class mail to me at the Property Address above or at a different address if I give the Note Holder a notice of my different address.

Unless the Note Holder requires a different method, any notice that must be given to the Note Holder under this Note will be given by mailing it by first class mail to the Note Holder at the address stated in Section 3(A) above or at a different address if I am given a notice of that different address.

**9. OBLIGATIONS OF PERSONS UNDER THIS NOTE**

If more than one person signs this Note, each person is fully and personally obligated to keep all of the promises made in this Note, including the promise to pay the full amount owed. Any person who is a guarantor, surety or endorser of this Note is also obligated to do these things. Any person who takes over these obligations, including the obligations of a guarantor, surety or endorser of this Note, is also obligated to keep all of the promises made in this Note. The Note Holder may enforce its rights under this Note against each person individually or against all of us together. This means that any one of us may be required to pay all of the amounts owed under this Note.

**10. WAIVERS**

I and any other person who has obligations under this Note waive the rights of Presentment and Notice of Dishonor. "Presentment" means the right to require the Note Holder to demand payment of amounts due. "Notice of Dishonor" means the right to require the Note Holder to give notice to other persons that amounts due have not been paid.

**11. UNIFORM SECURED NOTE**

This Note is a uniform instrument with limited variations in some jurisdictions. In addition to the protections given to the Note Holder under this Note, a Mortgage, Deed of Trust, or Security Deed (the "Security Instrument"), dated the same date as this Note, protects the Note Holder from possible losses that might result if I do not keep the promises that I make in this Note. That Security Instrument describes how and under what conditions I may be required to make immediate payment in full of all amounts I owe under this Note. Some of those conditions read as follows:

(A) Until my initial fixed interest rate changes to an adjustable interest rate under the terms stated in Section 4 above, Uniform Covenant 18 of the Security Instrument shall read as follows:

> **Transfer of the Property or a Beneficial Interest in Borrower.** As used in this Section 18, "Interest in the Property" means any legal or beneficial interest in the Property, including, but not limited to, those beneficial interests transferred in a bond for deed, contract for deed, installment sales contract or escrow agreement, the intent of which is the transfer of title by Borrower at a future date to a purchaser.
>
> If all or any part of the Property or any Interest in the Property is sold or transferred (or if Borrower is not a natural person and a beneficial interest in Borrower is sold or transferred) without Lender's prior written consent, Lender may require immediate payment in full of all sums secured by this Security Instrument. However, this option shall not be exercised by Lender if such exercise is prohibited by Applicable Law.

If Lender exercises this option, Lender shall give Borrower notice of acceleration. The notice shall provide a period of not less than 30 days from the date the notice is given in accordance with Section 15 within which Borrower must pay all sums secured by this Security Instrument. If Borrower fails to pay these sums prior to the expiration of this period, Lender may invoke any remedies permitted by this Security Instrument without further notice or demand on Borrower.

(B) When my initial fixed interest rate changes to an adjustable interest rate under the terms stated in Section 4 above, Uniform Covenant 18 of the Security Instrument described in Section 11(A) above shall then cease to be in effect, and Uniform Covenant 18 of the Security Instrument shall instead read as follows:

**Transfer of the Property or a Beneficial Interest in Borrower.** As used in this Section 18, "Interest in the Property" means any legal or beneficial interest in the Property, including, but not limited to, those beneficial interests transferred in a bond for deed, contract for deed, installment sales contract or escrow agreement, the intent of which is the transfer of title by Borrower at a future date to a purchaser.

If all or any part of the Property or any Interest in the Property is sold or transferred (or if Borrower is not a natural person and a beneficial interest in Borrower is sold or transferred) without Lender's prior written consent, Lender may require immediate payment in full of all sums secured by this Security Instrument. However, this option shall not be exercised by Lender if such exercise is prohibited by Applicable Law. Lender also shall not exercise this option if: (a) Borrower causes to be submitted to Lender information required by Lender to evaluate the intended transferee as if a new loan were being made to the transferee; and (b) Lender reasonably determines that Lender's security will not be impaired by the loan assumption and that the risk of a breach of any covenant or agreement in this Security Instrument is acceptable to Lender.

To the extent permitted by Applicable Law, Lender may charge a reasonable fee as a condition to Lender's consent to the loan assumption. Lender also may require the transferee to sign an assumption agreement that is acceptable to Lender and that obligates the transferee to keep all the promises and agreements made in the Note and in this Security Instrument. Borrower will continue to be obligated under the Note and this Security Instrument unless Lender releases Borrower in writing.

If Lender exercises the option to require immediate payment in full, Lender shall give Borrower notice of acceleration. The notice shall provide a period of not less than 30 days from the date the notice is given in accordance with Section 15 within which Borrower must pay all sums secured by this Security Instrument. If Borrower fails to pay these sums prior to the expiration of this period, Lender may invoke any remedies permitted by this Security Instrument without further notice or demand on Borrower.

WITNESS THE HAND(S) AND SEAL(S) OF THE UNDERSIGNED.

.................................................................. (Seal)
-Borrower

.................................................................. (Seal)
-Borrower

.................................................................. (Seal)
-Borrower

[Sign Original Only]

# Appendix G: Uniform Residential Loan Application

# Uniform Residential Loan Application

This application is designed to be completed by the applicant(s) with the Lender's assistance. Applicants should complete this form as "Borrower" or "Co-Borrower," as applicable. Co-Borrower information must also be provided (and the appropriate box checked) when ☐ the income or assets of a person other than the Borrower (including the Borrower's spouse) will be used as a basis for loan qualification or ☐ the income or assets of the Borrower's spouse or other person who has community property rights pursuant to state law will not be used as a basis for loan qualification, but his or her liabilities must be considered because the spouse or other person has community property rights pursuant to applicable law and Borrower resides in a community property state, the security property is located in a community property state, or the Borrower is relying on other property located in a community property state as a basis for repayment of the loan.

If this is an application for joint credit, Borrower and Co-Borrower each agree that we intend to apply for joint credit (sign below):

Borrower ______________________ Co-Borrower ______________________

## I. TYPE OF MORTGAGE AND TERMS OF LOAN

| **Mortgage Applied for:** ☐ VA ☐ FHA ☐ Conventional ☐ USDA/Rural Housing Service ☐ Other (explain): | | | Agency Case Number | Lender Case Number |
|---|---|---|---|---|
| Amount $ | Interest Rate % | No. of Months | **Amortization Type:** ☐ Fixed Rate ☐ GPM | ☐ Other (explain): ☐ ARM (type): |

## II. PROPERTY INFORMATION AND PURPOSE OF LOAN

| Subject Property Address (street, city, state & ZIP) | No. of Units |
|---|---|
| Legal Description of Subject Property (attach description if necessary) | Year Built |

| Purpose of Loan ☐ Purchase ☐ Refinance ☐ Construction ☐ Construction-Permanent ☐ Other (explain): | Property will be: ☐ Primary Residence ☐ Secondary Residence ☐ Investment |
|---|---|

***Complete this line if construction or construction-permanent loan.***

| Year Lot Acquired | Original Cost | Amount Existing Liens | (a) Present Value of Lot | (b) Cost of Improvements | Total (a + b) |
|---|---|---|---|---|---|
| | $ | $ | $ | $ | $ |

***Complete this line if this is a refinance loan.***

| Year Acquired | Original Cost | Amount Existing Liens | Purpose of Refinance | Describe Improvements ☐ made ☐ to be made |
|---|---|---|---|---|
| | $ | $ | | Cost: $ |

| Title will be held in what Name(s) | Manner in which Title will be held | Estate will be held in: ☐ Fee Simple ☐ Leasehold (show expiration date) |
|---|---|---|
| Source of Down Payment, Settlement Charges, and/or Subordinate Financing (explain) | | |

## III. BORROWER INFORMATION

| Borrower | | | | Co-Borrower | | | |
|---|---|---|---|---|---|---|---|
| Borrower's Name (include Jr. or Sr. if applicable) | | | | Co-Borrower's Name (include Jr. or Sr. if applicable) | | | |
| Social Security Number | Home Phone (incl. area code) | DOB (mm/dd/yyyy) | Yrs. School | Social Security Number | Home Phone (incl. area code) | DOB (mm/dd/yyyy) | Yrs. School |
| ☐ Married ☐ Unmarried (include single, divorced, widowed) ☐ Separated | | Dependents (not listed by Co-Borrower) no. ages | | ☐ Married ☐ Unmarried (include single, divorced, widowed) ☐ Separated | | Dependents (not listed by Borrower) no. ages | |
| Present Address (street, city, state, ZIP) ☐ Own ☐ Rent ___No. Yrs. | | | | Present Address (street, city, state, ZIP) ☐ Own ☐ Rent ___No. Yrs. | | | |
| Mailing Address, if different from Present Address | | | | Mailing Address, if different from Present Address | | | |

***If residing at present address for less than two years, complete the following:***

| Former Address (street, city, state, ZIP) ☐ Own ☐ Rent ___No. Yrs. | Former Address (street, city, state, ZIP) ☐ Own ☐ Rent ___No. Yrs. |
|---|---|

## IV. EMPLOYMENT INFORMATION

| Borrower | | Co-Borrower | |
|---|---|---|---|
| Name & Address of Employer ☐ Self Employed | Yrs. on this job | Name & Address of Employer ☐ Self Employed | Yrs. on this job |
| | Yrs. employed in this line of work/profession | | Yrs. employed in this line of work/profession |
| Position/Title/Type of Business | Business Phone (incl. area code) | Position/Title/Type of Business | Business Phone (incl. area code) |

***If employed in current position for less than two years or if currently employed in more than one position, complete the following:***

| Borrower | | IV. EMPLOYMENT INFORMATION (cont'd) | | Co-Borrower | |
|---|---|---|---|---|---|
| Name & Address of Employer | ☐ Self Employed | Dates (from – to) | Name & Address of Employer | ☐ Self Employed | Dates (from – to) |
| | | Monthly Income $ | | | Monthly Income $ |
| Position/Title/Type of Business | Business Phone (incl. area code) | | Position/Title/Type of Business | Business Phone (incl. area code) | |
| Name & Address of Employer | ☐ Self Employed | Dates (from – to) | Name & Address of Employer | ☐ Self Employed | Dates (from – to) |
| | | Monthly Income $ | | | Monthly Income $ |
| Position/Title/Type of Business | Business Phone (incl. area code) | | Position/Title/Type of Business | Business Phone (incl. area code) | |

## V. MONTHLY INCOME AND COMBINED HOUSING EXPENSE INFORMATION

| Gross Monthly Income | Borrower | Co-Borrower | Total | Combined Monthly Housing Expense | Present | Proposed |
|---|---|---|---|---|---|---|
| Base Empl. Income* | $ | $ | $ | Rent | $ | |
| Overtime | | | | First Mortgage (P&I) | | $ |
| Bonuses | | | | Other Financing (P&I) | | |
| Commissions | | | | Hazard Insurance | | |
| Dividends/Interest | | | | Real Estate Taxes | | |
| Net Rental Income | | | | Mortgage Insurance | | |
| Other (before completing, see the notice in "describe other income," below) | | | | Homeowner Assn. Dues | | |
| | | | | Other: | | |
| **Total** | $ | $ | $ | **Total** | $ | $ |

* **Self Employed Borrower(s) may be required to provide additional documentation such as tax returns and financial statements.**

**Describe Other Income**

*Notice:* **Alimony, child support, or separate maintenance income need not be revealed if the Borrower (B) or Co-Borrower (C) does not choose to have it considered for repaying this loan.**

| B/C | | Monthly Amount |
|---|---|---|
| | | $ |
| | | |
| | | |

## VI. ASSETS AND LIABILITIES

This Statement and any applicable supporting schedules may be completed jointly by both married and unmarried Co-Borrowers if their assets and liabilities are sufficiently joined so that the Statement can be meaningfully and fairly presented on a combined basis; otherwise, separate Statements and Schedules are required. If the Co-Borrower section was completed about a non-applicant spouse or other person, this Statement and supporting schedules must be completed about that spouse or other person also.

Completed ☐ Jointly ☐ Not Jointly

| ASSETS Description | Cash or Market Value |
|---|---|
| Cash deposit toward purchase held by: | $ |

**Liabilities and Pledged Assets.** List the creditor's name, address, and account number for all outstanding debts, including automobile loans, revolving charge accounts, real estate loans, alimony, child support, stock pledges, etc. Use continuation sheet, if necessary. Indicate by (*) those liabilities, which will be satisfied upon sale of real estate owned or upon refinancing of the subject property.

| *List checking and savings accounts below* | | LIABILITIES | Monthly Payment & Months Left to Pay | Unpaid Balance |
|---|---|---|---|---|
| Name and address of Bank, S&L, or Credit Union | | Name and address of Company | $ Payment/Months | $ |
| Acct. no. | $ | Acct. no. | | |
| Name and address of Bank, S&L, or Credit Union | | Name and address of Company | $ Payment/Months | $ |
| Acct. no. | $ | Acct. no. | | |
| Name and address of Bank, S&L, or Credit Union | | Name and address of Company | $ Payment/Months | $ |
| Acct. no. | $ | Acct. no. | | |

## VI. ASSETS AND LIABILITIES (cont'd)

| | | | | |
|---|---|---|---|---|
| Name and address of Bank, S&L, or Credit Union | | Name and address of Company | $ Payment/Months | $ |
| Acct. no. | $ | Acct. no. | | |
| Stocks & Bonds (Company name/ number & description) | $ | Name and address of Company | $ Payment/Months | $ |
| | | Acct. no. | | |
| Life insurance net cash value | $ | Name and address of Company | $ Payment/Months | $ |
| Face amount: $ | | | | |
| **Subtotal Liquid Assets** | $ | | | |
| Real estate owned (enter market value from schedule of real estate owned) | $ | | | |
| Vested interest in retirement fund | $ | | | |
| Net worth of business(es) owned (attach financial statement) | $ | Acct. no. | | |
| Automobiles owned (make and year) | $ | Alimony/Child Support/Separate Maintenance Payments Owed to: | $ | |
| Other Assets (itemize) | $ | Job-Related Expense (child care, union dues, etc.) | $ | |
| | | **Total Monthly Payments** | $ | |
| **Total Assets a.** | $ | Net Worth (a minus b) ▸ $ | **Total Liabilities b.** | $ |

**Schedule of Real Estate Owned** (If additional properties are owned, use continuation sheet.)

| Property Address (enter S if sold, PS if pending sale or R if rental being held for income) ▼ | | Type of Property | Present Market Value | Amount of Mortgages & Liens | Gross Rental Income | Mortgage Payments | Insurance, Maintenance, Taxes & Misc. | Net Rental Income |
|---|---|---|---|---|---|---|---|---|
| | | | $ | $ | $ | $ | $ | $ |
| | | | | | | | | |
| | | | | | | | | |
| | | Totals | $ | $ | $ | $ | $ | $ |

**List any additional names under which credit has previously been received and indicate appropriate creditor name(s) and account number(s):**

| Alternate Name | Creditor Name | Account Number |
|---|---|---|
| | | |
| | | |

## VII. DETAILS OF TRANSACTION

| | | |
|---|---|---|
| a. | Purchase price | $ |
| b. | Alterations, improvements, repairs | |
| c. | Land (if acquired separately) | |
| d. | Refinance (incl. debts to be paid off) | |
| e. | Estimated prepaid items | |
| f. | Estimated closing costs | |
| g. | PMI, MIP, Funding Fee | |
| h. | Discount (if Borrower will pay) | |
| i. | Total costs (add items a through h) | |

## VIII. DECLARATIONS

| **If you answer "Yes" to any questions a through i, please use continuation sheet for explanation.** | Borrower Yes | Borrower No | Co-Borrower Yes | Co-Borrower No |
|---|---|---|---|---|
| a. Are there any outstanding judgments against you? | □ | □ | □ | □ |
| b. Have you been declared bankrupt within the past 7 years? | □ | □ | □ | □ |
| c. Have you had property foreclosed upon or given title or deed in lieu thereof in the last 7 years? | □ | □ | □ | □ |
| d. Are you a party to a lawsuit? | □ | □ | □ | □ |
| e. Have you directly or indirectly been obligated on any loan which resulted in foreclosure, transfer of title in lieu of foreclosure, or judgment? (This would include such loans as home mortgage loans, SBA loans, home improvement loans, educational loans, manufactured (mobile) home loans, any mortgage, financial obligation, bond, or loan guarantee. If "Yes," provide details, including date, name, and address of Lender, FHA or VA case number, if any, and reasons for the action.) | □ | □ | □ | □ |

| VII. DETAILS OF TRANSACTION | |
|---|---|
| j. Subordinate financing | |
| k. Borrower's closing costs paid by Seller | |
| l. Other Credits (explain) | |
| m. Loan amount (exclude PMI, MIP, Funding Fee financed) | |
| n. PMI, MIP, Funding Fee financed | |
| o. Loan amount (add m & n) | |
| p. Cash from/to Borrower (subtract j, k, l & o from i) | |

**VIII. DECLARATIONS**

| If you answer "Yes" to any questions a through i, please use continuation sheet for explanation. | Borrower Yes | Borrower No | Co-Borrower Yes | Co-Borrower No |
|---|---|---|---|---|
| f. Are you presently delinquent or in default on any Federal debt or any other loan, mortgage, financial obligation, bond, or loan guarantee? | ☐ | ☐ | ☐ | ☐ |
| g. Are you obligated to pay alimony, child support, or separate maintenance? | ☐ | ☐ | ☐ | ☐ |
| h. Is any part of the down payment borrowed? | ☐ | ☐ | ☐ | ☐ |
| i. Are you a co-maker or endorser on a note? | ☐ | ☐ | ☐ | ☐ |
| j. Are you a U.S. citizen? | ☐ | ☐ | ☐ | ☐ |
| k. Are you a permanent resident alien? | ☐ | ☐ | ☐ | ☐ |
| **l. Do you intend to occupy the property as your primary residence?** | ☐ | ☐ | ☐ | ☐ |
| If Yes," complete question m below. | | | | |
| m. Have you had an ownership interest in a property in the last three years? | ☐ | ☐ | ☐ | ☐ |
| (1) What type of property did you own—principal residence (PR), second home (SH), or investment property (IP)? | ____ | | ____ | |
| (2) How did you hold title to the home— by yourself (S), jointly with your spouse (SP), or jointly with another person (O)? | ____ | | ____ | |

**IX. ACKNOWLEDGEMENT AND AGREEMENT**

Each of the undersigned specifically represents to Lender and to Lender's actual or potential agents, brokers, processors, attorneys, insurers, servicers, successors and assigns and agrees and acknowledges that: (1) the information provided in this application is true and correct as of the date set forth opposite my signature and that any intentional or negligent misrepresentation of this information contained in this application may result in civil liability, including monetary damages, to any person who may suffer any loss due to reliance upon any misrepresentation that I have made on this application, and/or in criminal penalties including, but not limited to, fine or imprisonment or both under the provisions of Title 18, United States Code, Sec. 1001, et seq.; (2) the loan requested pursuant to this application (the "Loan") will be secured by a mortgage or deed of trust on the property described in this application; (3) the property will not be used for any illegal or prohibited purpose or use; (4) all statements made in this application are made for the purpose of obtaining a residential mortgage loan; (5) the property will be occupied as indicated in this application; (6) the Lender, its servicers, successors or assigns may retain the original and/or an electronic record of this application, whether or not the Loan is approved; (7) the Lender and its agents, brokers, insurers, servicers, successors, and assigns may continuously rely on the information contained in the application, and I am obligated to amend and/or supplement the information provided in this application if any of the material facts that I have represented herein should change prior to closing of the Loan; (8) in the event that my payments on the Loan become delinquent, the Lender, its servicers, successors or assigns may, in addition to any other rights and remedies that it may have relating to such delinquency, report my name and account information to one or more consumer reporting agencies; (9) ownership of the Loan and/or administration of the Loan account may be transferred with such notice as may be required by law; (10) neither Lender nor its agents, brokers, insurers, servicers, successors or assigns has made any representation or warranty, express or implied, to me regarding the property or the condition or value of the property; and (11) my transmission of this application as an "electronic record" containing my "electronic signature," as those terms are defined in applicable federal and/or state laws (excluding audio and video recordings), or my facsimile transmission of this application containing a facsimile of my signature, shall be as effective, enforceable and valid as if a paper version of this application were delivered containing my original written signature.

Acknowledgement. Each of the undersigned hereby acknowledges that any owner of the Loan, its servicers, successors and assigns, may verify or reverify any information contained in this application or obtain any information or data relating to the Loan, for any legitimate business purpose through any source, including a source named in this application or a consumer reporting agency.

| Borrower's Signature X | Date | Co-Borrower's Signature X | Date |
|---|---|---|---|

**X. INFORMATION FOR GOVERNMENT MONITORING PURPOSES**

The following information is requested by the Federal Government for certain types of loans related to a dwelling in order to monitor the lender's compliance with equal credit opportunity, fair housing and home mortgage disclosure laws. You are not required to furnish this information, but are encouraged to do so. The law provides that a lender may not discriminate either on the basis of this information, or on whether you choose to furnish it. If you furnish the information, please provide both ethnicity and race. For race, you may check more than one designation. If you do not furnish ethnicity, race, or sex, under Federal regulations, this lender is required to note the information on the basis of visual observation and surname if you have made this application in person. If you do not wish to furnish the information, please check the box below. (Lender must review the above material to assure that the disclosures satisfy all requirements to which the lender is subject under applicable state law for the particular type of loan applied for.)

| BORROWER | CO-BORROWER |
|---|---|
| ☐ I do not wish to furnish this information | ☐ I do not wish to furnish this information |
| **Ethnicity:** ☐ Hispanic or Latino ☐ Not Hispanic or Latino | **Ethnicity:** ☐ Hispanic or Latino ☐ Not Hispanic or Latino |
| **Race:** ☐ American Indian or Alaska Native ☐ Asian ☐ Black or African American ☐ Native Hawaiian or Other Pacific Islander ☐ White | **Race:** ☐ American Indian or Alaska Native ☐ Asian ☐ Black or African American ☐ Native Hawaiian or Other Pacific Islander ☐ White |
| **Sex:** ☐ Female ☐ Male | **Sex:** ☐ Female ☐ Male |

**To be Completed by Loan Originator:**
This information was provided:
- ☐ In a face-to-face interview
- ☐ In a telephone interview
- ☐ By the applicant and submitted by fax or mail
- ☐ By the applicant and submitted via e-mail or the Internet

| Loan Originator's Signature X | | Date |
|---|---|---|
| Loan Originator's Name (print or type) | Loan Originator Identifier | Loan Originator's Phone Number (including area code) |
| Loan Origination Company's Name | Loan Origination Company Identifier | Loan Origination Company's Address |

**CONTINUATION SHEET/RESIDENTIAL LOAN APPLICATION**

| Use this continuation sheet if you need more space to complete the Residential Loan Application. Mark **B** f or Borrower or **C** for Co-Borrower. | Borrower: | Agency Case Number: |
|---|---|---|
| | Co-Borrower: | Lender Case Number: |

I/We fully understand that it is a Federal crime punishable by fine or imprisonment, or both, to knowingly make any false statements concerning any of the above facts as applicable under the provisions of Title 18, United States Code, Section 1001, et seq.

| Borrower's Signature | Date | Co-Borrower's Signature | Date |
|---|---|---|---|
| **X** | | **X** | |

# Appendix H: Request for Verification of Deposit

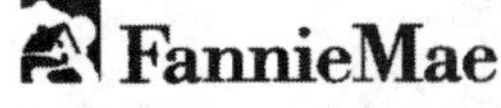


# Request for Verification of Deposit

**Privacy Act Notice:** This information is to be used by the agency collecting it or its assignees in determining whether you qualify as a prospective mortgagor under its program. It will not be disclosed outside the agency except as required and permitted by law. You do not have to provide this information, but if you do not your application for approval as a prospective mortgagor or borrower may be delayed or rejected. The information requested in this form is authorized by Title 38, USC, Chapter 37 (If VA); by 12 USC, Section 1701 et.seq. (If HUD/FHA); by 42 USC, Section 1452b (if HUD/CPD); and Title 42 USC, 1471 et.seq. or 7 USC, 1921 et.seq. (If USDA/FmHA).

**Instructions:** Lender – Complete Items 1 through 8. Have applicant(s) complete Item 9. Forward directly to depository named in Item 1.
Depository – Please complete Items 10 through 18 and return DIRECTLY to lender named in Item 2.
**The form is to be transmitted directly to the lender and is not to be transmitted through the applicant(s) or any other party.**

## Part I – Request

| 1. To (Name and address of depository) | 2. From (Name and address of lender) |
|---|---|
| | |

I certify that this verification has been sent directly to the bank or depository and has not passed through the hands of the applicant or any other party.

| 3. Signature of lender | 4. Title | 5. Date | 6. Lender's No. (Optional) |
|---|---|---|---|
| | | | |

7. Information To Be Verified

| Type of Account | Account in Name of | Account Number | Balance |
|---|---|---|---|
| | | | $ |
| | | | $ |
| | | | $ |

**To Depository:** I/We have applied for a mortgage loan and stated in my financial statement that the balance on deposit with you is as shown above. You are authorized to verify this information and to supply the lender identified above with the information requested in Items 10 through 13. Your response is solely a matter of courtesy for which no responsibility is attached to your institution or any of your officers.

| 8. Name and Address of Applicant(s) | 9. Signature of Applicant(s) |
|---|---|
| | |

## To Be Completed by Depository

## Part II – Verification of Depository

10. Deposit Accounts of Applicant(s)

| Type of Account | Account Number | Current Balance | Average Balance For Previous Two Months | Date Opened |
|---|---|---|---|---|
| | | $ | $ | |
| | | $ | $ | |
| | | $ | $ | |

11. Loans Outstanding To Applicant(s)

| Loan Number | Date of Loan | Original Amount | Current Balance | Installments (Monthly/Quarterly) | Secured By | Number of Late Payments |
|---|---|---|---|---|---|---|
| | | $ | $ | $ per | | |
| | | $ | $ | $ per | | |
| | | $ | $ | $ per | | |

12. Please include any additional information which may be of assistance in determination of credit worthiness. (Please include information on loans paid-in-full in Item 11 above.)

13. If the name(s) on the account(s) differ from those listed in Item 7, please supply the name(s) on the account(s) as reflected by your records.

**Part III – Authorized Signature** - Federal statutes provide severe penalties for any fraud, intentional misrepresentation, or criminal connivance or conspiracy purposed to influence the issuance of any guaranty or insurance by the VA Secretary, the U.S.D.A., FmHA/FHA Commissioner, or the HUD/CPD Assistant Secretary.

| 14. Signature of Depository Representative | 15. Title (Please print or type) | 16. Date |
|---|---|---|
| 17. Please print or type name signed in item 14 | 18. Phone No. | |

Fannie Mae
Form 1006 July 96

# Appendix I: Request for Verification of Employment

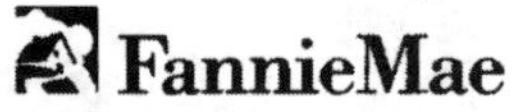


# Request for Verification of Employment

**Privacy Act Notice:** This information is to be used by the agency collecting it or its assignees in determining whether you qualify as a prospective mortgagor under its program. It will not be disclosed outside the agency except as required and permitted by law. You do not have to provide this information, but if you do not your application for approval as a prospective mortgagor or borrower may be delayed or rejected. The information requested in this form is authorized by Title 38, USC, Chapter 37 (if VA); by 12 USC, Section 1701 et. seq. (if HUD/FHA); by 42 USC, Section 1452b (if HUD/CPD); and Title 42 USC, 1471 et. seq., or 7 USC, 1921 et. seq. (if USDA/FmHA).

**Instructions:** **Lender** – Complete items 1 through 7. Have applicant complete item 8. Forward directly to employer named in item 1.
**Employer** – Please complete either Part II or Part III as applicable. Complete Part IV and return directly to lender named in item 2.
**The form is to be transmitted directly to the lender and is not to be transmitted through the applicant or any other party.**

## Part I – Request

| 1. To (Name and address of employer) | 2. From (Name and address of lender) |
|---|---|

I certify that this verification has been sent directly to the employer and has not passed through the hands of the applicant or any other interested party.

| 3. Signature of Lender | 4. Title | 5. Date | 6. Lender's Number (Optional) |
|---|---|---|---|

I have applied for a mortgage loan and stated that I am now or was formerly employed by you. My signature below authorizes verification of this information.

| 7. Name and Address of Applicant (include employee or badge number) | 8. Signature of Applicant |
|---|---|

## Part II – Verification of Present Employment

| 9. Applicant's Date of Employment | 10. Present Position | 11. Probability of Continued Employment |
|---|---|---|

12A. Current **Gross** Base Pay (Enter Amount and Check Period)
Annual / Hourly / Monthly / Other (Specify) / Weekly
$ ______

12B. **Gross** Earnings

| Type | Year To Date | Past Year | Past Year |
|---|---|---|---|
| Base Pay | Thru ______ $ | $ | $ |
| Overtime | $ | $ | $ |
| Commissions | $ | $ | $ |
| Bonus | $ | $ | $ |
| Total | $ 0.00 | $ 0.00 | $ 0.00 |

13. For Military Personnel Only
Pay Grade

| Type | Monthly Amount |
|---|---|
| Base Pay | $ |
| Rations | $ |
| Flight or Hazard | $ |
| Clothing | $ |
| Quarters | $ |
| Pro Pay | $ |
| Overseas or Combat | $ |
| Variable Housing Allowance | $ |

14. If Overtime or Bonus is Applicable, Is Its Continuance Likely?
Overtime [ Yes No
Bonus [ Yes [ No

15. If paid hourly – average hours per week

16. Date of applicant's next pay increase

17. Projected amount of next pay increase

18. Date of applicant's last pay increase

19. Amount of last pay increase

20.Remarks (If employee was off work for any length of time, please indicate time period and reason)

## Part III – Verification of Previous Employment

21. Date Hired
22. Date Terminated
23. Salary/Wage at Termination Per (Year) (Month) (Week)
Base ______ Overtime ______ Commissions ______ Bonus ______

| 24. Reason for Leaving | 25. Position Held |
|---|---|

**Part IV – Authorized Signature** - Federal statutes provide severe penalties for any fraud, intentional misrepresentation, or criminal connivance or conspiracy purposed to influence the issuance of any guaranty or insurance by the VA Secretary, the U.S.D.A., FmHA/FHA Commissioner, or the HUD/CPD Assistant Secretary.

| 26. Signature of Employer | 27. Title (Please print or type) | 28. Date |
|---|---|---|
| 29. Print or type name signed in Item 26 | 30. Phone No. | |

Fannie Mae
Form 1005 July 96

# Appendix J: Sample Credit Report

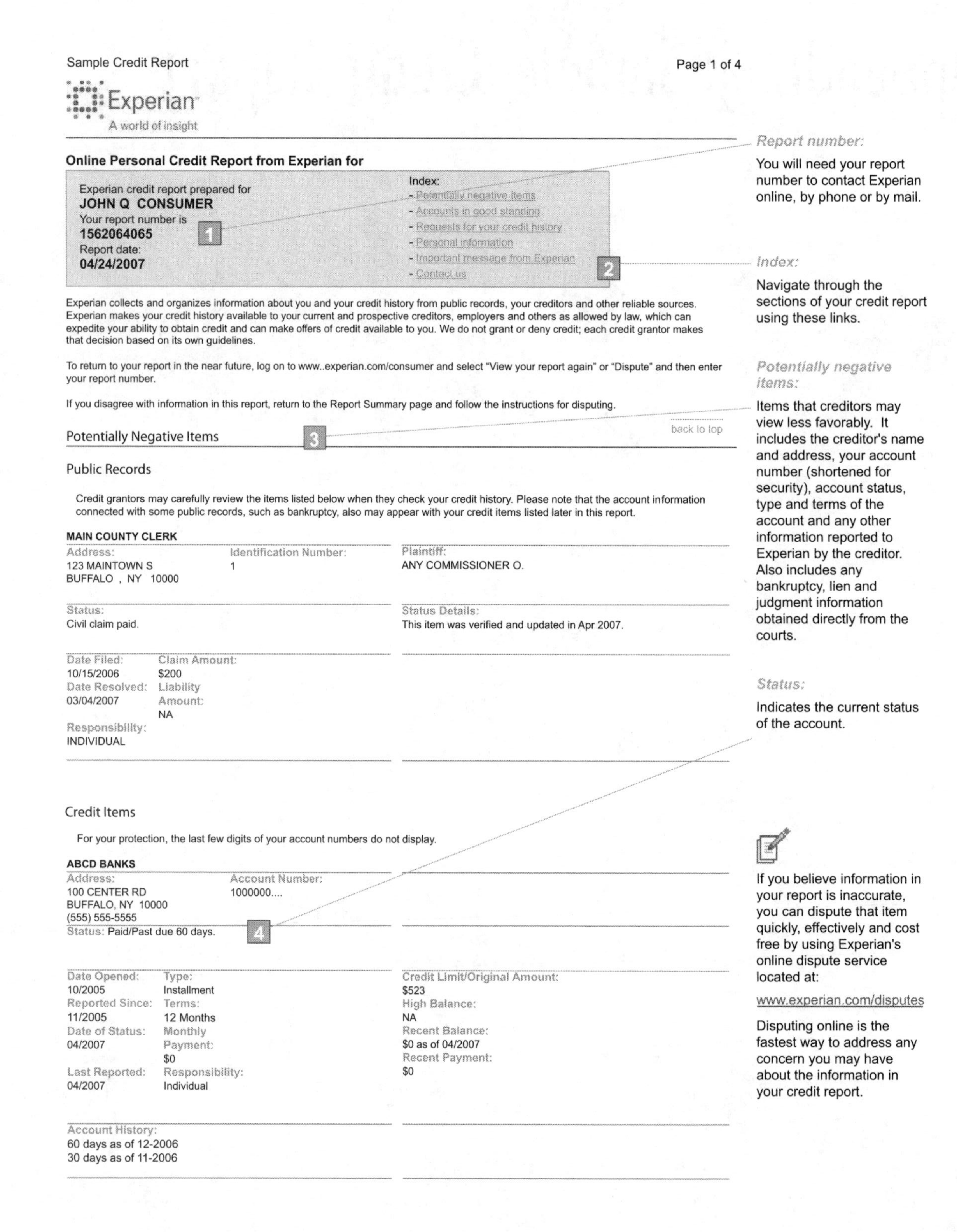

Sample Credit Report

Page 1 of 4

Experian
A world of insight

**Online Personal Credit Report from Experian for**

Experian credit report prepared for
**JOHN Q CONSUMER**
Your report number is
**1562064065**
Report date:
**04/24/2007**

Index:
- Potentially negative items
- Accounts in good standing
- Requests for your credit history
- Personal information
- Important message from Experian
- Contact us

Experian collects and organizes information about you and your credit history from public records, your creditors and other reliable sources. Experian makes your credit history available to your current and prospective creditors, employers and others as allowed by law, which can expedite your ability to obtain credit and can make offers of credit available to you. We do not grant or deny credit; each credit grantor makes that decision based on its own guidelines.

To return to your report in the near future, log on to www..experian.com/consumer and select "View your report again" or "Dispute" and then enter your report number.

If you disagree with information in this report, return to the Report Summary page and follow the instructions for disputing.

Potentially Negative Items — back to top

Public Records

Credit grantors may carefully review the items listed below when they check your credit history. Please note that the account information connected with some public records, such as bankruptcy, also may appear with your credit items listed later in this report.

**MAIN COUNTY CLERK**

Address:
123 MAINTOWN S
BUFFALO , NY 10000

Identification Number:
1

Plaintiff:
ANY COMMISSIONER O.

Status:
Civil claim paid.

Status Details:
This item was verified and updated in Apr 2007.

Date Filed:
10/15/2006
Date Resolved:
03/04/2007

Claim Amount:
$200
Liability Amount:
NA

Responsibility:
INDIVIDUAL

Credit Items

For your protection, the last few digits of your account numbers do not display.

**ABCD BANKS**

Address:
100 CENTER RD
BUFFALO, NY 10000
(555) 555-5555

Account Number:
1000000....

Status: Paid/Past due 60 days.

Date Opened:
10/2005
Reported Since:
11/2005
Date of Status:
04/2007
Last Reported:
04/2007

Type:
Installment
Terms:
12 Months
Monthly Payment:
$0
Responsibility:
Individual

Credit Limit/Original Amount:
$523
High Balance:
NA
Recent Balance:
$0 as of 04/2007
Recent Payment:
$0

Account History:
60 days as of 12-2006
30 days as of 11-2006

*Report number:*

You will need your report number to contact Experian online, by phone or by mail.

*Index:*

Navigate through the sections of your credit report using these links.

*Potentially negative items:*

Items that creditors may view less favorably. It includes the creditor's name and address, your account number (shortened for security), account status, type and terms of the account and any other information reported to Experian by the creditor. Also includes any bankruptcy, lien and judgment information obtained directly from the courts.

*Status:*

Indicates the current status of the account.

If you believe information in your report is inaccurate, you can dispute that item quickly, effectively and cost free by using Experian's online dispute service located at:

www.experian.com/disputes

Disputing online is the fastest way to address any concern you may have about the information in your credit report.

Source: www.experian.com

**MAIN COLL AGENCIES**

Address:
PO BOX 123
ANYTOWN, PA 10000
(555) 555-5555

Account Number:
0123456789

Original Creditor:
TELEVISE CABLE COMM.

Status: Collection account. $95 past due as of 4-2000.

Date Opened:
01/2005
Reported Since:
04/2005
Date of Status:
04/2005
Last Reported:
04/2005

Type:
Installment
Terms:
NA
Monthly Payment:
$0
Responsibility:
Individual

Credit Limit/Original Amount:
$95
High Balance:
NA
Recent Balance:
$95 as of 04/2005
Recent Payment:
$0

Your statement: ITEM DISPUTED BY CONSUMER

Account History:
Collection as of 4-2005

## Accounts in Good Standing 5

back to top

*Accounts in good standing:*

Lists accounts that have a positive status and may be viewed favorably by creditors. Some creditors do not report to us, so some of your accounts may not be listed.

**AUTOMOBILE AUTO FINANCE**

Address:
100 MAIN ST E
SMALLTOWN, MD 90001
(555) 555-5555

Account Number:
12345678998....

Status: Open/Never late.

*Type:*

Account type indicates whether your account is a revolving or an installment account.

Date Opened:
01/2006
Reported Since:
01/2006
Date of Status:
04/2007
Last Reported:
04/2007

Type: 6
Installment
Terms:
65 Months
Monthly Payment:
$210
Responsibility:
Individual

Credit Limit/Original Amount:
$10,355
High Balance:
NA
Recent Balance:
$7,984 as of 04/2007
Recent Payment:
$0

**MAIN**

Address:
PO BOX 1234
FORT LAUDERDALE, FL 10009

Account Number:
1234567899876

Status: Closed/Never late.

Date Opened:
03/1997
Reported Since:
03/1997
Date of Status:
08/2006
Last Reported:
08/2006

Type:
Revolving
Terms:
1 Months
Monthly Payment:
$0
Responsibility:
Individual

Credit Limit/Original Amount:
NA
High Balance:
$3,228
Recent Balance:
$0 /paid as of 08/2006
Recent Payment:
$0

Your statement:
Account closed at consumer's request

Sample Credit Report Page 3 of 4

## Requests for Your Credit History

7

back to top

### Requests Viewed By Others

We make your credit history available to your current and prospective creditors and employers as allowed by law. Personal data about you may be made available to companies whose products and services may interest you.

The section below lists all who have requested in the recent past to review your credit history as a result of actions involving you, such as the completion of a credit application or the transfer of an account to a collection agency, application for insurance, mortgage or loan application, etc. Creditors may view these requests when evaluating your creditworthiness.

**HOMESALE REALTY CO**

Address:
2000 S MAINROAD BLVD STE
ANYTOWN CA 11111
(555) 555-5555

Date of Request:
07/16/2006

Comments:
Real estate loan on behalf of 3903 MERCHANTS EXPRESS M. This inquiry is scheduled to continue on record until 8-2008.

**M & T BANK**

Address:
PO BOX 100
BUFFALO NY 10000
(555) 555-5555

Date of Request:
02/23/2006

Comments:
Permissible purpose. This inquiry is scheduled to continue on record until 3-2008.

**WESTERN FUNDING INC**

Address:
191 W MAIN AVE STE 100
INTOWN CA 10000
(559) 555-5555

Date of Request:
01/25/2006

Comments:
Permissible purpose. This inquiry is scheduled to continue on record until 2-2008.

### Requests Viewed Only By You

The section below lists all who have a permissible purpose by law and have requested in the recent past to review your information. You may not have initiated these requests, so you may not recognize each source. We offer information about you to those with a permissible purpose, for example, to:

- other creditors who want to offer you preapproved credit;
- an employer who wishes to extend an offer of employment;
- a potential investor in assessing the risk of a current obligation;
- Experian or other credit reporting agencies to process a report for you;
- your existing creditors to monitor your credit activity (date listed may reflect only the most recent request).

We report these requests **only to you** as a record of activities. We **do not** provide this information to other creditors who evaluate your creditworthiness.

**MAIN BANK USA**

Address:
1 MAIN CTR AA 11
BUFFALO NY 14203

Date of Request:
08/10/2006

**MYTOWN BANK**

Address:
PO BOX 825
MYTOWN DE 10000
(555) 555-5555

Date of Request:
08/05/2006

**INTOWN DATA CORPS**

Address:
2000 S MAINTOWN BLVD STE
INTOWN CO 11111
(555) 555-5555

Date of Request:
07/16/2006

*Requests for your credit history:*

Also called "inquiries," requests for your credit history are logged on your report whenever anyone reviews your credit information. There are two types of inquiries.

i.
Inquiries resulting from a transaction initiated by you. These include inquiries from your applications for credit, insurance, housing or other loans. They also include transfer of an account to a collection agency. Creditors may view these items when evaluating your creditworthiness.

ii.
Inquiries resulting from transactions you may not have initiated but that are allowed under the FCRA. These include preapproved offers, as well as for employment, investment review, account monitoring by existing creditors, and requests by you for your own report. These items are shown only to you and have no impact on your creditworthiness or risk scores.

Sample Credit Report



## Personal Information

8

The following information is reported to us by you, your creditors and other sources. Each source may report your personal information differently, which may result in variations of your name, address, Social Security number, etc. As part of our fraud prevention efforts, a notice with additional information may appear. As a security precaution, the Social Security number that you used to obtain this report is not displayed. The Name identification number and Address identification number are how our system identifies variations of your name and address that may appear on your report. The Geographical Code shown with each address identifies the state, county, census tract, block group and Metropolitan Statistical Area associated with each address.

Names:
JOHN Q CONSUMER
Name identification number: 15621

JONATHON Q CONSUMER
Name identification number: 15622

J Q CONSUMER
Name identification number: 15623

Social Security number variations:
999999999

Year of birth:
1959

Spouse or co-applicant:
JANE

Employers:
ABCDE ENGINEERING CORP

Telephone numbers:
(555) 555 5555 Residential

Address: 123 MAIN STREET
ANYTOWN, MD 90001-9999
Address identification number:
0277741504
Type of Residence: Multifamily
Geographical Code: 0-156510-31-8840

Address: 555 SIMPLE PLACE
ANYTOWN, MD 90002-7777
Address identification number:
0170086050
Type of Residence: Single family
Geographical Code: 0-176510-33-8840

Address: 999 HIGH DRIVE APT 15B
ANYTOWN, MD 90003-5555
Address identification number:
0170129301
Type of Residence: Apartment complex
Geographical Code: 0-156510-31-8840

9

## Your Personal Statement

10

No general personal statements appear on your report.

## Important Message From Experian

back to top

By law, we cannot disclose certain medical information (relating to physical, mental, or behavioral health or condition). Although we do not generally collect such information, it could appear in the name of a data furnisher (i.e., "Cancer Center") that reports your payment history to us. If so, those names display in your report, but in reports to others they display only as MEDICAL PAYMENT DATA. Consumer statements included on your report at your request that contain medical information are disclosed to others.

## Contacting Us

back to top

Contact address and phone number for your area will display here.



*Personal information:*

Personal information associated with your history that has been reported to Experian by you, your creditors and other sources.

May include name and Social Security number variations, employers, telephone numbers, etc. Experian lists all variations so you know what is being reported to us as belonging to you.

*Address information:*

Your current address and previous address(es)

*Personal statement:*

Any personal statement that you added to your report appears here.

Note - statements remain as part of the report for two years and display to anyone who has permission to review your report.

# Appendix K: Uniform Residential Appraisal Report

# Uniform Residential Appraisal Report

File #

The purpose of this summary appraisal report is to provide the lender/client with an accurate, and adequately supported, opinion of the market value of the subject property.

**SUBJECT**

Property Address | City | State | Zip Code

Borrower | Owner of Public Record | County

Legal Description

Assessor's Parcel # | Tax Year | R.E. Taxes $

Neighborhood Name | Map Reference | Census Tract

Occupant ☐ Owner ☐ Tenant ☐ Vacant | Special Assessments $ | ☐ PUD | HOA $ | ☐ per year ☐ per month

Property Rights Appraised ☐ Fee Simple ☐ Leasehold ☐ Other (describe)

Assignment Type ☐ Purchase Transaction ☐ Refinance Transaction ☐ Other (describe)

Lender/Client | Address

Is the subject property currently offered for sale or has it been offered for sale in the twelve months prior to the effective date of this appraisal? ☐ Yes ☐ No

Report data source(s) used, offering price(s), and date(s).

**CONTRACT**

I ☐ did ☐ did not analyze the contract for sale for the subject purchase transaction. Explain the results of the analysis of the contract for sale or why the analysis was not performed.

Contract Price $ | Date of Contract | Is the property seller the owner of public record? ☐ Yes ☐ No | Data Source(s)

Is there any financial assistance (loan charges, sale concessions, gift or downpayment assistance, etc.) to be paid by any party on behalf of the borrower? ☐ Yes ☐ No

If Yes, report the total dollar amount and describe the items to be paid.

**NEIGHBORHOOD**

**Note: Race and the racial composition of the neighborhood are not appraisal factors.**

| Neighborhood Characteristics | One-Unit Housing Trends | One-Unit Housing | Present Land Use % |
|---|---|---|---|
| Location ☐ Urban ☐ Suburban ☐ Rural | Property Values ☐ Increasing ☐ Stable ☐ Declining | PRICE AGE | One-Unit % |
| Built-Up ☐ Over 75% ☐ 25–75% ☐ Under 25% | Demand/Supply ☐ Shortage ☐ In Balance ☐ Over Supply | $ (000) (yrs) | 2-4 Unit % |
| Growth ☐ Rapid ☐ Stable ☐ Slow | Marketing Time ☐ Under 3 mths ☐ 3–6 mths ☐ Over 6 mths | Low | Multi-Family % |
| Neighborhood Boundaries | | High | Commercial % |
| | | Pred. | Other % |

Neighborhood Description

Market Conditions (including support for the above conclusions)

**SITE**

Dimensions | Area | Shape | View

Specific Zoning Classification | Zoning Description

Zoning Compliance ☐ Legal ☐ Legal Nonconforming (Grandfathered Use) ☐ No Zoning ☐ Illegal (describe)

Is the highest and best use of the subject property as improved (or as proposed per plans and specifications) the present use? ☐ Yes ☐ No If No, describe

| Utilities | Public | Other (describe) | | Public | Other (describe) | Off-site Improvements—Type | Public | Private |
|---|---|---|---|---|---|---|---|---|
| Electricity | ☐ | ☐ | Water | ☐ | ☐ | Street | ☐ | ☐ |
| Gas | ☐ | ☐ | Sanitary Sewer | ☐ | ☐ | Alley | ☐ | ☐ |

FEMA Special Flood Hazard Area ☐ Yes ☐ No | FEMA Flood Zone | FEMA Map # | FEMA Map Date

Are the utilities and off-site improvements typical for the market area? ☐ Yes ☐ No If No, describe

Are there any adverse site conditions or external factors (easements, encroachments, environmental conditions, land uses, etc.)? ☐ Yes ☐ No If Yes, describe

**IMPROVEMENTS**

| General Description | | Foundation | | Exterior Description materials/condition | | Interior materials/condition |
|---|---|---|---|---|---|---|
| Units ☐ One ☐ One with Accessory Unit | | ☐ Concrete Slab ☐ Crawl Space | | Foundation Walls | | Floors |
| # of Stories | | ☐ Full Basement ☐ Partial Basement | | Exterior Walls | | Walls |
| Type ☐ Det. ☐ Att. ☐ S-Det./End Unit | | Basement Area sq. ft. | | Roof Surface | | Trim/Finish |
| ☐ Existing ☐ Proposed ☐ Under Const. | | Basement Finish % | | Gutters & Downspouts | | Bath Floor |
| Design (Style) | | ☐ Outside Entry/Exit ☐ Sump Pump | | Window Type | | Bath Wainscot |
| Year Built | | Evidence of ☐ Infestation | | Storm Sash/Insulated | | Car Storage ☐ None |
| Effective Age (Yrs) | | ☐ Dampness ☐ Settlement | | Screens | | ☐ Driveway # of Cars |
| Attic | ☐ None | Heating ☐ FWA ☐ HWBB ☐ Radiant | | Amenities | ☐ Woodstove(s) # | Driveway Surface |
| ☐ Drop Stair | ☐ Stairs | ☐ Other | Fuel | ☐ Fireplace(s) # | ☐ Fence | ☐ Garage # of Cars |
| ☐ Floor | ☐ Scuttle | Cooling ☐ Central Air Conditioning | | ☐ Patio/Deck | ☐ Porch | ☐ Carport # of Cars |
| ☐ Finished | ☐ Heated | ☐ Individual | ☐ Other | ☐ Pool | ☐ Other | ☐ Att. ☐ Det. ☐ Built-in |

Appliances ☐ Refrigerator ☐ Range/Oven ☐ Dishwasher ☐ Disposal ☐ Microwave ☐ Washer/Dryer ☐ Other (describe)

Finished area **above** grade contains: | Rooms | Bedrooms | Bath(s) | Square Feet of Gross Living Area Above Grade

Additional features (special energy efficient items, etc.)

Describe the condition of the property (including needed repairs, deterioration, renovations, remodeling, etc.).

Are there any physical deficiencies or adverse conditions that affect the livability, soundness, or structural integrity of the property? ☐ Yes ☐ No If Yes, describe

Does the property generally conform to the neighborhood (functional utility, style, condition, use, construction, etc.)? ☐ Yes ☐ No If No, describe

# Uniform Residential Appraisal Report

**File #**

SALES COMPARISON APPROACH

There are comparable properties currently offered for sale in the subject neighborhood ranging in price from $ to $ .

There are comparable sales in the subject neighborhood within the past twelve months ranging in sale price from $ to $ .

| FEATURE | SUBJECT | COMPARABLE SALE # 1 | | COMPARABLE SALE # 2 | | COMPARABLE SALE # 3 | |
|---|---|---|---|---|---|---|---|
| Address | | | | | | | |
| Proximity to Subject | | | | | | | |
| Sale Price | $ | | $ | | $ | | $ |
| Sale Price/Gross Liv. Area | $ sq. ft. | $ sq. ft. | | $ sq. ft. | | $ sq. ft. | |
| Data Source(s) | | | | | | | |
| Verification Source(s) | | | | | | | |
| VALUE ADJUSTMENTS | DESCRIPTION | DESCRIPTION | +(-) $ Adjustment | DESCRIPTION | +(-) $ Adjustment | DESCRIPTION | +(-) $ Adjustment |
| Sale or Financing Concessions | | | | | | | |
| Date of Sale/Time | | | | | | | |
| Location | | | | | | | |
| Leasehold/Fee Simple | | | | | | | |
| Site | | | | | | | |
| View | | | | | | | |
| Design (Style) | | | | | | | |
| Quality of Construction | | | | | | | |
| Actual Age | | | | | | | |
| Condition | | | | | | | |
| Above Grade Room Count | Total / Bdrms. / Baths | Total / Bdrms. / Baths | | Total / Bdrms. / Baths | | Total / Bdrms. / Baths | |
| Gross Living Area | sq. ft. | sq. ft. | | sq. ft. | | sq. ft. | |
| Basement & Finished Rooms Below Grade | | | | | | | |
| Functional Utility | | | | | | | |
| Heating/Cooling | | | | | | | |
| Energy Efficient Items | | | | | | | |
| Garage/Carport | | | | | | | |
| Porch/Patio/Deck | | | | | | | |
| | | | | | | | |
| | | | | | | | |
| | | | | | | | |
| Net Adjustment (Total) | | ☐ + ☐ - | $ | ☐ + ☐ - | $ | ☐ + ☐ - | $ |
| Adjusted Sale Price of Comparables | | Net Adj. % Gross Adj. % | $ | Net Adj. % Gross Adj. % | $ | Net Adj. % Gross Adj. % | $ |

I ☐ did ☐ did not research the sale or transfer history of the subject property and comparable sales. If not, explain

My research ☐ did ☐ did not reveal any prior sales or transfers of the subject property for the three years prior to the effective date of this appraisal.

Data source(s)

My research ☐ did ☐ did not reveal any prior sales or transfers of the comparable sales for the year prior to the date of sale of the comparable sale.

Data source(s)

Report the results of the research and analysis of the prior sale or transfer history of the subject property and comparable sales (report additional prior sales on page 3).

| ITEM | SUBJECT | COMPARABLE SALE # 1 | COMPARABLE SALE # 2 | COMPARABLE SALE # 3 |
|---|---|---|---|---|
| Date of Prior Sale/Transfer | | | | |
| Price of Prior Sale/Transfer | | | | |
| Data Source(s) | | | | |
| Effective Date of Data Source(s) | | | | |

Analysis of prior sale or transfer history of the subject property and comparable sales

Summary of Sales Comparison Approach

Indicated Value by Sales Comparison Approach $

RECONCILIATION

**Indicated Value by: Sales Comparison Approach $ Cost Approach (if developed) $ Income Approach (if developed) $**

This appraisal is made ☐ "as is", ☐ subject to completion per plans and specifications on the basis of a hypothetical condition that the improvements have been completed, ☐ subject to the following repairs or alterations on the basis of a hypothetical condition that the repairs or alterations have been completed, or ☐ subject to the following required inspection based on the extraordinary assumption that the condition or deficiency does not require alteration or repair:

**Based on a complete visual inspection of the interior and exterior areas of the subject property, defined scope of work, statement of assumptions and limiting conditions, and appraiser's certification, my (our) opinion of the market value, as defined, of the real property that is the subject of this report is $ , as of , which is the date of inspection and the effective date of this appraisal.**

# Uniform Residential Appraisal Report

File #

ADDITIONAL COMMENTS

## COST APPROACH TO VALUE (not required by Fannie Mae)

Provide adequate information for the lender/client to replicate the below cost figures and calculations.

Support for the opinion of site value (summary of comparable land sales or other methods for estimating site value)

| | |
|---|---|
| ESTIMATED ☐ REPRODUCTION OR ☐ REPLACEMENT COST NEW | OPINION OF SITE VALUE ........ = $ |
| Source of cost data | Dwelling Sq. Ft. @ $ ........ =$ |
| Quality rating from cost service Effective date of cost data | Sq. Ft. @ $ ........ =$ |
| Comments on Cost Approach (gross living area calculations, depreciation, etc.) | |
| | Garage/Carport Sq. Ft. @ $ ........ =$ |
| | Total Estimate of Cost-New ........ = $ |
| | Less Physical \| Functional \| External |
| | Depreciation =$( ) |
| | Depreciated Cost of Improvements........ =$ |
| | "As-is" Value of Site Improvements........ =$ |
| Estimated Remaining Economic Life (HUD and VA only) Years | Indicated Value By Cost Approach ........ =$ |

## INCOME APPROACH TO VALUE (not required by Fannie Mae)

Estimated Monthly Market Rent $ X Gross Rent Multiplier = $ Indicated Value by Income Approach

Summary of Income Approach (including support for market rent and GRM)

## PROJECT INFORMATION FOR PUDs (if applicable)

Is the developer/builder in control of the Homeowners' Association (HOA)? ☐ Yes ☐ No Unit type(s) ☐ Detached ☐ Attached

Provide the following information for PUDs ONLY if the developer/builder is in control of the HOA and the subject property is an attached dwelling unit.

Legal name of project

Total number of phases Total number of units Total number of units sold

Total number of units rented Total number of units for sale Data source(s)

Was the project created by the conversion of an existing building(s) into a PUD? ☐ Yes ☐ No If Yes, date of conversion

Does the project contain any multi-dwelling units? ☐ Yes ☐ No Data source(s)

Are the units, common elements, and recreation facilities complete? ☐ Yes ☐ No If No, describe the status of completion.

Are the common elements leased to or by the Homeowners' Association? ☐ Yes ☐ No If Yes, describe the rental terms and options.

Describe common elements and recreational facilities

## Uniform Residential Appraisal Report

File #

This report form is designed to report an appraisal of a one-unit property or a one-unit property with an accessory unit; including a unit in a planned unit development (PUD). This report form is not designed to report an appraisal of a manufactured home or a unit in a condominium or cooperative project.

This appraisal report is subject to the following scope of work, intended use, intended user, definition of market value, statement of assumptions and limiting conditions, and certifications. Modifications, additions, or deletions to the intended use, intended user, definition of market value, or assumptions and limiting conditions are not permitted. The appraiser may expand the scope of work to include any additional research or analysis necessary based on the complexity of this appraisal assignment. Modifications or deletions to the certifications are also not permitted. However, additional certifications that do not constitute material alterations to this appraisal report, such as those required by law or those related to the appraiser's continuing education or membership in an appraisal organization, are permitted.

**SCOPE OF WORK:** The scope of work for this appraisal is defined by the complexity of this appraisal assignment and the reporting requirements of this appraisal report form, including the following definition of market value, statement of assumptions and limiting conditions, and certifications. The appraiser must, at a minimum: (1) perform a complete visual inspection of the interior and exterior areas of the subject property, (2) inspect the neighborhood, (3) inspect each of the comparable sales from at least the street, (4) research, verify, and analyze data from reliable public and/or private sources, and (5) report his or her analysis, opinions, and conclusions in this appraisal report.

**INTENDED USE:** The intended use of this appraisal report is for the lender/client to evaluate the property that is the subject of this appraisal for a mortgage finance transaction.

**INTENDED USER:** The intended user of this appraisal report is the lender/client.

**DEFINITION OF MARKET VALUE:** The most probable price which a property should bring in a competitive and open market under all conditions requisite to a fair sale, the buyer and seller, each acting prudently, knowledgeably and assuming the price is not affected by undue stimulus. Implicit in this definition is the consummation of a sale as of a specified date and the passing of title from seller to buyer under conditions whereby: (1) buyer and seller are typically motivated; (2) both parties are well informed or well advised, and each acting in what he or she considers his or her own best interest; (3) a reasonable time is allowed for exposure in the open market; (4) payment is made in terms of cash in U. S. dollars or in terms of financial arrangements comparable thereto; and (5) the price represents the normal consideration for the property sold unaffected by special or creative financing or sales concessions* granted by anyone associated with the sale.

*Adjustments to the comparables must be made for special or creative financing or sales concessions. No adjustments are necessary for those costs which are normally paid by sellers as a result of tradition or law in a market area; these costs are readily identifiable since the seller pays these costs in virtually all sales transactions. Special or creative financing adjustments can be made to the comparable property by comparisons to financing terms offered by a third party institutional lender that is not already involved in the property or transaction. Any adjustment should not be calculated on a mechanical dollar for dollar cost of the financing or concession but the dollar amount of any adjustment should approximate the market's reaction to the financing or concessions based on the appraiser's judgment.

**STATEMENT OF ASSUMPTIONS AND LIMITING CONDITIONS:** The appraiser's certification in this report is subject to the following assumptions and limiting conditions:

1. The appraiser will not be responsible for matters of a legal nature that affect either the property being appraised or the title to it, except for information that he or she became aware of during the research involved in performing this appraisal. The appraiser assumes that the title is good and marketable and will not render any opinions about the title.

2. The appraiser has provided a sketch in this appraisal report to show the approximate dimensions of the improvements. The sketch is included only to assist the reader in visualizing the property and understanding the appraiser's determination of its size.

3. The appraiser has examined the available flood maps that are provided by the Federal Emergency Management Agency (or other data sources) and has noted in this appraisal report whether any portion of the subject site is located in an identified Special Flood Hazard Area. Because the appraiser is not a surveyor, he or she makes no guarantees, express or implied, regarding this determination.

4. The appraiser will not give testimony or appear in court because he or she made an appraisal of the property in question, unless specific arrangements to do so have been made beforehand, or as otherwise required by law.

5. The appraiser has noted in this appraisal report any adverse conditions (such as needed repairs, deterioration, the presence of hazardous wastes, toxic substances, etc.) observed during the inspection of the subject property or that he or she became aware of during the research involved in performing this appraisal. Unless otherwise stated in this appraisal report, the appraiser has no knowledge of any hidden or unapparent physical deficiencies or adverse conditions of the property (such as, but not limited to, needed repairs, deterioration, the presence of hazardous wastes, toxic substances, adverse environmental conditions, etc.) that would make the property less valuable, and has assumed that there are no such conditions and makes no guarantees or warranties, express or implied. The appraiser will not be responsible for any such conditions that do exist or for any engineering or testing that might be required to discover whether such conditions exist. Because the appraiser is not an expert in the field of environmental hazards, this appraisal report must not be considered as an environmental assessment of the property.

6. The appraiser has based his or her appraisal report and valuation conclusion for an appraisal that is subject to satisfactory completion, repairs, or alterations on the assumption that the completion, repairs, or alterations of the subject property will be performed in a professional manner.

Freddie Mac Form 70 March 2005 Page 4 of 6 Fannie Mae Form 1004 March 2005

## Uniform Residential Appraisal Report

File #

**APPRAISER'S CERTIFICATION:** The Appraiser certifies and agrees that:

1. I have, at a minimum, developed and reported this appraisal in accordance with the scope of work requirements stated in this appraisal report.

2. I performed a complete visual inspection of the interior and exterior areas of the subject property. I reported the condition of the improvements in factual, specific terms. I identified and reported the physical deficiencies that could affect the livability, soundness, or structural integrity of the property.

3. I performed this appraisal in accordance with the requirements of the Uniform Standards of Professional Appraisal Practice that were adopted and promulgated by the Appraisal Standards Board of The Appraisal Foundation and that were in place at the time this appraisal report was prepared.

4. I developed my opinion of the market value of the real property that is the subject of this report based on the sales comparison approach to value. I have adequate comparable market data to develop a reliable sales comparison approach for this appraisal assignment. I further certify that I considered the cost and income approaches to value but did not develop them, unless otherwise indicated in this report.

5. I researched, verified, analyzed, and reported on any current agreement for sale for the subject property, any offering for sale of the subject property in the twelve months prior to the effective date of this appraisal, and the prior sales of the subject property for a minimum of three years prior to the effective date of this appraisal, unless otherwise indicated in this report.

6. I researched, verified, analyzed, and reported on the prior sales of the comparable sales for a minimum of one year prior to the date of sale of the comparable sale, unless otherwise indicated in this report.

7. I selected and used comparable sales that are locationally, physically, and functionally the most similar to the subject property.

8. I have not used comparable sales that were the result of combining a land sale with the contract purchase price of a home that has been built or will be built on the land.

9. I have reported adjustments to the comparable sales that reflect the market's reaction to the differences between the subject property and the comparable sales.

10. I verified, from a disinterested source, all information in this report that was provided by parties who have a financial interest in the sale or financing of the subject property.

11. I have knowledge and experience in appraising this type of property in this market area.

12. I am aware of, and have access to, the necessary and appropriate public and private data sources, such as multiple listing services, tax assessment records, public land records and other such data sources for the area in which the property is located.

13. I obtained the information, estimates, and opinions furnished by other parties and expressed in this appraisal report from reliable sources that I believe to be true and correct.

14. I have taken into consideration the factors that have an impact on value with respect to the subject neighborhood, subject property, and the proximity of the subject property to adverse influences in the development of my opinion of market value. I have noted in this appraisal report any adverse conditions (such as, but not limited to, needed repairs, deterioration, the presence of hazardous wastes, toxic substances, adverse environmental conditions, etc.) observed during the inspection of the subject property or that I became aware of during the research involved in performing this appraisal. I have considered these adverse conditions in my analysis of the property value, and have reported on the effect of the conditions on the value and marketability of the subject property.

15. I have not knowingly withheld any significant information from this appraisal report and, to the best of my knowledge, all statements and information in this appraisal report are true and correct.

16. I stated in this appraisal report my own personal, unbiased, and professional analysis, opinions, and conclusions, which are subject only to the assumptions and limiting conditions in this appraisal report.

17. I have no present or prospective interest in the property that is the subject of this report, and I have no present or prospective personal interest or bias with respect to the participants in the transaction. I did not base, either partially or completely, my analysis and/or opinion of market value in this appraisal report on the race, color, religion, sex, age, marital status, handicap, familial status, or national origin of either the prospective owners or occupants of the subject property or of the present owners or occupants of the properties in the vicinity of the subject property or on any other basis prohibited by law.

18. My employment and/or compensation for performing this appraisal or any future or anticipated appraisals was not conditioned on any agreement or understanding, written or otherwise, that I would report (or present analysis supporting) a predetermined specific value, a predetermined minimum value, a range or direction in value, a value that favors the cause of any party, or the attainment of a specific result or occurrence of a specific subsequent event (such as approval of a pending mortgage loan application).

19. I personally prepared all conclusions and opinions about the real estate that were set forth in this appraisal report. If I relied on significant real property appraisal assistance from any individual or individuals in the performance of this appraisal or the preparation of this appraisal report, I have named such individual(s) and disclosed the specific tasks performed in this appraisal report. I certify that any individual so named is qualified to perform the tasks. I have not authorized anyone to make a change to any item in this appraisal report; therefore, any change made to this appraisal is unauthorized and I will take no responsibility for it.

20. I identified the lender/client in this appraisal report who is the individual, organization, or agent for the organization that ordered and will receive this appraisal report.

# Uniform Residential Appraisal Report

File #

21. The lender/client may disclose or distribute this appraisal report to: the borrower; another lender at the request of the borrower; the mortgagee or its successors and assigns; mortgage insurers; government sponsored enterprises; other secondary market participants; data collection or reporting services; professional appraisal organizations; any department, agency, or instrumentality of the United States; and any state, the District of Columbia, or other jurisdictions; without having to obtain the appraiser's or supervisory appraiser's (if applicable) consent. Such consent must be obtained before this appraisal report may be disclosed or distributed to any other party (including, but not limited to, the public through advertising, public relations, news, sales, or other media).

22. I am aware that any disclosure or distribution of this appraisal report by me or the lender/client may be subject to certain laws and regulations. Further, I am also subject to the provisions of the Uniform Standards of Professional Appraisal Practice that pertain to disclosure or distribution by me.

23. The borrower, another lender at the request of the borrower, the mortgagee or its successors and assigns, mortgage insurers, government sponsored enterprises, and other secondary market participants may rely on this appraisal report as part of any mortgage finance transaction that involves any one or more of these parties.

24. If this appraisal report was transmitted as an "electronic record" containing my "electronic signature," as those terms are defined in applicable federal and/or state laws (excluding audio and video recordings), or a facsimile transmission of this appraisal report containing a copy or representation of my signature, the appraisal report shall be as effective, enforceable and valid as if a paper version of this appraisal report were delivered containing my original hand written signature.

25. Any intentional or negligent misrepresentation(s) contained in this appraisal report may result in civil liability and/or criminal penalties including, but not limited to, fine or imprisonment or both under the provisions of Title 18, United States Code, Section 1001, et seq., or similar state laws.

**SUPERVISORY APPRAISER'S CERTIFICATION:** The Supervisory Appraiser certifies and agrees that:

1. I directly supervised the appraiser for this appraisal assignment, have read the appraisal report, and agree with the appraiser's analysis, opinions, statements, conclusions, and the appraiser's certification.

2. I accept full responsibility for the contents of this appraisal report including, but not limited to, the appraiser's analysis, opinions, statements, conclusions, and the appraiser's certification.

3. The appraiser identified in this appraisal report is either a sub-contractor or an employee of the supervisory appraiser (or the appraisal firm), is qualified to perform this appraisal, and is acceptable to perform this appraisal under the applicable state law.

4. This appraisal report complies with the Uniform Standards of Professional Appraisal Practice that were adopted and promulgated by the Appraisal Standards Board of The Appraisal Foundation and that were in place at the time this appraisal report was prepared.

5. If this appraisal report was transmitted as an "electronic record" containing my "electronic signature," as those terms are defined in applicable federal and/or state laws (excluding audio and video recordings), or a facsimile transmission of this appraisal report containing a copy or representation of my signature, the appraisal report shall be as effective, enforceable and valid as if a paper version of this appraisal report were delivered containing my original hand written signature.

**APPRAISER**

Signature ____________________
Name ____________________
Company Name ____________________
Company Address ____________________
____________________
Telephone Number ____________________
Email Address ____________________
Date of Signature and Report ____________________
Effective Date of Appraisal ____________________
State Certification # ____________________
or State License # ____________________
or Other (describe) ____________ State # ____________
State ____________________
Expiration Date of Certification or License ____________

ADDRESS OF PROPERTY APPRAISED
____________________
____________________

APPRAISED VALUE OF SUBJECT PROPERTY $ ____________

LENDER/CLIENT
Name ____________________
Company Name ____________________
Company Address ____________________
____________________
Email Address ____________________

**SUPERVISORY APPRAISER (ONLY IF REQUIRED)**

Signature ____________________
Name ____________________
Company Name ____________________
Company Address ____________________
____________________
Telephone Number ____________________
Email Address ____________________
Date of Signature ____________________
State Certification # ____________________
or State License # ____________________
State ____________________
Expiration Date of Certification or License ____________

SUBJECT PROPERTY

☐ Did not inspect subject property
☐ Did inspect exterior of subject property from street
Date of Inspection ____________________
☐ Did inspect interior and exterior of subject property
Date of Inspection ____________________

COMPARABLE SALES

☐ Did not inspect exterior of comparable sales from street
☐ Did inspect exterior of comparable sales from street
Date of Inspection ____________________

# Appendix L: Loan Estimate

FICUS BANK
4321 Random Boulevard • Somecity, ST 12340

*Save this Loan Estimate to compare with your Closing Disclosure.*

# Loan Estimate

**DATE ISSUED** 2/15/2013
**APPLICANTS** Michael Jones and Mary Stone
123 Anywhere Street
Anytown, ST 12345
**PROPERTY** 456 Somewhere Avenue
Anytown, ST 12345
**SALE PRICE** $180,000

**LOAN TERM** 30 years
**PURPOSE** Purchase
**PRODUCT** Fixed Rate
**LOAN TYPE** ☒ Conventional ☐ FHA ☐ VA ☐ ____________
**LOAN ID #** 123456789
**RATE LOCK** ☐ NO ☒ YES, until 4/16/2013 at 5:00 p.m. EDT
*Before closing, your interest rate, points, and lender credits can change unless you lock the interest rate. All other estimated closing costs expire on **3/4/2013** at 5:00 p.m. EDT*



| **Loan Terms** | | **Can this amount increase after closing?** |
|---|---|---|
| **Loan Amount** | $162,000 | **NO** |
| **Interest Rate** | 3.875% | **NO** |
| **Monthly Principal & Interest** *See Projected Payments below for your Estimated Total Monthly Payment* | $761.78 | **NO** |
| | | **Does the loan have these features?** |
| **Prepayment Penalty** | | **YES** • **As high as $3,240** if you pay off the loan during the first 2 years |
| **Balloon Payment** | | **NO** |

## Projected Payments

| **Payment Calculation** | **Years 1-7** | **Years 8-30** |
|---|---|---|
| Principal & Interest | $761.78 | $761.78 |
| Mortgage Insurance | + 82 | + — |
| Estimated Escrow *Amount can increase over time* | + 206 | + 206 |
| **Estimated Total Monthly Payment** | $1,050 | $968 |

| | | | |
|---|---|---|---|
| **Estimated Taxes, Insurance & Assessments** *Amount can increase over time* | $206 a month | **This estimate includes** | **In escrow?** |
| | | ☒ Property Taxes | **YES** |
| | | ☒ Homeowner's Insurance | **YES** |
| | | ☐ Other: | |
| | | *See Section G on page 2 for escrowed property costs. You must pay for other property costs separately.* | |

## Costs at Closing

| | | |
|---|---|---|
| **Estimated Closing Costs** | $8,054 | Includes $5,672 in Loan Costs + $2,382 in Other Costs – $0 in Lender Credits. *See page 2 for details.* |
| **Estimated Cash to Close** | $16,054 | Includes Closing Costs. *See Calculating Cash to Close on page 2 for details.* |

Visit **www.consumerfinance.gov/mortgage-estimate** for general information and tools.

## Closing Cost Details

### Loan Costs

| A. Origination Charges | $1,802 |
|---|---|
| .25 % of Loan Amount (Points) | $405 |
| Application Fee | $300 |
| Underwriting Fee | $1,097 |

| B. Services You Cannot Shop For | $672 |
|---|---|
| Appraisal Fee | $405 |
| Credit Report Fee | $30 |
| Flood Determination Fee | $20 |
| Flood Monitoring Fee | $32 |
| Tax Monitoring Fee | $75 |
| Tax Status Research Fee | $110 |

| C. Services You Can Shop For | $3,198 |
|---|---|
| Pest Inspection Fee | $135 |
| Survey Fee | $65 |
| Title – Insurance Binder | $700 |
| Title – Lender's Title Policy | $535 |
| Title – Settlement Agent Fee | $502 |
| Title – Title Search | $1,261 |

| D. TOTAL LOAN COSTS (A + B + C) | $5,672 |
|---|---|

### Other Costs

| E. Taxes and Other Government Fees | $85 |
|---|---|
| Recording Fees and Other Taxes | $85 |
| Transfer Taxes | |

| F. Prepaids | $867 |
|---|---|
| Homeowner's Insurance Premium ( 6 months) | $605 |
| Mortgage Insurance Premium ( months) | |
| Prepaid Interest ( $17.44 per day for 15 days @ 3.875%) | $262 |
| Property Taxes ( months) | |

| G. Initial Escrow Payment at Closing | | $413 |
|---|---|---|
| Homeowner's Insurance | $100.83 per month for 2 mo. | $202 |
| Mortgage Insurance | per month for mo. | |
| Property Taxes | $105.30 per month for 2 mo. | $211 |

| H. Other | $1,017 |
|---|---|
| Title – Owner's Title Policy (optional) | $1,017 |

| I. TOTAL OTHER COSTS (E + F + G + H) | $2,382 |
|---|---|

| J. TOTAL CLOSING COSTS | $8,054 |
|---|---|
| D + I | $8,054 |
| Lender Credits | |

### Calculating Cash to Close

| | |
|---|---|
| Total Closing Costs (J) | $8,054 |
| Closing Costs Financed (Paid from your Loan Amount) | $0 |
| Down Payment/Funds from Borrower | $18,000 |
| Deposit | – $10,000 |
| Funds for Borrower | $0 |
| Seller Credits | $0 |
| Adjustments and Other Credits | $0 |
| **Estimated Cash to Close** | $16,054 |



LOAN ESTIMATE PAGE 2 OF 3 • LOAN ID # 123456789

## Additional Information About This Loan

| | | | |
|---|---|---|---|
| **LENDER** | Ficus Bank | **MORTGAGE BROKER** | |
| **NMLS/__ LICENSE ID** | | **NMLS/__ LICENSE ID** | |
| **LOAN OFFICER** | Joe Smith | **LOAN OFFICER** | |
| **NMLS/__ LICENSE ID** | 12345 | **NMLS/__ LICENSE ID** | |
| **EMAIL** | joesmith@ficusbank.com | **EMAIL** | |
| **PHONE** | 123-456-7890 | **PHONE** | |

| **Comparisons** | | **Use these measures to compare this loan with other loans.** |
|---|---|---|
| **In 5 Years** | $56,582 | Total you will have paid in principal, interest, mortgage insurance, and loan costs. |
| | $15,773 | Principal you will have paid off. |
| **Annual Percentage Rate (APR)** | 4.274% | Your costs over the loan term expressed as a rate. This is not your interest rate. |
| **Total Interest Percentage (TIP)** | 69.45% | The total amount of interest that you will pay over the loan term as a percentage of your loan amount. |

### Other Considerations

**Appraisal** — We may order an appraisal to determine the property's value and charge you for this appraisal. We will promptly give you a copy of any appraisal, even if your loan does not close. You can pay for an additional appraisal for your own use at your own cost.

**Assumption** — If you sell or transfer this property to another person, we
- ☐ will allow, under certain conditions, this person to assume this loan on the original terms.
- ☒ will not allow assumption of this loan on the original terms.

**Homeowner's Insurance** — This loan requires homeowner's insurance on the property, which you may obtain from a company of your choice that we find acceptable.

**Late Payment** — If your payment is more than *15* days late, we will charge a late fee of *5% of the monthly principal and interest payment.*

**Refinance** — Refinancing this loan will depend on your future financial situation, the property value, and market conditions. You may not be able to refinance this loan.

**Servicing** — We intend
- ☐ to service your loan. If so, you will make your payments to us.
- ☒ to transfer servicing of your loan.

### Confirm Receipt

By signing, you are only confirming that you have received this form. You do not have to accept this loan because you have signed or received this form.

Applicant Signature Date Co-Applicant Signature Date

LOAN ESTIMATE PAGE 3 OF 3 • LOAN ID #123456789

# Appendix M: Closing Disclosure

# Closing Disclosure

*This form is a statement of final loan terms and closing costs. Compare this document with your Loan Estimate.*

**Closing Information**

| | |
|---|---|
| **Date Issued** | 4/15/2013 |
| **Closing Date** | 4/15/2013 |
| **Disbursement Date** | 4/15/2013 |
| **Settlement Agent** | Epsilon Title Co. |
| **File #** | 12-3456 |
| **Property** | 456 Somewhere Ave<br>Anytown, ST 12345 |
| **Sale Price** | $180,000 |

**Transaction Information**

| | |
|---|---|
| **Borrower** | Michael Jones and Mary Stone<br>123 Anywhere Street<br>Anytown, ST 12345 |
| **Seller** | Steve Cole and Amy Doe<br>321 Somewhere Drive<br>Anytown, ST 12345 |
| **Lender** | Ficus Bank |

**Loan Information**

| | |
|---|---|
| **Loan Term** | 30 years |
| **Purpose** | Purchase |
| **Product** | Fixed Rate |
| **Loan Type** | ☒ Conventional ☐ FHA<br>☐ VA ☐ ______ |
| **Loan ID #** | 123456789 |
| **MIC #** | 000654321 |

## Loan Terms

| Loan Terms | | Can this amount increase after closing? |
|---|---|---|
| **Loan Amount** | $162,000 | **NO** |
| **Interest Rate** | 3.875% | **NO** |
| **Monthly Principal & Interest**<br>*See Projected Payments below for your Estimated Total Monthly Payment* | $761.78 | **NO** |
| | | **Does the loan have these features?** |
| **Prepayment Penalty** | | **YES** • **As high as $3,240** if you pay off the loan during the first 2 years |
| **Balloon Payment** | | **NO** |

## Projected Payments

| **Payment Calculation** | **Years 1-7** | **Years 8-30** |
|---|---|---|
| Principal & Interest | $761.78 | $761.78 |
| Mortgage Insurance | + 82.35 | + — |
| Estimated Escrow<br>*Amount can increase over time* | + 206.13 | + 206.13 |
| **Estimated Total Monthly Payment** | $1,050.26 | $967.91 |

| | | | |
|---|---|---|---|
| **Estimated Taxes, Insurance & Assessments**<br>*Amount can increase over time*<br>*See page 4 for details* | $356.13<br>a month | **This estimate includes** | **In escrow?** |
| | | ☒ Property Taxes | **YES** |
| | | ☒ Homeowner's Insurance | **YES** |
| | | ☒ Other: Homeowner's Association Dues | **NO** |

*See Escrow Account on page 4 for details. You must pay for other property costs separately.*

## Costs at Closing

| | | |
|---|---|---|
| **Closing Costs** | $9,712.10 | Includes $4,694.05 in Loan Costs + $5,018.05 in Other Costs – $0 in Lender Credits. *See page 2 for details.* |
| **Cash to Close** | $14,147.26 | Includes Closing Costs. *See Calculating Cash to Close on page 3 for details.* |

## Closing Cost Details

| Loan Costs | Borrower-Paid At Closing | Borrower-Paid Before Closing | Seller-Paid At Closing | Seller-Paid Before Closing | Paid by Others |
|---|---|---|---|---|---|
| **A. Origination Charges** | **$1,802.00** | | | | |
| 01 0.25 % of Loan Amount (Points) | $405.00 | | | | |
| 02 Application Fee | $300.00 | | | | |
| 03 Underwriting Fee | $1,097.00 | | | | |
| 04 | | | | | |
| 05 | | | | | |
| 06 | | | | | |
| 07 | | | | | |
| 08 | | | | | |
| **B. Services Borrower Did Not Shop For** | **$236.55** | | | | |
| 01 Appraisal Fee to John Smith Appraisers Inc. | | | | | $405.00 |
| 02 Credit Report Fee to Information Inc. | | $29.80 | | | |
| 03 Flood Determination Fee to Info Co. | $20.00 | | | | |
| 04 Flood Monitoring Fee to Info Co. | $31.75 | | | | |
| 05 Tax Monitoring Fee to Info Co. | $75.00 | | | | |
| 06 Tax Status Research Fee to Info Co. | $80.00 | | | | |
| 07 | | | | | |
| 08 | | | | | |
| 09 | | | | | |
| 10 | | | | | |
| **C. Services Borrower Did Shop For** | **$2,655.50** | | | | |
| 01 Pest Inspection Fee to Pests Co. | $120.50 | | | | |
| 02 Survey Fee to Surveys Co. | $85.00 | | | | |
| 03 Title – Insurance Binder to Epsilon Title Co. | $650.00 | | | | |
| 04 Title – Lender's Title Insurance to Epsilon Title Co. | $500.00 | | | | |
| 05 Title – Settlement Agent Fee to Epsilon Title Co. | $500.00 | | | | |
| 06 Title – Title Search to Epsilon Title Co. | $800.00 | | | | |
| 07 | | | | | |
| 08 | | | | | |
| **D. TOTAL LOAN COSTS (Borrower-Paid)** | **$4,694.05** | | | | |
| Loan Costs Subtotals (A + B + C) | $4,664.25 | $29.80 | | | |

| Other Costs | Borrower-Paid At Closing | Borrower-Paid Before Closing | Seller-Paid At Closing | Seller-Paid Before Closing | Paid by Others |
|---|---|---|---|---|---|
| **E. Taxes and Other Government Fees** | **$85.00** | | | | |
| 01 Recording Fees Deed: $40.00 Mortgage: $45.00 | $85.00 | | | | |
| 02 Transfer Tax to Any State | | | $950.00 | | |
| **F. Prepaids** | **$2,120.80** | | | | |
| 01 Homeowner's Insurance Premium ( 12 mo.) to Insurance Co. | $1,209.96 | | | | |
| 02 Mortgage Insurance Premium ( mo.) | | | | | |
| 03 Prepaid Interest ( $17.44 per day from 4/15/13 to 5/1/13 ) | $279.04 | | | | |
| 04 Property Taxes ( 6 mo.) to Any County USA | $631.80 | | | | |
| 05 | | | | | |
| **G. Initial Escrow Payment at Closing** | **$412.25** | | | | |
| 01 Homeowner's Insurance $100.83 per month for 2 mo. | $201.66 | | | | |
| 02 Mortgage Insurance per month for mo. | | | | | |
| 03 Property Taxes $105.30 per month for 2 mo. | $210.60 | | | | |
| 04 | | | | | |
| 05 | | | | | |
| 06 | | | | | |
| 07 | | | | | |
| 08 Aggregate Adjustment | – 0.01 | | | | |
| **H. Other** | **$2,400.00** | | | | |
| 01 HOA Capital Contribution to HOA Acre Inc. | $500.00 | | | | |
| 02 HOA Processing Fee to HOA Acre Inc. | $150.00 | | | | |
| 03 Home Inspection Fee to Engineers Inc. | $750.00 | | | $750.00 | |
| 04 Home Warranty Fee to XYZ Warranty Inc. | | | $450.00 | | |
| 05 Real Estate Commission to Alpha Real Estate Broker | | | $5,700.00 | | |
| 06 Real Estate Commission to Omega Real Estate Broker | | | $5,700.00 | | |
| 07 Title – Owner's Title Insurance (optional) to Epsilon Title Co. | $1,000.00 | | | | |
| 08 | | | | | |
| **I. TOTAL OTHER COSTS (Borrower-Paid)** | **$5,018.05** | | | | |
| Other Costs Subtotals (E + F + G + H) | $5,018.05 | | | | |

| | Borrower-Paid At Closing | Borrower-Paid Before Closing | Seller-Paid At Closing | Seller-Paid Before Closing | Paid by Others |
|---|---|---|---|---|---|
| **J. TOTAL CLOSING COSTS (Borrower-Paid)** | **$9,712.10** | | | | |
| Closing Costs Subtotals (D + I) | $9,682.30 | $29.80 | $12,800.00 | $750.00 | $405.00 |
| Lender Credits | | | | | |

## Calculating Cash to Close

**Use this table to see what has changed from your Loan Estimate.**

| | Loan Estimate | Final | Did this change? |
|---|---|---|---|
| Total Closing Costs (J) | $8,054.00 | $9,712.10 | **YES** • See **Total Loan Costs (D)** and **Total Other Costs (I)** |
| Closing Costs Paid Before Closing | $0 | – $29.80 | **YES** • You paid these Closing Costs **before closing** |
| Closing Costs Financed (Paid from your Loan Amount) | $0 | $0 | **NO** |
| Down Payment/Funds from Borrower | $18,000.00 | $18,000.00 | **NO** |
| Deposit | – $10,000.00 | – $10,000.00 | **NO** |
| Funds for Borrower | $0 | $0 | **NO** |
| Seller Credits | $0 | – $2,500.00 | **YES** • See Seller Credits in **Section L** |
| Adjustments and Other Credits | $0 | – $1,035.04 | **YES** • See details in **Sections K and L** |
| **Cash to Close** | $16,054.00 | $14,147.26 | |

## Summaries of Transactions

**Use this table to see a summary of your transaction.**

### BORROWER'S TRANSACTION

| **K. Due from Borrower at Closing** | **$189,762.30** |
|---|---|
| 01 Sale Price of Property | $180,000.00 |
| 02 Sale Price of Any Personal Property Included in Sale | |
| 03 Closing Costs Paid at Closing (J) | $9,682.30 |
| 04 | |
| **Adjustments** | |
| 05 | |
| 06 | |
| 07 | |
| **Adjustments for Items Paid by Seller in Advance** | |
| 08 City/Town Taxes to | |
| 09 County Taxes to | |
| 10 Assessments to | |
| 11 HOA Dues 4/15/13 to 4/30/13 | $80.00 |
| 12 | |
| 13 | |
| 14 | |
| 15 | |
| **L. Paid Already by or on Behalf of Borrower at Closing** | **$175,615.04** |
| 01 Deposit | $10,000.00 |
| 02 Loan Amount | $162,000.00 |
| 03 Existing Loan(s) Assumed or Taken Subject to | |
| 04 | |
| 05 Seller Credit | $2,500.00 |
| **Other Credits** | |
| 06 Rebate from Epsilon Title Co. | $750.00 |
| 07 | |
| **Adjustments** | |
| 08 | |
| 09 | |
| 10 | |
| 11 | |
| **Adjustments for Items Unpaid by Seller** | |
| 12 City/Town Taxes 1/1/13 to 4/14/13 | $365.04 |
| 13 County Taxes to | |
| 14 Assessments to | |
| 15 | |
| 16 | |
| 17 | |
| **CALCULATION** | |
| Total Due from Borrower at Closing (K) | $189,762.30 |
| Total Paid Already by or on Behalf of Borrower at Closing (L) | – $175,615.04 |
| **Cash to Close ☒ From ☐ To Borrower** | **$14,147.26** |

### SELLER'S TRANSACTION

| **M. Due to Seller at Closing** | **$180,080.00** |
|---|---|
| 01 Sale Price of Property | $180,000.00 |
| 02 Sale Price of Any Personal Property Included in Sale | |
| 03 | |
| 04 | |
| 05 | |
| 06 | |
| 07 | |
| 08 | |
| **Adjustments for Items Paid by Seller in Advance** | |
| 09 City/Town Taxes to | |
| 10 County Taxes to | |
| 11 Assessments to | |
| 12 HOA Dues 4/15/13 to 4/30/13 | $80.00 |
| 13 | |
| 14 | |
| 15 | |
| 16 | |
| **N. Due from Seller at Closing** | **$115,665.04** |
| 01 Excess Deposit | |
| 02 Closing Costs Paid at Closing (J) | $12,800.00 |
| 03 Existing Loan(s) Assumed or Taken Subject to | |
| 04 Payoff of First Mortgage Loan | $100,000.00 |
| 05 Payoff of Second Mortgage Loan | |
| 06 | |
| 07 | |
| 08 Seller Credit | $2,500.00 |
| 09 | |
| 10 | |
| 11 | |
| 12 | |
| 13 | |
| **Adjustments for Items Unpaid by Seller** | |
| 14 City/Town Taxes 1/1/13 to 4/14/13 | $365.04 |
| 15 County Taxes to | |
| 16 Assessments to | |
| 17 | |
| 18 | |
| 19 | |
| **CALCULATION** | |
| Total Due to Seller at Closing (M) | $180,080.00 |
| Total Due from Seller at Closing (N) | – $115,665.04 |
| **Cash ☐ From ☒ To Seller** | **$64,414.96** |

CLOSING DISCLOSURE

PAGE 3 OF 5 • LOAN ID # 123456789

## Additional Information About This Loan

### Loan Disclosures

**Assumption**
If you sell or transfer this property to another person, your lender
☐ will allow, under certain conditions, this person to assume this loan on the original terms.
☒ will not allow assumption of this loan on the original terms.

**Demand Feature**
Your loan
☐ has a demand feature, which permits your lender to require early repayment of the loan. You should review your note for details.
☒ does not have a demand feature.

**Late Payment**
If your payment is more than *15* days late, your lender will charge a late fee of *5% of the monthly principal and interest payment.*

**Negative Amortization** (Increase in Loan Amount)
Under your loan terms, you
☐ are scheduled to make monthly payments that do not pay all of the interest due that month. As a result, your loan amount will increase (negatively amortize), and your loan amount will likely become larger than your original loan amount. Increases in your loan amount lower the equity you have in this property.
☐ may have monthly payments that do not pay all of the interest due that month. If you do, your loan amount will increase (negatively amortize), and, as a result, your loan amount may become larger than your original loan amount. Increases in your loan amount lower the equity you have in this property.
☒ do not have a negative amortization feature.

**Partial Payments**
Your lender
☒ may accept payments that are less than the full amount due (partial payments) and apply them to your loan.
☐ may hold them in a separate account until you pay the rest of the payment, and then apply the full payment to your loan.
☐ does not accept any partial payments.
If this loan is sold, your new lender may have a different policy.

**Security Interest**
You are granting a security interest in
*456 Somewhere Ave., Anytown, ST 12345*

You may lose this property if you do not make your payments or satisfy other obligations for this loan.

**Escrow Account**
***For now,*** your loan
☒ will have an escrow account (also called an "impound" or "trust" account) to pay the property costs listed below. Without an escrow account, you would pay them directly, possibly in one or two large payments a year. Your lender may be liable for penalties and interest for failing to make a payment.

| Escrow | | |
|---|---|---|
| Escrowed Property Costs over Year 1 | $2,473.56 | Estimated total amount over year 1 for your escrowed property costs: *Homeowner's Insurance* *Property Taxes* |
| Non-Escrowed Property Costs over Year 1 | $1,800.00 | Estimated total amount over year 1 for your non-escrowed property costs: *Homeowner's Association Dues* You may have other property costs. |
| Initial Escrow Payment | $412.25 | A cushion for the escrow account you pay at closing. See Section G on page 2. |
| Monthly Escrow Payment | $206.13 | The amount included in your total monthly payment. |

☐ will not have an escrow account because ☐ you declined it ☐ your lender does not offer one. You must directly pay your property costs, such as taxes and homeowner's insurance. Contact your lender to ask if your loan can have an escrow account.

| No Escrow | | |
|---|---|---|
| Estimated Property Costs over Year 1 | | Estimated total amount over year 1. You must pay these costs directly, possibly in one or two large payments a year. |
| Escrow Waiver Fee | | |

***In the future,***
Your property costs may change and, as a result, your escrow payment may change. You may be able to cancel your escrow account, but if you do, you must pay your property costs directly. If you fail to pay your property taxes, your state or local government may (1) impose fines and penalties or (2) place a tax lien on this property. If you fail to pay any of your property costs, your lender may (1) add the amounts to your loan balance, (2) add an escrow account to your loan, or (3) require you to pay for property insurance that the lender buys on your behalf, which likely would cost more and provide fewer benefits than what you could buy on your own.

## Loan Calculations

| | |
|---|---|
| **Total of Payments.** Total you will have paid after you make all payments of principal, interest, mortgage insurance, and loan costs, as scheduled. | $285,803.36 |
| **Finance Charge.** The dollar amount the loan will cost you. | $118,830.27 |
| **Amount Financed.** The loan amount available after paying your upfront finance charge. | $162,000.00 |
| **Annual Percentage Rate (APR).** Your costs over the loan term expressed as a rate. This is not your interest rate. | 4.174% |
| **Total Interest Percentage (TIP).** The total amount of interest that you will pay over the loan term as a percentage of your loan amount. | 69.46% |

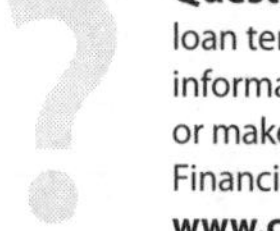

**Questions?** If you have questions about the loan terms or costs on this form, use the contact information below. To get more information or make a complaint, contact the Consumer Financial Protection Bureau at **www.consumerfinance.gov/mortgage-closing**

## Other Disclosures

**Appraisal**
If the property was appraised for your loan, your lender is required to give you a copy at no additional cost at least 3 days before closing. If you have not yet received it, please contact your lender at the information listed below.

**Contract Details**
See your note and security instrument for information about
- what happens if you fail to make your payments,
- what is a default on the loan,
- situations in which your lender can require early repayment of the loan, and
- the rules for making payments before they are due.

**Liability after Foreclosure**
If your lender forecloses on this property and the foreclosure does not cover the amount of unpaid balance on this loan,

☒ state law may protect you from liability for the unpaid balance. If you refinance or take on any additional debt on this property, you may lose this protection and have to pay any debt remaining even after foreclosure. You may want to consult a lawyer for more information.

☐ state law does not protect you from liability for the unpaid balance.

**Refinance**
Refinancing this loan will depend on your future financial situation, the property value, and market conditions. You may not be able to refinance this loan.

**Tax Deductions**
If you borrow more than this property is worth, the interest on the loan amount above this property's fair market value is not deductible from your federal income taxes. You should consult a tax advisor for more information.

## Contact Information

| | Lender | Mortgage Broker | Real Estate Broker (B) | Real Estate Broker (S) | Settlement Agent |
|---|---|---|---|---|---|
| **Name** | Ficus Bank | | Omega Real Estate Broker Inc. | Alpha Real Estate Broker Co. | Epsilon Title Co. |
| **Address** | 4321 Random Blvd. Somecity, ST 12340 | | 789 Local Lane Sometown, ST 12345 | 987 Suburb Ct. Someplace, ST 12340 | 123 Commerce Pl. Somecity, ST 12344 |
| **NMLS ID** | | | | | |
| **ST License ID** | | | Z765416 | Z61456 | Z61616 |
| **Contact** | Joe Smith | | Samuel Green | Joseph Cain | Sarah Arnold |
| **Contact NMLS ID** | 12345 | | | | |
| **Contact ST License ID** | | | P16415 | P51461 | PT1234 |
| **Email** | joesmith@ficusbank.com | | sam@omegare.biz | joe@alphare.biz | sarah@epsilontitle.com |
| **Phone** | 123-456-7890 | | 123-555-1717 | 321-555-7171 | 987-555-4321 |

## Confirm Receipt

By signing, you are only confirming that you have received this form. You do not have to accept this loan because you have signed or received this form.

Applicant Signature Date Co-Applicant Signature Date

CLOSING DISCLOSURE PAGE 5 OF 5 • LOAN ID # 123456789

# Glossary

**abstract of title** A condensed history of the title to a property, consisting of a summary of the original grant and all subsequent conveyances and encumbrances relating to the particular parcel of real estate.

**acceleration clause** The clause in a mortgage or trust deed that stipulates that the entire debt is due immediately if the borrower defaults under the terms of the contract.

**actual notice** Express information or fact; that which is known; direct knowledge.

**ad valorem** Property taxed according to its value.

**adjustable-rate mortgage (ARM)** A mortgage loan that has an interest rate that is changed (adjusted) periodically based upon an index agreed to between a borrower and a lender.

**administered price system** System by which Fannie Mae adjusts required yields in accordance with market factors and its financial needs.

**allowable closing costs** Costs of closing that follow FHA guidelines as to what may be charged to the borrower; the seller may contribute up to 6% of the sales price to cover points and other allowable closing costs.

**American Recovery and Reinvestment Act of 2009 (ARRA)** The first of the government's programs dedicated to restoring the American economy; also called the *Stimulus Act.*

**American Taxpayer Relief Act of 2012** This act retained some aspects of Taxpayer Relief Act of 1997, while eliminating others.

**amortization** The systematic repayment of a loan by periodic installments of principal and interest over the entire term of the loan agreement.

**annual percentage rate (APR)** The effective or actual interest rate, which may be higher or lower than the nominal or contract interest rate because it includes loan closing costs.

**appraisal** An estimate of value. An appraisal of real property value is based on a comparison of real estate prices as well as the current market for real estate.

**assets** All things of value owned by a person or corporation, whether encumbered or not.

**assumed** A loan that may be taken over (assumed) by a buyer when purchasing a parcel of real estate. Often requires the lender to approve the new buyer.

**baby boomers** Persons born between 1946 and 1964.

**balloon payment** A final payment of a mortgage loan that is considerably larger than the required periodic payments because the loan amount was not fully amortized.

**bearer bonds** Interest is paid to any person having the bonds in the person's possession.

**beneficiary** In a trust agreement, the entity in whom the property will vest at the completion of the trust term.

**blanket mortgage** A mortgage secured by pledging more than one property as collateral.

**boot** Money or property given to make up any difference in value or equity between two properties in a 1031 exchange.

**broker price opinion (BPO)** An opinion of real estate value commissioned by a bank or attorney and provided by a broker.

**buydown** A financing technique used to reduce the monthly payments for the first few years of a loan. Funds in the form of discount points are given to the lender by the builder or seller to buy down or lower the effective interest rate paid by the buyer, thus reducing the monthly payments for a set time.

**capitalization rate** The rate of return, based on purchase price, that would attract capital.

**carryback loan** The seller holds a portion of the sales price as a junior encumbrance.

**certificate of eligibility** A form issued by the VA that states the amount of loan guarantee entitlement for which the veteran is eligible.

**certificate of reasonable value (CRV)** A form indicating the appraised value of a property being financed with a VA loan.

**Closing Disclosure** A final account of all costs of a mortgage loan; it replaces the HUD-1 Settlement Statement.

**cloud on the title** Any document, claim, unreleased lien, or encumbrance that may impair the title to real property or make the title doubtful; usually revealed by a title search and removed by either a quitclaim deed or suit to quiet title.

**collateral** Property, real or personal, pledged as security to back up a promise to repay a debt.

**collateralized mortgage obligation (CMO)** A type of mortgage-backed security that creates separate pools of pass-through rates for different classes of bondholders with varying maturities, called tranches. The repayments from the pool of pass-through securities are used to retire the bonds in the order specified by the bonds' prospectus.

**commercial paper** Mortgage loans establishing commercial property as collateral.

**Community Development Block Grant Program (CDBG)** FHA program issuing grants to communities for economic development, job opportunities, and housing rehabilitation.

**Community Reinvestment Act (CRA)** Under the act, financial institutions are expected to meet the deposit and credit needs of their communities; became a significant factor in the growth of bank mergers starting in the 1990s.

**completion bond** A surety bond posted by a landowner or developer to guarantee that a proposed development will be completed according to specifications, free and clear of all mechanics' liens.

**conforming loan** Any mortgage loan that meets the qualifying standards set by Fannie Mae and Freddie Mac. The maximum loan limit is set each year by the Federal Housing Finance Agency.

**constructive notice** Notice given to the world by recorded documents.

**Consumer Financial Protection Bureau (CFPB)** Established in 2010 under the Wall Street Reform and Consumer Protection Act (Dodd-Frank Act) as an independent agency setting rules and regulations for any business providing financial services to consumers.

**contract for deed** A contract under which the purchase price is paid in installments over a period of time during which the purchaser has possession of the property but the seller retains title until the contract terms are completed; usually drawn between individuals. Also called a *land contract, installment contract,* or *agreement of sale.*

**correspondents** Another name for mortgage bankers who both originate and service mortgage loans on behalf of investors.

**cost approach** The process of appraising the value of a property by adding to the estimated value of the land the appraiser's calculations of the replacement cost of the building, less depreciation.

**coupon bonds** A type of corporate bond with interest coupons attached that may be cashed by the bearer of the bond.

**credit report** An itemization of the status of an individual's credit history.

**credit score** An objective method of assessing credit risk based on the statistical probability of debt repayment.

**cross-defaulting clause** A provision in a mortgage that triggers a default on a second mortgage if there is a default on the first mortgage.

**debentures** Unsecured bonds that are a claim against the general assets of a corporation.

**deed in lieu of foreclosure** To avoid a foreclosure action, a defaulting borrower may voluntarily convey the collateral to the lender.

**deed of trust** *See* trust deed.

**default** Nonperformance of a duty; failure to meet an obligation when due.

**defeasance clause** A clause used in leases and mortgages that cancels a specified right upon the occurrence of a certain condition, such as cancellation of a mortgage upon repayment of the mortgage loan.

**deficiency judgment** The difference in the amount received at an auction of defaulted property between the amount owed and the amount received as an award to the lender.

**demand deposits** Bank deposits that must be available on demand (e.g., checking accounts).

**depreciation** In appraisal, the loss of value due to physical deterioration, functional obsolescence, or economic obsolescence. In accounting, the allowable deduction for the recapture of the investment.

**Desktop Originator® (DO)** Fannie Mae's automated underwriting system for independent mortgage broker/agents.

**Desktop Underwriter® (DU)** Fannie Mae's automated underwriting system for lender services.

**direct endorsement program** Allows approved lenders to underwrite FHA loans; leaves the FHA with risk of default, but the FHA can remove the lender from the program.

**direct sales comparison approach** The process of estimating the value of a property by examining and comparing actual sales of comparable properties.

**discount rate** The rate of interest charged by the Federal Reserve to its member banks to borrow money.

**disintermediation** A situation when more funds are being withdrawn from financial institutions than are being deposited.

**draws** A system of payments made by a lender to a contractor as designated stages of a building's construction are completed.

**drive-by appraisal** Appraiser only observes exterior of the property, with no interior inspection.

**due-on-sale clause** A clause in a mortgage or trust deed that stipulates that a borrower cannot sell or transfer the property without prior written consent of the lender. Also called an *alienation clause.*

**echo boomers** Offspring of the baby boomer generation; suffering from current difficult economic times.

**encumbrance** Anything—such as a mortgage, tax, or judgment lien; an easement; a restriction on the use of the land; or an outstanding dower right—that may diminish the value or use and enjoyment of a property.

**Energy Efficient Mortgage (EEM)** Mortgage that includes funding for energy-efficient features to new or existing houses.

**entitlement** The amount of the sales price guaranteed by the VA for a VA mortgage loan.

**entitlement communities** Designated communities eligible for Community Development Block Grant (CDBG) funds.

**Equal Credit Opportunity Act (ECOA)** The federal law that prohibits discrimination in the extension of credit because of race, color, religion, national origin, sex, age, marital status, or source of income.

**equitable redemption period** Time granted before the sale of the property, allowing the borrower to make up late payments and charges; length varies by state.

**equitable right of redemption** The right of a defaulted property owner to recover the property prior to its sale by paying the appropriate fees and charges.

**equitable title** The interest held by a vendee under a contract for deed or an installment contract; the equitable right to obtain absolute ownership to property when legal title is held in another's name.

**equity loan** Money borrowed on accumulated equity.

**escrow funds** Funds collected by the lender to pay property taxes and homeowners insurance; also called *impound funds* in some states.

**eviction** The legal dispossession of an errant borrower or tenant.

**exculpatory clause** Stipulates that the borrower's liability is limited to the property designated in the legal description.

**Fannie Mae** A government-sponsored enterprise established to purchase any kind of mortgage loans in the secondary mortgage market from the primary lenders.

**Federal Deposit Insurance Corporation (FDIC)** A federal agency that provides insurance of $250,000 per depositor account and supervises the operations of banks and thrifts.

**federal funds rate** The rate recommended by the Federal Reserve for the member banks to charge each other on short-term loans. These rates form the basis on which the banks determine the percentage rate of interest they will charge their loan customers.

**Federal Home Loan Bank (FHLB)** Organized in 1932 to provide central clearing facilities and regulations for savings associations; now under supervision of Federal Housing Finance Agency (FHFA). Serves as secondary market for its members.

**Federal Housing Finance Agency (FHFA)** Created in 2008 under the Housing and Economic Recovery Act to oversee Fannie Mae, Freddie Mac, and the Federal Home Loan Banks; currently acting as conservator for Fannie Mae and Freddie Mac.

**FICO** System for determining credit score developed by Fair, Isaac & Company.

**fiduciary responsibility** A relationship that implies a position of trust or confidence wherein one person is usually entrusted to hold or manage property or money for another.

**financial intermediaries** Financial fiduciary institution that acts as an intermediary between savers and borrowers.

**financial statement** A standardized form listing all of an applicant's assets and liabilities.

**fixed-rate loan** A loan where the interest rate stays constant for the life of the loan.

**forbearance** An agreement by the lender for a full or partial waiver of payment for a set period of time.

**Freddie Mac** A government-sponsored enterprise established to purchase primarily conventional mortgage loans in the secondary mortgage market.

**funding fee** An amount charged on a VA loan to protect the VA in case of default by the borrower; amount varies according to time in service.

**general obligation bonds** System of financing in which the community is held responsible for making payments for capital improvements, usually included in property taxes.

**Generation X** Generally considered to be those born between 1965 and 1976; tend to marry later and have a higher divorce rate and lower remarriage rate, resulting in a higher percentage of persons living alone.

**Ginnie Mae** A government agency that plays an important role in the secondary mortgage market. It guarantees mortgage-backed securities using FHA and VA loans as collateral.

**Good Faith Estimate (GFE)** An estimate of all closing fees that must be provided to a borrower within three days of the loan application as required by the Real Estate Settlement Procedures Act (RESPA).

**government-sponsored enterprise (GSE)** Term used for Fannie Mae, Freddie Mac, and Federal Home Loan Bank—all independent entities receiving favorable tax benefits and line of credit with Department of the Treasury; now under supervision of Federal Housing Finance Agency.

**grace period** Time allowed by a lender before enforcing a penalty for late payment.

**granting clause** Words in a deed of conveyance that state the grantor's intention to convey the property at the present time. This clause is generally worded as "convey and warrant"; "grant"; "grant, bargain, and sell"; or the like.

**gross rent multiplier (GRM)** The figure used as a multiplier of the gross monthly income of a property to produce an estimate of the property's value.

**hazard insurance** Insurance that only covers physical hazards to the property.

**Home Affordable Modification Program (HAMP)** A program for modifying a mortgage loan in order for the payment to become within the borrower's ability to pay.

**Home Affordable Refinance Program (HARP)** A program of refinancing specifically designed for homeowners not eligible for the HAMP.

**Home Equity Conversion Mortgage (HECM)** FHA's reverse mortgage program designed to provide extra income for those 62 years of age or older.

**Home Equity Line of Credit (HELOC)** A version of a home equity loan where the borrower can draw down from an established line-of-credit amount, only paying interest on the amount of funds withdrawn.

**Home Mortgage Disclosure Act (HMDA)** A federal law that requires lenders to annually disclose the number of loan applications and loans in certain areas, thus eliminating the practice of redlining.

**homeowners insurance** A standardized package insurance policy that covers a residential real estate owner against financial loss from fire, theft, public liability, and other common risks.

**HOPE NOW** A special hotline number that borrowers at risk of foreclosure can call for advice.

**Housing and Economic Recovery Act of 2008 (HERA)** Created the Federal Housing Finance Agency to regulate the GSEs; also created the Neighborhood Stabilization Program to assist communities suffering from large number of foreclosures.

**Housing Choice Voucher Program** Provides rental assistance to eligible consumers and allows funds to be used towards mortgage payment. Formerly called *Section 8*.

**housing ratio** A percentage of gross monthly income set aside for total housing expense, including principal, interest, taxes, homeowners insurance, mortgage insurance, and any condominium or homeowners association fees.

**HUD-1 Settlement Statement** A form that itemizes fees and services charged to a borrower and seller during a real estate transaction.

**hypothecation** The act of pledging real estate as security without surrendering possession of the property.

**impound funds** Funds collected by the lender along with mortgage payment to pay for property taxes and homeowners insurance. Also called *escrow funds*.

**income approach** A process of estimating the value of an income-producing property by capitalization of its net operating income.

**industrial development bonds** Securities issued to pay for the development of a new industry, usually in the form of general obligation bonds.

**industrial revenue bonds (IRBs)** Bonds backed by a state's bonding credit to raise funds for the purchase and improvement of land for industrial and office parks.

**interest rate factor** The number of dollars it takes to pay down $1,000 of a loan based on the interest rate and term of the loan.

**interest-only loans** A loan that only requires the payment of interest for a stated period of time with the principal due at the end of the term.

**interim financing** An open-end mortgage loan, usually for a short term, obtained to finance the actual construction of buildings on a property.

**Internal Revenue Code Section 1031** Allows recognition of gain for tax purposes to be postponed by exchanging like kind income-producing properties.

**Interstate Land Sales Full Disclosure Act (ILSFDA)** A federal law that regulates interstate land sales by requiring registration of real property and disclosure of full and accurate information regarding the property to prospective buyers.

**involuntary lien** A lien placed on property without the consent of the property owner.

**judgment decree** Process by which a court orders the sale of property at public auction.

**judicial foreclosure** Foreclosure requiring court order and sale at public auction.

**jumbo loans** Any loan exceeding the current Fannie Mae/Freddie Mac conforming loan limit.

**junior financing** Any type of secondary (or tertiary) loan where there is a first mortgage in place.

**lease option** A lease under which the tenant has the right to purchase the property either during the lease term or at its end.

**lease purchase** The purchase of real property, the consummation of which is preceded by a lease, usually long-term, that is typically done for tax or financing purposes.

**leverage** Use of borrowed money to finance the purchase of an investment.

**liabilities** Debts incurred.

**lien theory** Some states interpret a mortgage as being purely a lien on real property. The mortgagee thus has no right of possession but must foreclose the lien and sell the property if the mortgagor defaults.

**lifting clause** A clause in a junior mortgage allowing a borrower to replace an existing first mortgage without disturbing the status of the junior mortgage.

**Loan Estimate** The required disclosure of all costs of obtaining a mortgage loan; it replaces the GFE and TILA disclosures.

**Loan Prospector®** Freddie Mac's automated underwriting system.

**loan-to-value (LTV) ratio** The relationship between the amount of the mortgage loan and the value of the real estate being pledged as collateral.

**M1** Measure of the total money supply; money easily available, such as cash, checking accounts, and demand deposits.

**M2** Measure of the total money supply; all of M1, plus money market funds, retirement accounts, and deposits under $100,000.

**M3** Measure of the total money supply; all of M2, plus deposits over $100,000, money on deposit overseas, and institutional money market funds.

**manufactured housing** Prefabricated homes built in a factory and transported to a lot for installation.

**market value** The highest price for which a property would sell, assuming a reasonable time for the sale and a knowledgeable buyer and seller acting without duress.

**moratorium** A temporary suspension of payments due under a financing agreement to help a distressed borrower recover and avoid a default and foreclosure.

**mortgage bankers** A financial intermediary who originates new mortgage loans, collects payments, inspects the collateral, and forecloses, if necessary.

**mortgage brokers** One who acts as an intermediary between borrower and lender for a real estate loan, thereby earning a placement fee.

**Mortgage Forgiveness Debt Relief Act of 2007** Relieves borrower from liability to pay taxes on any monies forgiven by a bank due to a short sale or foreclosure.

**mortgage insurance premium (MIP)** A fee paid to assure lenders that in the event a borrower does not make the required mortgage payments, the insurance company will.

**mortgage revenue bonds** Tax-exempt bonds used to make below-market interest rate loans to developers in redevelopment projects or for low-cost mortgages for first-time homebuyers.

**mortgage-backed securities (MBSs)** Packages of mortgage loans sold on the open market; some pools may be of the same type loans, while others may be multiple-issue pools.

**mortgagee** A lender in a mortgage loan transaction.

**mortgagor** A borrower in a mortgage loan transaction.

**municipal bonds** Bonds issued by a municipality, county, or state to finance community improvements.

**negative amortization** Less than interest-only loan payments, which cause the balance of a loan to increase by the amount of the deficient interest.

**Neighborhood Stabilization Program (NSP)** Part of the Housing and Economic Recovery Act of 2008 that provides grants to communities suffering from an excess number of foreclosures.

**net worth** Assets less liabilities.

**nonconforming loan** Any loan that does not conform to the Fannie Mae/Freddie Mac qualifying guidelines, including maximum loan amount.

**nonrecourse clause** Relieves the seller from liability if the borrower defaults.

**note** A signed instrument acknowledging a debt and promising repayment.

**note and mortgage** A note can stand alone, but a mortgage must be accompanied by a note in order to be legally enforceable.

**novation** Substituting a new obligation for an old one or substituting new parties to an existing obligation.

**open-market operations** The Fed's activities in buying and selling securities to control the money supply.

**origination fee** Fee charged by a lender to cover costs of originating the loan; frequently 1% of the loan amount.

**package mortgage** A real estate loan used to finance the purchase of both real property and personal property, such as in the purchase of a new home that includes carpeting, window coverings, and major appliances.

**par** With regard to mortgage loans, means bought at full-face value.

**partial entitlement** A veteran who has used the full entitlement in the past may be eligible for additional entitlement if the guarantee amount has increased; subtract the amount previously used from the current entitlement to obtain the partial entitlement. The bank will lend four times that amount with zero money down payment.

**participation certificates (PCs)** Another name for mortgage-backed securities sold by Freddie Mac.

**participation financing** When the lender requires an equity position in the property being financed.

**pass-through certificates** Mortgage-backed securities where the principal and interest payments are passed through to the investor in one of several different formats.

**piggy-back loan** When the borrower takes out a first and second mortgage simultaneously in order to avoid private mortgage insurance (there is no PMI as long as first mortgage is 80% or less).

**point** A percentage of the principal loan amount charged by the lender. Each point is equal to 1% of the loan amount.

**power of sale** In a deed of trust, authorizes the trustee to proceed with the sale of the property.

**power-of-sale method** A nonjudicial type of foreclosure usually performed by exercising the trustee rights under a deed of trust.

**predatory lending** The practice of charging excessive interest rates and fees to unsuspecting borrowers.

**premium** 1. In discounting, a payment of more than face value for a security. 2. In insurance, the fee paid for coverage.

**prepayment clause** A clause in a mortgage or trust deed that provides for a penalty to be levied against a borrower who repays a loan before the specified due date.

**primary lender** Institutions that make mortgage loans; primarily banks, savings associations, credit unions, mortgage brokers, and mortgage bankers.

**primary market** The mortgage market in which loans are originated and consisting of lenders such as commercial banks, savings associations, and mutual savings banks.

**prime rate** The interest rate a lender charges its most creditworthy customers.

**private mortgage insurance (PMI)** Mortgage insurance issued by companies not associated with the federal government.

**property report** The mandatory federal and state documents compiled by subdividers and developers to provide potential purchasers with facts about a property prior to their purchase.

**qualified residential mortgage (QRM)** A new standard of qualifying being considered by Fannie Mae and Freddie Mac where the lender must retain part of the risk for any mortgage loan with less than a 20% down payment.

**quantitative easing** A Fed program to purchase mortgage-backed securities and long-term Treasury notes.

**real estate cycle** Historically, real estate goes around in short-term (three to five years) and long-term (10 to 15 years) cycles. The ability to forecast future cycles is significant to investors.

**real estate investment trust (REIT)** An unincorporated trust set up to invest in real estate that must have at least 100 investors, with management, control, and title to the property in the hands of trustees.

**real estate mortgage investment conduits (REMICs)** A pool of mortgages in which investors may purchase proportionate interests.

**real estate mortgage trust (REMT)** A business trust, similar to a REIT, that invests in mortgage securities rather than in real estate.

**Real Estate Settlement Procedures Act (RESPA)** The federal law that requires certain disclosures to consumers about mortgage loan settlements. The law also prohibits the payment or receipt of kickbacks and certain kinds of referral fees.

**recast** A lender can reconfigure the remaining balance into a new loan over a new term, resulting in a reduction in the monthly payment.

**reconciliation** The final step in the appraisal process, in which the appraiser combines the estimates of value received from the sales comparison, cost, and income approaches to arrive at a final estimate of market value for the subject property.

**registered bonds** Bonds issued to a specific owner that cannot be transferred without the owner's endorsement; interest is paid to the last registered owner.

**Regulation Z** The truth-in-lending portion of the Consumer Credit Protection Act of 1968. It requires complete disclosure of the total costs involved in most credit activities.

**rehabilitation loan FHA 203(k)** A special type of FHA loan that provides funds to both purchase the property and make needed repairs and improvements.

**release clause** A clause included in a blanket mortgage that provides that on payment of a specific sum of money, the lien on a particular parcel or portion of the collateral will be released.

**release of liability** Releases the veteran seller from any remaining liability for a default on the loan.

**reserve requirements** The Fed requires its members to keep a certain percentage of the bank's total funds on deposit with its federal district bank. The Fed can change the amount of reserves requires to help control the flow of money in the country.

**residual income** On a VA loan, the lender must also take into account how much money will be left over (residual) after making the mortgage payment plus other fixed expenses. If the residual income is not considered sufficient, the loan will not be approved.

**revenue bonds** Bonds to be repaid by the fees charged for the use of the funded project.

**reverse annuity mortgage (RAM)** A loan under which the homeowner receives payments based on the accumulated equity; payment may be monthly, a lump sum, or established as a line-of-credit. The loan must be repaid at a prearranged date, upon the death of the owner, or upon the sale of the property. The FHA reverse mortgage is called a *Home Equity Conversion Mortgage (HECM)*.

**right of first refusal** The right of a person to have the first opportunity to either purchase or lease a specific parcel of real property.

**robo-signing** When a bank official signs off on numerous foreclosure papers without adequate research; blamed for some of the current foreclosure problems.

**second mortgage** Junior financing; a second mortgage issued on top of an existing first mortgage. Also called a *second deed of trust*.

**secondary market** A marketplace in which mortgages and trust deeds are traded. *See also* Fannie Mae, Freddie Mac, and Ginnie Mae.

**Secure and Fair Enforcement Mortgage Licensing Act (SAFE Act)** Designed to provide more control over those dealing with financial issues for the consumer.

**securities** Something given, deposited, or pledged to make secure the fulfillment of an obligation, usually the repayment of a debt. Generically, mortgages, trust deeds, and other financing instruments backed by collateral pledges are termed securities for investment purposes.

**shadow inventory** Homes that are delinquent or in foreclosure that do not appear on the open market.

**short sale** When a lender is willing to accept less than the total amount due on a mortgage.

**split loan** When a second mortgage is taken out in order to avoid private mortgage insurance. Also called a *piggy-back loan*.

**statement of record** An explanation and description of existing and proposed improvements and services planned for residential land to be sold intra-state.

**statutory period of redemption** Period of time allowed after the sale of property for the borrower to redeem the loan and the property.

**stop date** The date on which the entire principal balance on a term loan must be paid.

**streamline refinance** A faster way to refinance FHA loans with less documentation and underwriting.

**Streamlined Modification Program (SMP)** A loan modification program initiated in 2008 for at-risk borrowers with Fannie Mae and Freddie Mac loans.

**strict foreclosure** Court establishes a specific time for the balance of the loan to be paid off; if not paid, full legal title is awarded to the lender. Rare today except in case of land contract.

**subject to** Becoming responsible, but not assuming personal liability, for an existing loan.

**subordination** An existing mortgage can be placed in an inferior position to a new mortgage given to another mortgagee and secured by the same collateral.

**subprime lenders** Lenders specializing in loans for less than credit-worthy borrowers; blamed for much of the financial crisis starting in 2007 due to adjustable-rate loans that borrowers were not able to make payments on when the ARM reset after two or three years.

**subprime market** Lenders specializing in loans to less-than-credit-worthy borrowers. This market grew rapidly in the early 2000s and declined when the overall housing market began to decline in 2006.

**subrogation** Taking a lesser position or interest.

**substitution of entitlement** One veteran can substitute entitlement when purchasing another veteran's property, releasing the original veteran borrower from all liability on the loan.

**suit to quiet title** A court action intended to establish or settle the title to a particular property, especially when there is a cloud on the title.

**survey** The process by which boundaries are measured and land areas are determined; the on-site measurement of lot lines, dimensions, and position of a house on a lot, including the determination of any existing encroachments or easements.

**tax increment financing** Allocates increased property tax revenues to pay for debts incurred in improving an area.

**Taxpayer Relief Act of 1997 (TRA '97)** A sweeping revision of the income tax code providing homeowners with exemptions from capital gains tax on the sale of personal residences.

**thrifts** Savings associations or savings banks; may be organized as either stock or mutual companies.

**title insurance** A policy insuring an owner or mortgagee against loss by reason of defects in the title to a parcel of real estate.

**title report** A search of public records to determine all interests in the property.

**title theory** Some states interpret a mortgage to mean that the lender is the owner of mortgaged land. Upon full payment of the mortgage debt, the borrower becomes the landowner.

**Torrens Certificate** Includes the state as guarantor of the title in case of a claim.

**total obligations ratio** Percentage of gross monthly income allowed for all housing expense plus monthly debt payments. Also called the *back-end ratio.*

**Treasury bills** Department of the Treasury short-term securities.

**Treasury bonds** Department of the Treasury long-term securities that run more than ten years.

**Treasury notes** Department of the Treasury intermediate-term securities that run two to ten years.

**tri-merge credit report** Combines information from Experian, Equifax, and Trans-Union; required by most lenders.

**Troubled Asset Relief Program (TARP)** Establishes and manages a Treasury fund in an attempt to curb the ongoing financial crisis of 2007.

**trust deed** A financing instrument in which the borrower/trustor conveys title into the hands of a third-party trustee to be held for the beneficiary/lender. When the loan is repaid, title is reconveyed to the trustor. If default occurs, the trustee exercises the power of sale on behalf of the lender/beneficiary. Also called a *deed of trust.*

**trustee** The appointed third-party operator of a trust.

**trustor** The originator of a trust.

**Truth in Lending Act (TILA)** Federal government regulates the lending practices of mortgage lenders through Regulation Z of this act, which requires full disclosure of all terms of credit, including the annual percentage rate (APR).

**underwriting** The process of evaluating borrower credit, collateral value, and the risks involved in making a loan.

**upside down or underwater** When borrower owes more than the current value of a property.

**usury** Charging interest at a higher rate than the maximum rate established by state law. Does not apply to mortgage loans.

**value in exchange** When its power to purchase other objects defines a property's value.

**value in use** When a specific use defines a property's value.

**vendee** A buyer, usually under the terms of a land contract.

**vendor** A seller, usually under the terms of a land contract.

**voluntary lien** A lien placed on property with the knowledge and consent of the property owner.

**Wall Street Reform and Consumer Protection Act (Dodd-Frank Act)** Signed into law in July 2010; includes provisions anticipated to restore responsibility and accountability to the financial system, including establishing the Consumer Financial Protection Bureau.

**warehouse of funds** Funds committed by a commercial bank that mortgage brokers can draw on, enabling them to close individual home loans that may become part of a larger package.

**weighted average** An appraiser may assign percentages to illustrate the importance of one appraisal approach over another.

**workouts** Efforts made by a lender to avoid foreclosure, including payment waivers, refinancing, and loan modifications.

**zero-coupon bonds** A bond purchased at a discount and redeemed after a stated period of time for full value; patterned after World War II savings bonds.

# Answer Key

## REVIEW QUESTION ANSWERS

### Chapter 1: The Nature and Cycle of Real Estate Finance

1. c. The construction industry affects millions of people in related industries.
2. b. Disintermediation occurs when more funds are withdrawn than are deposited, resulting in a net loss of deposits, a cutback in lending, and a slowdown in the economy.
3. c. In the concept known as hypothecation, the borrower is the legal owner; the lender has rights only after a loan default.
4. a. Leverage makes use of borrowed funds to finance the major portion of a purchase.
5. d. Federal and related agencies are the largest holders of outstanding mortgage debt today.
6. c. The impact of local activities will always have the greatest effect on property values.
7. a. The majority of households are married couples, but a large number are single-person households.
8. b. A greater demand will generally lead to increased home prices.
9. d. The birth rate is actually lower.
10. b. In order to qualify for the capital gains tax exemption, an individual or couple must have lived in their home a total of two of the past five years.

### Chapter 2: Money and the Monetary System

1. c. The value of money is based on trust and confidence in the United States.
2. b. When interest rates are higher, the banks lend less money for spending.
3. b. Because rapid inflation or a slide into recession has the most impact on the economy, the Fed's primary short-term goal is to combat inflationary or deflationary pressures.
4. c. When the reserve requirements are lowered, commercial banks have more money available for lending.
5. b. The Federal Reserve discount rate is the amount of interest charged to banks for borrowed funds.
6. d. The Truth in Lending Act, also called TILA (Regulation Z), is administered by the Fed.
7. d. 8.00% + 0.75% = 8.75%.
8. b. Treasury departments are responsible for collecting funds and paying bills to keep federal agencies in operation.
9. c. Treasury bonds run for more than ten years; Treasury bills are less than one year; Treasury notes are two to ten years.
10. c. FDIC provides insurance for deposits in banks and thrifts.

## Chapter 3: Additional Government Influence

1. c. Fannie Mae is now under the control of the Federal Housing Finance Agency.
2. c. The Interstate Land Sales Act only pertains to land sales made out of state, not land marketed locally.
3. c. The Housing Choice Voucher Program allows the Public Housing Authority to use some of its allotted funds to provide mortgage payment assistance to qualified applicants.
4. b. The Equal Credit Opportunity Act (ECOA) forbids seeking information about childbearing capability.
5. d. Right of rescission is covered under the Truth in Lending Act rather than RESPA.
6. d. Regulation Z requires full disclosure of all aspects of financing if any one element is advertised.
7. b. Lenders are required to provide credit for all qualified persons in the community served.
8. b. IRBs are used to encourage incoming business to the community; an industrial or office park is an ideal application of IRB monies.
9. a. NSP grants are for the purchase and redevelopment of abandoned or foreclosed properties.
10. d. FCS provides credit in rural, not urban, areas.

## Chapter 4: The Secondary Mortgage Market

1. d. The sale of mortgage-backed securities using loan packages as collateral provides funds.
2. d. The administered price system replaced the free market auction system.
3. a. LTV higher than 80% requires mortgage insurance.
4. b. Any loan that does not meet Fannie Mae/Freddie Mac guidelines is nonconforming.
5. c. Ginnie Mae is administered by HUD and is not a GSE.
6. b. Freddie Mac was chartered to purchase conventional loans from savings associations and thrifts and now purchases both government and conventional loans.
7. d. As part of the Economic and Housing Recovery Act of 2008, Freddie Mac came under the supervision of the Federal Housing Finance Agency (FHFA) and in September 2008 was placed in conservatorship along with Fannie Mae.
8. d. Ginnie Mae guarantees payment to investors on FHA/VA mortgage-backed securities.
9. d. The FHA comes under the supervision of HUD, not FHFA.
10. c. A real estate mortgage investment conduit (REMIC) is made up of multiple classes of ownership interests in a single pass-through tax authority.

## Chapter 5: Sources of Funds: Institutional, Non-Institutional, and Other Lenders

1. d. Checking accounts provide more than savings accounts, loans, or equity.
2. c. Single-family home loans are generally issued for 30-year amortizations.
3. b. Commercial banks specialize in short-term construction loans.
4. b. Mutual savings banks originated in the early industrial areas of the Northeast.
5. c. Life insurance companies are more interested in larger, long-term projects, not home mortgage loans.
6. b. Mortgage brokers do not service the loan after settlement.
7. a. Mortgage bankers originate the loan and service the loan after settlement.
8. a. Through warehousing, the local commercial bank provides short-term financing to generate funds.
9. a. A real estate investment trust (REIT) provides income generated from the property itself.
10. b. A real estate mortgage trust (REMT) generates income from mortgage loans.
11. c. Municipal bonds are issued by a city, county, or state.
12. c. Registered bonds may be cashed in only by the registered owner.
13. c. If the market rate increases, the value of the lower interest rate bonds decreases.
14. c. Income from a REIT is taxed at the beneficiary level only.

## Chapter 6: Instruments of Real Estate Finance

1. a. The owner of the property chooses to place a mortgage lien.
2. d. Property taxes will take precedence over other liens.
3. a. The increased foreclosure power is very attractive to a lender.
4. c. An unsecured note is an independent debt instrument without collateral.
5. c. The defeasance clause provides the mortgagor with clear title when the loan is paid off.
6. c. In a contract for deed, title does not convey until all terms have been met.
7. a. A due-on-sale clause requires that the loan be paid off when the property is conveyed.
8. b. Purchasing subject to an existing loan leaves the seller with liability.
9. c. The release clause enables the developer to give clear title on each sale.
10. b. Lenders temporarily waiving payments run less risk that they will lose first rights.

## Chapter 7: Real Estate Financing Programs

1. b. Most people like the security of a fixed-rate loan and the lower monthly payment of a 30-year loan compared to a 15-year loan.
2. b. When the equity reaches 22% of the original value, the PMI must be dropped.
3. b. On the 80/15/5 split loan, the first mortgage will be $240,000, second mortgage $45,000, and down payment $15,000.
4. b. $80,000 ÷ 12 = $6,666.67 × 36% = $2,400.
5. d. Subprime lenders are not necessarily predatory but do make it possible for those with poor credit to obtain a mortgage loan, although at higher-than-market interest rates.
6. d. The cost of refinancing should be recoverable in two years.
7. c. The 2/6 cap limits to 6 the increase over the life of the loan: 3.5 + 6 = 9.5%.
8. b. The reverse annuity mortgage would provide the couple with income.
9. c. The lender disperses funds as the work is completed to protect the lender's interest.
10. c. The installment sale may provide a tax advantage for the individual.
11. b. In a lease-purchase, financial negotiations are often entered into prior to final settlement.
12. c. Under IRS Section 1031, equal value is not necessary, but equities in the property must be balanced.
13. d. In a joint venture, each party brings individual expertise to a specific project.

## Chapter 8: Government Loans

1. c. Because the government insured the full amount of the loan, lenders were willing to make loans with low down payments.
2. b. One of HUD's main functions is the administration of FHA.
3. c. A mortgage insurance premium provides funds to protect FHA from losses due to foreclosures.
4. d. The seller may not provide any part of the 3.5% required from the borrower.
5. b. The Home Equity Conversion Mortgage (HECM) was developed as an option for elderly homeowners.
6. c. The annual renewal payment is calculated as a percentage of the total loan, divided by 12 and added to the monthly PITI payment.
7. a. The FHA 203(k) loan covers both the purchase and rehabilitation of a property.
8. d. The lender considers the guaranteed VA entitlement the same as 25% down.
9. c. The Certificate of Eligibility is issued by the Department of Veterans Affairs on request.
10. b. Even if the seller opts to accept the CRV value as the sales price, the buyer is not obligated to purchase the property.
11. b. Current guarantee of $104,250 – $46,000 = $58,250 × 4 = $233,000.
12. c. The funding fee provides the VA a pool of money for costs due to foreclosure.

## Chapter 9: Processing Real Estate Loans

1. a. The borrower's ability to repay the loan is most important to the lender.
2. c. After seven or eight years, most people either sell or refinance.
3. a. The lender is very comfortable with a 2-to-1 assets-to-liabilities ratio.
4. a. High-income persons with a lax attitude about paying bills are a high risk.
5. a. The direct sales comparison approach is mostly used with residential properties.
6. b. As there are few comparables for churches, the cost approach is best.
7. b. All recorded instruments are considered to be constructive notice.
8. c. Most states require a mechanic's lien to be filed within less than a year.
9. c. The state maintains title records with the Torrens System.
10. b. If a seller is not able to resolve the problem, legal action in the form of a suit to quiet title may be taken.

## Chapter 10: Defaults and Foreclosures

1. c. Both borrower and lender gain as property increases in value.
2. b. Any breach may result in the lender accelerating the total loan due.
3. b. In using forbearance or moratorium, the lender anticipates that the borrower will solve the current financial problem.
4. b. The equitable redemption period allows the borrower to bring the payments current or pay off the total due.
5. b. The lender will make an opening bid when suing on terms of mortgage.
6. a. It is hoped that forbearance will enable the borrower to return to a secure financial position.
7. c. In receiving the top portion of the loan, the lender is paid—by the VA—the difference between present value and the loan balance.
8. c. Avoiding the judicial procedure enables the lender to foreclose more rapidly.
9. c. If the contract for deed is worded carefully, the vendor may be able to exercise strict foreclosure.
10. b. The IRS sees the defaulted loan as a gain to the borrower.

# Index

# Notes

# Notes

# Notes

# Notes

# Notes

# Notes

# Notes

# Notes

# Notes

Cooking Light

# Comfort Food

Cooking Light®

# Comfort Food

Home-Cooked,
Delicious Classics
Made Light

Oxmoor House®

ISBN-13: 978-0-8487-3464-0
ISBN-10: 0-8487-3464-5
Library of Congress Control Number: 2010933261
Printed in the United States of America
First printing 2011

Be sure to check with your health-care provider before making any changes in your diet.

**Oxmoor House**

VP, Publishing Director: Jim Childs
Editorial Director: Susan Payne Dobbs
Brand Manager: Michelle Turner Aycock
Senior Editor: Heather Averett
Managing Editor: Laurie S. Herr

**Cooking Light® Comfort Food**

Project Editor: Georgia Dodge
Senior Designer: Emily Albright Parrish
Test Kitchens Director: Elizabeth Tyler Austin
Assistant Directors, Test Kitchens: Julie Christopher, Julie Gunter
Test Kitchens Professionals: Wendy Ball, Allison E. Cox, Victoria E. Cox, Margaret Monroe Dickey, Allyson Moreland Haynes, Callie Nash, Kathleen Royal Phillips, Catherine Crowell Steele, Lean Van Deren
Photography Director: Jim Bathie
Senior Photo Stylist: Kay E. Clarke
Associate Photo Stylist: Katherine Eckert Coyne
Assistant Photo Stylist: Mary Louise Menendez
Senior Production Manager: Greg A. Amason
Production Manager: Tamara N. Wilder

**Contributors**

Copy Editor: Jacqueline Giovanelli
Proofreader: Lauren Brooks
Indexer: Mary Ann Laurens
Interns: Sarah Bélanger, Christine T. Boatwright, Blair Gillespie, Allison Sperando, Caitlin Watzke

**Cooking Light®**

Editor: Scott Mowbray
Creative Director: Carla Frank
Deputy Editor: Phillip Rhodes
Food Editor: Ann Taylor Pittman
Special Publications Editor: Mary Simpson Creel, MS, RD
Associate Food Editors: Timothy Q. Cebula, Julianna Grimes
Associate Editors: Cindy Hatcher, Brandy Rushing
Test Kitchens Director: Vanessa T. Pruett
Assistant Test Kitchens Director: Tiffany Vickers Davis
Chief Food Stylist: Charlotte Autry
Senior Food Stylist: Kellie Gerber Kelley
Recipe Testers and Developers: Robin Bashinsky, Adam Hickman, Deb Wise
Art Director: Fernande Bondarenko
Junior Deputy Art Director: Alexander Spacher
Associate Art Director: Rachel Lasserre
Designer: Chase Turberville
Photo Director: Kristen Schaefer
Senior Photographer: Randy Mayor
Senior Photo Stylist: Cindy Barr
Photo Stylist: Leigh Ann Ross
Copy Chief: Maria Parker Hopkins
Assistant Copy Chief: Susan Roberts
Research Editor: Michelle Gibson Daniels
Editorial Production Director: Liz Rhoades
Production Editor: Hazel R. Eddins
Art/Production Assistant: Josh Rutledge
Administrative Coordinator: Carol D. Johnson
CookingLight.com Editor: Allison Long Lowery
Nutrition Editor: Holley Johnson Grainger, MS, RD
Production Assistant: Mallory Daugherty

To order additional publications, call 1-800-765-6400 or 1-800-491-0551.

For more books to enrich your life, visit **oxmoorhouse.com**

To search, savor, and share thousands of recipes, visit **myrecipes.com**

**Cover:** Company Pot Roast (page 205)
**Back cover:** Coconut Banana Bread with Lime Glaze (page 70)

# about this book

**Welcome to a fresh and healthy approach to comfort food** from *Cooking Light,* America's leading food magazine. At *Cooking Light* we're passionate about making healthy taste great, and for years we've been helping our readers transform their favorite recipes into healthier versions that still retain all the memorable and enticing flavors that they've grown to love.

*Cooking Light Comfort Food* is an amazing assortment of over 200 classic recipes that fit into a well-balanced diet—yet no one will guess these dishes are light! Organized by Breakfast, Lunch, Dinner, and Sides & Desserts, this book makes it easy to choose a variety of flavorful recipes—from buttermilk biscuits to French onion soup, fried chicken, mashed potatoes, and strawberry shortcake!

There is something for everyone—no matter your craving—in this inviting book of light, warming comfort-food dishes that are equally as good for your body as they are for your soul. In addition to the classic comfort-food recipes, these additional features are woven within:

- **A beautiful color photograph** of every recipe showcases delicious food at its finest.
- **"5 Ways With..."** features recipes that provide you with five uniquely different variations of timeless classics like mashed potatoes, meat loaf, and mac and cheese.
- **"Recipe Makeovers"** highlights reader recipes and tells you how the *Cooking Light* staff made them healthier—while keeping the dish supremely satisfying at the same time.
- **"30 Minutes or Less"** icons flag all the super-quick and easy recipes.
- **"What Makes it Light?"** info shows you exactly what makes that particular recipe lighter than a traditional recipe, giving you ideas on how to lighten up your own recipes.
- **A nutritional analysis** for every recipe gives you confidence that it's healthy.

# breakfast
8

biscuits, muffins, waffles,
pancakes, cinnamon rolls,
sweet rolls, scones, casseroles,
omelets, quiches, grits, stratas,
French toast, coffee cakes...

# dinner
162

meat loaf, casseroles,
tetrazzini, pizzas, fettuccine,
fried chicken, lasagna,
pot pies, stroganoff, stews...

77

210

lunch 90

sandwiches, soups, chowders, chili, burgers, panini, po' boys, salads, grilled cheese sandwiches...

sides & desserts 236

fries, mashed potatoes, mac and cheese, slaw, hushpuppies, gratins, pies, cobblers, cakes, ice cream, cookies...

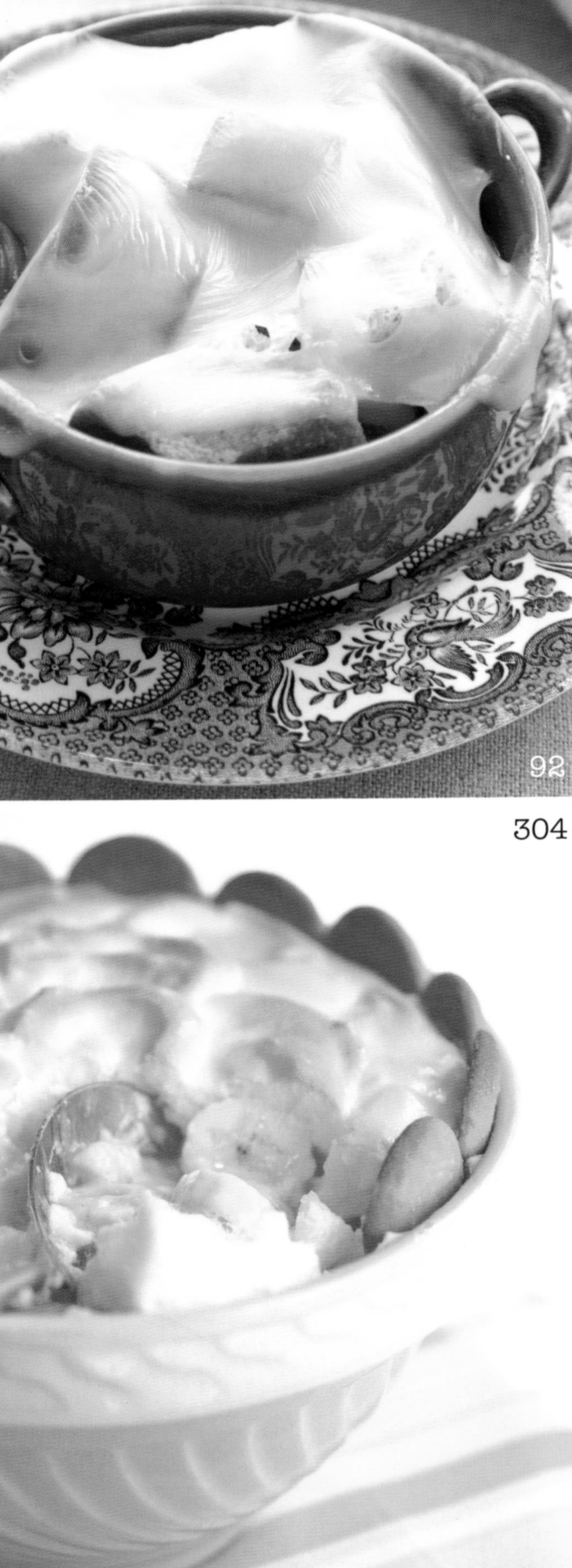

92

304

# breakfast

RECIPE MAKEOVERS



5 WAYS WITH



RECIPES

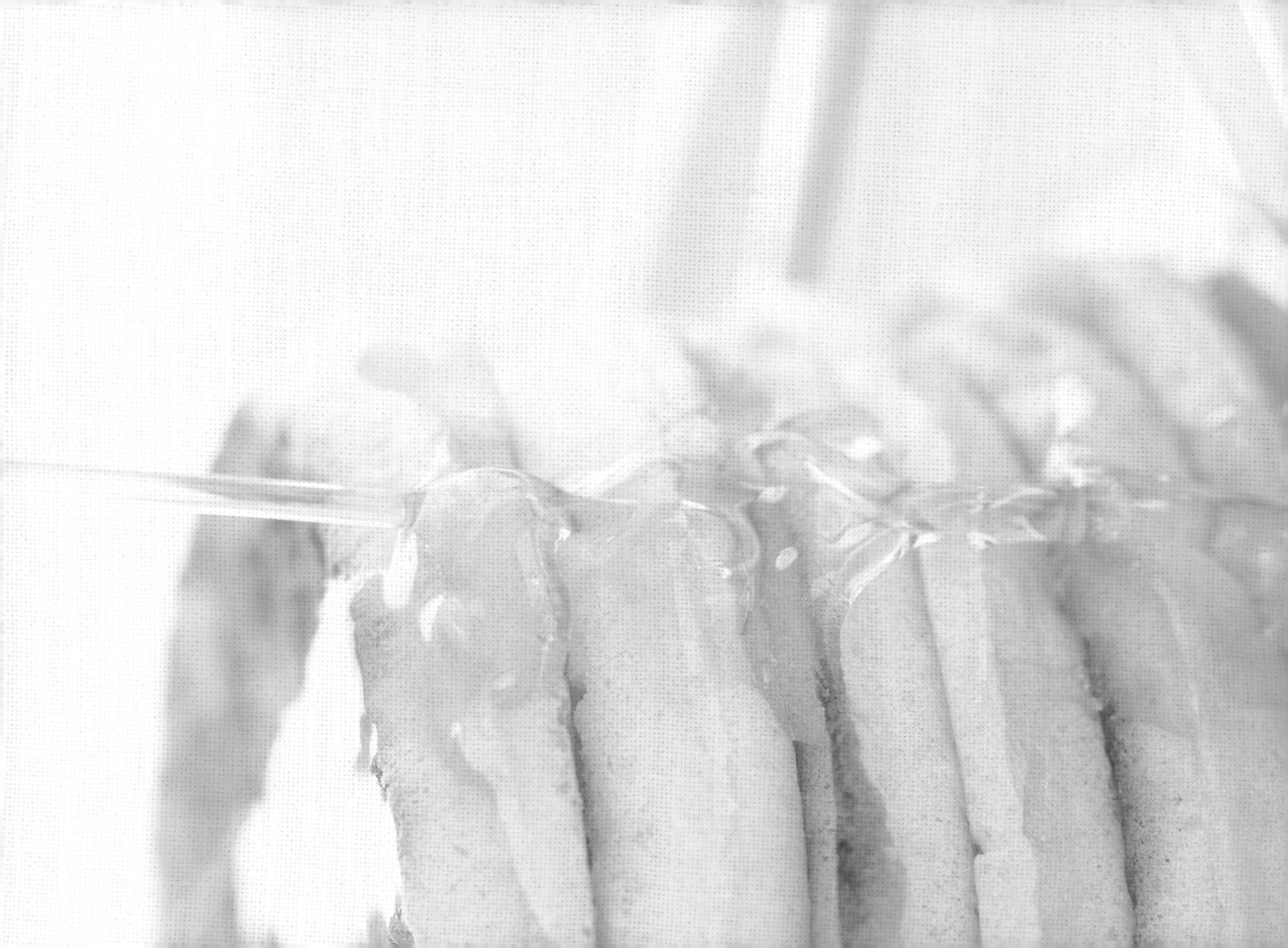

**Traditionally served for breakfast in Mexico,** huevos rancheros piles crisp corn tortillas with protein-rich eggs, spicy salsa, and shredded cheese. Serve your eggs whichever way you like them best—with fresh tomato salsa, salsa verde, or both. You can also use white, yellow, or blue corn tortillas to change things up.

# Huevos Rancheros

- 4 (6-inch) corn tortillas
- Cooking spray
- 1 cup chopped onion
- ½ cup chopped green bell pepper
- 3 garlic cloves, minced
- ¼ cup canned chopped green chiles
- 2 teaspoons New Mexico chile powder
- 1 teaspoon ground cumin
- 1 teaspoon dried oregano
- ½ teaspoon hot sauce
- 1 (14.5-ounce) can diced tomatoes, undrained
- 4 large eggs
- ¼ cup fresh salsa or ¼ cup salsa verde
- ¼ cup (1 ounce) shredded Monterey Jack cheese
- Cilantro sprigs (optional)

**1.** Preheat oven to 350°.

**2.** Coat tortillas with cooking spray; place on a baking sheet. Bake at 350° for 12 minutes or until crisp.

**3.** Heat a large nonstick skillet over medium-high heat. Coat pan with cooking spray. Add onion, bell pepper, and garlic; sauté 3 minutes. Add green chiles and next 5 ingredients. Bring to a boil; cook 3 minutes or until thick.

**4.** Heat a large nonstick skillet over medium-low heat. Coat pan with cooking spray. Add eggs to pan; cook 3 minutes or until done.

**5.** Place 1 tortilla on each of 4 plates. Top each tortilla with 1/2 cup tomato mixture and 1 egg. Spoon 1 tablespoon fresh salsa or salsa verde over each serving; sprinkle each serving with 1 tablespoon cheese. Garnish with cilantro sprigs, if desired. **YIELD:** 4 servings.

CALORIES 222; FAT 8.6g (sat 3.1g, mono 2.8g, poly 1.3g); PROTEIN 11.7g; CARB 26.7g; FIBER 5.5g; CHOL 219mg; IRON 2.5mg; SODIUM 376mg; CALC 174mg

## what makes it light

- uses baked, not fried, corn tortillas
- uses less cheese than traditional recipes
- uses cooking spray instead of butter or oil to fry eggs
- doesn't use refried beans, which can be high in fat, like many traditional recipes

**The creamy cheese and sour cream** add salty notes to these tacos. Round out your breakfast with fresh mango slices.

# Egg and Cheese Breakfast Tacos with Homemade Salsa

- 1 cup chopped tomato
- ¼ cup chopped red onion
- 2 tablespoons chopped fresh cilantro
- 1 teaspoon minced jalapeño pepper
- ¼ teaspoon kosher salt
- 4 teaspoons fresh lime juice, divided
- 1 teaspoon minced garlic, divided
- 1 cup organic refried beans
- ¼ teaspoon ground cumin
- 1 tablespoon 1% low-fat milk
- 6 large eggs, lightly beaten
- Cooking spray
- ¼ cup chopped green onions
- 8 (6-inch) corn tortillas
- ½ cup (2 ounces) shredded Monterey Jack cheese with jalapeño peppers
- 8 teaspoons reduced-fat sour cream

**1.** Combine first 5 ingredients in a small bowl. Stir in 2 teaspoons juice and ½ teaspoon garlic. Combine beans, remaining 2 teaspoons juice, remaining ½ teaspoon garlic, and cumin in another bowl.

**2.** Combine milk and eggs in a medium bowl; stir with a whisk. Heat a large nonstick skillet over medium-high heat. Coat pan with cooking spray. Add green onions to pan; sauté 1 minute, stirring frequently. Stir in egg mixture; cook 3 minutes or until soft-scrambled, stirring constantly. Remove from heat.

**3.** Warm tortillas according to package directions. Spread 1 tablespoon bean mixture on each tortilla. Spoon about 2 tablespoons egg mixture down center of each tortilla. Top each serving with 1 tablespoon tomato mixture, 1 tablespoon cheese, and 1 teaspoon sour cream. **YIELD:** 4 servings (serving size: 2 tacos).

CALORIES 334; FAT 13.3g (sat 5.5g, mono 4.2g, poly 2.3g); PROTEIN 19g; CARB 34g; FIBER 6.5g; CHOL 289mg; IRON 2.9mg; SODIUM 407mg; CALC 201mg

## what makes it light

- uses low-fat milk
- uses reduced-fat sour cream
- uses homemade salsa instead of bottled

**Perfect for either breakfast or a light dinner,** this dish uses white cornmeal for a creamy polenta. If you can find it, use imported Italian white polenta since the grain is very fine, resulting in a soft texture. Make an extra batch of salsa as a topping for bruschetta.

# Poached Eggs with White Corn Polenta

Salsa:

- 1/3 cup chopped bottled roasted red bell peppers
- 1 tablespoon chopped fresh basil
- 1/2 teaspoon extra-virgin olive oil
- 1/8 teaspoon salt
- 1 large plum tomato, seeded and diced (about 1/3 cup)

Polenta:

- 4 cups water
- 1 1/2 cups frozen white corn kernels, thawed
- 1 cup white cornmeal or dry polenta
- 1/2 teaspoon salt, divided
- 3 tablespoons grated fresh Parmesan cheese
- 1 teaspoon butter
- 1/4 teaspoon freshly ground black pepper

Eggs:

- 4 large eggs
- Cooking spray

Remaining Ingredients:

- 2 bacon slices, cooked and crumbled
- Freshly ground black pepper (optional)

**1.** To prepare salsa, combine bell pepper, basil, oil, 1/8 teaspoon salt, and tomato; set aside.
**2.** To prepare polenta, bring 4 cups water to a boil in a medium saucepan. Add corn, cornmeal, and 1/4 teaspoon salt. Cook 2 minutes or until cornmeal mixture returns to a boil, stirring constantly. Reduce heat to low; cook 20 minutes or until thick, stirring frequently. Stir in remaining 1/4 teaspoon salt, Parmesan cheese, butter, and black pepper. Cover and keep warm.
**3.** To prepare eggs, while polenta cooks, add water to a large skillet, filling two-thirds full; bring to a boil. Reduce heat; simmer. Break eggs into each of 4 (6-ounce) custard cups coated with cooking spray. Place custard cups in simmering water in pan. Cover pan; cook 6 minutes. Remove custard cups from water; carefully remove eggs from custard cups.
**4.** Spoon about 1 cup polenta onto each of 4 plates; top each serving with about 3 tablespoons salsa and 1 poached egg. Sprinkle evenly with bacon. Garnish with black pepper, if desired. **YIELD:** 4 servings.

CALORIES 307; FAT 10.3g (sat 3.4g, mono 4g, poly 1.6g); PROTEIN 14.2g; CARB 40.5g; FIBER 4.6g; CHOL 221mg; IRON 1.9mg; SODIUM 664mg; CALC 78mg

## what makes it light

- uses only ½ slice bacon per serving
- eggs are poached so no fat is used to cook them
- uses only 1 teaspoon butter in the polenta compared to several tablespoons in traditional recipes

**Here's an omelet that cooks up beautifully** and is chock-full of healthy vegetables wrapped in warm melted cheese.

# Mushroom and Bell Pepper Omelet with Fontina

- 1 teaspoon olive oil, divided
- Cooking spray
- ¼ cup chopped green onions
- ½ medium green bell pepper, thinly sliced
- 2 cups sliced shiitake mushrooms (about 6 ounces)
- ½ cup chopped seeded plum tomato
- ½ teaspoon salt, divided
- ⅛ teaspoon black pepper
- 2 teaspoons chopped fresh parsley
- 8 large eggs
- 2 large egg whites
- ½ teaspoon butter
- ½ cup (2 ounces) shredded fontina cheese
- ¼ cup reduced-fat sour cream
- Chopped fresh parsley (optional)

**1.** Heat 1/2 teaspoon oil in a large nonstick skillet coated with cooking spray over medium-high heat. Add green onions; sauté 1 minute. Add bell pepper; sauté 1 minute. Add mushrooms; cook 3 minutes, stirring frequently. Stir in tomato, 1/4 teaspoon salt, and black pepper; cook 30 seconds. Remove vegetable mixture from pan; cover and keep warm.

**2.** Place 1/4 teaspoon salt, parsley, eggs, and egg whites in a bowl; stir well with a whisk to combine.

**3.** Place 1/2 teaspoon oil and butter in skillet over medium-high heat until butter melts. Add egg mixture to pan; cook until edges begin to set (about 2 minutes). Slide front edge of a spatula between edge of omelet and pan. Gently lift edge of omelet, tilting pan to allow some uncooked egg mixture to come in contact with pan. Repeat procedure on opposite edge of omelet. Continue cooking until the center is just set (about 7 minutes).

**4.** Spoon vegetable mixture evenly over 1/2 of omelet; top vegetable mixture with cheese. Loosen omelet with a spatula; fold in half. Carefully slide omelet onto a serving platter. Cut omelet into 4 wedges; top with sour cream. Garnish with additional parsley, if desired. Serve immediately.

**YIELD:** 4 servings (serving size: 1 wedge and 1 tablespoon sour cream).

CALORIES 272; FAT 17.7g (sat 7.3g, mono 6.5g, poly 1.8g); PROTEIN 19.4g; CARB 7.1g; FIBER 1.3g; CHOL 448mg; IRON 2.4mg; SODIUM 576mg; CALC 145mg

## what makes it light

- uses a minimal amount of oil
- uses healthy vegetables
- uses some egg whites instead of all whole eggs
- uses reduced-fat sour cream
- uses creamy fontina instead of high-fat cheese

30
minutes
or
less

My family loves this dish. It is delicious, and after making it on a weekend for breakfast, we have **leftovers that are easy to heat up and enjoy during the week**. It is a great dish to serve when you have guests, too.

**from cookinglight.com**

# Garden Vegetable Crustless Quiche

- 1½ cups egg substitute
- 3 large eggs
- 1½ cups (6 ounces) shredded reduced-fat extrasharp cheddar cheese, divided
- 1½ cups (6 ounces) shredded reduced-fat Monterey Jack cheese, divided
- ½ cup 1% low-fat milk
- 2.25 ounces all-purpose flour (about ½ cup)
- 1 teaspoon baking powder
- ½ teaspoon salt
- 1 (16-ounce) carton fat-free cottage cheese
- Cooking spray
- 4 cups sliced zucchini (about 3)
- 2 cups diced potato with onion (such as Simply Potatoes)
- 1 cup finely chopped green bell pepper (about 1)
- 1 (8-ounce) package presliced mushrooms
- ½ cup chopped fresh parsley
- 2 tomatoes, thinly sliced

**1.** Preheat oven to 400°.

**2.** Beat egg substitute and eggs in a large bowl until fluffy. Add ¾ cup cheddar cheese, ¾ cup Jack cheese, milk, flour, baking powder, salt, and cottage cheese.

**3.** Heat a large nonstick skillet over medium-high heat. Coat pan with cooking spray. Add zucchini and next 3 ingredients; sauté 5 minutes or until tender. Add zucchini mixture and parsley to egg mixture. Pour mixture into a 3-quart casserole dish coated with cooking spray or 2 (10-inch) quiche pans. Top with remaining ¾ cup cheddar cheese and ¾ cup Jack cheese. Arrange tomato slices over cheese. Bake at 400° for 15 minutes. Reduce oven temperature to 350° (do not remove dish from oven), and bake 35 minutes or until lightly browned and set. **YIELD:** 10 servings.

CALORIES 230; FAT 7.7g (sat 4.6g, mono 1.3g, poly 0.3g); PROTEIN 23g; CARB 18.1g; FIBER 1.9g; CHOL 84mg; IRON 2.1mg; SODIUM 716mg; CALC 382mg

## what makes it light

- uses egg substitute
- uses reduced-fat extrasharp cheddar cheese
- uses reduced-fat Monterey Jack
- uses low-fat milk
- uses fat-free cottage cheese
- uses cooking spray instead of oil to sauté vegetables

Delicious! Rich, creamy, and satisfying. **I used a store-bought crust to save time** and added a shallot to the green onions since I had one on hand. I might add more shallots and spinach next time. The smoked Gouda was delicious!

**from cookinglight.com**

# Spinach, Green Onion, and Smoked Gouda Quiche

Crust:

- **6 tablespoons butter, softened**
- **2 tablespoons 1% low-fat milk**
- **¼ teaspoon salt**
- **1 large egg yolk**
- **5.6 ounces all-purpose flour (about 1¼ cups)**

Filling:

- **1 tablespoon extra-virgin olive oil**
- **½ cup thinly sliced green onions**
- **3 cups fresh baby spinach**
- **1 cup 1% low-fat milk**
- **¾ cup (3 ounces) grated smoked Gouda cheese**
- **¾ teaspoon salt**
- **Dash of grated nutmeg**
- **3 large eggs**

**1.** To prepare crust, place butter in a large bowl; beat with a mixer at medium speed until light and fluffy. Combine milk, salt, and egg yolk in a small bowl; stir well with a whisk. Add milk mixture to butter, 1 tablespoon at a time, beating well after each addition. Add flour; beat just until combined. Press mixture into a 4-inch circle on plastic wrap; cover. Chill 1 hour.

**2.** Preheat oven to 350°.

**3.** Unwrap and place chilled dough on a lightly floured surface. Roll dough into a 10-inch circle. Fit dough into a 9-inch pie plate. Freeze 15 minutes. Bake at 350° for 25 minutes or until lightly browned. Cool.

**4.** To prepare filling, heat oil in a large skillet over medium-high heat. Add onions; sauté 5 minutes or until tender. Add spinach; sauté 2 minutes.

**5.** Combine 1 cup milk and remaining ingredients in a bowl; stir well with a whisk. Stir in spinach mixture. Pour filling into crust. Bake at 350° for 35 minutes. Cut into 10 wedges.

**YIELD:** 10 servings (serving size: 1 wedge).

CALORIES 205; FAT 12.9g (sat 6.8g, mono 4.3g, poly 0.8g); PROTEIN 7.3g; CARB 15.4g; FIBER 1.1g; CHOL 113mg; IRON 1.5mg; SODIUM 405mg; CALC 120mg

## what makes it light

- uses butter instead of shortening in the crust
- uses low-fat milk in the filling
- uses a small amount of smoked Gouda cheese, which gives rich flavor

**Breakfast casseroles are ideal for overnight guests.** Assemble this one the night before, and bake in the morning.

# Mushroom, Bacon, and Swiss Strata

- 12 ounces ciabatta bread, cut into 1-inch cubes (about 7 cups)
- 2 tablespoons butter
- 2 cups chopped onion
- 2 (8-ounce) packages presliced mushrooms
- Cooking spray
- 1½ cups (6 ounces) shredded reduced-fat Swiss cheese
- 8 center-cut bacon slices, cooked and crumbled
- 3 cups 1% low-fat milk
- 1½ cups egg substitute
- 2 teaspoons chopped fresh thyme
- ½ teaspoon freshly ground black pepper
- ¼ teaspoon salt
- Thyme sprigs (optional)

**1.** Preheat oven to 350°.
**2.** Arrange bread in a single layer on a jelly-roll pan. Bake at 350° for 20 minutes or until toasted. Place bread cubes in a large bowl.
**3.** Melt butter in a large nonstick skillet over medium-high heat. Add onion and mushrooms to pan; sauté 10 minutes or until liquid evaporates and vegetables are tender. Add onion mixture to bread; toss well to combine. Arrange half of bread mixture in a 13 x 9–inch baking dish coated with cooking spray. Sprinkle with half of cheese and half of bacon; top with remaining bread mixture, cheese, and bacon.
**4.** Combine milk and next 4 ingredients, stirring with a whisk. Pour milk mixture over bread mixture. Cover and refrigerate 8 hours.
**5.** Preheat oven to 350°.
**6.** Remove strata from refrigerator; let stand at room temperature 15 minutes. Bake strata, covered, at 350° for 30 minutes. Uncover and bake an additional 15 minutes or until set. Let stand 10 minutes before serving. Garnish with thyme sprigs, if desired. **YIELD:** 8 servings.

CALORIES 313; FAT 10.4g (sat 5g, mono 4.2g, poly 0.8g); PROTEIN 21.7g; CARB 35.5g; FIBER 2.7g; CHOL 25mg; IRON 1.9mg; SODIUM 737mg; CALC 318mg

## what makes it light

- uses reduced-fat Swiss cheese
- uses low-fat milk
- uses egg substitute
- uses center-cut bacon, which is a leaner, lower-fat choice than regular bacon

This was a big hit at my brunch and was very simple to make. **I liked being able to do most of the work the night before.** Also, it was very light and the flavors were delicious. I didn't have any leftovers so I will be making it again soon so I can have more!

**from cookinglight.com**

# Brie and Egg Strata

- 2 teaspoons olive oil
- 2 cups chopped onion
- 1½ cups diced unpeeled Yukon gold potato (1 large)
- 1 cup chopped red bell pepper
- 1 cup halved grape tomatoes
- 1 teaspoon salt, divided
- ¾ pound ciabatta bread, cut into 1-inch cubes, toasted
- Cooking spray
- 4 ounces Brie cheese, rind removed and chopped
- 1 cup egg substitute
- 2 large eggs
- 1 teaspoon herbes de Provence
- ¼ teaspoon freshly ground black pepper
- 3 cups 1% low-fat milk
- 2 tablespoons chopped fresh parsley

**1.** Heat oil in a large nonstick skillet over medium-high heat. Add onion, potato, and bell pepper; sauté 4 minutes or until tender. Stir in tomatoes; sauté 2 minutes. Stir in 1/2 teaspoon salt. Combine onion mixture and bread.

**2.** Arrange half of bread mixture into a 13 x 9–inch baking dish coated with cooking spray. Sprinkle with half of Brie. Top with remaining bread mixture and remaining Brie.

**3.** Combine egg substitute and eggs in a medium bowl. Add remaining 1/2 teaspoon salt, herbes de Provence, and pepper. Add milk, stirring with a whisk until well blended. Pour egg mixture over bread mixture. Let stand 30 minutes.

**4.** Preheat oven to 350°.

**5.** Bake at 350° for 50 minutes or until set. Sprinkle with parsley. Serve immediately. **YIELD:** 12 servings (serving size: 1 piece).

CALORIES 205; FAT 6.9g (sat 2.7g, mono 3g, poly 0.8g); PROTEIN 10.8g; CARB 26.1g; FIBER 1.7g; CHOL 47mg; IRON 2mg; SODIUM 534mg; CALC 120mg

## what makes it light

- vegetables and potato add fiber and flavor
- uses a reduced amount of Brie
- uses low-fat milk

# recipe makeover
## breakfast casserole

**The Reader:** Lisanne Kaplan

**The Story:** Breakfast is a favorite meal in the Kaplan house, "enjoyed in pajamas with mugs of good coffee and lively conversation," Lisanne says. But with work, school, and activities with her children, Lisanne needs a make-ahead meal that will be a more healthful, energizing start to the day than the casserole she first found in one of her favorite cookbooks.

**The Dilemma:** This heavyweight casserole called for 1½ pounds pork sausage, 1½ cups full-fat cheese, and nine whole eggs. Each serving had 10 grams of saturated fat and a whopping 204 milligrams of cholesterol. And the sausage and cheese contributed about 900 milligrams of sodium (or 40 percent of the daily recommended intake) per serving.

**The Solution:** Since breakfast turkey sausage has about one-third the fat and half the calories of pork sausage, we use 12 ounces of the flavorful poultry sausage. This eliminates three grams of saturated fat, and using a bit less turkey sausage shaves 187 milligrams of sodium and 20 milligrams of cholesterol per serving. Instead of using nine large eggs, we combine three eggs with two cups egg substitute to offer a fluffy egg texture and taste without missing another two and a half grams of fat (one gram saturated) and 115 milligrams of cholesterol in each portion. The swap from whole milk to 1% low-fat milk trims another gram of fat. The last big change involves using a bit less cheese, and finely shredding reduced-fat extra-sharp cheddar to better distribute the smaller amount and perk up the flavor. Since we halved the original amount of salt, a bit of ground red pepper adds a little spiciness and zest to the casserole while shaving some sodium.

**The Feedback:** Without exception, the Kaplan family agrees—**their traditional casserole is improved,** with a fluffier texture and more pronounced egg and sausage flavor. No one missed the casserole's greasy edge. "Using finely shredded sharp cheese was a great tip; the flavorful cheese was more evenly distributed throughout the dish," Lisanne says.

| | BEFORE | AFTER |
|---|---|---|
| Calories per serving | 346 | 184 |
| Fat | 25.8g | 6.8g |
| Percent of total calories | 67% | 33% |

Fabulous recipe! Made this for Christmas breakfast and **it tasted exactly like my mom's full-fat version** made with cream and pork sausage. Everyone loved this casserole and was amazed that this was a lighter version of our traditional favorite. My husband has hinted that he would like this throughout the year. My new favorite breakfast casserole recipe!

**from cookinglight.com**

# Sausage and Cheese Breakfast Casserole

- Cooking spray
- 12 ounces turkey breakfast sausage
- 2 cups 1% low-fat milk
- 2 cups egg substitute
- 1 teaspoon dry mustard
- ¾ teaspoon salt
- ½ teaspoon freshly ground black pepper
- ¼ teaspoon ground red pepper
- 3 large eggs
- 16 (1-ounce) slices white bread
- 1 cup (4 ounces) finely shredded reduced-fat extrasharp cheddar cheese
- ¼ teaspoon paprika

**1.** Heat a large nonstick skillet over medium-high heat. Coat pan with cooking spray. Add sausage to pan; cook 5 minutes or until browned, stirring and breaking sausage to crumble. Remove from heat; cool.

**2.** Combine milk and next 6 ingredients in a large bowl, stirring with a whisk.

**3.** Trim crusts from bread. Cut bread into 1-inch cubes. Add bread cubes, sausage, and cheddar cheese to milk mixture, stirring to combine. Pour bread mixture into a 13 x 9–inch baking or 3-quart casserole dish coated with cooking spray, spreading egg mixture evenly in baking dish. Cover and refrigerate 8 hours or overnight.

**4.** Preheat oven to 350°.

**5.** Remove casserole from refrigerator; let stand 30 minutes. Sprinkle casserole evenly with paprika. Bake at 350° for 45 minutes or until set and lightly browned. Let stand 10 minutes.

**YIELD:** 12 servings (serving size: about 1 cup).

CALORIES 184; FAT 6.8g (sat 3.2g, mono 1.5g, poly 0.8g); PROTEIN 15.9g; CARB 14g; FIBER 0.6g; CHOL 76mg; IRON 2.2mg; SODIUM 636mg; CALC 181mg

"Wow! I was hesitant because the idea of tomatoes in this was not appealing to me, but this was great. **Only had hot Rotel, but my in-laws are from Texas and love hot.** It was great. They couldn't believe it was light. Can't wait to make again."

**from cookinglight.com**

# Southwestern Breakfast Casserole

- 1 (8½-ounce) package corn muffin mix
- 3 cups (½-inch) cubed white bread
- 8 ounces hot turkey Italian sausage
- 1 cup chopped onion
- 2½ cups fat-free milk
- 1 teaspoon ground cumin
- ⅛ teaspoon black pepper
- 1 (10-ounce) can diced tomatoes and green chiles, undrained
- 1 (8-ounce) carton egg substitute
- Cooking spray
- 1 cup (4 ounces) shredded reduced-fat Monterey Jack or mild cheddar cheese, divided

**1.** Prepare corn muffin mix according to package directions; cool. Crumble muffins into a large bowl; stir in bread. Set aside.

**2.** Remove casings from sausage. Cook sausage and onion in a large nonstick skillet over medium heat until browned, stirring to crumble. Drain.

**3.** Combine milk, cumin, pepper, tomatoes, and egg substitute; stir with a whisk until well blended. Add sausage mixture; stir well. Stir into bread mixture. Spoon half of bread mixture into an 11 x 7–inch baking dish coated with cooking spray. Top with 1/2 cup cheese. Spoon remaining bread mixture over cheese. Cover and refrigerate 8 hours or overnight.

**4.** Preheat oven to 350°.

**5.** Bake casserole at 350° for 20 minutes or until set. Top with 1/2 cup cheese, and bake an additional 20 minutes or until set. Let stand 10 minutes before serving. **YIELD:** 8 servings.

CALORIES 271; FAT 7.6g (sat 2.7g, mono 2.6g, poly 1.7g); PROTEIN 14.7g; CARB 33.9g; FIBER 1.6g; CHOL 22mg; IRON 2.1mg; SODIUM 700mg; CALC 290mg

## what makes it light

- uses turkey Italian sausage
- uses fat-free milk
- uses egg substitute
- uses reduced-fat Monterey Jack cheese

# recipe makeover

## stuffed french toast

**The Reader:** Kristi Wold

**The Story:** As a practice manager for a thriving medical group, Kristi knows the value of efficiency, which is partly why she loves this recipe. You can throw it together the night before and pop it into the oven shortly before brunch—perfect for a hectic schedule. With layers of smooth cream cheese stuffing and cinnamon-raisin bread, the puddinglike dish wins raves from coworkers whenever Kristi takes it to the office. The dish has only one drawback—its nutritional profile.

**The Dilemma:** The original recipe contained one pound of cream cheese, a quart of half-and-half, and eight eggs. Sure, it was delicious, but consuming 27 grams of fat in one sitting is no way to start the day.

**The Solution:** We knew this recipe could stand some serious downsizing. By combining fat-free and ⅓-less-fat cream cheeses to replace the regular cream cheese, we trimmed the fat by more than 100 grams without losing any richness. Reducing the half-and-half and making up the difference with 1% milk cut another 60 grams of fat, while using egg substitute instead of eggs brought the number down another 23 grams. The lightened version remained so rich and flavorful that it rated even higher than the original in our Test Kitchens.

**The Feedback:** Kristi gives the lightened dish an excellent review. She likes it better than the original, not only because the new version has a smoother consistency but also because she can enjoy it more since it isn't so heavy and filling. As for the folks at work who'd adored the original dish—they liked the lightened version more. One doctor told Kristi, "Your dessert was really good." When she replied that it wasn't really a dessert, he said, "Well, it could be." That's what we call creative management.

| | BEFORE | AFTER |
|---|---|---|
| Calories per serving | 502 | 340 |
| Fat | 27.3g | 11.3g |
| Percent of total calories | 49% | 30% |

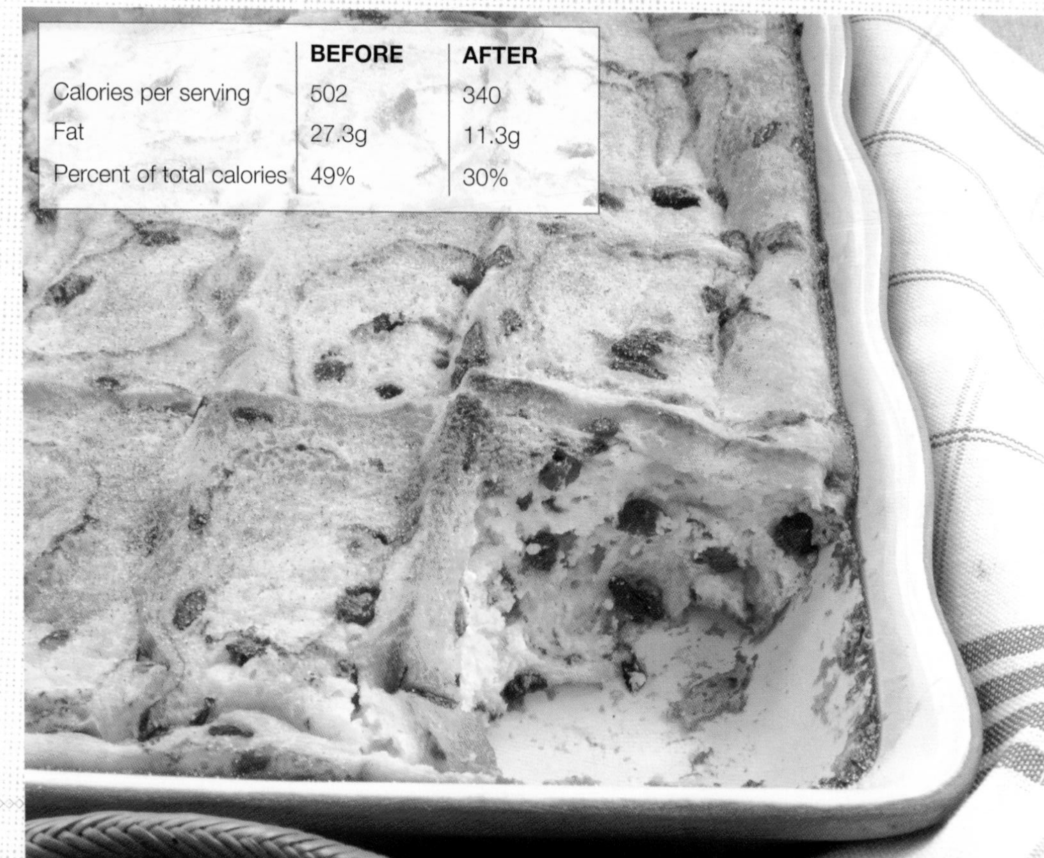

**This stuffed french toast is probably best described** as a combination of crème brulee, cheesecake, and bread pudding all wrapped up into one—only we recommend it for breakfast, not dessert!

# Stuffed French Toast

- 24 (1-ounce) slices cinnamon-raisin bread
- Cooking spray
- 3 cups 1% low-fat milk
- 2 cups egg substitute, divided
- 1 cup half-and-half
- 1 cup sugar, divided
- 1 tablespoon vanilla extract
- 1/8 teaspoon ground nutmeg
- 1 (8-ounce) block fat-free cream cheese, softened
- 1 (8-ounce) block 1/3-less-fat cream cheese, softened
- Bottled cinnamon-sugar (optional)

**1.** Trim crusts from bread. Arrange half of the bread in a 13 x 9–inch baking dish coated with cooking spray.
**2.** Combine milk, 1 1/2 cups egg substitute, half-and-half, and 1/2 cup sugar in a large bowl, stirring with a whisk. Pour half of milk mixture over bread in dish.
**3.** Place 1/2 cup egg substitute, 1/2 cup sugar, vanilla, nutmeg, and cheeses in a food processor or blender; process until smooth. Pour cream cheese mixture over moist bread in dish. Top with remaining bread; pour remaining milk mixture over bread. Cover and refrigerate 8 hours or overnight.
**4.** Preheat oven to 350°.
**5.** Uncover and bake at 350° for 55 minutes. Let stand 10 minutes before serving. Sprinkle with cinnamon-sugar, if desired. **YIELD:** 12 servings (serving size: 1 piece).

CALORIES 340; FAT 11.3g (sat 5.1g, mono 3.3g, poly 0.9g); PROTEIN 16.7g; CARB 43.2g; FIBER 1.5g; CHOL 26mg; IRON 3.7mg; SODIUM 447mg; CALC 197mg

# 5 ways with french toast

## Strawberry-Filled French Toast with Caramel and Pecans

Sauce:

- ½ cup granulated sugar
- 3 tablespoons water
- 1 tablespoon butter
- ½ cup evaporated fat-free milk
- ½ teaspoon vanilla extract
- ⅛ teaspoon salt

French Toast:

- Cooking spray
- 1 (12-ounce) loaf French bread, cut into 16 (¼-inch-thick) slices
- ½ cup strawberry preserves
- 2 cups fat-free milk
- ¾ cup egg substitute
- 1 tablespoon vanilla extract
- ⅛ teaspoon salt
- ¼ teaspoon ground cinnamon
- ⅛ teaspoon ground nutmeg
- 2 large eggs
- 3 tablespoons chopped pecans
- 2 tablespoons powdered sugar

**1.** To prepare sauce, combine granulated sugar and water in a medium, heavy saucepan. Cook over medium-low heat 5 minutes or until sugar dissolves. Cover and cook over medium heat 1 minute. Uncover and cook 3 minutes or until light golden (do not stir).

**2.** Remove from heat, and let stand 1 minute. Add butter; stir until melted. Add evaporated milk; stir constantly. Place pan over medium heat; cook 3 minutes or until caramel melts and mixture is smooth, stirring constantly. Remove from heat; stir in vanilla and salt.

**3.** To prepare French toast, pour sauce into a 13 x 9–inch baking dish coated with cooking spray. Arrange 8 bread slices in dish. Spread preserves evenly over bread; top with remaining bread.

**4.** Combine milk and next 6 ingredients. Pour milk mixture over bread; sprinkle with pecans.

**5.** Preheat oven to 350°.

**6.** Bake, uncovered, at 350° for 35 minutes or until top is golden. Let cool 5 minutes. Sprinkle with powdered sugar. **YIELD:** 8 servings (serving size: 1 piece).

CALORIES 332; FAT 6.7g (sat 1.7g, mono 2.9g, poly 1.5g); PROTEIN 11.9g; CARB 55.2g; FIBER 1.6g; CHOL 58mg; IRON 2mg; SODIUM 453mg; CALC 164mg

# Marmalade French Toast Casserole

Grapefruit or mixed fruit marmalade will work just as well as the orange marmalade called for in the recipe. Serve the casserole with honey or pancake syrup warmed with orange rind and a splash of orange juice (add one teaspoon rind and two tablespoons juice per ½ cup syrup). This easy casserole can be assembled in less than 15 minutes and stored in the refrigerator overnight.

- 3 tablespoons butter, softened
- 1 (16-ounce) sourdough French bread loaf, cut into 24 (½-inch) slices
- Cooking spray
- 1 (12-ounce) jar orange marmalade
- 2¾ cups 1% low-fat milk
- ⅓ cup sugar
- 1 teaspoon vanilla extract
- ¼ teaspoon ground nutmeg
- 6 large eggs
- ⅓ cup finely chopped walnuts

**1.** Spread softened butter on one side of each bread slice. Arrange 12 bread slices, buttered sides down, slightly overlapping in a single layer in a 13 x 9-inch baking dish coated with cooking spray. Spread marmalade evenly over bread; top with remaining 12 bread slices, buttered sides up.
**2.** Combine milk and next 4 ingredients, stirring with a whisk. Pour egg mixture over bread. Cover and refrigerate 8 hours or overnight.
**3.** Preheat oven to 350°.
**4.** Sprinkle casserole with walnuts. Bake at 350° for 45 minutes or until golden. Let stand 5 minutes before serving. **YIELD:** 12 servings (serving size: 1 piece).

CALORIES 293; FAT 9g (sat 3.2g, mono 2.2g, poly 2.3g); PROTEIN 9.1g; CARB 46.4g; FIBER 1.6g; CHOL 116mg; IRON 2.2mg; SODIUM 315mg; CALC 132mg

## Baked Coconut French Toast with Tropical Fruit Compote ▾

Compote:

1½ cups chopped fresh pineapple
1 cup chopped peeled mango
1 cup chopped peeled papaya
1 cup chopped peeled kiwifruit
3 tablespoons sugar
3 tablespoons fresh lime juice

French Toast:

16 (1-inch-thick) slices diagonally cut French bread baguette (about 10 ounces)
Cooking spray
1¼ cups light coconut milk
1¼ cups egg substitute
½ cup sugar
1 tablespoon vanilla extract
½ cup flaked sweetened coconut

**1.** To prepare compote, combine first 6 ingredients. Cover and chill 8 hours or overnight.
**2.** To prepare French toast, arrange bread in a single layer in a 13 x 9–inch baking dish coated with cooking spray. Combine light coconut milk, egg substitute, 1/2 cup sugar, and 1 tablespoon vanilla, stirring with a whisk, and pour evenly over bread. Turn bread over to coat. Cover and refrigerate 8 hours or overnight.
**3.** Preheat oven to 350°.
**4.** Remove bread mixture from refrigerator, and uncover. Turn bread slices over, and sprinkle evenly with flaked coconut. Let stand at room temperature 15 minutes. Bake, uncovered, at 350° for 30 minutes or until coconut is golden. Serve warm with fruit compote. **YIELD:** 8 servings (serving size: 2 french toast slices and 1/2 cup compote).

CALORIES 349; FAT 8.6g (sat 3.5g, mono 1.5g, poly 2.5g); PROTEIN 8.6g; CARB 60.3g; FIBER 4.1g; CHOL 0mg; IRON 1.8mg; SODIUM 309mg; CALC 44mg

## Easy French Toast Casserole ▾

⅔ cup packed dark brown sugar
2 tablespoons butter
2 tablespoons dark corn syrup
Cooking spray
1½ cups 1% low-fat milk
½ cup egg substitute
1 teaspoon vanilla extract
¼ teaspoon salt
⅛ teaspoon grated orange rind
2 large eggs
6 (1½-inch-thick) slices French bread
6 tablespoons frozen fat-free whipped topping, thawed
1 to 2 teaspoons Grand Marnier (orange-flavored liqueur)
2 tablespoons finely chopped pecans, toasted

**1.** Combine first 3 ingredients in a small, heavy saucepan over medium heat. Cook 5 minutes

or until bubbly and sugar dissolves, stirring constantly. Pour sugar mixture into bottom of a 13 x 9–inch baking dish coated with cooking spray. Spread mixture evenly over bottom of pan. Set aside; cool completely.

**2.** Combine milk and next 5 ingredients in a large shallow bowl; stir with a whisk. Dip 1 bread slice in milk mixture; arrange bread slice over sugar mixture in dish. Repeat procedure with remaining 5 bread slices. Pour any remaining egg mixture over bread slices. Cover and refrigerate overnight.

**3.** Preheat oven to 350°.

**4.** Bake at 350° for 30 minutes or until lightly browned.

**5.** While casserole bakes, combine whipped topping and Grand Marnier. Place 1 bread slice, caramel side up, on each of 6 plates; top each serving with 1 tablespoon topping and 1 teaspoon pecans. **YIELD:** 6 servings.

CALORIES 352; FAT 8.8g (sat 3.5g, mono 2.8g, poly 0.9g); PROTEIN 11.1g; CARB 58.1g; FIBER 1.2g; CHOL 83mg; IRON 2.6mg; SODIUM 466mg; CALC 191mg

## Overnight Caramel French Toast ▸

This is one of *Cooking Light* Test Kitchens Director Vanessa Pruett's favorite holiday brunch dishes. She adapted this recipe from an old family favorite by reducing the amount of butter and eggs, and switching to low-fat milk while still keeping it decadent and rich.

- **1 cup packed light brown sugar**
- **½ cup light-colored corn syrup**
- **¼ cup butter**
- **Cooking spray**
- **10 (1-ounce) slices French bread (soft bread such as Pepperidge Farm)**
- **2½ cups 1% low-fat milk**
- **1 tablespoon all-purpose flour**
- **1½ teaspoons vanilla extract**
- **¼ teaspoon salt**
- **2 large eggs**
- **2 tablespoons granulated sugar**
- **1 teaspoon ground cinnamon**

**1.** Combine first 3 ingredients in a small saucepan. Cook over medium heat 5 minutes or until mixture is bubbly, stirring constantly. Pour mixture evenly into a 13 x 9–inch baking dish coated with cooking spray.

**2.** Arrange bread slices in a single layer over syrup in dish.

**3.** Combine milk and next 4 ingredients in a large bowl, stirring with a whisk. Pour egg mixture over bread slices. Cover and refrigerate 8 hours or overnight.

**4.** Preheat oven to 350°.

**5.** Combine 2 tablespoons granulated sugar and cinnamon. Sprinkle evenly over bread.

**6.** Bake at 350° for 50 minutes or until golden. Let stand 5 minutes before serving.

**YIELD:** 10 servings (serving size: 1 piece).

CALORIES 314; FAT 7.2g (sat 3.2g, mono 2.8g, poly 0.6g); PROTEIN 6.2g; CARB 57.4g; FIBER 1.1g; CHOL 57mg; IRON 1.6mg; SODIUM 360mg; CALC 128mg

**To make ahead,** cook the grits, spoon them into the baking dish, and refrigerate overnight. Let the baking dish stand at room temperature while you prepare the mushroom topping; top the grits, and bake as directed.

# Grits Casserole with Mushrooms, Prosciutto, and Provolone

- 5 cups water
- 1¼ cups stone-ground yellow grits
- ¾ cup (3 ounces) shredded sharp provolone cheese, divided
- 1 teaspoon salt, divided
- Cooking spray
- 1½ teaspoons butter
- ¾ cup chopped onion
- 2 garlic cloves, minced
- 4 cups thinly sliced portobello mushrooms (about 6 ounces)
- 3 cups thinly sliced shiitake mushroom caps (about 4½ ounces)
- 1 teaspoon dried herbes de Provence
- ¼ teaspoon freshly ground black pepper
- 1 cup chopped prosciutto (about 3 ounces)
- ⅓ cup dry white wine
- 3 large eggs, lightly beaten
- 2 large egg whites, lightly beaten
- 1 tablespoon chopped fresh parsley

**1.** Bring water to a boil in a large saucepan; gradually stir in grits. Reduce heat, and simmer 30 minutes or until thick, stirring frequently. Remove from heat. Stir in 1/4 cup cheese and 1/2 teaspoon salt. Spoon grits mixture into an 11 x 7–inch baking dish coated with cooking spray.
**2.** Preheat oven to 350°.
**3.** Melt butter in a large nonstick skillet over medium-high heat. Add onion and garlic; sauté 3 minutes or until tender. Add remaining 1/2 teaspoon salt, mushrooms, herbes de Provence, and pepper; cook 6 minutes or until mushrooms are tender, stirring frequently. Stir in prosciutto and wine; cook 5 minutes or until liquid almost evaporates. Remove from heat; cool slightly. Stir in eggs and egg whites. Spread mushroom mixture over grits mixture; sprinkle with remaining 1/2 cup cheese. Bake at 350° for 30 minutes or until cheese melts and grits are thoroughly heated, and let stand 5 minutes before serving. Sprinkle with parsley. **YIELD:** 6 servings.

CALORIES 287; FAT 9.6g (sat 4.4g, mono 3.1g, poly 0.9g); PROTEIN 16.3g; CARB 35.7g; FIBER 2.3g; CHOL 131mg; IRON 2.9mg; SODIUM 832mg; CALC 136mg

## what makes it light

- uses a minimal amount of butter
- uses a combination of eggs and egg whites

30
minutes
or
less

"I was looking for something different for breakfast and I stumbled upon this recipe. **I have fallen in love, and I drool on the mornings that I know I will be making this.** The combination of the goat cheese and fig preserves is divine, and the lemon zest gives the combo just a touch of freshness. I don't always have basil on hand, but it is still dynamite without it. Try it. You will not be disappointed."

**from cookinglight.com**

# Goat Cheese Sandwiches with Fig and Honey

- 2 teaspoons honey
- ¼ teaspoon grated lemon rind
- 1 (4-ounce) package goat cheese
- 8 (1-ounce) slices cinnamon-raisin bread
- 2 tablespoons fig preserves
- 2 teaspoons thinly sliced fresh basil
- Cooking spray
- 1 teaspoon powdered sugar

**1.** Combine first 3 ingredients, stirring until well blended. Spread 1 tablespoon goat cheese mixture on each of 4 bread slices; top each slice with 1½ teaspoons preserves and ½ teaspoon basil. Top with remaining bread slices. Lightly coat outside of bread with cooking spray.
**2.** Heat a large nonstick skillet over medium heat. Add 2 sandwiches to pan. Place a cast-iron or heavy skillet on top of sandwiches; press gently to flatten. Cook 3 minutes on each side or until bread is lightly toasted (leave cast-iron skillet on sandwiches while they cook). Repeat with remaining sandwiches. Sprinkle with sugar. **YIELD:** 4 servings (serving size: 1 sandwich).

CALORIES 243; FAT 8.5g (sat 4.8g, mono 2.7g, poly 0.5g); PROTEIN 9.8g; CARB 33.1g; FIBER 2.5g; CHOL 13mg; IRON 2.2mg; SODIUM 326mg; CALC 78mg

## what makes it light

- uses cooking spray instead of oil to grill sandwiches

# 5 ways with pancakes

## Sweet Potato and Pecan Flapjacks

Cornmeal adds crunch, and mashed sweet potatoes lend creaminess to this weekend favorite. Yellow- or white-fleshed sweet potatoes have a dry and crumbly texture when baked and are not moist enough to make tender pancakes, so use the orange variety.

- 5.6 ounces all-purpose flour (about 1¼ cups)
- ¼ cup chopped pecans, toasted
- 3 tablespoons yellow cornmeal
- 2 teaspoons baking powder
- ½ teaspoon salt
- ½ teaspoon ground cinnamon
- 1 cup fat-free milk
- 1 cup mashed cooked sweet potato
- 3 tablespoons brown sugar
- 1 tablespoon canola oil
- ½ teaspoon vanilla extract
- 2 large egg yolks
- 2 large egg whites, lightly beaten
- Cooking spray

**1.** Weigh or lightly spoon all-purpose flour into dry measuring cups; level with a knife. Combine flour and next 5 ingredients in a large bowl, stirring with a whisk.

**2.** Combine milk, sweet potato, sugar, oil, vanilla, and egg yolks, stirring until smooth; add to flour mixture, stirring just until combined. Beat egg whites with a mixer at high speed until soft peaks form; then fold egg whites into batter. Let batter stand 10 minutes.

**3.** Heat a nonstick griddle or nonstick skillet over medium-high heat. Coat griddle or pan with cooking spray. Spoon about 1/4 cup batter per pancake onto griddle or pan. Cook 2 minutes or until tops are covered with bubbles and edges look cooked. Carefully turn pancakes over, and cook 2 minutes or until bottoms are lightly browned. **YIELD:** 6 servings (serving size: 2 pancakes).

CALORIES 276; FAT 7.9g (sat 1.1g, mono 4.1g, poly 2.1g); PROTEIN 7.7g; CARB 43.7g; FIBER 2.8g; CHOL 71mg; IRON 2.7mg; SODIUM 419mg; CALC 166mg

## Blueberry Pancakes

For variety, substitute sliced bananas or chocolate chips for the blueberries for a special treat. Since these pancakes reheat well in the toaster oven, consider making a big batch to enjoy throughout the week.

- 2.25 ounces all-purpose flour (about ½ cup)
- 2.38 ounces whole-wheat flour (about ½ cup)
- 1 tablespoon sugar
- 1 teaspoon baking powder
- ½ teaspoon baking soda
- ⅛ teaspoon salt
- ⅛ teaspoon ground nutmeg
- ¾ cup vanilla fat-free yogurt
- 2 tablespoons butter, melted
- 2 teaspoons fresh lemon juice
- ½ teaspoon vanilla extract
- 2 large eggs, lightly beaten
- 1 cup fresh blueberries

**1.** Weigh or lightly spoon flours into dry measuring cups; level with a knife. Combine flours and next 5 ingredients in a large bowl, stirring well with a whisk. Combine yogurt and next 4 ingredients in a small bowl; add to flour mixture, stirring until smooth.

**2.** Pour about ¼ cup batter per pancake onto a hot nonstick griddle or nonstick skillet. Top each pancake with 2 tablespoons blueberries. Cook 2 minutes or until tops are covered with bubbles and edges look cooked. Carefully turn pancakes over; cook 2 minutes or until bottoms are lightly browned. **YIELD:** 4 servings (serving size: 2 blueberry pancakes).

CALORIES 272; FAT 8.8g (sat 4.5g, mono 2.5g, poly 0.8g); PROTEIN 9.5g; CARB 40.1g; FIBER 3.2g; CHOL 122mg; IRON 2mg; SODIUM 403mg; CALC 192mg

## Buttermilk Pancakes ▼

To freeze any leftovers, place wax paper between pancakes, and wrap them tightly in foil.

- 4.5 ounces all-purpose flour (about 1 cup)
- 2 tablespoons sugar
- 1 teaspoon baking powder
- ½ teaspoon baking soda
- ¼ teaspoon salt
- 1 cup low-fat buttermilk
- 1 teaspoon vegetable oil
- 1 large egg, lightly beaten
- Cooking spray

**1.** Weigh or lightly spoon flour into a dry measuring cup; level with a knife. Combine flour and next 4 ingredients in a large bowl, and make a well in center of mixture. Combine buttermilk, oil, and egg; add to flour mixture, stirring until smooth.

**2.** Spoon about ¼ cup batter onto a hot nonstick griddle or nonstick skillet coated with cooking spray. Turn pancakes when tops are covered with bubbles and edges look cooked.

**YIELD:** 9 (4-inch) pancakes (serving size: 1 pancake).

CALORIES 99; FAT 2.9g (sat 0.8g, mono 0.9g, poly 1g); PROTEIN 3.2g; CARB 14.9g; FIBER 0.4g; CHOL 25mg; IRON 0.8mg; SODIUM 211mg; CALC 69mg

## Carrot Cake Pancakes ▼

These cakey flapjacks feature warm spices and bright carrot flavor. This lightened version uses low-fat buttermilk and a small dab of honey butter to top the pancakes versus a typical pat of butter.

- 5.6 ounces all-purpose flour (about 1¼ cups)
- ¼ cup chopped walnuts, toasted
- 2 teaspoons baking powder
- 1 teaspoon ground cinnamon
- ¼ teaspoon salt
- ⅛ teaspoon freshly ground nutmeg
- Dash of ground cloves
- Dash of ground ginger
- ¼ cup brown sugar
- ¾ cup low-fat buttermilk
- 1 tablespoon canola oil
- 1½ teaspoons vanilla extract
- 2 large eggs, lightly beaten
- 2 cups finely grated carrot (about 1 pound)
- Cooking spray
- 3 tablespoons butter, softened
- 2 tablespoons honey

**1.** Weigh or lightly spoon flour into dry measuring cups, and level with a knife. Combine flour

3

4

and next 7 ingredients in a large bowl, stirring with a whisk. Combine 1/4 cup brown sugar and next 4 ingredients; add sugar mixture to flour mixture, stirring just until moist. Fold in 2 cups carrot.

**2.** Heat a large nonstick skillet over medium heat. Coat pan with cooking spray. Spoon 4 (1/4-cup) batter mounds onto pan, spreading with a spatula. Cook 2 minutes or until tops are covered with bubbles and edges look cooked. Carefully turn pancakes over; cook 1 minute or until bottoms are lightly browned. Repeat procedure twice with remaining batter. Combine butter and honey in a small bowl; serve with pancakes. **YIELD:** 6 servings (serving size: 2 pancakes and about 2 teaspoons honey butter).

CALORIES 315; FAT 13.3g (sat 4.8g, mono 4.4g, poly 3.3g); PROTEIN 7.8g; CARB 41.6g; FIBER 2.2g; CHOL 78mg; IRON 2.3mg; SODIUM 381mg; CALC 177mg

## Hearty Pancakes ▸

Forget that these pancakes are supremely healthy—they are supremely satisfying! Any pancake aficionado will love to have these in the morning breakfast rotation. Ingredients such as whole-wheat flour, soy milk, golden raisins, and walnuts punch up the nutrition in these pancakes, making them heart-healthy.

- **4.75 ounces whole-wheat flour (about 1 cup)**
- **1.1 ounces all-purpose flour (about ¼ cup)**
- **⅓ cup uncooked farina (such as Cream of Wheat)**
- **⅓ cup sugar**
- **1 teaspoon baking soda**
- **1 teaspoon baking powder**
- **½ teaspoon salt**
- **1½ cups vanilla soy milk**
- **¼ cup applesauce**
- **1 large egg, lightly beaten**
- **Cooking spray**
- **½ cup golden raisins, divided**
- **½ cup coarsely chopped walnuts, divided**
- **¼ cup maple syrup**

**1.** Weigh or lightly spoon flours into dry measuring cups; level with a knife. Combine flours, farina, and next 4 ingredients in a large bowl, stirring with a whisk. Combine milk, applesauce, and egg in a medium bowl, stirring until well blended. Add milk mixture to flour mixture, stirring until well combined. Let batter stand 5 minutes.

**2.** Heat a nonstick griddle or skillet over medium heat; coat pan with cooking spray. Pour about 1/4 cup batter per pancake onto pan; sprinkle each with 2 teaspoons raisins and 2 teaspoons walnuts. Cook 1 minute or until tops are covered with bubbles and edges look cooked. Carefully turn pancakes over, and cook 1 minute or until bottoms are lightly browned. Repeat procedure with remaining batter, raisins, and walnuts. Serve with syrup. **YIELD:** 6 servings (serving size: 2 pancakes and 2 teaspoons maple syrup).

CALORIES 347; FAT 9g (sat 1g, mono 1.3g, poly 5.1g); PROTEIN 8.8g; CARB 61.1g; FIBER 4.3g; CHOL 35mg; IRON 4.8mg; SODIUM 537mg; CALC 142mg

# 5 ways with waffles

1

## Bacon Maple Waffles

Crumbled bacon is cooked into maple-sweetened waffles, so every bite contains that classic pairing. If you're using a Belgian waffle maker, spread about ½ cup batter per waffle onto the waffle iron; you'll get about eight waffles.

- **9 ounces all-purpose flour (about 2 cups)**
- **1 tablespoon baking powder**
- **½ teaspoon salt**
- **1¼ cups 2% reduced-fat milk**
- **3 tablespoons maple syrup**
- **2 tablespoons butter, melted**
- **4 bacon slices cooked, crumbled, and divided**
- **3 large eggs, lightly beaten**
- **Cooking spray**
- **⅓ cup maple syrup**

**1.** Weigh or lightly spoon flour into dry measuring cups; level with a knife. Place flour, baking powder, and salt in a bowl; stir with a whisk. Make a well in center of mixture. Combine milk, 3 tablespoons syrup, butter, 3 bacon slices, and eggs, stirring with a whisk. Add milk mixture to flour mixture; stir just until moist.

**2.** Coat a waffle iron with cooking spray; preheat. Spoon about ⅓ cup batter per waffle onto hot waffle iron, spreading batter to edges. Cook 4 to 5 minutes or until steaming stops; repeat procedure with remaining batter. Serve waffles with ⅓ cup syrup and remaining crumbled bacon. **YIELD:** 5 servings (serving size: 2 waffles and about 1 tablespoon syrup).

CALORIES 411; FAT 11.4g (sat 5.3g, mono 3.7g, poly 1.1g); PROTEIN 12.9g; CARB 64.5g; FIBER 1.4g; CHOL 149mg; IRON 3.7mg; SODIUM 754mg; CALC 284mg

## Banana-Cinnamon Waffles

Crown these lightly spiced waffles with cinnamon sugar, sliced bananas, and/or a drizzle of maple syrup. Buckwheat flour adds a somewhat tangy, robust nuttiness.

- 4.5 ounces all-purpose flour (about 1 cup)
- 2.38 ounces whole-wheat flour (about ½ cup)
- 1 ounce buckwheat flour (about ¼ cup)
- ¼ cup ground flaxseed
- 2 tablespoons sugar
- 1½ teaspoons baking powder
- ½ teaspoon ground cinnamon
- ¼ teaspoon salt
- 1½ cups fat-free milk
- 3 tablespoons butter, melted
- 2 large eggs, lightly beaten
- 1 large ripe banana, mashed
- Cooking spray

**1.** Weigh or lightly spoon flours into dry measuring cups; level with a knife. Combine flours, flaxseed, and next 4 ingredients in a medium bowl, stirring with a whisk.

**2.** Combine milk, butter, and eggs, stirring with a whisk; add milk mixture to flour mixture, stirring until blended. Fold in mashed banana.

**3.** Coat a waffle iron with cooking spray; preheat. Spoon about ¼ cup batter per 4-inch waffle onto hot waffle iron, spreading batter to edges. Cook 3 to 4 minutes or until steaming stops; repeat procedure with remaining batter.

**YIELD:** 8 servings (serving size: 2 waffles).

CALORIES 215; FAT 7.4g (sat 3.3g, mono 1.9g, poly 1.4g); PROTEIN 7.3g; CARB 31.1g; FIBER 3.4g; CHOL 65mg; IRON 1.9mg; SODIUM 205mg; CALC 133mg

## Citrus Waffles with Marmalade Compote

Compote:

- ¼ cup reduced-sugar orange marmalade (such as Smucker's)
- 1 tablespoon fresh orange juice
- 1 teaspoon fresh lemon juice
- 1 teaspoon honey
- 2 cups fresh orange sections (about 2 oranges)

Waffles:

- 3.75 ounces all-purpose flour (about ¾ cup)
- 3.5 ounces whole-wheat flour (about ¾ cup)
- ½ cup packed brown sugar
- ¼ cup toasted wheat germ
- 1¼ teaspoons baking powder
- 1 teaspoon baking soda
- ¼ teaspoon salt
- ¼ teaspoon nutmeg
- 1⅓ cups buttermilk
- ⅓ cup water
- 2 tablespoons canola oil
- 1 teaspoon grated orange rind
- 1 large egg, lightly beaten
- Cooking spray
- Powdered sugar

**1.** To prepare compote, place marmalade, orange juice, lemon juice, and honey in a small saucepan over medium-low heat; cook 2 minutes or until marmalade melts. Reduce heat, and gently stir in orange sections; keep warm.

**2.** To prepare waffles, weigh or lightly spoon flours into dry measuring cups, and level with a knife. Combine flours and next 6 ingredients in a large bowl, stirring with a whisk. Combine buttermilk, ⅓ cup water, canola oil, orange rind, and egg in a small bowl. Add milk mixture to flour mixture, stirring just until moist. Coat a waffle iron with cooking spray; preheat. Spoon about ⅓ cup batter per 4-inch waffle onto hot waffle iron, spreading batter to edges. Cook 5 minutes or until steaming stops, and repeat procedure with remaining batter. Sift powdered sugar over tops of waffles. Serve with orange compote. **YIELD:** 6 servings (serving size: 2 waffles and ⅓ cup compote).

CALORIES 309; FAT 8.3g (sat 1.9g, mono 3.7g, poly 2.1g); PROTEIN 8.5g; CARB 52.5g; FIBER 4.5g; CHOL 43mg; IRON 2.3mg; SODIUM 492mg; CALC 169mg

## French Toast Waffles ▾

A waffle maker creates a crisp, brown French toast without a skillet. Just make sure you start with slightly hardened bread so that the toast won't be soggy. Serve this toast with fresh raspberries and maple syrup.

Cooking spray
- 1 cup fat-free milk
- 1 tablespoon sugar
- 1 tablespoon butter, melted
- 1 teaspoon vanilla extract
- ½ teaspoon ground cinnamon
- 2 large eggs
- 16 (½-inch-thick) slices day-old French bread (about 7 ounces)

**1.** Coat waffle iron with cooking spray, and preheat.

**2.** Combine milk and next 5 ingredients, stirring well with a whisk. Place bread in a 13 x 9–inch baking dish; pour milk mixture over bread, turning to coat. Let stand 5 minutes.

**3.** Place 4 bread slices on hot waffle iron. Cook 3 to 5 minutes or until done; repeat procedure with remaining bread. **YIELD:** 4 servings (serving size: 4 waffles).

CALORIES 236; FAT 7g (sat 3g, mono 2.4g, poly 0.8g); PROTEIN 9.6g; CARB 32.5g; FIBER 1.6g; CHOL 115mg; IRON 1.7mg; SODIUM 395mg; CALC 129mg

## Honeyed Yogurt and Mixed Berries with Whole-Grain Waffles ▾

- 2 cups vanilla low-fat yogurt
- 2 tablespoons honey
- 2 cups fresh raspberries
- 1 cup quartered small strawberries
- 1 cup fresh blackberries
- ⅓ cup sugar
- 2 tablespoons fresh lemon juice
- 4 frozen whole-grain waffles, toasted
- 4 teaspoons toasted wheat germ

**1.** Drain yogurt in a fine sieve or colander lined with cheesecloth 10 minutes; spoon into a bowl. Add honey, stirring to combine.

**2.** Combine berries, sugar, and juice; let stand 5 minutes. Place 1 waffle on each of 4 plates; top each serving with 1 cup fruit mixture, about ⅓ cup yogurt mixture, and 1 teaspoon wheat germ. Serve immediately. **YIELD:** 4 servings (serving size: 1 waffle, 1 cup fruit mixture, about ⅓ cup yogurt mixture, and 1 teaspoon wheat germ).

CALORIES 377; FAT 6.8g (sat 2.3g, mono 2.3g, poly 1.6g); PROTEIN 11.5g; CARB 71.6g; FIBER 8.3g; CHOL 43mg; IRON 1.9mg; SODIUM 214 mg; CALC 345mg

This recipe falls into the 'dangerously good category.' For serving size it should say 'you will eat this until it is gone.' Highly recommended.

**from cookinglight.com**

# Sweet Potato and Canadian Bacon Hash

- 4 cups (¾-inch) diced peeled sweet potato (about 1 pound)
- 2 cups (¾-inch) diced red potato (about 8 ounces)
- 2 tablespoons vegetable oil
- 1 cup diced Canadian bacon (about 8 ounces)
- 1 cup chopped green bell pepper
- ⅔ cup chopped green onions
- ¾ teaspoon salt
- ½ teaspoon celery seed
- ½ teaspoon freshly ground black pepper
- ⅛ teaspoon grated whole nutmeg
- ¼ cup fat-free, lower-sodium chicken broth
- 1 tablespoon cider vinegar

**1.** Place potatoes in a saucepan, and cover with water. Bring to a boil. Reduce heat, and simmer 5 minutes. Drain.

**2.** Heat oil in a large nonstick skillet over medium heat. Add bacon; cook 4 minutes, stirring frequently. Add bell pepper and green onions; cook 2 minutes, stirring frequently. Add potatoes, salt, celery seed, pepper, and nutmeg; cook 4 minutes, gently stirring occasionally. Stir in broth and vinegar. Toss gently until liquid is absorbed. **YIELD:** 6 servings (serving size: about 1 cup).

CALORIES 207; FAT 6.8g (sat 1.4g, mono 2.1g, poly 3g); PROTEIN 8.8g; CARB 28g; FIBER 3g; CHOL 19mg; IRON 1.4mg; SODIUM 711mg; CALC 32mg

## what makes it light

- uses fat-free, lower-sodium chicken broth
- uses a minimal amount of salt
- uses Canadian bacon, which is a leaner choice than regular bacon

30
minutes
or
less

## what makes it light

- doesn't use butter like traditional recipes
- uses half the amount of cheese and sour cream as traditional recipes
- uses fat-free sour cream
- uses 30% reduced-sodium, 98% fat-free cream of mushroom soup

Here in the Midwest a popular side for Sunday dinners and potlucks is a hash brown casserole much like this one. There are probably five not-light versions in every local cookbook. I was asked to bring that dish for a huge family get-together, so I substituted a double recipe of this casserole. It was the first thing to disappear. Everyone loved the bacon (not included in the traditional recipes that are popular in this area) and **everyone thought they were getting a bonus version, not a light version.**

**from cookinglight.com**

# Hash Brown Casserole with Bacon, Onions, and Cheese

- 6 bacon slices
- 1 cup chopped onion
- 2 garlic cloves, minced
- 1 (32-ounce) package frozen Southern-style hash brown potatoes
- 1 cup (4 ounces) preshredded four cheese blend, divided (such as Kraft)
- ½ cup chopped green onions
- ½ cup fat-free sour cream
- ½ teaspoon salt
- ¼ teaspoon freshly ground black pepper
- 1 (10.75-ounce) can condensed 30% reduced-sodium, 98% fat-free cream of mushroom soup, undiluted
- Cooking spray

**1.** Cook bacon in a large nonstick skillet over medium heat until crisp. Remove bacon from pan, and crumble. Discard drippings. Add 1 cup onion and garlic to pan; cook 5 minutes or until tender, stirring frequently. Stir in potatoes; cover and cook 15 minutes, stirring occasionally.
**2.** Combine crumbled bacon, 1/4 cup cheese, green onions, sour cream, salt, pepper, and soup in a large bowl. Add potato mixture; toss gently to combine. Spoon mixture into an 11 x 7–inch baking dish coated with cooking spray. Sprinkle with remaining 3/4 cup cheese. Cover with foil coated with cooking spray. Refrigerate 8 hours or overnight.
**3.** Preheat oven to 350°.
**4.** Remove casserole from refrigerator; let stand at room temperature 15 minutes. Bake casserole, covered, at 350° for 30 minutes. Uncover and bake an additional 30 minutes or until bubbly around edges and cheese begins to brown. **YIELD:** 6 servings (serving size: about 1 cup).

CALORIES 293; FAT 10g (sat 4.8g, mono 3.3g, poly 0.7g); PROTEIN 12.2g; CARB 41.4g; FIBER 4.7g; CHOL 31mg; IRON 0.2mg; SODIUM 720mg; CALC 214mg

Super easy to make. **It is so much better than what you can buy in a box.** Much healthier, too! We've been eating a little of it each morning for breakfast with milk and sometimes as an after-workout snack with yogurt.

**from cookinglight.com**

# Three-Grain Breakfast Cereal with Walnuts and Dried Fruit

- ½ cup maple syrup
- ⅓ cup honey
- 3 tablespoons canola oil
- 1½ tablespoons vanilla extract
- 4½ cups regular oats
- 1 cup uncooked quick-cooking barley
- ¾ cup chopped walnuts or pecans
- ½ cup wheat germ
- 1 teaspoon ground cinnamon
- ¼ teaspoon ground nutmeg
- Cooking spray
- 1 (7-ounce) package dried mixed fruit, chopped (such as Sun-Maid brand)

**1.** Preheat oven to 325°.
**2.** Combine first 4 ingredients, stirring with a whisk.
**3.** Combine oats, barley, walnuts, wheat germ, cinnamon, and nutmeg in a large bowl. Add syrup mixture; stir well to coat. Spread oat mixture evenly onto a jelly-roll pan coated with cooking spray. Bake at 325° for 30 minutes or until browned, stirring every 10 minutes. Stir in dried fruit. Cool completely. **YIELD:** 24 servings (serving size: ⅓ cup).

CALORIES 185; FAT 5.8g (sat 0.6g, mono 1.7g, poly 2.8); PROTEIN 4.5g; CARB 31.3g; FIBER 4g; CHOL 0mg; IRON 1.6mg; SODIUM 4mg; CALC 24mg

## what makes it light

- uses canola oil, which is a healthy option
- doesn't use salt, which is in most store-bought cereals
- uses three types of whole grains to maximize health benefits

**This was a wonderful oatmeal and easy to make.** The dried cherries gave it a sweet-tart flavor, and the brown sugar–hazelnut topping added just the right amount of sweetness. The hazelnut oil gave it a rich creamy texture and a nutty kick. **Leftovers heated up nicely** with a little extra water. Will make again and again.

**from cookinglight.com**

# Cherry-Hazelnut Oatmeal

- 6 cups water
- 2 cups steel-cut (Irish) oats (such as McCann's)
- ⅔ cup dried Bing or other sweet cherries, coarsely chopped
- ¼ teaspoon salt
- 5 tablespoons brown sugar, divided
- ¼ cup chopped hazelnuts, toasted and divided
- ¼ teaspoon ground cinnamon
- 2 tablespoons toasted hazelnut oil

**1.** Combine first 4 ingredients in a medium saucepan; bring to a boil. Reduce heat, and simmer 20 minutes or until desired consistency, stirring occasionally. Remove from heat. Stir in 3 tablespoons sugar, 1 tablespoon nuts, and cinnamon. Place 1 cup oatmeal in each of 6 bowls; sprinkle each serving with 1 teaspoon sugar. Top each serving with 1½ teaspoon nuts; drizzle with 1 teaspoon oil. **YIELD:** 6 servings.

CALORIES 350; FAT 11.1g (sat 1.1g, mono 6.8g, poly 2g); PROTEIN 8.9g; CARB 56.1g; FIBER 6.8g; CHOL 0mg; IRON 3mg; SODIUM 112mg; CALC 52mg

## what makes it light

- uses cherries, cinnamon, and a small amount of brown sugar to add natural sweetness
- uses fiber-rich oats

30
minutes
or
less

what makes it light
• uses fat-free milk
• uses a minimal amount of salt

This makes an outstanding breakfast. I first had it at a trendy restaurant in Chicago and was able to locate the recipe to make at home. It can be made ahead and reheated for a later time. My family loves it!

from cookinglight.com

# Pan-Seared Oatmeal with Warm Fruit Compote and Cider Syrup

Syrup:

- 2 cups apple cider

Compote:

- 2 cups water
- ¼ cup packed brown sugar
- ½ teaspoon ground cinnamon
- 1 (7-ounce) package dried mixed fruit bits

Oatmeal:

- 3 cups water
- 1 cup fat-free milk
- ¼ cup packed brown sugar
- ½ teaspoon ground cinnamon
- ¼ teaspoon salt
- 1½ cups steel-cut (Irish) oats
- Cooking spray
- ¼ cup butter, divided

**1.** To prepare syrup, bring cider to a boil in a small saucepan over medium-high heat. Cook until reduced to 1/3 cup (about 20 minutes); set aside.
**2.** To prepare compote, combine 2 cups water, 1/4 cup sugar, 1/2 teaspoon cinnamon, and dried fruit in a medium saucepan; bring to a boil. Reduce heat, and simmer 20 minutes or until thick. Set aside, and keep warm.
**3.** To prepare oatmeal, combine 3 cups water, 1 cup milk, 1/4 cup brown sugar, 1/2 teaspoon cinnamon, and salt in a large saucepan. Bring to a boil over medium-high heat; stir in oats. Reduce heat, and simmer 20 minutes or until thick, stirring occasionally. Spoon oatmeal into an 11 x 7–inch baking dish coated with cooking spray; cool to room temperature. Cover and chill at least 1 hour or until set.
**4.** Using a sharp knife, cut oatmeal into 8 equal rectangles; cut each rectangle in half diagonally to form 16 triangles.
**5.** Melt 2 tablespoons butter in a large nonstick skillet over medium heat. Add 8 oatmeal triangles; cook 3 minutes on each side or until golden brown. Remove from pan; keep warm. Repeat procedure with remaining 2 tablespoons butter and oatmeal triangles. Place 2 oatmeal triangles on each of 8 plates, and top each serving with 3 1/2 tablespoons fruit compote and about 2 teaspoons syrup.

**YIELD:** 8 servings.

CALORIES 314; FAT 7.9g (sat 3.9g, mono 2.3g, poly 0.9g); PROTEIN 5.8g; CARB 58.7g; FIBER 2.8g; CHOL 16mg; IRON 2.4mg; SODIUM 167mg; CALC 76mg

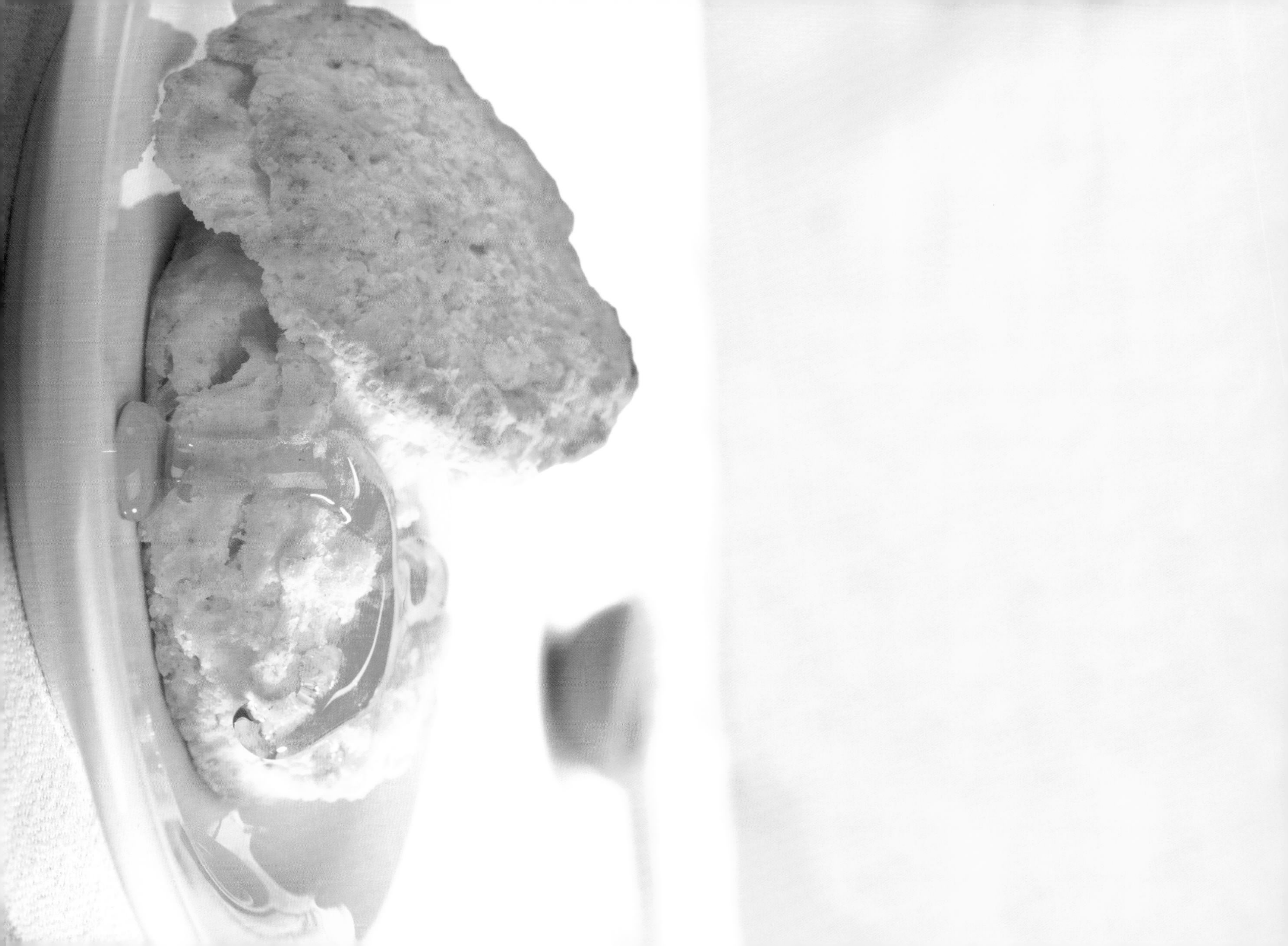

**It's important to measure the flour correctly.** We recommend weighing it. Also, keep this tip in mind when cutting your biscuits: Cut the dough with a biscuit cutter dipped in flour, but be careful not to twist it. Twisting it could seal the edges of the dough and hinder the biscuits from rising. The buttermilk adds flavor and tenderness so you don't have to use as much butter in these flaky melt-in-your-mouth biscuits.

# Buttermilk Biscuits

- 9 ounces all-purpose flour (about 2 cups)
- 2 teaspoons baking powder
- ¼ teaspoon baking soda
- ¼ teaspoon salt
- 3 tablespoons plus 1 teaspoon chilled butter, cut into small pieces
- ¾ cup low-fat or nonfat buttermilk
- Honey (optional)

**1.** Preheat oven to 450°.
**2.** Weigh or lightly spoon flour into dry measuring cups; level with a knife. Combine flour and next 3 ingredients in a bowl. Cut in butter with a pastry blender or 2 knives until mixture resembles coarse meal. Add buttermilk; stir just until dry ingredients are moist.
**3.** Turn dough out onto a lightly floured surface; knead 4 or 5 times. Roll dough to a 1/2-inch-thickness; cut with a 2 1/2-inch biscuit cutter. Place on a baking sheet. Bake at 450° for 12 minutes or until biscuits are golden. Drizzle biscuits with honey, if desired. **YIELD:** 1 dozen (serving size: 1 biscuit).

CALORIES 102; FAT 2.6g (sat 1.2g, mono 1g, poly 0.2g); PROTEIN 2.7g; CARB 16.9g; FIBER 0.6g; CHOL 6mg; IRON 1.1mg; SODIUM 189mg; CALC 67mg

## what makes it light

- uses low-fat buttermilk
- uses less butter than traditional recipes

**This recipe puts a surprising but delicious twist on a classic Southern breakfast.** Vegetarian sausage has a firmer texture than pork sausage. Crumbling it helps distribute it evenly throughout the gravy. The gravy boasts 3 grams of soy protein per serving and is far healthier than a traditional meat-based sausage gravy.

# Biscuits and Vegetarian Sausage Gravy

- 1 (16.3-ounce) can reduced-fat refrigerated biscuit dough
- 1 tablespoon vegetable oil
- ½ (14-ounce) package meatless fat-free sausage (such as Lightlife Gimme Lean)
- 1.1 ounces all-purpose flour (about ¼ cup)
- 3 cups 1% low-fat milk
- ½ teaspoon salt
- ¼ teaspoon freshly ground black pepper

**1.** Prepare biscuits according to package directions.

**2.** Heat oil in a large nonstick skillet over medium-high heat. Add sausage; cook 3 minutes or until browned, stirring to crumble.

**3.** Weigh or lightly spoon flour into a dry measuring cup; level with a knife. Combine flour and 1% low-fat milk, stirring with a whisk until smooth. Add milk mixture, salt, and freshly ground black pepper to pan; bring to a boil over medium-high heat. Cover, reduce heat, and simmer 3 minutes or until thick. Split biscuits in half. Place 2 biscuit halves on each of 8 plates; top each serving with about ⅓ cup gravy. Serve immediately. **YIELD:** 8 servings.

CALORIES 268; FAT 8.7g (sat 2.4g, mono 4g, poly 1g); PROTEIN 11.4g; CARB 36.9g; FIBER 0.6g; CHOL 4mg; IRON 1mg; SODIUM 910mg; CALC 131mg

## what makes it light

- uses vegetarian sausage instead of pork sausage
- uses low-fat milk
- uses reduced-fat refrigerated biscuits

30
minutes
or
less

**Best light scones ever!** I even added a couple tablespoons of ground flaxseed, and they were great.

**from cookinglight.com**

# Sour Cream Scones

- 6.75 ounces all-purpose flour (about 1½ cups)
- 3 ounces whole-wheat flour (about ⅔ cup)
- ⅓ cup packed brown sugar
- 2 tablespoons granulated sugar
- 2 teaspoons baking powder
- ½ teaspoon baking soda
- ¼ teaspoon salt
- ⅔ cup reduced-fat sour cream
- 3 tablespoons butter, melted and cooled
- 1 large egg white
- ⅓ cup dried currants or raisins
- Cooking spray
- 1 tablespoon granulated sugar
- ¼ teaspoon ground cinnamon
- Lemon curd (optional)

**1.** Preheat oven to 400°.

**2.** Weigh or lightly spoon flours into dry measuring cups; level with a knife. Combine flours and next 5 ingredients in a large bowl; stir well with a whisk.

**3.** Combine sour cream, butter, and egg white in a small bowl. Add sour cream mixture to flour mixture, stirring just until moist. Stir in currants.

**4.** Turn dough out onto a lightly floured surface; knead lightly 6 to 12 times with floured hands. (Dough will be crumbly.) Divide dough in half. Pat each half into a 6-inch circle on a baking sheet coated with cooking spray. Cut each circle into 6 wedges; do not separate.

**5.** Combine 1 tablespoon granulated sugar and cinnamon. Lightly coat top of dough with cooking spray. Sprinkle with cinnamon mixture. Bake at 400° for 15 minutes or until lightly browned. Serve with lemon curd, if desired. **YIELD:** 1 dozen (serving size: 1 scone).

CALORIES 175; FAT 4.8g (sat 2.9g, mono 1.3g, poly 0.3g); PROTEIN 3.6g; CARB 30.2g; FIBER 1.4g; CHOL 14mg; IRON 1.3mg; SODIUM 219mg; CALC 81mg

## what makes it light

- uses reduced-fat sour cream
- uses almost half the amount of butter as traditional recipes
- uses egg white

**This easy recipe turns out the most delicious, fluffy, rich-tasting scones.** My local bakery's full-fat version can't beat them! I've also substituted about ¾ cup chopped dill for the ham and have gotten nothing but rave reviews.

**from cookinglight.com**

# Ham and Cheese Scones

- 9 ounces all-purpose flour (about 2 cups)
- 1 tablespoon baking powder
- 2 teaspoons sugar
- ¼ teaspoon salt
- ¼ teaspoon ground red pepper
- 3 tablespoons chilled butter, cut into small pieces
- ¾ cup (3 ounces) shredded reduced-fat extrasharp cheddar cheese
- ¾ cup finely chopped 33%-less-sodium ham (about 3 ounces)
- ¾ cup nonfat buttermilk
- 2 large egg whites
- Cooking spray

**1.** Preheat oven to 400°.

**2.** Weigh or lightly spoon flour into dry measuring cups; level with a knife. Combine flour, baking powder, sugar, salt, and pepper in a large bowl; cut in butter with a pastry blender or 2 knives until mixture resembles coarse meal. Stir in cheese and ham. Combine buttermilk and egg whites, stirring with a whisk. Add to flour mixture, stirring just until moist.

**3.** Turn dough out onto a lightly floured surface; knead lightly 4 to 5 times with floured hands. Pat dough into an 8-inch circle on a baking sheet coated with cooking spray. Cut dough into 8 wedges, cutting into but not through dough. Bake at 400° for 20 minutes or until lightly browned. **YIELD:** 8 servings (serving size: 1 scone).

CALORIES 217; FAT 7.2g (sat 4.1g, mono 1.6g, poly 0.4g); PROTEIN 10.4g; CARB 27.1g; FIBER 0.9g; CHOL 26mg; IRON 1.8mg; SODIUM 519mg; CALC 235mg

## what makes it light

- uses reduced-fat extrasharp cheddar cheese
- uses 33%-less-sodium ham
- uses nonfat buttermilk
- uses egg whites
- uses almost half the amount of butter as traditional recipes

# 5 ways with muffins

## 1

## Strawberry-Cinnamon Muffins

- 6.75 ounces all-purpose flour (about 1½ cups)
- ½ cup sugar
- 2½ teaspoons baking powder
- 1 teaspoon ground cinnamon
- ¼ teaspoon salt
- ⅔ cup vanilla fat-free yogurt
- ¼ cup butter, melted
- 3 tablespoons 1% low-fat milk
- 1 large egg, lightly beaten
- Cooking spray
- ¼ cup strawberry jam
- 1 tablespoon sugar
- ½ teaspoon ground cinnamon

**1.** Preheat oven to 375°.

**2.** Weigh or lightly spoon flour into dry measuring cups, and level with a knife. Combine flour and next 4 ingredients in a large bowl, stirring well with a whisk. Make a well in center of flour mixture. Combine yogurt, butter, milk, and egg in a bowl, stirring well with a whisk. Add yogurt mixture to flour mixture, stirring just until moist.

**3.** Place 12 foil cup liners in muffin cups; coat liners with cooking spray. Spoon 1 tablespoon batter into each liner. Top each with 1 teaspoon jam. Top evenly with remaining batter. Combine 1 tablespoon sugar and ½ teaspoon cinnamon; sprinkle over batter. Bake at 375° for 15 minutes or until a wooden pick inserted in center comes out clean. Cool in pan on a wire rack 15 minutes. Remove from pan; place on wire rack. **YIELD:** 1 dozen (serving size: 1 muffin).

CALORIES 165; FAT 4.4g (sat 2.6g, mono 1.3g, poly 0.3g); PROTEIN 3g; CARB 29g; FIBER 0.6g; CHOL 28mg; IRON 1mg; SODIUM 206mg; CALC 94mg

# Raspberry-Cream Cheese Muffins

One of our cookinglight.com readers said she had a serious problem with this recipe—it was super easy to make and she couldn't stop eating them. We think you'll discover the same "problem."

- ⅔ cup (5 ounces) ⅓-less-fat cream cheese, softened
- ⅓ cup butter, softened
- 1½ cups sugar
- 1½ teaspoons vanilla extract
- 2 large egg whites
- 1 large egg
- 9 ounces all-purpose flour (about 2 cups)
- 1 teaspoon baking powder
- ¼ teaspoon baking soda
- ½ teaspoon salt
- ½ cup low-fat buttermilk
- 2 cups fresh or frozen raspberries
- ¼ cup finely chopped walnuts

**1.** Preheat oven to 350°.
**2.** Combine cream cheese and butter in a large bowl. Beat with a mixer at high speed until well blended. Add sugar; beat until fluffy. Add vanilla, egg whites, and egg; beat well.
**3.** Weigh or lightly spoon flour into dry measuring cups; level with a knife. Combine flour, baking powder, baking soda, and salt. With mixer on low speed, add flour mixture and buttermilk to cream cheese mixture, beginning and ending with flour mixture. Gently fold in raspberries and walnuts.
**4.** Place 24 foil cup liners in muffin cups. Spoon batter evenly into liners. Bake at 350° for 25 minutes or until a wooden pick inserted in center comes out clean. Remove from pans; cool on a wire rack. **YIELD:** 2 dozen (serving size: 1 muffin).

CALORIES 142; FAT 4.7g (sat 2.4g, mono 1.3g, poly 0.7g); PROTEIN 2.7g; CARB 22.6g; FIBER 1.1g; CHOL 19mg; IRON 0.7mg; SODIUM 138mg; CALC 31mg

## Sour Cream Muffins with Poppy Seed Streusel ▼

Keep these orange-scented muffins on hand for a quick breakfast or sweet snack.

Streusel:

- 3 tablespoons sugar
- 2 tablespoons all-purpose flour
- 1 tablespoon butter, melted
- 1 teaspoon poppy seeds

Muffins:

- 9 ounces all-purpose flour (about 2 cups)
- ¾ cup sugar
- 2 teaspoons baking powder
- 1 teaspoon baking soda
- ½ teaspoon salt
- ¾ cup nonfat buttermilk
- ¼ cup butter, melted
- 1 tablespoon grated orange rind
- 1 teaspoon vanilla extract
- 1 large egg, lightly beaten
- 1 (8-ounce) container reduced-fat sour cream
- Cooking spray

**1.** Preheat oven to 375°.

**2.** To prepare streusel, combine first 4 ingredients in a small bowl; set aside.

**3.** To prepare muffins, weigh or lightly spoon 9 ounces flour into dry measuring cups; level with a knife. Combine flour, 3/4 cup sugar, baking powder, baking soda, and salt in a medium bowl, stirring with a whisk. Make a well in center of mixture. Combine buttermilk and remaining ingredients except cooking spray in a small bowl; add to flour mixture, stirring just until moist. Spoon batter into 15 muffin cups coated with cooking spray. Sprinkle streusel evenly over batter. Bake at 375° for 18 minutes or until golden brown. Remove muffins from pans immediately; place on a wire rack. **YIELD:** 15 servings (serving size: 1 muffin).

CALORIES 180; FAT 6.3g (sat 3.2g, mono 2.3g, poly 0.4g); PROTEIN 3.3g; CARB 27.8g; FIBER 0.5g; CHOL 31mg; IRON 1mg; SODIUM 277mg; CALC 77mg

## Lemon-Blueberry Muffins ▼

- 9 ounces all-purpose flour (about 2 cups)
- ½ cup sugar
- 1 teaspoon baking powder
- ½ teaspoon baking soda
- ½ teaspoon salt
- ⅛ teaspoon ground nutmeg
- ¼ cup butter
- 1¼ cups low-fat buttermilk
- 1 large egg
- 1 tablespoon grated lemon rind
- 1 cup blueberries
- Cooking spray
- 1 tablespoon fresh lemon juice
- ½ cup powdered sugar

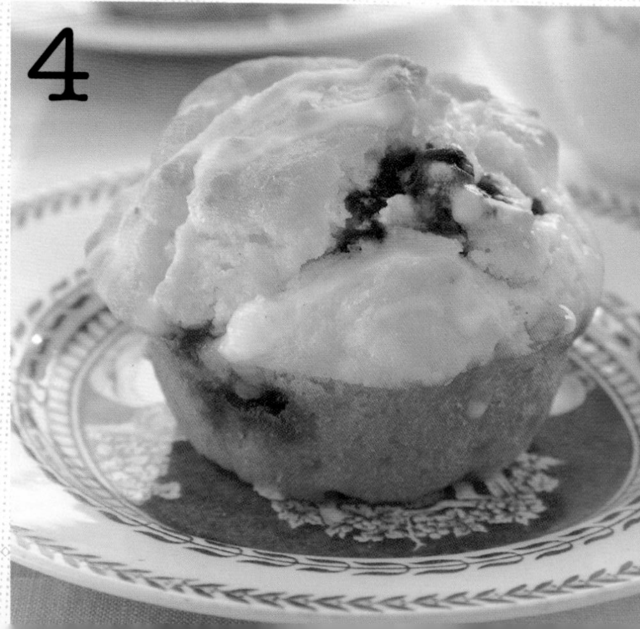

**1.** Preheat oven to 400°.
**2.** Weigh or lightly spoon flour into dry measuring cups; level with a knife. Combine flour and next 5 ingredients in a medium bowl; cut in butter with a pastry blender or 2 knives until mixture resembles coarse meal.
**3.** Combine buttermilk, egg, and rind; stir well with a whisk. Add to flour mixture; stir just until moist. Gently fold in blueberries.
**4.** Spoon batter into 12 muffin cups coated with cooking spray. Bake at 400° for 20 minutes or until muffins spring back when lightly touched. Remove muffins from pans immediately, and place on a wire rack to cool.
**5.** Combine lemon juice and powdered sugar in a small bowl. Drizzle glaze evenly over cooled muffins. **YIELD:** 1 dozen (serving size: 1 muffin).

CALORIES 187; FAT 4.8g (sat 2.7g, mono 1.4g, poly 0.3g); PROTEIN 3.7g; CARB 32.6g; FIBER 1g; CHOL 30mg; IRON 1.1mg; SODIUM 264mg; CALC 59mg

## Tropical Muffins with ▲ Coconut-Macadamia Topping

Muffins:

- 6 ounces all-purpose flour (about 1⅓ cups)
- 1 cup regular oats
- 1 teaspoon baking powder
- ½ teaspoon baking soda
- ½ teaspoon salt
- 1 cup mashed ripe banana (about 2 bananas)
- 1 cup low-fat buttermilk
- ½ cup packed brown sugar
- 2 tablespoons canola oil
- 1 teaspoon vanilla extract
- 1 large egg
- ½ cup canned crushed pineapple in juice, drained
- ⅓ cup flaked sweetened coconut
- 3 tablespoons finely chopped macadamia nuts, toasted
- Cooking spray

Topping:

- 2 tablespoons flaked sweetened coconut
- 1 tablespoon chopped macadamia nuts
- 1 tablespoon granulated sugar
- 1 tablespoon regular oats

**1.** Preheat oven to 400°.
**2.** To prepare muffins, weigh or lightly spoon flour into dry measuring cups; level with a knife. Combine flour and next 4 ingredients in a large bowl. Make a well in center of flour mixture. Combine banana and next 5 ingredients in a medium bowl; add to flour mixture, stirring just until moist. Stir in pineapple, ⅓ cup coconut, and 3 tablespoons nuts. Spoon batter into 12 muffin cups coated with cooking spray.
**3.** To prepare topping, combine coconut and remaining ingredients in a small bowl.
**4.** Sprinkle about 1 teaspoon topping over each muffin. Bake at 400° for 18 minutes or until muffins spring back when touched lightly in center. Remove muffins from pans immediately; place on a wire rack. **YIELD:** 1 dozen (serving size: 1 muffin).

CALORIES 205; FAT 6.7g (sat 1.7g, mono 3.4g, poly 1g); PROTEIN 4.3g; CARB 33.3g; FIBER 2g; CHOL 19mg; IRON 1.5mg; SODIUM 215mg; CALC 69mg

**I have made this recipe hundreds of times** since it first came out in **Cooking Light** in 2003. I've received nothing but rave reviews from the people I've made it for, and it's my favorite recipe to make! It also doubles well. Moist and flavorful.

**from cookinglight.com**

# Coconut Banana Bread with Lime Glaze

9 ounces all-purpose flour (about 2 cups)
¾ teaspoon baking soda
½ teaspoon salt
1 cup granulated sugar
¼ cup butter, softened
2 large eggs
1½ cups mashed ripe banana (about 3 bananas)
¼ cup plain low-fat yogurt
3 tablespoons dark rum
½ teaspoon vanilla extract
½ cup flaked sweetened coconut
Cooking spray
1 tablespoon flaked sweetened coconut
½ cup powdered sugar
1½ tablespoons fresh lime or lemon juice

**1.** Preheat oven to 350°.
**2.** Weigh or lightly spoon flour into dry measuring cups; level with a knife. Combine flour, baking soda, and salt, stirring with a whisk.
**3.** Place granulated sugar and butter in a large bowl; beat with a mixer at medium speed until well blended. Add eggs, 1 at a time, beating well after each addition. Add banana, yogurt, rum, and vanilla; beat until blended. Add flour mixture; beat at low speed just until moist. Stir in ½ cup coconut. Spoon batter into a 9 x 5–inch loaf pan coated with cooking spray; sprinkle with 1 tablespoon coconut. Bake at 350° for 1 hour or until a wooden pick inserted in center comes out clean. Cool in pan 10 minutes on a wire rack; remove from pan. Combine powdered sugar and juice, stirring with a whisk; drizzle over warm bread. Cool completely on wire rack.
**YIELD:** 1 loaf, 16 servings (serving size: 1 slice).

CALORIES 193; FAT 4.6g (sat 2.8g, mono 1.1g, poly 0.3g); PROTEIN 2.9g; CARB 35g; FIBER 1.1g; CHOL 35mg; IRON 1mg; SODIUM 179mg; CALC 15mg

## what makes it light

- uses half the amount of butter as traditional recipes

**Blueberries and lemon are a natural match,** and they come together nicely in this fruit-filled snack cake. Almond paste, a sweet mixture of ground almonds and sugar, contributes a mildly nutty flavor and moist texture. You can find almond paste in the baking section of the grocery store. (Don't substitute marzipan, which is sweeter and has a smoother texture.) If it is hard, soften it by microwaving at HIGH 10 to 15 seconds.

# Blueberry-Lemon Coffee Cake

Cake:
- 6.75 ounces all-purpose flour (about 1½ cups)
- 2 teaspoons baking powder
- ¼ teaspoon baking soda
- ½ teaspoon salt
- ½ cup sugar
- ⅓ cup almond paste
- 2 tablespoons chilled butter, cut into small pieces
- 1 large egg
- 1 tablespoon lemon juice
- ¾ cup fat-free milk
- 1½ cups blueberries
- 2 teaspoons grated lemon rind
- Cooking spray

Topping:
- ¼ cup sugar
- 3 tablespoons sliced almonds, chopped
- 1½ tablespoons butter, melted
- ½ teaspoon ground cinnamon

**1.** Preheat oven to 350°.
**2.** To prepare cake, weigh or lightly spoon flour into dry measuring cups, and level with a knife. Combine flour, baking powder, baking soda, and salt in a small bowl, stirring with a whisk.
**3.** Place 1/2 cup sugar, almond paste, and 2 tablespoons butter in a large bowl; beat with a mixer at medium speed until well blended. Add egg and lemon juice, beating well. Add flour mixture and fat-free milk alternately to sugar mixture, beginning and ending with flour mixture. Fold in blueberries and rind. Spoon batter into a 9-inch square baking pan coated with cooking spray.
**4.** To prepare topping, combine 1/4 cup sugar and remaining ingredients in a small bowl, tossing with a fork until moist. Sprinkle topping evenly over batter. Bake at 350° for 35 minutes or until a wooden pick inserted in center comes out clean. Cool in pan on a wire rack. **YIELD:** 12 servings (serving size: 1 piece).

CALORIES 196; FAT 6.5g (sat 2.1g, mono 3.2g, poly 0.8g); PROTEIN 3.8g; CARB 31.6g; FIBER 1.4g; CHOL 27mg; IRON 1.2mg; SODIUM 243mg; CALC 82mg

## what makes it light

- uses fat-free milk
- uses a reduced amount of butter

"Excellent low-fat coffee cake! **It has stayed fresh for over five days**—much longer than the full-fat sour cream coffee cake I used to make. This will be my new coffee cake recipe."

**from cookinglight.com**

# Sour Cream Coffee Cake

- ¾ cup old-fashioned rolled oats (about 2.5 ounces), divided
- Cooking spray
- 4.5 ounces all-purpose flour (about 1 cup)
- 1 ounce whole-wheat flour (about ¼ cup)
- 1 teaspoon baking powder
- ½ teaspoon baking soda
- ¼ teaspoon salt
- ½ cup granulated sugar
- ½ cup packed brown sugar, divided
- ⅓ cup butter, softened
- 2 large eggs
- 1 teaspoon vanilla extract
- 1 (8-ounce) carton light sour cream (such as Daisy)
- 2 tablespoons finely chopped walnuts, toasted
- ½ teaspoon ground cinnamon
- 1 tablespoon chilled butter, cut into small pieces

**1.** Preheat oven to 350°.
**2.** Spread oats in a single layer on a baking sheet. Bake at 350° for 6 minutes or until oats are barely fragrant and light brown.
**3.** Coat a 9-inch springform pan with cooking spray; set aside.
**4.** Reserve ¼ cup oats; set aside. Place remaining oats in a food processor; process 4 seconds or until finely ground. Weigh or lightly spoon flours into dry measuring cups; level with a knife. Combine processed oats, flours, baking powder, baking soda, and salt; stir with a whisk.
**5.** Place granulated sugar, ¼ cup brown sugar, and ⅓ cup butter in a large bowl. Beat with a mixer at medium speed 3 minutes or until light and fluffy. Add eggs, 1 at a time, beating well after each addition. Beat in vanilla. Add flour mixture to sugar mixture alternately with sour cream, beginning and ending with flour mixture. (Batter will be slightly lumpy because of oats.) Spoon batter into prepared pan; spread evenly.
**6.** Combine remaining ¼ cup oats, remaining ¼ cup brown sugar, nuts, and cinnamon in a bowl. Cut in 1 tablespoon butter with a pastry blender or 2 knives until well blended. Sprinkle top of batter evenly with nut mixture. Bake at 350° for 38 minutes or until a wooden pick inserted in center comes out clean, top is golden, and cake begins to pull away from sides of pan. Cool cake in pan 10 minutes; remove from pan. **YIELD:** 10 servings (serving size: 1 piece).

CALORIES 276; FAT 11.5g (sat 6.5g, mono 2.5g, poly 1.2g); PROTEIN 5.5g; CARB 38.5g; FIBER 1.4g; CHOL 61mg; IRON 1.5mg; SODIUM 247mg; CALC 59mg

what makes it light
• uses less sugar than traditional recipes

# recipe makeover

# pecan sticky rolls

**The Reader:** Angela Thompson

**The Story:** For more than 50 years, Angela Thompson's grandmother, Philomena Olivo, has delighted friends and family with her irresistible Pecan Sticky Rolls. These yeast-raised cinnamon buns are extravagant: The butter- and egg-enriched dough is formed into oversized bakery-style rolls smothered in a gooey brown sugar–butter sauce and topped with pecans. Angela recently had a private baking lesson with her grandmother during which Olivo divulged the secrets of this treasured family recipe. However, with the knowledge of just how much butter, sugar, and eggs go into the sweet pastry, Angela decided she needed an updated version to enjoy these special treats while adhering to her commitment to a healthful lifestyle.

**The Dilemma:** The dinner-plate-sized rolls contribute nearly half the 2,000 calories an average healthy adult needs in a day, according to the USDA Dietary Guidelines. Loaded with two cups sugar, one-half cup pecans, and nearly two sticks of butter, the rolls weighed in at more than 835 calories and about 36 grams of fat each, including 18 grams of saturated fat, about the maximum daily allotment, according to the USDA.

**The Solution:** Portion size was an issue here, so our first step was to increase the recipe's yield from six servings to 15 still generously sized rolls. Then we used fat-free milk instead of whole and one-half cup egg substitute in place of the egg to shave a few calories while maintaining the dough's richness. The filling and rich sauce are the high-fat and -calorie culprits, so we halved the butter in both components to trim 30 calories and five grams of fat (three grams saturated) per roll. To curb calories, we reduced the granulated sugar in the filling by one-third and the brown sugar in the sauce by one-fourth to drop another 20 calories per portion. Using dark brown sugar, which has a higher moisture content and stronger molasses flavor than light brown sugar offers richness and preserves the stickiness of the sauce. We also used fewer high-calorie pecans (and toasted them to intensify their flavor), cutting another 10 calories per serving.

| | BEFORE | AFTER |
|---|---|---|
| Calories per serving | 835 | 275 |
| Fat | 35.6g | 7.6g |
| Percent of total calories | 38% | 25% |

**The Feedback:** "They were fabulous," Angela says. She reports many family members found the lightened rolls just as tasty as the originals. Even her grandmother admits, "I think these might be better than mine."

**This recipe earned our Test Kitchens' highest rating.** The dough for these rolls rises twice before being shaped.

# Pecan Sticky Rolls

Dough:

- 3/4 cup warm fat-free milk (100° to 110°)
- 1/4 cup granulated sugar
- 1/2 teaspoon salt
- 1 package dry yeast (about 2 1/4 teaspoons)
- 1/4 cup warm water (100° to 110°)
- 1/2 cup egg substitute
- 3 tablespoons butter, melted and cooled
- 18 ounces all-purpose flour (about 4 cups), divided
- Cooking spray

Sauce:

- 3/4 cup packed dark brown sugar
- 3 tablespoons butter, melted
- 2 tablespoons hot water
- 1/3 cup finely chopped pecans, toasted

Filling:

- 2/3 cup granulated sugar
- 1 tablespoon ground cinnamon
- 1 1/2 tablespoons butter, melted

**1.** To prepare dough, combine first 3 ingredients in a large bowl.

**2.** Dissolve yeast in 1/4 cup warm water in a small bowl; let stand 5 minutes. Stir yeast mixture into milk mixture. Add egg substitute and 3 tablespoons melted butter; stir until well combined.

**3.** Weigh or lightly spoon flour into dry measuring cups; level with a knife. Add 16.8 ounces (about 3 3/4 cups) flour to yeast mixture; stir until smooth. Turn dough out onto a lightly floured surface. Knead until smooth and elastic (about 8 minutes); add enough of remaining flour, 1 tablespoon at a time, to prevent dough from sticking to hands (dough will feel slightly soft and tacky).

**4.** Place dough in a large bowl coated with cooking spray; turn to coat top. Cover and let rise in a warm place (85°), free from drafts, 45 minutes. Punch dough down and turn over in bowl; lightly coat with cooking spray. Cover and let rise another 45 minutes. Punch dough down; cover and let rest 5 minutes.

**5.** To prepare sauce, combine brown sugar, 3 tablespoons butter, and 2 tablespoons hot water in a small bowl; stir with a whisk until smooth. Scrape sugar mixture into a 13 x 9–inch baking pan coated with cooking spray, spreading evenly over bottom of pan with a spatula. Sprinkle sugar mixture evenly with pecans, and set aside.

**6.** To prepare filling, combine 2/3 cup granulated sugar and cinnamon in a small bowl. Turn dough out onto a lightly floured surface; pat dough into a 16 x 12–inch rectangle. Brush surface of dough with 1 1/2 tablespoons melted butter. Sprinkle sugar mixture evenly over dough, leaving a 1/2-inch border. Beginning with a long side, roll up dough jelly-roll fashion; pinch seam to seal (do not seal ends of roll). Cut roll into 15 slices (approximately 1 inch wide). Arrange slices, cut sides up, in prepared pan. Lightly coat rolls with cooking spray; cover and let rise in a warm place (85°), free from drafts, 30 minutes or until doubled in size.

**7.** Preheat oven to 350°.

**8.** Uncover rolls, and bake at 350° for 20 minutes or until lightly browned. Let stand 1 minute; carefully invert onto serving platter. **YIELD:** 15 servings (serving size: 1 roll).

CALORIES 275; FAT 7.6g (sat 3.8g, mono 2.6g, poly 0.8g); PROTEIN 4.9g; CARB 47g; FIBER 1.4g; CHOL 15mg; IRON 2.2mg; SODIUM 146mg; CALC 37mg

# 5 ways with cinnamon rolls

## Cinnamon Rolls

Rolls:

- 1 cup warm fat-free milk (100° to 110°)
- 6 tablespoons melted butter, divided
- ⅓ cup granulated sugar, divided
- 1 package quick-rise yeast
- 16.88 ounces all-purpose flour (about 3¾ cups)
- 1 large egg, lightly beaten
- ¼ teaspoon salt
- Cooking spray
- ⅔ cup packed brown sugar
- 1½ tablespoons ground cinnamon

Icing:

- 3 tablespoons butter, softened
- 2 tablespoons heavy cream
- ½ teaspoon vanilla extract
- 1 cup powdered sugar

1

**1.** To prepare rolls, combine milk, 3 tablespoons melted butter, 1 tablespoon granulated sugar, and yeast in a large bowl; let stand 5 minutes. Weigh or lightly spoon flour into dry measuring cups. Add egg and remaining granulated sugar to bowl. Stir in 4.5 ounces (1 cup) flour; let stand 10 minutes.
**2.** Add 11.25 ounces (about 2½ cups) flour and salt to milk mixture; stir until a soft dough forms (dough will be sticky). Turn out onto a lightly floured surface. Knead until smooth and elastic (about 6 minutes); add enough of remaining flour, 1 tablespoon at a time, to prevent dough from sticking to hands. Place dough in a large bowl coated with cooking spray; turn to coat top. Cover and let rise in a warm place (85°), free from drafts, 35 minutes or until doubled in size. (Gently press two fingers into dough. If indentation remains, dough has risen enough.) Punch dough down; cover and let rise 35 minutes or until doubled in size. Punch dough down; cover and let rest 5 minutes.
**3.** Combine brown sugar and cinnamon. Turn dough out onto a lightly floured surface; roll dough into an 18 x 11–inch rectangle. Brush remaining 3 tablespoons melted butter over dough; sprinkle evenly with brown sugar mixture. Beginning at one long side, roll up dough tightly, jelly-roll fashion; pinch seam to seal (do not seal ends of roll). Cut dough into 18 (1-inch) slices. Arrange 9 slices, cut sides up, in each of 2 (8-inch) square baking dishes coated with cooking spray. Cover and let rise 35 minutes or until doubled in size.
**4.** Preheat oven to 350°.
**5.** Uncover rolls. Bake at 350° for 22 minutes or until lightly browned. Cool 10 minutes in dishes on a wire rack. Turn rolls out onto wire rack; cool 5 minutes. Turn rolls over.
**6.** To prepare icing, combine 3 tablespoons softened butter and cream; stir with a whisk. Stir in vanilla. Gradually add powdered sugar; stir until blended. Spread icing over rolls; serve warm. **YIELD:** 18 servings (serving size: 1 roll).

CALORIES 234; FAT 6.8g (sat 4.1g, mono 1.8g, poly 0.4g); PROTEIN 3.8g; CARB 39.6g; FIBER 1.1g; CHOL 28mg; IRON 1.7mg; SODIUM 87mg; CALC 40mg

## Cinnamon-Date-Pecan Rolls with Maple Glaze

These frosted sweet rolls make a delectable breakfast or holiday brunch offering.

Dough:

- 1 teaspoon granulated sugar
- 1 package dry yeast (about 2¼ teaspoons)
- ¾ cup warm water (100° to 110°)
- ⅓ cup granulated sugar
- 3 tablespoons butter, melted
- ½ teaspoon salt
- 1 large egg
- 14.5 ounces all-purpose flour (about 3¼ cups)
- Cooking spray

Filling:

- ⅔ cup packed brown sugar
- 1 teaspoon ground cinnamon
- 1 teaspoon grated orange rind
- 2 tablespoons butter, melted
- ¾ cup chopped pitted dates
- ¼ cup chopped pecans, toasted

Glaze:

- 1 cup powdered sugar
- 2 tablespoons maple syrup
- 1 tablespoon fat-free milk

**1.** To prepare dough, dissolve 1 teaspoon granulated sugar and yeast in ¾ cup warm water; let stand 5 minutes. Combine ⅓ cup granulated sugar, 3 tablespoons butter, salt, and egg in a large bowl. Add yeast mixture; beat with a mixer at medium speed until blended.
**2.** Weigh or lightly spoon flour into dry measuring cups; level with a knife. Gradually add 3 cups flour to yeast mixture, beating mixture on low speed until a soft dough forms. Turn dough out onto a lightly floured surface. Knead until smooth and elastic (about 5 minutes); add enough of remaining flour, 1 tablespoon at a time, to prevent dough from sticking to hands. Place dough in a large bowl coated with cooking spray, turning to coat top. Cover and let rise in a warm place (85°), free from drafts, 1 hour or until doubled in size. Punch dough down; turn out onto a lightly floured surface.
**3.** To prepare filling, combine brown sugar, cinnamon, and rind in a small bowl. Roll dough into a 15 x 10–inch rectangle; brush with 2 tablespoons butter. Sprinkle brown sugar mixture over dough, leaving a ½-inch border. Sprinkle dates and pecans over sugar mixture. Beginning with a long side, roll up jelly-roll fashion; pinch seam to seal (do not seal ends of roll). Cut roll into 18 (½-inch) slices. Place slices, cut sides up, in a 13 x 9–inch baking pan coated with cooking spray. Cover and let rise in a warm place (85°), free from drafts, about 1 hour or until rolls have doubled in size.
**4.** Preheat oven to 375°.
**5.** Uncover dough. Bake at 375° for 20 minutes or until rolls are golden brown.
**6.** To prepare glaze, combine powdered sugar, syrup, and milk in a small bowl; stir with a whisk until smooth. Drizzle glaze over warm rolls. Serve immediately. **YIELD:** 18 rolls (serving size: 1 roll).

CALORIES 226; FAT 4.9g (sat 2.2g, mono 1.6g, poly 0.6g); PROTEIN 3.2g; CARB 43.4g; FIBER 1.5g; CHOL 20mg; IRON 1.5mg; SODIUM 96mg; CALC 21mg

# Cinnamon-Fruit Rolls

These rolls are good for busy mornings. Take them out of the freezer, let them stand 30 minutes, then bake 20 minutes.

Dough:

- 1 package dry yeast (about 2¼ teaspoons)
- ¼ cup warm water (100° to 110°)
- ½ cup fat-free milk
- ⅓ cup granulated sugar
- ¼ cup butter, melted
- 1 teaspoon vanilla extract
- ½ teaspoon salt
- 1 large egg, lightly beaten
- 16.88 ounces all-purpose flour (about 3¾ cups), divided
- Cooking spray

Filling:

- ⅔ cup packed brown sugar
- ½ cup golden raisins
- ½ cup chopped dried apricots
- ½ cup chopped pecans
- 1 tablespoon ground cinnamon
- 2 tablespoons butter, melted

Glaze:

- 1 cup powdered sugar
- 2 tablespoons fat-free milk

**1.** Dissolve yeast in warm water in a large bowl; let stand 5 minutes. Stir in 1/2 cup milk and next 5 ingredients. Weigh or lightly spoon flour into dry measuring cups; level with a knife. Add 3 1/2 cups flour to yeast mixture; stir until blended. Turn dough out onto a floured surface. Knead until smooth and elastic (about 10 minutes); add enough of remaining flour, 1 tablespoon at a time, to prevent dough from sticking to hands (dough will feel sticky).

**2.** Place dough in a large bowl coated with cooking spray, turning to coat top. Cover and let rise in a warm place (85°), free from drafts, 1 hour or until doubled in size. (Gently press two fingers into dough. If indentation remains, dough has risen enough.) Punch dough down; cover and let rest 5 minutes.

**3.** To prepare filling, combine brown sugar, raisins, dried apricots, chopped pecans, and cinnamon.

**4.** Roll dough into an 18 x 10–inch rectangle on a floured surface. Brush 2 tablespoons melted butter over dough; sprinkle with 1 1/2 cups filling, leaving a 1/2-inch border. Beginning with a long side, roll up jelly-roll fashion, and pinch seam to seal (do not seal ends of roll).

**5.** Place a long piece of dental floss under dough 3/4 inch from end of roll. Cross ends of floss over top of roll; slowly pull ends to cut through dough. Repeat procedure to make 24 rolls. Coat 2 (9-inch) square foil baking pans with cooking spray. Sprinkle 1/2 cup filling into bottom of each pan. Place 12 rolls, cut sides up, in each pan. Cover and let rise 1 1/2 hours or until doubled in size.

**6.** Preheat oven to 350°.

**7.** Uncover rolls. Bake at 350° for 20 minutes or until browned. Invert onto a serving platter.

**8.** To prepare glaze, combine powdered sugar and 2 tablespoons milk, stirring until smooth. Drizzle over warm rolls. **YIELD:** 24 servings (serving size: 1 roll).

CALORIES 193; FAT 5.1g (sat 2g, mono 1.9g, poly 0.8g); PROTEIN 3.1g; CARB 34.4g; FIBER 1.4g; CHOL 17mg; IRON 1.5mg; SODIUM 87mg; CALC 28mg

## Make-Ahead Ooey-Gooey Sticky Buns

- 1 package dry yeast (about 2¼ teaspoons)
- 1 teaspoon granulated sugar
- ¼ cup warm water (100° to 110°)
- 18 ounces all-purpose flour (about 4 cups), divided
- ¼ cup granulated sugar
- 1 teaspoon ground nutmeg
- ¾ teaspoon salt
- 1 cup evaporated fat-free milk, divided
- ¼ cup water
- 1 large egg, lightly beaten
- Cooking spray
- 1¼ cups packed dark brown sugar, divided
- ⅓ cup dark corn syrup
- 2 tablespoons butter
- ¾ cup chopped pecans
- 1 tablespoon ground cinnamon

**1.** Dissolve yeast and 1 teaspoon granulated sugar in 1/4 cup warm water in a small bowl; let stand 5 minutes. Weigh or lightly spoon flour into dry measuring cups; level with a knife. Place 3 3/4 cups flour, 1/4 cup granulated sugar, nutmeg, and salt in a food processor; pulse 2 times or until blended. Combine 2/3 cup milk, 1/4 cup water, and egg. With processor on, slowly add milk mixture and yeast mixture through food chute; process until dough forms a ball. Process for an additional minute. Turn dough out onto a lightly floured surface; knead until smooth and elastic (about 8 minutes); add enough of remaining flour, 1 tablespoon at a time, to prevent dough from sticking to hands.

**2.** Place dough in a large bowl coated with cooking spray, turning to coat top. Cover and let rise in a warm place (85°), free from drafts, 45 minutes or until doubled in size. Combine 1/3 cup milk, 1 cup brown sugar, corn syrup, and butter in a small saucepan; bring to a boil, stirring constantly. Remove from heat. Divide pecans evenly between 2 (9-inch) round cake pans coated with cooking spray. Top each with half of brown sugar mixture.

**3.** Punch dough down; let rest 5 minutes. Roll into a 24 x 10–inch rectangle on a lightly floured surface; coat entire surface of dough with cooking spray. Combine 1/4 cup brown sugar and cinnamon in a small bowl; sprinkle evenly over dough. Beginning with a long side, roll up jelly-roll fashion; pinch seam to seal (do not seal ends of roll). Cut roll into 24 (1-inch) slices, using string or dental floss. Arrange 12 slices, cut sides up, in each prepared pan. Cover with plastic wrap coated with cooking spray, and let rise in refrigerator 8 to 24 hours or until doubled in size.

**4.** Preheat oven to 375°.

**5.** Bake rolls at 375° for 23 minutes. Run a knife around outside edges of pans. Place a plate upside down on top of pan; invert onto plate.

**YIELD:** 2 dozen (serving size: 1 bun).

CALORIES 188; FAT 4g (sat 0.5g, mono 2.1g, poly 1g); PROTEIN 3.7g; CARB 35.1g; FIBER 1g; CHOL 10mg; IRON 1.5mg; SODIUM 110mg; CALC 51mg

# Pumpkin-Cinnamon Streusel Buns

Buns:

- 1 package dry yeast (about 2¼ teaspoons)
- ¼ cup warm water (100° to 110°)
- 13.5 ounces all-purpose flour (about 3 cups), divided
- ½ cup canned pumpkin puree
- ½ cup 1% low-fat milk
- ¼ cup butter, melted
- 1 tablespoon granulated sugar
- 1¼ teaspoons salt
- ¼ teaspoon ground nutmeg
- Cooking spray
- 3 tablespoons granulated sugar
- 3 tablespoons brown sugar
- 2 tablespoons all-purpose flour
- 1½ teaspoons ground cinnamon
- 2 tablespoons chilled butter, cut into small pieces

Glaze:

- ¾ cup sifted powdered sugar
- 1 tablespoon hot water
- ¼ teaspoon vanilla extract

**1.** To prepare buns, dissolve yeast in warm water in a large bowl; let stand 5 minutes. Weigh or lightly spoon flour into dry measuring cups, and level with a knife. Add 2¾ cups flour, pumpkin, and next 5 ingredients to yeast mixture; beat with a mixer at medium speed until smooth. Turn dough out onto a floured surface. Knead until smooth and elastic (about 10 minutes); add enough of remaining ¼ cup flour, 1 tablespoon at a time, to prevent dough from sticking to hands (dough will feel tacky).

**2.** Place dough in a large bowl coated with cooking spray, turning to coat top. Cover and let rise in a warm place (85°), free from drafts, for 45 minutes or until doubled in size. (Gently press two fingers into the dough. If an indentation remains, dough has risen enough.)

**3.** Combine 3 tablespoons granulated sugar, brown sugar, 2 tablespoons flour, and cinnamon in a small bowl. Cut in butter with a pastry blender or 2 knives until mixture resembles coarse meal.

**4.** Punch dough down; cover and let rest 5 minutes. Roll dough into a 12 x 10–inch rectangle on a floured surface. Sprinkle with brown sugar mixture. Roll up rectangle tightly, starting with a long edge, pressing firmly to eliminate air pockets; pinch seam and ends to seal. Cut roll into 12 (1-inch) slices. Place slices in a 9-inch square baking pan coated with cooking spray. Cover and let rise 25 minutes or until doubled in size.

**5.** Preheat oven to 375°.

**6.** Bake rolls at 375° for 20 minutes or until golden brown. Cool 15 minutes in pan on a wire rack.

**7.** To prepare glaze, combine powdered sugar, 1 tablespoon water, and vanilla extract in a small bowl, stirring with a whisk until smooth. Drizzle glaze over buns. Serve warm. **YIELD:** 12 servings (serving size: 1 bun).

CALORIES 219; FAT 6.2g (sat 3.7g, mono 1.8g, poly 0.3g); PROTEIN 3.8g; CARB 36.9g; FIBER 1.2g; CHOL 16mg; IRON 1.6mg; SODIUM 311mg; CALC 24mg

# Maple-Glazed Sour Cream Doughnut Holes

- 6 tablespoons warm water (100° to 110°)
- ¼ cup granulated sugar
- 1⅛ teaspoons dry yeast
- 6.75 ounces all-purpose flour (about 1½ cups), divided
- ⅛ teaspoon salt
- 3 tablespoons sour cream
- 1 large egg, lightly beaten
- Cooking spray
- 6 cups peanut oil
- 1½ cups powdered sugar
- 2 tablespoons maple syrup
- 2 tablespoons water

**1.** Combine first 3 ingredients in a large bowl. Let stand 5 minutes or until bubbly. Weigh or lightly spoon 5.63 ounces (about 1¼ cups) flour into dry measuring cups; level with a knife. Combine 5.63 ounces flour and salt. Add sour cream and egg to yeast mixture; stir until smooth. Add flour mixture; stir until a moist dough forms.

**2.** Turn dough out onto a lightly floured surface. Knead until smooth and elastic (about 3 minutes); add enough of remaining 1.13 ounces flour, 1 tablespoon at a time, to prevent dough from sticking to hands (dough will feel slightly sticky). Place dough in a clean bowl coated with cooking spray. Cover dough with plastic wrap. Let rise in a warm place (85°), free from drafts, 1 hour or until almost doubled in size.

**3.** Punch dough down. Divide dough into 36 equal portions; roll each portion into a ball. Cover dough with plastic wrap coated with cooking spray; let stand 30 minutes.

**4.** Clip a candy/fry thermometer onto side of a Dutch oven; add oil to pan. Heat oil to 375°. Combine powdered sugar, syrup, and 2 tablespoons water; stir until smooth. Place 9 dough balls in hot oil; fry 2 minutes or until golden and done, turning as necessary. Make sure oil temperature remains at 375°. Remove doughnut holes from pan; drain. Dip doughnut holes into syrup mixture; remove with a slotted spoon. Drain on a cooling rack over a baking sheet. Repeat procedure 4 times with remaining dough balls and syrup mixture. **YIELD**: 12 servings (serving size: 3 doughnut holes).

CALORIES 178; FAT 5.9g (sat 1.4g, mono 2.5g, poly 1.6g); PROTEIN 2.4g; CARB 29.3g; FIBER 0.5g; CHOL 19mg; IRON 0.9mg; SODIUM 33mg; CALC 11mg

# recipe makeover
## orange rolls

**The Reader:** Desiree Schneider

**The Story:** Ever since they began dating, Desiree had listened to her husband, Paul, reminisce about the gooey orange rolls of his childhood. So as a part of his 25th birthday celebration, she secretly obtained a copy of the recipe from her mother-in-law and surprised him by baking a batch of his favorite treat. Desiree describes them as "buttery yeast rolls drenched in a cooked sour cream glaze" and now understands why these delicious rolls were etched in Paul's memory.

**The Dilemma:** Desiree felt there was a good chance that Paul would overindulge in the rolls anytime she made them. We took her concerns to heart once we looked at the recipe and saw the ample amounts of sour cream and butter it called for.

**The Solution:** Our first alteration was simple, but it significantly lightened the rolls: Switching from regular to reduced-fat sour cream saved about 120 calories and 19 grams of fat in the recipe. Another 72 calories and almost 5 grams of fat were trimmed by using one egg instead of two. The biggest change occurred when we slashed the butter content, but we kept enough in the dough to maintain the original's tender, almost pillowlike texture. We kept most of the butter originally in the glaze because it imparts rich flavor at first bite. Still, the rolls contain only half the butter of the original recipe, which knocks out a whopping 792 calories and 91 grams of fat. All the modifications make for a rich-tasting baked delight with only 178 calories per serving and about half the fat of the original.

**The Feedback:** The **Cooking Light** staff awarded the new and improved orange rolls with our Test Kitchens' highest rating. Desiree found the new dough easier to work with, plus the lightened rolls "have the same decadent flavor with none of that heavy feeling after eating them. If I had not told Paul, I am certain he wouldn't have known any difference. Now when he's tempted to reach for a second roll, I won't feel nearly as bad knowing they've been lightened," she says.

| | BEFORE | AFTER |
|---|---|---|
| Calories per serving | 218 | 178 |
| Fat | 10.2g | 5.6g |
| Percent of total calories | 41% | 28% |

**Keep any remaining rolls in the baking pan.** Cover pan with foil, and store it in the refrigerator. To reheat, place foil-covered pan in a 300° oven for 15 minutes or until rolls are warm.

# Orange Rolls

Dough:

- 1 package dry yeast (about 2¼ teaspoons)
- ½ cup warm water (100° to 110°)
- 1 cup sugar, divided
- ½ cup reduced-fat sour cream
- 2 tablespoons butter, softened
- 1 teaspoon salt
- 1 large egg, lightly beaten
- 15.75 ounces all-purpose flour (about 3½ cups), divided
- Cooking spray
- 2 tablespoons butter, melted
- 2 tablespoons grated orange rind

Glaze:

- ¾ cup sugar
- ¼ cup butter
- 2 tablespoons fresh orange juice
- ½ cup reduced-fat sour cream

**1.** To prepare dough, dissolve yeast in warm water in a large bowl; let stand 5 minutes. Add 1/4 cup sugar, 1/2 cup sour cream, 2 tablespoons softened butter, salt, and egg, and beat with a mixer at medium speed until smooth. Weigh or lightly spoon flour into dry measuring cups; level with a knife. Add 9 ounces flour (about 2 cups) to yeast mixture; beat until smooth. Add 4.5 ounces flour (about 1 cup) to yeast mixture, stirring until a soft dough forms. Turn dough out onto a floured surface. Knead until smooth and elastic (about 10 minutes); add enough of remaining flour, 1 tablespoon at a time, to prevent dough from sticking to hands (dough will feel sticky).
**2.** Place dough in a large bowl coated with cooking spray, turning to coat top. Cover and let rise in a warm place (85°), free from drafts, 1 hour and 15 minutes or until doubled in size. (Gently press two fingers into dough. If indentation remains, dough has risen enough.)
**3.** Punch dough down; cover and let rest 5 minutes. Divide dough in half. Working with 1 portion at a time (cover remaining dough to prevent drying), roll each portion of dough into a 12-inch circle on a floured surface. Brush surface of each circle with 1 tablespoon melted butter. Combine 3/4 cup sugar and rind. Sprinkle half of sugar mixture over each circle. Cut each circle into 12 wedges. Roll up each wedge tightly, beginning at wide end. Place rolls, point sides down, in a 13 x 9–inch baking pan coated with cooking spray. Cover and let rise 25 minutes or until doubled in size.
**4.** Preheat oven to 350°.
**5.** Uncover dough. Bake at 350° for 25 minutes or until golden brown.
**6.** While rolls bake, prepare glaze. Combine 3/4 cup sugar, 1/4 cup butter, and orange juice in a small saucepan; bring to a boil over medium-high heat. Cook 3 minutes or until sugar dissolves, stirring occasionally. Remove from heat; cool slightly. Stir in 1/2 cup sour cream. Drizzle glaze over warm rolls; let stand 20 minutes before serving. **YIELD:** 2 dozen (serving size: 1 roll).

CALORIES 178; FAT 5.6g (sat 3.2g, mono 1.3g, poly 0.3g); PROTEIN 2.8g; CARB 30g; FIBER 0.6g; CHOL 24mg; IRON 1mg; SODIUM 146mg; CALC 23mg

what makes it light
• uses ⅓-less-fat cream cheese
• uses fat-free milk
• uses light sour cream

This is a wonderful recipe! **The bread is perfectly soft and sweet,** and the filling is a fantastic compliment—not to mention the beautiful presentation. I use seedless raspberry preserves at times and make this for all special occasions. A must try!

**from cookinglight.com**

# Apricot-Cream Cheese Bread

**Dough:**

- ½ cup granulated sugar
- ⅓ cup butter
- ½ teaspoon salt
- 1 (8-ounce) carton light sour cream
- 2 packages dry yeast (about 4½ teaspoons)
- ½ cup warm water (100° to 110°)
- 2 large eggs, lightly beaten
- 18 ounces all-purpose flour (about 4 cups)

**Filling:**

- ⅔ cup apricot preserves
- ¼ cup granulated sugar
- 1 teaspoon vanilla extract
- 2 (8-ounce) blocks ⅓-less-fat cream cheese, softened
- 1 large egg, lightly beaten
- Cooking spray

**Glaze:**

- 1½ cups sifted powdered sugar
- 2 tablespoons fat-free milk
- 1 teaspoon vanilla extract

**1.** To prepare dough, combine first 4 ingredients in a saucepan over medium heat, stirring until sugar dissolves. Remove from heat; cool. Dissolve yeast in warm water in a large bowl; let stand 5 minutes. Stir in sour cream mixture and 2 eggs. Weigh or lightly spoon flour into dry measuring cups; level with a knife. Gradually stir flour into sour cream mixture (dough will be soft and sticky). Cover dough; chill 8 hours or overnight.
**2.** To prepare filling, combine preserves and next 4 ingredients in a medium bowl; beat with a mixer at medium speed until well blended.
**3.** Divide dough into 4 equal portions. Turn each portion out onto a lightly floured surface; knead lightly 4 or 5 times. Roll each portion into a 12 x 8–inch rectangle. Spread one-fourth of filling over each portion, leaving a ½-inch border. Starting at a long side, carefully roll up each portion jelly-roll fashion; pinch seam and ends to seal.
**4.** Place 2 loaves on each of 2 baking sheets coated with cooking spray. Cut 4 (¼-inch-deep) "X"s in top of each loaf with scissors. Cover and let rise in a warm place (85°), free from drafts, 25 minutes or until doubled in size.
**5.** Preheat oven to 375°.
**6.** Place 1 baking sheet in oven (cover remaining loaves to keep from drying). Bake at 375° for 15 minutes or until lightly browned. Repeat procedure with remaining loaves. Cool loaves slightly.
**7.** To prepare glaze, combine powdered sugar, milk, and 1 teaspoon vanilla, stirring with a whisk. Drizzle warm loaves with glaze. **YIELD:** 4 loaves, 10 slices per loaf (serving size: 1 slice).

CALORIES 145; FAT 5g (sat 3g, mono 1.5g, poly 0.3); PROTEIN 3.3g; CARB 21.6g; FIBER 0.5g; CHOL 30mg; IRON 0.8mg; SODIUM 102mg; CALC 26mg

Wow, this breakfast braid was amazing. My husband couldn't get enough of it! We ate it as breakfast for dinner, and **the flavors and texture were so warm and comforting**. I will definitely be making this again!

**from cookinglight.com**

# Jalapeño, Sausage, Jack, and Egg Breakfast Braid

- 1 (13.8-ounce) can refrigerated pizza crust dough
- Cooking spray
- 1 tablespoon olive oil
- ¼ cup chopped onion
- 4 ounces chicken sausage with jalapeño peppers, chopped
- 2 large eggs, lightly beaten
- ½ cup (2 ounces) shredded Monterey Jack cheese
- ¼ cup shredded cheddar cheese
- ¼ cup chopped seeded jalapeño peppers
- 1 large egg white, lightly beaten

**1.** Preheat oven to 425°.
**2.** Unroll dough onto a baking sheet coated with cooking spray; pat into a 15 x 10–inch rectangle.
**3.** Heat oil in a large skillet over medium heat. Add onion and sausage; cook 9 minutes or until lightly browned. Stir in eggs; cook 1½ minutes or until set. Remove from heat.
**4.** Sprinkle Monterey Jack lengthwise down center of dough, leaving about a 2½-inch border on each side. Spoon egg mixture evenly over cheese. Sprinkle cheddar over egg mixture; top with jalapeño peppers.
**5.** Make 2-inch-long diagonal cuts about 1 inch apart on both sides of dough to within ½ inch of filling using a sharp knife or kitchen shears. Arrange strips over filling, alternating strips diagonally over filling. Press ends under to seal. Brush with egg white. Bake at 425° for 15 minutes or until golden brown. Let stand 5 minutes. Cut crosswise into slices. **YIELD:** 6 servings (serving size: 1 slice).

CALORIES 164; FAT 10.4g (sat 4.2g, mono 4.4g, poly 1g); PROTEIN 10.6g; CARB 7.3g; FIBER 0.1g; CHOL 98mg; IRON 0.8mg; SODIUM 344mg; CALC 115mg

## what makes it light

- uses chicken sausage
- uses pizza crust dough, which is lower in fat than crescent roll dough that is used for many breakfast braid recipes

# lunch

**RECIPE MAKEOVERS**



**5 WAYS WITH**



**RECIPES**

"This soup was very rich and flavorful—hard to believe it's a light recipe! I will definitely make this one again."

**from cookinglight.com**

# French Onion Soup

- 2 teaspoons olive oil
- 4 cups thinly vertically sliced Walla Walla or other sweet onion
- 4 cups thinly vertically sliced red onion
- ½ teaspoon sugar
- ½ teaspoon freshly ground black pepper
- ¼ teaspoon salt
- ¼ cup dry white wine
- 8 cups lower-sodium beef broth
- ¼ teaspoon chopped fresh thyme
- 8 (1-ounce) slices French bread, cut into 1-inch cubes
- 8 (1-ounce) slices reduced-fat, reduced-sodium Swiss cheese (such as Alpine Lace)

**1.** Heat olive oil in a Dutch oven over medium-high heat. Add onions to pan; sauté 5 minutes or until tender. Stir in sugar, pepper, and ¼ teaspoon salt. Reduce heat to medium; cook 20 minutes, stirring frequently. Increase heat to medium-high, and sauté 5 minutes or until onion is golden brown. Stir in wine, and cook 1 minute. Add broth and thyme; bring to a boil. Cover, reduce heat, and simmer 2 hours.
**2.** Preheat broiler.
**3.** Place bread in a single layer on a baking sheet; broil 2 minutes or until toasted, turning after 1 minute.
**4.** Place 8 ovenproof bowls on a jelly-roll pan. Ladle 1 cup soup into each bowl. Divide bread evenly among bowls; top each serving with 1 cheese slice. Broil 3 minutes or until cheese begins to brown. **YIELD:** 8 servings.

CALORIES 290; FAT 9.6g (sat 4.8g, mono 1.9g, poly 0.7g); PROTEIN 16.8g; CARB 33.4g; FIBER 3.1g; CHOL 20mg; IRON 1.6mg; SODIUM 359mg; CALC 317mg

## what makes it light

- uses lower-sodium beef broth
- uses reduced-fat, reduced-sodium Swiss cheese
- uses a minimal amount of oil to caramelize onions

# 5 ways with tomato soup

## Tomato Alphabet Soup

On chilly autumn afternoons, nothing warms more than a good bowl of creamy tomato soup and a grilled cheese sandwich. Pureed alphabet pasta, instead of cream, thickens the soup in this version.

- **2 tablespoons butter**
- **1 cup chopped onion**
- **1 cup chopped carrot**
- **⅓ cup chopped celery**
- **1½ cups vegetable broth**
- **1 teaspoon dried basil**
- **¼ teaspoon black pepper**
- **1 (28-ounce) can diced tomatoes, undrained**
- **2 cups cooked alphabet pasta (about 1 cup uncooked pasta), divided**
- **1 cup 2% reduced-fat milk**

**1.** Melt butter in a saucepan over medium-high heat. Add onion, carrot, and celery; sauté 4 minutes or until tender. Add broth, basil, pepper, and tomatoes, and bring to a boil. Reduce heat; simmer 15 minutes. Stir in 1/2 cup pasta. Remove from heat; let stand 5 minutes.

**2.** Place half of tomato mixture in a blender, and process until smooth. Pour pureed soup into a large bowl. Repeat procedure with remaining tomato mixture. Return pureed soup to pan; stir in remaining pasta and milk. Cook over medium-high heat 2 minutes or until thoroughly heated, stirring frequently (do not boil). **YIELD:** 6 servings (serving size: about 1 cup).

CALORIES 175; FAT 5.2g (sat 2.9g, mono 1.3g, poly 0.2g); PROTEIN 6.1g; CARB 27.9g; FIBER 4g; CHOL 13mg; IRON 1.3mg; SODIUM 492mg; CALC 93mg

# Creamy Tomato-Balsamic Soup

Cooking the vegetables at the high temperature of 500° caramelizes their natural sugars and deepens their flavor.

- 1 cup lower-sodium beef broth, divided
- 1 tablespoon brown sugar
- 3 tablespoons balsamic vinegar
- 1 tablespoon lower-sodium soy sauce
- 1 cup coarsely chopped onion
- 5 garlic cloves
- 2 (28-ounce) cans whole tomatoes, drained
- Cooking spray
- ¾ cup half-and-half
- Cracked black pepper (optional)

**1.** Preheat oven to 500°.

**2.** Combine 1/2 cup broth, sugar, vinegar, and soy sauce in a small bowl. Place onion, garlic, and tomatoes in a 13 x 9–inch baking pan coated with cooking spray. Pour broth mixture over tomato mixture. Bake at 500° for 50 minutes or until vegetables are lightly browned.

**3.** Place tomato mixture in a blender. Add remaining 1/2 cup broth and half-and-half, and process until smooth. Strain mixture through a sieve into a bowl; discard solids. Garnish with cracked black pepper, if desired. **YIELD:** 4 servings (serving size: about 1/2 cup).

CALORIES 120; FAT 4.7g (sat 3g, mono 1.5g, poly 0.1g); PROTEIN 3.8g; CARB 14.9g; FIBER 1.7g; CHOL 23mg; IRON 1.7mg; SODIUM 452mg; CALC 120mg

## Fresh Tomato Soup ▾

Six tablespoons plain of low-fat yogurt stands in for the half-and-half that's so prevalent in traditional tomato soup recipes. It still offers the creaminess without the fat and calories.

- **2 cups fat-free, lower-sodium chicken broth**
- **1 cup chopped onion**
- **¾ cup chopped celery**
- **1 tablespoon thinly sliced fresh basil**
- **1 tablespoon tomato paste**
- **2 pounds plum tomatoes, cut into wedges**
- **½ teaspoon salt**
- **¼ teaspoon freshly ground black pepper**
- **6 tablespoons plain low-fat yogurt**
- **3 tablespoons thinly sliced fresh basil**

**1.** Combine first 6 ingredients in a large saucepan; bring to a boil. Reduce heat, and simmer 30 minutes. Place half of tomato mixture in a blender. Remove center piece of blender lid (to allow steam to escape); secure lid on blender. Place a clean towel over opening in blender lid (to avoid splatters). Blend until smooth. Pour into a large bowl. Repeat procedure with remaining tomato mixture. Stir in salt and pepper. Ladle 3/4 cup soup into each of 6 bowls; top each serving with 1 tablespoon yogurt and 1 1/2 teaspoons basil. **YIELD:** 6 servings.

CALORIES 58; FAT 0.8g (sat 0.3g, mono 0.1g, poly 0.2g); PROTEIN 3.1g; CARB 11.3g; FIBER 2.8g; CHOL 1mg; IRON 1.1mg; SODIUM 382mg; CALC 49mg

## Tomato-Basil Soup ▾

Fresh tomato and basil are the stars of this classic summertime tomato soup recipe. Low-fat milk and light cream cheese keep it healthy. Refrigerate soup in an airtight container for up to one week.

- **4 cups chopped seeded peeled tomato (about 4 large)**
- **4 cups lower-sodium tomato juice**
- **⅓ cup fresh basil leaves**
- **1 cup 1% low-fat milk**
- **¼ teaspoon salt**
- **¼ teaspoon cracked black pepper**
- **½ cup (4 ounces) ⅓-less-fat cream cheese, softened**
- **Basil leaves, thinly sliced (optional)**
- **8 (½-inch-thick) slices diagonally cut French bread baguette**

**1.** Bring tomato and juice to a boil in a large saucepan. Reduce heat; simmer, uncovered, 30 minutes.

**2.** Place tomato mixture and basil in a blender or food processor; process until smooth. Return pureed mixture to pan; stir in milk, salt, and pepper. Add cream cheese, stirring well with a whisk, and cook over medium heat until thick (about 5 minutes). Ladle soup into individual bowls; garnish with sliced basil, if desired. Serve with bread. **YIELD:** 8 servings (serving size: 1 cup soup and 1 bread slice).

CALORIES 133; FAT 4.4g (sat 2.4g, mono 1.3g, poly 0.4g); PROTEIN 5.4g; CARB 18.7g; FIBER 1.9g; CHOL 12mg; IRON 1.5mg; SODIUM 310mg; CALC 77mg

## Tomato Garlic Soup with Parmesan Croutons

- 4 large tomatoes, cored (about 2½ pounds)
- 2 quarts water
- 2 quarts ice water
- 1¼ cups uncooked seashell pasta
- 4 teaspoons olive oil, divided
- ¾ cup finely chopped red onion
- 8 garlic cloves, thinly sliced
- 1 cup water
- 1 tablespoon chopped fresh flat-leaf parsley
- 1 tablespoon minced fresh chives
- 1 teaspoon minced fresh oregano
- 1 teaspoon minced fresh thyme
- 2 (14-ounce) cans fat-free, lower-sodium chicken broth
- 1 tablespoon red wine vinegar
- ½ teaspoon freshly ground black pepper
- 8 (½-ounce) slices diagonally cut French bread baguette (about 1 inch thick)
- ½ cup (2 ounces) grated fresh Parmesan cheese
- Fresh thyme sprigs (optional)

**1.** Score bottom of each tomato with an "X." Bring 2 quarts water to a boil in a Dutch oven. Add tomatoes; cook 30 seconds. Remove tomatoes with a slotted spoon; plunge tomatoes into 2 quarts ice water. Drain and peel. Cut each tomato in half crosswise. Push seeds out of tomato halves using the tip of a knife; discard seeds. Chop tomatoes.

**2.** Cook pasta according to package directions, omitting salt and fat; drain. Toss pasta with 1 teaspoon oil. Cool completely.

**3.** Heat 1 tablespoon oil in Dutch oven over medium-low heat. Add onion; cook 7 minutes, stirring occasionally. Add garlic; cook 3 minutes or until onion is tender, stirring frequently. Stir in tomatoes, 1 cup water, parsley, chives, oregano, thyme, and broth; bring to a boil. Reduce heat, and simmer 20 minutes, stirring occasionally. Add pasta, vinegar, and pepper; cook 1 minute or until thoroughly heated.

**4.** Preheat broiler.

**5.** Place bread slices on a baking sheet, and top each slice with 1 tablespoon cheese. Broil 1½ minutes or until lightly browned. Serve with soup. Garnish with thyme sprigs, if desired. **YIELD:** 4 servings (serving size: 1½ cups soup and 2 croutons).

CALORIES 335; FAT 9.9g (sat 3g, mono 3.8g, poly 1g); PROTEIN 15.3g; CARB 46.6g; FIBER 4.1g; CHOL 11mg; IRON 2.7mg; SODIUM 695mg; CALC 227mg

# recipe makeover

## broccoli and chicken noodle soup

**The Reader:** Amanda Farmer

**The Story:** A childhood favorite, this creamy soup is a go-to for Amanda. She received the recipe from her mother, Brenda Geiger, and wanted to give it to a friend for a cookbook project. Yet Amanda felt some guilt. "I know it's high in calories and fat, and I want a healthier recipe that's still satisfying," she wrote with her request to *Cooking Light* for an overdue makeover of the recipe.

**The Dilemma:** Several ingredients contributed to the soup's heavy nutritional report card: processed cheese, butter, whole milk, and half-and-half added a hefty amount of fat. Its canned cream of mushroom soup, regular chicken broth, and processed cheese added significant sodium.

**The Solution:** The soup's base warranted the bulk of our attention. We halved the amount of processed cheese and swapped to a lighter version, maintaining a satisfying taste and texture but cutting 79 calories, seven fat grams (five grams of which were saturated), and 286 milligrams of sodium per serving. We made a white sauce for the soup's base with just three tablespoons of butter and a little flour to thicken low-fat milk; omitting the can of soup cut 25 calories per bowlful. With half the rich half-and-half, we added an extra cup of 1% low-fat milk (instead of the full-fat type) to ensure a silky texture and saved 35 calories, four grams of fat, and two grams of saturated fat. Instead of using one-half cup butter to sauté the onion, we used cooking spray and added fresh mushrooms to enhance the taste. Reducing five tablespoons of butter (three tablespoons are used in the white sauce) shaved 50 calories and six grams of fat (3½ grams saturated) per serving. We switched regular chicken broth for the fat-free, lower-sodium type, and used less to shave 216 milligrams sodium. Since we broke the long noodles, which are easier to eat, we could also halve the amount to eliminate another 40 calories.

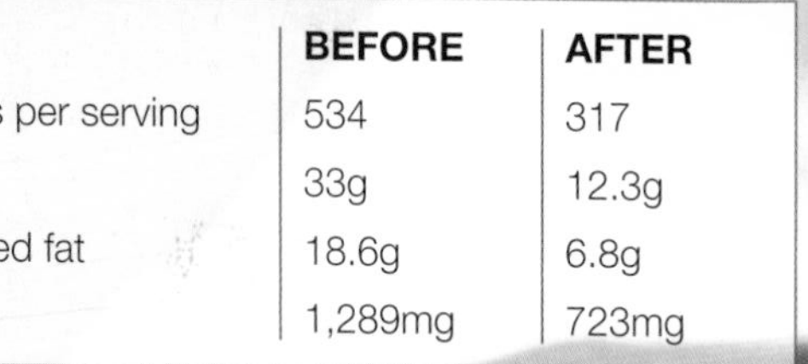

| | BEFORE | AFTER |
|---|---|---|
| Calories per serving | 534 | 317 |
| Fat | 33g | 12.3g |
| Saturated fat | 18.6g | 6.8g |
| Sodium | 1,289mg | 723mg |

**The Feedback:** Amanda and her husband, Lee, commend the revised recipe. **"None of the creaminess is sacrificed,** and the addition of fresh mushrooms enlivens the soup's flavor," she says. Amanda can feel good about preparing—and passing along—this restored childhood favorite.

**If the broccoli florets are large,** break into smaller pieces at the stalk instead of chopping them; they'll cook more quickly. Count on having dinner on the table in about 40 minutes, and serve this soup the moment it's done for the best results. In fact, if you wait, you'll find it gets thicker with time. If you have leftovers, you will want to thin the soup with a little chicken broth or milk to the desired consistency.

# Broccoli and Chicken Noodle Soup

Cooking spray
2 cups chopped onion
1 cup presliced mushrooms
1 garlic clove, minced
3 tablespoons butter
1.1 ounces all-purpose flour (about ¼ cup)
4 cups 1% low-fat milk
1 (14-ounce) can fat-free, lower-sodium chicken broth
4 ounces uncooked vermicelli, broken into 2-inch pieces
2 cups (8 ounces) shredded light processed cheese (such as Velveeta Light)
4 cups (1-inch) cubed cooked chicken breast
3 cups small broccoli florets (8 ounces)
1 cup half-and-half
1 teaspoon freshly ground black pepper
¾ teaspoon salt

**1.** Heat a Dutch oven over medium-high heat. Coat pan with cooking spray. Add onion, mushrooms, and garlic to pan; sauté 5 minutes or until liquid evaporates, stirring occasionally. Reduce heat to medium; add butter to mushroom mixture, stirring until butter melts. Sprinkle mushroom mixture with flour; cook 2 minutes, stirring occasionally. Gradually add milk and broth, stirring constantly with a whisk; bring to a boil. Reduce heat to medium-low; cook 10 minutes or until slightly thick, stirring constantly. Add pasta to pan; cook 10 minutes. Add cheese to pan, and stir until cheese melts. Add chicken and remaining ingredients to pan; cook 5 minutes or until broccoli is tender and soup is thoroughly heated. **YIELD:** 10 servings (serving size: 1 cup).

CALORIES 317; FAT 12.3g (sat 6.8g, mono 2.9g, poly 0.9g); PROTEIN 27.5g; CARB 23.8g; FIBER 1.9g; CHOL 74mg; IRON 1.6mg; SODIUM 723mg; CALC 179mg

30
minutes
or
less

Comfort food at its best! It's -3°F outside tonight, and this soup hits the spot!

from cookinglight.com

# Broccoli and Cheese Soup

Cooking spray
1 cup chopped onion
2 garlic cloves, minced
3 cups fat-free, lower-sodium chicken broth
1 (12-ounce) package broccoli florets
1.5 ounces all-purpose flour (about ⅓ cup)
2½ cups 2% reduced-fat milk
¼ teaspoon black pepper
8 ounces light processed cheese, cubed (such as Velveeta Light)

**1.** Heat a large nonstick saucepan over medium-high heat. Coat pan with cooking spray. Add onion and garlic; sauté 3 minutes or until tender. Add broth and broccoli. Bring broccoli mixture to a boil over medium-high heat. Reduce heat to medium; cook 10 minutes.
**2.** Weigh or lightly spoon flour into a dry measuring cup. Combine flour and milk, stirring with a whisk until well blended. Add milk mixture to broccoli mixture. Cook 5 minutes or until slightly thick, stirring constantly. Stir in pepper. Remove from heat; add cheese, stirring until cheese melts.
**3.** Place one-third of soup in a blender or food processor, and process until smooth. Return pureed soup mixture to pan. **YIELD**: 6 servings (serving size: 1⅓ cups).

CALORIES 203; FAT 6.3g (sat 4g, mono 1.8g, poly 0.4g); PROTEIN 15.6g; CARB 21.7g; FIBER 2.9g; CHOL 24mg; IRON 1.2mg; SODIUM 897mg; CALC 385mg

## what makes it light

- uses fat-free, lower-sodium chicken broth
- uses reduced-fat milk instead of cream
- uses light processed cheese
- uses cooking spray instead of butter or oil to sauté onion

# recipe makeover
## beer cheese soup

**The Reader:** Linda Vujnov

**The Story:** This soup became part of the Vujnov family Christmas Eve tradition 31 years ago, when they moved from Oregon back to California, and Linda's mother-in-law prepared a spread of cold cuts, relishes, cheese, breads, and this rich, savory soup. It's satisfying on its own or with a sandwich to take the chill off a winter day, notes Linda, and easy to pull together with a handful of aromatics, seasonings, cheese, and a bottle of beer. However, she said she was "disappointed to discover the nearly one pound of butter that contributed to the flavor." As an avid runner and mother of four children, she wants to choose wholesome foods and prepare them healthfully. She knew this recipe needed lightening to remain in the family's winter menu repertoire.

**The Dilemma:** Linda knew something had to be done about the ¾ pound of butter in the original recipe. The nearly two cups of shredded full-fat cheddar cheese contributed significant calories, cholesterol, and fat, including 31 grams of saturated fat. Chicken stock and a seasoning additive in the original recipe brought a bowl of soup to 1,767 milligrams of sodium.

**The Solution:** By sautéing the aromatics in cooking spray instead of butter, we shaved 300 calories, 34 grams of fat (most of which was saturated), 242 milligrams of sodium, and most of the cholesterol from each serving. To achieve buttery flavor and a smooth texture without butter, we cooked rich Yukon gold potatoes in fat-free, lower-sodium chicken broth, pureed the mixture, and added it back to the soup. The original soup called for flour as a thickening agent; we used the same amount of flour but added 1% low-fat milk for creaminess. Tinkering with the broth and milk in the soup cut 385 milligrams of sodium per portion. Instead of using all fat-free cheeses, which don't tend to melt well, we opted for a mixture of extrasharp reduced-fat cheddar and full-fat sharp cheddar to boost flavor. That cut four more grams of fat and 43 calories per serving. We omitted the artificial seasoning and used dry mustard, freshly ground black pepper, Worcestershire sauce, and a touch of salt to perk up the flavor—and shave another 40 milligrams of sodium per portion.

**The Feedback:** "I thought the blend of flavors was perfect and loved the thick consistency," Linda reports. **She also sprinkled on some crushed red pepper for added zing.**

| | BEFORE | AFTER |
|---|---|---|
| Calories per serving | 587 | 363 |
| Fat | 50g | 12.2g |
| Percent of total calories | 77% | 30% |

# Beer Cheese Soup

- 4½ cups fat-free, lower-sodium chicken broth, divided
- 1¼ cups cubed peeled Yukon gold potato (about 10 ounces)
- Cooking spray
- ½ cup finely diced onion
- ½ cup finely diced celery
- ½ cup finely diced carrot
- 1 teaspoon minced garlic
- 2.25 ounces all-purpose flour (about ½ cup)
- 2½ cups 1% low-fat milk
- ¾ cup (3 ounces) shredded sharp cheddar cheese
- ½ cup (2 ounces) shredded reduced-fat extrasharp cheddar cheese
- ½ teaspoon dry mustard
- ½ teaspoon Worcestershire sauce
- ¼ teaspoon freshly ground black pepper
- ⅛ teaspoon salt
- 1 (12-ounce) can beer
- Freshly ground black pepper (optional)

**1.** Simmer 2 cups broth and potato in a small saucepan. Cook 15 minutes or until potato is tender. Transfer potato mixture to a blender. Remove center piece of blender lid (to allow steam to escape); secure blender lid on blender. Place a clean towel over opening in blender lid (to avoid splatters). Blend until smooth. Set mixture aside.

**2.** Heat a large Dutch oven over medium heat. Coat pan with cooking spray. Add onion, celery, and carrot to pan; cook 5 minutes or until tender, stirring occasionally. Add garlic to pan; cook 30 seconds.

**3.** Weigh or lightly spoon flour into a dry measuring cup; level with a knife. Combine flour, remaining 2½ cups broth, and milk in a medium bowl; stir with a whisk. Add flour mixture to pan; bring to a boil. Cook 1 minute or until slightly thick; stir constantly with a whisk. Add potato mixture, sharp cheddar cheese, and next 5 ingredients to pan; cook 1 minute or until cheese melts, stirring constantly. Add beer to pan; bring to a simmer. Cook 15 minutes or until thoroughly heated. Garnish with black pepper, if desired. **YIELD:** 4 servings (serving size: 2 cups).

CALORIES 363; FAT 12.2g (sat 7.7g, mono 3.5g, poly 0.6g); PROTEIN 20.7g; CARB 41.8g; FIBER 3.4g; CHOL 39mg; IRON 2.1mg; SODIUM 884mg; CALC 480mg

# 5 ways with chicken and dumplings

## Chicken and Dumplings

This generous serving of soup is chock-full of vegetables and is hearty enough to pass as a complete meal.

**Broth:**

- 12 cups cold water
- 1 tablespoon whole black peppercorns
- 4 chicken leg quarters, skinned
- 3 celery stalks, sliced
- 2 medium carrots, peeled and sliced
- 2 bay leaves
- 1 large onion, peeled and cut into 8 wedges

**Dumplings:**

- 4.5 ounces all-purpose flour (about 1 cup), divided
- 1 teaspoon baking powder
- ¼ teaspoon salt
- ¼ cup chilled butter, cut into small pieces
- 3 tablespoons buttermilk

**Remaining Ingredients:**

- Cooking spray
- 1½ cups chopped onion
- 1 cup thinly sliced celery
- ¾ cup (¼-inch-thick) slices carrot
- ¾ teaspoon salt
- 1 tablespoon all-purpose flour
- 2 tablespoons finely chopped fresh chives

**1.** To prepare broth, combine first 7 ingredients in a large stockpot; bring to a boil. Reduce heat to medium-low, and simmer 2 hours, skimming as necessary. Remove chicken from broth; cool. Remove meat from bones. Shred meat; set aside. Discard bones. Strain broth through a sieve over a bowl; discard solids. Place broth in a large saucepan; bring to a boil. Cook until reduced to 6 cups (about 8 minutes).

**2.** To prepare dumplings, weigh or lightly spoon 4.5 ounces (about 1 cup) flour into a dry measuring cup; level with a knife. Combine 3.4 ounces (3/4 cup) flour, baking powder, and 1/4 teaspoon salt; stir with a whisk. Cut in butter with a pastry blender or 2 knives until mixture resembles coarse meal. Add buttermilk; stir to combine. Turn dough out onto a lightly floured surface; knead 5 times, adding remaining 1.1 ounces (1/4 cup) flour as needed. Divide mixture into 24 equal portions.

**3.** Heat a large Dutch oven over medium-high heat. Coat pan with cooking spray. Add chopped onion, 1 cup celery, and 3/4 cup carrot to pan; sauté 4 minutes, stirring occasionally. Add broth and 3/4 teaspoon salt; bring to a boil. Reduce heat, and simmer 20 minutes or until vegetables are tender. Drop dumplings into pan; cover and cook 10 minutes or until dumplings are done, stirring occasionally. Remove 1/4 cup liquid from pan; stir in 1 tablespoon flour. Return chicken to pan. Add flour mixture to pan; bring to a boil. Cook 1 minute or until slightly thick, stirring occasionally. Remove from heat; stir in chives. **YIELD:** 4 servings (serving size: about 2 cups).

CALORIES 457; FAT 19.7g (sat 9.6g, mono 5.7g, poly 2.4g); PROTEIN 31.8g; CARB 37.1g; FIBER 3.5g; CHOL 129mg; IRON 3.5mg; SODIUM 906mg; CALC 142mg

# Chicken and Rosemary Dumplings

Soup:

- 4 cups fat-free, lower-sodium chicken broth
- 3 cups water
- 1 pound chicken drumsticks, skinned
- 1 pound skinless, boneless chicken breast halves
- 2 fresh thyme sprigs
- 2 teaspoons olive oil
- 1½ cups diced carrots
- 1½ cups chopped celery
- 1 cup diced onion
- 2 garlic cloves, minced
- ½ teaspoon salt

Dumplings:

- 5.6 ounces all-purpose flour (about 1¼ cups)
- 1 tablespoon chopped fresh or ½ teaspoon dried rosemary
- 2 teaspoons baking powder
- ¼ teaspoon salt
- 2 tablespoons butter, softened
- ½ cup low-fat buttermilk
- 1 large egg
- 1.1 ounces all-purpose flour (about ¼ cup)
- ¼ cup water

Remaining Ingredient:

- Freshly ground black pepper

**1.** To prepare soup, combine first 5 ingredients in a large Dutch oven over medium-high heat; bring to a boil. Reduce heat, and simmer, uncovered, 15 minutes or until chicken is done. Remove pan from heat. Remove chicken pieces from broth; cool slightly. Strain broth through a sieve into a large bowl; discard solids. Remove chicken from bones. Discard bones; chop chicken into bite-sized pieces. Set chicken aside.

**2.** Heat oil in pan over medium-high heat. Add carrots, celery, onion, and garlic; sauté 6 minutes or until onion is tender. Add reserved broth mixture and ½ teaspoon salt; simmer 10 minutes. Keep warm.

**3.** To prepare dumplings, lightly spoon flour into dry measuring cups; level with a knife. Combine 5.6 ounces (1¼ cups) flour and next 3 ingredients in a large bowl. Cut in butter with a pastry blender or 2 knives until mixture resembles coarse meal. Combine buttermilk and egg, stirring with a whisk. Add buttermilk mixture to flour mixture, stirring just until combined.

**4.** Return chopped chicken to broth mixture; bring to a simmer over medium-high heat. Combine 1.1 ounces (¼ cup) flour and water, stirring with a whisk until well blended to form a slurry. Add flour mixture to pan; simmer 3 minutes. Drop dumpling dough, 1 tablespoon per dumpling, onto chicken mixture to form 12 dumplings. Cover and cook 7 minutes (do not boil). Sprinkle with pepper. **YIELD:** 6 servings (serving size: 2 dumplings and 1⅓ cups soup).

CALORIES 366; FAT 9.7g (sat 3.8g, mono 3.5g, poly 1.3g); PROTEIN 32.5g; CARB 35.1g; FIBER 2.9g; CHOL 115mg; IRON 3.3mg; SODIUM 936mg; CALC 169mg

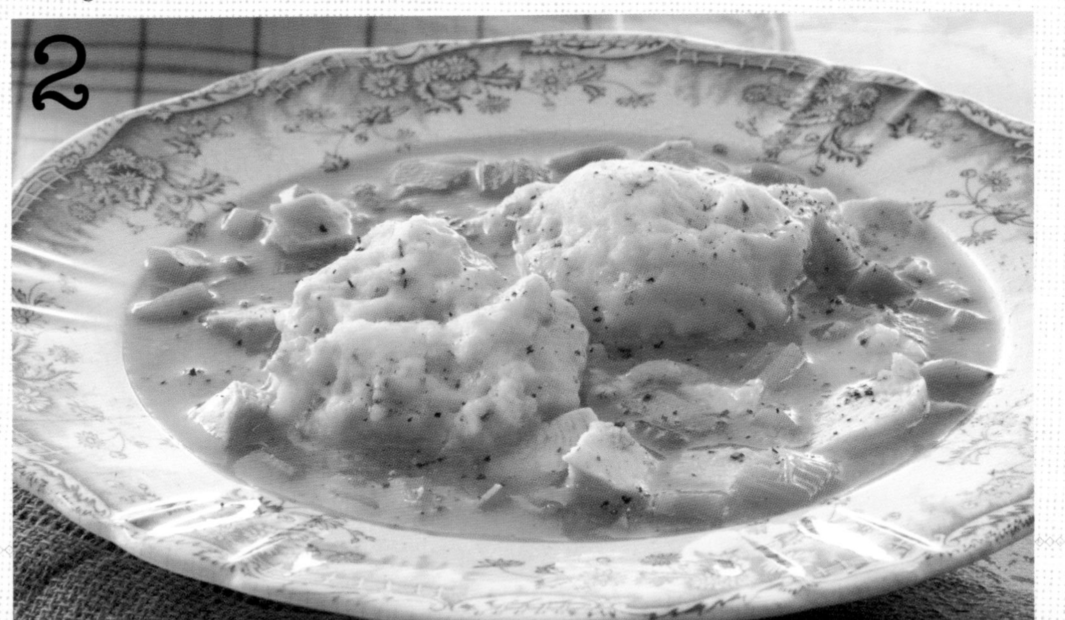

## Quick Chicken and Dumplings

In this recipe, flour tortillas stand in for the traditional biscuit dough. To quickly thaw frozen mixed vegetables, place them in a colander and rinse with warm water for about a minute.

- 1 tablespoon butter
- ½ cup prechopped onion
- 2 cups chopped roasted skinless, boneless chicken breast
- 1 (10-ounce) box frozen mixed vegetables, thawed
- 1½ cups water
- 1 tablespoon all-purpose flour
- 1 (14-ounce) can fat-free, lower-sodium chicken broth
- ¼ teaspoon salt
- ¼ teaspoon black pepper
- 1 bay leaf
- 8 (6-inch) flour tortillas, cut into ½-inch strips
- 1 tablespoon chopped fresh parsley

**1.** Melt butter in a large saucepan over medium-high heat. Add onion; sauté 5 minutes or until tender. Stir in chicken and vegetables; cook 3 minutes or until thoroughly heated, stirring constantly.

**2.** While chicken mixture cooks, combine water, flour, and broth. Gradually stir broth mixture into chicken mixture. Stir in salt, pepper, and bay leaf; bring to a boil. Reduce heat, and simmer 3 minutes. Stir in tortilla strips, and cook 2 minutes or until tortilla strips soften. Remove from heat; stir in parsley. Discard bay leaf. Serve immediately. **YIELD:** 4 servings (serving size: about 1½ cups).

CALORIES 366; FAT 9.3g (sat 3.1g, mono 3.9g, poly 1.4g); PROTEIN 29.8g; CARB 40.3g; FIBER 5.3g; CHOL 67mg; IRON 3.4mg; SODIUM 652mg; CALC 104mg

## Chicken and Dumplings from Scratch

Stew:

- 1 (4-pound) whole chicken
- 3 quarts water
- 3 cups chopped onion
- 1 cup chopped celery
- 1 cup chopped carrot
- 1 teaspoon salt
- ¼ teaspoon freshly ground black pepper
- 10 garlic cloves, peeled
- 4 fresh thyme sprigs
- 2 bay leaves
- 1.1 ounces all-purpose flour (about ¼ cup)
- 2 teaspoons cornstarch
- 3 tablespoons heavy cream

Dumplings:

- ¾ cup 1% low-fat milk
- 1 large egg
- 6.75 ounces all-purpose flour (about 1½ cups)
- 1 tablespoon baking powder
- 1 tablespoon cornmeal
- ½ teaspoon salt

Remaining Ingredients:

- 1 tablespoon chopped fresh parsley
- Freshly ground black pepper

**1.** To prepare stew, remove and discard giblets and neck. Rinse chicken with cold water, and place in an 8-quart stockpot. Add water and next 8 ingredients; bring to a simmer. Reduce heat, and simmer 45 minutes; skim surface occasionally, discarding solids. Remove chicken from pot; cool. Strain stock through a sieve into a large bowl; discard solids. Remove skin from chicken. Remove meat from bones; tear meat into 2-inch pieces, and store in refrigerator. Let stock cool to room temperature.

**2.** Pour stock into two zip-top plastic bags. Let stand 15 minutes. Working with one bag at a time, snip off a corner of bag; drain liquid into stockpot, stopping before fat layer reaches opening. Discard fat. Repeat procedure with remaining bag. Bring stock to a boil over medium-high heat; reduce heat, and simmer until reduced to 8 cups (about 15 minutes).

**3.** Heat a cast-iron skillet over medium-high heat. Lightly spoon 1.1 ounces (¼ cup) flour into a dry measuring cup; level with a knife. Add flour to pan; cook 1 minute or until lightly browned, stirring constantly. Combine browned flour and cornstarch in a large bowl; add ⅔ cup stock, stirring with a whisk until smooth. Add flour mixture to remaining stock in pan; bring to a boil over medium-high heat. Cook 2 minutes or until slightly thickened. Reduce heat; stir in cream. Add chicken; keep warm over low heat.

**4.** To prepare dumplings, combine milk and egg in a medium bowl. Lightly spoon 6.75 ounces (1½ cups) flour into dry measuring cups, and level with a knife. Combine flour and next 3 ingredients. Add flour mixture to milk mixture; stir with a fork until dry ingredients are moist.

**5.** Drop one-third of dumpling batter by 8 heaping teaspoonfuls onto chicken mixture. Cover and cook 3 minutes or until dumplings are done (do not allow chicken mixture to boil). Remove dumplings with a slotted spoon; place in a bowl or on a platter; keep warm. Repeat twice with remaining dumpling batter.

**6.** Remove pan from heat; slowly pour stew over dumplings. Sprinkle with parsley and pepper. Serve immediately. **YIELD:** 6 servings (serving size: 1⅓ cups stew and 4 dumplings).

CALORIES 334; FAT 7.9g (sat 3.2g, mono 2.4g, poly 1.2g); PROTEIN 31.4g; CARB 32.2g; FIBER 1.2g; CHOL 130mg; IRON 3.3mg; SODIUM 755mg; CALC 211mg

5

## Herbed Chicken and Dumplings

Fluffy herb-flecked dumplings, tender vegetables, and rich dark-meat chicken combine in this soul-satisfying classic. Garnish with parsley sprigs, if desired.

- Cooking spray
- 8 ounces skinless, boneless chicken thighs, cut into bite-sized pieces
- ¾ cup (¼-inch) diagonally cut celery
- ½ cup (¼-inch) diagonally cut carrot
- ½ cup chopped onion
- ⅛ teaspoon dried thyme
- 3 fresh parsley sprigs
- 1 bay leaf
- 3 cups fat-free, lower-sodium chicken broth
- 2.25 ounces all-purpose flour (about ½ cup)
- 1 tablespoon chopped fresh parsley
- ¼ teaspoon baking powder
- ¼ teaspoon salt
- ¼ cup 1% low-fat milk

**1.** Heat a large saucepan over medium-high heat. Coat pan with cooking spray. Add chicken to pan; cook 4 minutes, browning on all sides. Remove chicken from pan; keep warm. Add celery and next 5 ingredients to pan; sauté 5 minutes or until onion is tender. Return chicken to pan; cook 1 minute. Add broth to pan; bring mixture to a boil. Cover, reduce heat, and simmer 30 minutes.

**2.** Weigh or lightly spoon 2.25 ounces (about 1/2 cup) flour into a dry measuring cup; level with a knife. Combine flour, chopped parsley, baking powder, and salt in a medium bowl. Add milk, stirring just until moist. Spoon by heaping teaspoonfuls into broth mixture; cover and simmer 10 minutes or until dumplings are done. Discard parsley sprigs and bay leaf. **YIELD:** 2 servings (serving size: 2 cups).

CALORIES 285; FAT 5.2g (sat 1.5g, mono 1.9g, poly 1.2g); PROTEIN 25g; CARB 35.2g; FIBER 3.1g; CHOL 55mg; IRON 3.4mg; SODIUM 596mg; CALC 133mg

# Simple Clam Chowder

- 2 bacon slices
- 2 cups chopped onion
- 1¼ cups chopped celery
- ½ teaspoon salt
- ½ teaspoon dried thyme
- 2 garlic cloves, minced
- 6 (6½-ounce) cans chopped clams, undrained
- 5 cups diced peeled baking potato (about 1 pound)
- 4 (8-ounce) bottles clam juice
- 1 bay leaf
- 2.25 ounces all-purpose flour (about ½ cup)
- 3 cups fat-free milk
- Thyme sprig (optional)

**1.** Cook bacon in a large Dutch oven over medium heat until crisp. Remove bacon from pan, reserving 1 teaspoon drippings in pan. Crumble bacon; set aside. Add onion, celery, salt, dried thyme, and garlic to drippings in pan; cook 4 minutes or until vegetables are tender.
**2.** Drain clams, reserving liquid. Add clam liquid, potato, clam juice, and bay leaf to pan; bring to a boil. Reduce heat, and simmer 15 minutes or until potato is tender. Discard bay leaf.
**3.** Weigh or lightly spoon flour into a dry measuring cup. Combine 2.25 ounces (about 1/2 cup) flour and milk, stirring with a whisk until smooth. Add flour mixture to pan; bring to a boil. Cook 12 minutes or until thick, stirring constantly. Add clams; cook 2 minutes. Sprinkle with bacon. Garnish with thyme, if desired. **YIELD**: 12 servings (serving size: 1 cup).

CALORIES 257; FAT 2.9g (sat 0.6g, mono 0.6g, poly 0.7g); PROTEIN 28.5g; CARB 27.9g; FIBER 2g; CHOL 67mg; IRON 26.6mg; SODIUM 475mg; CALC 242mg

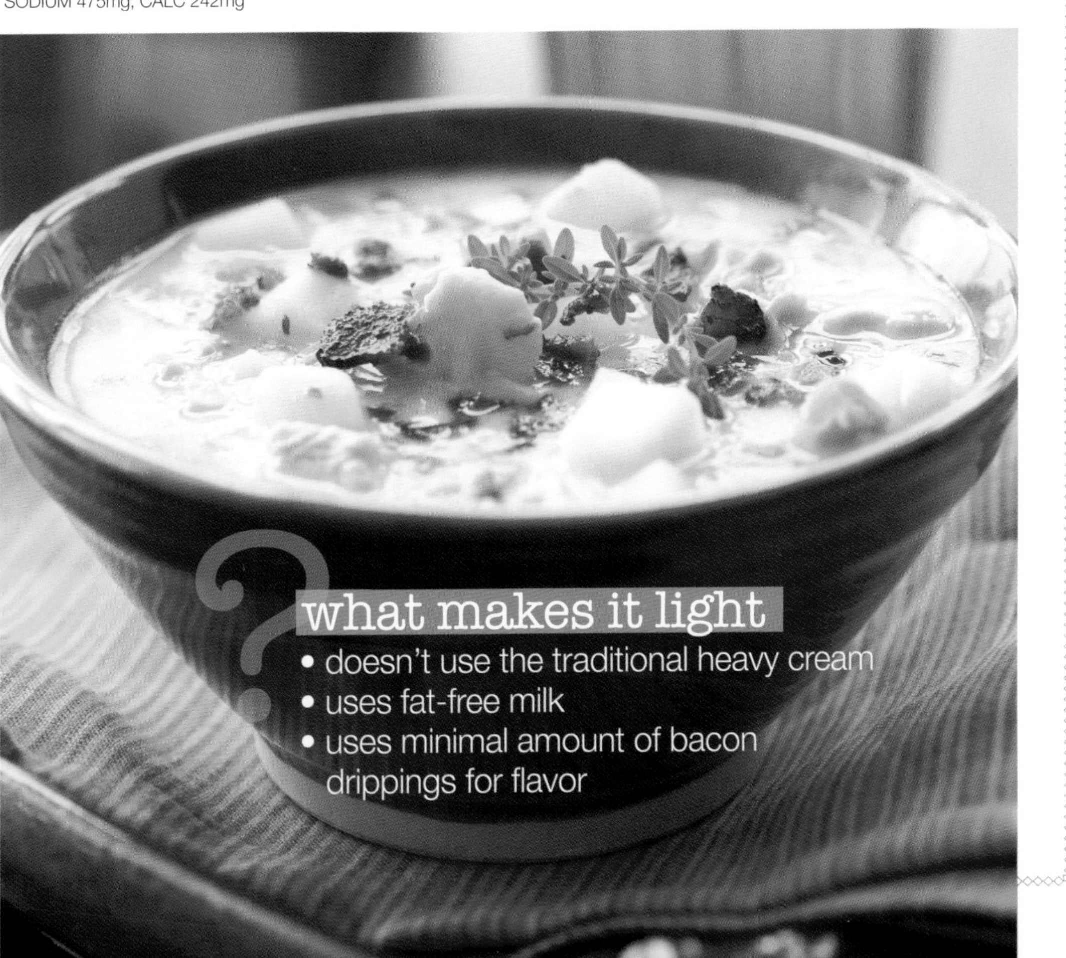

## what makes it light

- doesn't use the traditional heavy cream
- uses fat-free milk
- uses minimal amount of bacon drippings for flavor

# recipe makeover

## scallop clam chowder

**The Reader:** Patty Garcia

**The Story:** Patty clipped the original version of this recipe from a newspaper. She and her husband liked the idea of fresh thyme and Pernod (licorice-flavored liqueur) in a creamy, scallop-studded soup. However, since her husband had heart surgery, they have both altered their eating habits to focus on low-fat, low-cholesterol foods. So Patty sent the recipe to *Cooking Light* for a healthful makeover.

**The Dilemma:** The original recipe's six cups of heavy cream produced a velvety broth, and the fat balanced assertive flavors from black pepper, Pernod, and fresh thyme. The cream, however, also contributed an astounding 615 calories, 66 grams of fat, and 245 milligrams of cholesterol per serving. A serving of soup contained twice the daily recommendation for saturated fat intake and nearly all the daily allotment of dietary cholesterol.

**The Solution:** To cut calories and fat from the chowder's base, we used 2% reduced-fat milk and clam juice thickened with a little flour to offer creaminess at a fraction of the fat. Finishing the soup with 1½ cups of half-and-half imparts enough richness to round out the flavors. These changes slashed 502 calories, 60 grams of fat, and most of the cholesterol per serving. We used Yukon gold potatoes, which have a buttery flavor; the potatoes' starch also thickens the chowder. With the fat drastically reduced, we added a little garlic and celery to the onion, and sautéed them in a prudent pat of butter to add flavor to the soup. Also, we reduced the amount of Pernod because, with less fat to temper its assertive flavor, a tablespoon of the liqueur was plenty. To manage sodium, we chose flavorful kosher salt and used a bit less.

**The Feedback:** Patty prepared the newly lightened chowder for a dinner party. "Everyone wanted the recipe—it was a great success."

| | BEFORE | AFTER |
|---|---|---|
| Calories per serving | 909 | 349 |
| Fat | 70.1g | 8.1g |
| Percent of total calories | 69% | 21% |

**We liked the flavor of the clam juice in this soup,** but you could substitute fat-free, lower-sodium chicken broth. If you don't have Pernod on hand, or prefer to omit the alcohol, substitute one teaspoon anise extract or finely ground aniseed. Serve with crackers.

# Scallop Clam Chowder

- 2 teaspoons butter
- Cooking spray
- 1½ cups chopped onion (about 1 medium)
- ¼ cup chopped celery
- 1 teaspoon minced garlic
- 4½ cups (½-inch) cubed peeled Yukon gold or red potato (about 1½ pounds)
- 1¼ teaspoons kosher salt, divided
- 1 teaspoon freshly ground black pepper, divided
- 1.1 ounces all-purpose flour (about ¼ cup)
- 2½ cups clam juice
- 2½ cups 2% reduced-fat milk
- 1 tablespoon Pernod (licorice-flavored liqueur)
- 1½ teaspoons chopped fresh thyme
- 1½ pounds sea scallops, cut into 1-inch chunks
- 1½ cups half-and-half
- ¼ cup chopped fresh chives

**1.** Melt 2 teaspoons butter in a Dutch oven coated with cooking spray over medium-high heat. Add chopped onion and celery; sauté 5 minutes or until tender. Add 1 teaspoon garlic, and sauté 1 minute. Add potato, 1 teaspoon salt, and ¾ teaspoon pepper; cook 2 minutes. Weigh or lightly spoon 1.1 ounces (about ¼ cup) flour into a dry measuring cup; level with a knife. Sprinkle flour over potato mixture, and cook 1 minute, stirring frequently. Add clam juice and milk; bring to a boil, stirring constantly. Cover, reduce heat, and simmer 20 minutes or until potato is tender. Partially mash potato using a potato masher. Stir in remaining ¼ teaspoon salt, remaining ¼ teaspoon pepper, Pernod, and thyme; simmer 10 minutes. Add scallops and half-and-half; cook 5 minutes or until scallops are done. Sprinkle with chives. **YIELD:** 8 servings (serving size: about 1¼ cups chowder and 1½ teaspoons chives).

CALORIES 349; FAT 8.1g (sat 4.6g, mono 2.2g, poly 0.2g); PROTEIN 33.8g; CARB 32.7g; FIBER 2.1g; CHOL 94mg; IRON 1.3mg; SODIUM 842mg; CALC 220mg

# 5 ways with chili

## 1

## White Bean and Turkey Chili

- 1 tablespoon canola oil
- 2 cups diced yellow onion (about 2 medium)
- 1½ tablespoons chili powder
- 1 tablespoon minced garlic
- 1½ teaspoons ground cumin
- 1 teaspoon dried oregano
- 3 (15.8-ounce) cans Great Northern beans, rinsed and drained
- 4 cups fat-free, lower-sodium chicken broth
- 3 cups chopped cooked turkey
- ½ cup diced seeded plum tomato (about 1)
- ⅓ cup chopped fresh cilantro
- 2 tablespoons fresh lime juice
- ½ teaspoon salt
- ½ teaspoon freshly ground black pepper
- 8 lime wedges (optional)

**1.** Heat oil in a large Dutch oven over medium-high heat. Add onion; sauté 10 minutes or until tender and golden. Add chili powder, garlic, and cumin; sauté 2 minutes. Add oregano and beans; cook 30 seconds. Add broth; bring to a simmer. Cook 20 minutes.

**2.** Place 2 cups bean mixture in a blender or food processor, and process until smooth. Return pureed mixture to pan. Add turkey, and cook 5 minutes or until thoroughly heated. Remove from heat. Add diced tomato, chopped cilantro, lime juice, salt, and pepper, stirring well. Garnish with lime wedges, if desired.

**YIELD:** 8 servings (serving size: about 1 cup).

CALORIES 286; FAT 6g (sat 1.2g, mono 2.1g, poly 1.6g); PROTEIN 32.4g; CARB 24.3g; FIBER 5.5g; CHOL 85mg; IRON 4.8mg; SODIUM 435mg; CALC 105mg

# All-American Chili

- 6 ounces hot turkey Italian sausage
- 2 cups chopped onion
- 1 cup chopped green bell pepper
- 8 garlic cloves, minced
- 1 pound ground sirloin
- 1 jalapeño pepper, chopped
- 2 tablespoons chili powder
- 2 tablespoons brown sugar
- 1 tablespoon ground cumin
- 3 tablespoons tomato paste
- 1 teaspoon dried oregano
- ½ teaspoon freshly ground black pepper
- ¼ teaspoon salt
- 2 bay leaves
- 1¼ cups Merlot or other fruity red wine
- 2 (28-ounce) cans whole tomatoes, undrained and coarsely chopped
- 2 (15-ounce) cans kidney beans, drained
- ½ cup (2 ounces) shredded reduced-fat sharp cheddar cheese

**1.** Heat a large Dutch oven over medium-high heat. Remove casings from sausage. Add sausage, onion, and next 4 ingredients to pan; cook 8 minutes or until sausage and beef are browned, stirring to crumble.
**2.** Add chili powder and next 7 ingredients, and cook 1 minute, stirring constantly. Stir in wine, tomatoes, and kidney beans; bring to a boil. Cover, reduce heat, and simmer 1 hour, stirring occasionally.
**3.** Uncover and cook 30 minutes, stirring occasionally. Discard bay leaves. Sprinkle each serving with cheddar cheese. **YIELD**: 8 servings (serving size: 1¼ cups chili and 1 tablespoon cheese).

CALORIES 375; FAT 12g (sat 4.6g, mono 4.1g, poly 1.1g); PROTEIN 28.9g; CARB 33.7g; FIBER 8.2g; CHOL 59mg; IRON 5mg; SODIUM 969mg; CALC 165mg

## Chunky Vegetarian Chili ▾

This vegetarian chili recipe is a great way to get kids to eat fiber-rich foods. It can be taken on camping trips and in school lunches in a thermos.

- 1 tablespoon vegetable oil
- 2 cups chopped onion
- ½ cup chopped yellow bell pepper
- ½ cup chopped green bell pepper
- 2 garlic cloves, minced
- 1 tablespoon brown sugar
- 1½ tablespoons chili powder
- 1 teaspoon ground cumin
- 1 teaspoon dried oregano
- ½ teaspoon salt
- ½ teaspoon black pepper
- 2 (14.5-ounce) cans stewed tomatoes, undrained
- 2 (15-ounce) cans black beans, rinsed and drained
- 1 (15-ounce) can kidney beans, rinsed and drained
- 1 (16-ounce) can pinto beans, rinsed and drained

**1.** Heat oil in a Dutch oven over medium-high heat. Add onion, bell peppers, and garlic; sauté 5 minutes or until tender. Add sugar and remaining ingredients, and bring to a boil. Reduce heat, and simmer 30 minutes. **YIELD:** 8 servings (serving size: 1 cup).

CALORIES 257; FAT 2.7 g (sat 0.3g, mono 0.5g, poly 1.2g); PROTEIN 12.8g; CARB 48.8g; FIBER 14.2g; CHOL 0mg; IRON 4.5mg; SODIUM 876mg; CALC 150mg

3

## Cincinnati Turkey Chili ▾

- 4 ounces uncooked spaghetti
- Cooking spray
- 8 ounces lean ground turkey
- 1½ cups prechopped onion, divided
- 1 cup chopped green bell pepper
- 1 tablespoon bottled minced garlic
- 1 tablespoon chili powder
- 2 tablespoons tomato paste
- 1 teaspoon ground cumin
- 1 teaspoon dried oregano
- ¼ teaspoon ground cinnamon
- ⅛ teaspoon ground allspice
- ½ cup fat-free, lower-sodium chicken broth
- 1 (15-ounce) can kidney beans, rinsed and drained
- 1 (14.5-ounce) can diced tomatoes, undrained
- 2½ tablespoons chopped semisweet chocolate
- ¼ teaspoon salt
- ¾ cup (3 ounces) shredded sharp cheddar cheese

**1.** Cook pasta according to package directions, omitting salt and fat. Drain; set aside.
**2.** Heat a Dutch oven over medium-high heat. Coat pan with cooking spray. Add turkey; cook 3 minutes, stirring to crumble. Add 1 cup onion, bell pepper, and garlic; sauté 3 minutes. Stir in chili powder and next 5 ingredients; cook 1 minute. Add broth, beans, and tomatoes;

4

bring to a boil. Cover, reduce heat, and simmer 20 minutes, stirring occasionally. Remove from heat; stir in chocolate and salt. Serve chili over spaghetti; top with remaining 1/2 cup onion and cheese. **YIELD**: 4 servings (serving size: about 1/2 cup spaghetti, 1 1/2 cups chili, 2 tablespoons onion, and 3 tablespoons cheese).

CALORIES 408; FAT 13.8g (sat 6.6g, mono 4.3g, poly 1.7g); PROTEIN 24.5g; CARB 47.4g; FIBER 7.9g; CHOL 67mg; IRON 3.7mg; SODIUM 765mg; CALC 237mg

## Mexican Black Bean Sausage Chili ▸

Sausage:

1½ tablespoons Hungarian sweet paprika
2 tablespoons minced garlic
3 tablespoons dry red wine
2 tablespoons sherry vinegar
2 teaspoons ancho chili powder
1 teaspoon ground cumin
½ teaspoon dried oregano
½ teaspoon ground coriander
½ teaspoon black pepper
Dash of kosher salt
¾ pound lean ground pork
¾ pound ground turkey breast

Chili:

2 tablespoons olive oil
2 cups diced onion (about 2 medium)
1 tablespoon ground cumin
1 tablespoon finely minced garlic
2 teaspoons dried oregano
3 canned chipotle chiles in adobo sauce, minced
4 (15-ounce) cans black beans, rinsed and drained, divided
3 cups fat-free, lower-sodium chicken broth, divided
3 cups water
2 (14.5-ounce) cans no salt-added diced tomatoes, drained
¼ cup freshly squeezed lime juice
¼ cup very finely chopped cilantro
Low-fat sour cream (optional)
Sliced green onions (optional)

**1.** To prepare sausage, combine first 12 ingredients in a large bowl. Cover and refrigerate overnight.

**2.** To prepare chili, heat oil in a large saucepan over medium-high heat. Add sausage mixture; cook 7 minutes or until browned, stirring to crumble. Add onion, 1 tablespoon cumin, 1 tablespoon garlic, 2 teaspoons oregano, and chiles; cook 4 minutes or until onion is tender. Place 1 1/2 cups black beans and 1 cup broth in a food processor; process until smooth. Add pureed beans, remaining beans, remaining 2 cups broth, water, and tomatoes to pan; bring to a boil. Reduce heat, and simmer, partially covered, 45 minutes or until slightly thick. Stir in juice and cilantro. Ladle about 1 3/4 cups chili into each of 6 bowls. Garnish each serving with sour cream and sliced green onions, if desired. **YIELD**: 6 servings.

CALORIES 395; FAT 11g (sat 2.9g, mono 6g, poly 2.1g); PROTEIN 35.3g; CARB 40.4g; FIBER 13.7g; CHOL 78mg; IRON 6mg; SODIUM 989mg; CALC 128mg

**Bacon, blue cheese, avocado, and chicken** are all ingredients in the classic Cobb salad. Serve with a chilled summer soup or a sandwich for a light and refreshing meal.

# Chicken Cobb Salad

- **Cooking spray**
- **1½ pounds skinless, boneless chicken breast cutlets**
- **¼ teaspoon salt**
- **¼ teaspoon black pepper**
- **8 cups mixed greens**
- **1 cup cherry tomatoes, halved**
- **⅓ cup diced peeled avocado**
- **2 tablespoons sliced green onions**
- **⅓ cup fat-free Italian dressing**
- **2 tablespoons crumbled blue cheese**
- **1 bacon slice, cooked and crumbled**

**1.** Heat a large nonstick skillet over medium-high heat. Coat pan with cooking spray. Sprinkle chicken with salt and pepper. Add chicken to pan; cook 5 minutes on each side or until done. Cut into ½-inch slices.

**2.** Combine greens, tomatoes, avocado, and onions in a large bowl. Drizzle greens mixture with dressing; toss gently to coat. Arrange about 2 cups greens mixture on each of 4 salad plates. Top each serving with 4 ounces chicken, 1½ teaspoons cheese, and about ½ teaspoon bacon. **YIELD**: 4 servings.

CALORIES 263; FAT 8g (sat 2.4g, mono 3.2g, poly 1.4g); PROTEIN 37.9g; CARB 8.9g; FIBER 3.7g; CHOL 99mg; IRON 2.6mg; SODIUM 606mg; CALC 89mg

## what makes it light

- uses skinless chicken breast cutlets
- uses fat-free Italian dressing instead of traditional creamy ranch-style or blue cheese dressing
- uses less of the traditional ingredients that are high in calories
- doesn't use boiled eggs

30
minutes
or
less

30
minutes
or
less

This is my absolute favorite **Cooking Light** recipe. Be sure and use real maple syrup, as pancake syrup will not do this recipe justice. Guests are wowed by it. It is all I can do not to lick the dressing left over on my plate.

from cookinglight.com

# Spinach Salad with Maple-Dijon Vinaigrette

- ¼ cup maple syrup
- 3 tablespoons minced shallots (about 1 medium)
- 2 tablespoons red wine vinegar
- 1 tablespoon canola oil
- 1 tablespoon country-style Dijon mustard
- ¼ teaspoon salt
- ¼ teaspoon freshly ground black pepper
- 1 garlic clove, minced
- 1 cup sliced mushrooms
- ½ cup vertically sliced red onion
- ½ cup chopped Braeburn apple
- 4 bacon slices, cooked and crumbled
- 1 (10-ounce) package fresh spinach

**1.** Combine first 8 ingredients in a large bowl, stirring with a whisk. Add mushrooms and remaining ingredients; toss well to coat. **YIELD**: 8 servings (serving size: about 1½ cups).

CALORIES 80; FAT 3.3g (sat 0.6g, mono 1.6g, poly 0.7g); PROTEIN 2.6g; CARB 11.1g; FIBER 1.2g; CHOL 3mg; IRON 1.2mg; SODIUM 219mg; CALC 43mg

## what makes it light

- uses less canola oil than a traditional vinaigrette
- uses only ½ slice bacon per serving
- doesn't use boiled eggs
- uses chopped apple to boost fiber and flavor without fat

**This fun, kid-friendly indulgence** was a hit at taste testing and received our highest rating. The recipe can easily be multiplied to make as many sandwiches as you need.

# Grilled Peanut Butter and Banana Split Sandwich

- 2 (1-ounce) slices firm white sandwich bread, divided
- 1 teaspoon butter, softened
- 1 tablespoon creamy peanut butter
- 2 teaspoons honey
- ½ teaspoon semisweet chocolate minichips
- 1 large strawberry, thinly sliced
- ½ small banana, cut lengthwise into 3 slices (about 2 ounces)
- 1 tablespoon pineapple jam

**1.** Spread one side of each white bread slice with 1/2 teaspoon butter. Combine peanut butter and honey; spread over plain side of 1 bread slice. Sprinkle with chocolate chips; top evenly with strawberry slices and banana slices.
**2.** Spread pineapple jam over plain side of remaining bread slice. Carefully assemble sandwich.
**3.** Heat a small nonstick skillet over medium-high heat. Add sandwich; cook 2 minutes on each side or until lightly browned. **YIELD:** 1 serving (serving size: 1 sandwich).

CALORIES 436; FAT 14.5g (sat 4.2g, mono 6g, poly 3.2g); PROTEIN 9.4g; CARB 72g; FIBER 4.6g; CHOL 10mg; IRON 3mg; SODIUM 497mg; CALC 100mg

## what makes it light

- uses a combination of peanut butter and honey to reduce calories and fat
- uses fresh fruit instead of jelly

30
minutes
or
less

# 5 ways with grilled cheese

## All-American Grilled Cheese with a Twist

- 8 (1-ounce) slices country white bread
- 2 cups (4 ounces) shredded sharp cheddar cheese
- 12 (¼-inch-thick) slices plum tomato (about 3 tomatoes)
- ¼ cup thinly sliced fresh basil
- Cooking spray

**1.** Place 4 bread slices on a work surface; arrange 1/2 cup cheddar cheese on each slice. Top each slice with 3 tomato slices and 1 tablespoon basil. Top with remaining 4 bread slices.

**2.** Heat a large nonstick skillet over medium heat. Coat pan with cooking spray. Add sandwiches to pan; cook 4 minutes or until lightly browned. Turn sandwiches over; cover and cook 2 minutes or until cheese melts.

**YIELD:** 4 servings (serving size: 1 sandwich).

CALORIES 247; FAT 10.5g (sat 6.3g, mono 3.4g, poly 0.6g); PROTEIN 11.6g; CARB 30g; FIBER 3.2g; CHOL 30mg; IRON 1.1mg; SODIUM 464mg; CALC 233mg

## Grilled Tomato and Brie Sandwiches ▾

- 8 (1-ounce) slices 100% whole-grain bread (about ¼ inch thick)
- 1 teaspoon olive oil
- 1 garlic clove, halved
- 2 teaspoons country-style Dijon mustard
- 4 ounces Brie cheese, thinly sliced
- 1⅓ cups packaged baby arugula and spinach greens (such as Dole)
- 8 (¼-inch-thick) slices beefsteak tomato
- Cooking spray

**1.** Preheat grill to high heat.
**2.** Brush one side of each bread slice with oil; rub cut sides of garlic over oil. Spread ½ teaspoon mustard on each of 4 bread slices, oil side down. Top each bread slice with 1 ounce cheese, ⅓ cup greens, and 2 tomato slices. Top each with remaining 4 bread slices, oil side up.
**3.** Place sandwiches on grill rack coated with cooking spray; grill 2 minutes on each side or until lightly toasted and cheese melts. **YIELD:** 4 servings (serving size: 1 sandwich).

CALORIES 234; FAT 10.1g (sat 5.1g, mono 3.1g, poly 1g); PROTEIN 11g; CARB 26.9g; FIBER 6.5g; CHOL 28mg; IRON 1.8mg; SODIUM 445mg; CALC 210mg

## Grilled Tomato, Smoked Turkey, and Muenster Sandwiches ▾

- 1 tablespoon minced red onion
- 3 tablespoons fat-free sour cream
- 1 tablespoon Dijon mustard
- 1 teaspoon chopped fresh or ¼ teaspoon dried thyme
- 4 teaspoons butter, softened
- 4 (1½-ounce) slices sourdough bread
- 6 (1-ounce) slices fat-free, honey-roasted smoked turkey breast
- 4 (½-inch-thick) slices tomato
- 2 (½-ounce) slices Muenster cheese

**1.** Combine first 4 ingredients in a bowl. Spread 1 teaspoon butter on one side of each bread slice. Spread 2 tablespoons mustard mixture over unbuttered side of each of 2 bread slices; top each with 3 turkey slices, 2 tomato slices, 1 cheese slice, and 1 bread slice (with buttered side up).
**2.** Heat a large nonstick skillet over medium heat until hot. Add sandwiches; cover and cook 3 minutes on each side or until golden brown. **YIELD:** 2 sandwiches (serving size: 1 sandwich).

CALORIES 451; FAT 14.2g (sat 8g, mono 4.5g, poly 0.9g); PROTEIN 27.9g; CARB 48.7g; FIBER 1.8g; CHOL 65mg; IRON 2.4mg; SODIUM 913mg; CALC 238mg

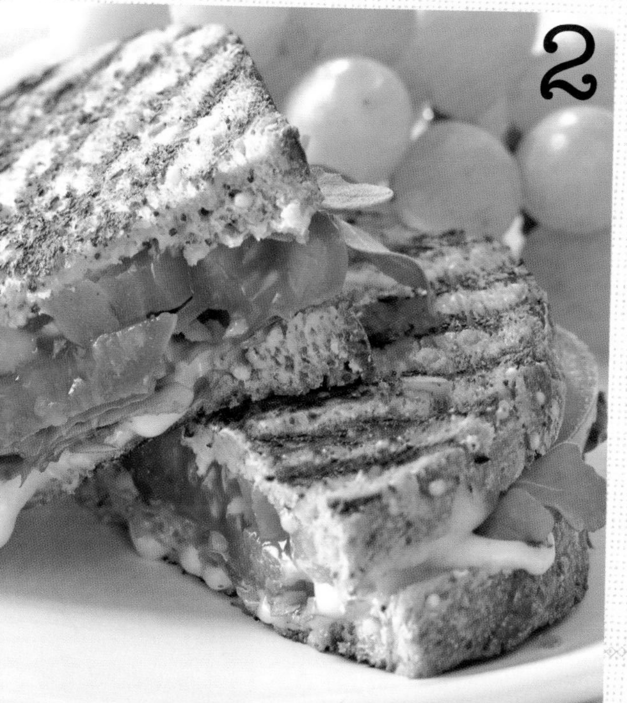

# Tomato-Provolone Sandwiches with Pesto Mayo

- 3 tablespoons organic canola mayonnaise (such as Spectrum)
- 5 teaspoons refrigerated pesto
- 8 (1½-ounce) slices sourdough bread
- 4 (½-ounce) slices provolone cheese
- 1 cup arugula leaves
- 8 (¼-inch-thick) slices tomato
- ¼ teaspoon freshly ground black pepper
- ⅛ teaspoon salt

**1.** Preheat broiler.

**2.** Combine mayonnaise and pesto in a bowl, stirring well.

**3.** Arrange bread in a single layer on a baking sheet. Broil bread 2 minutes or until toasted. Turn bread over; place 1 cheese slice on each of 4 bread slices. Broil 1 minute or until cheese is bubbly. Spread about 2 teaspoons pesto mixture over each cheese-topped bread slice. Arrange ¼ cup arugula and 2 tomato slices over pesto mixture; sprinkle tomato slices evenly with pepper and salt. Spread about 1½ teaspoons remaining pesto mixture evenly over one side of each remaining 4 bread slices; place 1 slice, pesto-side down, on top of each sandwich.

**YIELD:** 4 servings (serving size: 1 sandwich).

CALORIES 329; FAT 16.7g (sat 3.4g, mono 5.8g, poly 6.3g); PROTEIN 11g; CARB 35.7g; FIBER 2.9g; CHOL 16mg; IRON 3.3mg; SODIUM 630mg; CALC 194mg

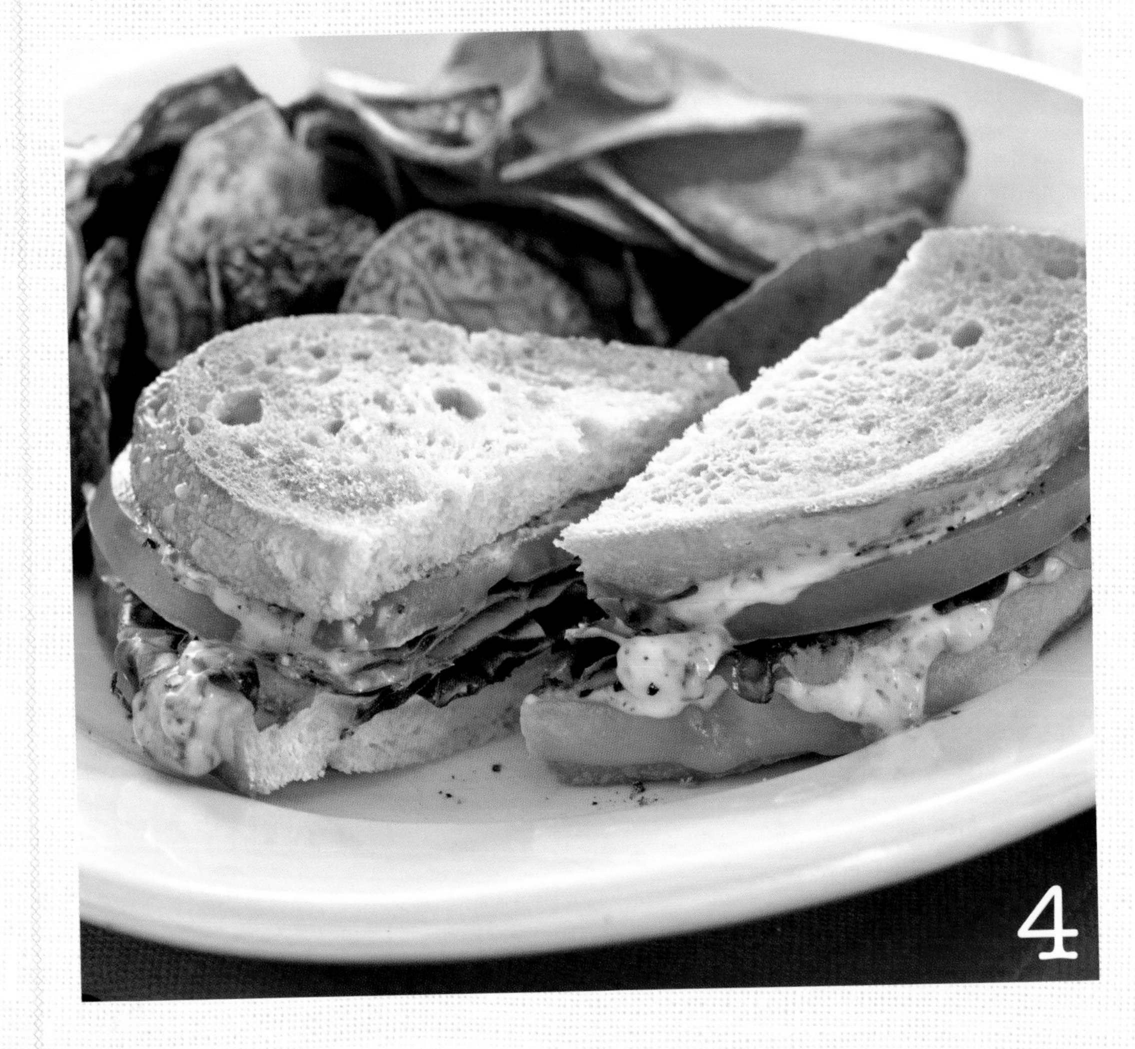

5

## Grown-Up Grilled Cheese Sandwiches

A new take on a familiar favorite pairs grilled cheese with a BLT for a luscious veggie-packed sandwich that feels like an indulgence. Serve with zesty dill pickle spears. If you have extra room in your budget, pair with a sweet-tart hard cider.

**Cooking spray**
- **1 cup vertically sliced red onion**
- **1 large garlic clove, minced**
- **1 cup (4 ounces) shredded reduced-fat sharp white cheddar cheese (such as Cracker Barrel)**
- **8 (1½-ounce) slices hearty white bread (such as Pepperidge Farm)**
- **2 cups fresh spinach leaves**
- **8 (¼-inch-thick) slices tomato**
- **6 center-cut bacon slices, cooked**

**1.** Heat a large nonstick skillet over medium-low heat. Coat pan with cooking spray. Add 1 cup onion and garlic; cook 10 minutes or until tender and golden brown, stirring occasionally.

**2.** Sprinkle 2 tablespoons cheese over each of 4 bread slices. Top each slice with $^{1}/_{2}$ cup spinach, 2 tomato slices, 2 tablespoons onion mixture, and $1^{1}/_{2}$ bacon slices. Sprinkle each with 2 tablespoons cheese; top with remaining 4 bread slices.

**3.** Heat skillet over medium heat. Coat pan with cooking spray. Place sandwiches in pan, and cook 3 minutes on each side or until golden brown and cheese melts. **YIELD:** 4 servings (serving size: 1 sandwich).

CALORIES 376; FAT 11g (sat 5.3g, mono 4.8g, poly 0.6g); PROTEIN 20.2g; CARB 50.3g; FIBER 3.3g; CHOL 24mg; IRON 2.9mg; SODIUM 876mg; CALC 308mg

# Pimiento Cheese Sandwiches

- 2 tablespoons block-style fat-free cream cheese, softened
- ¼ cup reduced-fat mayonnaise
- ¼ teaspoon finely grated onion
- ⅛ teaspoon Worcestershire sauce
- ⅛ teaspoon salt
- Dash of ground red pepper
- 1 cup (4 ounces) shredded reduced-fat extrasharp cheddar cheese
- 1 tablespoon chopped pecans, toasted
- ½ (2-ounce) jar diced pimiento, undrained
- ⅛ teaspoon smoked paprika (optional)
- 8 (1-ounce) slices white bread

**1.** Beat together cream cheese and next 5 ingredients. Stir in cheese, pecans, pimiento, and smoked paprika, if desired. Cover and chill up to 3 hours.
**2.** Spread ¼ cup cheese mixture over 4 bread slices. Top with remaining 4 bread slices. **YIELD:** 4 servings (serving size: 1 sandwich).

CALORIES 296; FAT 14g (sat 5.3g, mono 1.1g, poly 1.1g); PROTEIN 12.2g; CARB 29.1g; FIBER 1.7g; CHOL 26mg; IRON 2.2mg; SODIUM 819mg; CALC 301mg

## what makes it light

- uses fat-free cream cheese
- uses reduced-fat mayonnaise
- uses reduced-fat extrasharp cheddar cheese

30
minutes
or
less

This was a big hit, which is saying a lot in my family. My son wanted seconds, which is rare for anything he thinks is healthy.

from cookinglight.com

# Tuna Melts

- 3 tablespoons finely chopped red onion
- 3 tablespoons organic canola mayonnaise
- 1 teaspoon grated lemon rind
- ¼ teaspoon fennel seeds, crushed
- ¼ teaspoon freshly ground black pepper
- 3 center-cut bacon slices, cooked and crumbled
- 2 (5-ounce) cans albacore tuna in water, drained and flaked
- 8 (1½-ounce) slices sourdough bread
- 4 (½-ounce) slices provolone cheese
- Cooking spray

**1.** Combine first 7 ingredients in a medium bowl, stirring well to coat. Place 4 bread slices on a flat surface; top each bread slice with 1 cheese slice. Divide tuna mixture evenly among bread slices; top each serving with 1 remaining bread slice.

**2.** Heat a large skillet over medium heat. Lightly coat sandwiches with cooking spray. Place sandwiches in pan; top with another heavy skillet. Cook 3 minutes on each side or until lightly browned (leave skillet on sandwiches as they cook). **YIELD**: 4 servings (serving size: 1 sandwich).

CALORIES 405; FAT 17.7g (sat 4g, mono 5.1g, poly 6.9g); PROTEIN 28.3g; CARB 33.3g; FIBER 2.3g; CHOL 49mg; IRON 3.6mg; SODIUM 872mg; CALC 182mg

## what makes it light

- uses canola mayonnaise, which is healthier than regular mayonnaise
- uses less mayonnaise than traditional recipes
- uses center-cut bacon instead of regular bacon
- uses cooking spray instead of butter or oil to cook sandwiches

**Fish tacos with a Baja flair** are flavorful partners to the cabbage slaw, which adds crunch and a peppery bite.

# Baja Fish Tacos

- 2 tablespoons taco seasoning
- 1 tablespoon fresh lime juice
- 1 tablespoon fresh orange juice
- 1 pound mahimahi or other firm white fish fillets, cut into bite-sized pieces
- 1 tablespoon vegetable oil
- 2 cups presliced green cabbage
- ½ cup chopped green onions
- ½ cup reduced-fat sour cream
- 8 (6-inch) corn tortillas
- 8 lime wedges (optional)
- Cilantro sprigs (optional)

**1.** Combine first 3 ingredients in a medium bowl. Add fish; toss to coat.
**2.** Heat oil in a large nonstick skillet over medium-high heat. Add fish; sauté 5 minutes or until fish is done.
**3.** Combine cabbage, onions, and sour cream in a medium bowl.
**4.** Warm tortillas according to package directions. Spoon about ¼ cup cabbage mixture down center of each tortilla. Divide fish evenly among tortillas; fold in half. Serve with lime wedges and cilantro, if desired. **YIELD**: 4 servings (serving size: 2 fish tacos and 2 lime wedges).

CALORIES 327; FAT 9.4g (sat 3.3g, mono 1.3g, poly 2.8g); PROTEIN 26g; CARB 35.8g; FIBER 4.6g; CHOL 98mg; IRON 2.4mg; SODIUM 624mg; CALC 182mg

## what makes it light

- uses reduced-fat sour cream
- fish isn't battered and deep-fried
- uses a minimal amount of oil to sauté fish

30
minutes
or
less

30
minutes
or
less

**A New Orleans specialty,** this sandwich is often made with deep-fried shrimp. Broiling the shrimp, which are coated in garlicky breadcrumbs, delivers big flavor without the fat.

# Shrimp Po'Boys with Spicy Ketchup

- 3 tablespoons dry breadcrumbs
- 1/4 teaspoon salt
- 1/4 teaspoon black pepper
- 1 garlic clove, minced
- 1 tablespoon olive oil
- 1 pound large shrimp, peeled and deveined
- 1/4 cup ketchup
- 1 1/2 teaspoons fresh lemon juice
- 1/2 teaspoon Worcestershire sauce
- 1/4 teaspoon chili powder
- 1/4 teaspoon hot sauce
- 2 (10-inch) submarine rolls, split
- 2 cups torn curly leaf lettuce
- 1/2 cup thinly sliced red onion

**1.** Preheat broiler.

**2.** Line a baking sheet with heavy-duty aluminum foil. Combine breadcrumbs, salt, pepper, and garlic in a medium bowl, stirring with a fork. Combine oil and shrimp; toss well. Place half of shrimp in breadcrumb mixture; toss well to coat. Place breaded shrimp in a single layer on prepared baking sheet. Repeat procedure with remaining shrimp and breadcrumb mixture. Broil 4 minutes or until shrimp are done.

**3.** Combine ketchup, juice, Worcestershire, chili powder, and hot sauce in a small bowl, stirring with a whisk.

**4.** Spread 2 tablespoons ketchup mixture over cut sides of each roll half. Place 1 cup lettuce over bottom half of each roll; top with 1/4 cup onion. Arrange 1 cup shrimp on each roll half; top with remaining roll half. Cut sandwiches in half. **YIELD:** 4 servings (serving size: 1 sandwich half).

CALORIES 401; FAT 9.1g (sat 1.7g, mono 4.6g, poly 1.7g); PROTEIN 30g; CARB 48.9g; FIBER 3g; CHOL 172mg; IRON 5.3mg; SODIUM 864mg; CALC 183mg

## what makes it light

- shrimp are broiled, not deep-fried
- uses a lower-calorie spicy ketchup instead of a mayonnaise-laden tartar sauce

**Bright citrus and licorice notes from the fennel** complement the sweet, tarragon-flecked lobster meat. We use New England–style hot dog buns, which are top-split and have an open crumb on the sides.

# Lobster Salad Rolls with Shaved Fennel and Citrus

3 cups coarsely chopped cooked lobster meat (about 3 [1¼-pound] lobsters)
3 tablespoons canola mayonnaise
2 teaspoons chopped fresh tarragon
½ teaspoon kosher salt, divided
2 cups thinly sliced fennel bulb (about 1 medium)
½ teaspoon grated orange rind
1 tablespoon fresh orange juice
1 tablespoon fresh lemon juice
1 tablespoon rice wine vinegar
2 teaspoons extra-virgin olive oil
¼ teaspoon freshly ground black pepper
Cooking spray
6 (1½-ounce) hot dog buns
Lemon wedges (optional)

**1.** Combine lobster, mayonnaise, 2 teaspoons tarragon, and 1/4 teaspoon salt; cover and refrigerate.
**2.** Combine fennel, remaining 1/4 teaspoon salt, orange rind, and next 5 ingredients.
**3.** Heat a large nonstick skillet over medium heat. Coat pan with cooking spray. Add buns to pan; cook 2 minutes on each side or until lightly browned. Place 1/3 cup fennel salad in each bun. Top each serving with 1/2 cup lobster salad. Serve with lemon wedges, if desired. **YIELD**: 6 servings (serving size: 1 lobster roll).

CALORIES 238; FAT 6.2g (sat 0.8g, mono 3g, poly 1.9g); PROTEIN 19.4g; CARB 24.9g; FIBER 1.9g; CHOL 52mg; IRON 1.9mg; SODIUM 699mg; CALC 120mg

## what makes it light

- uses less mayonnaise than traditional recipes
- doesn't call for a buttered, toasted bun like most traditional recipes

**This is also called a patty melt:** ground meat and cheese nestled between slices of bread (any kind will do) and grilled. Prewrapped slices of processed cheddar cheese are the only way to go, as they melt better. We do it here far lighter than you're likely to find it on the road.

# Grilled Sourdough Cheddar Melts

- 2 teaspoons butter, divided
- Cooking spray
- 2 cups coarsely chopped onion
- 1 pound ground round
- ¼ teaspoon freshly ground black pepper
- ⅛ teaspoon salt
- 4 (¾-ounce) slices 2% reduced-fat processed sharp cheddar cheese
- 8 (1½-ounce) slices sourdough or white bread

**1.** Melt 1 teaspoon butter in a large nonstick skillet coated with cooking spray over medium-high heat. Add onion, and cook 4 minutes or until golden brown, stirring frequently. Reduce heat; cook 10 minutes or until tender, stirring occasionally. Set aside.

**2.** Preheat broiler.

**3.** Combine beef, pepper, and salt in a medium bowl. Divide beef mixture into 4 equal portions, shaping each into a ¼-inch-thick oval patty. Place patties on a broiler pan coated with cooking spray; broil 4 minutes on each side or until done.

**4.** Place 1 cheese slice over each of 4 bread slices; top each slice with 1 patty and 3 tablespoons onion mixture. Cover with remaining bread slices. Melt ½ teaspoon butter in pan coated with cooking spray over medium heat; add 2 sandwiches to pan. Cook 4 minutes on each side until browned and cheese melts. Repeat procedure with ½ teaspoon butter and remaining sandwiches. **YIELD**: 4 servings (serving size: 1 sandwich).

CALORIES 462; FAT 11.5g (sat 5.3g, mono 3.1g, poly 0.9g); PROTEIN 38.5g; CARB 49.3g; FIBER 3g; CHOL 80mg; IRON 5.2mg; SODIUM 909mg; CALC 357mg

## what makes it light

- uses ground round
- uses reduced-fat cheese
- uses a minimal amount of butter to grill sandwiches

# 5 ways with burgers

## Stilton Burgers

- 2 teaspoons olive oil
- 4 cups sliced onion (about 12 ounces)
- ½ teaspoon salt, divided
- 1 pound ground sirloin
- 2 tablespoons grated onion
- 2 tablespoons Worcestershire sauce
- ⅛ teaspoon ground black pepper
- 2 garlic cloves, minced
- Cooking spray
- ¼ cup crumbled Stilton cheese
- 4 (2-ounce) French hamburger rolls, split
- 4 green leaf lettuce leaves
- 4 (¼-inch-thick) slices tomato

**1.** Preheat grill to medium-high heat.

**2.** Heat a large skillet over medium heat. Add oil to pan. Add sliced onion and ¼ teaspoon salt; cook 18 minutes or until golden, stirring occasionally.

**3.** Combine ¼ teaspoon salt, beef, and next 4 ingredients; toss gently. Divide mixture into 4 equal portions, shaping each into a ½-inch-thick patty.

**4.** Place patties on grill rack lightly coated with cooking spray; grill 4 minutes on each side or until desired degree of doneness. Top each patty with 1 tablespoon cheese during last 2 minutes of cooking.

**5.** Place cut sides of rolls on grill rack; grill 1 minute. Place bottom halves of rolls on 4 plates; top each serving with 1 lettuce leaf, 1 tomato slice, 1 patty, ¼ cup onion mixture, and 1 roll top. **YIELD:** 4 servings (serving size: 1 burger).

CALORIES 393; FAT 15g (sat 6.3g, mono 6g, poly 0.6g); PROTEIN 28.3g; CARB 35.3g; FIBER 2.1g; CHOL 75mg; IRON 5.1mg; SODIUM 849mg; CALC 142mg

## Southwestern Turkey-Cheddar Burgers with Grilled Onions

Wheat germ adds a nuttiness that complements the turkey and spices. For more spicy heat, use Monterey Jack cheese with jalapeño peppers.

- ¾ cup finely chopped Maui or other sweet onion
- ⅓ cup wheat germ
- 1½ teaspoons ancho chile powder
- ¾ teaspoon ground cumin
- ½ teaspoon salt
- ¼ teaspoon ground red pepper
- 1½ pounds ground turkey breast
- Cooking spray
- 4 ounces extrasharp cheddar cheese, thinly sliced
- 6 (½-inch-thick) slices Maui or other sweet onion
- 6 (2-ounce) Kaiser rolls, split
- 6 tablespoons Chipotle-Poblano Ketchup

**1.** Prepare grill.
**2.** Combine first 7 ingredients in a large bowl. Divide mixture into 6 equal portions, shaping each into a 1/2-inch-thick patty.
**3.** Place patties on grill rack coated with cooking spray; grill 5 minutes. Turn patties over; grill 2 minutes. Divide cheese evenly over patties; grill an additional 5 minutes or until a thermometer registers 165°. Remove from grill; let stand 5 minutes.
**4.** Place onion slices on grill rack coated with cooking spray; grill 4 minutes on each side or until browned and tender.
**5.** Place rolls, cut sides down, on grill rack; grill 1 minute or until toasted. Place 1 patty on bottom half of each roll; top each serving with 1 onion slice, 1 tablespoon Chipotle-Poblano Ketchup, and top half of roll. **YIELD:** 6 servings (serving size: 1 burger).

CALORIES 395; FAT 10.7g (sat 4.8g, mono 2.5g, poly 1.6g); PROTEIN 32.8g; CARB 42.6g; FIBER 3.3g; CHOL 54mg; IRON 3.4mg; SODIUM 853mg; CALC 211mg

## Chipotle-Poblano Ketchup

- 1 poblano chile (about 5 ounces)
- 1 cup ketchup
- 2 tablespoons minced seeded chipotle chiles, canned in adobo sauce (about 2 chiles)
- ½ teaspoon ground cumin

**1.** Preheat broiler.
**2.** Pierce poblano two times with the tip of a knife. Place poblano on a foil-lined baking sheet; broil 10 minutes or until blackened, turning occasionally. Place in a zip-top plastic bag; seal. Let stand 15 minutes. Peel and discard skins. Cut a lengthwise slit in poblano; discard seeds and stem. Finely chop poblano.
**3.** Combine poblano and remaining ingredients. Refrigerate in an airtight container for up to 2 weeks. **YIELD:** 1¼ cups (serving size: 1 tablespoon).

CALORIES 15; FAT 0.2g (sat 0g, mono 0g, poly 0.1g); PROTEIN 0.3g; CARB 3.6g; FIBER 0.4g; CHOL 0mg; IRON 0.2mg; SODIUM 150mg; CALC 3mg

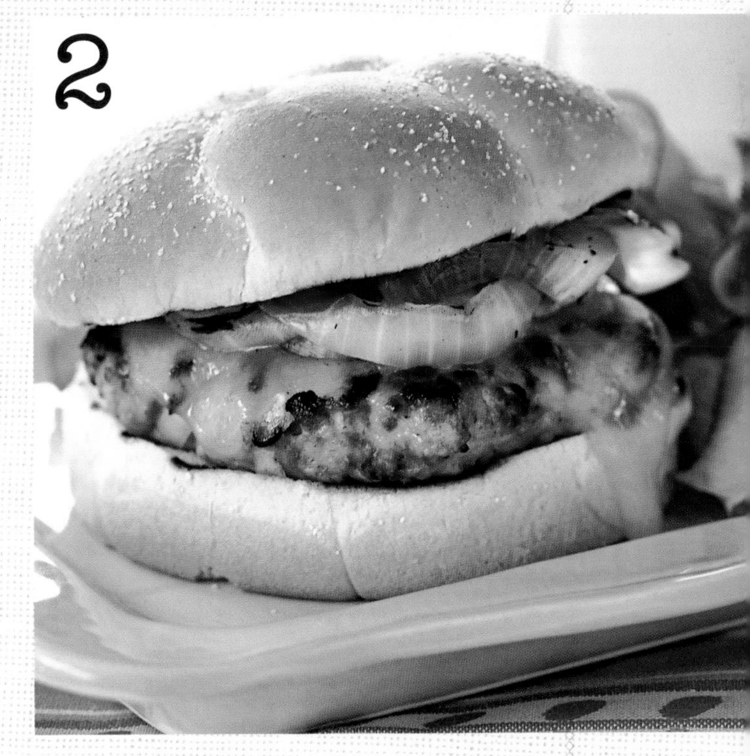

## Italian Meatball Burgers ▼

- 8 ounces sweet turkey Italian sausage
- 1 teaspoon dried oregano
- 1 teaspoon dried basil
- ½ teaspoon salt
- ½ teaspoon fennel seeds, crushed
- ⅛ teaspoon garlic powder
- 1 pound ground sirloin
- Cooking spray
- 2 ounces fresh mozzarella cheese, thinly sliced
- 6 (2-ounce) Italian bread rolls, split
- ¾ cup fat-free tomato-basil pasta sauce (such as Muir Glen)

**1.** Prepare grill.
**2.** Remove casings from sausage. Combine sausage, oregano, basil, salt, fennel seeds, garlic powder, and ground sirloin. Divide beef mixture into 6 equal portions, shaping each into a ½-inch-thick patty.
**3.** Place patties on grill rack coated with cooking spray; grill 5 minutes. Turn patties over; grill 2 minutes. Divide fresh mozzarella cheese evenly over patties, and grill an additional 5 minutes or until a thermometer registers 165°. Remove from grill; let stand 5 minutes.
**4.** Place rolls, cut sides down, on grill rack; grill 1 minute or until toasted. Place 1 patty on bottom half of each roll; top each serving with 2 tablespoons sauce and top half of roll. **YIELD:** 6 servings (serving size: 1 burger).

CALORIES 375; FAT 13.9g (sat 5.3g, mono 4.4g, poly 1.7g); PROTEIN 28.1g; CARB 32.7g; FIBER 1.8g; CHOL 80mg; IRON 4.5mg; SODIUM 894mg; CALC 130mg

## Portobello Burgers ▼

- ¼ cup lower-sodium soy sauce
- ¼ cup balsamic vinegar
- 2 tablespoons olive oil
- 3 garlic cloves, minced
- 4 (4-inch) portobello mushroom caps
- 1 small red bell pepper
- Cooking spray
- ¼ cup reduced-fat mayonnaise
- ½ teaspoon olive oil
- ⅛ teaspoon ground red pepper
- 4 (2-ounce) onion sandwich buns
- 4 (¼-inch-thick) slices tomato
- 4 curly leaf lettuce leaves

**1.** Combine first 4 ingredients in a large zip-top plastic bag; add mushrooms to bag. Seal and marinate at room temperature 2 hours, turning bag occasionally. Remove mushrooms from bag; discard marinade.
**2.** Prepare grill to medium heat.
**3.** Cut bell pepper in half lengthwise; discard

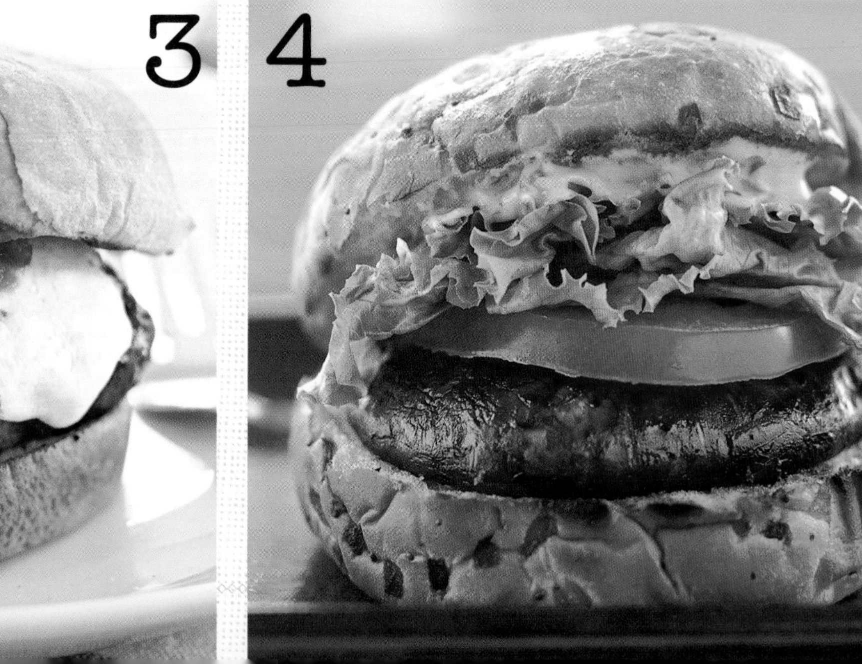

seeds and membranes. Place pepper halves on grill rack coated with cooking spray; grill 15 minutes or until blackened, turning occasionally. Place in a zip-top plastic bag; seal. Let stand 10 minutes. Peel. Reserve 1 pepper half for another use. Finely chop 1 pepper half; place in a small bowl. Add mayonnaise, 1/2 teaspoon oil, and ground red pepper; stir well.
**4.** Place mushrooms, gill sides down, on grill rack coated with cooking spray; grill 4 minutes on each side. Place buns, cut sides down, on grill rack coated with cooking spray; grill 30 seconds on each side or until toasted. Spread 2 tablespoons mayonnaise mixture on top half of each bun. Place 1 mushroom on bottom half of each bun. Top each mushroom with 1 tomato slice and 1 lettuce leaf; cover with top halves of buns. **YIELD:** 4 servings (serving size: 1 burger).

CALORIES 251; FAT 8.4g (sat 2.3g, mono 3.7g, poly 2.1g); PROTEIN 7.3g; CARB 37.9g; FIBER 2.4g; CHOL 0mg; IRON 2.2mg; SODIUM 739mg; CALC 81mg

## Chipotle Salmon Burgers ▲

Mayonnaise:

- 1 tablespoon chopped fresh cilantro
- 3 tablespoons light mayonnaise
- 2 tablespoons finely chopped fresh mango
- 1 tablespoon finely chopped fresh pineapple
- 1/8 teaspoon finely grated lime rind

Burgers:

- 1/3 cup chopped green onions
- 1/4 cup chopped fresh cilantro
- 1 tablespoon finely chopped chipotle chile, canned in adobo sauce
- 2 teaspoons fresh lime juice
- 1/4 teaspoon salt
- 1 (1 1/4-pound) salmon fillet, skinned and cut into 1-inch pieces
- Cooking spray
- 4 English muffins
- 4 butter lettuce leaves

**1.** To prepare mayonnaise, place first 5 ingredients in a food processor or blender; process until smooth. Transfer to a bowl; cover and chill.
**2.** To prepare burgers, place onions, 1/4 cup cilantro, chile, and juice in a food processor; process until finely chopped. Add salt and salmon; pulse 4 times or until salmon is coarsely ground and mixture is well blended.
**3.** Divide salmon mixture into 4 equal portions; shape each portion into a (1-inch-thick) patty. Cover and chill 30 minutes.
**4.** Heat a grill pan over medium-high heat. Coat pan with cooking spray. Add patties to pan; cook 6 minutes on each side or until desired degree of doneness.
**5.** Wipe skillet with paper towels; recoat with cooking spray. Place 2 muffins, cut sides down, in pan; cook 2 minutes or until lightly toasted. Repeat procedure with cooking spray and remaining muffins.
**6.** Place 1 muffin bottom on each of 4 plates; top each serving with 1 lettuce leaf and 1 patty. Spread about 1 tablespoon mayonnaise mixture over each patty; place 1 muffin top on each serving. **YIELD:** 4 servings (serving size: 1 burger).

CALORIES 408; FAT 15g (sat 2.6g, mono 4.5g, poly 6.6g); PROTEIN 37.4g; CARB 28.9g; FIBER 2.9g; CHOL 94mg; IRON 3.8mg; SODIUM 595mg; CALC 124mg

30
minutes
or
less

# Spicy Bistro Steak Subs

- 1 tablespoon butter
- 2 garlic cloves, minced
- 1 pound thinly sliced lean deli roast beef
- 2 tablespoons ketchup
- 4 teaspoons Worcestershire sauce
- ½ teaspoon dried basil
- ½ teaspoon dried oregano
- ¼ teaspoon ground red pepper
- 1 (12-ounce) can dark beer
- 6 (2½-ounce) hoagie rolls with sesame seeds, cut in half lengthwise

**1.** Melt butter in a large nonstick skillet over medium-high heat. Add minced garlic, and sauté 2 minutes. Add roast beef and next 6 ingredients, and bring to a boil. Reduce heat, and simmer 2 minutes, stirring frequently. Drain roast beef in a colander over a bowl, reserving sauce. Divide roast beef evenly among roll bottoms, and top with roll tops. Serve sandwiches with reserved sauce. **YIELD:** 6 servings (serving size: 1 sandwich and 3 tablespoons sauce).

CALORIES 345; FAT 10.6g (sat 3.4g, mono 4.5g, poly 1.6g); PROTEIN 21.4g; CARB 40.6g; FIBER 1.6g; CHOL 2mg; IRON 3.8mg; SODIUM 938mg; CALC 67mg

## what makes it light

- uses lean deli roast beef instead of prime rib
- doesn't include cheese like many traditional recipes

# Memphis Pork Sandwiches

Pork:

- 8 hickory wood chunks (about 4 pounds)
- 2 tablespoons paprika
- 1 tablespoon freshly ground black pepper
- 1 tablespoon turbinado sugar
- 1½ teaspoons kosher salt
- 1½ teaspoons garlic powder
- 1½ teaspoons onion powder
- 1½ teaspoons dry mustard
- 1 (5-pound) bone-in pork shoulder (Boston butt)
- ⅓ cup white vinegar
- 1 tablespoon Worcestershire sauce
- 1 teaspoon canola oil
- 1 (12-ounce) can beer
- 2 cups water
- Cooking spray

Slaw:

- ¼ cup finely chopped onion
- 1½ tablespoons prepared mustard
- 1½ tablespoons white vinegar
- 1 tablespoon reduced-fat mayonnaise
- 1½ teaspoons granulated sugar
- ¼ teaspoon salt
- 6 cups chopped green cabbage

Remaining Ingredients:

- 13 hamburger buns
- 1⅔ cups Memphis Barbecue Sauce

**1.** To prepare pork, soak wood chunks in water about 16 hours; drain.
**2.** Combine paprika and next 6 ingredients; reserve 1 tablespoon paprika mixture. Rub half of remaining paprika mixture onto pork. Place in a large zip-top plastic bag; seal and refrigerate overnight.
**3.** Remove pork from refrigerator; let stand at room temperature 30 minutes. Rub remaining half of paprika mixture onto pork.
**4.** Combine reserved 1 tablespoon paprika mixture, 1/3 cup vinegar, Worcestershire, oil, and beer in a small saucepan; cook over low heat 5 minutes or until warm.
**5.** Remove grill rack; set aside. Prepare grill for indirect grilling, heating one side to medium-low and leaving one side with no heat. Maintain temperature at 225°. Pierce bottom of a disposable aluminum foil pan several times with the tip of a knife. Place pan on heated side of grill; add half of wood chunks to pan. Place another disposable aluminum foil pan (do not pierce pan) on unheated side of grill. Pour 2 cups water in pan. Coat grill rack with cooking spray; place grill rack on grill.
**6.** Place pork on grill rack over foil pan on unheated side. Close lid; cook 4 1/2 hours or until a thermometer registers 170°, gently brushing pork with beer mixture every hour (avoid brushing off sugar mixture). Add additional wood chunks halfway during cooking time. Discard any remaining beer mixture.
**7.** Preheat oven to 250°.
**8.** Remove pork from grill. Wrap pork in several layers of aluminum foil, and place in a baking pan. Bake at 250° for 2 hours or until a thermometer registers 195°. Remove from oven. Let stand, still wrapped, 1 hour or until pork easily pulls apart. Unwrap pork; trim and discard fat. Shred pork with 2 forks.
**9.** While pork bakes and rests, prepare slaw. Combine onion and next 5 ingredients in a large bowl. Add cabbage, and toss to coat. Cover and chill 3 hours before serving. Serve pork and slaw on buns with Memphis Barbecue Sauce. **YIELD:** 13 servings (serving size: 1 bun, 3 ounces pork, about 1/3 cup slaw, and about 1 1/2 tablespoons sauce).

CALORIES 387; FAT 15.2g (sat 5.1g, mono 6.3g, poly 2.2g); PROTEIN 26.6g; CARB 33.7g; FIBER 2.3g; CHOL 74mg; IRON 3.5mg; SODIUM 843mg; CALC 120mg

## Memphis Barbecue Sauce

- 1 cup ketchup
- ¾ cup white vinegar
- 2 tablespoons brown sugar
- 1 tablespoon onion powder
- 2 tablespoons Worcestershire sauce
- 2 tablespoons prepared mustard
- ½ teaspoon freshly ground black pepper
- ¼ teaspoon salt
- ⅛ teaspoon ground red pepper

**1.** Combine all ingredients in a medium saucepan; bring to a simmer. Cook 5 minutes; serve warm. **YIELD**: 2 cups (serving size: 2 tablespoons).

CALORIES 25; FAT 0.1g (sat 0g, mono 0.1g, poly 0g); PROTEIN 0.4g; CARB 6.4g; FIBER 0.2g; CHOL 0mg; IRON 0.3mg; SODIUM 247mg; CALC 10mg

### what makes it light

- uses reduced-fat mayonnaise
- fat is trimmed from pork before it's shredded unlike many restaurant recipes
- uses a minimal amount of mayonnaise in slaw

30
minutes
or
less

# Grilled Cuban Sandwiches

- 2 tablespoons Dijon mustard
- 1 (8-ounce) loaf French bread, cut in half horizontally
- 6 ounces reduced-fat Swiss cheese, thinly sliced (such as Alpine Lace)
- 6 ounces deli-sliced ham (such as Hillshire Farms)
- 8 sandwich-sliced dill pickles
- Cooking spray
- Sandwich-sliced dill pickles (optional)

**1.** Spread mustard evenly over cut sides of bread. Arrange half of cheese and half of ham on bottom half of loaf; top with pickle slices. Repeat layer with remaining cheese and ham; cover with top half of loaf. Cut into quarters.

**2.** Heat a large, heavy skillet over medium-high heat. Coat pan with cooking spray. Add sandwiches; press with a heavy skillet (such as cast-iron). Cook 2 minutes on each side. Garnish with dill pickles, if desired. **YIELD:** 4 servings (serving size: 1 sandwich).

CALORIES 335; FAT 11g (sat 5.3g, mono 2.1g, poly 0.9g); PROTEIN 23.1g; CARB 36g; FIBER 3g; CHOL 43mg; IRON 2.8mg; SODIUM 1,301mg; CALC 318mg

## what makes it light

- uses reduced-fat Swiss cheese
- not grilled with oil or butter
- uses less amounts of traditional high-fat ingredients

**Double-breading the tomato slices** gives them a crunchy coating. Soaking the tomatoes in hot water draws out their moisture, which helps keep them crisp when cooked. On their own, the fried green tomatoes in this recipe are a classic Southern side dish.

# Open-Faced Bacon, Lettuce, and Fried Green Tomato Sandwiches

- 2 medium green tomatoes, cut into 12 (¼-inch-thick) slices (about 1 pound)
- 2 tablespoons fat-free milk
- 4 large egg whites, lightly beaten
- 1½ cups yellow cornmeal
- ¾ teaspoon salt
- ¼ teaspoon freshly ground black pepper
- 2 tablespoons olive oil, divided
- 5 tablespoons light mayonnaise
- 1 teaspoon fresh lemon juice
- ¼ teaspoon hot sauce
- 6 (1½-ounce) slices white bread, toasted
- 6 Bibb lettuce leaves
- 9 bacon slices, cooked and cut in half
- 2 tablespoons fresh chives

**1.** Place tomato slices in a large bowl; cover with hot water. Let stand 15 minutes. Drain and pat dry with paper towels. Combine milk and egg whites, stirring with a whisk. Combine cornmeal, salt, and pepper in a shallow dish, stirring with a whisk. Dip each tomato slice in milk mixture; dredge in cornmeal mixture. Return tomato slices, one at a time, to milk mixture; dredge in cornmeal mixture.

**2.** Heat 1 tablespoon oil in a large nonstick skillet over medium-high heat. Add half of tomato slices; cook 4 minutes on each side or until crisp and golden. Repeat procedure with remaining oil and tomato slices.

**3.** Combine mayonnaise, juice, and hot sauce, stirring with a whisk. Spread about 1 tablespoon mayonnaise mixture onto each bread slice; top with 1 lettuce leaf, 3 bacon pieces, and 2 tomato slices. Sprinkle each sandwich with 1 teaspoon chives. Serve immediately. **YIELD:** 6 servings (serving size: 1 sandwich).

CALORIES 386; FAT 12.8g (sat 2.8g, mono 4.5g, poly 2.6g); PROTEIN 12.2g; CARB 56.2g; FIBER 3.9g; CHOL 16mg; IRON 2.2mg; SODIUM 834mg; CALC 44mg

## what makes it light

- uses fat-free milk
- uses egg whites
- pan-fried, not deep-fried, in a minimal amount of olive oil
- uses olive oil
- uses light mayonnaise

# Pork and Pinto Bean Nachos

Meat:

1 (1-pound) pork tenderloin, trimmed
2 tablespoons olive oil, divided
½ teaspoon salt, divided
¼ teaspoon black pepper
Cooking spray
2 tablespoons fresh lime juice
1 teaspoon minced garlic

Beans:

1 can chipotle chiles in adobo sauce
2 tablespoons water
2 teaspoons fresh lime juice
1 teaspoon chili powder
¼ teaspoon salt
2 (15-ounce) cans pinto beans, rinsed and drained
4 applewood-smoked bacon slices, cooked and crumbled

Topping:

1½ cups chopped plum tomato
1 cup diced avocado
½ cup chopped jícama
⅓ cup chopped onion
2 tablespoons fresh lime juice
1 tablespoon olive oil
¼ teaspoon salt

Remaining Ingredients:

6 ounces sturdy tortilla chips (8 cups)
1¼ cups (5 ounces) shredded reduced-fat Colby and Monterey Jack cheese blend
¼ cup chopped fresh cilantro
1 jalapeño pepper, thinly sliced

**1.** Preheat oven to 500°.
**2.** To prepare meat, rub pork with 1 tablespoon oil, 1/4 teaspoon salt, and black pepper. Place pork in a shallow roasting pan coated with cooking spray. Bake at 500° for 23 minutes or until a thermometer registers 160°. Remove from pan; cool 10 minutes. Shred pork with 2 forks to measure 2 cups; place in a small bowl. Stir in remaining 1 tablespoon oil, remaining 1/4 teaspoon salt, 2 tablespoons juice, and garlic.
**3.** To prepare beans, remove 2 chipotle chiles and 1 teaspoon adobo sauce from can; reserve remaining chiles and sauce for another use. Drop chiles through food chute with food processor on; pulse 3 times or until coarsely chopped. Add adobo sauce, water, and next 4 ingredients; process 5 seconds or until smooth. Stir in bacon.
**4.** Preheat broiler.
**5.** To prepare topping, combine plum tomato and next 6 ingredients; toss well to coat.
**6.** Arrange tortilla chips in a single layer on a large rimmed baking sheet. Top evenly with bean mixture; top with meat mixture, and sprinkle with cheese. Broil 4 minutes or until cheese melts. Top evenly with topping, cilantro, and jalapeño. Serve immediately. **YIELD:** 6 servings (serving size: 1 ounce chips, 1/2 cup beans, 1/3 cup pork, and 1/2 cup topping).

CALORIES 517; FAT 26.9g (sat 6.8g, mono 12.4g, poly 3.3g); PROTEIN 31.4g; CARB 38.4g; FIBER 8.9g; CHOL 66mg; IRON 3.3mg; SODIUM 991mg; CALC 248mg

## what makes it light

- uses lean pork tenderloin
- uses reduced-fat cheese
- smaller portion size than traditional recipes

# Muffuletta

Grilled Vegetables:

- ¼ cup reduced-fat Italian dressing
- 8 (½-inch-thick) slices eggplant (about 1 pound)
- 2 (½-inch-thick) slices Vidalia or other sweet onion
- 1 medium yellow squash, thinly sliced
- 1 medium red bell pepper, cut into 4 wedges
- Cooking spray

Olive Salad:

- 1 cup chopped tomato or quartered cherry tomatoes
- ⅓ cup chopped pepperoncini peppers
- ¼ cup sliced pimiento-stuffed olives
- 2 tablespoons pepperoncini juice
- ½ teaspoon dried thyme
- ½ teaspoon cracked black pepper

Remaining Ingredients:

- 1 (16-ounce) loaf French bread, cut in half horizontally
- 2 ounces thinly sliced provolone cheese
- 2 ounces thinly sliced reduced-fat hard salami (such as Franklin)

**1.** To prepare grilled vegetables, combine first 5 ingredients in a zip-top plastic bag; seal and marinate in refrigerator 2 hours, turning bag occasionally.
**2.** Prepare grill.
**3.** Remove vegetables from plastic bag; place vegetables on grill rack coated with cooking spray. Grill 5 minutes on each side or until vegetables are tender.
**4.** To prepare olive salad, combine tomato and next 5 ingredients.
**5.** Hollow out bottom half of bread, leaving a 1-inch-thick shell; reserve torn bread for another use. Arrange cheese in bottom half of the bread. Top with salami, grilled vegetables, olive salad, and top half of bread. Wrap loaf with plastic wrap; refrigerate up to 24 hours. Cut into 4 pieces just before serving. **YIELD:** 4 servings (serving size: 1 piece).

CALORIES 384; FAT 11.9g (sat 4.3g, mono 3.4g, poly 1.9g); PROTEIN 16.3g; CARB 55.1g; FIBER 7.9g; CHOL 23mg; IRON 3.4mg; SODIUM 1,313mg; CALC 204mg

## what makes it light

- uses reduced-fat Italian dressing
- uses reduced-fat hard salami
- grilled vegetables replace the bulk of meat that's in a traditional muffuletta
- doesn't use oil in the olive salad like traditional recipes

Yummy, yummy. **Best egg salad I've ever eaten, and adding it to BLT is just genius.** Can't wait for my leftovers today at lunch. My husband is not a big fan of egg salad, but he loved it, too. We will definitely make this again.

**from cookinglight.com**

# Egg Salad BLTs

- ¼ cup fat-free mayonnaise
- 3 tablespoons thinly sliced green onions
- 3 tablespoons reduced-fat sour cream
- 2 teaspoons whole-grain Dijon mustard
- ½ teaspoon freshly ground black pepper
- ¼ teaspoon grated lemon rind
- 8 hard-cooked large eggs
- 8 (1½-ounce) slices peasant bread or firm sandwich bread, toasted
- 4 center-cut bacon slices, cooked and cut in half crosswise
- 8 (¼-inch-thick) slices tomato
- 4 large Boston lettuce leaves

**1.** Combine first 6 ingredients in a medium bowl, stirring well.
**2.** Cut 2 eggs in half lengthwise; reserve 2 yolks for another use. Coarsely chop remaining egg whites and whole eggs. Add eggs to mayonnaise mixture; stir gently to combine.
**3.** Arrange 4 bread slices on a cutting board or work surface. Top each bread slice with ½ cup egg mixture, 2 bacon pieces, 2 tomato slices, 1 lettuce leaf, and 1 bread slice. Serve sandwich immediately. **YIELD**: 4 servings (serving size: 1 sandwich).

CALORIES 371; FAT 11.7g (sat 4.1g, mono 4.4g, poly 1.4g); PROTEIN 21.9g; CARB 44g; FIBER 2.4g; CHOL 329mg; IRON 4mg; SODIUM 892mg; CALC 70mg

## what makes it light

- uses fat-free mayonnaise
- uses reduced-fat sour cream
- uses fewer egg yolks than traditional recipes
- uses center-cut bacon, which is lower in fat than regular bacon

30
minutes
or
less

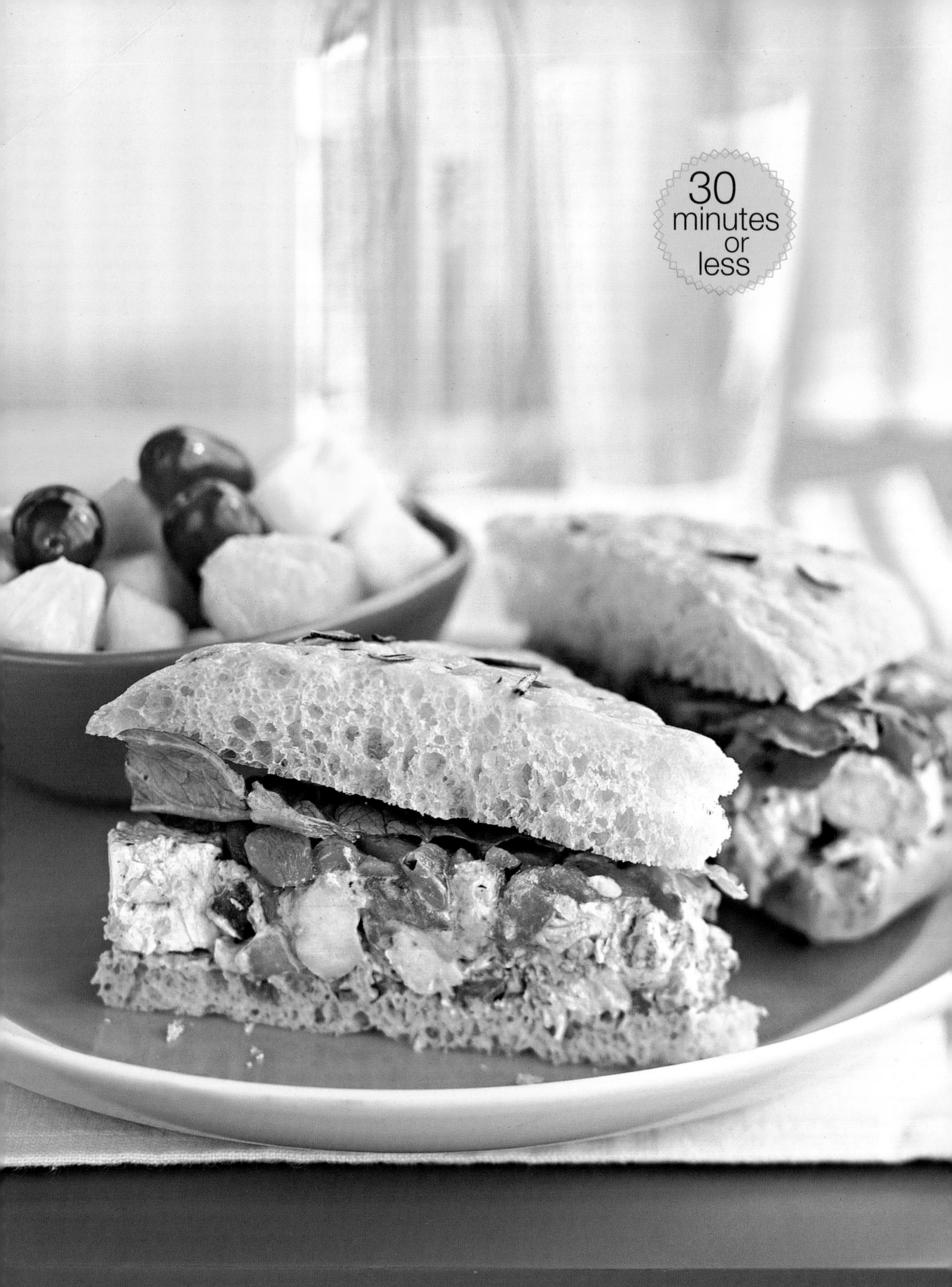
30
minutes
or
less

**This hearty sandwich** is a filling lunch option. Prepare the chicken salad at home the night before, and then assemble the sandwich at work the next day. Substitute baguettes for focaccia if you want.

# Pesto Chicken Salad Sandwiches

- ½ cup reduced-fat mayonnaise
- ⅓ cup plain fat-free yogurt
- ⅓ cup commercial pesto (such as Buitoni)
- 1½ tablespoons fresh lemon juice
- ½ teaspoon salt
- ½ teaspoon black pepper
- 4 cups cubed skinless, boneless rotisserie chicken breast
- 1 cup diced celery
- ⅓ cup chopped walnuts, toasted
- 1 (1-pound) focaccia bread, cut in half horizontally, toasted, and cut into 20 slices
- 1 (12-ounce) bottle roasted red bell peppers, drained and chopped
- 10 romaine lettuce leaves

**1.** Combine first 6 ingredients in a large bowl, stirring with a whisk. Stir in chicken, celery, and walnuts.

**2.** Spread ½ cup salad onto each of 10 bread slices. Top each slice with about 2 tablespoons bell pepper, 1 lettuce leaf, and 1 bread slice. **YIELD**: 10 servings (serving size: 1 sandwich).

CALORIES 324; FAT 10g (sat 1.2g, mono 0.6g, poly 2.2g); PROTEIN 26.4g; CARB 31.6g; FIBER 1.6g; CHOL 55mg; IRON 2.3mg; SODIUM 725mg; CALC 39mg

## what makes it light

- uses low-fat mayonnaise
- uses fat-free yogurt

Wow! These were delicious! My son and husband love Reuben sandwiches, and **I was happy to find a way to make these a healthier choice.**

**from cookinglight.com**

# Turkey Reuben Panini

- 8 (½-ounce) slices thin-slice rye bread
- ¼ cup fat-free Thousand Island dressing
- 8 (½-ounce) thin slices reduced-fat Swiss cheese
- ¼ cup refrigerated sauerkraut, rinsed and drained
- 8 ounces low-sodium deli turkey breast (such as Boar's Head)
- Cooking spray

**1.** Spread one side of each bread slice evenly with 1½ teaspoons dressing. Place 1 cheese slice on dressed side of each of 4 bread slices; top each with 1 tablespoon sauerkraut and 2 ounces turkey. Top each sandwich with 1 cheese slice and 1 bread slice, dressed side down. Coat outside of each sandwich (top and bottom) with cooking spray. Heat a large skillet over medium-high heat. Add sandwiches to pan. Place a cast-iron or other heavy skillet on top of sandwiches; press gently to flatten sandwiches (leave cast-iron skillet on sandwiches while they cook). Cook 2 minutes on each side or until browned and cheese melts. **YIELD:** 4 servings (serving size: 1 sandwich).

CALORIES 268; FAT 7.5g (sat 3g, mono 0.6g, poly 0.4g); PROTEIN 25.2g; CARB 25.7g; FIBER 3.1g; CHOL 35mg; IRON 1.7mg; SODIUM 819mg; CALC 304mg

## what makes it light

- uses fat-free Thousand Island dressing
- uses reduced-fat Swiss cheese
- uses turkey, which is lower in sodium and fat than the traditional corned beef or pastrami

30
minutes
or
less

# recipe makeover

## spinach-cheese bake

**The Reader:** Joyce Keil

**The Story:** Joyce's sister-in-law, Judy Wipf, gave her this egg, cheese, and spinach casserole recipe 30 years ago, and it has been a family favorite since. However, Joyce eats more healthfully these days by preparing *Cooking Light* recipes and eating plenty of fruits and vegetables. While she enjoyed the dish's rich cheese and spinach combination, she knew the recipe needed to be revamped. "You can see the fat glistening" on the baked casserole, she wrote to us.

**The Dilemma:** This original recipe's short ingredient list belied its heavy nutrition profile. One pound of cheese, one-quarter cup of butter, three eggs, and a cup of whole milk contributed a hefty amount of fat and most of the dish's calories. One serving contained more than half of a day's worth of saturated fat, as well as one-third of the dietary cholesterol for someone on a 2,000-calorie diet.

**The Solution:** We reduced the butter to one tablespoon, which was melted and used to grease the pan and maintain the casserole's buttery back note. And we reduced the total amount of cheese and substituted a lower-fat yet tasty cheese to keep fat in check: We combined ¾ cup Monterey Jack cheese with 1¼ cups of more assertive-tasting reduced-fat sharp cheddar cheese. These changes cut more than 13 grams of fat (nearly 9 grams saturated) and 135 calories per portion. The butter, cheese, and eggs contributed most of the original's cholesterol count, but by using less butter, mostly reduced-fat cheese, and 1 cup of fat-free and cholesterol-free egg substitute (in place of the original's three whole eggs), we slashed 89 milligrams of cholesterol per serving. Adding a bit more spinach improved the fiber and iron content. And to compensate for this addition, we increased the flour-milk mixture with minimal extra calories by using fat-free milk instead of whole. Adding a little mustard and a few spices further boosted the savory quality of the casserole.

**The Feedback:** When Joyce prepared the recipe for her daughter, she feared reducing the butter so drastically wouldn't work. But her daughter was "pleased and frankly amazed" by the trimmed-down recipe and deemed the lightened casserole's texture and taste comparable to the original.

| | BEFORE | AFTER |
|---|---|---|
| Calories per serving | 286 | 157 |
| Fat | 21.2g | 6g |
| Percent of total calories | 34% | 67% |

**You can assemble the casserole in less than 10 minutes** by using preshredded cheeses. Pair this dish with a fresh berry salad and mini muffins for a lovely Mother's Day or graduation brunch.

# Spinach-Cheese Bake

- 1 tablespoon butter, melted
- Cooking spray
- 2 (6-ounce) packages fresh baby spinach
- 1¼ cups (5 ounces) shredded reduced-fat sharp cheddar cheese
- ¾ cup (3 ounces) shredded Monterey Jack cheese
- 6 ounces all-purpose flour (about 1⅓ cups)
- 1½ cups fat-free milk
- 1 cup egg substitute
- 1 teaspoon salt
- 1 teaspoon baking powder
- 2 teaspoons Dijon mustard
- ¼ teaspoon freshly ground black pepper
- ⅛ teaspoon ground nutmeg
- ⅛ teaspoon ground red pepper

**1.** Preheat oven to 350°.

**2.** Pour butter into bottom of a 13 x 9–inch baking dish coated with cooking spray; tilt dish to coat. Place spinach evenly in bottom of dish; sprinkle evenly with cheeses.

**3.** Weigh or lightly spoon 6 ounces (about 1⅓ cups) flour into dry measuring cups; level with a knife. Combine flour and remaining ingredients in a medium bowl; stir with a whisk until blended. Pour milk mixture over cheese. Bake at 350° for 40 minutes or until lightly browned. Serve immediately. **YIELD**: 12 servings.

CALORIES 157; FAT 6g (sat 3.7g, mono 1.7g, poly 0.4g); PROTEIN 10.8g; CARB 15.1g; FIBER 1.6g; CHOL 18mg; IRON 2.6mg; SODIUM 494mg; CALC 263mg

# dinner

## RECIPE MAKEOVERS



## 5 WAYS WITH



## RECIPES

This is one of my favorite **Cooking Light** recipes of all time! It has outstanding texture and flavor for a lightened soup! Truly delicious! This soup actually won a "cook off" contest at work, and when I told everyone it was from **Cooking Light** they couldn't believe it!!

**from cookinglight.com**

# Baked Potato Soup

- 4 baking potatoes (about 2½ pounds)
- 3 ounces all-purpose flour (about ⅔ cup)
- 6 cups 2% reduced-fat milk
- 1 cup (4 ounces) reduced-fat shredded extrasharp cheddar cheese, divided
- 1 teaspoon salt
- ½ teaspoon freshly ground black pepper
- 1 cup reduced-fat sour cream
- ¾ cup chopped green onions, divided
- 6 bacon slices, cooked and crumbled
- Cracked black pepper (optional)

**1.** Preheat oven to 400°.
**2.** Pierce potatoes with a fork; bake at 400° for 1 hour or until tender. Cool. Peel potatoes; coarsely mash.
**3.** Weigh or lightly spoon flour into a dry measuring cup; level with a knife. Place flour in a large Dutch oven; gradually add milk, stirring with a whisk until blended. Cook over medium heat until thick and bubbly (about 8 minutes). Add mashed potatoes, ¾ cup cheese, salt, and ½ teaspoon pepper, stirring until cheese melts. Remove from heat.
**4.** Stir in sour cream and ½ cup onions. Cook over low heat 10 minutes or until thoroughly heated (do not boil). Ladle 1½ cups soup into each of 8 bowls. Sprinkle each serving with 1½ teaspoons cheese, 1½ teaspoons onions, and about 1 tablespoon bacon. Garnish with cracked pepper, if desired. **YIELD:** 8 servings (serving size: about 1½ cups soup, 1½ teaspoons cheese, 1½ teaspoons onions, and about 1 tablespoon bacon).

CALORIES 329; FAT 10.8g (sat 5.9g, mono 3.5g, poly 0.7g); PROTEIN 13.6g; CARB 44.5g; FIBER 2.8g; CHOL 38mg; IRON 1.1mg; SODIUM 587mg; CALC 407mg

## what makes it light

- uses reduced-fat milk rather than cream for the base
- uses extrasharp reduced-fat cheese for maximum flavor
- uses reduced-fat sour cream

# 5 ways with pizza

## Chicago Deep-Dish Pizza

- 2 teaspoons sugar
- 1 package dry yeast (about 2¼ teaspoons)
- 1 cup warm water (100° to 110°)
- 1 tablespoon extra-virgin olive oil
- 12.38 ounces all-purpose flour (about 2¾ cups), divided
- ¼ cup yellow cornmeal
- ½ teaspoon salt
- Cooking spray
- 2 cups (8 ounces) shredded part-skim mozzarella cheese, divided
- 2 precooked mild Italian chicken sausages (about 6 ounces), casings removed, chopped
- 1 (28-ounce) can whole tomatoes, drained
- 1½ teaspoons chopped fresh oregano
- 1½ teaspoons chopped fresh basil
- 2 cups thinly sliced mushrooms (about 6 ounces)
- ¾ cup chopped green bell pepper
- ¾ cup chopped red bell pepper

**1.** Dissolve sugar and yeast in warm water in a large bowl; let stand 5 minutes. Stir in olive oil.
**2.** Weigh or lightly spoon flour into dry measuring cups; level with a knife. Combine 11.25 ounces (about 2½ cups) flour, cornmeal, and salt in a bowl. Stir flour mixture into yeast mixture until dough forms a ball. Turn dough out onto a lightly floured surface. Knead until smooth and elastic (about 5 minutes); add enough of remaining flour, 1 tablespoon at a time, to prevent dough from sticking to hands (dough will feel sticky).
**3.** Place dough in a large bowl coated with cooking spray, turning to coat top. Cover and let rise in a warm place (85°), free from drafts, 45 minutes or until doubled in size. (Gently press two fingers into dough. If indentation remains, dough has risen enough.) Punch dough down; cover and let rest 5 minutes. Roll dough into an 11 x 15–inch rectangle on a lightly floured surface. Place dough in a 13 x 9–inch baking dish coated with cooking spray; press dough up sides of dish. Spread 1½ cups cheese evenly over dough. Arrange chopped sausage evenly over cheese.
**4.** Preheat oven to 400°.
**5.** Chop tomatoes; place in a sieve. Stir in oregano and basil; drain tomato mixture 10 minutes.
**6.** Heat a large nonstick skillet over medium heat. Coat pan with cooking spray. Add mushrooms to pan; cook 5 minutes, stirring occasionally. Stir in peppers; cook 8 minutes or until tender, stirring occasionally. Arrange vegetables over sausage; spoon tomato mixture evenly over vegetables and sausage. Sprinkle evenly with remaining ½ cup cheese. Bake at 400° for 25 minutes or until crust browns and cheese bubbles. Cool 5 minutes before cutting. **YIELD:** 8 servings (serving size: 1 piece).

CALORIES 330; FAT 9.2g (sat 4.6g, mono 3.2g, poly 1g); PROTEIN 17.8g; CARB 44g; FIBER 3.2g; CHOL 31mg; IRON 3.9mg; SODIUM 365mg; CALC 244mg

## Pizza Margherita

Because this classic Neapolitan-style pizza is so simple, it depends on quality ingredients. Use the best fresh mozzarella and basil you can find.

- 1 cup warm water (100° to 110°), divided
- 10 ounces bread flour (about 2 cups plus 2 tablespoons)
- 1 package dry yeast (about 2¼ teaspoons)
- 4 teaspoons olive oil
- ¾ teaspoon kosher salt, divided
- Cooking spray
- 1 tablespoon yellow cornmeal
- ¾ cup Pizza Sauce
- 1¼ cups (5 ounces) thinly sliced fresh mozzarella cheese
- ⅓ cup small fresh basil leaves

**1.** Pour 3/4 cup warm water in the bowl of a stand mixer with dough hook attached. Weigh or lightly spoon flour into dry measuring cups and spoons; level with a knife. Add flour to 3/4 cup water; mix until combined. Cover; let stand 20 minutes. Combine remaining 1/4 cup water and yeast in a small bowl; let stand 5 minutes or until bubbly. Add yeast mixture, oil, and 1/2 teaspoon salt to flour mixture; mix 5 minutes or until a soft dough forms. Place dough in a large bowl coated with cooking spray; cover surface of dough with plastic wrap lightly coated with cooking spray. Refrigerate 24 hours.
**2.** Remove dough from refrigerator. Let stand, covered, 1 hour or until dough comes to room temperature. Punch dough down. Press dough out to a 12-inch circle on a lightly floured baking sheet, without raised sides, sprinkled with cornmeal. Crimp edges to form a 1/2-inch border. Cover dough loosely with plastic wrap.
**3.** Position an oven rack in the lowest setting. Place a pizza stone on lowest rack. Preheat oven to 500°. Preheat pizza stone for 30 minutes before baking dough.
**4.** Remove plastic wrap from dough. Sprinkle dough with remaining 1/4 teaspoon salt. Spread Pizza Sauce evenly over dough, leaving a 1/2-inch border. Arrange cheese slices evenly over pizza. Slide pizza onto preheated pizza stone, using a spatula as a guide. Bake at 500° for 15 minutes or until crust is golden. Cut pizza into 10 wedges, and sprinkle evenly with basil. **YIELD:** 5 servings (serving size: 2 wedges).

CALORIES 421; FAT 10.9g (sat 4.7g, mono 4.7g, poly 1g); PROTEIN 16.9g; CARB 62.8g; FIBER 6.5g; CHOL 22mg; IRON 4.4mg; SODIUM 754mg; CALC 267mg

## Pizza Sauce

- 2 tablespoons extra-virgin olive oil
- 5 garlic cloves, minced
- 1 (28-ounce) can San Marzano tomatoes
- ½ teaspoon kosher salt
- ½ teaspoon dried oregano

**1.** Heat oil in a medium saucepan over medium heat. Add garlic to pan; cook 1 minute, stirring frequently. Remove tomatoes from can using a slotted spoon, reserving juices. Crush tomatoes. Stir tomatoes, juices, salt, and oregano into garlic mixture; bring to a boil. Reduce heat, and simmer 30 minutes, stirring occasionally. **YIELD:** 6 servings (serving size: about 1/3 cup).

CALORIES 66; FAT 4.7g (sat 0.7g, mono 3.3g, poly 0.6g); PROTEIN 1.2g; CARB 6.2g; FIBER 1.4g; CHOL 0mg; IRON 1.4mg; SODIUM 175mg; CALC 48mg

## Pepperoni Pizza

Cooking spray
2 cups thinly sliced cremini mushrooms (about 4 ounces)
Basic Pizza Dough
2 teaspoons olive oil
Basic Pizza Sauce (recipe on page 169)
1½ cups (6 ounces) shredded part-skim mozzarella cheese
2 tablespoons grated fresh Parmesan cheese
2 ounces sliced turkey pepperoni (such as Hormel)

**1.** Position one oven rack in the middle setting. Position another rack in the lowest setting, and place a rimless baking sheet on the bottom rack. Preheat oven to 500°.
**2.** Heat a large nonstick skillet over medium-high heat. Coat pan with cooking spray. Add sliced mushrooms to pan, and sauté 5 minutes or until moisture evaporates.
**3.** Remove plastic wrap from Basic Pizza Dough; discard. Brush oil over dough. Remove preheated baking sheet from oven; close oven door. Slide dough onto preheated baking sheet, using a spatula as a guide. Bake on lowest oven rack at 500° for 8 minutes. Remove from oven.
**4.** Spread Basic Pizza Sauce in an even layer over crust, leaving a ¼-inch border. Top sauce with mushrooms. Sprinkle mushrooms evenly with mozzarella and Parmesan. Arrange pepperoni on top of cheese. Bake on middle rack an additional 10 minutes or until crust is golden brown and cheese melts. Cut into 12 wedges.

**YIELD:** 6 servings (serving size: 2 wedges).

CALORIES 346; FAT 8.2g (sat 3.8g, mono 3g, poly 0.8g); PROTEIN 18.1g; CARB 49.5g; FIBER 3.6g; CHOL 29mg; IRON 4mg; SODIUM 692mg; CALC 249mg

## Basic Pizza Dough

2 teaspoons honey
1 package active dry yeast (about 2¼ teaspoons)
¾ cup warm water (100° to 110°)
10 ounces all-purpose flour (about 2¼ cups), divided
½ teaspoon salt
Cooking spray
2 tablespoons stone-ground yellow cornmeal

**1.** Dissolve honey and yeast in ¾ cup warm water in a large bowl. Let stand 5 minutes or until bubbly. Weigh or lightly spoon flour into dry measuring cups; level with a knife. Add 2 cups flour and salt to yeast mixture; stir until a soft dough forms. Turn dough out onto a lightly floured surface. Knead until smooth

and elastic (about 6 minutes); add enough of remaining flour, 1 tablespoon at a time, to prevent dough from sticking to hands (dough will feel slightly sticky).

**2.** Place dough in a large bowl coated with cooking spray, turning to coat top. Cover and let rise in a warm place (85°), free from drafts, 30 minutes or until doubled in size. (Gently press two fingers into dough. If indentation remains, dough has risen enough.)

**3.** Roll dough into a 12-inch circle (about 1/4 inch thick) on a lightly floured surface. Place dough on a rimless baking sheet sprinkled with cornmeal. Crimp edges of dough with fingers to form a rim. Lightly spray surface of dough with cooking spray, and cover with plastic wrap. Place dough in refrigerator up to 30 minutes. Bake according to recipe directions. **YIELD**: 1 (12-inch) crust.

CALORIES 1,155; FAT 3.4g (sat 0.6g, mono 0.5g, poly 1.3g); PROTEIN 33.8g; CARB 242.5g; FIBER 10.8g; CHOL 0mg; IRON 14.3mg; SODIUM 1,195mg; CALC 49mg

## Basic Pizza Sauce

Cooking spray
- ¼ cup finely chopped onion
- 1 garlic clove, minced
- ¼ cup white wine
- 2 tablespoons tomato paste
- 1 teaspoon dried oregano
- ⅛ teaspoon freshly ground black pepper
- 1 (14.5-ounce) can crushed tomatoes, undrained
- 1 tablespoon chopped fresh basil
- ½ teaspoon balsamic vinegar

**1.** Heat a large saucepan over medium-high heat. Coat pan with cooking spray. Add onion to pan; sauté 3 minutes or until tender. Add garlic to pan; sauté 30 seconds. Stir in wine; cook 30 seconds. Add tomato paste, oregano, pepper, and tomatoes. Reduce heat, and simmer 20 minutes or until thick. Remove from heat; stir in basil and vinegar. Cool. **YIELD**: 1 1/3 cups.

CALORIES 203; FAT 0.3g (sat 0.1g, mono 0.1g, poly 0.1g); PROTEIN 9.6g; CARB 42.2g; FIBER 10.1g; CHOL 0mg; IRON 7.3mg; SODIUM 953mg; CALC 201mg

## Chicken, Red Grape, and Pesto Pizza ▲

- 1 (11-ounce) can refrigerated thin-crust pizza dough

Cooking spray
- ⅓ cup refrigerated pesto
- 1½ cups seedless red grapes, halved
- 8 ounces shredded skinless, boneless rotisserie chicken breast
- 3 garlic cloves, thinly sliced
- 4 ounces fresh mozzarella cheese, thinly sliced
- 3 tablespoons grated Romano cheese
- ¼ teaspoon black pepper
- ¼ cup sliced green onions

**1.** Preheat oven to 425°.

**2.** On a lightly floured surface, pat dough into a 12-inch circle; place dough on a pizza pan coated with cooking spray. Spread pesto evenly over dough, leaving a 1/2-inch border around edges. Arrange grapes evenly over dough; top with chicken. Top with garlic and mozzarella; sprinkle with Romano and pepper. Bake at 425° for 20 minutes or until crust is golden brown. Sprinkle with onions. Cut into 12 wedges. **YIELD**: 6 servings (serving size: 2 wedges).

CALORIES 364; FAT 14.4g (sat 4.8g, mono 6.3g, poly 1.4g); PROTEIN 22.6g; CARB 34.6g; FIBER 1.7g; CHOL 55mg; IRON 2.5mg; SODIUM 562mg; CALC 191mg

# Herbed Cheese Pizza

Dough:

- 9.5 ounces bread flour (about 2 cups), divided
- 2 cups warm water (100° to 110°), divided
- 1 teaspoon sugar
- 2 packages dry yeast (about 4½ teaspoons)
- 14.6 ounces all-purpose flour (about 3¼ cups), divided
- 1 teaspoon salt
- 2 teaspoons olive oil
- Cooking spray

Topping:

- 2 teaspoons dried oregano
- 2 teaspoons ground cumin
- 1 teaspoon hot paprika
- ¾ teaspoon coarsely ground black pepper, divided
- 1 teaspoon olive oil
- 1 cup finely chopped onion
- ½ teaspoon salt
- 5 garlic cloves, minced
- 1 bay leaf
- 1 (28-ounce) can diced tomatoes
- 10 ounces sliced kasseri cheese
- 3 tablespoons minced fresh parsley

**1.** To prepare dough, weigh or lightly spoon bread flour into dry measuring cups; level with a knife. Combine 4.75 ounces (about 1 cup) bread flour, 1 cup warm water, sugar, and yeast in a bowl; let stand 15 minutes.

**2.** Weigh or lightly spoon all-purpose flour into dry measuring cups; level with a knife. Combine 13.5 ounces (about 3 cups) all-purpose flour, remaining 4.75 ounces (about 1 cup) bread flour, and 1 teaspoon salt in a large bowl; make a well in center. Add yeast mixture, remaining 1 cup warm water, and 2 teaspoons oil to flour mixture; stir well. Turn dough out onto a floured surface. Knead until smooth and elastic (about 10 minutes); add enough of remaining flour, 1 tablespoon at a time, to prevent dough from sticking to hands.

**3.** Place dough in a large bowl coated with cooking spray, turning to coat top. Cover and let rise in a warm place (85°), free from drafts, 45 minutes or until doubled in size. (Press two fingers into dough. If indentation remains, dough has risen enough.) Punch dough down; divide dough into 8 equal portions. Cover and let rest 20 minutes.

**4.** To prepare topping, combine oregano, cumin, paprika, and 1/2 teaspoon black pepper. Heat a large skillet over medium-high heat. Add olive oil to pan. Add onion; sauté 3 minutes. Add salt, remaining 1/4 teaspoon black pepper, garlic, bay leaf, and tomatoes; bring to a boil. Reduce heat, and simmer 15 minutes or until thick. Remove from heat; discard bay leaf.

**5.** Preheat oven to 450°.

**6.** Working with one dough portion at a time (cover remaining dough to keep from drying), roll each portion into a 6-inch circle on a lightly floured surface; place circle on a baking sheet coated with cooking spray. Repeat procedure with remaining dough portions. Top each crust with 1/4 cup tomato mixture, 1 1/4 ounces cheese, and 1/2 teaspoon oregano mixture. Bake at 450° for 12 minutes or until crusts are lightly browned. Sprinkle evenly with parsley.

**YIELD**: 8 servings (serving size: 1 pizza).

CALORIES 493; FAT 13.7g (sat 7.9g, mono 1.4g, poly 0.4g); PROTEIN 19.4g; CARB 73.9g; FIBER 5.1g; CHOL 38mg; IRON 5.2mg; SODIUM 917mg; CALC 296mg

# Easy Meatless Manicotti

- 2 cups (8 ounces) shredded part-skim mozzarella cheese, divided
- 1 (16-ounce) carton fat-free cottage cheese
- 1 (10-ounce) package frozen chopped spinach, thawed, drained, and squeezed dry
- ¼ cup (1 ounce) grated fresh Parmesan cheese
- 1½ teaspoons dried oregano
- ¼ teaspoon salt
- ¼ teaspoon black pepper
- 1 (8-ounce) package manicotti (14 shells)
- 1 (26-ounce) jar fat-free tomato-basil pasta sauce
- Cooking spray
- 1 cup water

**1.** Preheat oven to 375°.

**2.** Combine 1½ cups mozzarella, cottage cheese, and next 5 ingredients in a medium bowl. Spoon about 3 tablespoons cheese mixture into each uncooked manicotti. Pour half of tomato-basil pasta sauce into a 13 x 9–inch baking dish coated with cooking spray. Arrange stuffed shells in a single layer over sauce, and top with remaining sauce. Pour 1 cup water into dish. Sprinkle remaining ½ cup mozzarella evenly over sauce. Cover tightly with foil. Bake at 375° for 1 hour or until shells are tender. Let stand 10 minutes before serving. **YIELD:** 7 servings (serving size: 2 manicotti).

CALORIES 328; FAT 9g (sat 4.8g, mono 2.2g, poly 0.5g); PROTEIN 23.8g; CARB 38.3g; FIBER 3.9g; CHOL 23mg; IRON 3mg; SODIUM 891mg; CALC 451mg

# recipe makeover
## spinach fettuccine

**The Reader:** Kathy Gordon

**The Story:** The spinach, bacon, and Parmesan pasta recipe was a family favorite Kathy inherited about 15 years ago from her mom, Sharon, who clipped it from a newspaper. "My mom prepared it when we had company, and it was a big hit because it's so delicious," recalls Kathy. But she stopped making the dish about 10 years ago, when she and her husband, Mike, started eating more healthfully.

**The Dilemma:** "This recipe is easy and delicious but so full of fat," she says. The original butter-, cream-, and bacon-laden dish was as heavy on the palate as the waistline. A single serving contributed nearly a full day's worth of sodium, a whopping 27 grams of saturated fat, and more than half the suggested daily cholesterol intake.

**The Solution:** We modified several components yet still created a rich, creamy, and bacon-crisped result. The original sauce included one egg, 1 1/2 cups heavy cream, 1/2 cup butter, and 2 cups Parmesan cheese, which contributed a total of 34 grams of fat per serving.

Sodium was another concern with the original recipe. Almost half the dish's sodium and one-third of its fat came from a pound of bacon. We were able to keep about 1/2 pound by switching to leaner center-cut bacon, which shaved 194 calories, 15 grams of fat, and 823 milligrams of sodium per portion. To keep the lightened recipe's sodium level in check, we halved the amount of salt added to the final product and omitted salt from the pasta cooking water, shaving an additional 325 milligrams of sodium per serving. A few small but significant adjustments enhanced the taste of the lighter version. For example, a minced garlic clove and additional freshly ground black pepper boosted the flavor.

**The Feedback:** "I like the lighter version better," says Kathy. One big difference, she notes, is that "you can actually taste the spinach and bacon now," whereas before, the fat masked other flavors in the dish. And what did Mom—who clipped the recipe to begin with—think? "She approved of the lightened version," says Kathy, remarking that there were no leftovers.

| | BEFORE | AFTER |
|---|---|---|
| Calories per serving | 800 | 365 |
| Fat | 53.2g | 12.2g |
| Percent of total calories | 60% | 30% |

**You can use Asiago cheese** for a slightly sweeter flavor, or Parmigiano-Reggiano for a sharper flavor than the pecorino Romano.

# Spinach Fettuccine

- 1 pound uncooked fettuccine
- 1 tablespoon butter
- 1 garlic clove, minced
- ¼ cup (2 ounces) ⅓-less-fat cream cheese
- ¾ cup fat-free, lower-sodium chicken broth
- 3 tablespoons all-purpose flour
- ¾ cup (3 ounces) grated fresh pecorino Romano cheese
- ¾ cup half-and-half
- 1 teaspoon salt
- ½ teaspoon freshly ground black pepper
- 1 (10-ounce) package frozen chopped spinach, thawed, drained, and squeezed dry
- 10 center-cut bacon slices, cooked and crumbled (about 1¼ cups)
- Parsley sprigs (optional)

**1.** Cook pasta according to package instructions, omitting salt and fat. Drain pasta, reserving ½ cup pasta water.
**2.** Melt butter in a large nonstick skillet over medium-high heat. Add garlic; sauté 30 seconds. Add reserved pasta water and cream cheese, stirring with a whisk until smooth.
**3.** Combine broth and flour in a small bowl, stirring with a whisk until smooth. Add flour mixture to pan, stirring with a whisk to combine; bring to a boil. Cook 2 minutes or until mixture thickens, stirring constantly. Remove from heat; add pecorino Romano, stirring until smooth. Add half-and-half, salt, and pepper. Stir in spinach. Combine cheese mixture and pasta in a large bowl, tossing to coat. Place about 1 cup pasta mixture in each of 8 bowls; top each serving with 2½ tablespoons bacon. Garnish with parsley, if desired. **YIELD:** 8 servings.

CALORIES 365; FAT 12.2g (sat 6.3g, mono 3.3g, poly 0.6g); PROTEIN 15.9g; CARB 46.6g; FIBER 2.3g; CHOL 34mg; IRON 1.8mg; SODIUM 681mg; CALC 188mg

# 5 ways with mac and cheese

## Bacon, Ranch, and Chicken Mac and Cheese

- 8 ounces uncooked elbow macaroni
- 1 applewood-smoked bacon slice
- 8 ounces skinless, boneless chicken breast, cut into ½-inch pieces
- 1 tablespoon butter
- 1 tablespoon all-purpose flour
- 1½ cups fat-free milk
- ⅓ cup condensed 45% reduced-sodium 98% fat-free cream of mushroom soup, undiluted
- ¾ cup (3 ounces) shredded six-cheese Italian blend (such as Sargento)
- ½ teaspoon onion powder
- ½ teaspoon garlic powder
- ½ teaspoon chopped fresh dill
- ½ teaspoon salt
- Cooking spray
- ½ cup (2 ounces) shredded colby-Jack cheese

**1.** Cook pasta according to package directions, omitting salt and fat; drain.

**2.** Cook bacon in a large nonstick skillet over medium heat until crisp. Remove bacon from pan, reserving drippings in pan. Finely chop bacon; set aside. Increase heat to medium-high. Add chicken to drippings in pan; sauté 6 minutes or until done.

**3.** Melt butter in a large saucepan over medium heat; sprinkle flour evenly into pan. Cook 2 minutes, stirring constantly with a whisk. Combine milk and soup, stirring with a whisk; gradually add milk mixture to saucepan, stirring with a whisk. Bring to a boil; cook 2 minutes or until thick. Remove from heat; let stand 4 minutes or until sauce cools to 155°. Add Italian cheese blend, onion powder, garlic powder, dill, and salt, stirring until cheese melts. Stir in pasta and chicken.

**4.** Preheat broiler. Spoon mixture into an 8-inch square baking dish coated with cooking spray. Sprinkle evenly with reserved bacon and colby-Jack cheese. Broil 3 minutes or until cheese melts. **YIELD:** 4 servings (serving size: about 2 cups).

CALORIES 497; FAT 17g (sat 9.2g, mono 4.7g, poly 1.4g); PROTEIN 33.3g; CARB 51.7g; FIBER 2g; CHOL 74mg; IRON 2.4mg; SODIUM 767mg; CALC 368mg

## Macaroni and Cheese with Roasted Tomatoes ▼

- 3 cups halved cherry tomatoes
- Cooking spray
- ¼ teaspoon black pepper
- 3 ounces sourdough bread, torn into pieces
- 1 teaspoon butter, melted
- 12 ounces uncooked large elbow macaroni
- 2 cups (8 ounces) shredded extrasharp cheddar cheese
- ¼ cup egg substitute
- 1½ teaspoons kosher salt
- ¼ teaspoon ground red pepper
- 1 (12-ounce) can evaporated low-fat milk

**1.** Preheat oven to 375°.
**2.** Place tomatoes in a 13 x 9-inch baking dish coated with cooking spray. Sprinkle with black pepper. Bake at 375° for 30 minutes or until browned, stirring occasionally.
**3.** While tomatoes cook, place bread in a food processor; pulse 2 times or until crumbly. Toss crumbs with melted butter. Sprinkle the crumbs on a baking sheet, and bake at 375° for 12 minutes or until golden, stirring frequently.
**4.** Cook macaroni in boiling water 7 minutes; drain. Return macaroni to pan; place over medium-low heat. Add cheese and remaining ingredients; cook 4 minutes or until cheese melts, stirring constantly. Stir in tomatoes. Sprinkle each serving with about 3 tablespoons breadcrumbs. **YIELD:** 8 servings (serving size: 1 cup).

CALORIES 357; FAT 11.4g (sat 6.6g, mono 3.1g, poly 0.8g); PROTEIN 18.1g; CARB 45.2g; FIBER 2g; CHOL 33mg; IRON 2.7mg; SODIUM 669mg; CALC 350mg

## Sausage Mac and Cheese ▲

- 4 ounces chicken and sun-dried tomato sausage (such as Gerhard's), chopped
- 1¼ cups fat-free milk
- 2 tablespoons all-purpose flour
- ¾ cup (3 ounces) shredded reduced-fat sharp cheddar cheese
- ⅓ cup (about 1⅓ ounces) shredded Monterey Jack cheese
- ¼ cup (2 ounces) ⅓-less-fat cream cheese
- ½ teaspoon onion powder
- ¼ teaspoon garlic salt
- 5 cups hot cooked elbow macaroni (about 8 ounces uncooked pasta)
- Chopped fresh parsley (optional)

**1.** Heat a large nonstick saucepan over medium-high heat. Add sausage; sauté 4 minutes or until browned. Combine milk and flour in a small bowl, stirring well with a whisk. Add milk mixture to pan; bring to a boil, stirring constantly. Reduce heat to medium. Stir in cheeses, onion powder, and garlic salt; cook 3 minutes or until cheeses melt, stirring constantly. Stir in pasta. Garnish with parsley, if desired. Serve immediately. **YIELD:** 4 servings (serving size: about 1¼ cups).

CALORIES 433; FAT 13.9g (sat 7.8g, mono 3.8g, poly 0.9g); PROTEIN 23.6g; CARB 53.1g; FIBER 2.7g; CHOL 56mg; IRON 2.4mg; SODIUM 538mg; CALC 340mg

## Chipotle Macaroni and Cheese

This macaroni and cheese is a favorite of ours because it is incredibly tasty and easy to prepare. You don't even have to make a white sauce for this creamy dish. The acidic tomatoes counter the richness of the cheeses.

- 1 (7-ounce) can chipotle chiles in adobo sauce
- 1 tablespoon butter
- ½ cup finely chopped onion
- ½ cup finely chopped green bell pepper
- 1 garlic clove, minced
- 2 tablespoons all-purpose flour
- 1 (14½-ounce) can diced tomatoes and green chiles, undrained
- 4 cups hot cooked elbow macaroni (about 2 cups uncooked)
- 2 cups (8 ounces) shredded reduced-fat sharp cheddar cheese
- 1 cup 1% low-fat cottage cheese
- 1 cup 2% reduced-fat milk
- ¼ cup (1 ounce) grated fresh Parmesan cheese
- 1 large egg, lightly beaten
- Cooking spray
- 3 tablespoons dry breadcrumbs

**1.** Preheat oven to 350°.

**2.** Remove 1 teaspoon adobo sauce from can; set aside. Remove 2 chipotle chiles from can; finely chop to measure 1 tablespoon. Reserve remaining chiles and adobo sauce for another use.

**3.** Melt butter in a Dutch oven over medium-high heat. Add chopped chiles, onion, bell pepper, and garlic; cook 4 minutes or until onion is tender, stirring frequently. Sprinkle with flour; cook 30 seconds, stirring constantly. Reduce heat to medium; add tomatoes. Cook 3 minutes or until thickened. Add reserved 1 teaspoon adobo sauce, pasta, cheddar cheese, cottage cheese, milk, Parmesan, and egg; stir to combine. Spoon pasta mixture into a 2-quart baking dish coated with cooking spray; top with breadcrumbs. Bake at 350° for 30 minutes or until bubbly. **YIELD:** 6 servings (serving size: about 1 cup).

CALORIES 324; FAT 8.5g (sat 4.6g, mono 2.4g, poly 0.6g); PROTEIN 34.2g; CARB 39.6g; FIBER 2g; CHOL 56mg; IRON 2.4mg; SODIUM 756mg; CALC 307mg

# Three-Cheese Macaroni and Cheese

Try this rich and creamy three-cheese macaroni and cheese for the ultimate feel-good meal. "If I go more than a day or two without pasta, watch out, because I get nasty," jokes one cookinglight.com user. Other users admit hankering for high-quality cheese. Keep a close eye on the flour while it cooks so it doesn't burn.

- **1 teaspoon olive oil**
- **1 cup finely chopped onion (about 1 medium)**
- **2 tablespoons all-purpose flour**
- **1 garlic clove, minced**
- **1½ cups 1% low-fat milk**
- **1 bay leaf**
- **½ cup (2 ounces) crumbled Gorgonzola cheese**
- **¾ cup (3 ounces) grated Parmigiano-Reggiano cheese, divided**
- **¼ teaspoon salt**
- **2 cups uncooked elbow macaroni (about 8 ounces)**
- **Cooking spray**
- **⅔ cup (about 2½ ounces) shredded part-skim mozzarella cheese**
- **⅔ cup panko (Japanese breadcrumbs)**
- **⅛ teaspoon freshly ground black pepper**

**1.** Heat oil in a medium saucepan over medium heat. Add onion to pan; cook 8 minutes or until tender, stirring occasionally. Add flour and garlic; cook 1 minute, stirring constantly. Stir in milk and bay leaf; bring to a boil. Cook 2 minutes or until thick, stirring constantly with a whisk. Add Gorgonzola, 1/2 cup Parmigiano-Reggiano, and salt; stir until cheeses melt. Discard bay leaf.

**2.** Preheat oven to 375°.

**3.** Cook pasta in boiling water 5 minutes or until almost tender, omitting salt and fat; drain well. Add pasta to cheese mixture, stirring well. Place about 1/2 cup pasta mixture into each of 6 (1-cup) ramekins coated with cooking spray. Sprinkle evenly with mozzarella. Top evenly with remaining pasta mixture. Combine remaining 1/4 cup Parmigiano-Reggiano and panko; sprinkle evenly over pasta mixture. Spray lightly with cooking spray; sprinkle with black pepper. Bake at 375° for 25 minutes or until heated. **YIELD:** 6 servings (serving size: about 1 ramekin).

CALORIES 321; FAT 9.9g (sat 5.6g, mono 2.3g, poly 0.9g); PROTEIN 17.4g; CARB 40.8g; FIBER 2.4g; CHOL 26mg; IRON 1.5mg; SODIUM 487mg; CALC 332mg

30
minutes
or
less

"Very tasty. Reminds me of my dad's fried catfish, but much less mess and fat! We enjoyed it with creamy coleslaw, which was the first coleslaw I've made in years. I chose to serve both with plain roasted green beans. Awesome nostalgia. Definitely to be repeated!"

**from cookinglight.com**

# Cornmeal-Crusted Catfish

- 3 bacon slices
- ⅓ cup yellow cornmeal
- 2 teaspoons salt-free Cajun seasoning
- ½ teaspoon salt
- 4 (6-ounce) catfish fillets

**1.** Cook bacon in a large nonstick skillet over medium heat until crisp. Remove bacon from pan; reserve 2 teaspoons drippings in pan. Crumble bacon; reserve for another use.
**2.** Combine cornmeal, seasoning, and salt in a shallow dish. Dredge fillets in cornmeal mixture, shaking off excess.
**3.** Heat reserved drippings in pan over medium-high heat. Add fillets; cook 5 minutes on each side or until fish flakes easily when tested with a fork or until desired degree of doneness.
**YIELD**: 4 servings (serving size: 1 fillet).

CALORIES 277; FAT 13.7g (sat 3.4g, mono 6.9g, poly 2.3g); PROTEIN 27.5g; CARB 8.9g; FIBER 0.9g; CHOL 93mg; IRON 1.6mg; SODIUM 412mg; CALC 13mg

## what makes it light

- uses salt-free Cajun seasoning
- pan-seared, not deep-fried
- uses minimal amount of bacon drippings

> My fish was crisp on the outside and flaky in the middle. My husband is a fried catfish fiend, and he loved this. **Next time I will make more hush puppies, because we were fighting over them they were so good.**
>
> **from cookinglight.com**

# Fried Catfish with Hush Puppies and Tartar Sauce

Tartar Sauce:

- ¼ cup organic canola mayonnaise (such as Spectrum)
- 1 tablespoon dill pickle relish
- 1 tablespoon chopped fresh flat-leaf parsley
- 1 teaspoon prepared horseradish
- ¾ teaspoon fresh lemon juice
- ⅛ teaspoon salt

Catfish:

- 8 cups peanut oil
- 6 (6-ounce) catfish fillets
- ½ teaspoon salt
- 9 ounces all-purpose flour (about 2 cups), divided
- 1¼ cups cornmeal
- 1 teaspoon freshly ground black pepper
- 2 cups buttermilk
- 2 large eggs, lightly beaten

Hush Puppies:

- 3.4 ounces all-purpose flour (about ¾ cup)
- ⅓ cup cornmeal
- ⅓ cup buttermilk
- 3 tablespoons grated onion
- 1 teaspoon baking powder
- ¼ teaspoon salt
- ¼ teaspoon ground red pepper
- 1 large egg, lightly beaten

**1.** To prepare tartar sauce, combine first 6 ingredients. Cover and chill.
**2.** To prepare catfish, clip a candy/fry thermometer to a Dutch oven; add oil to pan. Heat oil to 385°.
**3.** Sprinkle fillets evenly with ½ teaspoon salt. Place 4.5 ounces (1 cup) flour in a shallow dish. Combine remaining 4.5 ounces (1 cup) flour, cornmeal, and black pepper in a shallow dish. Combine 2 cups buttermilk and 2 eggs in a shallow dish. Dredge fillets in flour; dip in buttermilk mixture. Dredge in cornmeal mixture; shake off excess breading. Place 2 fillets in hot oil; cook 5 minutes or until done, turning occasionally. Make sure oil temperature does not drop below 375°. Remove fillets from pan using a slotted spoon; drain on paper towels. Return oil temperature to 385°. Repeat procedure twice with remaining fillets.
**4.** To prepare hush puppies, weigh or lightly spoon 3.4 ounces (¾ cup) flour into a dry measuring cups; level with a knife. Combine 3.4 ounces flour and remaining ingredients. Drop batter 1 tablespoonful at a time into pan; fry at 375° for 5 minutes or until browned, turning frequently. Remove hush puppies from pan using a slotted spoon; drain on paper towels. **YIELD**: 6 servings (serving size: 1 fillet, 2 hush puppies, and 4 teaspoons tartar sauce).

CALORIES 507; FAT 23.8g (sat 4.1g, mono 8.4g, poly 9.4g); PROTEIN 29.4g; CARB 43g; FIBER 2.6g; CHOL 153mg; IRON 3.6mg; SODIUM 846mg; CALC 171mg

I grew up eating tuna noodle casserole and had to beg my husband to try it when I made this recipe. He was hooked after one bite. **I stuck to the recipe, and it came out delicious.** Overall, a keeper for a weeknight dinner.

**from cookinglight.com**

# Tuna Noodle Casserole

- 8 ounces uncooked wide egg noodles
- 2 tablespoons olive oil
- ½ cup chopped yellow onion
- ⅓ cup chopped carrot
- 2 tablespoons all-purpose flour
- 2¾ cups fat-free milk
- ½ cup (4 ounces) ⅓-less-fat cream cheese, softened
- 2 tablespoons Dijon mustard
- ½ teaspoon salt
- ½ teaspoon freshly ground black pepper
- 1 cup frozen peas, thawed
- ½ cup (2 ounces) grated Parmigiano-Reggiano cheese, divided
- 2 (5-ounce) cans albacore tuna in water, drained and flaked
- Cooking spray

**1.** Preheat broiler.

**2.** Cook noodles according to package directions, omitting salt and fat. Drain. Heat a large skillet over medium heat. Add oil to pan; swirl to coat. Add onion and carrot; cook 6 minutes or until carrot is almost tender, stirring occasionally. Sprinkle with flour; cook 1 minute, stirring constantly. Gradually stir in milk; cook 5 minutes, stirring constantly with a whisk until slightly thick. Stir in cream cheese, mustard, salt, and pepper; cook 2 minutes, stirring constantly.

**3.** Remove pan from heat. Stir in noodles, peas, 1/4 cup Parmigiano-Reggiano cheese, and tuna. Spoon mixture into a shallow broiler-safe 2-quart baking dish coated with cooking spray; top with remaining 1/4 cup Parmigiano-Reggiano cheese. Broil 3 minutes or until golden and bubbly. Let stand 5 minutes before serving. **YIELD**: 6 servings (serving size: 1 1/3 cups).

CALORIES 422; FAT 16.5g (sat 7.1g, mono 6.3g, poly 1.8g); PROTEIN 27.4g; CARB 40.6g; FIBER 3g; CHOL 88mg; IRON 2.4mg; SODIUM 756mg; CALC 293mg

## what makes it light

- uses fat-free milk
- uses ⅓-less-fat cream cheese
- uses only a small amount of Parmigiano-Reggiano cheese, which is a more flavorful option than regular Parmesan or cheddar cheese that's used in traditional recipes

I have made this several times—as little appetizers and as a full entrée. **Everyone—I mean everyone—I make this for says they're the best crab cakes they have ever eaten.** If you want to win over the crowd, this recipe is a slam dunk.

**from cookinglight.com**

# Louisiana Crab Cakes with Creole Tartar Sauce

Tartar Sauce:

- ½ cup reduced-fat mayonnaise
- 3 tablespoons sweet pickle relish
- 2 tablespoons capers, drained and rinsed
- 1 teaspoon Creole mustard
- ¼ teaspoon salt-free Cajun-Creole seasoning (such as The Spice Hunter)
- ¼ teaspoon hot pepper sauce (such as Tabasco)

Crab Cakes:

- 4 (1-ounce) slices white bread
- ¼ cup finely chopped onion
- ¼ cup finely chopped red bell pepper
- 1 tablespoon chopped fresh parsley
- 1 tablespoon fresh lemon juice
- 1 tablespoon hot pepper sauce (such as Tabasco)
- ¼ teaspoon freshly ground black pepper
- 1 pound lump crabmeat, shell pieces removed
- 1 large egg, lightly beaten
- 1 large egg white, lightly beaten
- 4 teaspoons vegetable oil, divided
- Parsley sprigs (optional)
- Lemon wedges (optional)

**1.** To prepare tartar sauce, combine first 6 ingredients, stirring with a whisk. Let stand 10 minutes.
**2.** To prepare crab cakes, place bread in a food processor; pulse 10 times or until coarse crumbs measure 2 cups. Combine 1 cup breadcrumbs, onion, and next 8 ingredients; mix well. Divide crab mixture into 8 equal portions. Form each portion into a ½-inch-thick patty. Place 1 cup breadcrumbs in a shallow dish. Dredge patties, one at a time, in breadcrumbs.
**3.** Heat 2 teaspoons oil in a large nonstick skillet over medium-high heat. Add 4 patties; cook 3 minutes on each side or until golden brown. Repeat procedure with remaining oil and patties. Serve with tartar sauce. Garnish with parsley sprigs and lemon wedges, if desired. **YIELD**: 4 servings (serving size: 2 crab cakes and 2 tablespoons tartar sauce).

CALORIES 331; FAT 11g (sat 1.8g, mono 2.6g, poly 5.3g); PROTEIN 28.2g; CARB 29.1g; FIBER 1.4g; CHOL 167mg; IRON 2.5mg; SODIUM 992mg; CALC 163mg

## what makes it light

- uses reduced-fat mayonnaise
- uses salt-free Cajun-Creole seasoning
- uses minimal amount of oil to sauté crab cakes

30
minutes
or
less

**One (8-ounce) container select oysters**, undrained, can be substituted for crawfish, if desired.

# Gulf of Mexico Gumbo

- 4.5 ounces all-purpose flour (about 1 cup)
- 1 teaspoon canola oil
- 2 cups chopped onion
- 1 cup chopped green bell pepper
- ½ cup chopped celery
- 4 garlic cloves, minced
- 1 cup sliced okra
- 1 cup chopped tomato
- 1½ cups water
- 1 teaspoon Cajun-Creole Seasoning
- 4 (8-ounce) bottles clam juice
- 2 bay leaves
- ½ pound skinned red snapper or other firm white fish fillet, cut into 1-inch pieces
- ¼ cup thinly sliced green onions
- ¾ pound crawfish, peeled
- ¼ pound medium shrimp, peeled and deveined
- ½ teaspoon hot sauce
- 4½ cups hot cooked long-grain rice

**1.** Place flour in a 9-inch cast-iron skillet; cook over medium heat 20 minutes or until browned, stirring constantly with a whisk. (If flour browns too fast, remove it from heat, and stir until it cools down.) Remove from heat; set aside.
**2.** Heat oil in a large Dutch oven over medium heat. Add onion, bell pepper, celery, and garlic; sauté 8 minutes or until vegetables are tender. Add okra and tomato; cover and cook 5 minutes, stirring occasionally. Add 1½ cups water, Cajun-Creole Seasoning, clam juice, and bay leaves, and bring to a boil. Gradually add browned flour, stirring with a whisk. Reduce heat; simmer, uncovered, 45 minutes, stirring occasionally.
**3.** Add snapper; cook 5 minutes. Add green onions, crawfish, and shrimp; cook 10 minutes or until seafood is done. Stir in hot sauce; discard bay leaves. Serve gumbo over rice. **YIELD:** 9 servings (serving size: 1 cup gumbo and ½ cup rice).

CALORIES 254; FAT 1.8g (sat 0.3g, mono 0.3g, poly 0.7g); PROTEIN 16.8g; CARB 41.8g; FIBER 2.4g; CHOL 59mg; IRON 3.1mg; SODIUM 447mg; CALC 73mg

## Cajun-Creole Seasoning

- 1 tablespoon salt
- ¾ teaspoon ground red pepper
- ½ teaspoon garlic powder
- ½ teaspoon black pepper

**1.** Combine all ingredients in a bowl; stir well. **YIELD:** about 1½ tablespoons.

CALORIES 0; FAT 0g (sat 0g, mono 0g, poly 0g); PROTEIN 0g; CARB 0g; FIBER 0g; CHOL 0mg; IRON 0mg; SODIUM 97mg; CALC 0mg

what makes it light
• uses a minimal amount of oil compared to traditional recipes
• doesn't use oil to brown the flour like a traditional roux

# recipe makeover
## shrimp étouffée

**The Reader:** Katharine O'Hara McIntyre

**The Story:** Katharine began dating her Louisiana-native husband, Charles Aaron, while attending law school in New Orleans. He introduced her to "some wonderful foods," including shrimp étouffée, a spicy Cajun classic made with a rich, nutty roux. After much trial and error, Katharine perfected a recipe for the dish that easily adjusts to accommodate a dinner for two or a hungry crowd of 10. Unfortunately, the expansion of her culinary repertoire with such indulgent dishes, combined with the stresses of a recent move to Maryland and intense study for the bar exam, began to stretch the couple's waistlines, as well. They have since adopted more healthful cooking habits, but Katharine would like to treat Charles to his beloved Louisiana fare on a more regular basis.

**The Dilemma:** *Étouffée* is the French word for "smothered," and this dish swims in two sticks of butter and sodium-laden ingredients. With 32 grams total fat and 1,200 milligrams of sodium per serving, the original contains nearly half the recommended daily intakes of both.

**The Solution:** We trimmed the ¾ cup butter originally used in the roux to ¼ cup, shaving 134 calories, 15 grams of total fat, and 12 grams of saturated fat per serving. Since we used less butter, we also cut down on the flour so the roux achieved an appropriately thick, nutty consistency that contributes to a pleasing, silky étouffée. To further reduce fat, we sautéed what Louisianans call "the trinity of aromatics" (bell pepper, onion, and celery) in just one tablespoon of butter to stretch the rich flavor and add body to the finished dish. This change trimmed another five grams of fat (three grams of it saturated) and another 50 calories per portion.

**The Feedback:** Katharine is pleased with our improvements. In fact, except for the addition of the red bell pepper, the couple **"couldn't tell the difference between the regular and the lightened version,"** says Katharine. They're delighted to re-introduce this much-loved taste of home to their dinner table.

| | BEFORE | AFTER |
|---|---|---|
| Calories per serving | 623 | 395 |
| Fat | 32.5g | 12.2g |
| Percent of total calories | 47% | 28% |

"I am from New Orleans and must say this recipe is just fantastic! **It preserves the authentic flavor of an étouffée using a roux, spices, and seasoning, while eliminating the fat.** I may cut back on amount of tomato paste next time to see if the sauce is a little darker, but otherwise bravo **Cooking Light**!!"

**from cookinglight.com**

# Shrimp Étouffée

- 4 cups fat-free, less-sodium chicken broth
- 1 teaspoon dried thyme
- 1 teaspoon dried basil
- 1 bay leaf
- 1/3 cup butter, divided
- 1/2 cup all-purpose flour (about 2 1/4 ounces)
- Cooking spray
- 1 1/2 cups chopped onion
- 2/3 cup diced celery
- 1/2 cup chopped red bell pepper
- 1/2 cup chopped green bell pepper
- 3/4 cup water
- 1/4 cup tomato paste
- 1 tablespoon salt-free Cajun seasoning
- 1 1/2 teaspoons minced garlic
- 1/4 teaspoon salt
- 1/4 teaspoon black pepper
- 1/4 teaspoon ground red pepper
- 1 teaspoon Worcestershire sauce
- 1/2 cup chopped green onions
- 1/2 cup chopped fresh flat-leaf parsley, divided
- 1 pound medium shrimp, peeled and deveined (about 30 shrimp)
- 4 cups hot cooked long-grain rice

**1.** Combine first 4 ingredients in a small saucepan over medium heat; bring to a simmer. Cover and remove from heat.

**2.** Melt 1/4 cup butter in a medium saucepan over medium heat. Lightly spoon flour into a dry measuring cup; level with a knife. Add flour to pan; cook 8 minutes or until very brown, stirring constantly with a whisk. Remove from heat. Add 1 cup broth mixture to pan; stir with a whisk until smooth. Add remaining 3 cups broth mixture, stirring with a whisk until smooth; set aside.

**3.** Melt remaining 1 tablespoon plus 1 teaspoon butter in a large Dutch oven coated with cooking spray over medium-high heat. Add 1 1/2 cups onion, celery, and bell peppers to pan; cook 10 minutes or until vegetables are tender and onion is golden brown, stirring occasionally. Stir in 3/4 cup water, scraping pan to loosen browned bits. Add tomato paste, Cajun seasoning, garlic, salt, black pepper, and red pepper to onion mixture; cook 1 minute, stirring constantly. Add reserved broth-flour mixture and Worcestershire sauce to pan, stirring well to combine; bring to a simmer. Cook 10 minutes, stirring occasionally. Add green onions, 1/4 cup parsley, and shrimp; cook 3 minutes or until shrimp are done. Discard bay leaf. Serve over rice. Sprinkle each serving with 2 teaspoons remaining parsley, if desired. **YIELD:** 6 servings (serving size: about 1 1/4 cups étouffée and 2/3 cup rice).

CALORIES 395; FAT 12.2g (sat 6.9g, mono 3g, poly 1.1g); PROTEIN 22.6g; CARB 47.9g; FIBER 3.6g; CHOL 142mg; IRON 4.9mg; SODIUM 655mg; CALC 102mg

**Using both andouille sausage and juicy pink shrimp,** jambalaya is like a spicy surf-and-turf. To save time, buy frozen peeled shrimp and thaw in the refrigerator or under cold, running water.

# Jambalaya with Shrimp and Andouille Sausage

- 1 tablespoon olive oil
- 1 cup chopped onion
- 1 cup chopped red bell pepper
- 1 tablespoon minced garlic
- 6 ounces andouille sausage, sliced
- 1 cup uncooked long-grain white rice
- 1 teaspoon paprika
- 1 teaspoon freshly ground black pepper
- 1 teaspoon dried oregano
- ½ teaspoon onion powder
- ½ teaspoon dried thyme
- ¼ teaspoon garlic salt
- 1 bay leaf
- 2 cups fat-free, lower-sodium chicken broth
- ¾ cup water
- 1 tablespoon tomato paste
- ½ teaspoon hot pepper sauce
- 1 (14.5-ounce) can no-salt-added diced tomatoes, undrained
- ½ pound peeled and deveined medium shrimp
- 2 tablespoons chopped fresh parsley

**1.** Heat olive oil in a large Dutch oven over medium-high heat. Add chopped onion, chopped bell pepper, minced garlic, and sausage; sauté 5 minutes or until vegetables are tender.
**2.** Add rice and next 7 ingredients; cook 2 minutes. Add broth, water, tomato paste, hot pepper sauce, and diced tomatoes; bring to a boil. Cover, reduce heat, and simmer 20 minutes. Add shrimp; cook 5 minutes. Let stand 5 minutes. Discard bay leaf. Stir in parsley. **YIELD:** 4 servings (serving size: 1½ cups).

CALORIES 426; FAT 12.7g (sat 3.9g, mono 2.8g, poly 1g); PROTEIN 25g; CARB 52.7g; FIBER 4.9g; CHOL 117mg; IRON 5.1mg; SODIUM 763mg; CALC 99mg

## what makes it light

- uses a smaller amount of andouille sausage than traditional recipes

# 5 ways with meat loaf

1

## Italian Meat Loaf with Fresh Basil and Provolone

In addition to providing the lift in cakes, egg whites act as a binder for dishes such as crab cakes, salmon patties, and meat loaf. Serve this dish with your favorite mashed potato recipe.

- 1 cup boiling water
- ½ cup sun-dried tomatoes, packed without oil
- ½ cup ketchup
- 1 cup seasoned breadcrumbs
- ¾ cup finely chopped onion
- ¾ cup chopped fresh basil
- ½ cup (2 ounces) shredded sharp provolone cheese
- 2 large egg whites
- 2 garlic cloves, minced
- 1 pound ground round
- Cooking spray
- ⅓ cup ketchup

**1.** Combine boiling water and tomatoes in a bowl; let stand 30 minutes or until soft. Drain tomatoes; finely chop.

**2.** Preheat oven to 350°.

**3.** Combine ½ cup ketchup, breadcrumbs, and next 6 ingredients in a large bowl. Add tomatoes to meat mixture. Shape meat mixture into a 9 x 5–inch loaf on a broiler pan coated with cooking spray. Spread ⅓ cup ketchup over meat loaf. Bake at 350° for 1 hour or until a thermometer registers 160°. Let stand 10 minutes before slicing. Cut into 12 slices. **YIELD:** 6 servings (serving size: 2 slices).

CALORIES 294; FAT 8.7g (sat 3.6g, mono 3.2g, poly 0.7g); PROTEIN 24.3g; CARB 30.8g; FIBER 2.5g; CHOL 53mg; IRON 3.9mg; SODIUM 893mg; CALC 149mg

## Classic Meat Loaf

Combining three types of ground meat lends more depth to the overall flavor of this meat loaf recipe. Serve with roasted carrots and onions.

- 1 (1½-ounce) slice white bread
- 2 tablespoons fat-free milk
- ½ cup ketchup, divided
- ⅔ pound ground beef, extra lean (raw)
- ½ pound lean ground veal
- 6 ounces lean ground pork
- ½ cup chopped onion
- ⅓ cup chopped fresh parsley
- 1 tablespoon Dijon mustard
- 1 teaspoon dried basil
- ¾ teaspoon salt
- ¼ teaspoon black pepper
- 2 large egg whites
- Cooking spray

**1.** Preheat oven to 350°.
**2.** Place bread in a food processor; pulse 10 times or until coarse breadcrumbs measure 1½ cups.
**3.** Combine breadcrumbs and milk in a large bowl; let stand 5 minutes. Add 2 tablespoons ketchup and remaining ingredients except cooking spray.
**4.** Shape meat mixture into a 9 x 5–inch loaf on a broiler pan coated with cooking spray. Spread remaining 6 tablespoons ketchup over top of meat loaf. Bake at 350° for 1 hour or until a thermometer registers 160°. Let stand 10 minutes. Cut loaf into 12 slices. **YIELD:** 6 servings (serving size: 2 slices).

CALORIES 231; FAT 7.9g (sat 3.1g, mono 3.2g, poly 0.8g); PROTEIN 26.7g; CARB 13.2g; FIBER 0.9g; CHOL 79mg; IRON 2.3mg; SODIUM 764mg; CALC 49mg

## Barbecue Meat Loaf ▼

This easy meat loaf recipe gets its great flavor from barbecue sauce.

- 1½ pounds ground beef, extra lean (raw)
- ½ cup dry breadcrumbs
- ½ cup chopped onion
- ⅓ cup barbecue sauce, divided
- 1 tablespoon prepared mustard
- 1½ teaspoons chili powder
- 1 teaspoon garlic powder
- ½ teaspoon salt
- ½ teaspoon freshly ground black pepper
- 2 large egg whites
- Cooking spray

**1.** Preheat oven to 350°.
**2.** Combine beef, breadcrumbs, onion, 1 tablespoon barbecue sauce, and remaining ingredients except cooking spray in a large bowl.
**3.** Shape meat mixture into a 9 x 5–inch loaf on a broiler pan coated with cooking spray. Spread remaining barbecue sauce over top of meat loaf. Bake at 350° for 1 hour or until a thermometer registers 160°. Let stand 10 minutes. Cut loaf into 12 slices. **YIELD:** 6 servings (serving size: 2 slices).

CALORIES 203; FAT 5.4g (sat 2.2g, mono 2.2g, poly 0.5g); PROTEIN 27.3g; CARB 10.5g; FIBER 1.1g; CHOL 61mg; IRON 3.2mg; SODIUM 517mg; CALC 26mg

## Mini Meat Loaves ▼

- ½ cup ketchup
- 1½ tablespoons Dijon mustard
- 1 pound ground sirloin
- ¾ cup finely chopped onion
- ¼ cup seasoned breadcrumbs
- ½ teaspoon salt
- ½ teaspoon dried oregano
- ⅛ teaspoon black pepper
- 1 large egg, lightly beaten
- Cooking spray

**1.** Preheat oven to 400°.
**2.** Combine ketchup and mustard, stirring well with a whisk. Reserve 2½ tablespoons ketchup mixture. Combine remaining ketchup mixture, beef, and next 6 ingredients in a large bowl, stirring to combine.
**3.** Divide beef mixture into 4 equal portions. Shape each portion into a 4 x 2½–inch loaf; place loaves on a jelly-roll pan coated with cooking spray.
**4.** Spread about 2 teaspoons reserved ketchup mixture evenly over each loaf. Bake at 400° for 25 minutes or until done. **YIELD:** 4 servings (serving size: 1 mini loaf).

CALORIES 255; FAT 7.9g (sat 2.8g, mono 3.2g, poly 0.4g); PROTEIN 27.4g; CARB 15.7g; FIBER 0.9g; CHOL 120mg; IRON 2.7mg; SODIUM 944mg; CALC 31mg

## Diner Meat Loaf Muffins

This delicious mini meat loaf muffin recipe allows you to sit down to a meat loaf in a half hour. Serve with steamed green beans and roasted potato wedges for an at-home version of a blue-plate special.

- 1 teaspoon olive oil
- 1 cup finely chopped onion
- ½ cup finely chopped carrot
- 1 teaspoon dried oregano
- 2 garlic cloves, minced
- 1 cup ketchup, divided
- 1½ pounds ground beef, extra lean (raw)
- 1 cup finely crushed fat-free saltine crackers (about 20)
- 2 tablespoons prepared mustard
- 1 teaspoon Worcestershire sauce
- ¼ teaspoon freshly ground black pepper
- 2 large eggs
- Cooking spray

**1.** Preheat oven to 350°.
**2.** Heat olive oil in a large nonstick skillet over medium-high heat. Add chopped onion, chopped carrot, dried oregano, and minced garlic; sauté 2 minutes. Cool.
**3.** Combine onion mixture, 1/2 cup ketchup, and remaining ingredients except cooking spray in a large bowl.
**4.** Spoon meat mixture into 12 muffin cups coated with cooking spray. Top each with 2 teaspoons ketchup. Bake at 350° for 25 minutes or until a thermometer registers 160°. Let stand 5 minutes. **YIELD**: 6 servings (serving size: 2 muffins).

CALORIES 276; FAT 8.6g (sat 3g, mono 4g, poly 0.8g); PROTEIN 28.7g; CARB 21.7g; FIBER 1.8g; CHOL 131mg; IRON 3.9mg; SODIUM 759mg; CALC 48mg

If you like a classic beef stroganoff (and I do) this is perfect! **What-ever is 'missing' to make this light, I didn't miss it!**

**from cookinglight.com**

# Beef Stroganoff

- 1 pound boneless sirloin steak, trimmed
- Cooking spray
- 3 cups sliced cremini mushrooms (about 8 ounces)
- ½ cup chopped onion
- 1 tablespoon butter
- 2 tablespoons all-purpose flour
- 1 cup fat-free, lower-sodium beef broth
- ¼ cup dry sherry
- ½ teaspoon salt
- ⅛ teaspoon freshly ground black pepper
- ¾ cup reduced-fat sour cream
- 4 cups hot cooked egg noodles (8 ounces uncooked)
- 3 tablespoons minced fresh flat-leaf parsley
- Parsley sprigs (optional)

**1.** Cut beef diagonally across grain into 1/4-inch-wide strips; cut strips into 2-inch pieces.
**2.** Heat a large nonstick skillet over medium-high heat. Coat pan with cooking spray. Add beef to pan; sauté 2 minutes or until lightly browned. Remove beef from pan; place in a medium bowl, and keep warm. Add cremini mushrooms and onion to pan; sauté 4 minutes. Add cremini mushroom mixture to beef.
**3.** Melt butter in pan over medium heat. Add flour. Cook 1 minute, stirring with a whisk. Gradually add broth, stirring constantly. Cook 1 minute or until thickened and bubbly, stirring constantly.
**4.** Add beef mixture, sherry, salt, and pepper to pan; bring to a boil. Reduce heat, and simmer 4 minutes. Remove from heat; let stand 30 seconds. Stir in sour cream.
**5.** Combine noodles and minced parsley. Serve beef mixture over noodles. Garnish with parsley sprigs, if desired. **YIELD:** 6 servings (serving size: about 2/3 cup beef mixture and 2/3 cup noodles).

CALORIES 352; FAT 11.7g (sat 5.3g, mono 3.9g, poly 1g); PROTEIN 24.2g; CARB 36g; FIBER 1.8g; CHOL 87mg; IRON 3.1mg; SODIUM 355mg; CALC 40mg

## what makes it light

- uses a minimal amount of butter
- uses fat-free, lower-sodium beef broth
- uses reduced-fat sour cream
- uses a smaller amount of meat than normal for six servings
- uses earthy mushrooms to replace a bulk of the meat

## what makes it light

- uses fat-free milk
- uses egg whites
- uses less oil than traditional recipes

This has become my go-to recipe. **It satisfies my husband's craving for steak and gravy, and it satisfies my need for lighter fare.** By using a no-salt-added beef broth you can lower the sodium even more. It absolutely has the taste of down-home comfort food, but it only takes minutes to make. I usually have my husband do the potatoes, and I do the steaks. Add a vegetable, and you are done! It's great for company because it's so quick and easy.

**from cookinglight.com**

# Country-Fried Steak with Mushroom Gravy

- 3 tablespoons fat-free milk
- 2 large egg whites
- 1.5 ounces all-purpose flour (about ⅓ cup)
- ½ teaspoon onion powder
- ½ teaspoon salt
- ¼ teaspoon garlic powder
- ¼ teaspoon black pepper
- 4 (4-ounce) sirloin cubed steaks
- 2 teaspoons vegetable oil
- 2⅔ cups frozen mashed potatoes (such as Ore Ida)
- 1⅓ cups fat-free milk
- 2 cups mushrooms, quartered
- 2½ tablespoons all-purpose flour
- ¼ teaspoon salt
- 1 (14.5-ounce) can fat-free, lower-sodium beef broth (such as Swanson)

**1.** Combine 3 tablespoons milk and egg whites in a shallow dish, stirring with a whisk. Combine 1.5 ounces flour and next 4 ingredients in a shallow dish. Working with one steak at a time, dip in egg mixture; dredge in flour mixture. Repeat procedure with remaining steaks, egg mixture, and flour mixture.

**2.** Heat oil in a large nonstick skillet over medium-high heat. Add steaks; cook 3 minutes on each side or until browned. Remove steaks from pan; keep warm.

**3.** While steaks cook, prepare mashed potatoes according to package directions, using 1⅓ cups milk. Keep warm.

**4.** Add mushrooms to pan; sauté 3 minutes. Combine 2½ tablespoons flour, ¼ teaspoon salt, and broth, stirring with a whisk. Add broth mixture to pan. Bring to a boil; cook 1 minute, stirring constantly. Spoon over steaks. Serve with mashed potatoes. **YIELD**: 4 servings (serving size: 1 steak, about ⅓ cup gravy, and about 1 cup mashed potatoes).

CALORIES 436; FAT 14.7g (sat 5.1g, mono 4.8g, poly 2.2g); PROTEIN 38.2g; CARB 34.7g; FIBER 1.9g; CHOL 189mg; IRON 4.6mg; SODIUM 759mg; CALC 147mg

I am a stew lover, and this one ranks with the best, even the venerable Julia! I made it for guests, and they all raved about it. The raisins combined with the Guinness provide a subtle hint of sweetness.

**from cookinglight.com**

# Beef and Guinness Stew

- 2 tablespoons canola oil, divided
- 1 tablespoon butter, divided
- 1.1 ounces all-purpose flour (about ¼ cup)
- 2 pounds boneless chuck roast, trimmed and cut into 1-inch cubes
- 1 teaspoon salt, divided
- 5 cups chopped onion (about 3 onions)
- 1 tablespoon tomato paste
- 4 cups fat-free, lower-sodium beef broth
- 1 (11.2-ounce) bottle Guinness Draught
- 1 tablespoon raisins
- 1 teaspoon caraway seeds
- ½ teaspoon black pepper
- 1½ cups (½-inch-thick) diagonal slices carrot (about 8 ounces)
- 1½ cups (½-inch-thick) diagonal slices parsnip (about 8 ounces)
- 1 cup (½-inch) cubed peeled turnip (about 8 ounces)
- 2 tablespoons finely chopped fresh flat-leaf parsley

**1.** Heat 1 tablespoon oil in a Dutch oven over medium-high heat. Add 1½ teaspoons butter to pan. Place flour in a shallow dish. Sprinkle beef with ½ teaspoon salt; dredge beef in flour. Add half of beef to pan; cook 5 minutes, turning to brown on all sides. Remove beef from pan with a slotted spoon. Repeat procedure with remaining 1 tablespoon oil, 1½ teaspoons butter, and beef. **2.** Add onion to pan; cook 5 minutes or until tender, stirring occasionally. Stir in tomato paste; cook 1 minute, stirring frequently. Stir in broth and beer, scraping pan to loosen browned bits. Return meat to pan. Stir in remaining ½ teaspoon salt, raisins, caraway seeds, and pepper; bring to a boil. Cover, reduce heat, and simmer 1 hour, stirring occasionally. Uncover and bring to a boil. Cook 50 minutes, stirring occasionally. Add carrot, parsnip, and turnip. Cover, reduce heat to low, and simmer 30 minutes, stirring occasionally. Uncover and bring to a boil; cook 10 minutes or until vegetables are tender. Sprinkle with parsley. **YIELD**: 8 servings (serving size: about 1 cup).

CALORIES 365; FAT 19.4g (sat 6.8g, mono 8.6g, poly 1.7g); PROTEIN 25.3g; CARB 18.8g; FIBER 3.6g; CHOL 62mg; IRON 2.6mg; SODIUM 454mg; CALC 52mg

## what makes it light

- uses minimal amount of canola oil and butter to brown two pounds of meat
- lower-sodium broth keeps the sodium lower than most stews

**Are you kidding me? This is unbelievably good!** I followed the recipe exactly and was just blown away by the results. The meat was so tender you could cut it with a fork, and the flavor was awesome. Adding cloves took it to a whole other level. I served this with Yorkshire pudding and almost licked my plate. By far, the best **Cooking Light** recipe I've made to date.

**from cookinglight.com**

# Beef Daube Provençal

- 2 teaspoons olive oil
- 12 garlic cloves, crushed
- 1 (2-pound) boneless chuck roast, trimmed and cut into 2-inch cubes
- 1½ teaspoons salt, divided
- ½ teaspoon freshly ground black pepper, divided
- 1 cup red wine
- 2 cups chopped carrot
- 1½ cups chopped onion
- ½ cup lower-sodium beef broth
- 1 tablespoon tomato paste
- 1 teaspoon chopped fresh rosemary
- 1 teaspoon chopped fresh thyme
- Dash of ground cloves
- 1 (14.5-ounce) can diced tomatoes
- 1 bay leaf
- 3 cups cooked medium egg noodles (about 4 cups uncooked noodles)

**1.** Preheat oven to 300°.

**2.** Heat oil in a small Dutch oven over low heat. Add garlic; cook 5 minutes or until garlic is fragrant, stirring occasionally. Remove garlic with a slotted spoon, and set aside. Increase heat to medium-high. Add beef to pan; sprinkle with 1/2 teaspoon salt and 1/4 teaspoon pepper. Cook 5 minutes, browning on all sides. Remove beef from pan. Add wine to pan; bring to a boil, scraping pan to loosen browned bits. Add garlic, beef, 1 teaspoon salt, 1/4 teaspoon pepper, carrot, and next 8 ingredients, and bring to a boil.

**3.** Cover and bake at 300° for 2 1/2 hours or until beef is tender. Discard bay leaf. Serve over noodles.

**YIELD:** 6 servings (serving size: about 3/4 cup stew and 1/2 cup noodles).

**Note:** To make in a slow cooker, prepare through Step 2. Place beef mixture in an electric slow cooker. Cover and cook on HIGH 5 hours.

CALORIES 367; FAT 12.8g (sat 4.3g, mono 5.8g, poly 0.9g); PROTEIN 29.1g; CARB 33.4g; FIBER 3.9g; CHOL 105mg; IRON 4.3mg; SODIUM 776mg; CALC 76mg

## what makes it light

- uses minimal amount of oil to sauté meat

what makes it light
• serving size is smaller than traditional recipes
• uses lower-sodium soy sauce
• no added salt keeps total sodium lower than normal

This recipe was OUTSTANDING! I have tried making roasts in the slow cooker time and time again and have always failed. Often the meat is so overcooked it is inedible. **This roast is delicious and the meat is super juicy.** The vegetables at the bottom make for a wonderful side. This is a VERY HIGH recommendation and has already become a favorite.

**from cookinglight.com**

# Company Pot Roast

- 1 (2-pound) boneless chuck roast, trimmed and cut in half
- 1/4 cup lower-sodium soy sauce
- 2 garlic cloves, minced
- 1 cup beef broth
- 1 (.35-ounce) package dried morel mushrooms
- 1 tablespoon cracked black pepper
- 3 tablespoons sun-dried tomato paste
- 2 medium onions (about 3/4 pound), quartered
- 1 (16-ounce) package carrots, cut into 2-inch pieces
- 16 small red potatoes (about 2 pounds), halved
- 1 tablespoon vegetable oil
- 1 1/2 tablespoons all-purpose flour
- 3 tablespoons water
- Chopped fresh parsley (optional)

**1.** Combine roast, soy sauce, and garlic in a large zip-top plastic bag; seal bag, and marinate in refrigerator at least 8 hours, turning bag occasionally.
**2.** Bring broth to a boil in a small saucepan; add mushrooms. Remove from heat; cover and let stand 20 minutes. Drain mushrooms through a cheesecloth-lined colander over a bowl, reserving broth mixture.
**3.** Remove roast from bag, reserving marinade. Sprinkle roast with pepper, gently pressing pepper into roast. Combine reserved marinade, mushroom broth mixture, and tomato paste; stir well, and set aside.
**4.** Place mushrooms, onion, carrot, and potato in a 6-quart electric slow cooker; toss gently.
**5.** Heat oil in a large skillet over medium-high heat. Add roast, browning well on all sides. Place roast over vegetables in slow cooker. Pour tomato paste mixture into pan, scraping to loosen browned bits. Pour tomato paste mixture over roast and vegetables. Cover with lid; cook on high-heat setting 1 hour. Reduce to low-heat setting, and cook 8 hours or until roast is tender. Place roast and vegetables on a serving platter; keep warm. Reserve liquid in slow cooker; increase to high-heat setting.
**6.** Place flour in bowl. Gradually add water, stirring with a whisk until well blended. Add flour mixture to liquid in slow cooker. Cook, uncovered, 15 minutes or until slightly thick, stirring frequently. Serve gravy with roast and vegetables. Garnish with parsley, if desired. **YIELD**: 8 servings (serving size: 3 ounces roast, 1 onion wedge, about 3 carrot pieces, 4 potato halves, and about 1/4 cup gravy).

CALORIES 384; FAT 12.5g (sat 4.2g, mono 0g, poly 0g); PROTEIN 27.4g; CARB 40g; FIBER 5.6g; CHOL 76mg; IRON 5mg; SODIUM 488mg; CALC 49mg

**A rich sauce with plenty of meat** feels like the old-world Italian dish but fits in the new-world nutrition sense. A little liquid remaining in the sauce helps coat the pasta.

# Spaghetti with Pork Bolognese

- 1½ tablespoons extra-virgin olive oil
- 2 cups finely chopped onion
- ½ cup finely chopped carrot (about 1 medium)
- ½ cup finely chopped celery (about 1 stalk)
- 1½ teaspoons chopped garlic
- 1 teaspoon kosher salt, divided
- 1 bay leaf
- 1 pound ground pork tenderloin
- ¾ pound ground pork
- 2 ounces pancetta, finely diced
- ¼ cup tomato paste
- 2 cups chopped plum tomato (about ½ pound)
- 1½ cups organic vegetable broth (such as Swanson)
- 1 cup dry white wine
- 1 cup 1% low-fat milk
- ⅛ teaspoon grated whole nutmeg
- 1 (2-ounce) piece Parmigiano-Reggiano rind
- 1 (3-inch) cinnamon stick
- ½ teaspoon freshly ground black pepper
- 8 cups hot cooked spaghetti (about 16 ounces uncooked)
- ½ cup (2 ounces) grated fresh Parmigiano-Reggiano
- ½ cup chopped fresh parsley

**1.** Heat olive oil in a large Dutch oven over medium heat. Add onion, carrot, celery, garlic, ¼ teaspoon salt, and bay leaf to pan; cook 8 minutes or until vegetables are tender, stirring occasionally. Increase heat to medium-high. Add ground pork tenderloin, ground pork, pancetta, and ¼ teaspoon salt; sauté 8 minutes or until pork loses its pink color. Stir in tomato paste; cook 1 minute. Add tomato and next 5 ingredients; bring to a boil. Reduce heat, and simmer 45 minutes. Add cinnamon; simmer 30 minutes or until most of liquid evaporates. Discard bay leaf, rind, and cinnamon stick; stir in remaining ½ teaspoon salt and pepper. Arrange 1 cup noodles on each of 8 plates; top each with about ¾ cup sauce. Sprinkle each serving with 1 tablespoon grated cheese and 1 tablespoon parsley. **YIELD:** 8 servings.

CALORIES 512; FAT 18g (sat 6.8g, mono 6.8g, poly 1.6g); PROTEIN 34.5g; CARB 51.4g; FIBER 4.5g; CHOL 79mg; IRON 4mg; SODIUM 770mg; CALC 205mg

## what makes it light

- uses low-fat milk
- uses more lean pork tenderloin than ground pork, which cuts down on fat
- uses a small amount of pancetta, which adds big flavor without a lot of fat

30
minutes
or
less

**Excellent!** These were literally the best pork chops I've ever made. I will never buy barbecue sauce again.

**from cookinglight.com**

# Barbecued Pork Chops

Sauce:

¼ cup packed brown sugar
¼ cup ketchup
1 tablespoon Worcestershire sauce
1 tablespoon lower-sodium soy sauce

Remaining Ingredients:

6 (6-ounce) bone-in center-cut pork chops (about ½ inch thick)
1 teaspoon dried thyme
1 teaspoon garlic salt
¼ teaspoon ground red pepper
Cooking spray

**1.** Preheat grill or broiler.
**2.** To prepare sauce, combine first 4 ingredients in a small bowl. Place 1/4 cup sauce in a small bowl, and set aside.
**3.** Trim fat from pork. Combine thyme, garlic salt, and pepper; sprinkle over pork. Place pork on grill rack or broiler pan coated with cooking spray; cook 6 minutes on each side, basting with remaining sauce. Serve pork chops with reserved 1/4 cup sauce. **YIELD**: 6 servings (serving size: 1 pork chop and 1 1/2 tablespoons sauce).

CALORIES 244; FAT 11.3g (sat 3.9g, mono 5g, poly 1.4g); PROTEIN 24.6g; CARB 9.9g; FIBER 0.2g; CHOL 77mg; IRON 1.5mg; SODIUM 649mg; CALC 22mg

## what makes it light

- uses a homemade sauce, which is lower in calories and sodium than a commerical sauce

**This recipe will definitely be on repeat!** Sometimes eating something like lasagna leaves you feeling heavy, but this is a great, lightened version that is just as flavorful.

**from cookinglight.com**

# Tomato-Basil Lasagna with Prosciutto

- 5 garlic cloves
- 1 (16-ounce) carton 1% low-fat cottage cheese
- ½ cup (4 ounces) block-style fat-free cream cheese
- ¼ cup (1 ounce) grated fresh Romano cheese, divided
- 2½ teaspoons dried basil
- ½ teaspoon crushed red pepper
- 1 large egg
- 1 (26-ounce) bottle fat-free tomato-basil pasta sauce (such as Muir Glen)
- Cooking spray
- 12 cooked lasagna noodles
- 1 cup (4 ounces) chopped prosciutto or ham
- 1 cup (4 ounces) shredded part-skim mozzarella cheese

**1.** Preheat oven to 375°.

**2.** Drop garlic through food chute with food processor on, and process until minced. Add cottage cheese; process 2 minutes or until smooth. Add cream cheese, 2 tablespoons Romano, basil, pepper, and egg; process until well blended.

**3.** Spread 1/2 cup pasta sauce in bottom of a 13 x 9–inch baking dish coated with cooking spray. Arrange 3 noodles over pasta sauce; top with 1 cup cheese mixture, 1/3 cup prosciutto, and 3/4 cup pasta sauce. Repeat layers two times, ending with noodles. Spread remaining pasta sauce over noodles. Sprinkle with 2 tablespoons Romano and mozzarella.

**4.** Cover and bake at 375° for 45 minutes or until sauce is bubbly. Uncover and bake an additional 15 minutes. Let lasagna stand 5 minutes. **YIELD**: 9 servings.

CALORIES 272; FAT 5.6g (sat 2.8g, mono 1.8g, poly 0.6g); PROTEIN 20.8g; CARB 33g; FIBER 2.1g; CHOL 47mg; IRON 2.3mg; SODIUM 775mg; CALC 213mg

## what makes it light

- uses fat-free tomato-basil pasta sauce
- uses part-skim mozzarella
- uses low-fat cottage cheese and fat-free cream cheese to replace full-fat ricotta used in traditional recipes

This was a deliciously salty-and-sweet dish that was a huge hit at my house! My husband was skeptical and wanted to stick with traditional meat and spaghetti for dinner but was impressed with the end result. **The pasta was creamy and rich like a homemade mac 'n' cheese,** and the bacon added an incredible flavor to the otherwise overly indulgent dish.

**from cookinglight.com**

# Roasted Butternut Squash and Bacon Pasta

- ¾ teaspoon salt, divided
- ½ teaspoon dried rosemary
- ¼ teaspoon freshly ground black pepper
- 3 cups (1-inch) cubed peeled butternut squash
- Cooking spray
- 6 sweet hickory-smoked bacon slices (raw)
- 1 cup thinly sliced shallots
- 8 ounces uncooked mini penne (tube-shaped pasta)
- 1.1 ounces all-purpose flour (about ¼ cup)
- 2 cups 2% reduced-fat milk
- ¾ cup (3 ounces) shredded sharp provolone cheese
- ⅓ cup (1½ ounces) grated fresh Parmesan cheese

**1.** Preheat oven to 425°.

**2.** Combine ¼ teaspoon salt, rosemary, and pepper. Place squash on a foil-lined baking sheet coated with cooking spray; sprinkle with salt mixture. Bake at 425° for 45 minutes or until tender and lightly browned. Increase oven temperature to 450°.

**3.** Cook bacon in a large nonstick skillet over medium heat until crisp. Remove bacon from pan, reserving 1½ teaspoons drippings in pan; crumble bacon. Increase heat to medium-high. Add shallots to pan; sauté 8 minutes or until tender. Combine squash mixture, bacon, and shallots; set aside.

**4.** Cook pasta according to package directions, omitting salt and fat. Drain well.

**5.** Combine flour and ½ teaspoon salt in a Dutch oven over medium-high heat. Gradually add milk, stirring constantly with a whisk; bring to a boil. Cook 1 minute or until slightly thick, stirring constantly. Remove from heat. Add provolone, stirring until cheese melts. Add pasta to cheese mixture, tossing well to combine. Spoon pasta mixture into an 11 x 7–inch baking dish lightly coated with cooking spray; top with squash mixture. Sprinkle evenly with Parmesan cheese. Bake at 450° for 10 minutes or until cheese melts and begins to brown. **YIELD:** 5 servings.

CALORIES 469; FAT 14.4g (sat 7.3g, mono 4.4g, poly 0.9g); PROTEIN 22.1g; CARB 66.6g; FIBER 6.8g; CHOL 40mg; IRON 3.5mg; SODIUM 849mg; CALC 443mg

## what makes it light

- uses reduced-fat milk
- uses cooking spray instead of oil to roast squash
- uses a minimal amount of reserved bacon drippings to sauté shallots
- uses sharp provolone for big flavor impact

**The luxurious, velvety texture** of a good pasta carbonara is ephemeral at best, so you must enjoy it right away. Tempering the egg with hot pasta water keeps the sauce creamy by preventing it from curdling. For a smoky taste, use bacon in place of pancetta.

# Linguine Carbonara

- 4 ounces uncooked linguine
- ½ cup 1% low-fat milk
- 3 tablespoons grated fresh Parmesan cheese
- 1 tablespoon chopped fresh parsley
- ⅛ teaspoon salt
- ⅛ teaspoon freshly ground black pepper
- Cooking spray
- ⅓ cup chopped pancetta (about 1½ ounces)
- ¼ cup finely chopped onion
- 1 garlic clove, minced
- 1 large egg

**1.** Cook pasta according to package directions, omitting salt and fat. Drain pasta in a colander over a bowl, reserving 1/4 cup cooking liquid.
**2.** Combine milk and next 4 ingredients in a small bowl; set milk mixture aside.
**3.** Heat a medium nonstick skillet over medium-high heat. Coat pan with cooking spray. Add pancetta to pan; sauté 3 minutes or until lightly browned. Add onion and garlic to pan; sauté 3 minutes or until onion is lightly browned. Reduce heat to medium-low. Add milk mixture and pasta to pan; toss gently to coat.
**4.** Place egg in a small bowl; stir with a whisk. Gradually add 1/4 cup reserved hot cooking liquid, stirring constantly with a whisk. Gradually add egg mixture to pan, stirring constantly; cook 4 minutes or until sauce is thick and creamy. **YIELD**: 2 servings (serving size: about 1 1/4 cups).

CALORIES 387; FAT 13g (sat 5.8g, mono 4.5g, poly 1.3g); PROTEIN 19.2g; CARB 48.2g; FIBER 2.3g; CHOL 130mg; IRON 2.6mg; SODIUM 682mg; CALC 192mg

## what makes it light

- uses low-fat milk instead of the traditional heavy cream
- uses reserved pasta water to develop creaminess instead of depending on cream, cheese, and more eggs

# 5 ways with potpie

## Individual Chicken Potpies

Because the piecrust topping cooks on a baking sheet and is then placed over the filling, you don't need to use ovenproof bowls for the pies. Use a bowl or ramekin as a guide for cutting the dough. You can use 2 cups chopped leftover chicken in place of chicken breast tenders.

**½ (14.1-ounce) package refrigerated pie dough (such as Pillsbury)**
**Cooking spray**
**⅛ teaspoon salt**
**2 tablespoons all-purpose flour**
**1 teaspoon dried rubbed sage**
**¼ teaspoon salt**
**¼ teaspoon black pepper**
**8 ounces chicken breast tenders, cut into bite-sized pieces**
**1¼ cups water**
**1½ cups frozen mixed vegetables**
**1 cup mushrooms, quartered**
**1 (10¾-ounce) can condensed reduced-fat, reduced-sodium cream of chicken soup**

**1.** Preheat oven to 425°.
**2.** Cut 3 (4-inch) circles out of dough; discard remaining dough. Place dough circles on a baking sheet coated with cooking spray. Lightly coat dough with cooking spray; sprinkle evenly with ⅛ teaspoon salt. Pierce top of dough with a fork. Bake dough at 425° for 8 minutes or until golden.
**3.** Combine flour, sage, ¼ teaspoon salt, and pepper in a zip-top plastic bag; add chicken. Seal bag, and toss to coat. Heat a large non-stick skillet over medium-high heat. Coat pan with cooking spray. Add chicken mixture; cook 5 minutes, browning on all sides. Stir in water, scraping pan to loosen browned bits. Stir in vegetables, mushrooms, and soup; bring to a boil. Reduce heat, and cook 10 minutes. Spoon 1 cup chicken mixture into each of 3 (1-cup) ramekins or bowls; top each serving with 1 piecrust. **YIELD:** 3 servings (serving size: 1 pie).

CALORIES 452; FAT 18g (sat 7.6g, mono 7.5g, poly 2.2g); PROTEIN 24g; CARB 49g; FIBER 2.8g; CHOL 54mg; IRON 1.3mg; SODIUM 1,027mg; CALC 30mg

## Barbecued-Chicken Potpie

- 1 teaspoon butter
- Cooking spray
- 2 cups chopped onion
- ½ cup chopped green bell pepper
- ⅓ cup diced seeded poblano chile or 1 (4.5-ounce) can chopped green chiles, drained
- 1 small garlic clove, minced
- 1½ teaspoons cumin seeds
- 1 teaspoon ground coriander
- ¼ cup cider vinegar
- 4 cups shredded cooked chicken breast (about 1½ pounds)
- 2 tablespoons brown sugar
- 1 ounce unsweetened chocolate, grated
- 1 (12-ounce) bottle chili sauce
- 1½ cups lower-sodium chicken broth (such as Swanson Natural Goodness)
- 1 (8-ounce) can refrigerated breadsticks
- ½ cup cornmeal

**1.** Preheat oven to 375°.

**2.** Melt butter in a large nonstick skillet coated with cooking spray over medium-high heat. Add onion, peppers, and garlic, and sauté 5 minutes. Stir in cumin and coriander, and cook 2 minutes. Stir in vinegar, scraping skillet to loosen browned bits. Add chicken and next 4 ingredients, and cook 15 minutes or until thick, stirring occasionally. Spoon chicken mixture into 11 x 7–inch baking dish coated with cooking spray.

**3.** Unroll breadstick dough, separating into strips; press cornmeal into strips. Place strips in a lattice fashion over chicken mixture. Bake at 375° for 25 minutes or until golden brown; let stand 15 minutes before serving. **YIELD**: 8 servings.

CALORIES 371; FAT 7.3g (sat 3.2g, mono 2.2g, poly 1.1g); PROTEIN 31.3g; CARB 44.3g; FIBER 2.2g; CHOL 74mg; IRON 3.1mg; SODIUM 862mg; CALC 37mg

3

## Biscuit-Topped Chicken Potpie

Serve a homemade potpie for dinner tonight. It tastes just like Mom's, but cooks in a fraction of the time.

- 1 tablespoon butter
- 2 cups chopped leek
- ¼ cup chopped shallot
- ¾ teaspoon chopped fresh or ¼ teaspoon dried thyme
- 1½ cups refrigerated diced potatoes with onions (such as Simply Potatoes)
- ⅓ cup dry white wine
- 1 teaspoon Dijon mustard
- 1 (14-ounce) can fat-free, lower-sodium chicken broth
- 2 cups chopped roasted chicken breast
- 1½ cups frozen mixed vegetables
- ¼ teaspoon salt
- ¼ teaspoon freshly ground black pepper
- 1½ tablespoons cornstarch
- 2 tablespoons water
- ⅔ cup half-and-half
- Cooking spray
- 1¼ cups low-fat baking mix (such as Bisquick Heart Smart)
- ½ cup fat-free milk
- 1 large egg white, lightly beaten

**1.** Preheat oven to 425°.

**2.** Melt butter in a large nonstick skillet over medium-high heat. Add leek, shallot, and thyme; sauté 2 minutes. Add potatoes; sauté 2 minutes. Add wine; cook 1 minute or until liquid evaporates. Stir in mustard and broth; bring to a boil. Cook 4 minutes, stirring occasionally. Stir in chicken, mixed vegetables, salt, and pepper; cook 1 minute. Combine cornstarch and 2 tablespoons water in a small bowl, stirring with a whisk. Add cornstarch mixture and half-and-half to pan. Reduce heat, and simmer 2 minutes, stirring constantly. Spoon mixture into a 13 x 9–inch baking dish coated with cooking spray.

**3.** Lightly spoon baking mix into dry measuring cups; level with a knife. Combine baking mix, milk, and egg in a medium bowl, stirring with a whisk. Spoon batter over chicken mixture; spread evenly to cover. Bake at 425° for 20 minutes or until topping is golden and filling is bubbly. Let stand 10 minutes. **YIELD:** 6 servings (serving size: 1½ cups).

CALORIES 348; FAT 9.2g (sat 4.1g, mono 2.2g, poly 0.9g); PROTEIN 23.5g; CARB 43.3g; FIBER 4.4g; CHOL 55mg; IRON 3.1mg; SODIUM 634mg; CALC 131mg

## Speedy Chicken Potpie

Though you have to hustle, you really can get this chicken potpie on the table in 20 minutes. Start browning the chicken and bringing the broth to a boil right away, and get the pie dough in the oven as soon as it reaches 425°. Strips of pastry are a quick stand-in for the traditional crust on top.

- Cooking spray
- 1 pound skinless, boneless chicken breast, cut into ½-inch pieces
- ¼ teaspoon salt
- 3 cups fat-free, lower-sodium chicken broth, divided
- 1 bay leaf
- 2 cups refrigerated diced potatoes with onion (such as Simply Potatoes)
- ⅔ cup frozen green peas and diced carrot blend
- 3 tablespoons all-purpose flour
- ½ teaspoon chopped fresh thyme
- ¼ teaspoon black pepper
- ¼ teaspoon dried rubbed sage
- ¼ (15-ounce) package refrigerated pie dough

**1.** Preheat oven to 425°.

**2.** Heat a large nonstick skillet over medium-high heat. Coat pan with cooking spray. Add chicken to pan; sprinkle with salt. Sauté 5 minutes or until browned and done.

**3.** While chicken cooks, bring 2½ cups broth and bay leaf to a boil in a large saucepan. Add potatoes; cover and cook over medium-high heat 8 minutes. Stir in peas and carrots; cover and cook 2 minutes. Stir in chicken. Combine remaining ½ cup broth and flour; stir into potato mixture. Reduce heat to medium; cook 2 minutes or until bubbly and thick. Remove bay leaf. Stir in thyme, pepper, and sage.

**4.** While potato mixture cooks, cut dough crosswise into 12 strips. Arrange on a parchment-lined baking sheet. Bake at 425° for 7 minutes or until browned and puffy. Top chicken mixture with dough strips. **YIELD**: 4 servings (serving size: 1¼ cups chicken mixture and 3 piecrust strips).

CALORIES 341; FAT 8.5g (sat 2.9g, mono 2.5g, poly 0.7g); PROTEIN 30.4g; CARB 33.6g; FIBER 2.5g; CHOL 69mg; IRON 1.7mg; SODIUM 813mg; CALC 20mg

## Chicken Potpie

- 2 tablespoons butter
- 2 tablespoons olive oil
- 3 cups diced red potato (about 1 pound)
- 2 cups diced onion
- 2 cups sliced mushrooms (about 8 ounces)
- 1 cup diced celery
- 1 cup diced carrot
- ¼ cup chopped fresh parsley
- 2 teaspoons chopped fresh thyme
- 6½ tablespoons all-purpose flour
- 3 cups fat-free milk
- ½ cup fat-free, lower-sodium chicken broth
- 2 cups chopped cooked chicken breast (about 12 ounces)
- 1 cup frozen green peas
- 1 teaspoon salt
- ½ teaspoon freshly ground black pepper
- 6 (14 x 9–inch) sheets frozen phyllo dough, thawed
- Cooking spray

**1.** Preheat oven to 375°.

**2.** Melt butter in a large Dutch oven over medium-high heat; add oil. Add potato and next 6 ingredients, and sauté 5 minutes. Reduce heat to medium-low; sprinkle flour over vegetables. Cook 5 minutes, stirring frequently. Stir in milk and broth. Increase heat to medium-high; bring to a boil. Reduce heat, and simmer 5 minutes or until thickened. Add chicken, peas, salt, and pepper.

**3.** Spoon mixture into a 3-quart baking dish. Place 1 phyllo sheet on a large cutting board or work surface (cover remaining dough to keep from drying); lightly spray with cooking spray. Repeat layers with cooking spray and remaining phyllo. Place phyllo layers loosely on top of mixture in dish. Place dish on a baking sheet. Bake at 375° for 30 minutes or until top is golden. **YIELD**: 6 servings.

CALORIES 354; FAT 11.2g (sat 3.8g, mono 5.3g, poly 1.2g); PROTEIN 24.2g; CARB 40g; FIBER 4.4g; CHOL 52mg; IRON 2.5mg; SODIUM 680mg; CALC 209mg

# Quick Chicken Noodle Soup

- 2 cups water
- 1 (32-ounce) carton fat-free, lower-sodium chicken broth
- 1 tablespoon olive oil
- ½ cup prechopped onion
- ½ cup prechopped celery
- ½ teaspoon salt
- ½ teaspoon freshly ground black pepper
- 1 medium carrot, chopped
- 6 ounces uncooked fusilli pasta
- 2½ cups shredded skinless, boneless rotisserie chicken breast
- 2 tablespoons chopped fresh flat-leaf parsley

**1.** Combine 2 cups water and chicken broth in a microwave-safe dish, and microwave at HIGH 5 minutes.

**2.** While broth mixture heats, heat a large saucepan over medium-high heat. Add oil to pan; swirl to coat. Add onion, celery, salt, pepper, and carrot; sauté 3 minutes or until almost tender, stirring frequently. Add hot broth mixture and pasta; bring to a boil. Cook 7 minutes or until pasta is almost al dente. Stir in chicken; cook 1 minute or until thoroughly heated. Stir in parsley.

**YIELD:** 6 servings (serving size: about 1 cup).

CALORIES 237; FAT 4.8g (sat 1g, mono 2.4g, poly 0.9g); PROTEIN 22.9g; CARB 23.9g; FIBER 1.7g; CHOL 50mg; IRON 1.8mg; SODIUM 589mg; CALC 28mg

## what makes it light

- uses skinless rotisserie chicken breast, which is low fat

This is great for wintertime when you want a nice easy meal that is filling and **makes you feel warm inside**. My husband didn't know it was light!

**from cookinglight.com**

# Creamy Chicken-and-Rice Casserole

- 1 (6.9-ounce) package one-third-less-salt chicken-flavored rice-and-vermicelli mix with chicken broth and herbs (such as Rice-A-Roni)
- 1 tablespoon butter
- 2¼ cups hot water
- Cooking spray
- 1½ pounds skinless, boneless chicken breast, cut into bite-sized pieces
- 1 cup presliced fresh mushrooms
- ½ teaspoon garlic powder
- ¾ cup fat-free sour cream
- ¼ teaspoon pepper
- 1 (10¾-ounce) can condensed reduced-fat, reduced-sodium cream of mushroom soup, undiluted
- ¼ cup crushed multigrain crackers (about 6 crackers)
- 1 tablespoon butter, melted
- ½ teaspoon poppy seeds

**1.** Preheat oven to 350°.
**2.** Cook rice mix in a large nonstick skillet according to package directions, using 1 tablespoon butter and 2¼ cups hot water. Remove mixture from pan; set aside. Wipe pan with a paper towel.
**3.** Heat skillet over high heat. Coat pan with cooking spray. Add chicken, mushrooms, and garlic powder; sauté 6 minutes or until chicken loses its pink color. Combine rice mixture, chicken mixture, sour cream, pepper, and soup in a bowl; stir well. Spoon mixture into a 2-quart casserole coated with cooking spray. Combine cracker crumbs, butter, and poppy seeds; stir well, and sprinkle over chicken mixture. Bake at 350° for 35 minutes or until thoroughly heated. **YIELD**: 6 servings (serving size: 1⅓ cups).

CALORIES 373; FAT 9.1g (sat 3.5g, mono 2.9g, poly 2.3g); PROTEIN 32.1g; CARB 39.9g; FIBER 1.9g; CHOL 81mg; IRON 2mg; SODIUM 896mg; CALC 77mg

## what makes it light

- uses one-third-less-salt chicken-flavored rice-and-vermicelli mix
- uses less butter than traditional recipes
- uses fat-free sour cream
- uses reduced-fat, reduced-sodium condensed cream of mushroom soup
- uses multigrain crackers, which are healthier than traditional crackers (usually Ritz)

# recipe makeover
# cheesy chicken enchiladas

**The Reader:** Anna Marie "Rie" Lotti

**The Story:** "My son-in-law, Marc, is from a traditional Mexican family, and we're Italian. This is a dish we all love because it's cheesy and good," Rie says of this recipe that's been in her family for two decades. Rie notes their lifestyle has changed a lot since she started making the casserole: Both she and her husband, Tom, keep tabs on sodium, saturated fat, and calories since Tom was diagnosed with type 2 diabetes a few years ago. "I'm glad my daughter, Dawn, sent the recipe to *Cooking Light* for a makeover," she says.

**The Dilemma:** Plenty of cheese and sour cream, as well as canned cream of chicken soup, contributed to the hefty 773 calories per serving of this filling entrée. Plus, the soup and abundant 2 pounds of cheese added to the dish's sodium content.

**The Solution:** Using half the amount of cheese and opting for a reduced-fat Mexican blend in the filling cut 149 calories, 13.4 grams of fat (8.4 grams saturated), and 126 milligrams of sodium per serving. We topped the casserole with one-fourth the original amount of cheese and employed a sharp reduced-fat cheddar to trim 97 calories, 8.3 grams of fat (5.2 grams saturated), and 134 milligrams of sodium per serving.

In place of 2 cups of the full-fat sour cream, we used a combination of 1⅔ cups low-fat plain yogurt and ⅓ cup butter to shave 29 calories and about 4 grams of fat (2.4 grams saturated) per serving. We substituted a reduced-fat, reduced-sodium version of canned cream of chicken soup for a savings of 1.5 grams of fat and 102 milligrams of sodium per serving. And, instead of frying the tortillas in oil, we brushed them with a prudent 1 tablespoon canola oil to keep fat and calories in check and pan-toasted them.

**The Feedback:** "The family thoroughly enjoyed the new version of the enchiladas," says Rie. **"The tortillas were tender, and the filling was flavorful and creamy with extra onion and garlic and the combined sour cream and butter."**

| | BEFORE | AFTER |
|---|---|---|
| Calories per serving | 773 | 454 |
| Fat | 53.4g | 20.3g |
| Percent of total calories | 38% | 25% |

**Trade the traditional enchilada** sauce for a creamy, cheesy topping on this Mexican chicken recipe. Your family will never know they're enjoying a lightened meal. Serve with a salad of fresh mango, jícama, and shredded lettuce topped with a lime vinaigrette.

# Cheesy Chicken Enchiladas

2½ cups chopped cooked chicken breast
2 cups (8 ounces) preshredded reduced-fat 4-cheese Mexican blend cheese
1⅔ cups plain low-fat yogurt
⅓ cup butter, melted
¼ cup chopped onion
1 teaspoon minced garlic
¼ teaspoon freshly ground black pepper
1 (10¾-ounce) can condensed reduced-fat, reduced-sodium cream of chicken soup (such as Healthy Request), undiluted
1 (4.5-ounce) can chopped green chiles, drained
8 (8-inch) flour tortillas
1 tablespoon canola oil
Cooking spray
½ cup (2 ounces) finely shredded reduced-fat sharp cheddar cheese
¼ cup chopped green onions

**1.** Preheat oven to 350°.
**2.** Combine first 9 ingredients in a large bowl. Remove 1 cup chicken mixture; set mixture aside.
**3.** Heat a large skillet over medium-high heat. Working with 1 tortilla at a time, brush oil over both sides of tortilla. Add tortilla to pan; cook 5 seconds on each side or until toasted and soft. Remove from pan; arrange ½ cup chicken mixture down center of tortilla. Roll jelly-roll style; place filled tortilla, seam side down, in a 13 x 9–inch baking dish coated with cooking spray. Repeat procedure with remaining 7 tortillas, remaining oil, and remaining chicken mixture. Spread reserved 1 cup chicken mixture evenly over enchiladas. Cover and bake at 350° for 20 minutes. Uncover; sprinkle evenly with cheddar cheese and green onions; bake an additional 5 minutes or until cheese melts.
**YIELD**: 8 servings (serving size: 1 enchilada).

CALORIES 454; FAT 20.3g (sat 10.4g, mono 6.7g, poly 1.5g); PROTEIN 30.8g; CARB 36.6g; FIBER 2.2g; CHOL 73mg; IRON 2.3mg; SODIUM 757mg; CALC 347mg

**Serve a classic family-favorite** for an easy weeknight meal in minutes. Pair with a quick starch and a small green salad.

# Oven-Fried Chicken Parmesan

- 1.1 ounces all-purpose flour (about ¼ cup)
- ½ teaspoon dried oregano
- ¼ teaspoon salt
- 2 large egg whites, lightly beaten
- ¾ cup panko (Japanese breadcrumbs)
- 4 (6-ounce) skinless, boneless chicken breast halves
- 2 tablespoons olive oil, divided
- Cooking spray
- ½ cup tomato-basil pasta sauce
- ½ cup (2 ounces) grated Parmigiano-Reggiano cheese
- ¾ cup (3 ounces) shredded part-skim mozzarella cheese

**1.** Preheat oven to 450°.
**2.** Combine first 3 ingredients in a shallow dish; place egg whites in a bowl. Place panko in a shallow dish. Dredge 1 breast half in flour mixture. Dip in egg whites; dredge in panko. Repeat procedure with remaining chicken, flour mixture, egg whites, and panko.
**3.** Heat 1 tablespoon oil in a large ovenproof skillet over medium-high heat. Add chicken to pan; cook 2 minutes. Add remaining 1 tablespoon oil. Turn chicken over; cook 2 minutes. Coat chicken with cooking spray; place pan in oven. Bake at 450° for 5 minutes. Turn chicken over; top each breast half with 2 tablespoons sauce, 2 tablespoons Parmigiano-Reggiano, and 3 tablespoons mozzarella. Bake 6 minutes or until chicken is done. **YIELD:** 4 servings (serving size: 1 breast half).

CALORIES 401; FAT 16.9g (sat 6.4g, mono 7.6g, poly 1.3g); PROTEIN 44.4g; CARB 15.9g; FIBER 0.6g; CHOL 95mg; IRON 1.8mg; SODIUM 719mg; CALC 352mg

## what makes it light

- uses less oil to brown the chicken before baking than traditional recipes
- uses less cheese on top than traditional recipes

# 5 ways with fried chicken

## Pan-Fried Chicken

The key to success with this recipe is even heat. If the oil gets too hot, the chicken may brown too quickly before fully cooking. If the oil is not hot enough, the chicken will absorb too much of it. You can lower the heat, or brown the chicken on the stovetop and then cook in a 350° oven until done.

**4.5 ounces all-purpose flour (about 1 cup)**
**2.38 ounces whole-wheat flour (about ½ cup)**
**1 teaspoon ground ginger**
**½ teaspoon hot paprika**
**½ teaspoon ground cinnamon**
**½ teaspoon freshly ground nutmeg**
**½ teaspoon fine sea salt**
**2 bone-in chicken breast halves, skinned**
**2 bone-in chicken thighs, skinned**
**2 chicken drumsticks, skinned**
**¼ cup peanut oil**

**1.** Sift together first 6 ingredients; place mixture in a large zip-top plastic bag. Sprinkle salt evenly over chicken. Add chicken, one piece at a time, to bag; seal. Shake bag to coat chicken. Remove chicken from bag, shaking off excess flour. Place chicken on a cooling rack; place rack in a jelly-roll pan. Reserve remaining flour mixture. Loosely cover chicken; chill 1½ hours. Let chicken stand at room temperature 30 minutes. Return chicken, one piece at a time, to flour mixture, shaking bag to coat chicken. Discard excess flour mixture.

**2.** Heat peanut oil in a large skillet over medium-high heat. Add chicken to pan. Reduce heat to medium-low, and cook 25 minutes or until done, carefully turning every 5 minutes.

**3.** Line a clean cooling rack with brown paper bags; arrange chicken in a single layer on bags. Let stand 5 minutes. **YIELD:** 4 servings (serving size: 1 chicken breast half, or 1 thigh and 1 drumstick).

CALORIES 245; FAT 10.1g (sat 2g, mono 4.1g, poly 3g); PROTEIN 28.2g; CARB 9g; FIBER 0.8g; CHOL 87mg; IRON 1.8mg; SODIUM 240mg; CALC 17mg

## Lemon-Ginger Fried Chicken

- 1 teaspoon grated lemon rind
- 1 cup fresh lemon juice (about 4 lemons)
- 2 teaspoons minced peeled fresh ginger
- 1½ teaspoons minced garlic
- 2 bone-in chicken breast halves, skinned
- 2 bone-in chicken thighs, skinned
- 2 chicken drumsticks, skinned
- 4.5 ounces all-purpose flour (about 1 cup)
- 2 teaspoons ground ginger
- 1 teaspoon paprika
- ½ teaspoon ground red pepper
- 1 teaspoon kosher salt
- ½ teaspoon freshly ground black pepper
- ¼ cup peanut oil
- ¼ cup fat-free, lower-sodium chicken broth
- 2 tablespoons brown sugar
- 1 lemon, thinly sliced

**1.** Place rind, juice, and next 5 ingredients in a large zip-top plastic bag; seal and shake to coat. Marinate in refrigerator 1 hour, turning bag occasionally.
**2.** Sift together flour and next 3 ingredients. Place flour mixture in a large zip-top plastic bag. Remove chicken from marinade bag, reserving marinade. Sprinkle salt and black pepper evenly over chicken. Add chicken, one piece at a time, to flour mixture; seal bag and shake to coat chicken. Remove chicken from bag, shaking off excess flour mixture. Reserve remaining flour mixture. Place chicken on a wire rack; place rack in a jelly-roll pan. Cover and refrigerate $1^1/_2$ hours. Let stand at room temperature 30 minutes.
**3.** Preheat oven to 350°.
**4.** Return chicken, one piece at a time, to flour mixture; seal bag and shake to coat chicken. Remove chicken from bag, shaking off excess flour mixture. Discard remaining flour mixture.
**5.** Heat oil in a large skillet over medium-high heat. Add chicken to pan; cook 3 minutes or until golden, turning once. Arrange chicken in a single layer in a shallow roasting pan. Combine broth and reserved marinade in a small bowl; carefully pour broth mixture into pan. Sprinkle chicken evenly with sugar, and top with lemon slices. Bake at 350° for 45 minutes or until golden and a thermometer registers 165°. **YIELD**: 4 servings (serving size: 1 breast half, or 1 thigh and 1 drumstick).

CALORIES 375; FAT 15.5g (sat 3.3g, mono 6.6g, poly 4.7g); PROTEIN 30.8g; CARB 30.5g; FIBER 2.4g; CHOL 85mg; IRON 2.6mg; SODIUM 578mg; CALC 48mg

2

## Oven-Fried Chicken ▾

- 1 cup low-fat buttermilk
- 2 large egg whites, beaten
- 4.5 ounces all-purpose flour (about 1 cup)
- ⅓ cup cornmeal
- 1 teaspoon salt, divided
- ¾ teaspoon freshly ground black pepper
- ¼ teaspoon ground red pepper
- 2 chicken breast halves, skinned (about 1 pound)
- 2 chicken thighs, skinned (about ½ pound)
- 2 chicken drumsticks, skinned (about ½ pound)
- 2 tablespoons canola oil
- Cooking spray

**1.** Preheat oven to 425°.

**2.** Cover a large baking sheet with parchment paper. Combine buttermilk and egg whites in a shallow dish; stir well with a whisk. Combine flour, cornmeal, ½ teaspoon salt, black pepper, and red pepper in a separate shallow dish; stir well. Sprinkle chicken evenly with remaining ½ teaspoon salt. Dip chicken in buttermilk mixture; dredge in flour mixture.

**3.** Heat oil in a large nonstick skillet over medium-high heat. Add chicken to pan; cook 4 minutes on each side or until lightly browned. Place chicken on prepared baking sheet; lightly coat chicken with cooking spray. Bake at 425° for 30 minutes or until chicken is done. **YIELD:** 4 servings (serving size: 1 chicken breast half, or 1 drumstick and 1 thigh).

CALORIES 450; FAT 13.8g (sat 2.5g, mono 6.1g, poly 3.6g); PROTEIN 43.5g; CARB 35.3g; FIBER 1.7g; CHOL 109mg; IRON 3.2mg; SODIUM 803mg; CALC 88mg

## Buttermilk Oven-Fried Chicken with Coleslaw ▾

Coleslaw:

- 4 cups packaged coleslaw
- 3 tablespoons fat-free mayonnaise
- 1½ teaspoons sugar
- ½ teaspoon celery seeds
- 1½ teaspoons cider vinegar
- ⅛ teaspoon salt

Chicken:

- 1 cup low-fat buttermilk
- 4 (8-ounce) bone-in chicken breast halves, skinned
- 1.5 ounces all-purpose flour (about ⅓ cup)
- ⅓ cup cracker meal
- ½ teaspoon salt
- ½ teaspoon freshly ground black pepper
- 2 tablespoons butter

**1.** To prepare coleslaw, combine first 6 ingredients; toss to coat. Cover and chill.
**2.** Preheat oven to 425°.
**3.** To prepare chicken, combine buttermilk and chicken in a shallow dish, turning to coat.
**4.** Combine flour and cracker meal in a shallow dish. Transfer chicken from buttermilk to a work surface. Sprinkle chicken evenly with 1/2 teaspoon salt and pepper. Working with one chicken breast half at a time, dredge chicken in flour mixture, shaking off excess; set aside. Repeat procedure with remaining chicken and flour mixture.
**5.** Melt butter in a large ovenproof nonstick skillet over medium-high heat. Add chicken to pan, meat side down; cook 4 minutes or until golden brown. Turn chicken over, and bake at 425° for 32 minutes or until a thermometer registers 165°. **YIELD:** 4 servings (serving size: 1 chicken breast half and 3/4 cup slaw).

CALORIES 342; FAT 8.8g (sat 4.5g, mono 2.2g, poly 0.8g); PROTEIN 45.1g; CARB 18.5g; FIBER 2.6g; CHOL 123mg; IRON 2.3mg; SODIUM 672mg; CALC 95mg

## Oven-Fried Coconut Chicken ▸

The marinade infuses dark-meat chicken with a light coconut flavor; flaked coconut in the breading heightens the nutty taste. Find panko in your supermarket's ethnic food aisle.

**1 tablespoon fresh lime juice**
**1 tablespoon hot pepper sauce**
**1 (13.5-ounce) can light coconut milk**
**4 (4-ounce) chicken thighs, skinned**
**4 (4-ounce) chicken drumsticks, skinned**
**¾ cup panko (Japanese breadcrumbs)**
**½ cup flaked sweetened coconut**
**½ teaspoon salt**
**¼ teaspoon freshly ground black pepper**
**Cooking spray**

**1.** Combine first 3 ingredients in a large zip-top plastic bag. Add chicken to bag; seal. Marinate in refrigerator 1 1/2 hours, turning bag occasionally.
**2.** Preheat oven to 400°.
**3.** Combine panko, flaked coconut, salt, and black pepper in a shallow dish. Remove chicken from marinade; discard marinade. Dredge chicken, one piece at a time, in panko mixture. Place chicken on a baking sheet lined with parchment paper. Lightly coat chicken with cooking spray. Bake at 400° for 30 minutes or until golden brown. Carefully turn chicken over; bake an additional 30 minutes or until done. **YIELD:** 4 servings (serving size: 1 thigh and 1 drumstick).

CALORIES 256; FAT 8.6g (sat 4.4g, mono 1.6g, poly 1.2g); PROTEIN 27.7g; CARB 15.6g; FIBER 0.8g; CHOL 103mg; IRON 1.6mg; SODIUM 464mg; CALC 18mg

**This recipe first ran in the May 2005 issue of *Cooking Light* magazine** that profiled Chuck Williams, founder of Williams-Sonoma, and it's our hands-down best roast chicken.

# Roasted Chicken with Onions, Potatoes, and Gravy

- 1 (4-pound) roasting chicken
- 1¼ teaspoons salt, divided
- ¾ teaspoon freshly ground black pepper, divided
- 4 fresh oregano sprigs
- 1 lemon, quartered
- 1 celery stalk, cut into 2-inch pieces
- Cooking spray
- 2 tablespoons butter, melted
- 2 pounds medium yellow onions, peeled and each cut into 8 wedges
- 2 pounds small red potatoes, cut into (1-inch) wedges
- 1.1 ounces all-purpose flour (about ¼ cup)
- 1 (14-ounce) can fat-free, lower-sodium chicken broth, divided
- Lemon wedges (optional)
- Oregano sprigs (optional)

**1.** Preheat oven to 425°.

**2.** Remove and discard giblets and neck from chicken. Trim excess fat. Starting at neck cavity, loosen skin from breast and drumsticks by inserting fingers, gently pushing between skin and meat. Combine ½ teaspoon salt and ½ teaspoon black pepper; rub under loosened skin and over breast and drumsticks. Place oregano sprigs, quartered lemon, and celery pieces into body cavity. Lift wing tips up and over back; tuck under chicken. Tie legs together with string. Place chicken, breast side up, on the rack of a broiler pan coated with cooking spray.

**3.** Combine ½ teaspoon salt, remaining ¼ teaspoon pepper, melted butter, onions, and potatoes in a large bowl, and toss well to coat. Arrange onion mixture around chicken on rack. Place rack in pan. Bake at 425° for 20 minutes. Reduce oven temperature to 325° (do not remove pan from oven); bake an additional 1 hour and 10 minutes or until onions and potatoes are tender and a thermometer inserted into meaty part of chicken thigh registers 165°. Set chicken, onions, and potatoes aside; cover and keep warm.

**4.** Place a zip-top plastic bag inside a 2-cup glass measure. Pour pan drippings into bag; let stand 10 minutes (fat will rise to the top). Seal bag; carefully snip off 1 bottom corner of bag. Drain drippings into a small saucepan, stopping before fat layer reaches opening; discard fat. Combine remaining ¼ teaspoon salt, flour, and ½ cup chicken broth in a small bowl, stirring with a whisk. Add flour mixture and remaining chicken broth to saucepan. Bring to a boil over medium-high heat. Reduce heat to medium; cook 5 minutes or until gravy thickens, stirring frequently with a whisk. Carve chicken; serve with gravy and onion mixture. Garnish with lemon wedges and oregano sprigs, if desired. **YIELD:** 6 servings (serving size: about 4 ounces chicken, 1⅓ cups onion mixture, and ⅓ cup gravy).

CALORIES 430; FAT 11.6g (sat 4.5g, mono 3.8g, poly 2g); PROTEIN 36.9g; CARB 43.7g; FIBER 5.2g; CHOL 113mg; IRON 3.4mg; SODIUM 753mg; CALC 71mg

## what makes it light

- fat is removed from the broth before making the gravy
- portion size serves six instead of the usual four

This dish was delicious! My family loved it—**great comfort food that kept them coming back for seconds!** It is also a great dish to prepare ahead of time when entertaining.

**from cookinglight.com**

# Turkey Tetrazzini

- 10 ounces uncooked vermicelli
- 2 teaspoons vegetable oil
- 1 pound turkey breast cutlets
- ¾ teaspoon onion powder, divided
- ½ teaspoon salt, divided
- ¼ teaspoon black pepper, divided
- 2 tablespoons dry sherry
- 2 (8-ounce) packages presliced mushrooms
- ¾ cup frozen green peas, thawed
- ¾ cup fat-free milk
- ⅔ cup fat-free sour cream
- ⅓ cup (about 1½ ounces) grated fresh Parmesan cheese
- 1 (10¾-ounce) can reduced-fat cream of chicken soup (such as Healthy Choice)
- Cooking spray
- ⅓ cup dry breadcrumbs
- 2 tablespoons butter, melted

**1.** Preheat oven to 450°.
**2.** Cook pasta according to package directions, omitting salt and fat. Drain.
**3.** Heat oil in a large nonstick skillet over medium-high heat. Sprinkle turkey with 1/2 teaspoon onion powder, 1/4 teaspoon salt, and 1/8 teaspoon pepper. Add turkey to pan; cook 2 minutes on each side or until done. Remove turkey from pan.
**4.** Add 1/4 teaspoon onion powder, sherry, and mushrooms to pan. Cover and cook 4 minutes or until mushrooms are tender.
**5.** Combine peas, milk, sour cream, cheese, and soup in a large bowl. Chop turkey. Add 1/4 teaspoon salt, 1/8 teaspoon pepper, pasta, turkey, and mushroom mixture to soup mixture, tossing gently to combine. Spoon mixture into a 13 x 9–inch baking dish coated with cooking spray.
**6.** Combine breadcrumbs and butter, tossing to combine. Sprinkle over pasta mixture. Bake at 450° for 12 minutes or until bubbly. **YIELD**: 6 servings (serving size: about 1 2/3 cups).

CALORIES 459; FAT 14.8g (sat 5.9g, mono 4.4g, poly 2.8g); PROTEIN 30.5g; CARB 48.1g; FIBER 3.1g; CHOL 69mg; IRON 4mg; SODIUM 716mg; CALC 199mg

## what makes it light

- uses turkey breast, which is leaner than the traditional light-and-dark-meat mixed versions
- uses fat-free milk
- uses fat-free sour cream
- uses reduced-fat cream of chicken soup
- uses a minimal amount of butter

# sides & desserts

**RECIPE MAKEOVERS**



**5 WAYS WITH**



**RECIPES**

**Cook the fruit unpeeled to add flavor** and a pink hue. Then pass through a sieve to remove the peels. If you have a food mill, use it instead of a sieve. Or cool the fruit slightly, remove and discard the peels, and pulse in a food processor. Refrigerate for up to five days.

# Pear Applesauce

- ½ cup apple juice
- 2 pounds Fuji apples, cored and cut into wedges
- 2 pounds red Bartlett pears, cored and cut into wedges
- 2 (3-inch) cinnamon sticks
- ½ lemon, cut into 2 pieces
- ¼ cup packed brown sugar

**1.** Combine first 5 ingredients in a large saucepan; bring to a boil. Cover, reduce heat, and simmer 45 minutes or until fruit is tender. Discard cinnamon sticks and lemon. Press fruit mixture through a sieve over a bowl using the back of a spoon, and discard peels. Stir in brown sugar. Serve sauce at room temperature or chilled. **YIELD:** 16 servings (serving size: 1/4 cup).

CALORIES 80; FAT 0.4g (sat 0.1g, mono 0.1g, poly 0.1g); PROTEIN 0.3g; CARB 20.7g; FIBER 1.6g; CHOL 0mg; IRON 0.2mg; SODIUM 2.1mg; CALC 12mg

## what makes it light

- uses much less sugar than traditional recipes

This slaw is a healthier version of an original family recipe. It is creamy and delicious, and **takes about five minutes to make.**

**from cookinglight.com**

# New-Fashioned Apple and Raisin Slaw

- ½ cup light sour cream
- 3 tablespoons reduced-fat mayonnaise
- 1½ tablespoons white balsamic vinegar
- 1 teaspoon sugar
- ½ teaspoon black pepper
- ¼ teaspoon salt
- 2 cups unpeeled chopped Rome apple (about 1 medium)
- 1 cup golden raisins
- 1 (16-ounce) package cabbage-and-carrot coleslaw

**1.** Combine first 6 ingredients in a large bowl, stirring with a whisk. Add chopped apple, 1 cup raisins, and coleslaw; toss to combine. **YIELD:** 8 servings (serving size: 1 cup).

CALORIES 120; FAT 2.2g (sat 1.2g, mono 0.8, poly 0.2g); PROTEIN 2.3 g; CARB 25.3g; FIBER 3.3g; CHOL 0mg; IRON 0.8mg; SODIUM 162mg; CALC 31mg

## what makes it light

- uses light sour cream
- uses reduced-fat mayonnaise

30
minutes
or
less

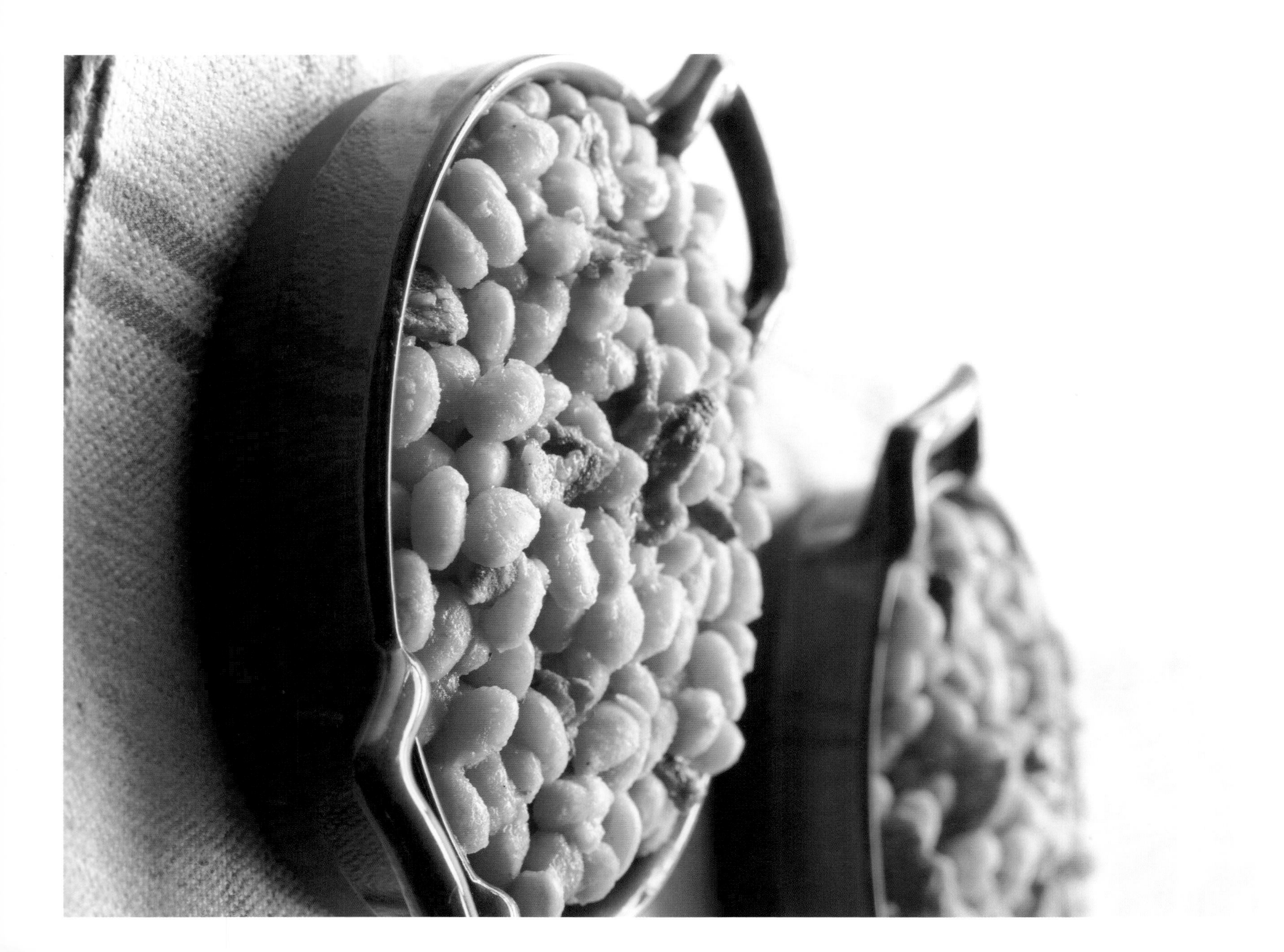

**Check the beans 10 to 15 minutes ahead of time** to make sure they're not drying out.

# Bourbon Baked Beans

- 1 pound dried navy beans (about 2½ cups)
- 3 applewood-smoked bacon slices
- 1 cup finely chopped onion
- 5 cups water, divided
- ½ cup maple syrup, divided
- ¼ cup plus 2 tablespoons bourbon, divided
- ¼ cup Dijon mustard
- 1½ teaspoons Worcestershire sauce
- ¼ teaspoon freshly ground black pepper
- 1 tablespoon cider vinegar
- 1 teaspoon salt

**1.** Sort and wash beans; place in a large Dutch oven. Cover with water to 2 inches above beans; cover and let stand 8 hours or overnight. Drain beans. Wipe pan dry with a paper towel.
**2.** Preheat oven to 350°.
**3.** Heat pan over medium-high heat. Add bacon to pan, and cook 4 minutes or until crisp. Remove from pan, reserving 1½ tablespoons drippings in pan; crumble bacon. Add onion to drippings in pan; cook 5 minutes or until onion begins to brown, stirring frequently. Add beans, bacon, 4 cups water, ¼ cup maple syrup, ¼ cup bourbon, and next 3 ingredients to pan. Bring to a boil; cover and bake at 350° for 2 hours.
**4.** Stir in remaining 1 cup water, remaining ¼ cup maple syrup, and remaining 2 tablespoons bourbon. Cover and bake 1 hour or until beans are tender and liquid is almost absorbed. Stir in vinegar and salt. **YIELD:** 6½ cups (serving size: ½ cup).

CALORIES 199; FAT 3.1g (sat 1.1g, mono 0.7g, poly 0.5g); PROTEIN 7.8g; CARB 31.8g; FIBER 5.6g; CHOL 4mg; IRON 2.1mg; SODIUM 307mg; CALC 66mg

## what makes it light

- uses much less sugar than traditional recipes
- uses less bacon than traditional recipes
- uses much less salt than traditional recipes

# recipe makeover
## broccoli casserole

**The Reader:** Trisha Prenger

**The Story:** Trisha has enjoyed this cheesy, simple casserole since childhood, when her mother prepared it for family meals. "My mother has had this recipe for at least 20 years. As children, my brother and I always liked the crunch of the water chestnuts in the casserole," she says. Since the recipe is easily assembled using ingredients found in most kitchens, Trisha says the casserole is now one of her family's favorites as a side dish for weeknight dinners. But as the mother of a two-year-old daughter, and with another baby on the way, she knows how important it is to make healthful food choices. "My husband, Eric, and I are trying to eat better overall and watch our fat intake," she notes. It's also important for her to cook dishes that are quick, easy, and tasty.

**The Dilemma:** "I knew my mom's version of the casserole was fattening because of the cream and mayonnaise," she says. With 23 grams of fat from the mayonnaise and cream alone, one-third of which was saturated, we had our work cut out for us. Furthermore, the original version contained about 20 percent of the American Heart Association's recommended daily dietary cholesterol intake (less than 300 milligrams) per serving.

**The Solution:** The mayonnaise, Miracle Whip, cream, and cheese added the bulk of the fat and calories to the original recipe. To match the sweet "tang" the Miracle Whip provided, we substituted fat-free mayonnaise, which also imparts a slightly sweet flavor, and shaved 118 calories and nearly 14 grams of fat per serving. Instead of using the cream, we cooked fat-free milk with flour and seasoned the mixture with a bit of salt and pepper to make a thick, rich-tasting sauce. A little fat-free cream cheese stirred into the milk sauce added more body and flavor. Swapping a homemade sauce for the cream cut another 11 grams of fat and 77 calories per portion. These changes also lowered the cholesterol to a manageable 15 milligrams per serving. Creative tweaking—like substituting flavorful sharp cheddar cheese for the original's milder Colby and adding a bit more chopped onion—allowed us to use several fat-free dairy products to cut calories, fat, and cholesterol without compromising taste. One final update: We used crispy panko (Japanese breadcrumbs) tossed with a little butter for a nice golden, crunchy topping.

**The Feedback:** Trisha prepared the heavy and light casseroles for a side-by-side family taste-testing. **"My husband, mother, and I were very impressed and actually liked the lightened version better than the original recipe,"** Trisha says. They preferred the cheddar flavor of the lightened casserole over the "tangy-zesty" taste of the original. One other bonus, according to Trisha, was that there was more sauce in the lighter version, so the healthier version seemed creamier. This cheesier but lighter casserole, which is still quick to assemble, will remain a weeknight favorite for the Prenger family.

| | BEFORE | AFTER |
|---|---|---|
| Calories per serving | 351 | 141 |
| Fat | 30.9g | 4.9g |
| Percent of total calories | 79% | 31% |

# Zesty Broccoli Casserole

- 3 (10-ounce) packages frozen broccoli florets, thawed
- Cooking spray
- 1½ cups fat-free milk
- 2½ tablespoons all-purpose flour
- ½ teaspoon salt
- ¼ teaspoon freshly ground black pepper
- ¾ cup (3 ounces) shredded sharp cheddar cheese
- ½ cup (4 ounces) fat-free cream cheese, softened
- 1 cup fat-free mayonnaise
- ¾ cup chopped onion (about ½ medium)
- 1 (8-ounce) can sliced water chestnuts, rinsed and drained
- ¾ cup panko (Japanese breadcrumbs)
- 2 teaspoons butter, melted

**1.** Preheat oven to 375°.
**2.** Arrange broccoli in an even layer in an 11 x 7–inch baking dish coated with cooking spray; set aside.
**3.** Combine milk, flour, salt, and pepper in a large saucepan over medium-high heat; bring to a boil. Cook 1 minute or until thick, stirring constantly. Remove from heat. Add cheddar and cream cheeses; stir until smooth. Stir in mayonnaise, onion, and water chestnuts. Spoon cheese mixture evenly over broccoli.
**4.** Place panko in a small bowl. Drizzle with butter, and toss. Sprinkle breadcrumb mixture evenly over cheese mixture. Lightly spray breadcrumb layer with cooking spray. Bake at 375° for 25 minutes or until mixture begins to bubble and breadcrumbs brown. **YIELD:** 10 servings (serving size: about ¾ cup).

CALORIES 141; FAT 4.9g (sat 2.6g, mono 1.3g, poly 0.7g); PROTEIN 8.6g; CARB 17.9g; FIBER 4.1g; CHOL 15mg; IRON 1mg; SODIUM 484mg; CALC 173mg

This is now 'my' coleslaw recipe! **Anyone who doesn't normally like coleslaw loves this!** Perfect combo of vinegar and mayo to satisfy the old debate of whether a vinegar- or mayo-based slaw is best. This is now my go-to recipe for company in the summer, and I always make this for the family at the beach. Doubles very easily for large groups, too.

**from cookinglight.com**

# Tangy Mustard Coleslaw

- 7 cups finely shredded green cabbage (about ½ head)
- 1 cup thinly vertically sliced red onion
- 1 cup grated carrot
- ¼ cup white wine vinegar
- 2 tablespoons sugar
- 2 tablespoons whole-grain mustard
- 2 tablespoons reduced-fat mayonnaise
- ⅛ teaspoon salt
- ⅛ teaspoon black pepper
- ⅛ teaspoon ground red pepper

**1.** Combine cabbage, onion, and 1 cup carrot in a large bowl. Combine white wine vinegar, sugar, mustard, mayonnaise, salt, black pepper, and red pepper in a small bowl; stir well with a whisk. Add mustard mixture to cabbage mixture, and toss well to coat. Cover and chill 20 minutes. Stir before serving. **YIELD:** 7 servings (serving size: about 1 cup).

CALORIES 58; FAT 0.8g (sat 0.1g, mono 0.1g, poly 0.3g); PROTEIN 1.5g; CARB 12.3g; FIBER 3g; CHOL 0mg; IRON 0.5mg; SODIUM 172mg; CALC 43mg

## what makes it light

- uses reduced-fat mayonnaise
- uses less salt than traditional recipes

30
minutes
or
less

Yum! This is delicious. **It doesn't taste overly heavy, but it's not obviously light, either.** Was a hit at two dinners for my family and very easy. Nothing fancy—just good comfort food.

**from cookinglight.com**

# Corn Fritter Casserole

- 3 tablespoons butter, softened
- 3 large egg whites
- 1 (8-ounce) block fat-free cream cheese, softened
- ½ cup finely chopped onion
- ½ cup finely chopped red bell pepper
- 1 (15¼-ounce) can whole-kernel corn, drained
- 1 (14¾-ounce) can cream-style corn
- 1 (8½-ounce) package corn muffin mix (such as Jiffy)
- ¼ teaspoon black pepper
- Cooking spray

**1.** Preheat oven to 375°.

**2.** Combine first 3 ingredients in a large bowl, stirring with a whisk until smooth. Stir in onion, bell pepper, whole-kernel corn, and cream-style corn; mix well. Add muffin mix and black pepper, stirring until well combined. Pour into an 11 x 7–inch baking dish coated with cooking spray. Bake at 375° for 50 minutes or until a wooden pick inserted in center comes out clean. **YIELD:** 9 servings (serving size: about ⅔ cup).

CALORIES 247; FAT 8.4g (sat 3.7g, mono 2.7g, poly 0.7g); PROTEIN 8.6g; CARB 36.7g; FIBER 1.9g; CHOL 31mg; IRON 1.3mg; SODIUM 629mg; CALC 72mg

## what makes it light

- uses egg whites
- uses fat-free cream cheese

I give this recipe five stars because we can't live without it! I don't make conventional pickles like Mama used to do, but I have to have a jar of these in the refrigerator at all times during cuke season! **They are fantastic either with a sandwich or as a side-dish.** My husband, who refuses to touch a cucumber in any other form, wants them with just about every meal!

**from cookinglight.com**

# Easy Refrigerator Pickles

- 6 cups thinly sliced pickling cucumbers (about 2 pounds)
- 2 cups thinly sliced onion
- 1½ cups white vinegar
- ¾ cup sugar
- ¾ teaspoon salt
- ½ teaspoon mustard seeds
- ½ teaspoon celery seeds
- ½ teaspoon ground turmeric
- ½ teaspoon crushed red pepper
- ¼ teaspoon freshly ground black pepper
- 4 garlic cloves, thinly sliced

**1.** Place 3 cups cucumber in a medium glass bowl; top with 1 cup onion. Repeat procedure with remaining 3 cups cucumber and remaining 1 cup onion.

**2.** Combine vinegar and remaining ingredients in a small saucepan; stir well. Bring to a boil; cook 1 minute. Pour over cucumber mixture; let cool. Cover and chill at least 4 days. **YIELD:** 7 cups (serving size: ¼ cup).

CALORIES 28; FAT 0.1g (sat 0g, mono 0g, poly 0.1g); PROTEIN 0.3g; CARB 7g; FIBER 0.3g; CHOL 0mg; IRON 0.1mg; SODIUM 64mg; CALC 7mg

## what makes it light

- uses a lot less sugar than traditional recipes
- naturally low fat

**Fried okra is a southern treat.** This version produces a crisp coating without frying.

# Oven-Fried Okra

- 1½ cups yellow cornmeal
- ¾ teaspoon kosher salt, divided
- ½ teaspoon freshly ground black pepper
- Dash of ground red pepper
- ½ cup nonfat buttermilk
- 1 large egg, lightly beaten
- 1 pound fresh okra pods, trimmed and cut into ¾-inch slices (about 3 cups)
- Cooking spray

**1.** Preheat oven to 450°.

**2.** Combine cornmeal, 1/2 teaspoon salt, black pepper, and red pepper in a shallow dish; set aside.

**3.** Combine buttermilk and egg in a large bowl, stirring with a whisk. Add okra; toss to coat. Let stand 3 minutes.

**4.** Dredge okra in cornmeal mixture. Place okra on a jelly-roll pan coated with cooking spray. Lightly coat okra with cooking spray. Bake at 450° for 35 to 40 minutes, stirring once. Sprinkle with remaining 1/4 teaspoon salt. **YIELD:** 8 servings (serving size: about 1/2 cup).

CALORIES 144; FAT 0.7g (sat 0.2g, mono 0.3g, poly 0.1g); PROTEIN 4.5g; CARB 29.3g; FIBER 2.6g; CHOL 27mg; IRON 1.3mg; SODIUM 204mg; CALC 68mg

## what makes it light

- uses kosher salt to keep sodium low
- uses nonfat buttermilk
- oven-fried, not deep-fried

This is exactly what you want potato salad to be. **The simple flavors all meld well together to create that taste we all expect and love.** Using low-fat mayo definitely did not compromise the flavor. Yet another great **Cooking Light** recipe where you don't even notice it's light.

**from cookinglight.com**

# Potato Salad 101

- 2 pounds small all-purpose white or red potatoes
- 3 tablespoons white vinegar
- 1 tablespoon canola oil
- ½ cup chopped celery
- ½ cup finely chopped red onion
- 2 tablespoons sweet pickle relish, drained
- 3 hard-cooked large eggs, chopped
- ¾ cup reduced-fat mayonnaise
- 2 tablespoons prepared mustard
- ½ teaspoon salt
- ¼ teaspoon freshly ground black pepper

**1.** Place potatoes in a saucepan, and cover with water. Bring to a boil. Reduce heat; simmer 10 minutes or until tender. Drain. Cool and peel. Cut potatoes into 1/2-inch cubes. Place potatoes in a large bowl; sprinkle with vinegar and oil. Add celery, onion, pickle relish, and eggs; toss gently.
**2.** Combine mayonnaise, mustard, salt, and pepper. Spoon mayonnaise mixture over potato mixture; toss gently to coat. Cover and chill 1 to 24 hours. **YIELD:** 7 servings (serving size: 1 cup).

CALORIES 215; FAT 6.1g (sat 1.1g, mono 2.5g, poly 2g); PROTEIN 4.9g; CARB 35.9g; FIBER 1.9g; CHOL 91mg; IRON 0.9mg; SODIUM 536mg; CALC 26mg

## what makes it light

- uses reduced-fat mayonnaise
- uses canola oil, which is a healthy option

# 5 ways with mashed potatoes

## Buttermilk-Parmesan Mashed Potatoes

Be sure to purchase a crumbly wedge of Parmigiano-Reggiano for this superquick potato side dish.

- **2 pounds russet potatoes**
- **⅔ cup fat-free milk**
- **3 tablespoons butter**
- **½ cup buttermilk**
- **⅓ cup (1½ ounces) grated fresh Parmigiano-Reggiano cheese**
- **½ teaspoon salt**
- **¼ teaspoon freshly ground black pepper**

**1.** Prick each potato several times with a fork. Place potatoes in microwave, and cook at HIGH 16 minutes or until tender, turning after 8 minutes. Let stand 2 minutes. Cut each potato in half lengthwise; scoop out flesh with a large spoon, and transfer to a bowl.

**2.** Combine milk and butter in a microwave-safe bowl, and microwave at HIGH 2 minutes or until butter melts. Add milk mixture to potatoes; mash with a potato masher to desired consistency. Stir in buttermilk and remaining ingredients. **YIELD:** 6 servings (serving size: ¾ cup).

CALORIES 240; FAT 7.9g (sat 4.9g, mono 1.9g, poly 0.3g); PROTEIN 7.5g; CARB 35.2g; FIBER 3.5g; CHOL 22mg; IRON 1.7mg; SODIUM 366mg; CALC 117mg

## Creamy Herbed Mashed Potatoes

Yukon golds make brilliant mashed potatoes, thanks to their balance of waxiness and starch. Because yellow potatoes are more flavorful than others, they don't need a lot of fat to taste rich. Mash them just until creamy—overworking the potatoes will make them gummy.

- 4 cups cubed peeled Yukon gold potato (about 2 pounds)
- ½ cup 2% reduced-fat milk
- ¼ cup low-fat sour cream
- 3 tablespoons butter
- 3 tablespoons chopped fresh chives
- 2 tablespoons chopped fresh parsley
- ½ teaspoon salt
- ¼ teaspoon freshly ground black pepper

**1.** Place potato in a saucepan; cover with water. Bring to a boil; cover, reduce heat, and simmer 10 minutes or until tender. Drain. Return potato to pan. Add milk and remaining ingredients; mash with a potato masher to desired consistency. **YIELD:** 6 servings (serving size: ¾ cup).

CALORIES 215; FAT 7.1g (sat 4.5g, mono 1.8g, poly 0.3g); PROTEIN 4.5g; CARB 34.5g; FIBER 2.4g; CHOL 20mg; IRON 0.7mg; SODIUM 280mg; CALC 51mg

## Camembert Mashed Potatoes ▼

The buttery taste and creamy texture of Camembert cheese glorifies these potatoes. Camembert is similar in flavor and texture to Brie, which makes a fine substitute.

**1½ (8-ounce) rounds Camembert cheese**
**11 cups cubed peeled Yukon gold potato (about 4½ pounds)**
**½ cup 1% low-fat milk**
**¾ teaspoon salt**
**¾ teaspoon freshly ground black pepper**
**Chopped fresh chives (optional)**
**Freshly ground black pepper (optional)**

**1.** Cut cheese into 6 wedges. Carefully remove rind from cheese; discard rind. Chop cheese; let stand at room temperature while potato cooks.
**2.** Place potato in a large Dutch oven; cover with water. Bring to a boil. Reduce heat; simmer 12 minutes or until tender. Drain in a colander; return potato to pan. Add cheese, milk, salt, and 3/4 teaspoon pepper; mash with a potato masher until smooth. Garnish with chives and additional pepper, if desired. **YIELD:** 12 servings (serving size: about 2/3 cup).

CALORIES 198; FAT 4.4g (sat 2.8g, mono 1.3g, poly 0.1g); PROTEIN 7.9g; CARB 30.7g; FIBER 2g; CHOL 13mg; IRON 1.5mg; SODIUM 310mg; CALC 82mg

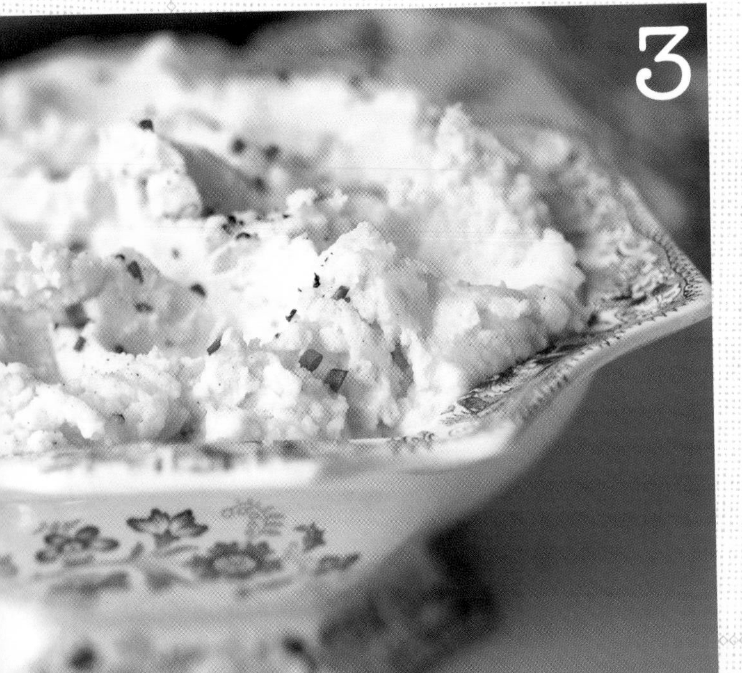

## Mashed Honey-Roasted Sweet Potatoes ▲

Prepare this dish up to a day ahead, and store, covered, in the refrigerator. To reheat, bake at 350°, covered, for 45 minutes.

**6 pounds sweet potatoes, peeled and cut into (1-inch) cubes**
**Cooking spray**
**5 tablespoons honey, divided**
**4 tablespoons unsalted butter**
**¾ teaspoon salt**

**1.** Preheat oven to 375°.
**2.** Place potato in a single layer on 2 large baking sheets coated with cooking spray. Lightly spray potato with cooking spray. Bake at 375° for 1 hour or until tender, stirring occasionally. Place potato, 1/4 cup honey, butter, and salt in a large bowl, and beat with a mixer at medium speed until smooth. Drizzle with 1 tablespoon honey. **YIELD:** 12 servings (serving size: 1/2 cup).

CALORIES 140; FAT 3.9g (sat 2.4g, mono 1.1g, poly 0.2g); PROTEIN 1.4g; CARB 26.2g; FIBER 2.4g; CHOL 10mg; IRON 0.4mg; SODIUM 154mg; CALC 24mg

## Mashed Yukon Gold Potatoes with Horseradish Butter

Horseradish is such a pungent ingredient that a little goes a long way. If you don't have a ricer or food mill, gently mash the potatoes with a potato masher. Just be sure not to overmash, or they will become rubbery.

Horseradish Butter:

- Cooking spray
- 1 tablespoon minced shallots
- ¼ cup butter, softened
- 1 tablespoon chopped fresh parsley
- 2 teaspoons prepared horseradish

Potatoes:

- 6½ cups cubed peeled Yukon gold potato (about 2½ pounds)
- 1 bay leaf
- ¼ cup 1% low-fat milk
- ¼ cup fat-free, lower-sodium chicken broth
- ¼ cup reduced-fat sour cream
- 1 teaspoon salt
- ¼ teaspoon freshly ground black pepper

**1.** To prepare horseradish butter, heat a small nonstick skillet over medium heat. Coat pan with cooking spray. Add shallots to pan; cook 1 minute. Remove from heat; cool.

**2.** Combine shallots, butter, parsley, and horseradish in a small bowl; blend well. Transfer butter mixture to a sheet of plastic wrap. Shape butter mixture into a 3-inch-long log, using plastic wrap to help mold. Wrap log tightly in plastic wrap, and refrigerate until firm.

**3.** To prepare potatoes, place potato and bay leaf in a large saucepan; cover with water. Bring to a boil. Cover, reduce heat, and simmer 20 minutes or until tender; drain. Discard bay leaf. Press potato through a ricer or food mill into a large bowl. Combine milk and broth in a microwave-safe dish. Microwave at HIGH 1 minute or until warm. Add milk mixture, sour cream, salt, and pepper to potato, stirring until well blended. Serve with horseradish butter.

**YIELD:** 8 servings (serving size: ½ cup potatoes and 1½ teaspoons horseradish butter).

CALORIES 182; FAT 6.7g (sat 4.2g, mono 1.8g, poly 0.3g); PROTEIN 4g; CARB 26.1g; FIBER 1.8g; CHOL 18mg; IRON 1.3mg; SODIUM 369mg; CALC 21mg

**This recipe was a great change from the usual potato au gratin!** I was concerned that our kids would think it was 'icky' because of the strong flavor of the Gorgonzola, but they devoured it!

**from cookinglight.com**

# Potato-Gorgonzola Gratin

- 2 tablespoons butter
- 2½ tablespoons all-purpose flour
- 1 teaspoon chopped fresh thyme
- 2½ cups fat-free milk
- ¾ cup (3 ounces) crumbled Gorgonzola or other blue cheese
- 1½ teaspoons salt
- ¼ teaspoon freshly ground black pepper
- 3 pounds baking potatoes, peeled and cut into ⅛-inch-thick slices
- Cooking spray
- ⅓ cup (1½ ounces) grated Parmigiano-Reggiano cheese

**1.** Preheat oven to 375°.

**2.** Melt butter in a small saucepan over medium-high heat. Add flour, and cook 2 minutes, stirring constantly with a whisk. Stir in thyme. Gradually add milk, stirring with a whisk; cook over medium heat until slightly thick (about 3 minutes), stirring constantly. Stir in Gorgonzola; cook 3 minutes or until cheese melts, stirring constantly. Stir in salt and pepper. Remove from heat.

**3.** Arrange one-fourth of potato in bottom of a 13 x 9–inch baking dish coated with cooking spray; spoon about 3/4 cup sauce over potato. Repeat layers twice; arrange remaining potato over sauce. Sprinkle with Parmigiano-Reggiano. Cover and bake at 375° for 30 minutes. Uncover and bake an additional 40 minutes or until potatoes are tender. Remove from oven; let stand 10 minutes before serving. **YIELD:** 8 servings (serving size: about 1 cup).

CALORIES 254; FAT 7.9g (sat 5g, mono 2g, poly 0.2g); PROTEIN 10.6g; CARB 36.8g; FIBER 2.8g; CHOL 22mg; IRON 1.5mg; SODIUM 751mg; CALC 228mg

## what makes it light

- uses a minimal amount of butter
- uses fat-free milk
- uses two strong cheeses, which makes it possible to use less cheese to get great flavor

# 5 ways with fries

## Garlic Fries

These fries stand out. First, they're roasted at high heat until crisp and golden. Then they're tossed in melted butter, shredded Parmesan cheese, and chopped fresh parsley for a tasty finishing touch.

- **4 teaspoons canola oil**
- **¾ teaspoon salt**
- **3 pounds peeled baking potatoes, cut into ¼-inch-thick strips**
- **Cooking spray**
- **2 tablespoons butter**
- **8 garlic cloves, minced (about 5 teaspoons)**
- **2 tablespoons finely chopped fresh parsley**
- **2 tablespoons freshly grated Parmesan cheese**

**1.** Preheat oven to 400°.

**2.** Combine first 3 ingredients in a large zip-top plastic bag, tossing to coat. Arrange potato in a single layer on a baking sheet coated with cooking spray. Bake at 400° for 50 minutes or until potato is tender and golden brown, turning after 20 minutes.

**3.** Place butter and garlic in a large nonstick skillet, and cook over low heat 2 minutes, stirring constantly. Add potato, parsley, and Parmesan cheese to pan; toss to coat. Serve immediately. **YIELD:** 6 servings.

CALORIES 256; FAT 7.7g (sat 3.3g, mono 2g, poly 2g); PROTEIN 5.9g; CARB 42.3g; FIBER 3.5g; CHOL 12mg; IRON 1.9mg; SODIUM 386mg; CALC 55mg

1

# Oven Fries with Crisp Sage Leaves

As beautiful to look at as they are great to eat, these golden slices of potato are scented and subtly flavored with crisp cooked sage. They are an incredible snack or a perfect savory side to any meal, from chicken to filet mignon. You can double this recipe and use two baking sheets. For even browning, rotate the baking sheets halfway through the first 40 minutes of baking.

**2 small baking potatoes (about 1 pound)**
**1 tablespoon extra-virgin olive oil**
**½ teaspoon kosher salt**
**12 fresh sage leaves**

**1.** Preheat oven to 400°.
**2.** Cut each baking potato lengthwise into 6 equal slices. Place potato slices in a large bowl, and drizzle with olive oil. Sprinkle with salt; toss well to coat potato slices. Remove potato slices from bowl. Reserve remaining olive oil and salt in bowl; set aside. Arrange potato slices in a single layer on a baking sheet.
**3.** Bake at 400° for 40 minutes or until potato slices are golden brown on the bottom. Remove potato slices from oven (leave oven at 400°).
**4.** Add sage leaves to reserved olive oil and salt in bowl. Gently rub sage leaves along bottom of bowl, coating both sides with olive oil and salt. Working with one potato slice at a time, lift potato slice from baking sheet with a thin spatula. Lay 1 sage leaf on baking sheet, and cover with potato slice, browned side down. Repeat with remaining potato slices and sage leaves.
**5.** Bake at 400° for 10 minutes. Remove from heat. Using a thin spatula, carefully turn potato slices over with leaves on top. Bake at 400° for an additional 10 minutes or until bottoms begin to brown. Serve immediately.
**YIELD:** 3 servings (serving size: 4 potato slices).

CALORIES 205; FAT 4.7g (sat 0.7g, mono 3.3g, poly 0.4g); PROTEIN 3.5g; CARB 38.2g; FIBER 3.6g; CHOL 0mg; IRON 2.1mg; SODIUM 326mg; CALC 15mg

## Spicy Steak Fries ▾

Best served with burgers or steaks, these thick fries are a welcome change from deep-fried French fries.

- **1 tablespoon vegetable oil**
- **2 large baking potatoes, each cut lengthwise into 12 wedges (about 1½ pounds)**
- **2 teaspoons seasoning blend (such as Paul Prudhomme's Seafood Magic)**
- **¼ teaspoon salt**

**1.** Preheat oven to 400°.

**2.** Spread oil on a jelly-roll pan. Place potato wedges on pan. Sprinkle with seasoning; toss gently to coat. Bake at 400° for 40 minutes or until tender. Sprinkle with salt. **YIELD:** 4 servings (serving size: 6 wedges).

CALORIES 216; FAT 3.6g (sat 0.7g, mono 1g, poly 1.7g); PROTEIN 3.7g; CARB 42.9g; FIBER 3.1g; CHOL 0mg; IRON 2.3mg; SODIUM 275mg; CALC 17mg

## Herbed Sweet Potato Fries ▾

We guarantee you can't eat just one. And that's a good thing: Sweet potatoes are rich in beta carotene, vitamin C, and vitamin E.

- **2 cups frozen sweet potato fries (such as Alexia)**
- **Cooking spray**
- **1 teaspoon chopped fresh thyme**
- **1 teaspoon chopped fresh rosemary**
- **¼ teaspoon salt**
- **¼ teaspoon freshly ground black pepper**

**1.** Preheat oven to 425°.

**2.** Arrange fries in a single layer on a baking sheet coated with cooking spray. Coat fries evenly with cooking spray; sprinkle remaining ingredients evenly over fries, tossing to coat.

**3.** Bake at 425° for 14 minutes or until golden. **YIELD:** 4 servings (serving size: ½ cup).

CALORIES 86; FAT 3g (sat 0.3g, mono 0g, poly 0g); PROTEIN 1.2g; CARB 13.8g; FIBER 1.8g; CHOL 0mg; IRON 0.5mg; SODIUM 225mg; CALC 25mg

5

## Spicy Sweet Potato Fries

- 2½ cups frozen sweet potato fries
- Butter-flavored cooking spray
- ¼ teaspoon kosher salt
- ⅛ teaspoon ground red pepper

**1.** Preheat oven to 425°.
**2.** Place potatoes in a single layer on a large baking sheet coated with cooking spray. Coat potatoes with cooking spray.
**3.** Bake at 425° for 16 minutes or until crisp and golden.
**4.** Combine salt and ground pepper in a small bowl. Remove fries from oven, and sprinkle with salt mixture. **YIELD:** 4 servings (serving size: ½ cup).

CALORIES 202; FAT 8.2g (sat 1.7g, mono 3.7g, poly 2.3g); PROTEIN 2.7g; CARB 32.1g; FIBER 4.1g; CHOL 0mg; IRON 1mg; SODIUM 304mg; CALC 54mg

This dish was amazing! Took it to a dinner party, and everyone loved it! **This was my first time making a sweet potato casserole, and it was surprisingly simple.** Make sure to not skip the broiling part—it gives the crumble on top the perfect crunch! This is definitely a keeper! Thanks for another good recipe CL!

**from cookinglight.com**

# Sweet Potato Casserole

Potatoes:

- 2 pounds sweet potatoes, peeled and chopped
- ¾ cup granulated sugar
- ¼ cup evaporated low-fat milk
- 3 tablespoons butter, melted
- ½ teaspoon salt
- 1 teaspoon vanilla extract
- 2 large eggs
- Cooking spray

Topping:

- 1.5 ounces all-purpose flour (about ⅓ cup)
- ⅔ cup packed brown sugar
- ⅛ teaspoon salt
- 2 tablespoons melted butter
- ½ cup chopped pecans

**1.** Preheat oven to 350°.
**2.** To prepare potatoes, place potato in a Dutch oven; cover with water. Bring to a boil. Reduce heat, and simmer 20 minutes or until tender; drain. Cool 5 minutes.
**3.** Place potato in a large bowl; add granulated sugar, evaporated milk, 3 tablespoons melted butter, 1/2 teaspoon salt, and vanilla. Beat with a mixer at medium speed until smooth. Add eggs; beat well. Pour potato mixture into a 13 x 9–inch baking pan coated with cooking spray.
**4.** To prepare topping, weigh or lightly spoon flour into a dry measuring cup; level with a knife. Combine flour, brown sugar, and 1/8 teaspoon salt; stir with a whisk. Stir in 2 tablespoons melted butter. Sprinkle flour mixture evenly over potato mixture; arrange pecans evenly over top. Bake at 350° for 25 minutes or just until golden. Remove casserole from oven.
**5.** Preheat broiler.
**6.** Broil casserole 45 seconds or until topping is bubbly. Let stand 10 minutes before serving.
**YIELD:** 12 servings (serving size: about 2/3 cup).

CALORIES 258; FAT 9.2g (sat 3.6g, mono 3.6g, poly 1.5g); PROTEIN 3.3g; CARB 42g; FIBER 2.5g; CHOL 43mg; IRON 1.2mg; SODIUM 199mg; CALC 54mg

## what makes it light

- uses less sugar than traditional recipes
- uses evaporated low-fat milk
- uses a minimal amount of butter

**Easy to prepare and rich in flavor,** the casserole pairs fabulously with roasted chicken, ham, or pork chops. This simple dish has become a staff favorite, and we believe it will be in your home, too.

# Squash-Rice Casserole

- 8 cups sliced zucchini (about 2½ pounds)
- 1 cup chopped onion
- ½ cup fat-free, lower-sodium chicken broth
- 2 cups cooked rice
- 1 cup (4 ounces) shredded reduced-fat sharp cheddar cheese
- 1 cup fat-free sour cream
- ¼ cup (1 ounce) grated fresh Parmesan cheese, divided
- ¼ cup Italian-seasoned breadcrumbs
- 1 teaspoon salt
- ¼ teaspoon black pepper
- 2 large eggs, lightly beaten
- Cooking spray

**1.** Preheat oven to 350°.
**2.** Combine first 3 ingredients in a Dutch oven; bring to a boil. Cover, reduce heat, and simmer 20 minutes or until tender. Drain; partially mash with a potato masher.
**3.** Combine zucchini mixture, rice, cheddar cheese, sour cream, 2 tablespoons Parmesan cheese, breadcrumbs, salt, pepper, and eggs in a bowl; stir gently. Spoon mixture into a 13 x 9–inch baking dish coated with cooking spray; sprinkle with remaining 2 tablespoons Parmesan cheese. Bake at 350° for 30 minutes or until bubbly. Remove casserole from oven.
**4.** Preheat broiler. Broil 1 minute or until lightly browned. **YIELD:** 8 servings (serving size: 1 cup).

CALORIES 197; FAT 5.5g (sat 2.7g, mono 1.5g, poly 0.4g); PROTEIN 12.7g; CARB 24g; FIBER 1.4g; CHOL 65mg; IRON 1.5mg; SODIUM 623mg; CALC 209mg

## what makes it light

- uses fat-free, lower-sodium chicken broth
- uses reduced-fat sharp cheddar cheese
- uses fat-free sour cream

**Here's our lightened rendition of a traditional yellow squash casserole;** it's just as delicious, just minus the guilt. Meat-and-three casseroles are usually laden with mayo, cream, butter, cheese, or any combination of the four.

# Yellow Squash Casserole

- 8 cups sliced yellow squash (about 2 pounds)
- 1 tablespoon water
- 6 ounces hot turkey Italian sausage (about 2 links)
- ½ cup chopped onion
- 2 garlic cloves, minced
- 2 (1-ounce) slices day-old white bread
- ½ cup fat-free sour cream
- ⅓ cup (1½ ounces) diced provolone cheese
- ¼ teaspoon salt
- ¼ teaspoon black pepper
- 1 (10¾-ounce) can condensed reduced-fat, reduced-sodium cream of mushroom soup, undiluted
- Cooking spray

**1.** Preheat oven to 350°.
**2.** Combine squash and water in a large microwave-safe bowl. Cover with plastic wrap; vent. Microwave at HIGH 6 to 10 minutes or until tender. Drain well.
**3.** Remove casing from sausage. Cook sausage, onion, and garlic in a large nonstick skillet over medium-high heat until browned, stirring to crumble. Drain.
**4.** Place bread in a food processor, and pulse 10 times or until coarse crumbs form to measure 1 cup. Combine squash, sausage mixture, ½ cup breadcrumbs, sour cream, cheese, salt, pepper, and soup. Spoon squash mixture into a 2-quart casserole coated with cooking spray.
**5.** Top with remaining ½ cup breadcrumbs. Spray breadcrumbs with cooking spray. Bake at 350° for 30 minutes. **YIELD:** 12 servings (serving size: ⅔ cup).

CALORIES 85; FAT 2.9g (sat 1.2g, mono 0.5g, poly 0.6g); PROTEIN 4.8g; CARB 10.3g; FIBER 1.8g; CHOL 12mg; IRON 0.7mg; SODIUM 279mg; CALC 91mg

## what makes it light

- uses turkey Italian sausage
- uses fat-free sour cream
- uses reduced-fat, reduced-sodium cream of mushroom soup

# 5 ways with cookies

## Snickerdoodles

Extremely easy to make, these cookies are just as good for a special occasion as they are an everyday snack.

- **7.9 ounces all-purpose flour (about 1¾ cups)**
- **½ teaspoon baking soda**
- **½ teaspoon cream of tartar**
- **1 cup sugar**
- **¼ cup butter, softened**
- **1 tablespoon corn syrup**
- **1 teaspoon vanilla**
- **1 large egg**
- **3 tablespoons sugar**
- **2 teaspoons ground cinnamon**
- **Cooking spray**

**1.** Preheat oven to 375°.

**2.** Weigh or lightly spoon flour into dry measuring cups; level with a knife. Combine flour, baking soda, and cream of tartar, stirring with a whisk.

**3.** Combine 1 cup sugar and butter in a large bowl, and beat with a mixer at medium speed until well blended. Add corn syrup, vanilla, and egg; beat well. Gradually add flour mixture to sugar mixture, beating just until combined. Cover and chill 10 minutes.

**4.** Combine 3 tablespoons sugar and cinnamon, stirring with a whisk.

**5.** With moist hands, shape dough into 42 (1-inch) balls. Roll balls in sugar mixture. Place balls 2 inches apart onto baking sheets coated with cooking spray. Flatten balls with bottom of a glass. Bake at 375° for 5 minutes (cookies will be slightly soft). Cool on baking sheets 2 minutes. Remove cookies from pans; cool completely on wire racks. **YIELD:** 42 cookies (serving size: 1 cookie).

CALORIES 54; FAT 1.3g (sat 0.7g, mono 0.1g, poly 0.4g); PROTEIN 0.7g; CARB 10.1g; FIBER 0.2g; CHOL 8mg; IRON 0.3mg; SODIUM 28mg; CALC 3mg

1

## Lemon-Honey Drop Cookies

One cookinglight.com reader describes these cookies as "little lemony morsels of loveliness." We think you'll wholeheartedly agree.

- ½ cup granulated sugar
- 7 tablespoons butter, softened
- 2 teaspoons grated lemon rind
- ⅓ cup honey
- ½ teaspoon lemon extract
- 1 large egg
- 7.9 ounces all-purpose flour (about 1¾ cups)
- 1 teaspoon baking powder
- ½ teaspoon salt
- ¼ cup plain fat-free yogurt
- Cooking spray
- 1 cup powdered sugar
- 2 tablespoons fresh lemon juice
- 2 teaspoons grated lemon rind

**1.** Preheat oven to 350°.

**2.** Beat first 3 ingredients with a mixer at medium speed until light and fluffy. Add honey, extract, and egg; beat until well blended. Weigh or lightly spoon flour into dry measuring cups; level with a knife. Combine flour, baking powder, and salt, stirring well with a whisk. Add flour mixture to sugar mixture alternately with yogurt, beginning and ending with flour mixture. Drop by level tablespoons 2 inches apart onto baking sheets coated with cooking spray. Bake at 350° for 12 minutes or until lightly browned.

**3.** Combine powdered sugar and juice in a small bowl; stir with a whisk. Brush powdered sugar mixture evenly over hot cookies. Sprinkle evenly with 2 teaspoons rind. Remove cookies from pan; cool on wire racks. **YIELD:** 32 cookies (serving size: 1 cookie).

CALORIES 89; FAT 2.8g (sat 1.6g, mono 0.8g, poly 0.2g); PROTEIN 1.1g; CARB 15.3g; FIBER 0.2g; CHOL 14mg; IRON 0.4mg; SODIUM 81mg; CALC 15mg

## Chocolate Chip Cookies ▼

Store up to one week in an airtight container—if they last that long. We suggest keeping a dozen in the freezer for emergencies.

- **10 ounces all-purpose flour (about 2¼ cups)**
- **1 teaspoon baking soda**
- **¼ teaspoon salt**
- **1 cup packed brown sugar**
- **¾ cup granulated sugar**
- **½ cup butter, softened**
- **1 teaspoon vanilla extract**
- **2 large egg whites**
- **¾ cup semisweet chocolate chips**
- **Cooking spray**

**1.** Preheat oven to 350°.

**2.** Weigh or lightly spoon flour into dry measuring cups; level with a knife. Combine flour, baking soda, and salt, stirring with a whisk.

**3.** Combine sugars and butter in a large bowl; beat with a mixer at medium speed until well blended. Add vanilla and egg whites; beat 1 minute. Add flour mixture and chips; beat until blended.

**4.** Drop dough by level tablespoons 2 inches apart onto baking sheets coated with cooking spray. Bake at 350° for 10 minutes or until lightly browned. Cool on pans 2 minutes. Remove from pans; cool completely on wire racks. **YIELD:** 4 dozen (serving size: 1 cookie).

CALORIES 88; FAT 3g (sat 1.8g, mono 0.5g, poly 0.1g); PROTEIN 1g; CARB 14.6g; FIBER 0.2g; CHOL 5mg; IRON 0.4mg; SODIUM 56mg; CALC 5mg

## Peanut Butter Icebox Cookies ▼

For a chocolate-peanut butter variation add one ounce of grated semisweet chocolate to the flour mixture.

- **4.5 ounces all-purpose flour (about 1 cup)**
- **¼ teaspoon baking soda**
- **⅛ teaspoon salt**
- **3 tablespoons butter, softened**
- **2 tablespoons chunky peanut butter**
- **½ cup packed brown sugar**
- **¼ cup granulated sugar**
- **1 teaspoon vanilla extract**
- **1 large egg white**
- **Cooking spray**

**1.** Weigh or lightly spoon flour into a dry measuring cup; level with a knife. Combine flour, baking soda, and salt; set aside. Beat butter and peanut butter at medium speed of a mixer until light and fluffy. Gradually add sugars, beating at medium speed until well blended. Add vanilla and egg white, and beat well. Add flour mixture; stir well. Turn dough out onto wax paper; shape into a 6-inch log. Wrap log in wax paper; freeze 3 hours.
**2.** Preheat oven to 350°.
**3.** Cut log into 24 (1/4-inch) slices, and place slices 1 inch apart on a baking sheet coated with cooking spray. Bake at 350° for 8 to 10 minutes. Remove from pan, and cool on wire racks. **YIELD:** 2 dozen (serving size: 1 cookie).

CALORIES 69; FAT 2.4g (sat 0.4g, mono 0.7g, poly 0.5g); PROTEIN 1.2g; CARB 10.8g; FIBER 0.2g; CHOL 9mg; IRON 0.4mg; SODIUM 53mg; CALC 7mg

5

## Oatmeal-Raisin Cookies ▸

Fast, simple, and satisfying, oatmeal-raisin cookies are a sure-to-please staple in the American home. They're easy to prepare because they're made with ingredients you probably have on hand.

- ½ cup granulated sugar
- ½ cup packed brown sugar
- ⅓ cup butter, softened
- 1 teaspoon vanilla extract
- ⅛ teaspoon salt
- 1 large egg
- 4.5 ounces all-purpose flour (about 1 cup)
- 1 cup regular oats
- ½ cup raisins
- Cooking spray

**1.** Preheat oven to 350°.
**2.** Beat first 6 ingredients at medium speed of a mixer until light and fluffy. Weigh or lightly spoon flour into a dry measuring cup, and level with a knife. Add flour and oats to egg mixture; beat until blended. Stir in raisins. Drop by level tablespoons 2 inches apart onto baking sheets coated with cooking spray. Bake at 350° for 15 minutes or until golden brown. Cool on pan 3 minutes. Remove cookies from pan; cool on wire racks. **YIELD:** 2 dozen (serving size: 1 cookie).

CALORIES 101; FAT 3.1g (sat 1.7g, mono 0.9g, poly 0.2g); PROTEIN 1.5g; CARB 17.3g; FIBER 0.6g; CHOL 16mg; IRON 0.6mg; SODIUM 43mg; CALC 10mg

These are perfect!!! They remind me of my childhood and those muggy southern summer afternoons spent by my neighbor's pool. They are smooth and sweet and tangy, finishing with an unexpected crunch. **The combination of textures is addictive if the flavor isn't already enough to hook you.** I finished them with a light dusting of powdered sugar. Next time I will use a doily as a stencil before I powder them up for added elegance.

**from cookinglight.com**

# Easy Lemon Squares

Crust:

- ¼ cup granulated sugar
- 3 tablespoons butter, softened
- 4.5 ounces all-purpose flour (about 1 cup)

Topping:

- 3 large eggs
- ¾ cup granulated sugar
- 2 teaspoons grated lemon rind
- ⅓ cup fresh lemon juice
- 3 tablespoons all-purpose flour
- ½ teaspoon baking powder
- ⅛ teaspoon salt
- 2 teaspoons powdered sugar

**1.** Preheat oven to 350°.

**2.** To prepare crust, beat 1/4 cup granulated sugar and butter at medium speed of a mixer until creamy. Weigh or lightly spoon 4.5 ounces flour into a dry measuring cup; level with a knife. Gradually add flour to sugar mixture, beating at low speed until mixture resembles fine crumbs. Gently press mixture into bottom of an 8-inch square baking pan. Bake at 350° for 15 minutes; cool on a wire rack.

**3.** To prepare topping, beat eggs at medium speed until foamy. Add 3/4 cup granulated sugar and next 5 ingredients, and beat until well blended. Pour mixture over partially baked crust. Bake at 350° for 20 to 25 minutes or until set. Cool on wire rack. Sift powdered sugar evenly over top.

**YIELD:** 16 servings (serving size: 1 square).

CALORIES 118; FAT 3.2g (sat 1.7g, mono 1g, poly 0.3g); PROTEIN 2.2g; CARB 20.5g; FIBER 0.3g; CHOL 47mg; IRON 0.6mg; SODIUM 68mg; CALC 16mg

## what makes it light

- uses less butter than traditional recipes
- uses fewer eggs than traditional recipes

# recipe makeover
## butterscotch bars

**The Reader:** Carol Bischoff

**The Story:** Carol has always had a sweet tooth. She says these rich butterscotch bars, with a buttery crust and gooey-nutty center, are irresistible. But she and her husband now have goals to stay fit and eat more healthfully, so she sent the recipe to *Cooking Light* for a makeover.

**The Dilemma:** Plenty of butter, butterscotch chips, sweetened condensed milk, and walnuts contributed to the hefty 223 calories per serving. One bar had 5 grams of saturated fat per serving, about one-third the daily allotment per American Heart Association diet recommendations.

**The Solution:** We started with the middle layer. First, we swapped fat-free sweetened condensed milk for the regular version to maintain sweetness and richness with fewer calories. Then we reduced the amount of butterscotch chips by a third and omitted 2 tablespoons butter in this part of the recipe without compromising flavor or texture. These three changes trimmed 42 calories and 2½ grams of fat (nearly 2 grams saturated) per serving. We also slightly tweaked the base layer, which serves double-duty as the crumb topping. Eliminating 3 tablespoons of butter and ½ cup brown sugar shaved 20 calories and 1 gram of fat per bar. Lastly, to keep calories in check, we used fewer walnuts and finely chopped and toasted them to extend their flavor and crunch. This cut another 10 calories and about 1 gram of fat.

**The Feedback:** Carol and her husband liked the lighter bars. Her husband thought the oatmeal was more prominent, which added a pleasingly hearty texture to the dessert. "There were many excellent changes, and **I like this healthier version of my longtime dessert favorite,**" Carol says.

| | BEFORE | AFTER |
|---|---|---|
| Calories per serving | 223 | 148 |
| Fat | 9.8g | 5.1g |
| Percent of total calories | 5.4% | 2.7% |

**A small square of these rich bars is enough to satisfy a dessert craving.** The flour and oats mixture is somewhat dry after combining, but it serves as both a solid base for the soft butterscotch chip layer and a crumbly, streusel-like topping.

# Butterscotch Bars

- 1 cup packed brown sugar
- 5 tablespoons butter, melted
- 1 teaspoon vanilla extract
- 1 large egg, lightly beaten
- 9 ounces all-purpose flour (about 2 cups)
- 2½ cups quick-cooking oats
- ½ teaspoon salt
- ½ teaspoon baking soda
- Cooking spray
- ¾ cup fat-free sweetened condensed milk
- 1¼ cups butterscotch morsels (about 8 ounces)
- ⅛ teaspoon salt
- ½ cup finely chopped walnuts, toasted

**1.** Preheat oven to 350°.

**2.** Combine sugar and butter in a large bowl. Stir in vanilla and egg. Weigh or lightly spoon flour into dry measuring cups; level with a knife. Combine flour, oats, 1/2 teaspoon salt, and baking soda in a bowl. Add oat mixture to sugar mixture; stir with a fork until combined (mixture will be crumbly). Place 3 cups oat mixture into the bottom of a 13 x 9–inch baking pan coated with cooking spray; press into bottom of pan. Set aside.

**3.** Place sweetened condensed milk, butterscotch morsels, and 1/8 teaspoon salt in a microwave-safe bowl; microwave at HIGH 1 minute or until butterscotch morsels melt, stirring every 20 seconds. Stir in walnuts. Scrape mixture into prepared pan, spreading evenly over crust. Sprinkle evenly with remaining oat mixture, gently pressing into butterscotch mixture. Bake at 350° for 30 minutes or until topping is golden brown. Place pan on a wire rack; run a knife around outside edge. Cool completely. **YIELD:** 36 servings (serving size: 1 bar).

CALORIES 148; FAT 5.1g (sat 2.7g, mono 0.9g, poly 1.1g); PROTEIN 2.6g; CARB 23.4g; FIBER 0.8g; CHOL 11mg; IRON 0.8mg; SODIUM 87mg; CALC 31mg

The hard thing to remember is this: just because they're lower in fat, doesn't mean you can eat half the pan. Hahaha! These are very tasty brownies, and have been a big hit every time I've made them.

from cookinglight.com

# Ooey-Gooey Peanut Butter-Chocolate Brownies

- ¾ cup fat-free sweetened condensed milk, divided
- ¼ cup butter, melted and cooled
- ¼ cup fat-free milk
- 1 (18.25-ounce) package devil's food cake mix
- 1 large egg white, lightly beaten
- Cooking spray
- 1 (7-ounce) jar marshmallow creme (about 1¾ cups)
- ½ cup peanut butter morsels

**1.** Preheat oven to 350°.

**2.** Combine 1/4 cup condensed milk, butter, and next 3 ingredients in a bowl (batter will be very stiff). Coat bottom of a 13 x 9–inch baking pan with cooking spray. Press two-thirds of batter into prepared pan using floured hands; pat evenly (layer will be thin).

**3.** Bake at 350° for 10 minutes. Combine 1/2 cup condensed milk and marshmallow creme in a bowl; stir in morsels. Spread marshmallow mixture evenly over brownie layer. Carefully drop remaining batter by spoonfuls over marshmallow mixture. Bake at 350° for 27 to 30 minutes. Cool completely in pan on a wire rack. **YIELD:** 2 dozen (serving size: 1 brownie).

CALORIES 176; FAT 5g (sat 2.1g, mono 1.6g, poly 1.1g); PROTEIN 2.6g; CARB 29.9g; FIBER 0.8g; CHOL 6mg; IRON 0.8mg; SODIUM 212mg; CALC 30mg

## what makes it light

- uses fat-free sweetened condensed milk
- uses a minimal amount of butter
- uses fat-free milk
- uses an egg white instead of a whole egg

bottled on our farm
in Strafford, Vermont.
"Know Better Milk"
VERMONT
ORGANIC
CERTIFIED
Return for Deposit

what makes it light
• uses a minimal amount of butter compared to traditional recipes
• uses less sugar than traditional recipes
• uses fat-free cottage cheese
• uses ⅓-less-fat cream cheese
• uses fat-free sour cream

Having been raised on 'the real thing,' with gobs of eggs and full-fat cream cheese, I was skeptical—but this was fabulous! **The texture was right on, and the taste was wonderful.** For cheesecake I'll use this recipe exclusively from now on. If you make this for guests they probably will never know it's low fat unless you tell them!

**from cookinglight.com**

# New York Cheesecake

Crust:

- 3 ounces all-purpose flour (about ⅔ cup)
- 3 tablespoons sugar
- 2 tablespoons chilled butter, cut into small pieces
- 1 tablespoon ice water
- Cooking spray

Filling:

- 4 cups fat-free cottage cheese
- 2 cups sugar
- 2 (8-ounce) blocks ⅓-less-fat cream cheese, softened
- 1.1 ounces all-purpose flour (about ¼ cup)
- ½ cup fat-free sour cream
- 1 tablespoon grated lemon rind
- 1 tablespoon vanilla extract
- ¼ teaspoon salt
- 5 large eggs

**1.** Preheat oven to 400°.
**2.** To prepare crust, weigh or lightly spoon 3 ounces flour into a dry measuring cup; level with a knife. Place flour and 3 tablespoons sugar in a food processor; pulse 2 times or until combined. Add butter; pulse 6 times or until mixture resembles coarse meal. With processor on, slowly pour ice water through food chute, processing just until blended (do not allow dough to form a ball).
**3.** Firmly press mixture into bottom of a 9-inch springform pan coated with cooking spray. Bake at 400° for 10 minutes or until lightly browned; cool on a wire rack.
**4.** Reduce oven temperature to 325°.
**5.** To prepare filling, strain cottage cheese through a cheesecloth-lined sieve for 10 minutes; discard liquid. Place cottage cheese in food processor; process until smooth.
**6.** Place 2 cups sugar and cream cheese in a large bowl; beat with a mixer at medium speed until smooth. Weigh or lightly spoon 1.1 ounces flour into a dry measuring cup; level with a knife. Add flour, sour cream, and remaining ingredients to cream cheese mixture; beat well. Add cottage cheese, stirring until well blended. Pour mixture into prepared crust.
**7.** Bake at 325° for 1 hour and 30 minutes or until almost set. Turn oven off. Cool cheesecake in closed oven 1 hour. Remove cheesecake from oven; run a knife around outside edge. Cool to room temperature. Cover and chill at least 8 hours. **YIELD:** 16 servings (serving size: 1 wedge).
**Note:** You can also make the cheesecake in a 10 x 2½–inch springform pan. Bake at 300° for 1 hour and 30 minutes or until almost set. Turn oven off. Cool cheesecake in closed oven 30 minutes.

CALORIES 291; FAT 9.8g (sat 5.7g, mono 3g, poly 0.5g); PROTEIN 12.9g; CARB 37.7g; FIBER 0.2g; CHOL 98mg; IRON 0.7mg; SODIUM 410mg; CALC 93mg

# recipe makeover
## sour cream pound cake

**The Reader:** Don Milburn

**The Story:** Don loves to cook and has always enjoyed the recipe for this cake, given to him by his mother. But he came to us for help because "all the old-time recipes never considered calories or fat content."

**The Dilemma:** This cake was indeed heavy, weighed down by 2½ sticks of butter and a cup of sour cream.

**The Solution:** We didn't want to lose any lushness in the cake, so we only slightly decreased the amount of butter from 1 cup to ¾ cup—cutting about 30 calories and 3 grams of fat from each slice. Switching to fat-free sour cream removed another 3 grams of fat from each serving. Using only 1½ tablespoons of butter instead of 4 tablespoons for the glaze shaved almost 2 grams of fat per serving. To replace flavor lost in the glaze, we switched from granulated sugar to brown sugar, which has a rich, full caramel-like flavor.

**The Feedback:** Don enjoyed our version so much that he made it for a family celebration. He didn't tell anyone in the family that it was a light adaptation, and "no one knew there was a difference."

| | BEFORE | AFTER |
|---|---|---|
| Calories per serving | 427 | 325 |
| Fat | 19.4g | 11g |
| Percent of total calories | 41% | 30% |

# Sour Cream Pound Cake with Rum Glaze

Cake:

- Cooking spray
- 3 tablespoons dry breadcrumbs
- 12 ounces cake flour (about 3 cups)
- 1 teaspoon baking powder
- ¼ teaspoon baking soda
- ¼ teaspoon salt
- ¾ cup butter, softened
- 2 cups granulated sugar
- 3 large eggs
- ¼ cup fat-free milk
- 1 tablespoon dark rum
- 2 teaspoons vanilla extract
- 1 cup fat-free sour cream

Glaze:

- ½ cup packed brown sugar
- 2 tablespoons dark rum
- 2 tablespoons water
- 1½ tablespoons butter

**1.** Preheat oven to 350°.

**2.** To prepare cake, coat a 10-inch tube pan with cooking spray; dust with breadcrumbs. Set aside.

**3.** Weigh or lightly spoon flour into dry measuring cups; level with a knife. Combine flour, baking powder, baking soda, and salt, stirring well with a whisk. Place butter and granulated sugar in a large bowl; beat with a mixer at medium speed until light and fluffy. Add eggs, 1 at a time, beating well after each addition. Add milk, 1 tablespoon rum, and vanilla; beat until combined. Beating at low speed, add flour mixture and sour cream alternately to sugar mixture, beginning and ending with flour mixture; beat until just combined.

**4.** Spoon batter into prepared pan. Bake at 350° for 1 hour or until a wooden pick inserted in center comes out clean. Cool in pan 10 minutes. Loosen cake from sides of pan using a narrow metal spatula. Place a plate upside down on top of cake; invert onto plate. Invert cake again. Pierce cake liberally with a wooden pick.

**5.** While cake bakes, prepare glaze. Combine brown sugar, 2 tablespoons rum, and water in a small saucepan; bring to a boil, stirring until sugar dissolves. Add 1½ tablespoons butter, stirring until butter melts. Drizzle half of warm glaze evenly over warm cake; allow mixture to absorb into cake. Drizzle remaining glaze over cake. Cool cake completely. **YIELD:** 16 servings (serving size: 1 slice).

CALORIES 325; FAT 11g (sat 6.3g, mono 3.2g, poly 0.5g); PROTEIN 3.6g; FIBER 0.6g; CHOL 68mg; IRON 1.5mg; SODIUM 232mg; CALC 58mg

# 5 ways with cakes

## Texas Sheet Cake

Rich in chocolate, this easy charmer boasts a sweet, fudgy icing that would melt in your mouth if not for the pecans.

- Cooking spray
- 2 teaspoons all-purpose flour
- 9 ounces all-purpose flour (about 2 cups)
- 2 cups granulated sugar
- 1 teaspoon baking soda
- 1 teaspoon ground cinnamon
- ¼ teaspoon salt
- ¾ cup water
- ½ cup butter
- ½ cup unsweetened cocoa, divided
- ½ cup low-fat buttermilk
- 1 tablespoon vanilla extract, divided
- 2 large eggs
- 6 tablespoons butter
- ⅓ cup fat-free milk
- 3 cups powdered sugar
- ¼ cup chopped pecans, toasted

**1.** Preheat oven to 375°.

**2.** Coat a 13 x 9–inch pan with cooking spray, and dust with 2 teaspoons flour. Set aside.

**3.** Weigh or lightly spoon 9 ounces flour into dry measuring cups; level with a knife. Combine flour and next 4 ingredients in a large bowl, stirring well with a whisk. Combine 3/4 cup water, 1/2 cup butter, and 1/4 cup cocoa in a small saucepan; bring to a boil, stirring frequently. Add to flour mixture. Beat at medium speed with an electric mixer until well blended. Add buttermilk, 1 teaspoon vanilla, and eggs; beat well. Pour batter into prepared pan. Bake at 375° for 22 minutes or until a wooden pick inserted in center comes out clean. Place on a wire rack.

**4.** Combine 6 tablespoons butter, fat-free milk, and remaining 1/4 cup cocoa in a saucepan; bring to a boil, stirring constantly. Remove from heat. Gradually stir in powdered sugar and remaining 2 teaspoons vanilla. Spread over hot cake. Sprinkle cake with pecans. Cool completely on wire rack. **YIELD:** 20 servings (serving size: 1 piece).

CALORIES 298; FAT 10g (sat 5.5g, mono 3.2g, poly 0.7g); PROTEIN 3.1g; CARB 49.8g; FIBER 0.5g; CHOL 44mg; IRON 1.1mg; SODIUM 188mg; CALC 25mg

# Cranberry Upside-Down Coffee Cake

Serve this buttery cake for a make-ahead brunch dish or at the end of a casual meal.

Cake:

- Cooking spray
- 1 tablespoon all-purpose flour
- 1 cup fresh cranberries
- ½ cup coarsely chopped pitted dates
- 2 tablespoons chopped walnuts
- 1 teaspoon grated orange rind
- ½ cup butter, softened and divided
- ½ cup packed dark brown sugar
- 2 tablespoons fresh orange juice
- ¼ teaspoon ground cinnamon
- 6.75 ounces all-purpose flour (about 1½ cups)
- 1 teaspoon baking powder
- ½ teaspoon salt
- 1 cup granulated sugar
- 1 teaspoon vanilla
- 1 large egg
- ½ cup nonfat buttermilk

Glaze:

- 1 cup powdered sugar
- 1 teaspoon butter, melted
- 2 tablespoons fresh orange juice

**1.** Preheat oven to 350°.

**2.** To prepare cake, coat a 9-inch square baking pan with cooking spray; dust with 1 tablespoon flour. Combine cranberries, dates, walnuts, and rind in a bowl. Melt 2 tablespoons butter in a small saucepan over medium heat. Stir in brown sugar, 2 tablespoons juice, and cinnamon; cook 3 minutes, stirring constantly. Pour brown sugar mixture into prepared pan. Sprinkle cranberry mixture evenly over brown sugar mixture.

**3.** Weigh or lightly spoon 6.75 ounces flour into dry measuring cups; level with a knife. Combine flour, baking powder, and salt in a bowl, stirring well with a whisk. Place granulated sugar and remaining 6 tablespoons butter in a large bowl; beat with a mixer at medium speed until well blended. Add vanilla and egg; beat well. Add flour mixture and buttermilk alternately to granulated sugar mixture, beginning and ending with flour mixture. Spoon batter over cranberry mixture.

**4.** Bake at 350° for 40 minutes or until a wooden pick inserted in center comes out clean. Cool in pan 5 minutes on a wire rack; run a knife around outside edges. Invert cake onto a plate; cool.

**5.** To prepare glaze, combine powdered sugar and remaining ingredients in a small bowl, stirring until smooth. Drizzle over cake. Cut cake into squares. **YIELD:** 12 servings (serving size: 1 square).

CALORIES 312; FAT 9.1g (sat 5.1g, mono 1g, poly 2.3g); PROTEIN 3g; CARB 55.7g; FIBER 1.4g; CHOL 39mg; IRON 1.2mg; SODIUM 236mg; CALC 32mg

## Carrot Cake with Toasted Coconut Cream Cheese Frosting

This cake keeps for up to three days in the refrigerator and also freezes well.

**Cake:**

- **3.4** ounces all-purpose flour (about ¾ cup)
- **¼** cup quick-cooking oats
- **1½** teaspoons ground cinnamon
- **1** teaspoon baking powder
- **½** teaspoon baking soda
- **¼** teaspoon salt
- **1** cup granulated sugar
- **¼** cup canola oil
- **1** (2½-ounce) jar carrot baby food
- **2** large eggs, lightly beaten
- **1¼** cups finely grated carrot (about 4 ounces)
- **½** cup golden raisins
- Cooking spray

**Frosting:**

- **⅓** cup (3 ounces) ⅓-less-fat cream cheese, softened
- **1** tablespoon butter, softened
- **1¼** cups powdered sugar, sifted
- **½** teaspoon vanilla extract
- **¼** cup flaked sweetened coconut, toasted

**1.** Preheat oven to 325°.

**2.** To prepare cake, weigh or lightly spoon flour into a dry measuring cup; level with a knife. Place flour and next 5 ingredients in a food processor; pulse 6 times or until well blended. Place flour mixture in a large bowl. Combine granulated sugar, canola oil, baby food, and eggs; stir with a whisk. Add to flour mixture; stir just until moist. Stir in grated carrot and raisins. Spoon batter into an 8-inch square baking pan coated with cooking spray.

**3.** Bake at 325° for 40 minutes or until a wooden pick inserted in center comes out clean. Cool in pan on a wire rack.

**4.** To prepare frosting, combine cream cheese and butter in a large bowl. Beat with a mixer at high speed until creamy. Gradually add powdered sugar and vanilla, beating at low speed until smooth (do not overbeat). Spread over cake; sprinkle with coconut. Cover and chill. **YIELD:** 12 servings (serving size: 1 piece).

CALORIES 262; FAT 8.8g (sat 2.7g, mono 3.6g, poly 1.6g); PROTEIN 3.2g; CARB 44.1g; FIBER 1.2g; CHOL 44mg; IRON 0.9mg; SODIUM 201mg; CALC 47mg

# Old-Fashioned Caramel Layer Cake

Hands down, this is one of the best-tasting cake recipes we have ever created. The caramel frosting is sweet perfection.

Cake:

- Cooking spray
- 1 tablespoon all-purpose flour
- 1½ cups granulated sugar
- ½ cup butter, softened
- 2 large eggs
- 1 large egg white
- 10.1 ounces all-purpose flour (about 2¼ cups)
- 2½ teaspoons baking powder
- ½ teaspoon salt
- 1¼ cups fat-free milk
- 2 teaspoons vanilla extract

Frosting:

- 1 cup packed dark brown sugar
- ½ cup evaporated fat-free milk
- 2½ tablespoons butter
- 2 teaspoons light-colored corn syrup
- Dash of salt
- 2 cups powdered sugar
- 2½ teaspoons vanilla extract

**1.** Preheat oven to 350°.
**2.** To prepare cake, coat 2 (9-inch) round cake pans with cooking spray; line bottoms with wax paper. Coat wax paper with cooking spray; dust with 1 tablespoon flour.
**3.** Beat granulated sugar and 1/2 cup butter at medium speed of a mixer until well blended (about 5 minutes). Add eggs and egg white, 1 at a time, beating well after each addition. Weigh or lightly spoon 10.1 ounces flour into dry measuring cups; level with a knife. Combine flour, baking powder, and salt; stir well with a whisk. Add flour mixture to sugar mixture alternately with 1 1/4 cups milk, beginning and ending with flour mixture. Stir in 2 teaspoons vanilla.
**4.** Pour batter into prepared pans, and sharply tap pans once on counter to remove air bubbles. Bake at 350° for 30 minutes or until a wooden pick inserted in center comes out clean. Cool in pans 10 minutes on a wire rack; remove from pans. Carefully peel off wax paper; cool completely on wire rack.
**5.** To prepare frosting, combine brown sugar and next 4 ingredients in a medium saucepan, and bring to a boil over medium-high heat, stirring constantly. Reduce heat, and simmer until thick (about 5 minutes), stirring occasionally. Remove from heat. Add powdered sugar and 2 1/2 teaspoons vanilla; beat at medium speed of a mixer until smooth and slightly warm. Cool 2 to 3 minutes (frosting will be thin but thickens as it cools).
**6.** Place 1 cake layer on a plate; spoon 1/2 cup frosting on to cake layer spreading to cover. Top with remaining cake layer. Frost top and sides of cake. Store cake loosely covered in refrigerator. **YIELD:** 18 servings (serving size: 1 slice).

CALORIES 307; FAT 7.5g (sat 4.4g, mono 2.2g, poly 0.4g); PROTEIN 3.8g; CARB 56.7g; FIBER 0.4g; CHOL 43mg; IRON 1.2mg; SODIUM 251mg; CALC 97mg

## Red Velvet Cupcakes

Throw out that old recipe that calls for shortening. This version is healthier—and even more delicious. As one cookinglight.com reader says, "The icing is to die for."

**Cupcakes:**

- Cooking spray
- 10 ounces cake flour (about 2½ cups)
- 3 tablespoons unsweetened cocoa
- 1 teaspoon baking soda
- 1 teaspoon baking powder
- 1 teaspoon kosher salt
- 1½ cups granulated sugar
- 6 tablespoons unsalted butter, softened
- 2 large eggs
- 1¼ cups nonfat buttermilk
- 1½ teaspoons white vinegar
- 1½ teaspoons vanilla extract
- 2 tablespoons red food coloring (about 1 ounce)

**Frosting:**

- 5 tablespoons butter, softened
- 4 teaspoons nonfat buttermilk
- 1 (8-ounce) block cream cheese, softened
- 3½ cups powdered sugar (about 1 pound)
- 1¼ teaspoons vanilla extract

**1.** Preheat oven to 350°.

**2.** To prepare cupcakes, place 30 paper muffin cup liners in muffin cups; coat with cooking spray.

**3.** Weigh or lightly spoon cake flour into dry measuring cups; level with a knife. Combine cake flour, unsweetened cocoa, baking soda, baking powder, and salt in a medium bowl; stir with a whisk. Place granulated sugar and unsalted butter in a large bowl; beat with a mixer at medium speed until well blended (about 3 minutes). Add eggs, 1 at a time, beating well after each addition. Add flour mixture and 1¼ cups nonfat buttermilk alternately to sugar mixture, beginning and ending with flour mixture. Add white vinegar, 1½ teaspoons vanilla, and food coloring; beat well.

**4.** Spoon batter into prepared muffin cups. Bake at 350° for 20 minutes or until a wooden pick inserted in center comes out clean. Cool in pan 10 minutes on a wire rack; remove from pan. Cool completely on wire racks.

**5.** To prepare frosting, beat 5 tablespoons butter, 4 teaspoons nonfat buttermilk, and cream cheese with a mixer at high speed until fluffy. Gradually add powdered sugar; beat until smooth. Add 1¼ teaspoons vanilla; beat well. Spread frosting evenly over cupcakes.

**YIELD:** 30 cupcakes (serving size: 1 cupcake).

CALORIES 205; FAT 7.3g (sat 4.5g, mono 2g, poly 0.3g); PROTEIN 2.3g; CARB 33.5g; FIBER 0.3g; CHOL 34mg; IRON 0.9mg; SODIUM 168mg; CALC 35mg

# Maple-Walnut Apple Crisp

- 1.5 ounces all-purpose flour (about ⅓ cup)
- ½ cup packed light brown sugar
- ⅓ cup regular oats
- ¼ teaspoon ground cinnamon
- ¼ cup chilled butter, cut into small pieces
- 3 tablespoons chopped walnuts
- 7 cups sliced peeled Rome apple (about 3 pounds)
- ¼ cup maple syrup
- ½ teaspoon ground cinnamon

**1.** Preheat oven to 375°.

**2.** Weigh or lightly spoon flour into a dry measuring cup; level with a knife. Combine flour, sugar, oats, and 1/4 teaspoon cinnamon in a medium bowl; cut in butter with a pastry blender or 2 knives until mixture is crumbly. Stir in walnuts.

**3.** Combine apple and remaining ingredients in a large bowl; toss well. Spoon apple mixture into an 8-inch square baking dish or 1 1/2-quart casserole. Sprinkle with crumb mixture. Bake at 375° for 45 minutes or until golden brown. Serve warm. **YIELD:** 9 servings.

CALORIES 208; FAT 7.1g (sat 3.4g, mono 1.9g, poly 1.3g); PROTEIN 1.8g; CARB 36.5g; FIBER 2.3g; CHOL 14mg; IRON 0.9mg; SODIUM 58mg; CALC 27mg

Amazing!!! Made this on Father's Day for my very picky, quadruple bypass father-in-law who is a strawberry shortcake expert. **He LOVED it and never even knew it was light!** Worked great for make ahead and will definitely make it again!

**from cookinglight.com**

# Old-Fashioned Strawberry Shortcakes

- 3½ cups halved strawberries, divided
- ⅓ cup sugar
- ⅓ cup orange juice
- 2 teaspoons vanilla extract
- 1 teaspoon lemon juice
- 5.6 ounces all-purpose flour (about 1¼ cups)
- 3 tablespoons sugar
- 1 teaspoon baking powder
- ¼ teaspoon baking soda
- ⅛ teaspoon salt
- 3 tablespoons chilled butter, cut into small pieces
- ½ cup low-fat buttermilk
- Cooking spray
- 6 tablespoons frozen reduced-calorie whipped topping, thawed
- Whole strawberries (optional)

**1.** Combine 1 cup strawberry halves, 1/3 cup sugar, orange juice, vanilla, and lemon juice in a bowl, and mash with a potato masher. Stir in 2 1/2 cups strawberry halves. Cover and chill.
**2.** Preheat oven to 425°.
**3.** Weigh or lightly spoon flour into dry measuring cups; level with a knife. Combine flour, 3 tablespoons sugar, baking powder, baking soda, and salt in a bowl; cut in butter with a pastry blender or 2 knives until mixture resembles coarse meal. Add buttermilk, stirring just until moist (dough will be sticky).
**4.** Turn dough out onto a lightly floured surface, and knead lightly 4 times with floured hands. Pat dough into a 6 x 4-inch rectangle. Cut dough into 6 squares. Place 1 inch apart on a baking sheet coated with cooking spray. Bake at 425° for 12 minutes. Cool on a wire rack.
**5.** Split shortcakes in half horizontally using a serrated knife; place each bottom half on a dessert plate. Spoon 1/4 cup strawberry mixture over each bottom half. Top with shortcake tops; spoon 1/4 cup strawberry mixture over each top. Top each serving with 1 tablespoon whipped topping; garnish with whole strawberries, if desired. **YIELD:** 6 servings.

CALORIES 270; FAT 7.2g (sat 1.9g, mono 2.7g, poly 2.1g); PROTEIN 4.3g; CARB 47.3g; FIBER 3g; CHOL 0mg; IRON 1.7mg; SODIUM 183mg; CALC 93mg

what makes it light
• uses less sugar than traditional recipes
• uses low-fat buttermilk
• uses reduced-calorie whipped topping

**For extra-delicious decadence** add a scoop of vanilla low-fat ice cream to your warm serving of cobbler.

# Lattice-Topped Blackberry Cobbler

- 1 cup granulated sugar, divided
- 6 tablespoons butter, softened
- 1 large egg yolk
- ½ teaspoon vanilla extract
- ¾ cup whole almonds, toasted
- 6 ounces all-purpose flour (about 1⅓ cups)
- ¼ teaspoon baking powder
- ¼ teaspoon salt
- 3 tablespoons ice water
- 10 cups fresh blackberries
- 3 tablespoons cornstarch
- 1 tablespoon fresh lemon juice
- Cooking spray
- 2 tablespoons turbinado sugar

**1.** Place 1/3 cup granulated sugar and butter in a large bowl; beat with a mixer until combined (about 1 minute). Add egg yolk, beating well. Stir in vanilla.
**2.** Place almonds in a food processor; pulse 10 times or until finely ground. Weigh or lightly spoon flour into dry measuring cups; level with a knife. Combine nuts, flour, baking powder, and salt, stirring well with a whisk. Gradually add nut mixture to butter mixture, beating at low speed just until a soft dough forms, adding 3 tablespoons ice water, as necessary. Turn dough out onto a lightly floured surface; knead lightly 6 times or until smooth. Divide dough into 2 equal portions; wrap each portion in plastic wrap. Chill 1 hour or until firm.
**3.** Preheat oven to 375°.
**4.** Combine remaining 2/3 cup granulated sugar, blackberries, cornstarch, and lemon juice; toss gently. Arrange berry mixture in a 13 x 9–inch glass or ceramic baking dish coated with cooking spray.
**5.** Unwrap dough. Roll each dough portion into a 13 x 9–inch rectangle on a lightly floured surface. Cut one rectangle, crosswise, into (1-inch-wide) strips. Cut remaining rectangle, lengthwise, into (1-inch-wide) strips. Arrange strips in a lattice pattern over fruit mixture; sprinkle dough with turbinado sugar. Bake at 375° for 50 minutes or until golden. Let stand 10 minutes.
**YIELD:** 12 servings (serving size: about 2/3 cup).

CALORIES 301; FAT 11.5g (sat 4.1g, mono 4.6g, poly 1.8g); PROTEIN 5.7g; CARB 47g; FIBER 8.6g; CHOL 32mg; IRON 2mg; SODIUM 103mg; CALC 75mg

## what makes it light

- uses a lot less sugar for the amount of blackberries than traditional recipes

**mply good. Nothing says summer like fresh, juicy peaches,** nd here's a fantastic application that pairs down-home flavor with a ealthy twist.

# Peach Cobbler

- 9 ounces all-purpose flour (about 2 cups)
- 1 tablespoon granulated sugar
- 1/4 teaspoon salt
- 6 tablespoons chilled butter, cut into 6 pieces
- 6 tablespoons ice water
- Cooking spray
- 6 cups sliced peeled peaches (about 3 3/4 pounds)
- 3/4 cup packed brown sugar, divided
- 2 1/2 tablespoons all-purpose flour
- 1 tablespoon vanilla extract
- 1 teaspoon ground cinnamon
- 1/4 cup slivered almonds
- 1 large egg
- 1 teaspoon water
- 1 tablespoon granulated sugar

**1.** Preheat oven to 375°.

**2.** Weigh or lightly spoon 9 ounces flour into dry measuring cups; level with a knife. Place flour, sugar, and salt in a food processor; pulse 2 to 3 times. Add butter pieces; pulse 10 times or until mixture resembles coarse meal. With processor on, slowly add ice water through food chute, processing just until combined (do not form a ball).

**3.** Gently press dough into a 4-inch circle. Slightly overlap 2 lengths of plastic wrap on a slightly damp surface. Place dough on plastic wrap; cover with 2 additional lengths of overlapping plastic wrap. Roll dough, still covered, into a 15 x 13–inch rectangle. Place in freezer 5 minutes or until plastic wrap can be easily removed; remove top sheets. Fit dough, uncovered side down, into a rectangular 2-quart baking dish coated with cooking spray, allowing dough to extend over edges; remove remaining plastic wrap.

**4.** Combine peaches, 1/2 cup brown sugar, 2 1/2 tablespoons flour, vanilla, and cinnamon in a large bowl; toss gently. Spoon into prepared dish; fold edges of dough over peach mixture. Sprinkle 1/4 cup brown sugar over mixture; sprinkle with almonds.

**5.** Combine egg and water in a small bowl. Brush egg mixture over dough; sprinkle with granulated sugar. Bake at 375° for 45 minutes or until filling is bubbly and crust is lightly browned. Let stand 30 minutes before serving. **YIELD:** 10 servings.

CALORIES 302; FAT 9.2g (sat 1.6g, mono 4.3g, poly 2.7g); PROTEIN 4.5g; CARB 51.5g; FIBER 2.8g; CHOL 11mg; IRON 1.9mg; SODIUM 149mg; CALC 39mg

## what makes it light

- uses much less sugar than traditional recipes
- uses less fat to make the crust than traditional recipes

This pie is absolutely amazing! **I was a little unsure whether it would taste good with all the fat-free and low-cal ingredients. It turned out so good, and everyone I served it to raved about it!** In fact, the lighter ingredients made the pie so much better, and I think this type of pie could be too sweet if full-fat ingredients were used. The chocolate shavings were the perfect touch! I have made it a bunch of times and plan on doing so again this weekend!

**from cookinglight.com**

# Frozen Peanut Butter Pie

- **1⅔ cups chocolate graham cracker crumbs (about 8½ cookie sheets)**
- **7 tablespoons sugar, divided**
- **2 large egg whites, lightly beaten**
- **Cooking spray**
- **1¼ cups fat-free milk**
- **⅔ cup reduced-fat crunchy peanut butter**
- **½ teaspoon vanilla**
- **½ cup (4 ounces) fat-free cream cheese, softened**
- **1 (8-ounce) container frozen fat-free whipped topping, thawed**
- **3 tablespoons finely chopped salted, dry-roasted peanuts**
- **¼ cup shaved milk chocolate (about 1 ounce)**

**1.** Preheat oven to 350°.

**2.** Combine crumbs, 3 tablespoons sugar, and egg whites; toss with a fork until moist. Press into bottom and up sides of a 9-inch deep-dish pie plate coated with cooking spray. Prick crust with a fork before baking. Bake at 350° for 10 minutes. Remove from oven; cool on a wire rack.

**3.** Combine milk and remaining 1/4 cup sugar in a heavy saucepan over medium-low heat. Cook 2 minutes or until sugar dissolves, stirring constantly; transfer mixture to a bowl. Add peanut butter and vanilla, stirring with a whisk until combined. Cover and chill 30 minutes.

**4.** Place cream cheese in a large bowl, and beat with a mixer at medium speed until light and fluffy. Add milk mixture, beating on low speed until combined. Fold in whipped topping; pour mixture into prepared piecrust. Freeze, uncovered, 8 hours or overnight or until hard. Sprinkle with peanuts and shaved chocolate. Transfer pie to refrigerator 30 minutes before slicing. **YIELD:** 10 servings (serving size: 1 wedge).

CALORIES 259; FAT 8.7g (sat 1.9g, mono 3.8g, poly 2g); PROTEIN 9.4g; CARB 35.5g; FIBER 1.6g; CHOL m2g; IRON 0.6mg; SODIUM 249mg; CALC 136mg

## what makes it light

- uses fat-free milk
- uses reduced-fat crunchy peanut butter
- uses fat-free cream cheese
- uses fat-free whipped topping
- uses egg whites instead of butter to bind the crumbs together for the crust

# 5 ways with pies

## Apple Pie

This traditional pie calls for Cortland apples, but we found that Pacific Rose apples also work well.

- **11.25** ounces all-purpose flour (about 2½ cups)
- **¾** teaspoon salt
- **6** tablespoons chilled butter, cut into small pieces
- **2** tablespoons vegetable shortening, cut into small pieces
- **1** tablespoon fresh lemon juice
- **¾** cup ice water
- **2½** cups thinly sliced peeled Braeburn apple (about 1 pound)
- **2½** cups thinly sliced peeled Cortland apple (about 1 pound)
- **1** cup sugar
- **1.1** ounces all-purpose flour (about ¼ cup)
- **¼** teaspoon ground cinnamon
- **⅛** to ¼ teaspoon ground allspice
- Cooking spray
- **1** tablespoon chilled butter, cut into small pieces
- **½** teaspoon vanilla extract
- **1** tablespoon whole milk

**1.** Weigh or lightly spoon 11.25 ounces flour into dry measuring cups; level with a knife. Combine flour and salt in a large bowl; cut in 6 tablespoons butter and vegetable shortening with a pastry blender or 2 knives until mixture resembles coarse meal. Add lemon juice. Sprinkle surface with ice water, 1 tablespoon at a time, and toss with a fork until moist and crumbly. Shape dough into a ball, and wrap in plastic wrap. Chill 1 hour.

**2.** Divide dough into 2 equal portions. Gently press each portion into a 1-inch-thick circle on heavy-duty plastic wrap; cover and freeze 10 minutes.

**3.** Preheat oven to 350°.

**4.** Place apples in a large bowl. Combine sugar, 1.1 ounces flour, cinnamon, and allspice in a small bowl. Sprinkle sugar mixture over apples; toss well to coat.

**5.** Working with 1 dough portion at a time, roll dough into a 12-inch circle on a lightly floured surface. Fit dough circle into a 9-inch pie plate coated with cooking spray, allowing dough to extend over the edge. Roll remaining dough portion into a 10-inch circle on a lightly floured surface. Spoon apple mixture into prepared pie plate, and dot with 1 tablespoon butter. Drizzle

apple mixture with 1/2 teaspoon vanilla. Top with 10-inch dough circle. Press edges of dough together. Fold edges under, and flute. Brush surface of dough with milk. Cut 3 (1-inch) slits in the top of dough to allow steam to escape. Bake at 350° for 1 hour or until apples are tender. **YIELD:** 10 servings (serving size: 1 wedge).

CALORIES 326; FAT 10.8g (sat 6g, mono 2.8g, poly 1.2g); PROTEIN 3.8g; CARB 54.1g; FIBER 2.3g; CHOL 21mg; IRON 1.7mg; SODIUM 233mg; CALC 14mg

## Coconut Cream Pie ▸

This pie takes a brief turn under the broiler to brown the peaks of the Italian meringue.

Crust:

- **½ (15-ounce) package refrigerated pie dough (such as Pillsbury)**

Filling:

- **1.1 ounces all-purpose flour (about ¼ cup)**
- **½ cup sugar**
- **⅛ teaspoon salt**
- **2 large eggs**
- **¾ cup 2% reduced-fat milk**
- **¾ cup light coconut milk**
- **¼ teaspoon coconut extract**
- **¼ teaspoon vanilla extract**

Meringue:

- **3 large egg whites**
- **⅔ cup sugar**
- **¼ cup water**
- **1 tablespoon flaked sweetened coconut, toasted**

**1.** Prepare and bake piecrust in a 10-inch deep-dish pie plate. Cool completely on a wire rack.

**2.** To prepare filling, weigh or lightly spoon flour into a dry measuring cup; level with a knife. Combine flour, 1/2 cup sugar, salt, and eggs in a large bowl; stir well with a whisk.

**3.** Heat milk and coconut milk over medium-high heat in a small, heavy saucepan to 180° or until tiny bubbles form around edge (do not boil). Gradually add hot milk mixture to sugar mixture, stirring constantly with a whisk. Place mixture in pan; cook over medium heat until thick and bubbly (about 10 minutes), stirring constantly.

**4.** Remove from heat. Spoon custard into a bowl; place bowl in a large ice-filled bowl 10 minutes or until custard comes to room temperature, stirring occasionally. Remove bowl from ice. Stir in extracts; spoon mixture into prepared crust. Cover and chill 8 hours or until firm.

**5.** Preheat broiler with rack in middle of oven.

**6.** To prepare meringue, place egg whites in a large bowl; beat with a mixer at high speed until soft peaks form. Combine 2/3 cup sugar and water in a saucepan; bring to a boil. Cook, without stirring, until candy thermometer registers 238°. Pour hot sugar syrup in a thin stream over egg whites, beating at high speed until stiff peaks form.

**7.** Spread meringue over chilled pie, and sprinkle with coconut. Broil 1 minute or until meringue is lightly browned; cool 5 minutes on a wire rack. Serve immediately. **YIELD:** 10 servings (serving size: 1 wedge).

CALORIES 281; FAT 9.3g (sat 5.6g, mono 2.6g, poly 0.4g); PROTEIN 5.3g; CARB 45.6g; FIBER 0.6g; CHOL 63mg; IRON 1.4mg; SODIUM 208mg; CALC 28mg

## Key Lime Pie ▾

Key lime pie is traditionally made with egg yolks, sweetened condensed milk, and lime juice from yellowish green Key limes. We guarantee that this lightened version will be a family favorite.

- 2 large eggs
- 2 large egg whites
- ½ cup Key lime juice (such as Nellie and Joe's Famous Key West Lime Juice)
- 1 teaspoon grated lime rind
- 1 (14-ounce) can fat-free sweetened condensed milk
- 1 (6-ounce) reduced-fat graham cracker crust
- 1½ cups frozen reduced-calorie whipped topping, thawed
- Grated lime rind (optional)

**1.** Preheat oven to 350°.

**2.** Beat eggs and egg whites at medium speed of a mixer until well blended. Gradually add juice, rind, and milk to egg mixture, beating until well blended. Spoon mixture into crust, and bake at 350° for 20 minutes or until almost set (the center will not be firm but will set up as it chills). Cool pie on a wire rack. Cover loosely, and chill 4 hours. Spread whipped topping evenly over filling. Garnish with grated lime rind, if desired. **YIELD:** 8 servings (serving size: 1 wedge).

CALORIES 288; FAT 5.9g (sat 3g, mono 1.5g, poly 1.1g); PROTEIN 7.6g; CARB 49.2g; FIBER 0.8g; CHOL 56mg; IRON 0.6mg; SODIUM 198mg; CALC 141mg

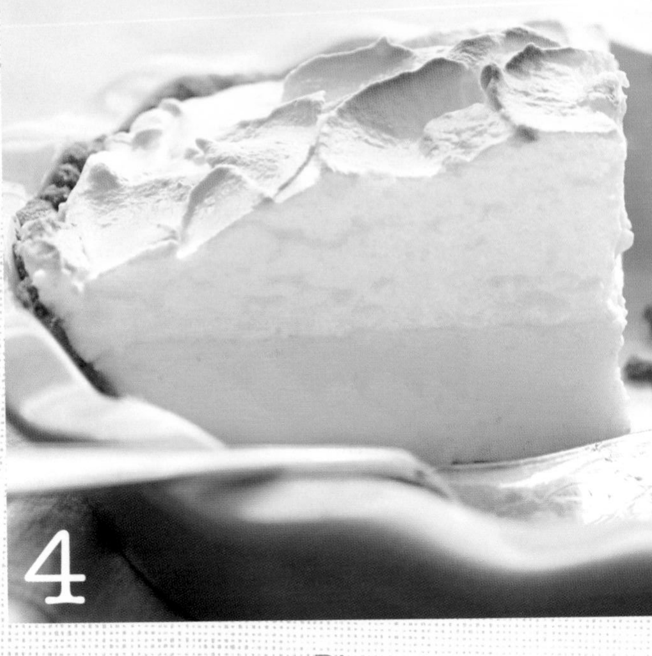


## Lemon Meringue Pie ▴

Crust:

- 1¼ cups graham cracker crumbs (about 8 cookie sheets)
- 2 tablespoons sugar
- 1 tablespoon butter, melted
- 1 large egg white, lightly beaten
- Cooking spray

Filling:

- 2 teaspoons grated lemon rind
- ½ cup fresh lemon juice (about 3 lemons)
- 1 (14-ounce) can fat-free sweetened condensed milk
- 1 (6-ounce) carton lemon fat-free yogurt (such as Yoplait)
- 1½ teaspoons unflavored gelatin
- 3 tablespoons water

Meringue:

- ⅔ cup sugar
- ¼ cup water
- 3 large egg whites
- ¼ teaspoon cream of tartar

**1.** Preheat oven to 325°.

**2.** To prepare crust, combine first 4 ingredients in a bowl; toss with a fork until moist. Press into a 9-inch pie plate coated with cooking spray. Bake at 325° for 15 minutes or until lightly browned; cool on a wire rack.

**3.** To prepare filling, combine lemon rind and next 3 ingredients in a medium bowl, and set aside. Sprinkle gelatin over 3 tablespoons water in a small microwave-safe bowl; let stand 1 minute. Microwave at HIGH 15 seconds, stirring until gelatin dissolves. Stir gelatin mixture thoroughly into yogurt mixture. Spoon filling into prepared crust. Press plastic wrap onto surface of filling; chill 1 hour or until almost firm.
**4.** To prepare meringue, combine 2/3 cup sugar and 1/4 cup water in a small saucepan; bring to a boil. Cook, without stirring, until candy thermometer registers 240°. Beat egg whites and cream of tartar at high speed of a mixer until foamy. Pour hot sugar syrup in a thin stream over egg white mixture, beating at high speed until stiff peaks form. Remove plastic wrap from filling. Spread meringue evenly over filling, sealing to edge of crust.
**5.** Preheat broiler with rack in middle of oven.
**6.** Broil 1 minute or until meringue is lightly browned, and cool pie on wire rack. Chill until set. **YIELD:** 9 servings (serving size: 1 wedge).

CALORIES 293; FAT 2.9g (sat 1.1g, mono 0.9g, poly 0.6g); PROTEIN 6.8g; CARB 59.9g; FIBER 0.1g; CHOL 9mg; IRON 0.6mg; SODIUM 178mg; CALC 141mg

## Classic Pecan Pie ▸

Crust:

- 4.5 ounces all-purpose flour (about 1 cup)
- 2 tablespoons granulated sugar
- ½ teaspoon baking powder
- ¼ teaspoon salt
- ¼ cup fat-free milk
- 1 tablespoon butter, melted
- Cooking spray

Filling:

- 1 large egg
- 4 large egg whites
- 1 cup light or dark-colored corn syrup
- ⅔ cup packed dark brown sugar
- ¼ teaspoon salt
- 1 cup pecan halves
- 1 teaspoon vanilla extract

**1.** To prepare crust, weigh or lightly spoon flour into a dry measuring cup; level with a knife. Combine flour, granulated sugar, baking powder, and 1/4 teaspoon salt in a bowl. Add milk and butter; toss with a fork until moist.
**2.** Press mixture gently into a 4-inch circle on heavy-duty plastic wrap; cover with additional plastic wrap. Roll dough, still covered, to an 11-inch circle. Freeze 10 minutes or until plastic wrap can be easily removed.
**3.** Remove 1 sheet of plastic wrap; fit dough into a 9-inch pie plate coated with cooking spray. Remove top sheet of plastic wrap. Fold edges under; flute.
**4.** Preheat oven to 350°.
**5.** To prepare filling, beat egg and next 4 ingredients at medium speed of a mixer until well blended. Stir in pecan halves and vanilla extract. Pour mixture into prepared crust. Bake at 350° for 20 minutes, then cover with foil. Bake an additional 20 minutes or until a knife inserted 1 inch from the edge comes out clean. Do not overbake. Cool pie on a wire rack. **YIELD:** 10 servings (serving size: 1 wedge).

CALORIES 288; FAT 9.2g (sat 1.5g, mono 5.1g, poly 2g); PROTEIN 4.3g; CARB 48.1g; FIBER 1g; CHOL 25mg; IRON 1.1mg; SODIUM 253mg; CALC 52mg

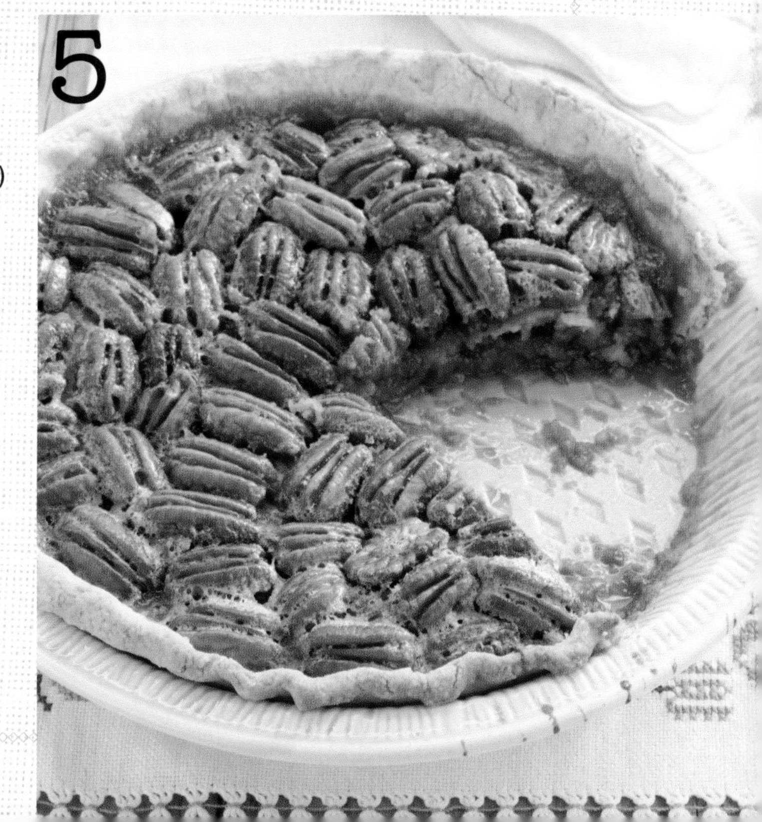

Awesome! **I have had some delicious banana puddings in my day, and this recipe ranks right up there.** It's great out of the oven or out of the fridge. You have to try this recipe!

**from cookinglight.com**

# Banana Pudding

- 1.5 ounces all-purpose flour (about ⅓ cup)
- Dash of salt
- 2½ cups 1% low-fat milk
- 1 (14-ounce) can fat-free sweetened condensed milk
- 2 large egg yolks
- 2 teaspoons vanilla extract
- 3 cups sliced ripe banana, divided
- 45 reduced-fat vanilla wafers, divided
- 4 large egg whites (at room temperature)
- ¼ cup sugar

**1.** Preheat oven to 325°.
**2.** Combine flour and salt in a medium saucepan. Gradually add milks and yolks; stir well. Cook over medium heat 8 minutes or until thick, stirring constantly. Remove from heat; stir in vanilla.
**3.** Arrange 1 cup banana slices in bottom of a 2-quart baking dish. Spoon one-third of pudding mixture over banana. Arrange 15 wafers on top of pudding. Repeat layers twice, arranging last 15 wafers around edge of dish. Push cookies into pudding.
**4.** Beat egg whites at high speed of a mixer until foamy. Gradually add sugar, 1 tablespoon at a time, beating until stiff peaks form. Spread meringue evenly over pudding, sealing to edge of dish. Bake at 325° for 25 minutes or until golden. **YIELD:** 10 servings (serving size: 3/4 cup).

CALORIES 255; FAT 2.9g (sat 1g, mono 0.9g, poly 0.2g); PROTEIN 7.9g; CARB 49.5g; FIBER 0.1g; CHOL 51mg; IRON 0.4mg; SODIUM 155mg; CALC 161mg

## what makes it light

- uses low-fat milk
- uses fat-free sweetened condensed milk
- uses reduced-fat vanilla wafers

**Adding cornstarch to this homey pudding lessens the possibility of its curdling.** To prevent the custard from tipping and taking on ice water, make sure the bowl you use for the ice bath is only slightly larger than the custard bowl.

# Bittersweet Chocolate Pudding

- ½ cup granulated sugar
- ⅓ cup unsweetened cocoa
- 3 tablespoons cornstarch
- 3 tablespoons dark brown sugar
- ⅛ teaspoon salt
- 4 cups 2% reduced-fat milk
- 3 large egg yolks, lightly beaten
- 2 ounces bittersweet chocolate, chopped
- 1 teaspoon vanilla extract

**1.** Combine first 5 ingredients in a large saucepan. Gradually add milk, stirring with a whisk. Bring to a boil over medium heat, stirring constantly. Cook 1 minute, stirring constantly.
**2.** Place egg yolks in a bowl. Gradually add hot milk mixture to egg yolks, stirring constantly. Return milk mixture to pan. Cook over medium heat 5 minutes or until mixture is thick, stirring constantly. Remove mixture from heat, and add chopped chocolate and vanilla extract, stirring until chocolate melts. Spoon pudding into a small bowl. Place bowl in a large ice-filled bowl 15 minutes or until pudding is cool, stirring occasionally. Remove bowl from ice; cover and chill. **YIELD:** 6 servings (serving size: 3/4 cup).

CALORIES 282; FAT 9.5g (sat 5.1g, mono 2.4g, poly 0.5g); PROTEIN 8.4g; CARB 43g; FIBER 2.4g; CHOL 119mg; IRON 1.2mg; SODIUM 138mg; CALC 222mg

## what makes it light

- uses reduced-fat milk
- uses less sugar than traditional recipes
- doesn't use butter, which some puddings do

**Raisin-studded bread pudding and buttery,** bourbon-spiked sauce combine in this time-honored dessert.

# New Orleans Bread Pudding with Bourbon Sauce

Pudding:

- ¼ cup raisins
- 2 tablespoons bourbon
- 1¼ cups 2% reduced-fat milk
- ½ cup sugar
- 1 tablespoon vanilla extract
- ½ teaspoon ground cinnamon
- ¼ teaspoon ground nutmeg
- Dash of salt
- 3 large eggs, lightly beaten
- 4½ cups (½-inch) cubed French bread (about 8 ounces)
- Cooking spray

Sauce:

- ½ cup sugar
- ¼ cup light-colored corn syrup
- ¼ cup butter
- ¼ cup bourbon

**1.** To prepare pudding, combine raisins and 2 tablespoons bourbon in a bowl. Let stand 30 minutes. Drain mixture in a sieve over a bowl, reserving liquid.

**2.** Combine reserved liquid, milk, and next 6 ingredients in a large bowl, stirring well with a whisk. Add bread, tossing gently to coat. Spoon mixture into an 8-inch square baking dish coated with cooking spray. Sprinkle evenly with raisins, pressing gently into bread mixture. Cover with foil; chill 30 minutes or up to 4 hours.

**3.** Preheat oven to 350°.

**4.** Place dish in a 13 x 9–inch baking pan; add hot water to pan to a depth of 1 inch. Bake, covered, at 350° for 20 minutes. Uncover and bake an additional 10 minutes or until a knife inserted in center comes out clean.

**5.** To prepare sauce, combine 1/2 cup sugar, corn syrup, and butter in a small saucepan over medium heat. Bring to a simmer; cook 1 minute, stirring constantly. Remove from heat; stir in 1/4 cup bourbon. Serve each bread pudding piece warm with about 1 tablespoon sauce. **YIELD:** 9 servings.

CALORIES 309; FAT 8.2g (sat 4.3g, mono 2.7g, poly 0.6g); PROTEIN 5.6g; CARB 47.6g; FIBER 1g; CHOL 87mg; IRON 1.1mg; SODIUM 272mg; CALC 74mg

## what makes it light

- uses reduced-fat milk
- uses fewer eggs than traditional recipes
- uses less butter than traditional recipes
- uses less sugar than traditional recipes

**Nutty caramel coats delicate baked custard in this rich dessert, also referred to as "flan."** Although we specify cooking the caramel until golden, you can cook it longer for a deep amber color; the bitter notes of the darker caramel add a nice contrast to the sweet custard.

# Classic Crème Caramel

- 4 cups 2% reduced-fat milk
- 1 vanilla bean, split lengthwise
- Cooking spray
- 1⅔ cups sugar, divided
- ¼ cup water
- ¼ teaspoon kosher salt
- 6 large eggs
- 3 tablespoons heavy whipping cream

**1.** Preheat oven to 225°.
**2.** Heat milk and vanilla bean over medium-high heat in a medium, heavy saucepan to 180° or until tiny bubbles form around edge (do not boil); remove pan from heat. Cover and set aside.
**3.** Coat 10 (6-ounce) custard cups with cooking spray; arrange cups on a jelly-roll pan.
**4.** Combine 1 cup sugar and 1/4 cup water in a small, heavy saucepan; cook over medium-high heat until sugar dissolves, stirring frequently. Continue cooking 7 minutes or until golden (do not stir). Immediately pour into prepared custard cups, tipping quickly until caramelized sugar coats bottom of cups.
**5.** Combine remaining 2/3 cup sugar, salt, and eggs in a large bowl, stirring with a whisk. Remove vanilla bean from milk mixture; reserve bean for another use. Gradually pour warm milk mixture into egg mixture, stirring constantly with a whisk; stir in cream. Strain egg mixture through a sieve into a large bowl; pour about 1/2 cup egg mixture over caramelized sugar in each custard cup. Bake at 225° for 2 hours or until custards are just set. Remove from oven; cool to room temperature. Place plastic wrap on surface of custards; chill overnight.
**6.** Loosen edges of custards with a knife or rubber spatula. Place a dessert plate, upside down, on top of each cup; invert onto plate. Drizzle any remaining caramelized syrup over custards. **YIELD:** 10 servings (serving size: 1 custard).

CALORIES 236; FAT 6.5g (sat 3.1g, mono 2.2g, poly 0.5g); PROTEIN 7.1g; CARB 38.4g; FIBER 0g; CHOL 140mg; IRON 0.6mg; SODIUM 139mg; CALC 138mg

## what makes it light

- uses reduced-fat milk
- uses less heavy cream than traditional recipes

This recipe is fantastic, very easy, and full of peach flavor. **It's simple but not too sweet** like commercial ice cream. Would recommend this to anyone who loves a taste of summer.

**from cookinglight.com**

# Peach Ice Cream

- 3 cups sliced peeled peaches (about 1½ pounds)
- 1 cup half-and-half
- ½ cup sugar
- ½ cup whole milk
- 1 teaspoon vanilla extract

**1.** Place peaches in a blender or food processor; process until finely chopped. Combine peaches and remaining ingredients in a large bowl. Pour peach mixture into freezer can of an ice-cream freezer; freeze according to manufacturer's instructions. Spoon ice cream into a freezer-safe container; cover and freeze 2 hours or until firm. **YIELD:** 8 servings (serving size: ½ cup).

CALORIES 125; FAT 4g (sat 2.5g, mono 1.2g, poly 0.2g); PROTEIN 1.8g; CARB 21.3g; FIBER 1.2g; CHOL 13mg; IRON 0.1mg; SODIUM 20mg; CALC 53mg

## what makes it light

- uses less sugar than traditional recipes
- uses less cream than traditional recipes by substituting a mix of milk and half-and-half

# Nutritional Analysis

## How to Use It and Why

Glance at the end of any *Cooking Light* recipe, and you'll see how committed we are to helping you make the best of today's light cooking. With chefs, registered dietitians, home economists, and a computer system that analyzes every ingredient we use, *Cooking Light* gives you authoritative dietary detail like no other magazine. We go to such lengths so you can see how our recipes fit into your healthful eating plan. If you're trying to lose weight, the calorie and fat figures will probably help most. But if you're keeping a close eye on the sodium, cholesterol, and saturated fat in your diet, we provide those numbers, too. And because many women don't get enough iron or calcium, we can also help there, as well. Finally, there's a fiber analysis for those of us who don't get enough roughage.

Here's a helpful guide to put our nutritional analysis numbers into perspective. Remember, one size doesn't fit all, so take your lifestyle, age, and circumstances into consideration when determining your nutrition needs. For example, pregnant or breast-feeding women need more protein, calories, and calcium. And women older than 50 need 1,200mg of calcium daily, 200mg more than the amount recommended for younger women and men.

## We Use These Abbreviations in Our Nutritional Analysis

| | | | |
|---|---|---|---|
| sat | saturated fat | CHOL | cholesterol |
| mono | monounsaturated fat | CALC | calcium |
| poly | polyunsaturated fat | g | gram |
| CARB | carbohydrates | mg | milligram |

### Daily Nutrition Guide

| | Women Ages 25 to 50 | Women over 50 | Men over 24 |
|---|---|---|---|
| **Calories** | 2,000 | 2,000 or less | 2,700 |
| **Protein** | 50g | 50g or less | 63g |
| **Fat** | 65g or less | 65g or less | 88g or less |
| **Saturated Fat** | 20g or less | 20g or less | 27g or less |
| **Carbohydrates** | 304g | 304g | 410g |
| **Fiber** | 25g to 35g | 25g to 35g | 25g to 35g |
| **Cholesterol** | 300mg or less | 300mg or less | 300mg or less |
| **Iron** | 18mg | 8mg | 8mg |
| **Sodium** | 2,300mg or less | 1,500mg or less | 2,300mg or less |
| **Calcium** | 1,000mg | 1,200mg | 1,000mg |

The nutritional values used in our calculations either come from The Food Processor, Version 8.9 (ESHA Research), or are provided by food manufacturers.

# Metric Equivalents

The information in the following charts is provided to help cooks outside the United States successfully use the recipes in this book. All equivalents are approximate.

## Cooking/Oven Temperatures

| | Fahrenheit | Celsius | Gas Mark |
|---|---|---|---|
| **Freeze Water** | 32° F | 0° C | |
| **Room Temp.** | 68° F | 20° C | |
| **Boil Water** | 212° F | 100° C | |
| **Bake** | 325° F | 160° C | 3 |
| | 350° F | 180° C | 4 |
| | 375° F | 190° C | 5 |
| | 400° F | 200° C | 6 |
| | 425° F | 220° C | 7 |
| | 450° F | 230° C | 8 |
| **Broil** | | | Grill |

## Liquid Ingredients by Volume

| | | | | | | | | |
|---|---|---|---|---|---|---|---|---|
| ¼ tsp | = | 1 ml | | | | | | |
| ½ tsp | = | 2 ml | | | | | | |
| 1 tsp | = | 5 ml | | | | | | |
| 3 tsp | = | 1 tbl | = | ½ fl oz | = | 15 ml | | |
| 2 tbls | = | ⅛ cup | = | 1 fl oz | = | 30 ml | | |
| 4 tbls | = | ¼ cup | = | 2 fl oz | = | 60 ml | | |
| 5⅓ tbls | = | ⅓ cup | = | 3 fl oz | = | 80 ml | | |
| 8 tbls | = | ½ cup | = | 4 fl oz | = | 120 ml | | |
| 10⅔ tbls | = | ⅔ cup | = | 5 fl oz | = | 160 ml | | |
| 12 tbls | = | ¾ cup | = | 6 fl oz | = | 180 ml | | |
| 16 tbls | = | 1 cup | = | 8 fl oz | = | 240 ml | | |
| 1 pt | = | 2 cups | = | 16 fl oz | = | 480 ml | | |
| 1 qt | = | 4 cups | = | 32 fl oz | = | 960 ml | | |
| | | | | 33 fl oz | = | 1000 ml | = | 1 l |

## Dry Ingredients by Weight

(To convert ounces to grams, multiply the number of ounces by 30.)

| | | | | |
|---|---|---|---|---|
| 1 oz | = | 1/16 lb | = | 30 g |
| 4 oz | = | ¼ lb | = | 120 g |
| 8 oz | = | ½ lb | = | 240 g |
| 12 oz | = | ¾ lb | = | 360 g |
| 16 oz | = | 1 lb | = | 480 g |

## Equivalents for Different Types of Ingredients

| Standard Cup | Fine Powder (ex. flour) | Grain (ex. rice) | Granular (ex. sugar) | Liquid Solids (ex. butter) | Liquid (ex. milk) |
|---|---|---|---|---|---|
| 1 | 140 g | 150 g | 190 g | 200 g | 240 ml |
| ¾ | 105 g | 113 g | 143 g | 150 g | 180 ml |
| ⅔ | 93 g | 100 g | 125 g | 133 g | 160 ml |
| ½ | 70 g | 75 g | 95 g | 100 g | 120 ml |
| ⅓ | 47 g | 50 g | 63 g | 67 g | 80 ml |
| ¼ | 35 g | 38 g | 48 g | 50 g | 60 ml |
| ⅛ | 18 g | 19 g | 24 g | 25 g | 30 ml |

## Length

(To convert inches to centimeters, multiply the number of inches by 2.5.)

| | | | | | | | | |
|---|---|---|---|---|---|---|---|---|
| 1 in | = | | | | | 2.5 cm | | |
| 6 in | = | ½ ft | | | = | 15 cm | | |
| 12 in | = | 1 ft | | | = | 30 cm | | |
| 36 in | = | 3 ft | = | 1 yd | = | 90 cm | | |
| 40 in | = | | | | | 100 cm | = | 1 m |

# index